ROBERT L. SHURTER

Professor of English
Case Western Reserve University

WRITTEN
COMMUNICATION
IN
BUSINESS

WRITTEN COMMUNICATION IN BUSINESS

third edition

MCGRAW-HILL BOOK COMPANY

New York	Kuala Lumpur	Panama
St. Louis	London	Rio de Janeiro
San Francisco	Mexico	Singapore
Düsseldorf	Montreal	Sydney
Johannesburg	New Delhi	Toronto

WRITTEN COMMUNICATION IN BUSINESS

Library of Congress Catalog Card Number 71-136183
ISBN 07-057325-5

90 HDBP 798765

This book was set in Patina by University Graphics, Inc., printed on permanent paper by Halliday Lithograph Corporation, and bound by The Book Press, Inc. The designer was Paula Tuerk; the drawings were done by John Cordes, J. & R. Technical Services, Inc. The editors were R. Bruce Kezer and John M. Morriss. Matt Martino supervised production.

CONTENTS

PART FOUR   THE REPORT AND MEMORANDUM

PART FIVE   SELF-DEVELOPMENT ON THE JOB

CASES

REFERENCE SECTION

PREFACE

Written Communication in Business is intended for two types of readers: college students taking formal courses in the various forms of business writing and readers who are already engaged in their business careers. The book is designed to present a comprehensive treatment of the major principles of business communication, an analysis of the most widely used forms of business writing—the letter, the report, and the memorandum—and a discussion of the associated skills of dictation and reading. It includes a reference section with a commentary on "Writing Correctly" as well as a conveniently organized treatment to provide answers to the specific questions about currect usage which frequently confront both students and business writers. The book is organized to present the general principles of effective communication in the first section and to apply these principles to specific types of writing—business letters, reports, memoranda—in subsequent sections.

In the third edition, I have tried to give equal emphasis to business communication both as a very important activity of business management and as an invaluable skill or technique for the individual whose career goal is a position in business or industry. The result, I hope, is a book which will prove useful both to those students who are primarily concerned with business administration, as well as those who are concerned with the techniques of writing, and to businessmen familiar with management viewpoint who seek to improve their own or their employees' communication skills. To that end, a number of actual business problems have been added which deal with the management thinking and analysis which must precede and accompany the writing of a business communication. A number of the new problems also deal with situations in the academic community so that students may use their background knowledge to write about subjects with which they are familiar, as in the chapter "The Report Writing Process—An Example," where the entire process of writing a report, from original assignment to finished report, is followed through in terms of a subject about which all college students have specific knowledge.

Other changes in the third edition involve a new chapter on "Words— Their Use and Abuse," a greatly expanded treatment of reports in Part Three, a number of exercises and cases which stress business's role as a part of our total society in the 1970s, and the inclusion of a great many new exercises designed to force students to think creatively. It should perhaps be added that I have had the good fortune to serve for the past twenty years as consultant, lecturer, and coworker on communication problems for many of America's largest corporations, and the problems and exercises in this book derive from actual business problems I have encountered. Many of them have been specifically selected to stress the opportunity which business provides for original rather than routine writing, for the imaginative rather than the repetitive treatment. For that reason, for example, the exercises at the end of Chapter 1 have been deliberately chosen to disabuse the student of notions such as "anyone can write for business" or "business communication is dull." The section on Cases presents a number of new problems in considerable detail; these are intended to show the interchange of memos, letters, and reports frequently involved in one communication situation. Above all else, I have tried to present a realistic approach to what actually goes on in the practical forms of writing which are so vital to American business.

In writing this third edition, I have been influenced by two questions that business executives have frequently asked:

1. Why don't our employees attain higher standards of performance in their writing?
2. Why are so many people in business reluctant to write?

Both these questions deserve answers in any book dealing with business communication—and the answers naturally depend, in large measure, on the background of the author's thinking and experience. For instance, one answer, advanced by many writers and executives, is that the key to communication problems can be found in devising an organization pattern or organization chart which will maintain a flow of written communication up, down, and across all levels of the organization. It is certainly true that even the best writer cannot communicate effectively in a rigidly authoritarian organization; but it is equally true that communication will not rise above the mediocrity of poorly prepared writers even in the most "open" organization. I am convinced, therefore, that the best way to improve business communication is by teaching individual writers—whether they be in college or on the job—the principles and techniques of effective writing. Since this book provides one approach to communication, readers, quite properly, should expect some insight into my own thinking about the two questions which executives ask so frequently and how this thinking has been incorporated into this book.

Why don't business writers achieve higher standards of performance? I think there is only one answer—that the real goals of business writing have not been clearly set for them. Too many writers have had only the hackneyed letters in the incoming mail basket or the wordy reports in the files to "guide" them. That is why the early chapters of this book are devoted to a discussion of the goals for business writers and subsequent chapters stress continual measurement of individual performance against these goals. Just as the golfer who plays against par will develop a better game than the one who plays haphazardly without any measure of performance, the college student or business writer who measures his writing against his instructor's comments or the specified goals will learn to approach "par" for the course.

Why are so many people in business reluctant to write? There is nearly universal agreement that of all the forms of communication writing is the most difficult. But the real reason why it is difficult—and why people dislike to write—is that writing forces people to think or, worse, exposes the fact that they have not thought. Because of that belief, this book places a heavy emphasis on the patterns of thinking which must precede all forms of writing. Particularly in the section on report writing, stress is placed on the fundamental thought processes and logical organizational patterns which undergird effective reports. Similarly, in the sections on letters and memorandums, I have emphasized thinking—about the purpose, about the reader, and about the material itself.

For two salient aspects of this edition, I have relied on experts in related disciplines. For the careful background of thinking which goes into management decisions, I have retained much of the viewpoint of Professor J. Peter Williamson, who was my coauthor in the second edition and who is Professor of Business Administration at The Amos Tuck School of Business Administration, Dartmouth College. Since an important part of business writing involves the use of charts and graphic presentation—a specialized field in which few people are really expert—I have asked Mr. Kenneth W. Haemer, formerly Manager, Presentation Research, American Telephone and Telegraph Company, to prepare the chapter on "Conveying Information Graphically" in the section on report writing.

I am indebted to many business executives for helpful suggestions and for the many useful examples they have supplied as a follow-up to my consulting activities with their corporations. To my students and to my colleagues in that most useful organization, The American Business Communication Association, and to its director, Professor Francis Weeks, I am grateful for many helpful suggestions and much assistance. Specific acknowledgments for the use of various printed materials are made throughout the text, but I particularly want to express my gratitude to the many editors and publishers who have generously made these materials available.

Robert L. Shurter

PART ONE

PRINCIPLES OF BUSINESS COMMUNICATION

In a society where "machines talk to machines" and electronic gadgets bid fair to replace humans, it is comforting to remember one basic fact: like water in its natural state, communication never rises above its source. And that source is a human being. Simply stated, this means that the quality of any written message can never rise above the ability of the human being who wrote it.

At first glance, these statements appear to be so obvious as not to require repeating. But the emerging technology associated with today's communication explosion, with its array of automatic typewriters, computers, and electronic devices, has created the erroneous notion that emphasis on the medium has somehow replaced emphasis on the message. It is a little like concluding that a stupid speaker, given all the resources of television with its vast audience, will be anything but stupid, when, in fact, he will only be so for more listeners.

Part One of this book, as well as subsequent chapters, is based on two fundamental convictions about written communication:

1. The ability to express one's thoughts clearly and concisely in writing is one of the most sought-after skills in business—and will continue to be.
2. The quality of written communication is always a result of the writer's knowledge of the basic principles of communication.

For the student or businessman, therefore, it would be fatuous to "write off writing" for the 1970s because of computers or mechanical devices. No evidence exists to indicate that written communication will play a less important role in the future business world than it has in the past. Plenty of evidence *does* exist, however, to indicate that it will play a changed role, brought about in part by the appalling costs of today's written word (which are discussed in Chapter 1) and in part by the electronic and mechanized devices now available.

This changed role will undoubtedly involve a technique widely used—and taught—in the business community called "management by exception." Under this principle, routine and repetitive situations are treated routinely by a carefully planned method of dealing with them, thus freeing executives—and writers—to concentrate on the unusual, the creative, and the original. In essence, therefore, tomorrow's business writer will require greater skill, broader knowledge, and more flexibility. As the widely quoted advertisement of IBM describes it: "Machines should work; people should think."

An interesting glimpse of things to come as they affect the writer in a computerized world is provided by William C. Greenough, Chairman and President of Teachers Insurance and Annuity Association, as reported in the *Bulletin* of the American Business Communication Association:

Recently I received an abacus as a graduation present. I got it for graduating

3

from IBM school early in 1966. Graduating with me were other executives who wanted to know more about how the machine can help their organization.

We studied very thoroughly all of the new-generation machines. We learned the utility and service potentials of their fantastic speeds and capabilities. We programmed them ourselves to answer simple questions, then watched them boom out answers, demonstrating their ability to compute in moments what would take humans years to figure out. We programmed to find out when Mexico will exceed the United States in population; and how much the $24 the Indians paid for Manhattan Island would be worth now had it been put out at 1%, 2%, 3%, and 4% interest on the day of purchase.

These modern machines can pour out data so fast (1,100 lines per minute) that they literally can inundate the user with paper. So the problems of paper work, always very great, are becoming greater and greater.

Recently, I instructed all TIAA departments to move into the new generation of machines in such a way as to eliminate use of paper wherever possible. We aim to get rid of every bit of paper work we can; to make letter writing as nearly obsolete as possible. . . .

We want communication with the policyholder to be more direct instead of through a lot of intermediate steps and shuffling of paper back and forth among departments. . . .

In such a setup, the communications job will be much more interesting, complex and fascinating. . . . The communicator, far from being obsolete, will be the key figure—right smack in the middle of the operation.

As Mr. Greenough indicates, the obsolete hand of past communication practices is being lifted—and to the advantage of today's writer who wants to deal with original and creative problems. One has only to recall the maxims about communication which we have inherited in our folklore and which we unthinkingly repeat to recognize how erroneous the past has been: "Silence is golden"; "Talk is cheap"; "No news is good news"; "What you don't know won't hurt you."

Equally nonsensical is today's frightened assumption that tomorrow's written business communication will involve dehumanized, impersonal interchange between machines in which English has been replaced by *Fortran* or *Cobol*. Certainly tomorrow's business writer will have at his command the greatest arsenal of methods and techniques—computers, tapes, dictating equipment—that any communicator has ever had, and he will have the responsibility of choosing the quickest or the most appropriate or the least expensive among them, depending on his purpose. But these are servants which provide him with the time and opportunity for the challenging and interesting aspects of communication.

Finally, before we begin our discussion of the principles of business communication, we ought appropriately to make a statement which startles many students and businessmen:

If you are now paid (or will be paid) to write in business, you are in a very real sense a professional writer.

Most businessman back away from his statement out of modesty—"Come on now. I'm no Hemingway."—or out of mild shock—"Oh, I don't write that much on the job." (Actually myriads of businessmen do more writing during their careers than many novelists, if we consider simply the amount of their writing; numerous surveys show that business executives spend the major part of their day communicating.)

The alternative to being a *professional* is to be a hack writer, turning out words just to make money without concern for ethics or principles or self-improvement. Of course there are hacks in business as in every other facet of our society. But there are professionals too—and if you are now an "apprentice" in college, you should aim at professionalism in your writing. In the chapters of this book, we have tried to emphasize professionalism by raising questions and providing exercises dealing with ethical aspects of business writing; we have tried to select as many examples of creative, original, and humorous business writing as possible to underscore the belief that writing in business does not necessarily have to be drab and stereotyped. Consider, for the moment, how to define or describe a car: it can be "more than 25,000 separate pieces of metal, plastic, rubber, and other materials assembled into . . ." or "a body placed on four wheels propelled by . . ." But then consider this:

A car is to tie shoes on and go off to start a new life in.

A professional has left his mark here, as he has in the beautifully worded letter, just to cite one example, from Yeck & Yeck which is reproduced on page 100.

What is it that distinguishes professionalism in communication from hack writing? A lot of things, but the essence of professionalism is *to keep endlessly trying to improve.* This means seizing every opportunity to write; using every chance to read and to learn how other writers express themselves; and studying the generally accepted principles of effective writing. These principles and techniques are set forth in the pages which follow.

CHAPTER 1

THE INFORMATION EXPLOSION AND THE BUSINESS WRITER

Before we go on to discuss the meaning and purposes of business writing, we ought briefly to examine the conditions which affect communication in today's business community. The phenomenon in our society conventionally labeled "the information explosion" has had a profound impact on both the form and the substance of business communication, and it leads to a logical question of "Why put it in writing?" The answer derives from two conditions which are uniquely characteristic of the seventies:

1. Never before has the businessman had so wide a choice of media for his message.
2. The cost of business communication has become astronomical.

Just as the Victorian era of the quill pen gave way to the typewriter in the early twentieth century, today's technology provides the businessman with a myriad of choices beyond the conventional writing it down or talking face to face. Shall he telephone, teletype, televise by closed circuit, use electronic taping or video taping, or employ some other method to get his message across? The age-old dream of instantaneous communication regardless of distance has become a reality. In fact, this dream may well become a nightmare induced by the very abundance of our technical ability to communicate: one estimate, for example, of the rate at which we are adding to the existing store of knowledge in the form of reports, trade journals, letters, documents, and seminar proceedings places it at 500,000 pages per minute.

Here is an excerpt from one of IBM's ads in 1969 carrying the headline IT'S NOT THE COMMUNICATION EXPLOSION THAT'S BURYING AMERICAN BUSINESS. IT'S WRITING IT DOWN.

> American business is in the computer age when it comes to collecting and processing information. And, for the most part, in the pencil age when it comes to communicating it.
>
> The time it takes to sort and process the most complex information has been cut from weeks, even years, down to minutes and seconds.
>
> But it can still take a man and a secretary working with pencils and a typewriter the better part of a morning to get ridiculously few pages of normal business communication written and out the door. . . .
>
> Right now it costs $2.49 to get one business letter from one businessman's head to another businessman's hands. [By 1970, the cost of the average letter had risen to $3.15.]
>
> Maybe that doesn't sound like a lot. But if you have 100 people in your office, each writing five letters a day, it sounds frightening.
>
> Because then it's costing you $298,000 a year. [By 1970, $409,500.]
>
> There is so much paperwork to be done today, and so much coming, that it's actually going to reach a point where no matter how much you're willing to increase your salaries, or pay overtime, or pay part time help, you're just not going to get the work out.
>
> We are running out of people to process paper.

The statistics associated with this paper deluge are staggering: more than 82 billion pieces of mail were sent in 1969—51.1 billion of them letters—and Ronald B. Lee, Assistant Postmaster General for Planning and Marketing, projects 166.5 billion pieces of mail by 1991. The House Post Office and Civil Service Committee Report in 1965 put the cost of paper work to the federal government at $8 billion a year, and it is much higher now. The National Stationery and Office Equipment Association estimates that it costs 4 cents to file a business letter, $7\frac{1}{2}$ cents just to maintain it for a year, and $74.15 in clerical time if it is misfiled for a year. One estimate is that American business now stores 1 trillion pieces of paper in filing cabinets and adds 250 million pieces each year. What was probably a unique event in business history was chronicled by the *Wall Street Journal* (May 23, 1968) when it headlined the demise of a brokerage house under the ominous title "Pickard Collapses from Heavy Flow of Paperwork."

Shall we then conclude that business should, as one corporation suggests,

"Call, don't write—not at $3.15 a letter"? The best way of handling our original question "Why put it in writing?" is, first, to consider whether some alternative medium—like the telephone—would better serve the purpose and the reader's or listener's need and, second, to pay attention to the relative costs of the potential media. While there have been tongue-in-check advertisements by manufacturers of dictating equipment and telephone companies warning that IT IS NOW VITAL THAT AMERICAN BUSINESSMEN FORGET HOW TO WRITE, one needs only to recall the stagnation and inactivity of the business community at the time of the March, 1970, postal strike if he doubts the basic necessity for writing in business.

It is realistic to assume that oral communication will probably play a larger role in future business communication than it has in the past, but writing will always be with us. Certainly the telephone is personal, immediate, and two-way, and it provides an opportunity to discuss questions or interpretations as they arise. In many instances, telephoning is less expensive than writing.

On the other hand, a written communication leaves a permanent record to be referred to; that is why, even when oral methods of communication are used, we so often conclude by saying "I wish you'd put that in writing" or "I'd like to see it in black and white." A written business communication gives its writer a chance to consider and to organize his thoughts; it provides the chance to reread and to revise; and it offers a choice of various forms and styles in which the message can be couched. It is foolish to think, therefore, that reports or memos or letters will be replaced as integral parts of the communication process in business, and it is absurd to use the cost of the letter, for instance, as the sole reason for considering it obsolete. Instead, business is making a sensible, cost-conscious attempt to use the kind of communication best suited to the message, the purpose, and the reader or listener. And since written communication is often the most effective method, it also becomes the least expensive way of getting the job done.

Admittedly, the fantastic potential of the varying communications choices is not altogether an unmixed blessing. The fact that we can produce more words on paper more quickly does not provide any assurance that the *quality* of our communication will improve; the danger is that we may become so enamored of the techniques and media of communication that we forget the substance of communication. In a brilliant article in *Saturday Review* (March 12, 1966) the poet Stephen Spender reminds us that the capacity to speak, think, and write clearly should be at the core of all education. In his title Spender supplies us with an apt description of the dangers implicit in communication during the last third of the twentieth century—"The Age of Overwrite and Underthink."

In the rest of this chapter, we will examine the elements and purposes involved in communication. An understanding of these fundamentals is essential for business writers who want to avoid the twin dangers of thinking too little and writing too much.

THE ELEMENTS IN WRITTEN COMMUNICATION

What do we mean by "communication"? We can define it quite simply as *imparting or exchanging thoughts or information*, and since we are dealing with only one form of business communication, we must add *in writing* to pay our respects to the medium of communication. But such a definition really doesn't help very much. We come closer to the fundamentals of written communication by thinking of it as a process which always includes:

1. A writer
2. The material or message—facts, ideas, information, recommendations, conclusions—which he wants to communicate
3. A medium of expression—which for our purposes can be generally described as typewritten words in the form of reports, memos, or letters
4. A reader or, more realistically in the case of reports, group of readers

This analysis may be oversimplified, but it is better than the impersonal tone of our first definition because it puts human beings—a writer and reader(s)—into the process of communicating. "It takes two to speak the truth," said Thoreau; "one to speak and another to hear."

In this two-person relationship let there be no doubt about who bears the responsibility for effective communication. The responsibility rests on you, as the writer. You might as well accept this responsibility right now. It will be forced on you in business. You will have to abandon certain alibis you may have used in the past. You won't be able to blame misunderstandings on "a stupid reader"; you'll have to make every effort to write with such clarity and simplicity that he can understand. You can't say that he is stubborn or pig-headed or narrow-minded because he doesn't agree with you; you'll have to use tact and persuasion and evidence to make him see your point of view. Of course, you may still fail to get your ideas across; it would be unrealistic to think that you can always succeed with your reader. But if you fail, you have at least done so with the knowledge that you did your best—and that is the essence of responsibility in writing, as in anything else.

Fulfilling your responsibility requires that you *think*. Think *before* you write, *when* you write—and then think about how you can improve or revise *after* you have written. Writing which serves your particular purpose requires that you think the purpose through. Clear writing stems from thoughtful planning. Concise writing results from thinking your way through to essentials, eliminating the extraneous and irrelevant. And writing which is correct and appropriate in style reveals that you have thought of how the reader will react and have designed your communication to produce the reactions you want.

We can sum up these observations on thinking, and at the same time state a major theme of this book, by saying that you must have your reader always in mind. You must always be thinking of what *he* wants to learn, what you want *him* to learn, what reactions you want to produce in *him* and what you want to avoid, and how your writing can accomplish this.

The more you can learn about orderly habits of thought and the logical sequence of events and ideas, the better you can organize your material. The more you can learn about psychology and human relations and people, the more you can know about your readers. These habits of thought and a broad knowledge of people are the most useful background you can have for writing in business. They will enable you to avoid the pitfalls of "thought-less" writing and accomplish the particular purposes you have in mind for a communication. You will, of course, have to supplement this background with a knowledge of the techniques of writing which are discussed in this book as they apply to the specific problems of writing letters, reports, memorandums, and other forms of business communication. But whatever the form, the fundamentals remain the same.

When business writers forget the fundamentals of the communication process and ignore the thinking behind it, a phenomenon known to electrical engineers as *noise* or *interference* occurs. In their diagrams of mechanical or electronic communication, the engineers show messages from source to destination like this:

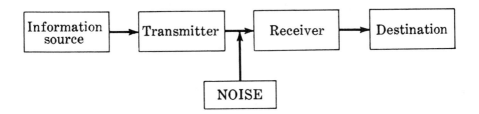

The noise here is static on your radio, "snow" or fading on your television screen—in short, anything which blocks or impedes the transmission of sound or sight. Unfortunately, human beings are probably even more ingenious when it comes to producing noise or interference in their written communications. The noise caused by thoughtlessness—whether in the form of ambiguity, tedious wordiness, inappropriate style, distracting irrelevancies, or any of a number of writing faults—damages the impression you are trying to plant in your reader's mind.

For the most part, good business writing is just good writing. But if your education until now has involved only nonbusiness writing—essays and short stories, for example—you may be disappointed by your first attempts at business writing. We have stressed the importance in business writing of having your purpose clearly in mind, and this, of course, applies to all writing. If you really understand the elements of good writing and are aware of the particular purposes they serve, then you will be successful whether you are writing an essay, short story, magazine article, scholarly article, or a business letter or report. But if what you have learned is how to write a good essay or short story without understanding the techniques involved and knowing *why* they are suitable, then you will have trouble with business writing, just as a person trained to write business communications without understanding the *why* of what he is doing will have trouble with essays and short stories.

Some distinctions between business and literary writing are quite apparent. The reader of a business communication is generally in much more of a hurry than is the reader of a literary work. Conciseness, brevity, and devices such as headings and summary sentences or paragraphs are more important to business than to literary writing. At the same time, the reader of a business communication is rarely looking for entertainment. Witticisms, clever allusions, and paradoxes may add much to the enjoyment of literary writing, but they are more apt to annoy the business reader.

These distinctions are rather obvious. We will explore many less obvious purposes in business writing. The materials in the four chapters of Part One are designed to relate the "how" to the "why" of business writing. Our intention is not to persuade you to write in a certain way because it is *the* way to write in business, but to help you to decide the purposes to be served by what you write and to learn the techniques appropriate to serving them.

One aspect of business writing that you can learn only on the job concerns the particular forms, procedures, and even writing style that have been established by the business organization you work for. Many companies have a single acceptable form for letters, for example. Some companies insist that letters and reports conform to a particular style manual, such as the *New York Times Style Book*. These details should not concern you now. It will be easy to adapt your writing to them if you understand the fundamentals of good business writing and the purposes they serve.

THE PURPOSE OF A WRITTEN COMMUNICATION

If we were to coin a slogan for this chapter, it would be "Think now; write later." Before you can begin to plan the "how" of business writing, you have to understand the "why." Until you have established just what purposes a written communication is to serve—both your own and your readers' purpose—you cannot decide what is the most appropriate form of presentation. The failure of writers to think through their purposes causes more frustration to readers than any other writing fault. Nor is this frustration lessened by the thought-less writer's stereotyped, lame excuse "I thought you wanted something different."

In all fairness, we should add that such misunderstandings frequently arise because readers or executives do not know, or do not express clearly, what they want. One executive, for example, has the irritating custom of sending the letters or memos he receives on to his subordinates with a cryptic penciled notation such as "Noodle something more on this" or "Supply more info by the fifteenth." College students who are baffled by what some of their instructors want in their assignments will understand the bewilderment which ensues. They will also recognize the "solution"—to try to include every possible purpose in a kind of shotgun approach so that they will be protected from the accusation "This isn't what I wanted."

Here are a few examples taken from both business and government of the waste generated by the failure to think about purposes or to define them sharply:

A senior officer in the Federal government complained that all the reports written for him were five or six times as long as he thought they should be, vague, and hard to read. It turned out that the men writing these reports simply did not know exactly what purposes the reports were to serve. Consequently, they tried to serve every possible purpose, writing long and largely irrelevant reports.

A senior partner in a management consulting firm was considering a training program to improve the writing of the firm's engineers. The reports these men were writing to the firm's clients were eliciting a lukewarm response, yet the partner knew his men were highly competent engineers. A little investigation revealed that the engineers were accustomed to writing a routine report describing the work they had done and the recommendations they had come up with. It had never occurred to them that their readers were unlikely to adopt a recommendation that involved changing methods of operating a business unless they were shown clearly and emphatically what they had to gain by change. A client who was not "sold" on the consultant's recommendations rarely adopted them, and the reputation of the consulting firm suffered. The engineers had simply never been aware that one of the purposes of their reports was to "sell" the client on their recommendations.

A production manager was dissatisfied with the reports of an assistant, a recent graduate of a business school. The assistant had been asked to write a series of reports on the advisability of acquiring various kinds of new production equipment. The production manager intended to use these reports to justify to the top management his recommendations that the equipment be purchased. He felt the reports did a poor job of persuasion. It turned out that the assistant was not aware that the manager had already decided to recommend the purchases. He had assumed his reports were to serve as a basis for the manager's decisions; consequently, he had tried to present an objective and balanced analysis of the pros and cons.

In all three of these cases a writer was making an unsatisfactory impression simply because he did not understand the purpose of his writing.

Every written communication should serve its own particular set of purposes. A letter may be designed to sell goods or services, to collect an overdue account, to obtain a job, to build good will by expressing appreciation, or to retain good will while denying a request. The point is that you must know precisely what the purposes are before you begin to write. We are going to discuss in this chapter one purpose that will be served by almost everything you write: demonstrating your business ability.

Demonstrating ability is especially important for a young and inexperienced writer who has not yet earned the confidence and respect of his business organization. It may not seem to you very important to convince others in business that you are able to write well. But your writing conveys more than your ability to write well. It demonstrates your ability to think, to analyze, and to make sound judgments. Most people react unfavorably to a badly written report, but relatively few are able to tell exactly what is wrong with it. If you write an inadequate report, your readers are just as likely to blame you for poor thinking as for poor writing. In fact, there is a very common belief that bad writing *always* results from bad thinking. Ineffective writing, then, can gain you a reputation for illogical thinking and bad judgment. The fact that this conclusion may be unjustified will be small consolation to you.

What you write in business may well go to people with whom you have no other contact. This provides both an opportunity and a risk. Your letters, memorandums, or reports may be passed on by a superior to people further up the line; because of this, you may be able to demonstrate your ability to people who are in a position to affect your promotions and the kind of work assigned to you but who are generally inaccessible to you. Even the routine writing you do for an immediate superior may be handed on to other people without your expecting it. This means that a piece of work hastily or carelessly done, which you did not expect to go beyond the man with whom you are already on pretty good terms, may actually reach some influential people who have no other knowledge of you. The result inevitably is that they form a low opinion of your ability.

It is obvious to a college student that the principal purpose of his written work is to demonstrate his knowledge and ability to an instructor. Yet many people forget this purpose when they start writing reports, letters, or memorandums in business. You cannot afford to forget how important your writing is to your personal success.

If you remember the personal importance of your writing, you will have made a good beginning. You will next have to identify the specific purposes you should be trying to serve in any particular writing situation. For example, you may be attempting to persuade someone to do something, providing information to help someone do or decide something, or trying to build good will for your company. It may surprise you that anyone could have trouble identifying purposes such as these, but recall the examples quoted in this chapter. It is crucial to have the correct set of purposes in mind.

We will deal in some detail with the purposes peculiar to reports in Part Four and with the special purposes of letters in Part Three. This chapter will continue with a discussion of general purposes and principles, so that when we move to specific features of good communication it will be possible to relate these to the purposes of the communication.

Sometimes the purpose of a written communication is very clear, or seems so. A person who has bought an electrical appliance, had trouble with it, and received poor service takes up his pen to give the manufacturer his opinions about the company, its products, and its personnel. If asked for the purpose of his letter, he would probably answer, "I'm going to blast this company." But is this really his purpose? On reflection, he may decide that what he actually wants is a replacement for his defective appliance or, at least, adequate repairs. The satisfaction gained by "blasting" the company is less important than achieving these results.

If the real purpose of the letter is to obtain a replacement, then the manufacturer must be made to feel that a customer has suffered unreasonably, that the company is responsible, and that it would be good business to replace the appliance. Now we are developing a rather specific set of purposes, or perhaps subpurposes, since the principal purpose is still to obtain a replacement. And now we can begin to see what content and attitude the letter requires. It must, for example, be reasonable. It may display annoyance but it must not appear to be the letter of a crank. It should quickly convince the reader that the writer is not exaggerating his troubles, that he is intelligent enough to treat an electrical appliance properly, that he does not expect every appliance to be perfect, and that his complaint is justified. At this point the writer may decide that if he has to go to all this trouble to get a new appliance, he'd rather have the satisfaction of blasting the company. Nevertheless, the choice of purpose should be a conscious one. Don't "blast" the company and then complain that they didn't replace your appliance.

Here are some questions you might ask yourself as you try to identify the purposes of any written communication:

1. Who is going to read this—one person? several? a clerk? a responsible manager?
2. What do I want him to do, or say, or decide?
3. What sort of feeling must I produce in him in order to persuade him to do as I wish?
4. What has the reader asked me to tell him?
5. What does he intend to do with what I tell him?

In any particular situation you can probably think of more questions, questions more specifically related to the letter, report, or whatever it is you have to write. If you can ask the right questions as to purpose and answer them, you will find that deciding on the form of your writing is easier and there will be a much greater probability of your communication accomplishing what you really want it to.

Closely related to the determination of purpose in a communication is the fundamental question of whether the communication should even be in writing. This book deals only with written communication, but behind every written communication lies a decision that writing, in that particular case, is more appropriate than speaking. This is a decision that should rest on the purpose of the communication and, of course, on the policies of the company.

Most of us prefer to talk rather than to write. Writing well is hard work, and a poorly written document may survive as evidence of our deficiencies. But no one expects our conversation to be as well-organized and smooth-flowing as our writing. And no one remembers exactly how we spoke. This can lead to all kinds of rationalization for choosing to speak rather than to write. The usual reason is that a speaker can adapt what he has to say to his listeners' reactions. He can repeat when they are puzzled; he can speed up when they show boredom; he can move to another topic when they fail to respond as he wishes. And, of course, he can get a reaction to a question or a suggestion before he decides what to say next. Some purposes are certainly best served by oral communication. A coach's pep talk in writing would hardly inspire a football team, and most teachers would be out of work if education could be achieved entirely through written instruction. But before you decide that it will be easier to convey your thoughts orally, be sure your purpose is really served by oral communication.

Consider the case of an office manager who is bothered by the fact that too many employees are arriving late for work and that too much time is being spent on coffee breaks. He decides to remind all the employees that they are expected to be at their desks by 9 A.M. and that the morning and afternoon coffee breaks are limited to fifteen minutes. He begins to draft a memorandum to be distributed to the employees or posted on a notice board. He grapples with the problem of how to appear firm and get results while at the same time avoiding the impression that he is treating the employees like children or, perhaps even worse, that he is participating in a sort of game in which he tries to get the employees to work hard and they try to avoid work. After starting two or three times and tearing up each draft, he begins to think it would be much better just to talk to the employees. There are too many to talk to all at once, so he speaks to groups and individuals.

A day or two later all, or almost all, have been told. There is an embarrassing incident when the manager angrily asks an employee arriving at 9:15, "Didn't I remind you just yesterday that we begin work at 9:00?" and the answer is a bewildered, "No." The manager thought he had spoken to everyone, but apparently he had missed a few. One stenographer is about to quit because the manager spoke to her alone and she concluded that she had been singled out as the only employee who came late and took too long for coffee breaks, and this, she feels, was quite unfair. A few employees believe that the office is now opening earlier than it used to, others say the coffee break has been abolished, and still others say that only the afternoon break is to be done away with. Six weeks later the employees have forgotten the whole incident, and the manager is bothered by the fact that too many employees are arriving late for work and that too much time is being spent on coffee breaks.

If the manager had given adequate thought to the purpose of his communication, he might have decided that it was this: to eliminate or greatly reduce tardiness and overlong coffee breaks, to accomplish this for as long a time as possible, and to avoid confusion and resentment. In deciding how to achieve this purpose he would probably, but not necessarily, have chosen a written communication. At least he would have foreseen the dangers in an oral communication and might have taken special care to avoid them.

It is appropriate to say, in conclusion, that we have purposely kept this discussion brief so that students may concentrate on the exercises. They illustrate one fact which does not communicate well in generalities—that it is often *very* difficult to decide on the central purpose of a communication because the choice is affected and limited by a complex of personalities, alternative decisions, and unknown factors. The central purpose of the exercises is to underscore the fact that in selecting a purpose and medium there is often no one right answer.

EXERCISES

1. As a college senior, you have been interviewed and have made a visit to the executive offices and manufacturing plant of Lincoln Enterprises Corporation. They have offered you a position at an attractive salary, but have been quite insistent that they must have your acceptance or rejection of their job offer by April 15. On April 12 you unexpectedly receive an offer at $100 a month more from the Washington Company, with whose college recruiter you once had a casual interview but about which you know nothing substantial. You are naturally interested in the higher salary, but you feel under some obligation to Lincoln Enterprises.

   Assume that it is April 14, after you have been torn by indecision for two days. Which of the following purposes would you try to achieve?
   a. Play for time by trying to get Lincoln Enterprises to let you defer your decision long enough to visit the Washington Company.
   b. Decide that your obligation is to Lincoln Enterprises, and that therefore you will accept their offer but will let them know that you have had a more lucrative offer from the Washington Company.
   c. Reject Lincoln Enterprises and arrange to visit the Washington Company.
   d. Think up any other solution that you consider more desirable than the three listed. Once you have decided on what you want to do, indicate what medium of communication you should use—letter, phone call, telegram, personal interview (Lincoln is close enough for you to get there in one day, but Washington will require longer). Give the reasons for your choice. Then *write* the necessary messages involved in the solution of your choice, or *describe* exactly what you would say to achieve your purpose by way of phone or interview.

2. For some time, large numbers of undergraduates in your business school have felt that the courses they are studying are too theoretical. As one campus spokesman put it, "We want practical studies that are relevant to the jobs we will hold after graduation." The attitude of the Faculty Committee on Curriculum has been that since no one can predict the exact needs of graduates, it is better to teach broad theory, leaving the practical and specific aspects to on-the-job training programs.

   At this point, a survey by Industrial Trainers, Inc., which furnishes training programs for industry, has appeared, showing that a large percentage of middle management wants to have further training courses in practical decision making, how to write reports, everyday human relations, and leadership training. When the survey was shown to the chairman of the curriculum committee, his reaction was, "That's exactly what should be taught in on-the-job courses, and it shows that we are right in stressing broad theory in our program."

   As spokesman for the students, you have as your purpose one of two things—to influence the faculty committee to change to all practical courses or to work out a compromise between the practical and the theoretical. Write out the statement by which you would attempt to convince the five-member faculty committee that (1) a change in curriculum is desirable, and (2) the changes you recommend are the best solution.

3. The Rowan Company comprises a number of small manufacturing plants in rural areas which produce components for assembling in the major plant. One of these small plants, located in Blueville, was acquired just a year ago; its acquisition has produced considerable resentment among the local citizenry, since it had long been a closely held company owned by a prominent Blueville family, which had employed only local people for labor. Because of increased production, the Rowan Company has had to recruit outside labor, and this has added to the resentment between what Blueville citizens call "foreigners" and the natives. Now the manager of the plant, who was brought in from outside, has reported that pilferage of small precision tools has cost the Rowan Company more than $11,000 in six months. The plant manager has asked you to "give him a guideline as to what action to take."

What should be your major purpose in handling this situation?
a. Stop the pilferage regardless of consequences to morale?
b. Try somehow to maintain employee morale? How?
c. Adopt some middle-of-the-road plan which will reduce pilferage without damage to morale? If so, what?

4. You are now to assume that investigation in the Rowan Company pilferage case (Exercise 3) is finished and the findings are complete. (Note that these findings are mutually exclusive, so you must consider each one of them as a *separate* result of the investigation.)
   1. A metal-detecting device that you have rented conclusively proves that four veteran local workers have been responsible for the pilferage.
   2. A detective agency has proved that 20 of the "foreign" help are members of an organized group who steal tools and sell them as a black-market operation.
   3. A group of "foreign" help have conducted their own investigation secretly, have accused three veteran foremen of the thefts, and have sent you a letter making this accusation.
   4. There is no pattern except that a large number of employees have indulged in petty pilfering.

Assume that your two chosen purposes are (a) to prevent future pilferage and (b) to maintain employee morale. How would the results of each "case" above affect your choice? (Give four separate answers.)

Applying the same two purposes to each of the four cases above, what would you consider the most satisfactory method of communication among the following? Why?
a. To say nothing
b. To say nothing, but discharge those who are guilty
c. To send out a memo for posting on all plant bulletin boards announcing what has been discovered
d. To tell the editor of the local paper, which is read by everyone in Blueville, and thus get a news story published next week

e.   To hold small group meetings with all employees to explain and discuss the situation

f.   To instruct all supervisors to have personal interviews with all of their subordinates to inform the employees that any act of pilferage will result in the immediate firing of those responsible

g.   Any other method of communication which you consider appropriate and effective

5.   You have now been working for three years for the Gloucester Management Company as a salesman. During that period you have had to move three times to a new territory, and your wife is disgruntled about what she calls "this rootless existence." Now another position with the identical salary and responsibility has been offered to you by the York Company with the assurance that you can settle permanently where you are now located. You have made up your mind to inform Jack Scofield, sales manager for Gloucester, of the new offer. Decide what purpose you want to achieve in this situation, then decide what medium you will use (phone, letter, interview) to achieve that purpose with Mr. Scofield, whose office is 500 miles away. Write out what you would sent in a written communication, or describe what you would say in a personal interview or a telephone conversation.

6.   Two years ago your company was in serious danger of bankruptcy. The management persuaded some investors to provide badly needed funds and called on all employees to accede to a reduction in pay. When the employees agreed, they were told that the reduction would stay in effect until the company "is out of danger." This year the company is finally earning a small profit, and, although this has not been made public, rumors have begun to spread and many employees are talking confidently of pay raises this year.

Assume you are the assistant to the treasurer. He has told you there will be no pay raises this year and has asked you to write a letter or memorandum to the employees telling them this. His reasons for not granting pay raises are these:

Although the company is finally showing a profit, the current year may turn out not to be profitable.

The company is still heavily in debt, and all available cash must be used to reduce debts in case of more bad times ahead.

The investors who helped the company two years ago expect to see it in sound financial condition before any pay raises are granted. It may take two or three years to reach this state. These investors are in a position to remove the management if their wishes are not carried out.

What purposes must the communication to the employees accomplish? What must it avoid? Write the letter or memorandum for the treasurer's signature.

7.   Assume you are assistant to the president of a small steel company. The company's earnings have shown steady growth for the past several years and dividends on the common shares have been increased, as the following table shows:

	5 years ago	4 years ago	3 years ago	2 years ago	Last year
Annual earnings per share	$1.10	$1.25	$1.34	$1.38	$1.49
Dividends per share	$0.40	$0.40	$0.50	$0.55	$0.55

This year earnings per share will probably be about $1.55, but the company's directors have decided to reduce the dividend to 30 cents.

The directors believe that the next few years will prove difficult for the company. They foresee a great increase in competition and a consequent need to reduce production costs drastically. Cost reduction can come only from modernization of the company's plant, and this will be expensive. The directors expect to borrow a large amount of capital for new plant construction but they feel that the borrowing must be supplemented by greater retention of the company's earnings, which will mean a reduction in dividends.

The treasurer has prepared the following data and future estimates:

	2 years ago	Last year	This year	Next year	Year after next
Expenditure on new plant (in millions)	$32.0	$38.0	$65.0	$75.0	$65.0
Earnings retained (in millions)	$16.6	$18.8	$25.0		
Earnings paid out in dividends (in millions)	$11.0	$11.0	$ 6.0		

The directors hope that earnings will increase during the next few years and that the dividend can be restored to 55 cents or even raised above that figure. They see no prospect of a dividend above 30 cents next year or the year after, however. And they do not want to encourage the shareholders to expect a higher dividend even in the succeeding year or two, because they are apprehensive that increased competition may reduce earnings.

The company's stock is held by about 35,000 shareholders. Some are sophisticated professional investors, and some are widows and orphans with little understanding of corporate finance. The president of the company feels that an explanation to the shareholders should accompany the notice that the dividend for the current year will be only 30 cents.

What purposes should the explanation be designed to accomplish? Write, for the president's signature, a letter to the shareholders announcing and explaining the 30-cent dividend.

8. Assume that you are working for a company with 1,000 employees, all located in the same building, and all of whose customers are easily accessible by telephone. The organization chart divides into five levels, as follows:

President and two vice-presidents
6 division heads

24 department heads

97 section heads

870 unclassified employees reporting directly to section heads

For each of the following, describe what purposes a communication should accomplish and what method of communication is most appropriate:

a. An announcement by the president that the company has initiated an employee stock-purchase plan by which all employees can buy company stock at a 15 percent discount from the market price. No employee may buy, at the discounted price, stock amounting to more than 12 percent of his annual wages.

b. A statement from a section head to the head of the personnel division that three of his unclassified employees are doing unsatisfactory work.

c. A rejection by a department head of a section head's request for raises in pay for two of his unclassified employees.

d. Information from the head of the collection department to the head of the credit department about a change in procedure within the collection department. This change will have some effect on the sales and accounting departments.

e. An announcement that all employees will take their vacations this year during the first two weeks of August so that the plant can be completely shut down for inventory during that period. Studies by similar companies show that this "one-vacation plan" results in greater efficiency because work is not disrupted by sporadic vacations throughout the year. The date is now March 15, and the plan will go into effect this August.

f. An answer by a department head to a customer's complaint letter. The answer will involve considerable checking of records in two other departments before the complaint can be settled.

g. A notice from a department head firing a section head for irresponsible behavior.

h. An announcement by a section head that the 42 employees he supervises will be required to work until 7 P.M. on Friday, July 3, because shipments of orders are behind schedule.

i. A request to a department head from an unclassified employee that he be transferred to another section because he cannot get along with his section head.

j. An announcement of a new plan under which the company will pay for hospital insurance for all employees who have been with the company at least two years. There are 600 such employees.

k. An answer by a section head to a telephone request from the director of the office services division for complete information about the advantages of metered mail.

l. A statement by the head of a department in the personnel division to the head of personnel in another company, answering a request for information about a former employee who is seeking a job at the other company. The employee was fired ostensibly for carelessness, but really because the department head was sure he was stealing although no proof was ever obtained. The employee was never told the real reason.

m. A statement of appreciation from the head of the sales division to the purchasing agent of a new customer who has just placed a large order with the company. This is the agent's first purchase from the company.

9. Colossal Stores, a nationwide chain, has decided to close its downtown store in your city because of falling sales and because it has a highly profitable outlet in nearby Braxton. Facts in this situation are as follows:

    a. The closed outlet has 137 clerks, about 40 of whom can be usefully employed at the Braxton store, 20 miles away.

    b. Records show that when other outlets in the chain have been closed, 60 percent of the clerks transfer to another Colossal store if it is within 25 miles.

    c. Severance pay will be granted at the rate of one week's pay for each year of service.

    d. The executive committee has agreed to offer a comparable position at comparable pay to anyone who wants it, but its chairman has also informed you that "if all 137 clerks take jobs in Braxton, we won't know what to do with them. In fact, we'll have trouble finding places for more than 40 of them."

    You are now to choose (1) the method by which you will inform the 137 clerks of this situation, and (2) the purpose you will aim at. Write down the major points you would use to achieve that purpose.

10. Because of your own education and interest in art, you have been reading with great excitement the magazine and newspaper articles describing the large number of executive offices, banks, and professional buildings which display good art. As one newspaper columnist described it, "Some of the best firms in this area are looking like galleries of contemporary art—and about time, too. Business finally awoke to the fact that not only is good art a good investment, but, more importantly, it means prestige and the look of being alive to today's world."

    Your excitement stems from your own desire for a career as an art dealer to serve this need. Furthermore, you know several established dealers who will let you specialize in the needs of business for a good commission. For contemporary art, you have available the paintings of many of your classmates in art school whose reputations are not yet established but whose paintings show great promise in your judgment. You can operate quite inexpensively from your own small studio, where you can display paintings for sale and make appointments to see executives in their offices. Your main problem is how to make the initial contacts. Shall you use telephone, an advertisement in the local publication of the Chamber of Commerce and Industry, a letter to selected executives, or some other medium?

    Write what you would say in such an advertisement and such a letter. What are the advantages and disadvantages of written communication in such a situation?

CHAPTER 2

CLARITY AND COHERENCE

Clarity is usually assumed to be essential to all forms of communication, but occasionally there may be reasons for being deliberately unclear. Historians still disagree as to Calvin Coolidge's meaning when he uttered his famous words concerning his possible candidacy in 1928: "I do not choose to run." Were his words an outright denial of further presidential aspirations? Was he merely stating a personal preference which would change in the face of urgent demands? When we comment that "the answer is not clear," we are saying that Coolidge's six-monosyllable sentence lacks the quality which we are calling clarity.

Another incident illustrates deliberate and very effective ambiguity. There is a story to the effect that the management of a British steamship company once decided that the officers of its passenger ships should wear swords. This, the management felt, would add to the glamour of a transatlantic crossing and appeal to the passengers. But because the wearing of swords might make company personnel resemble naval officers, the management decided to request permission of the British Admiralty before making the change. The Admiralty was not enthusiastic about the idea and yet did not wish to say no. Finally a reply was drafted, saying that the Admiralty had no objection to the company's proposal provided that the swords were worn "on the right side."

This put the company in a dilemma. Did the letter mean the Admiralty insisted that swords be worn on the *correct* side, which is the left side, or were the company's officers to wear their swords on the *right-hand* side, to distinguish themselves from naval officers? Too embarrassed to ask for clarification, the management dropped the whole idea, and the Admiralty achieved a quiet triumph.

You will rarely run into a situation calling for lack of clarity. But it is important to think of clarity, or any other attribute of writing, as serving some purpose in a particular piece of writing, rather than as an end in itself.

Many elements of writing contribute to clarity, and we shall discuss two of them—correctness and style—in subsequent chapters. But probably the most important aspect of clarity is coherence. Coherence refers to connections between words, sentences, or paragraphs, or between topics or ideas. In a coherent presentation each sentence is connected in some logical way with both the preceding and the following sentences. Each topic or idea appears to follow logically from the preceding topic, and a reader is never led to expect a discussion of one topic only to find that the writer has chosen another.

You should regard every statement you make in a written communication, from the title onward, as involving a sort of contract with your reader in which you undertake to discuss certain topics and ideas. If the title of a report you write is "Company Policy in Hiring College Graduates," then you have promised your reader that this is what you will talk about, this and nothing else. If you deviate from this topic your reader may quite properly be surprised and annoyed. But promises are made in almost every statement you write, not just in titles. If you begin a paragraph with the sentence "We have found several small colleges in the Midwest to be good sources for new employees," then you have led your reader to believe that you will go on to discuss the usefulness, as sources of employees, of small colleges in the Midwest, or at least the usefulness of small colleges generally. If you immediately switch to a discussion of what beginning salaries the company should offer in New York City, the reader is surprised and confused. Your writing is incoherent.

Coherence usually depends on good organization—arranging your topics and ideas in the proper sequence and linking them by logical transitions. This involves giving *structure* to your writing and a logical *sequence* to the development of your ideas. This sequence is especially important in organizing sentences as we shall see in the next section of this chapter. To emphasize the inseparable connection between clarity and structure, you should think of your writing as if you are taking your reader on a journey. The analogy is sound, because a piece of writing is dynamic—it moves; it carries the reader from one place to another. You are, therefore, the means by which he will make the journey; every word you write should be organized in the proper sequence to get him to his destination. Start by telling him what you are going to tell him about; avoid detours and unnecessary bypaths along the way; put your ideas and sentences in the sequence to get your reader to journey's end as expeditiously as possible. Remember, you are the planner, the driver, the mechanic, and the organizer of this expedition in words, and your slogan for the trip is "proper things in proper places."

ORGANIZATION OF A SENTENCE

SCHOOL BOARD BANS SEX BEHIND CLOSED DOORS

You have probably seen statements similar to this newspaper headline. Their humor lies in the location of a modifying phrase—in this case "behind closed doors"—next to a noun it was never intended to modify. A reader tends to link in his mind ideas and words that are located together, so that although a little thought leads to the conclusion that the writer meant to refer to a closed school board meeting, the first impression is of something quite different.

Here's an example of instructions to photographers at an important luncheon showing unfortunate linkage of words:

Do not photograph the speakers while they are addressing the audience; shoot them as they approach the platform.

Even worse is this misleading modifier from a university newspaper, because it says something quite different from what was intended:

SDS also attacked Blank Corporation for its "war profiteering." As the seventh leading defense contractor, SDS claims that last year 20% of its $159 million profit came from military work.

Here is a more complex example:

He is aware that he should uphold the authority to fire workers of his supervisors who disobey orders whenever possible as a management representative.

The sentence begins fairly well but soon degenerates into an incoherent scramble of thoughts. We will try to put the writer's meaning into coherent form. First we'll isolate the satisfactory beginning: "He is aware that he should uphold the authority to fire workers." This is coherent and expresses the main thought of the sentence. *Of his supervisors* is out of place because it appears to refer to *workers* although it seems clear that the writer intended it to refer to *authority*. Otherwise there would be nothing to tell us whose authority he is talking about. So we move *of his supervisors* up to follow *authority*. Now we have:

> He is aware that he should uphold the authority of his supervisors to fire
> workers who disobey orders whenever possible as a management representative.

This is better: *who disobey orders* has now fallen in place after *workers*, the word to which it was evidently intended to refer, instead of seeming to refer to *supervisors*.

But *whenever possible* and *as management representative* still seem wrongly placed. *As a management representative* seems at first glance to refer to *workers* but it can really refer only to *he;* there is no other single person mentioned in the sentence. To make the reference quite clear we could shift this phrase to precede or follow *he.* The expression "He, as a management representative, is aware" is correct but a little awkward, especially as the beginning of a rather long and involved sentence. "As a management representative, he is aware" is better.

We now have to decide what to do with *whenever possible.* There is genuine doubt here as to what the writer meant. Did he really mean to refer to workers who disobey orders whenever possible? Probably not, because this would limit the application of the whole sentence to an insignificant number of situations. There are only three verbs in the sentence to which *whenever possible* could refer. If it doesn't refer to *disobey*, then it can refer only to *should uphold* or to *to fire.* Probably the writer intended it to refer to *should uphold.* On this assumption we rewrite the sentence as follows:

> As a management representative he is aware that he should uphold whenever
> possible the authority of his supervisors to fire workers who disobey orders.

What we have done is to reconstruct the sentence so that the apparent references—apparent because of their location—are the correct ones. The reader is no longer temporarily or even permanently confused by apparent references that the writer never intended.

We shall have more to say about clarity in later sections of this book, since it is probably the most important single quality that business writing can have. For the moment, we can best describe it as a means of getting your ideas across so that they cannot possibly be misunderstood. As an example of unclear writing and consequent misunderstanding, *Training Manual No. 7* of the Federal Security Agency cites the following sentence, which was sent to at least 100,000 inquirers over a seven-year period:

> In order to be fully insured, an individual must have earned $50 or more in
> covered employment for as many quarters of coverage as half the calendar quarters elapsing between 1936 and the quarter in which he reaches age 65 or dies,
> whichever first occurs.

The *Manual* laconically comments that the response of one mystified citizen was "I am no longer in covered employment. I have an outside job now."

Here is a sentence sent out by the clerk of a Board of Education which particularly wanted clear reports of school activities sent to all taxpayers because a new school levy was soon to be voted upon:

> Current topics of interest are reported through films, reading, and discussion in a class made up of the combined student body from Mr. Green's and Mr. Brown's classes not included in choir or industrial arts on the day they meet.

Since it is impossible to detect what this sentence is intended to convey, we cannot correct it. Its lack of clarity and emphasis stems from trailing too many items along in haphazard order, ending with the mysterious phrase *not included*, and misusing the pronoun *they*, whose reference remains an enigma. Beyond grammatical and rhetorical technicalities, what the sentence really proves is that vague and unclear minds produce vague and unclear communications.

Emphasis

An important element of clarity is proper emphasis. This means simply that important ideas should be emphasized, less important ones subordinated. In a paragraph or a report, position may indicate importance. The topic sentence, at the beginning of the paragraph, will introduce the central idea. Or the paragraph may lead up to the important topic, which is given an emphatic position at the end. In a report, the same rule holds true. Central ideas or recommendations should not be buried in the text, but should be given an eye-catching place at the beginning or the end.

The way of achieving proper emphasis on the sentence level is slightly different. The general rule is that the important point should be in the main, or independent, clause. As an example, let us look at the sentence we rewrote in the previous section:

> As a management representative he is aware that he should uphold whenever possible the authority of his supervisors to fire workers who disobey orders.

As this sentence stands, its dominant idea is *he is aware*. If we want the reader to be struck by the importance of *a management representative should uphold the authority of his supervisors*, we will have to remove this thought from its subordinate position. If we consider awareness equally important to our message, we will have to construct our sentence with two independent clauses, separated by a semicolon:

> A management representative should, whenever possible, uphold the authority of his supervisors to fire workers who disobey orders; he is aware of this.

Normally, readers expect the subject of the sentence to be featured, and to be followed by the action (verb) and then the receiver of the action (object). Normally, they do not want to indulge in mental gymnastics to rearrange your sentence or to locate these important parts. (We have to put our own emphasis here on "normally," since variety in sentence structure is desirable so that this reader will not be lulled into boredom by an endless succession of subject-verb-object sentences.) But notice the roundabout wordiness of the following:

> There have been developed by the local branch of the Management Association seven new methods for reducing the amount of papers in company files. (Say: The local Management Association has developed, etc.)

> Three trips are made to the warehouse each day by our truck drivers in order to replace supplies. (Say: Our truck drivers make three trips daily, etc.)

A complete lack of emphasis and an undercutting of the total effect of the sentence occur when we use for the ending some unimportant comment or afterthought. Note how these sentences trail off into nothingness instead of leading up to a clear-cut ending:

> Our new computerized typewriter saves time, eliminates mistakes, and reduces costs, we are sure.

> Tomorrow's business will offer more opportunity for civic responsibility and a greater share in national problems than ever before, I think.

If these sentences let you down with a thump as you read them, you know how readers react when you use an important part of the sentence for trivia.

Parallel Constructions

One of the most useful devices for achieving clarity and emphasis is parallelism—*expressing parallel ideas in parallel form.* Parallelism helps readers by employing both form and substance to establish relationships. We can fall back on one of the techniques of intelligence and vocabulary tests to illustrate the discordance that results when logical relationships are violated:

Which of these words has nothing in common with the rest?

a.   report
b.   memorandum
c.   vice-president
d.   letter

And which of these?

a.   to write
b.   to speak
c.   to listen
d.   a commentator on the radio

In these oversimplified examples, *vice-president* offends the logical mind because it has nothing in common with the other three words: in the second group, *a commentator on the radio* is jarring because its form is not parallel to the three infinitives. This discordant, illogical effect is what you produce in your reader when you connect facts, words, or thoughts which do not belong together (such as "vice-president"); it is equally illogical to use a parallel form to group together thoughts which have no relationship.

When you present two or more ideas and want to emphasize a similarity or a contrast to make them clear, avoid such misleading sentences as these:

Salesmen are expected to travel at least four days a week, to send in daily reports, and must make out weekly expense account vouchers.

All typists are given instruction in handling office equipment and how to serve as receptionists.

It was not only Smith's poor forecasting of market conditions but also he didn't seem to provide adequate production facilities.

Either the executive has the ability to plan or getting things done.

By putting ideas that logically belong together in the same form, you can achieve clarity and emphasis:

Salesmen are expected *to travel* four days a week, *to send* in daily reports, and *to make out* weekly expense-account vouchers. (Since the first two items use infinitives, the third should be an infinitive form.)

All typists are given instruction in *handling* office equipment and in *serving* as receptionists. (*Handling* is a participle; therefore, *how to serve* should be changed to a participial form.)

It was not only Smith's poor *forecasting* of market conditions but also his *providing* of inadequate production facilities. (A participle parallel with a participle.)

The executive has the ability either *to plan* or *to get* things done. (Parallel infinitives)

or

The executive is responsible either for *planning* or for *getting* things done. (Parallel participles)

Notice that when you use connectives like *either . . . or, not only . . . but also*, you are signaling your reader that you are expressing similarities or contrasts and that he can expect parallel forms. In long sentences, you can underscore this parallelism by repeating the key word which leads into the parallel structure:

We must teach our students everything *about* preparing for the interview with the company's representative, *about* actually meeting and greeting the person it sends, and *about* following up the interview with a letter of thanks.

Notice how the parallelism* of the following sentence is doubly emphasized by repetition:

The Widget Electronic Company *offers* years of experience *but* remains at the cutting edge of research, *offers* the most precise quality control *but* always has the most competitive prices, and *offers* the fastest service in the industry *but* never sacrifices quality for speed.

In the final analysis, you should regard parallelism as a means not merely of attaining grammatical consistency but of writing clearly and emphatically. One has only to cite a few of the best-known sentences of our heritage to see how effective and memorable this device can be:

But, in a larger sense, we cannot dedicate, we cannot consecrate, we cannot hallow this ground.

—Abraham Lincoln,
The Gettysburg Address

For thine is the kingdom, and the power, and the glory, for ever.

—*The Lord's Prayer*

---

*You will find more information on parallel constructions in the reference section at the back of this book.

As Caesar loved me, I weep for him;
As he was fortunate, I rejoice at it;
As he was valiant, I honour him;
But as he was ambitious, I slew him.

—William Shakespeare,
Julius Caesar

ORGANIZATION OF PARAGRAPHS

Paragraphs, like sentences, demand carefully arranged sequences of topics and ideas. But paragraph construction makes two demands that rarely concern you in building sentences. A paragraph must be built around a single theme or major topic, and the ideas or minor topics that are discussed in the paragraph must be connected with each other by logical transitions.* A sentence is usually short enough for every part to deal with a single topic or theme, and you rarely find so many ideas in a sentence that it is difficult to connect them up.

Most writing texts will tell you that a paragraph should deal with a *single topic.* This is fine as long as you know what a single topic is. Probably the best test to use is this: Put yourself in your reader's place, read over your paragraph, and decide whether there is a central theme or major topic that runs through the entire paragraph. If there is not *some* such theme or topic, then you do not have a satisfactory paragraph. Either it should be broken into two or more paragraphs or it should be rewritten.

The first sentence of your paragraph should indicate the major topic of that paragraph. You may use a *topic sentence,* one that states the topic explicitly, or you may merely imply in your first sentence what your major topic is. In any case, your reader is going to decide on the basis of this sentence what *he* thinks the major topic is, and he will expect you to stick to that topic. It is this consistency that is called *unity* in a paragraph.

Unity requires that the minor topics of your paragraph—what you have to say about the major topic—all be part of the major topic or be closely related to it. To achieve this unity, once you have selected your minor topics you must establish a logical sequence for them, as in the construction of sentences, and once the sequence is established you must devise transitions to carry the reader's attention from one minor topic to the next in what appears to him a logical way.

We will turn now to some examples illustrating the importance of unity and how to achieve it by the selection of minor topics within a paragraph. At the same time, we will deal with the logical sequence of these topics. Following this will be a discussion of transitions among the topics.

* Transitions between paragraphs are discussed in Chapters 15 and 16.

Unity and Logical Sequence

The following excerpts are from a report written to three young men planning to open a repertory theater. They had very little business experience and turned to a businessman for advice. His report began:

> (1) I think that the idea of forming a repertory theater is excellent. However, you should consider starting the project on a smaller scale.

This seems to be a good beginning. The writer has come directly to the point and offers a specific recommendation. What do you expect will follow these two sentences? Probably a discussion of why or how the theater should be started on a smaller scale. Small-scale operation seems to be the major topic of the paragraph. Here is how the report actually progressed:

> (2) I think that the idea of forming an experimental repertory theater is excellent. However, you should consider starting the project on a smaller scale. The statement of the general manager of a similar venture attributed its failure to inexperienced management.

The third sentence, instead of dealing with small scale, has switched to inexperience. Is there any connection between the first two sentences and the third? Perhaps, but the writer certainly hasn't told us what it is. We are left wondering whether the topic of small-scale operations has been abandoned and why inexperience has been introduced. Now we add the writer's fourth and fifth sentences:

> (3) I think that the idea of forming an experimental repertory theater is excellent. However, you should consider starting the project on a smaller scale. The statement of the general manager of a similar venture attributed its failure to inexperienced management. The man who is to be your business manager has not the experience to operate such a large enterprise as you are planning. Besides, the rest of the group have had little theatrical experience and are not well known.

At last we know why inexperience was brought in. The writer apparently believes this group has the experience necessary to run a small operation (at least he implies this), but not a large one. But we had to read through one distracting and apparently irrelevant sentence to find this out. And even now we are not sure why that third sentence was included. Was it intended to prove that inexperience dooms a large venture but not a small one? It certainly doesn't say so. It simply tells us that the failure of another venture, which may have been large or small, has been attributed to inexperience.

The fifth sentence, too, has added a new topic. The writer says the members of the group are not well known. Is this intended to strengthen the argument for small-scale operations? Probably, but the writer doesn't tell us why. He seems to have dragged in another topic that may or may not be relevant. He certainly doesn't show why it is relevant.

His next two sentences, still in the same paragraph, were the following:

(4) You intend to invest $20,000 to rebuild an old factory building in a city populated by people you regard as "Philistines." As your repertoire will be experimental theater, how can you appeal to this group of people?

What has happened to the theme of small-scale operation? It seems to have been dropped completely when the writer switched to the "Philistines." He gives us no explanation for the switch, and in fact he seems to be arguing against any theatrical venture, large or small. Probably what he intended to say was that a very small part of the city's population would patronize the proposed theater and hence it should be kept small. But he didn't say this.

We might rewrite the entire paragraph as follows, keeping to the theme of optimism but small-scale operation, which is what the writer presumably had in mind.

I think that the idea of forming an experimental repertory theater is excellent. However, you should consider starting the project on a smaller scale. Your business manager does not have the experience necessary to operate the large enterprise you are planning, and the rest of the group is inexperienced as well. Lack of experience has been blamed for the failure of a venture similar to yours. Another reason for small-scale operation is the probability that only a small segment of the city's population will be interested in experimental theater. You yourselves characterize this population as "Philistine."

Notice that we have preserved the theme, or major topic, throughout the paragraph. And we have arranged the sequence of ideas so that each one seems to follow logically from the one before.

All of this may seem picayune to you. A common reaction of a sloppy writer to a reader's complaint is: "But you know what I mean." And in fact we were able to deduce what the writer probably had in mind even when he seemed to be wandering hopelessly. But your job as a writer in business is not to provide guessing games for your reader. Let him know very quickly when you begin a paragraph what that paragraph is about. And then stick to your topic. Make sure not only that each sentence is related to your topic but also that this is obvious to your reader. The writer of the paragraph we have been discussing may have known perfectly well why a "Philistine" population indicated a small theater. But he didn't bother to show us why, and we had to puzzle it out.

At least we were able to puzzle out that paragraph and reconstruct it in coherent form. But can you do the same for the next three paragraphs in the report?

(5) The general idea of your project is to fuse the American and English traditions in a repertory theater. Therefore my suggestion is the following:
We know about a successful repertory theater established seven years ago in your city operating in a tiny building.
As you want to stay in the city, I suggest you rent a small place there.

What do you expect after reading the first of these three paragraphs (5)? Surely a suggestion as to how the three men may accomplish their objective of fusing the American and English theater traditions. But what actually comes next is a statement about another theater operating in a very small building. Is there any logical connection at all? There doesn't seem to be. The writer has apparently returned to the theme of small-scale operations, pointing out that another repertory theater is successfully operating on a small scale, and concluding that this group should rent a small place too.

The first of the three paragraphs in (5) is simply incomprehensible as it stands. The author may have believed it to be relevant, but there is no clue from which we could deduce the relevance. This is writing at its most incoherent. You can probably see why a reader of this report might conclude that the writer just couldn't think clearly.

Transitions

Transitions make a paragraph "hang together." You can think of transitions in two senses, as *logical connections* among ideas or as *mechanical aids* in linking these ideas. Consider the example:

(6) We do not have the experience necessary to operate a large theater; we shall have to be content with a small one.

There is a logical connection between the topics of lack of experience and limitation to only small-scale operations. One is the cause of the other. We can add a mechanical transition—the word *therefore*—to obtain the following:

(7) We do not have the experience necessary to operate a large theater; therefore, we shall have to be content with a small one.

We have in fact discussed logical connections already, as part of the arrangement of topics in a logical sequence. In this section we shall be concerned with mechanical transitions.

Mechanical transitions may be words, phrases, clauses, or whole sentences. Typical transition words are: *and, but, also, therefore, however, since, moreover, first, next, finally*. Transition phrases that are often useful are: *in addition, at the same time, as well*. None of these expressions is new to you, nor is the idea of mechanical transitions. In fact, the subject is important because of the common overuse and misuse of transitions, not because of widespread failure to use them. To begin with, if your sequence of topics is not logical, so that you are placing topics with no logical connection next to one another, no mechanical transition will create a connection that seems reasonable to your reader. And even if there is a logical connection among your topics, you may find yourself using the wrong transitions or using transitions where none are needed.

Consider the following example. It comes from a letter sent to its customers by an investment banking firm:

(8) Net long-term capital gains are taxable at a maximum effective rate of 25% That is, only half of the net long-term gain is added to ordinary income in computing the tax.

Even if you are not familiar with the taxation of long-term capital gains under the Internal Revenue Code, you should be able to see that something is wrong here. If you are familiar with the tax rules, you know that there are two significant aspects to the taxation of long-term capital gains: Only half the gain is added to ordinary income in computing income tax, and the effective rate on the gain is limited to 25 percent. These two aspects are not the same or even interdependent. They are logically related only because together they account for the special way in which long-term capital gains are taxed. The example above uses what we might call a false transition. The writer has used *that is* to provide a mechanical connection between his two topics, implying that the second somehow explains the first. There is no such logical relationship here. Only a conjunction which does not connote dependence—for example, *and, in addition*—can link the two ideas.

It is natural to prefer a transition implying logical connection to one that is simply a conjunction, such as *and*. This is probably why you so often find expressions such as *that is* or *therefore* used to begin a paragraph that has no causal connection with the one that went before.

Transitions can be overdone. If a connection between two topics or ideas is perfectly clear to a reader, the addition of a transition will not contribute to his understanding and will probably slow him down and give an impression of childish writing. Compare the following two paragraphs. Do the transitions added in the second serve any purpose?

(9) A large-scale operation can be successful only if it is well financed and the management is experienced. Your manager is not experienced, and you have little capital. You should limit yourselves to small-scale operation.

A large-scale operation can be successful only if it is well financed and the management is experienced. But your manager is not experienced, and second, you have little capital. Therefore, you should limit yourselves to small-scale operations.

In the following example at least one transition is used in each sentence following the first. (The transitions are italicized.) Which do you think are useful in guiding a reader? Which are unnecessary because they only point out what is obvious? And which are actually false, in that they imply logical connections which do not exist?

(10) I think that the idea of forming a repertory theater is excellent. *However,* you should consider starting the project on a smaller scale. *This is because* your business manager does not have the experience necessary to operate the large enterprise you are planning. *Therefore,* he is qualified to run only a small-scale operation. *Also,* lack of experience has been blamed for the failure of a venture similar to yours. *Another* reason for small-scale operation is the probability that only a small segment of the city's population will be interested in experimental theater. *This is because* you yourselves characterize this population as "Philistine."

However is useful in signaling a qualification to the statement made in the first sentence. Without it the second sentence may seem to contradict the first. *This is because* is probably superfluous, although it is not incorrect. *Therefore,* on the other hand, is probably incorrect. The fact that a man is not experienced enough to operate a large enterprise does not prove that he is qualified to run a small one. He may or may not be.

Also is not false (it does not imply a nonexistent logical relation) but it is temporarily misleading to a reader. He expects *also* to be followed by another reason for small-scale operation, but instead he is told why experience is important.

Another helps to bring the reader's mind back to reasons for small-scale operation after a brief digression to show why experience is important. You cannot avoid occasional digressions, and you may have to provide reminders of your principal topic.

This is because is false. The probability described in the preceding sentence is not caused by anyone's characterization. The writer's guess that certain things are probable is consistent with the readers' characterization, and this consistency may help convince the readers that the writer is correct, but there is no causal relationship involved.

Compare the example with the rewritten paragraph on page 34.

EXERCISES

1. Rewrite the following sentences, using the principle of parallelism to make them more clear:
    a. Receptionists are employed to receive callers, to answer the telephone, and a variety of miscellaneous assignments must be handled by them.
    b. All the salesmen were given training in writing letters, in using the telephone, and how to keep all our various products classified.
    c. We found it useful not only to locate information but also for providing a list of place names.
    d. It was not only the poor planning in the collection department, but they also seemed to have no idea of the way to write a courteous letter to customers.
    e. The officer finally decided to support the research expenditure rather than being the only one opposed.

2. Criticize the following, and make it clearer and more emphatic:

    Three good reasons exist for us to change our policy, I think. There is a lot of study of this program needed, particularly in the area of plant development, in my judgment, so that two of the reasons—namely, increased efficiency and lowered costs—can really be brought about. The study of which I speak should, therefore, focus on these two factors primarily.

    Another reason is that employment conditions in our area have changed. Here again I suggest a long-range study of trends in employment so that we'll know where we're going if one hasn't already been made. Maybe the local Chamber of Commerce could help us out, if they do that kind of thing, as I imagine they do. But in summary, the three reasons seem to add up to the fact that we ought to change and locate the new plant right next to the old one as a kind of addition. This will give us better efficiency, different costs, and better possibility for skilled employees, I am sure.

3. Use paragraphs and any other changes to make the following memorandum clearer and more emphatic:

    This is in response to your inquiry of February 27 inquiring about the possibility of employing young engineers who graduate from college this June. It is worthy of noting that competition for this type of graduate is unprecedented and that visits to three representative engineering colleges accomplished nothing in the way of results. The feeling and reaction of the placement officers in these *three institutions was that it would be necessary for us to institute a training program for employees if our offers of employment were to be made sufficiently attractive. It was further felt that our starting salaries were approximately $15 below the monthly average and that until a new salary policy is considered, efforts by us to contact further institutions of technological learning would be wasted and futile. Several instances were cited of industrial organizations which have been pursuing a policy of offering summer employment to engineering students in the expectation that on graduation this would constitute an inducement for these students to become permanently connected with the enterprise with which they obtain summer employment. In this connection, one organization reported that almost 50 percent of such summer employees joined the company upon graduation, and this would seem to indicate one possibility to be considered by our company. It is a matter of regret, therefore, that this report on the situation seems so unpromising and that because of this, your request for definite recommendations cannot be complied with. If any further information pertaining to this subject is required, do not hesitate to get in touch with me at your convenience.*

4. How would you change the following examples to make them clearer and more coherent?

   a. It is necessary, therefore, that you have the three carbons signed by you or your agent, notarized, and keeping one for your files, return one to us and send the other to the bank which is the transfer agent along with the stock certificate which must be signed by you and sent preferably by registered mail.

   b. This is the report which you requested on May 4. Its subject is "The Need for Coordinated Recruiting of College Graduates." It, therefore, deals with a matter of real importance to the White Company and all supervisory employees. For that reason, it should be read with care and especially because we have spent two months in interviews and assembling data. Last year, for example, we employed 11 recent college graduates against our projected needs, as you know, for 35. This shows the importance of the report and why something should be done about it. That decision is not our prerogative since the authorization for our investigation asked us to institute "a fact-finding survey," as you will recall.

   c. In answer to your request for information to send on to our sales representatives about the development of Marsynex, I would say its chief advantages are its resiliency, its impermeability, and its longevity. While its price is slightly higher than that of competitive products, these advantages more than offset the price factor, a fact which should be obvious to our sales representatives. With increased volume, it is entirely possible that production costs can be reduced, although this is contingent on further developments in the polymerization process. For the time being, therefore, our representatives should stress the many uses of Marsynex in the home.

5. The following are paragraphs from a report entitled "The Future Needs of the Blankville Community Library" and written for the library's board of trustees. What changes would you make in it?

On the basis of our study, we have concluded that the future needs of the Blankville Library are:

    1. An addition to the present building

    2. A larger appropriation for the purchase of books

As you know, the history of our library dates back some 76 years, and if we do say so, it has had a distinguished record of community service. Unfortunately, during the past two years, the circulation of books has dropped off, a fact which we hope will be disregarded and there is the expectation that our two recommendations will change that.

Our definition of "future" is approximately the next ten years—or what is sometimes referred to as the "foreseeable" future, even though it is difficult in such fast-moving times as ours to foresee very much.

The addition to the present building—and incidentally the study for this was made by a local architect and our head librarian—will serve the needs of community children. We studied these for six months and found them inadequate. Trustees have certainly heard comments from local teachers on this, we are certain.

In conclusion, we need a larger appropriation for books if we are to reverse the circulation trend. Users complain frequently that we don't have the books they want and we could get them with more money. For the moment, we think it inappropriate to discuss joining the Tri-County Library System which has a combined total of over 700,000 books. We, therefore, urge the trustees to consider these recommendations carefully and acting upon them promptly.

6.   Rewrite the following to make them clear and emphatic:

   a. The personnel department has never had an adequate staff according to the vice-president which was set up the year the company was founded.

   b. Diversification of products to avoid backruptcy will only enable the company if undertaken right away.

   c. The company must decide whether to replace the equipment by next fall now rendered obsolete by new products discovered this year, immediately.

   d. The sales manager considers both the fixed and variable costs of production and distribution for a new product in setting a price as well as the company's investment in the product usually, but mainly he is guided by his estimate of how much customers are willing to pay.

7.   What changes would you make in the sequence and transitions of the following letter to give it greater clarity?

> Dear Mr. Jones:
>
> We're so sorry. If we had only known about it in time we could have done two or three things. But your letter just didn't get here in time. It should have been here by the 31st of the month, that being the time when the premium expired. Finally, we did not receive your letter until the 3rd of the month following.
>
> If we had received your payment, we could have kept the policy active. As it is, we

might have been able to get a loan or to extend it for 30 days, these being the things we mentioned we might have done above.

Now we can do one other thing—write a new policy, which will cost you a little more but give you the same coverage as the one you let lapse. As a matter of fact, it will cost you $8.43 more monthly, but it's worth it to be covered, we think. Shall we write it? Let us know. You know how sorry we are that the other one lapsed, don't you?

Very truly yours,

CHAPTER 3

WORDS — THEIR USE
AND ABUSE

"There is magic in words properly used," says the excellent *Monthly Letter* of the Royal Bank of Canada, "and to give them this magic is the purpose of discipline of language." The emphasis here is on "discipline," and a younger generation of writers who insist on "telling it like it is" must sooner or later recognize the inescapable fact that accuracy and precision in language stem only from the disciplined knowledge which enables us to put "proper words in proper places with the thoughts in proper order."

The English language is unusually rich in words whose shades of meaning differ only slightly. We thus have at our command an extremely sensitive instrument by which to express the finest distinctions of meaning. Such delicate distinctions, however, make it very easy for the undisciplined writer to mislead and confuse his readers.

Sometimes the poor choice of a word stems simply from the writer's misunderstanding of its meaning. When the author of a current text on financial management wrote, "There are several pragmatic reasons which mitigate against sharply drawn lines of distinction," he confused *mitigate*, which means to reduce the severity of, with *militate*, which means to have force or effect for or against. His mistake is perhaps less embarrassing than that of the consultant who wrote, "This is an important decision and must be approached with levity," under the impression that *levity* meant seriousness, when in fact it means frivolity.

The confusion of one word with another which resembles it in some way is labeled a *malapropism*, a name derived from Mrs. Malaprop, a character in Sheridan's *The Rivals*, who makes such outrageous errors as "an allegory on the banks of the Nile." Her misuse of words has probably never been matched—unless, perhaps, by a contemporary mayor of a large American city, who was reported in the press to have originated such abuses as "Together we must rise to ever higher and higher platitudes" and "I resent the insinuendos."

You can test your own sensitivity to the distinctions of meaning in words which sound alike by making the correct choice in the following sentences:

1. He (appraised, apprised) his department head of the situation.
2. She made an (illusion, allusion) to what had happened the week before.
3. We need a witness who is completely (uninterested, disinterested).
4. After hearing the evidence, we were (incredible, incredulous).
5. Because he was related to the (principal, principle), he was (accepted, excepted) from testifying.

The remedy for confusion about the word which precisely conveys your meaning is to know the meaning of the word before you use it or to look it up in a dictionary. (If you can't conveniently use a dictionary at the time, use another word of whose meaning you are sure.)

The confusion of one word with another which looks or sounds like it can at least be called "an honest mistake"; but increasinly, in our society, the use and abuse of words must be ascribed to other and less forgivable causes. Among these are the following, which we will discuss in the rest of this chapter.

Showing off the latest fashion in words
Using specialized language
Making simple things sound complex
Using jargon

SHOWING OFF THE LATEST FASHION IN WORDS

As everyone knows, our language grows by coinage, by adding new words, and by joining old words in new combinations. "Splashdown," for instance, is a beautifully accurate description of the return of a space vehicle—a word with the ring of the last third of the twentieth century. By contrast, large numbers of parrotlike nonthinkers in our stereotyped society hear a word used by someone else, adopt it as their own "fashionable" expression, and use it to impress their listeners. One could list hundreds of such tired expressions of the past few years, of which these are but a few:

Viable   For the past three years no one could describe a program, an economy, or a trend without calling it "viable."

Charisma   This obscure term, derived from the Greek, suddenly represented the *sine qua non* of every American politician.

Dichotomy   To say "a split," "a division of opinion," is, of course, not as impressive. Since dichotomy is now worn thin, let's try a new fashion—a bifurcation of thought.

Dialogue   This used to be a part of drama, but for three years no two people or groups have been able simply to talk or discuss. They must have a dialogue. It's even more *de rigueur* in socioeconomic-political contexts pertaining to ethnic differences and peer groups.

Expertise   Just to know something, to be expert, is old hat in a world where only a man's expertise can put him in the front ranks of knowledge.

These verbal attempts to identify with the "in" group, to follow the fad of the word-of-the-moment, mark their users as pompous and pretentious—stuffed shirts who think in clichés, which—as someone once remarked—should be "avoided like the plague."

USING SPECIALIZED LANGUAGE

We have an admirably descriptive phrase in English to denote clear, concise communication; we say of a speaker or writer, "He speaks my language." Actually, however, in a highly specialized society, most educated people speak not one language but two—the general language of their society and the specialized one of their business or profession. When metallurgist communicates with metallurgist, for example, physician with physician, educator with educator, specialist with specialist, their expertness finds expression in the finely honed words evolved by their profession.

    Fog descends on cat feet to becloud communication, however, when specialists use technical language to communicate with nontechnical readers or listeners. It is as if two of your friends suddenly shifted into Norwegian in the middle of a conversation with you. Your reaction? "They're showing off; they don't want me to know what they're saying; they're making fun of me." And out of frustration, you want to say what every baffled reader ought to say, "Will you please say that in plain English?"

    When a patient is told he has agrypnia instead of insomnia or cephalalgia instead of a headache, we would suggest therapy not for the patient but for the language. When a parent is told by the educator that his children should take "enrichment courses in a properly structured sequential summer program," he should ask, "Why does he have to go to summer school?" And when the taxpayer or citizen is confronted at income tax time with instructions like these, we should ask for a change *fast*:

> A detailed and contemporaneous recording of an expenditure, supported by sufficient documentary evidence, has a high degree of credibility not present with respect to a statement prepared subsequent to the incurrence of an expenditure where there may be a lack of accurate recall. Thus, the corroborative evidence required to support a noncontemporaneous statement must have a high degree of probative value to elevate such statement and evidence to the level of credibility reflected by a detailed and contemporaneous record supported by sufficient documentary evidence.

This kind of specialized language has even infested the sports world, where for football coaches and voluntary members of Touchdown Clubs it may be appropriate. But the television viewer deserves better for his enjoyment of the game than "a safety blitz pressuring a scrambler who has run out of his pocket waiting for the split end to cross in front of the slotback while they flood a zone." Innocent football fans who simply want to enjoy the game deserve protection (in the form of "red-dogging"?) from such pretentious language.

Stephen Spender, the poet, has some words of wisdom on the subject of specialization:*

> Whether what scientists have to explain to us is communicable, or whether they have to explain that it is incommunicable, the fact is that the present breakdown in communication is due at least partly to the neglect of English. It is slovenly to accept without question the cliché that we cannot communicate because we live in "an age of specialization."

The most sensible procedure in business writing is to estimate the level of your reader's understanding and to write on that level, keeping these two points in mind:

1. If you know your reader is a specialist and speaks your technical language, you can communicate in your common shoptalk to your heart's content. In fact, if you do not, he may feel you are talking down to him and failing to appreciate his understanding.

2. If you are not sure of your reader's familiarity with your special language, stick to simple, everyday English. If you can't avoid technical terms, define or explain them carefully.

*Stephen Spender, "The Age of Overwrite and Underthink," *Saturday Review*, March 12, 1966, p. 22. Copyright © Saturday Review, Inc.

MAKING SIMPLE THINGS SOUND COMPLEX

One of the qualities we associate with profound thinkers is their ability to explain highly complex matters in clear simple language. The opposite is characteristic of the shallow mind, which continually tries to make relatively simple things appear complex by the use of what can only be described as dishonest language. Unfortunately, this fault is often manifested by young employees in business, who think that by using polysyllabic words they will impress their superiors. Similarly, they bulk out their reports and memos under the mistaken belief that long communications convey the impression of intensive work and profound thought.

The fact is that any simple process or idea can be arrayed in language that makes it seem complex and difficult, as the following actual instance shows: A consultant on communication was being escorted through the offices of a company by its vice-president when they came to the room which housed the central files of the company. Turning to a file clerk, the consultant asked, "How long do you keep things in these files?" "Normally we don't keep forms no more than three years," she said. "Then you can either tear them up yourself or give them to the janitor." The visitor turned to the vice-president. "When we get back to your office, let's see how this situation is described in the Procedures Manual," he suggested. Here is what the manual said:

> At the end of the established retention period, which is normally three years, mutilate the forms or carbons to be destroyed by tearing them into small bits or pieces or by shredding them, and dispose of the resulting waste in accordance with the procedures established for the Maintenance Department.

Whoever wrote that statement was attempting to make a relatively simple task sound impressive and complex. The words of the file clerk, despite her bad grammar, are a far more effective explanation, because she tried to express an idea rather than to impress a listener.

What, for instance, does this sentence, taken from an actual report, mean?

> We will make a judgment on this once we have had time to crank in the intangibles.

What it really means is that the writer does not know what he's talking about and is playing for time.

Here's a sentence from a young social scientist to a business man who wanted to know what his company could do to help improve education in the community so that better employees could be attracted by way of good schools for their children:

> Acceptance of the postulate framework and its resultant conceptualized statement diagramming the functioning of the education system within the community leads to an analysis of the system as well as of the potential impacts and implications of the consequence of the process.

At a recent meeting of the American Management Association's annual personnel conference in New York, Alan L. Rudell, a vice-president of Honeywell, Inc., came up with a handy pocket card device called a "buzzword generator." When fed with any three-digit number at random—say 478—the gadget would select from its three columns such weighty phrases as "balanced transitional time-phase" and "functional incremental hardware." Said Mr. Rudell of the latter phrase, "This, of course, has no meaning whatsoever, but you'll find that no one, not even the most knowledgeable technician, will dare challenge the use of such a profound term." Said the reporter describing the meeting, "For collectors of verbal bushwa, the meeting of personnel officers was a goldmine. Indeed, so glittering were its specimens that it was hard to tell Mr. Rudell's parody from the real thing."

USING JARGON

"Jargon" is a derogatory term implying unintelligibility or the use of wordy, worn-out, often meaningless expressions peculiar to those who share the same work or way of life. It encompasses most of the faults we have thus far discussed—and more. Jargon is a form of vagueness, of loose thinking, and it is the worst enemy of clarity and conciseness. Called by various names —gobbledygook, bafflegab, and businessese—it is characterized by vague general words instead of precise, informative ones, and its prevalence in business stems from a thoughtless reaching for words which have always been used or which everyone else uses.

Over the years, strange, meaningless, trite, and pompous expressions have persisted in business writing, although in the past five or ten years there has been a great deal of progress in eliminating business jargon, thanks to the efforts of progressive teachers in our business colleges and universities. Furthermore, businessmen themselves have become conscious of the cost—in both dollars and unintelligibility—of language misused. No longer, therefore, do we find much of the jargon which for so long survived as a hangover of so-called courtesy, in which a letter was called a "favor" (Thanking you for your favor of the 7th inst.), or one "begged to state" or "begged to remain."

Seldom nowadays do we encounter such pompous statements as "The writer thanks you kindly for your favor and the remittance." Such windy techniques persisted too long, however, because untrained writers sat down to write letters with only the incoming correspondence and the hackneyed reports in the files to guide them.

George Orwell, author of *1984*, once compared using jargon to the process of picking up ready-made and worn-out strips of words and gluing them together as an easy way to avoid the thought required for original writing. Here are a few examples of gummed strips of business jargon, with equivalents in simple English:

Met with the approval of the Council of Executives . . .	The Executive Council approved . . .
He was able to reach a decision.	He decided.
The discussion by the committee was on the subject of the underutilization of recreational facilities.	The committee discussed why recreational facilities were used so little.
After a dialogue with the representatives of the sales department, it was decided that a dichotomy of interests would prevent implementing the policy.	After talking with men from the sales department, we found the policy would not work because of different interests.

Instead of using obsolete language, present-day jargon often reflects a desire to avoid the responsibility of making a direct and clear statement. It also reflects the muddy thinking of its users, of course. Consider that overworked word *finalize*, which purists have objected to because it contorts an adjective into a verb. But language grows by such methods, and we should not object on that score. The real objection is that the word doesn't tell us anything which can't be said more clearly by other words—*end, finish, conclude, terminate, stop,* to cite a few. When a businessman writes that he is going to *finalize* an advertisement this afternoon, he may mean that he is going to make a final decision on the content of the advertisement or obtain someone else's final decision, or that he is going to complete the layout of the advertisement, or that he is going to place an order for the running of the advertisement, or that he is going to approve the running of the advertisement or obtain someone else's approval, or probably any one of several other things that will complete some stage in the preparation and running of an advertisement. Instead of finding and using the term that describes precisely what he is going to do, he reaches for a vague word that gives a general idea of the kind of activity that will occupy him for the afternoon.

The indiscriminate use of the suffix *-wise* is an all too obvious instance of the way jargon spreads. To tack *-wise* onto an endless number of words is to substitute mechanics for thought—to telescope a thought which could be better conveyed by well-established words. Hence we have such horrendous combinations as "prestige-wise," "customer-wise," and "sales-wise." When a businessman says "Tax-wise, that would be a good course of action," does he mean that the action will reduce taxes, postpone them, eliminate them, cause a shift from one form of tax to another, or make it easier to pay the tax? Here we see the real objection to jargon—it does not fill any real need other than a sloppy or lazy writer's desire to avoid thinking. As one tongue-in-cheek editor wrote of a hopeless piece of "creative" writing: "Story-wise it is lacking surprise-wise." Or as a newspaper editor reprimanded a correspondent by telegram: WORDWISE "WEATHERWISE" UNWISE.

Similar poverty of language can be illustrated by too many specific examples, of which these are but a few:

make a judgment
vary the mix
hardware, software
a survey in depth
togetherness
implement a decision
the interface of the systems
I'm for it 120 percent
touch all the bases
a can of worms

Students should listen and read with careful attention to make their own lists of these modern equivalents of yesterday's girls who were pretty as pictures, mails slow as molasses in January, things that look like something the cat dragged in, and—to coin a phrase—minds that are dull as dishwater.

Much of jargon is simply showing off by writers who hold the mistaken notion that the longer and more obscure their words are the more impressive they will be.

Here's a clever satire, called "Syllable Happy," by Franklin N. Turner of Shell Oil Company, which appeared in *The Wall Street Journal.**

How often we've been told to write, at college age and less,
In terms as plain as Mr. Lincoln's Gettysburg Address—
Avoiding phrases erudite where simple ones are clearer,
The better to express the thought, not just impress the hearer.

*Reprinted by permission of the author and *The Wall Street Journal.*

Though few dispute this sound advice, inside a corporation
The common touch in writing is a victim of inflation:
The language of the office walks on stilts the long way 'round,
Discarding easy words whenever hard ones can be found.

We find the sub-executive whose eye is on advancement
Proclaiming that the net return reflected some enhancement
(A mouthful meaning neither more nor less than PROFITS ROSE,
And gaining nothing from the gilt of ostentatious prose).

To say ABOUT is frowned upon—APPROXIMATELY's better—
While LATER must be SUBSEQUENTLY in the business letter.
BEFORE is out, since PRIOR TO sounds more sophisticated,
And no one writes EXPECTED who can spell ANTICIPATED.

Disguising CAUSE as CAUSATIVE FACTOR shows one's on the move,
And words like OPTIMUM, for MOST, are really in the groove.
INAUGURATE and FINALIZE are favored, though, in truth,
BEGIN and END are more exact and not at all uncouth.

Sir Winston's famed BLOOD, SWEAT AND TEARS, that sparked the English nation,
Would never have endured with SWEAT dressed up as PERSPIRATION
So here's a plea for plain words that more clearly tell the story
Than polysyllable displays of verbal repertory.

Some well-established words are also used frequently in business writing
to convey only vague, general impressions. *Problem*, for instance, is a favorite
word of those who cannot be bothered to think of the right words to express
their thoughts precisely. Here is an example:

> In trying to increase his company's efficiency, Mr. Withers faces the problems
> of union opposition, what to do with employees no longer needed, not knowing
> how much money is available for modernization, and that after he is all through
> his products may be obsolete.

Problems are something we *solve*. A union's opposition is not a problem; it
is an obstacle, or perhaps a difficulty that we try to *overcome*. What to do
with superfluous employees is a question, something that must be *answered*.
Not knowing how much money is available is probably an obstacle or difficulty, and that the products may be obsolete is a risk that Mr. Withers must
run. The following version is much more precise in thought and language:

> In trying to increase his company's efficiency, Mr. Withers faces the obstacle
> of union opposition and the difficulty of not knowing how much money is avail-

able for modernization; he must answer the question of what to do with employees no longer needed; and he runs the risk that after he is all through his products may be obsolete.

Phase is another word that is often used as a sort of fill-in when a writer can't think of the right word to express his meaning:

All phases of the company are currently moving to a position of optimum efficiency, productivity, and organization.

A phase is an aspect of something whose appearance changes. A company can go through phases as its characteristics change. But here, presumably, what the writer had in mind were not different stages through which the company was moving but different parts of the company, perhaps divisions or departments. Exactly what he had in mind we don't know.

The word *area*, commonly used to describe a body of knowledge or a specialty, can be confusing when it is used in conjunction with a concept of space:

In the area of plant location there is still need for planning.

"The area of plant location" suggests a physical area reserved for the location of a plant, but the rest of the sentence indicates that this is not the kind of area that the writer had in mind. He is referring to the topic or job of plant location.

These examples indicate the need to examine your writing constantly to see if you are taking refuge in vague, fuzzy expressions when you should be selecting precise words to tell your reader exactly what you mean. It is very easy to slip into trite generalities, but a reader who is looking for useful analysis or information will soon realize that he is not finding it. Like Hamlet's answer to the question "What do you read, my lord?", the result is "words, words, words" but not meaning.

For the writer who wishes to inform rather than to impress, who wants to use precise tools of thought rather than worn-out blunted and overworked instruments, who feels responsible for his reader's understanding, the best words on words are these four principles from H. W. Fowler's *The King's English:*

Prefer the familiar word to the far-fetched.
Prefer the concrete word to the abstract.
Prefer the single word to the circumlocution.
Prefer the short word to the long.

The choice of words is a large topic and an important one. But beyond giving the advice contained in this chapter, it is difficult to provide useful guidance without discussing a great many individual words and writing an entire book on the subject. Fortunately, several writers have done just that; a number of their books are listed in the bibliography in Chapter 22.

TRITE AND OUTWORN EXPRESSIONS TO AVOID

The following is a list of the more common expressions found in business jargon. Beginning students should consider them as warnings of bad habits that writers may fall into; experienced writers may use them as a yardstick against which they can measure the effectiveness of their work.

Acknowledge receipt of   as in "We wish to acknowledge receipt of your letter." Forget it; say "Thank you for your letter."

Advise   as in "In answer to your letter of August 7, we wish to advise that shipment has been made." "Advise" is a perfectly good word, but it means "to give advice"; in general, it should be replaced by "inform" when information is being conveyed.

Allow me to   as in "Allow me to express our appreciation for." A pompous method of saying "Thank you for."

Along these lines   as in "We are carrying on research along these lines." A meaningless phrase. Make it specific.

As per   as in "As per our records," "As per your report," etc. Another barbarous mixture; say "According to."

Attached please find   No hunting is necessary if your check or order is attached. Say "We are attaching" or "We enclose our check" and let it go at that.

At an early date, at the earliest possible moment   Say "soon" and save yourself some words.

At hand   as in "I have your letter of May 9 at hand." Omit it entirely since "at hand" adds nothing. "Thank you for your letter of May 9" or better "Your letter of May 9 . . ."

At the present writing, at this time   Overworked and roundabout jargon for "now."

At your earliest convenience   Say "soon" and save yourself some words.

Awaiting your favor   This might make a song title, but you probably mean "We hope to hear from you soon" or "Please let us hear from you."

Beg   as in "Beg to inform," "Beg to acknowledge," "Beg to state," "Beg to remain," etc. Omit "beg" entirely. Go ahead and inform, acknowledge, state, or remain; it is absurd for perfectly solvent firms to go around begging in their business letters.

Dictated but not read   Of all the insulting notations on letters, this is the worst. Readers who receive them should immediately write back "Received but not read."

Enclosed please find as in "Enclosed please find our check for $25." He won't have to hunt for your check if it *is* enclosed; simply say "We enclose" or "We are enclosing."

For your information Tactless. Everything in the report or letter is for his information. Omit it.

Hand you as in "We herewith hand you our check for $37.10." A meaningless and outworn expression—and what long arms you have, Grandma! Say "We enclose our check for $37.10."

I have your letter, I have received your report A thoughtless warm-up for starting letters or memos. Since you are answering, he knows you have the letter. Say "Thank you for your report" or "We appreciate your letter of February 15."

In receipt of as in "We are in receipt of your check." Say "We have received your check" or "Thank you for your check."

In (or to or for) the amount of as in "We enclose our check in the amount of $33.16." Simply say "for" as in "We enclose our check for $33.16."

In the near future Be specific, or save words with "soon."

Permit me to say Go on and say it; no permission is needed.

Replying to yours of December 12 a sure way of showing your reader that you want to avoid thinking. Omit it and refer to the date of his letter indirectly.

Thanking you in advance as in "Thanking you in advance for any information you may send." Poor psychology because it antagonizes the reader by too obviously assuming that he is going to do what you want him to. Say "We shall be grateful for any information you may care to send."

Thank you kindly An absurd statement. Why are you being kind in thanking him? Just say "Thank you."

The writer as in "The writer believes" or "It is the opinion of the writer." An obvious and pompous attempt to give the impression of modesty by avoiding the use of "I" or "we." Don't be afraid to use "I believe" or "We think."

This letter is for the purpose of requesting Why all this preliminary? Go ahead and ask. When you write effective letters, their purpose is clear.

This will acknowledge receipt of your letter Another wasted warm-up.

Under separate cover as in "We are sending under separate cover." This should be used very sparingly; wherever possible be specific. "We are sending by parcel post" (or express or air mail).

The undersigned See comments on "the writer." Say "I."

Up to this writing Say "Up to now."

We regret to inform you that we are in error Wordy and hackneyed. Say "We are sorry for our mistake."

You claim, you state, you say Avoid these wherever possible because they antagonize the reader by implying that his statement is not true. Recast the sentence to eliminate them.

Yours as in "Yours of recent date." Say "Your letter" or "Your order."

These are the specters that haunt business communication. But the jargoneer has other devices to assure pompousness. Above all else, he enjoys using several words where one or two are necessary, and he likes to say the same thing twice by using what are known as *doublets*. Just as he prefers *in the amount of* to *for*, he selects the following wordy expressions in the left-hand column rather than those in the right, which efffective writers use.

Answer in the affirmative	say *yes*
At a later date	*later*
At the present time	*now*
Despite the fact that	*though, although*
Due to the fact that	*since, because*
For the purpose of	*to, for*
For the reason that	*since, because*
In accordance with your request	*as you requested*
In addition	*also*
Inasmuch as	*since*
In order that	*so*
In order to	*to*
In the event that	*if*
In the nature of	*like*
In the neighborhood of	*about*
In the normal course of our procedure	*normally*
In the very near future	*soon*
In this connection	omit
In this day and age	*today*
In view of the fact that	*since, because*
Of the order of magnitude of	*about*
On the grounds that	*because*
On the occasion of	*when, on*
Prior to	*before*
Pursuant to our agreement	*as we agreed*
Subsequent to	*after*
The reason is due to	*because*
Under date of	*on*
We are not in a position to	*we cannot*
Will you be kind enough to	*please*
With a view to	*to*
Without further delay	*now, immediately*
With reference to	*about*
With regard to	*about*
With respect to	*about*
With the result that	*so that*

Equally dear to the hearts of jargoneers are redundant phrases. Here are a few examples.

Absolutely complete	*complete*
Agreeable and satisfactory	just one
Anxious and eager	one or the other
Basic fundamentals	*fundamentals*, being basic, will suffice
Consensus of opinion	*consensus* can't be anything but opinion; say just *consensus*
Courteous and polite	one or the other, not both
Each and every one of us	*each of us, every one of us, all of us*
Exactly identical	*identical*
First and foremost	either one, not both
Full and complete	just one
Hope and trust	*hope*
If and when	either one
Insist and demand	choose one
My personal opinion	*my opinion;* it can't be anything but personal
Right and proper	don't say the same thing twice
Sincere and earnest	select one
Thought and consideration	only one
True facts	since facts are true, omit the adjective
Unique—as "the most unique," "very unique," etc.	*unique* cannot be qualified; it means one of a kind, without equal

EXERCISES

1. In a thoughtful article called "A Rationale for the Use of Common Business-Letter Expressions" (*The Journal of Business Communication*, October, 1966), Professor J. Harold Janis of New York University presents a different point of view from that suggested in the previous chapter and one which is worth considering. His aim is "to provide a rational basis for the use of stock words and phrases in business letters. This aim follows the hypothesis that such expressions can, under controlled conditions, serve the needs of business and at the same time avoid criticism on stylistic grounds."

   While it is perhaps unfair to lift Professor Janis's comments out of context, here are some of his more important reasons for using "common business-letter expressions" which he abbreviates as CBE's and which we have labeled "cliches," "jargon," "stereotyped," and "gobbledygook" in the previous chapter.

   Among what he calls "the organizational factors favoring the use of CBE's," Professor Janis lists the following:

   1. Letter writing in business is highly repetitive. The same kinds of situations occur again and again, providing the writers with ample precedent for both the substance and phrasing of the letters. If this were not so—if each situation were unique or had to be treated as if it were—business correspondence on a large scale would take a disproportionate amount of the organization's energies.

2. CBE's increase efficiency by providing ready clues to rhetorical patterns and consequently reducing the uncertainties of expression. For example, given the initial phrase with reference to your letter of, *the writer is easily able to begin not just one letter, but a great many. When the writer is required to begin the letter in less redundant (less predictable) fashion, e.g.,* We don't know how we mislaid your order, *he is left completely to his own devices and, furthermore, cannot rely on such phrasing to provide any assistance in composing other letters.*

3. CBE's help to reduce the uncertainties of response. From the point of view of the writer's superior, any new language treatment increases the risk of message failure, including misunderstanding and legal liability. He is therefore inclined to reject originality in favor of phrasing proved by experience. Conformity is thus enforced by the threat of non-acceptance.

4. CBE's permit the correspondent to be impersonal in the many instances when he does not have any personal involvement in his subject or considers it desirable to avoid personal responsibility. In many instances the correspondent has had only a small part in the transaction about which he is writing, or he may be writing for some other person's signature. The tradition of the particular company or department for which the writer works may also encourage his self-effacement. The use of CBE's like receipt is acknowledged, the undersigned, *and* our records indicate *becomes more understandable in the light of this explanation.*

Insofar as stylistic considerations are concerned, Professor Janis says, "The test of a cliché, then, is not that it is common, but that it is both common and unsuitable for its context."

Later he comments, "Much of the prejudice against CBE's is really a prejudice against the use of official or formal language in situations that would be more appropriately handled by informal language. This is legitimate criticism. The following letter, for example, is needlessly stilted, as the writer himself seems to sense in the postscript:

> Gentlemen:
>
> We are carrying you on our mailing list as follows: . . . Will you please return this notice with any corrections shown thereon which should be made. If the above information is correct, we would appreciate advice from you to that effect so that our records will be complete.
>
> Yours truly,
>
> P. S. In other words, we would appreciate having your correct mailing address.

After saying, among other things, that "any excesses in the use of CBE's are bad style" and "some CBE's are hard to justify in any circumstances" (examples are *and oblige, we remain, per,* and *favor* for *letter*), Professor Janis concludes:

In summary, (1) use of the common business expressions (CBE's) most often as-sociated with routine business letters is a normal consequence of the business culture, (2) such use is not inconsistent with the need for effectiveness, (3) CBE's are not necessarily clichés and may therefore be exempt from criticism on esthetic grounds, and (4) the criterion of good usage in a CBE is its appropriateness to the business situation and to the formality of the context.

On the basis of Professor Janis's article and the chapter you have just read, answer the following questions:

a. Does the repetitiveness of business situations justify the repeating of certain words and phrases?

b. Is CBE itself a cliché? Or is it a more neutral word than such other forms as "busi-ness argon" or "stereotyped expressions"?

c. What are the main points of disagreement toward clichés as presented in this book and in Professor Janis's article?

d. Do you agree that lack of personal involvement on the part of the letter writer en-courages and justifies an impersonal form of writing?

e. Is the fact that CBE's are familiar to readers a good reason for using them?

f. How would you go about justifying the use of some CBE's and not others? Or should all such clichés be avoided?

g. While Professor Janis is discussing only letter writing, would you be willing to ar-gue that his convictions apply with equal force to other forms of written business communication? To conversation? To public speaking?

h. Do you object to clichés or CBE's because they are, as Professor Janis says, official or formal language used where informal language is more appropriate? Or because they are overworked and monotonous? Or because there is a better way of express-ing what they say? Or for what other reason?

i. Why do you think the writer of the letter about the mailing list added the post-script? Is it an effective letter?

j. Do you agree with Professor Janis's second conclusion that use of CBE's "is not in-consistent with the need for effectiveness"?

2. Which word ought to be changed in the following sentences:

a. She certainly evaded the truth, and in some of her statements she was disingenious.

b. We hardly believe that such evasions will rebound to her credit.

c. The difficulty was that she kept defending her attitude with what could only be called spacious reasoning.

d. When customers started writing in, we learned that she had been very depilatory in answering their correspondence.

e. The assumption that she worked only for money was a gratuity.

3. Do you object to the phraseology of any of the following sentences? Why? Because it is overworked and tired, or because it does not communicate? How would you change those sentences to which you object?

a. We'll make a judgment on that after we've arrived at a consensus, and then we can finalize the agenda.

b. The underutilization of material forced us to reorient our thinking production-wise.

c. This major breakthrough constitutes a giant step forward toward a more viable research posture.

d. Man, we had a blast. It was a real fun party, and we had a ball until some guys, strictly from Squaresville, made us douse the lights.

e. Let's face it now and get with it. We're being bugged by production problems. So we'd better touch all the bases with our department heads and see what we can do to change our posture costwise.

f. It is unquestionably the case that in most communications of whatever sort, regarding any and all topical material involving wordage, the redundancy and overexpression employed in verbal usage could, by effort particularly on the part of those engaged in such communication, whether written or verbal, be effectively reduced to a degree which would, as a consequence, add immeasurably to the understandability and clarity of the aforementioned subject in question.

g. Wordwise, this writer is strictly from Phoneysville; he authored a book with that three-sided liaison bit and all that ball of wax. He should reorient his thinking, get more tie-in plotwise, and more carry-over by some in-depth research for his next book.

h. What is needed is more innovational research planning, new pilot projects with an aggressive thrust—in short, some new dimensions in the educational awareness experience. Top priority must be given to help those climbing the socioeconomic ladder and to fixing the parameters of the problem.

i. Today's "breakthrough," is tomorrow's commonplace and the next day's cliché.

j. Let's put this in the proper frame of reference context-wise and then make a judgment about what guidelines to postulate for charting new facilities.

4. Rewrite the following sentences to eliminate jargon and to make them direct and forceful:

a. We are in receipt of yours of the 19th, and in reply we regret exceedingly our mistake in sending you a collection letter for a bill which you had already paid.

b. Your letter of 7-11-70 addressed to the undersigned was received and in due course was referred to our shipping department. You will hear from them in the near future relative to the reasons for the delay in the shipment of the merchandise you ordered.

c. Due to the fact that our shipping department has been undergoing a reorganization, it is my personal opinion that your request has been delayed until sometime in the near future.

d. In the event that this does not meet your approval, please notify the writer as to your wishes.

e. In order to obtain absolutely complete information which will be agreeable and satisfactory to you, it is the consensus of our staff's opinion that we should conduct a survey and notify you of the results.

5.   Make a list of the words or phrases or expressions which grate on your ears because they are overworked or attempting to impress. Then translate them into simple, concise, meaningful English. Here are a few examples to guide you:

	Translation
Our recent centralization and streamlining of organization will indubitably provide us advantages in the market. (From a company's annual report.)	We got rid of a lot of dead wood and now can sell at competitive prices.
George's social adjustment hasn't been quite what we had hoped. (A teacher's report to a parent.)	All the children dislike George.
Early retirement is a significant factor in one's physical development, pecuniary success, and intellectual attainment.	Early to bed and . . .

6.   Your boss, James Forthwright, who is a direct, down-to-earth personality with a drive to "get something done," has called you into his office to discuss the work of George Flowers, a young man with a master's degree in sociology. Flowers has been employed to advise your company on problems of urban renewal and, particularly, the upgrading of the neighborhood in which your major manufacturing plant is located.

"I don't know what he's talking about. And when he writes me a report, I don't know what he's saying," Forthwright tells you, as he reaches for one of Flowers's reports. "Now just listen to this:

> *The danger of scapegoating must be avoided by an insightful view of the commonalities in the ethnicity of our area.*

"Look at these words: 'ego-integrative action orientation'; 'universalistic-specific achievement patterns'; and 'gratification-deprivation balance;' The fact is, I don't know whether I'm stupid, whether he's just using a lot of high falutin words to impress men, or what.

"He came in yesterday to give me another report, and after a lot of conversation I finally told him I just didn't know what he was talking about. Now, you tell me what to do because we've got to get our phase of urban renewal started—and soon."

As you have been taught to do, you list all of the alternatives and possibilities in this impasse between Forthwright and Flowers:

1.   Forthwright is actually stupid.
2.   Flowers is just trying to impress him.
3.   Flowers doesn't really know what he is talking about and tries to cover it up with pompous language.
4.   Flowers learned these terms in graduate school, and this language offers him a precise medium in which to express his thoughts.

5. Such people have some kind of psychological problems and motivations which lead them to use language that makes other people feel inadequate.
6. If people can't say what they mean simply and clearly, they just don't know the subject they are trying to talk about.
7. Other explanations?

Choose one or more of these alternatives and write a memo to Mr. Forthwright which will be helpful to him.

CHAPTER 4

STYLED TO THE READER'S TASTE

We have discussed in the last three chapters the importance of thinking through the purpose of everything you write, and we have gone through the elements of clarity and correctness. Once you know what you are doing, once your writing is clear and correct, isn't this adequate? For many purposes, it may be. But if your aim is to persuade your reader to your point of view, to make him act, to impress him with your knowledge or your reasoning powers or the effort you have put into your work, you must first capture his attention. The quality in writing which compels attention we call *style*.

Written communication must be a two-way street. It does not do you much good to write if no one is going to read. One subject on which we need a great deal more research is how writing is read. Normally, as in this book, emphasis is placed on how good writing is written; yet the real test of its quality is how it is read. Does the message get across to the reader in the way the writer intended?

Young business writers need to be reminded that many times their readers will misunderstand them. The reasons? Conventionally—and generally quite properly—we blame such failures on incompetent writers. Nonetheless, it is perfectly true that what sometimes appears to be a clear message ends up in the reader's mind as something different from what the writer meant. *What has the reader done to it?* We need to know not only a lot more about how to get readers to understand our writing but also *why* they misunderstand. It is interesting to note that about ninety out of a hundred of our aphorisms, maxims, and precepts on the subject of communication deal with what the writer does or should do; those that are concerned with reading tend to be in the nature of tributes to reading as a means of education, like Bacon's "Reading maketh a full man. . . ." Apparently the weight of the past is on the side of making writers responsible for misunderstanding; nevertheless, since we want you to think, to question, and to find out about all the basic principles of communication, here are a few of these oft-repeated precepts for class discussion or for your own consideration:

Attention has a narrow mouth; we must pour into it what we say very carefully, and as it were, drop by drop.

—Joubert

If you want me to weep, you must grieve.

—Horace

Slow beginnings put readers to sleep.

—A textbook on writing

Words are like leaves; and where they most abound
Much fruit of sense beneath is rarely found.

—Pope

When you don't know what you mean, use big words—that often fools little people.

—Facetious comment by a speech teacher

A conversation is always going on inside your reader's head—about himself.

—Advice by a communications consultant

A picture is worth a thousand words.

—Old Chinese proverb

Write the way you talk and your reader will understand.

—Advice in a letter-writing manual

Learn to write for the reader who knows less about the subject than the author, but who doesn't want to know all.

—S. I. Hayakawa

It would be misleading to overemphasize the concept that readers seem always to be armed with the writer's two worst enemies—lack of interest and an infinite capacity to misunderstand; as a matter of fact, in business writing it is fair to assume that what you have written *will* be read, or, at least, that someone will *begin* to read it. Most of your writing will concern things your reader wants to know about.

While business writers can generally assume that a ready-made interest exists, however, they must also remember this: When we ask a reader to pay too dearly for what he is getting, we not only lose his interest but we also squander his principal, the time he invests. Exorbitant demands by writers result in skimming, skipping, and frustration and reflect anything but credit on the writer.

An effective writer learns to capitalize on the reader's initial interest and to hold it throughout his communication. To do this, the writer must understand his reader. The degree of understanding will, of course, vary in different situations. If you are writing reports and memorandums for the same people frequently, you will come to know a good deal about your readers, and you will have the added advantage of feedback—their comments on how well you are doing.

Such personal contact occurs less frequently when you write business letters. Often you will know very little about your reader, and you may never receive a reaction to your letter. But lack of familiarity with your reader is no excuse for ignoring him when you write. In fact, it is additional reason for thinking through carefully what a reader probably is looking for in your writing and what the probable effect of what you have written will be on most readers.

Understanding your reader does not require any elaborate feats of psychology. It is a good idea to steer clear of such theories as the one which holds that American people have an average mental age of twelve years. Except in special situations, such as when you are trying to decide whether to use technical language, it is safest to assume that your reader thinks somewhat as you do: that his understanding is about the same, that he appreciates clarity and conciseness much as you do, and that he objects to condescension as much as you would.

You may miss your mark occasionally. When you do, remember that the reaction of readers can at times be totally unexpected. The collection agent for a furniture store learned this when he sent the following letter to a delinquent debtor:

Dear Mr. Smith:

What would your neighbors think if we have to send our truck out to your house to repossess that furniture on which you have not met your last three payments?

Sincerely yours,

The Acme Furniture Co.

A week later he received this answer:

> Dear Sir:
> I have discussed the matter you wrote me about with all of my neighbors and every one
> of them thinks it would be a mean, low-down trick.
> > Yours truly,
> > John Smith

In a previous chapter on "Words—Their Use and Abuse" we discussed some of the reasons why such misunderstandings arise: inappropriate use of highly technical language, attempts to impress, and overindulgence in jargon. The following 10 specific principles have a common goal of styling your writing to your reader's taste and, more importantly, to his understanding:

1. Be concise.
2. Watch your pace.
3. Keep your sentences short.
4. Put your qualifying ideas in separate sentences.
5. Use paragraphs to break your text into readable units.
6. Avoid too much use of the passive voice.
7. Use action verbs.
8. Be direct.
9. Keep your tone appropriate.
10. Be specific.

BE CONCISE

Good writing, says an old adage, is the art of speaking volumes without writing them. In business writing, you should write not only so your reader will understand, but also so he will understand as quickly and easily as possible. Don't tax his attention with a sentence such as this:

> During the past two weeks, we have been wondering if you have as yet found yourself in a position to give us an indication of whether you have been able to come to a decision on our offer.

This statement uses too many words to say: "Have you decided on our offer?"

Being concise is not the same as being brief. A 37-page report can be concise, and many a one-page letter lacks conciseness. A concise piece of writing is efficient; it conveys all that the writer wishes to say and all that his reader needs to know in the shortest, most direct way. The difference between being too brief and being concise is well illustrated by the wire a nosy and overly aggressive columnist sent to ascertain a star's age:

HOW OLD CARY GRANT?

Back came the reply:

OLD CARY GRANT FINE. HOW YOU?

Here is a sentence from a letter written in response to an inquiry as to when a very expensive piece of equipment could be delivered:

> As you probably know, we just recently received approval of drawings to permit our proceeding with engineering details on this installation, and as you can understand it is difficult at this early date to determine a more definite delivery schedule than our originally quoted promise.

This obese statement is a compound of evasion, padding, and nonthinking. What it says is:

> The drawings have been approved, and we can now start the actual engineering. But right now we can't give you a more specific delivery date than the one we originally quoted.

Lack of conciseness creates boredom and inattention along with the same feeling of frustration that a bright student in a group of slow learners endures. Here's a supposedly humorous satire on the way business procedures are written with step-by-step instructions; but notice, as you read it, that it stops being funny and irritates you to the point of saying "Why doesn't he get on with it?"

> Consider my procedure in putting on my shoes in the morning.
> First I have to sit down, then select the right shoe for the right foot, adjust my socks so there are no wrinkles, bend down and pick up the shoe, insert my foot in it, put my foot on the floor, wiggle my toes to be sure that I am comfortable, bend down and lace the shoe, frequently having to straighten the lace, and invariably going through the motion of making a knot first, then a bow, then getting up.
> And now I proceed to the left foot. . . .

Irrelevancy is a major enemy of conciseness. A writer almost always tends to go on at great length about the things that interest him. And most of us are vain enough to wish to display our knowledge of the subject we are discussing. The result may be that much of what is written appears quite irrelevant to the reader, whose needs do not necessarily fit the writer's interests and who has no desire to wade through a display of proficiency.

Here is a portion of an auditor's report to a comptroller on incorrect procedures he discovered in a company's payroll department:

> I have discovered what is, in effect, a mishandling of funds. Employees are permitted to authorize payroll deductions for savings bonds, in accordance with a decision reached during the Korean conflict, when the Board of Directors decided to encourage bond purchases as a patriotic gesture. At the end of that crisis no change was made in the policy, probably because many employees were purchasing bonds and the company likes to see them building security for emergencies and their old age. The deductions are posted to savings bond accounts and, when an employee's account is large enough, a bond is purchased for him. Some employees have discovered that the payroll is actually made up quite early in the month and that the savings bond deductions are posted at this time to the employees' savings bond accounts. It has always been company policy to permit an employee to withdraw from his account any savings bond deductions that have not yet actually been used to buy bonds. This policy was established at the insistence of the Treasurer, who has been with the company for twenty-three years and has worked in every one of our plants. He felt the money in the accounts was still the employees' and that they should be able to do as they like with it. The employees referred to above, who have learned of the posting procedure, withdraw amounts from their savings bond accounts as soon as the postings are made, long before payday. Thus they obtain, in effect, an advance salary payment.

It seems unlikely that the comptroller needed to know the history of the payroll deduction plan or the details of the treasurer's past life. What he did need to know was: (1) that employees were allowed to authorize payroll deductions for bond purchases, (2) that the deductions were posted to individual accounts well before payday, (3) that withdrawals were permitted as soon as postings had been made, and (4) that some employees were making these withdrawals and in effect receiving advance payments of salary. The preceding 50 words convey all that is relevant to the comptroller's needs, out of the 255-word statement. You may feel that the 50-word summary is a little too abbreviated, but you can expand it considerably without coming close to the length of the original. The trouble with the example is not merely its length but also the way in which the reader is distracted—taken away from what he wants to know more about and forced to read information he has no use for.

The causes of a lack of conciseness are so numerous that they can hardly be listed; but among them are many of the things we have talked about—attempts to impress, unnecessary technical language, jargon, inability to think about purposes, and failure to consider readers. For *their* part, readers of such windy writing can fervently subscribe to George Eliot's words: "Blessed is the man who, having nothing to say, abstains from giving in words evidence of the fact."

WATCH YOUR PACE

Inside the doors of buses in a certain city appears this cryptic statement: "Pay enter East Pay leave West." Habitual riders are accustomed to seeing strangers to the city snarled at by bus drivers when they try to find out when to pay their fare or when, still worse, they drop it into the box at the wrong time. There is both a complete failure of communication and a ducking of responsibility by irritated drivers, who wearily point to the signs as if the instructions were simple English. What the signs really mean is: When you are on a bus going east, pay when you enter the bus; when you are going west, pay when you leave. Since strangers usually can't figure out what the signs mean and don't even know whether the buses are going east or west, utter confusion results. Contrast the statement with the sign one bus driver lettered on his fare box: "Don't fumble while others grumble. Please pay exact fare 18¢ when you get on," and you have the difference between inadequate and effective communication.

The first example is an illustration of poor pacing—trying to say too much in too few words. Whenever you see someone puzzling over how to operate a vending machine, how to follow a receptionist's instructions for getting from one office to another, or how to run an automatic elevator, poor pacing may be responsible. The instructions go too fast for the reader; they attempt to say too much in too few words, or they wrongly assume that everyone understands the short cuts in language. Occasionally, terseness and compression of several ideas in one sentence are effective changes of pace, but this sort of writing requires great skill. Here is an example from *Time:*

> In Chilliwack, B.C., Mrs. Edna Fenton walked into police headquarters and asked the desk constable how she might get herself jailed to escape her angry husband, was advised to hit a cop, did, was.

Unless you are a very able writer, you will do well to avoid trying to pack too much information into your sentences. The potential result of such tight packing is a sense of irritated frustration on the reader's part. Test your own reaction to this instruction on the changed income tax forms for 1970:

> If line 15a is under $5,000 and consisted only of wages subject to withholding and not more than $200 of dividends, and you are not claiming any adjustments on line 15b, you can have IRS figure your tax by omitting lines 16, 17, 18, 20, 21, 22, 23, 24, 25 and 26 (but complete line 19).

The opposite fault in pacing occurs when a few meager facts or ideas are strung out on a long clothesline of words. Slow pacing occurs more frequently in business writing than fast pacing. Here's an example from a business report which moves at a snail's pace:

> Since the beginning of large-scale research programs on automatic controls, there has been a need for simple but rapid tests to evaluate these controls. These methods of evaluation must be easy to use and fast. They should also give a definite answer. What is needed is a method which says "yes" or "no" to a specific problem of using automatic controls. The current emphasis on these controls has posed a difficult problem in the field of their evaluation. We, therefore, need evidence which will give us a method of deciding when to use them.

Such slow-paced writing creates a knotty problem for the reader. The first time he reads it, he gets a vague impression that the writer is actually saying something significant. Then, if he is patient and goes back to examine what has been said, he finds that 6 sentences and 95 words have been expended to express one simple idea:

> Because of the widespread use of automatic controls, we need to develop a simple, fast, and definite method of evaluating their use.

Here is another example from a text on financial management:

> Financial management is the responsibility for obtaining and effectively utilizing the funds necessary for the efficient operation of an enterprise. The finance function centers about the *management* of funds—raising and using them effectively. But the dimensions of financial management are much broader than simply obtaining funds. Planning is one of the most important activities of the financial manager.

This writer started out with what he thought was a fairly good definition of financial management, and he put it in the first sentence. But evidently he was not satisfied that he had made himself clear, so he said the same thing again, in different words, in his second sentence. He seems then to have decided that his definition was not really complete. In his third sentence, he prepared to expand on it, but in doing so he partly recapitulated his original definition, so that the reader doesn't know whether more repetition or a new thought is on the way. Finally, in his fourth sentence, he completed his definition. What the whole paragraph seems to mean is:

> The financial manager has the responsibility for obtaining and effectively utilizing the funds necessary for the efficient operation of an enterprise. Planning is one of his most important activities.

KEEP YOUR SENTENCES SHORT

How short is "short"? No simple answer will suffice; Dr. Rudolph Flesch, who wrote *The Art of Plain Talk*, believes that an *average* sentence length of 17 words makes high readability. Writers in business should aim at variety in both the length and pattern of their sentences. They should occasionally check the average length of sentences in their letters and reports to see that it falls somewhere between 15 and 20 words. If not, they should employ a very useful device—the period—more frequently; most long sentences lend themselves logically to this chopping-up process.

> I should greatly appreciate your letting me know what your decision is so that I can send the report to Mr. Jones in our Memphis office with a request for more information which we will need to make our plans for the coming year and to encourage him to make any suggestions he may want to incorporate. (*One sentence, 57 words*)

> I should greatly appreciate your letting me know your decision. I can then send the report to Mr. Jones in our Memphis office requesting more information. We will need his suggestions for next year's plans. (*Three sentences, 35 words*)

Perhaps the best analysis of why sentences should be kept short and clear is this statement by Herbert Spencer in his *Philosophy of Style:*

> A reader or listener has at each moment but a limited amount of mental power available. To recognize and interpret the symbols presented to him requires part of this power; to arrange and combine the images suggested requires a further part; and only that part which remains can be used for realizing the thought conveyed. Hence, the more time and attention it takes to receive and understand each sentence, the less time and attention can be given to the contained idea; and the less vividly will that idea be conceived. . . .

This analysis of what happens when the reader reads is a good argument for carrying the reader along step by step. Don't force him to go along until he is breathless from the sheer length of your sentences. By doing so, you merely divert the small amount of attention he has left for comprehending.

One of the major causes of excessive sentence length in business writing stems from the techniques of dictation, which are discussed in Chapter 20. We can highlight the difficulty here by calling attention to the danger of rambling along in the oral process of dictating without sufficient regard for the length of sentences. Since you can't actually *see* how long the sentence is in this process, the transcriber or typist can help by calling attention to the fact that a sentence is too long, too involved, or too cumbersome, and that it will be more effective if it is broken into shorter units.

PUT YOUR QUALIFYING IDEAS IN SEPARATE SENTENCES

Paradoxically, one of the worst attributes of business writing stems from an admirable human quality—the desire to write the exact, absolute, and final truth in a sentence. But since a sentence follows a pattern of one thought at a time, it is impossible to express all kinds of qualifications and conditions without producing a long, complex, and highly involved sentence. "And you become obscure," said Aristotle, "if, in seeking to introduce a number of details in the middle of a sentence, you do not complete the sense before you mention them." As we noted earlier, this zeal for accuracy throws ideas or information at the reader at too fast a pace. Notice this example:

> The result of this study is a recommendation that our hiring policies should be changed during the coming year but it should be remembered that this recommendation may not be sound if there is an appreciable change in the labor market during that period or if changing circumstances affect our own company's level of operations so that we need to increase or decrease the total number of employees.

You can always spot this kind of long-windedness by such words as *under certain circumstances, under different conditions*, and similar phrases. They are almost inevitable in these sentences because that is just what the writer attempts to do—to take care of all the possible contingencies, conditions, or variable elements in one sentence. As we have suggested, the cause may be his own intellectual honesty or it may be the opposite—a desire to hedge, to avoid committing himself unequivocally. Whatever the cause, don't clutter your sentences with too many qualifying ideas. Break such sentences as the one cited above like this:

> The result of our study is a recommendation to change our hiring policies during the coming year. This recommendation may not be sound if the labor market changes in the next year or if unforeseen business conditions affect our company's level of operations. If that happens, we will have to change the number of employees.

The classic definition of the sentence is *a group of words to convey a single thought*. Too many writers in business err on the side of putting qualifying phrases and clauses into their sentences and hence lengthen them to a point which passeth understanding. Aim at conciseness, at clean-cut sentences, and put the qualifiers in separate sentences.

> Usually we find that our refrigerators give maximum efficiency when they are stored in a very dry place until they are used, but occasionally we hear of a case

where such storage has resulted in a drying out of the insulation around the door in which case we recommend that it be treated by applying a damp cloth so that the moisture in the rubber may be replaced. (*One sentence, 68 words*)

We find that our refrigerators give maximum efficiency when they are stored in a very dry place. Occasionally, this results in drying out the insulation around the door. We then recommend applying a damp cloth to the insulation to replace the moisture in the rubber. (*Three sentences, 45 words*)

Schopenhauer expressed the reaction of most readers when he commented: "In these long sentences rich in involved parentheses, like a box of boxes within one another, and padded out like roast geese stuffed with apples, it is really the memory that is chiefly taxed."

Fundamentally, the sentence is the basic test of how clearly you think. It can be a hazy, vague, flabby collection of words or a functional, well-designed garb for a thought. The result will depend on how much thinking you have done before you write. Great writers have always recognized this inexorable link between clear thinking and effective writing. Perhaps the best illustration of this concerns Richard Brinsley Sheridan, the famous dramatist who wrote *The School for Scandal* and *The Rivals*. A friend asked him how his new play was coming along. "It's finished," said Sheridan. "When can I read the script?" asked his friend. "Oh, I haven't written a word yet," Sheridan replied. And that is where good sentences are "written" first—in your mind.

USE PARAGRAPHS TO BREAK YOUR TEXT INTO READABLE UNITS

Readers in the twentieth century have become accustomed to seeing material in smaller units than those used a century ago. Advertisers, journalists, and other writers have, therefore, learned to break text into shorter and more readable units. You can test this practice on the basis of your own habits when you read a novel. If you are typical, the chances are that you read most of the conversation and skim over most of the description. You do this not because the conversation is necessarily more interesting than the description but because it generally comes in shorter units of text.

When you write reports, letters, or memorandums, you should remember that long paragraphs, heavy chunks of typing or print, have an eye-repelling quality for today's reader. They should be divided into more easily comprehended bits by a technique which advertising men call "letting daylight into the copy."

No one can say authoritatively how long a paragraph should be; that will depend entirely on how thoroughly or in how much detail you are trying to develop an idea or a topic. It will also depend on the reader, whose preferences in business writing we have already indicated. Certainly you will be exacting too high a payment of attention from most business readers if you write paragraphs which cover a whole page. At the opposite extreme, you don't want paragraphs averaging only a sentence or two because you then won't be developing your ideas as you should.

To be completely practical, most long paragraphs in business communication can be broken up without any loss of their logic; in fact, most of these paragraphs are written because the writer has lost sight of his reader and of the way he reads. In reports and memorandums, therefore, you can use an arbitrary rule of thumb by trying to break the text into at least three or four paragraphs on a page.

In business letters, you can often disregard the literary definition of the paragraph as "a group of related sentences forming a unit of thought." Think of it, instead, as a device for making the message easier to read and as a method of dividing the message into functional parts. For instance, as we shall see later, the sales letter usually has four functions—attracting attention, creating desire for the product or service, convincing the reader, and motivating action. To each of these functions within the letter, a paragraph is devoted. The following two letters illustrate how the paragraph can contribute to the ease of reading:

Dear Mr. Potter:

We are glad to tell you, in answer to your letter of May 4, that our service department has found nothing seriously wrong with your Blank Camera, Model 12 A. A few comparatively inexpensive repairs and adjustments are needed, the chief of which are replacement of one part of the shutter mechanism and readjustment of the timing. The camera appears to have been dropped or seriously jarred. Our guarantee covers "any defect of workmanship or materials within one year of normal use," but, as you doubtless realize, it does not cover careless handling. If you will send us your check for $5.50, we will put your camera in first-class condition and renew our guarantee on workmanship and materials for another year. Just as soon as you sign and mail the enclosed, stamped, addressed post card, we'll return your camera as good as new—ready to catch that picture ahead that you'll treasure as a moment of happiness recaptured.

Sincerely yours,

Dear Mr. Potter:

We are glad to tell you, in answer to your letter of May 4, that our service department has found nothing seriously wrong with your Blank Camera, Model 12 A.

A few comparatively inexpensive repairs and adjustments are needed, the chief of which are replacement of one part of the shutter mechanism and readjustment of the timing. The camera appears to have been dropped or seriously jarred.

Our guarantee covers "any defect of workmanship or materials within one year of normal use," but, as you doubtless realize, it does not cover careless handling. If you will

send us your check for $5.50, we will put your camera in first-class condition and re-
new our guarantee on workmanship and materials for another year.

Just as soon as you sign and mail the enclosed, stamped, addressed post card, we'll return your camera as good as new—ready to catch that picture ahead that you'll treasure as a moment of happiness recaptured.

Sincerely yours,

A glance shows how much more inviting to the eye the second version of
this letter is than the first, which repels the eye by its lack of paragraphing.
Furthermore, the second letter helps the reader by using paragraphs to divide
the message into its logical functions. Thus, in the four-paragraph letter above,
the division is made on the following basis:

Paragraph 1: A reference to the date of the letter being answered and a statement of
what this letter is about
Paragraph 2: A statement of what is wrong with the camera and why
Paragraph 3: An explanation of why the guarantee does not cover this situation and
a statement of the cost
Paragraph 4: An incentive to action

To present these subdivisions of the thought in the most readable fashion,
the paragraphs of the business letter should be kept short. In using paragraphs
to suit such functions, we are actually returning to the original meaning and
use of the word. For *paragraph* is composed of two Greek words: *graph* from
graphein, "to write," and *para*, "beside." At one time, a paragraph was a mark,
usually ¶, written beside the text of a manuscript to mark a unit or subdivision of the text for the reader. While we have replaced the mark with indentions or arrangements of single and double spacing, the purpose of the paragraph is unchanged—to help the reader by breaking the text and to arrange
clusters of sentences in logical units. There are exceptions to every principle—
William Faulkner, for instance, wrote paragraphs which extend over several
pages—but for the purposes of business writing, short paragraphs are more
readable. If you combine this shortness with a logical or functional grouping
of ideas expressed by the sentences within the paragraph, you will achieve the
two purposes of the paragraph in business communication.

AVOID TOO MUCH USE OF THE PASSIVE VOICE

Excessive use of the passive voice results in more wordiness in business writing
than almost any other form of expression. It results, too, in monotony, vagueness, and complete lack of vigor. The passive has its uses. You may find that
older readers, and technically trained men such as engineers and accountants,

prefer an impersonal, passive style because they were schooled in that tradition. The tradition, however, is breaking down. A better reason for using the
passive voice is to achieve an unemphatic, impersonal style in the specific
cases where this suits your purpose. Rather than point a finger of accusation,
for example, you may prefer to be a little vague. Compare these two examples:

> The sales manager has permitted unauthorized expenditures on advertising.

> Unauthorized expenditures have been made on advertising.

To a reader who understands the company's organization, the two sentences
may mean the same thing. The first is vigorous, very explicit, and would be
recommended by most text writers. However, the second may suit your purposes better.

   Note that it is all too easy to take refuge in the passive to avoid admitting your own responsibilities:

> An overestimate of sales last year has produced an inventory level higher than
> normal.

> I made a bad estimate of sales last year and now our inventory is too high.

You might prefer to write the first sentence, but a reader who understands your
responsibilities will quickly see your attempt to cover up.

   On the whole there is far too much use of the passive in business writing.
Writers get into the habit of using the passive voice, perhaps because of a constant unwillingness to be specific and commit themselves emphatically, perhaps because they have read so much business and technical material written
in the passive. Here is an unfortunately typical construction from a business
report:

> When our employees are subjected to long work hours which are necessitated
> by storms, it is expected that a higher rate of accidents will prevail.

What this writer means is:

> When storms force our employees to work long hours, we can expect a higher
> accident rate.

   Unless you have a specific need for the passive voice, stick to the active
except for occasional variation. But let the passive be the variation, not the
theme. Here are examples in which the active voice improves a statement:

> *Passive:* It is noted that the sales volume has been increasing.
> *Active:* We note that the sales volume has increased.

Passive: It is believed that this policy will be beneficial to our personnel.

Active: We believe this policy will benefit our personnel.

Passive: Consideration is being given to this matter by our Sales Department.

Active: Our Sales Department will consider this matter.

Passive: It is occasionally found that one of our customers has been unintentionally missed by our representative.

Active: Occasionally, our representative unintentionally misses one of our customers.

USE ACTION VERBS

We have seen how the active voice can put life and vigor into your writing and cut away excess verbiage. Much the same can be accomplished by making verbs carry the load of what you have to say. The vividness of Sir Winston Churchill's writing is due in large part to his reliance on verbs and to his choice of strong, expressive verbs. Participles, infinitives, and adjectives carry much less force than active verbs. Even nouns are frequently less effective than well-chosen verbs. Notice this statement of conclusions from a report:

> It was found that by selection of the proper test conditions it was possible to duplicate the actual use of the machine by the housewife. Under these conditions, there was a definite tendency for the fan mechanism to deteriorate or to break down completely after usage which was equivalent to 3½ years of service in the home. It is believed, therefore, that it is desirable to replace the fan mechanism by substituting the larger motor which is capable of 6 years of service under the same conditions.

These 87 words virtually stand still, but by inserting some strong verbs, and especially by replacing infinitives, we can give the paragraph both conciseness and forward movement.

> By selecting proper test conditions, we duplicated the housewife's actual use of the machine. These tests showed that the fan mechanism deteriorated or broke down after the equivalent of 3½ years of service in the home. We believe the larger motor should be used because our tests show it can give 6 years of service under the same conditions.

Notice how these sentences from letters and memorandums can be improved by putting verbs to work:

Instead of: Application of these principles is the best way for us to obtain the cooperation of our retailers.

Say: By applying these principles, we can get our retailers to cooperate.

Instead of: This sales message is something of vital concern to all our personnel.
       Say: This sales message vitally concerns all our personnel.
Instead of: This contract has a requirement that it be signed by you.
       Say: This contract requires your signature.
Instead of: This makes it necessary for us to refuse your request with regret.
       Say: We regret that we must, therefore, refuse your request.
Instead of: This does have a direct bearing on the possibilities for future sales.
       Say: This directly affects future sales.

Some of this wordiness stems from the passive; some of it comes from round-about expressions like *is something of vital concern*, where one verb will express the idea; and some of it results from abstract words like *application*, which can usually be replaced by verbs.

Remember the advice of John Hookham Frere, an English diplomat and writer of the nineteenth century:

> *And don't confound the language of the nation*
> *With long-tailed words in* osity *and* ation.

Two things you can do to pack more action into your sentences:

1.   Change words like *requirement, selection,* and *application* to verbs: *require, select,* and *apply.*
2.   Use expressions such as *it is* and *there is* sparingly.

These expressions lead to such awkward and cumbersome sentences as "It is to introduce our new products that we are sending this brochure," when you can cut out the deadwood by saying "We are sending you this brochure to introduce our new products." Wordiness inevitably results in writing which overuses these expressions:

Instead of: It is my personal opinion that . . .
       Say: I think . . .
Instead of: There are certain problems which confront us . . .
       Say: Certain problems confront us . . .
Instead of: It was our understanding that . . .
       Say: We understood that . . .
Instead of: It is the responsibility of our Production Department to see that it meets the requirements of our Sales Division. (Note that the first *it* is indefinite and the second refers to Production Department, making a very confusing sentence.)
       Say: Our Production Department must meet the requirements of our Sales Division.

BE DIRECT

Directness results from choosing and arranging words to convey your meaning precisely and economically. To write direct sentences, therefore, you have to know what you want to say and how to use words exactly. If you can't do this the first time you try, you have to rearrange your sentences until they *are* *direct*.

Here's a bad example from a memorandum issued to call employees' attention to the importance of concise reports:

> Due to the fact that the production of reports involves considerable cost to our organization, it can easily be seen that the reduction of the time spent in writing and reading them, a shortening of the reports themselves, would represent an appreciable gain in reducing our general operating expenses, although the matter of the length of the report should naturally be considered in relation to the complexity of the material and its adequate coverage keeping in mind the necessary requirements of the specific situation.

What, we may ask somewhat breathlessly, is this man trying to say? Had he asked himself that, he could have decided on these three ideas and produced two direct sentences:

> Because our reports cost money (1), we should cut the time to write and read them and shorten the reports (2). Their length, however, will depend on how complex the material is and how adequate the coverage ought to be for a speciific situation (3).

The first step toward writing direct sentences is knowing what you want to say and then using the words which convey that meaning precisely and concisely. Notice how the changes in the following sentences improve them:

Wordy: We must, therefore, keep each method of paying our salesmen a matter of information to be known only to those affected.

Improved: We must, therefore, keep each method of paying our salesmen confidential.

Wordy: There are changes in the organization of the department to be expected; no one as yet knows what changes will take place.

Improved: No one can anticipate what changes will be made in the organization of the department.

Wordy: His report discussed the risks to workers involved in leaving this equipment on our production line unguarded because this unguarded equipment increases the possibility of accidents and undermines employees' morale because of their fear of injury.

Improved: He reported that unguarded equipment on our production line increased the possibility of accidents and undermined our employees' morale.

Wordy: He explained that their methods of handling inquiries were antiquated and out-of-date and that their whole procedure of answering inquiry letters should be considered as one of the first methods of operation to be changed as soon as possible.

Improved: He explained that their methods of handling inquiries were obsolete and should be changed immediately.

KEEP YOUR TONE APPROPRIATE

When you write, tone is particularly important. You can't convey your feeling by a smile, a gesture, or an inflection; you must rely completely on written words. And when you write in business, particularly when you write letters, the tone of your writing expresses not only your own personality but that of your company. The customer who receives a discourteous, pompous, or abrupt letter may well decide that this represents the tone of the whole company. We can give so many shades of tone to our communications—positive or negative, helpful or indifferent, courteous or impertinent—that it is impossible to discuss all of them. Only a highly skilled writer has complete control over the tone of his writing, but here, too, the key is understanding the reader's point of view. Here are two examples:

Please investigate this matter and *submit* a report as soon as possible.

Please *do not hesitate to* call upon us if we can be of help.

The word *submit*, which has connotations of yielding, surrendering, and showing humility, is likely to arouse resentment and hostility even though the reader may not be able to identify just what it is about the request he doesn't like. The expression *do not hesitate* suggests that the writer is so full of self-importance that he believes his reader will pause before daring to disturb him. You can improve the tone of the first sentence by substituting *let me have* or *give me* for *submit*. In the second sentence, simply delete *do not hesitate to*.

Here are two sentences from the report of an accountant on what he regarded as an improper procedure in a department of his company. Each sentence is followed by a revision written by a "writing expert." The expert believed he was improving the readability of the original without changing its meaning. Do you agree?

Mr. Smith feels there have been no violations of any company policy in his department.

Mr. Smith denies that anyone in his department has violated any company policies.

I am sure you will agree that these people's actions were not within the results we desired our policies to achieve.

I am sure you will agree that these people perverted our policies.

Test your own reactions to these sentences from letters and reports:

Since you misunderstood the proposal in our last report, the only intelligent thing to do is to abandon the project.

We do not handle inquiries from retail customers at the Central Office, but if you are still interested you can get in touch with our local dealer.

You state that your contention about a late shipment is correct, but our records do not verify your contention.

We again apologize for the dissatisfaction you had and regret our failure to correct the unfortunate error.

BE SPECIFIC

There are occasions in business when general statements are advantageous— but such occasions are comparatively rare. Just to illustrate one such situation where general language is preferable to specific, let's assume that your company's distribution committee has received a request for funds from a church in the area. Although you have considerable money available, a rigid policy has been established to support only educational and health and welfare institutions. Instead of going into the specifics, a general statement such as the following is probably better:

> Dear Reverend McCullough:
>
> You will understand, I'm sure, that each year we receive innumerable requests for funds from very worthy organizations like yours. We wish that we could support every one of them and we regret that we cannot.
>
> We're sorry that we cannot contribute the support that you requested, and we sincerely hope that you will get it from some other source.
>
> Sincerely yours,

The principle here is clear: use general words and statements where detail and specific statements are not helpful, although usually readers do want the specifics and the details.

Look at this report of an important meeting by a company secretary:

The meeting opened with a discussion of some of the company's sales and production problems. This discussion was followed by a proposal from the research staff for a considerable increase in budget for fiscal 1971. Several objections were raised to this increase, but in the long run it was approved with certain modifications.

There seems to be a reason for secrecy, because these minutes tell readers little or nothing. What are the problems connected with sales and production? What was the specific proposal of the research staff? How much was the "considerable" increase asked for? What were the specific objections and by whom were they made? And after what modifications? Interested readers of these minutes are simply being tantalized by generalities which may cause them to read the worst into such nonspecific expressions.

The business writer who says, "In this report I will attempt to analyze some of the major problems in the Alpha Window Washer company's present situation. I will give the reasons for these problems, along with my recommendations for solving them," is running an unnecessary risk. He isn't presenting a definition or a theory which has to be expressed in general terms, if he has enough information on tap to be able to say:

The Alpha Window Washer company has suffered a 60 percent decline in sales for three reasons:
1. The fierce competition offered by Beta throwaway windows
2. The 30 percent rise in martinis consumed by Alpha salesmen during expense account lunches
3. The high rate of loss of window washers caused by the increasing use of narrow window-ledge construction

As we have said earlier, there may be reasons for wanting to be unspecific about a given situation, but they do not include winning the attention of your reader.

Notice how specifically directions about "How to Write a Check" are given in the material displayed on p. 81 taken from an excellent little pamphlet published by the Public Information Department of the Federal Reserve Bank of New York.* This booklet deals cartoon-style and in very specific terms with such usually abstruse subjects as the history of checkbook money, the clearing-house operation, and the role of the Federal Reserve System, and it takes a look into the future of checks in 1975, when an estimated 30 billion of them will be written.

---

* Federal Reserve Bank of New York, *The Story of Checks*, 3d ed., New York, 1966, p. 21.

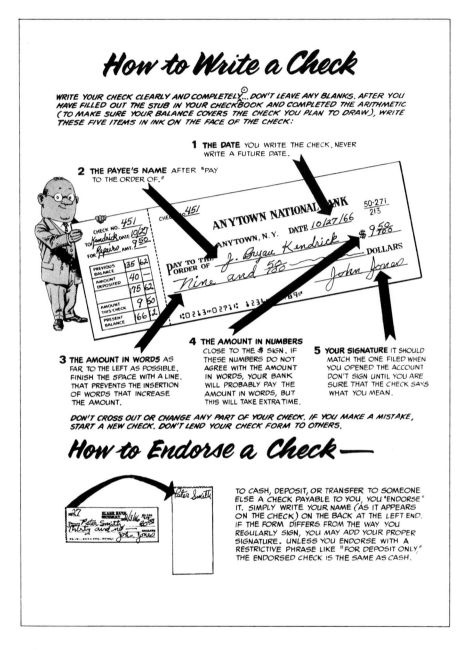

How to Write a Check

WRITE YOUR CHECK CLEARLY AND COMPLETELY... DON'T LEAVE ANY BLANKS. AFTER YOU HAVE FILLED OUT THE STUB IN YOUR CHECKBOOK AND COMPLETED THE ARITHMETIC (TO MAKE SURE YOUR BALANCE COVERS THE CHECK YOU PLAN TO DRAW), WRITE THESE FIVE ITEMS IN INK ON THE FACE OF THE CHECK:

1 THE DATE YOU WRITE THE CHECK. NEVER WRITE A FUTURE DATE.

2 THE PAYEE'S NAME AFTER "PAY TO THE ORDER OF."

3 THE AMOUNT IN WORDS AS FAR TO THE LEFT AS POSSIBLE. FINISH THE SPACE WITH A LINE. THAT PREVENTS THE INSERTION OF WORDS THAT INCREASE THE AMOUNT.

4 THE AMOUNT IN NUMBERS CLOSE TO THE $ SIGN. IF THESE NUMBERS DO NOT AGREE WITH THE AMOUNT IN WORDS, YOUR BANK WILL PROBABLY PAY THE AMOUNT IN WORDS, BUT THIS WILL TAKE EXTRA TIME.

5 YOUR SIGNATURE IT SHOULD MATCH THE ONE FILED WHEN YOU OPENED THE ACCOUNT DON'T SIGN UNTIL YOU ARE SURE THAT THE CHECK SAYS WHAT YOU MEAN.

DON'T CROSS OUT OR CHANGE ANY PART OF YOUR CHECK. IF YOU MAKE A MISTAKE, START A NEW CHECK. DON'T LEND YOUR CHECK FORM TO OTHERS.

How to Endorse a Check —

TO CASH, DEPOSIT, OR TRANSFER TO SOMEONE ELSE A CHECK PAYABLE TO YOU, YOU "ENDORSE" IT. SIMPLY WRITE YOUR NAME (AS IT APPEARS ON THE CHECK) ON THE BACK AT THE LEFT END. IF THE FORM DIFFERS FROM THE WAY YOU REGULARLY SIGN, YOU MAY ADD YOUR PROPER SIGNATURE. UNLESS YOU ENDORSE WITH A RESTRICTIVE PHRASE LIKE "FOR DEPOSIT ONLY," THE ENDORSED CHECK IS THE SAME AS CASH.

EXERCISES

1. If readers did not understand the following sentences, to what would you ascribe their difficulty? Rewrite each sentence so that it cannot be misunderstood:

    a. On the day following the executive session which had been stormy, a lot of people left the convention on account of the weather and because it was poorly organized.

b. When Mr. Fewsmith saw the advertising, which John gave him, he told him that he had better keep it a few days more.

c. It is of considerable significance, in my judgment, that this sales presentation be handled in a way which will do credit to the company and, under certain circumstances, will be tried out on a selected group first assuming, of course, that such a trial could be made without diverting too many people from their daily routine in which case it should be avoided.

d. A few reductions in cost were achieved by the San Francisco group last month, but in general it was a quarter in which inflation was a major factor in the limitation of earnings.

e. The matter in question has given rise to considerable offense on the part of certain employees who think it inexcusable, evasive, and dilatory and adding fuel to the flames of their repugnance for such management decisions.

2. What changes will make the following more direct and concise?

   a. These new regulations were promulgated with the intention of providing a few guidelines which were requested by employees who have been employed by the company for ten years or more.

   b. Since this new manual is of particular interest to college freshmen, it is our hope and expectation to put it in the college bookstore where it will be on sale for $1.95.

   c. Since it is part of our policy to practice recognition of employees for superior performance, it is believed that an occasion once a year might be instituted in which such employees are honored in front of the entire company.

   d. Once the ownership of this property was transferred to the new owner, the latter was immediately informed that in view of the extraordinarily high interest rates he should develop it with as great speed as possible so that income would be forthcoming within a year, if not sooner.

   e. The salient importance of this new method of transporting our products was a consideration by which we were influenced to change to transport by ship rather than by train.

3. Rewrite the following to give them a more appropiate tone:

   a. Dear Mr. Jones:

   After most detailed consideration, we cannot possibly grant your request for admission to next year's freshman class at the university.

   Your high school grades were so low that we doubt your ability to meet our high academic standards. It seems to us that you really belong in an institution with less rigorous intellectual discipline than ours.

   Thank you so much for your application.

   Sincerely yours,

   b. Dear Mr. Smith:

   When we granted you credit of up to $500 on our six-month account, we expected you to pay us promptly.

   Now it is only the second month, and you have paid us a mere $50. Don't you know that the interest of $1\frac{1}{2}\%$ a month on your unpaid balance of \$437.91 really mounts up and pretty soon you'll be over your credit limit?

You're not being fair to us. So send us a check for this month's payment of \$71.22 and then let's keep up the payments regularly from there on in.

Very truly yours,

c.   Dear Mr. Miller:

We can't really understand why anyone wants one of our large name signs which we use in advertising the J. Q. Miller Company, even though your name happens to be exactly the same as ours.

At first, we thought your letter was some kind of gag until we noted the identity of names and realized that you wanted to acquire an inexpensive symbol for the barn on your country place.

We're reluctant to do this and we earnestly hope that there aren't a lot of J. Q. Millers to make similar requests. Anyway, we finally decided to send you one of our signs and you will have to pay the express charges collect. We hope you will call your guests' attention to the fact that we gave you the sign.

Sincerely yours,

d.   Dear Mr. Jones:

Enclosed is the annual report of this company which you requested. It will undoubtedly supply you with the information you wanted as a potential investor in the stock of our company.

If there is other material needed, do not hesitate to get in touch with us.

Sincerely,

e.   Dear Mr. Blue:

Words cannot convey our joy at learning that your store has now passed its 20th birthday.

You must feel ineffable satisfaction and happiness that for 20 years you have met the challenges and triumphed over the manifold problems of establishing a business.

May continued success be yours. True merit is always rewarded in the competition of the marketplace, and your rewards are truly merited.

Very truly yours,

P.S. We enclose our latest catalog and order blank for your convenience.

f.   Dear Mr. Green:

We received your request for a 2% discount on future orders, considered it, even asked our president, but we can't grant it. How about 1%?

Cordially yours,

g.   Dear Mrs. Whiteway:

Your letter asking us to donate merchandise worth more than \$15 for auction at the annual fair of the Community Ladies' Auxiliary must regretfully be turned down.

Your see, if we granted all such requests, we would really be in trouble.

We know that you and many other members of your organization are good customers. We hope all of you will understand this policy of ours.

Truly yours,

4. Assuming that you are the reader involved in each of the following situations, which would you consider effective and which ineffective? Why? Rewrite them to make them acceptable to the reader.

 a. (Response to your application for summer work.)

 Unfortunately it is not our policy to employ students during the summer. We have found it to be much more efficient if only permanent employees are employed. Should you be interested in permanent employment, please use the enclosed form.

 b. (Letter sent to you because you have purchased records from a department store which has put you on its mailing list.)

 Come on, man! Let's get out of Squaresville!

 On July 10, we're opening our new Teen Shop with a blast. Music by the Moss Gatherers. Free drinks and sandwiches. And the biggest selection of records in town.

 Get out of that pad, bring your chick, and meet the beautiful people who know that Blanco's is the place to go . . . go . . . go!

 c. (Response to your request for a memo explaining why Blanco was able to employ only 9 college graduates this year when for the past five years the average has been 21.)

 It seems advisable in connection with the question raised in the memo of May 1 to the writer to consider the various factors pertaining to the employment of college graduates and the recent decline in the number employed to say that changing conditions in our colleges and universities have resulted in attitudes which are occasionally unsympathetic to the activities of this company.

 d. (A different response to the same situation as c.)

 You've got something in that question. And the answer is—they don't like business, their professors don't like business, and we're lucky to get nine because next year it may be only three. What to do? Increase starting salaries, stress the service we render to people and the community, and then *hope*. Maybe that way we'll get seven next year.

 e. (Another response to c.)

 It is apparent that this request indicates some undercurrent of dissatisfaction with the results of recruiting efforts on behalf of this company—and quite properly so. Nonetheless, the fact that we employed nine college graduates this year should be put in the proper frame of reference. As for example, our competitors, the Nocorp people, were able to put only seven on their employment rolls. Hence it would appear that a reexamination of our employment practices and perquisites would be in order, and perhaps this study in depth should be made in collaboration with the Nocorp people, since industry-wise the problem seems to be the same.

    f. (Response to your request for a prospectus giving information about vacations on a small Caribbean island.)

        Here it is. We hope you like it. We do.

    g. (Response to an error you have made in paying a bill.)

        We're returning your check for $86.70. If you will look at your bill, you'll see it is for $68.70.

        Will you send us the right amount this time, please.

    h. (Response to the same situation as **g.**)

        You made a natural error in transposing the figures from $68.70 to $86.70. It happens frequently. Here's your check. Now send us one for $68.70 and we'll all be happy.

    i. (Response to a new booklet you have sent out explaining the services of your firm of management consultants.)

        It's a great job and it hit us right between the eyes that someday—maybe soon, maybe late—we'll need these services. Right now we're on a do-it-yourself kick. But the best of us—and I do mean *us*—make mistakes. That's when we may need you.

    j. (Response to the situation in **i.**)

        Thank you for the brochure explaining your services. It's really an impressive list of aids to companies. Right now, we seem to be reasonably self-sufficient. But if the need arises, we shall certainly get in touch with you.

5. By using action verbs, make the following sentences more concise and readable:

    a. In the discussion of this problem, it was our belief that the employment of new staff members would not be the solution.

    b. The content of this report is, by its very nature, a subject of varied interpretation and it is, therefore, a subject worthy of discussion at the next departmental meeting.

    c. It is a matter of considerable importance to me that this application be acted upon as soon as possible since the decision will have a direct effect on whether my graduate school studies should be pursued and my registration is needed within two weeks.

    d. The attention of all employees is directed to the forthcoming House and Garden Show at which a display of our company's products is planned. Tickets of admission for our employees are available at the Employee Services Department, Room 714, upon showing of company identification cards by which each employee is to receive two free tickets. In the expectation that there will be considerable demand for these tickets, the Employee Services Department will be open from 8:30 until 5:30 on Friday, May 4. It is hoped that employees will avail themselves of this opportunity.

    e. In the administration of these policies, the suggestion is made that attention be given to the fact that they are effective as of December 15.

6. What changes should be made in the following sentences to make them clear, concise, and appropriate in tone?

a. We asked our research department to check the materials you returned and, contrary to your claims, they report that there is absolutely nothing wrong.

b. This is the situation which we reported in our quarterly Evaluation Analysis which was submitted to the committee on February 2 when this matter was first discussed.

c. You will discover by a comparison of these price lists which are the most economical buys.

d. We cannot understand why you decided to send your service request direct to the main office instead of our local representative.

e. May we take the liberty of pointing out that this discount is not permissible in this instance, the remittance having been sent in after the 10th of the month.

f. I am disturbed that you have not answered my letter of application which has left me in a state of indecision because I have another job offer but wanted to work for your company.

g. Our regret that this mistake occurred is beyond mere words, particularly because your patronage has been so highly valued in the past and we had hoped for better relations in the future.

h. This failure to comply with the regulation concerning prompt payment has disappointed us greatly and we hope that you will keep it in mind in subsequent orders.

i. Despite the fact that we found nothing wrong with this merchandise, we are willing to let you return it to us for credit.

j. Keeping in mind that he is a new employee, he recommended that he be transferred to another department which his education and abilities suited him for.

7. Rewrite the following notice which was sent to all departments of a large company:

In order that the controller's office may achieve a more rapid liquidation of currently outstanding accounts, and thus maintain more effective relationships with vendors, it would be appreciated if all personnel in all departments would hereafter process all purchase requisitions through the purchasing department.

It is recognized that this procedure has heretofore been adhered to in most cases; however, due to the occurrence of certain exceptions, it is believed that there will be a valuable saving of time and avoidance of duplication if all purchase requisitions are hereafter processed by the purchasing department.

8. Change the following sentences to show the relative importance of the ideas and to make them more concise:

a. The meeting was called at 10 A.M. and ended at 3 P.M., by which time the decision to merge with the Household Co. was made.

b. This technique is very useful and it is certain to lower production costs.

c. This department is constantly working to expand sales activities and it gets little publicity.

d. We were approaching the main office when the explosion occurred.

e. The office is very large and it accommodates the entire stenographic department.

9. Indicate how you would break the following material into paragraphs for a business letter:

   a. We are sending in today's mail our latest catalogue of electrical appliances which you requested recently. We hope you will find it as helpful and informative as thousands of our customers already have. You will notice on page 41 a description of our latest model electric stove, the Economiser, which incorporates the newest techniques in design and construction. The Economiser carries a five-year guarantee against any defect in workmanship or materials. Since we are now in full production of this type of stove, we can make delivery within two weeks of your order. A convenient order blank is enclosed in our catalogue. With prices on electrical appliances due for a rise within the next few months, you can save money by acting now.

   b. At this time of the year, our certified public accountants are making preparations for their annual audit of our books and analysis of the condition of accounts. Since we notice that your account is overdue, we suggest that payment be made immediately so that you will not be listed among those considered in arrears. We know that you will wish to protect your credit rating. Please return this letter with your check for $120 in the enclosed convenient envelope.

10. Rewrite the following sentences to make them more readable:

    a. It is obvious that it is becoming more and more important that top management should be furnished with timely and up-to-date reports. It is therefore necessary that the methods of getting information from our branch offices be improved.

    b. Many of our dealers have advanced the thought that it was better at present to hold accounts in the local office and try to collect them rather than to turn them over to the main office where they might possibly be handled by the legal department.

    c. Another advantage of the use of prepunched form cards is that by reducing the time required for the processing of a credit transaction, the next customer to be served will not be kept waiting as long as he normally would be under the present system.

    d. This safety policy is called to your attention because our day-to-day experience seems to indicate that a review of the facts from a safety point of view is advisable and that our policy should be finalized in the light of these facts.

    e. There is a strong probability that tax-wise our present situation renders us liable to a precarious position in the event of a diminution of sales.

11. The following letter is an exact transcript of a communication sent to the placement director of one college. How would you rewrite it to interest your fellow students in working during the Christmas holidays?

   Dear Sir:

   May I take the liberty of respectfully requesting you to announce to the student body that those who are interested in modestly augmenting their personal allowances, reducing accumulated incidental expenses, replenishing and increasing their bank accounts, may secure, during the Christmas period of December 15th to January 1st, temporary employment at our Main Plant, located at 630 Blank Street.

Applications are now being accepted and honored at this unit for temporary positions at $1.75 an hour for a 40–48 hour week.

It would be of material assistance to us if applicants possessed knowledge and could advise when their services would be available.

Please accept, in advance, my deep and humble gratitude for your kind cooperation.

                                                          Respectfully,

PART TWO

TECHNIQUES OF BUSINESS LETTERS

Everything that we have said thus far about the fundamental principles and purposes of communication and about the need for readable and correct writing applies with equal force to the business letter. Now we make a transition from the discussion of general principles to their specific application in the business letter.

Many people are inclined to deprecate this utilitarian form of communication. They say such things as "If I know how to write, I'll be able to turn out a good business letter." They are probably right *if* they really know how to write (and the emphasis in on *if*). Curiously one seldom hears the reverse of this statement—"If I can write good business letters, I'll be able to write good essays or articles"—although it has equal validity.

Why learn to write business letters? First, because more people will use the practical skills of expression required in the business letter than any other writing skills. You probably won't write many essays or "research papers" after you get out of college—and we're not deprecating the usefulness of these forms. We're merely saying that more people (housewives, artisans, professional men, bakers, candlestick makers, as well as businessmen) will have occasion to express their thoughts, appreciation, disagreement, information, or whatever in business letters than in any other form of writing. To write them well is, therefore, a skill which everyone should have.

Second, because the business letter is generally short, it forces the writer to think about how he can express himself concisely yet completely, to organize his thoughts logically so that his reader can follow them. If one were trying to make comparisons, one might suggest that the letter does not encourage the flabbiness of language, the padding, or the repetition which often characterize those favorite academic exercises known as "5,000-word research reports" or "25-page term papers."

In sum, then, we can say of the business letter that you will undoubtedly write it the rest of your life and that you can learn a great deal about writing by practicing its principles and methods. Furthermore, for those who plan to work in business, writing effective letters is an indispensable professional skill which contributes immeasurably to your career for two important reasons.

First, of all forms of business writing, the letter plays the most vital role in a company's public relations because *it goes outside the company* to a person who may base his judgment of the whole organization on just one letter he receives. No one can condone cold, impersonal, or incorrect writing in reports or memos—but at least such faults are being aired "within the family." But a letter with these faults is inexcusable because it adversely affects the opinion of those who count most—readers who are potential customers, clients, users of services, or just the mythical man-on-the-street whose combined opinion adds up to good or ill will toward a business organization.

Second, as we said in the Introduction to Part One, business has become acutely conscious of communication costs, in which letters play a major share. As we have indicated, analyses put the average cost of the business letter today at around $3.15 (IBM says $3.05 in its advertising; the New York Telephone Company quotes a figure of $3.15). An interesting historical survey by the Dartnell Corporation of Chicago reveals the cost trend—1953, $1.17; 1957, $1.70; 1960, $1.89; 1962, $1.97; 1964, $2.32; 1968, $2.49; 1970, $3.15. These figures include the dictator's and transcriber's time, overhead costs, postage, printing, and paper and envelopes. The one uncertain factor is the number of business letters sent in a given year. If we assume that around 50 billion pieces of mail go first class (which is realistic and which will increase each year) and that one out of five is a business letter—which is probably conservative—at a cost of $3.15, we have some idea of the astronomical sums American business invests in this one form of business communication. One guesstimate that can be made with reasonable certainty is that the cost of the individual letter, like everything else in our society, will surely increase.

WHAT THE BUSINESS LETTER IS

Considered in its most fundamental terms and from its writer's viewpoint, the *business letter* may be defined as *a message that attempts to influence its reader to take some action or attitude desired by the writer.* In other words, the correspondent tries to get his reader to agree with him. This attempt at agreement should always be part of the letter—in fact, it is its central purpose. Often that purpose is specific and immediate—to get the reader to pay a bill, to send necessary information, to buy a product or service. Sometimes the purpose is less tangible—to get the reader to accept a refusal as fair, to maintain an attitude of good will, to decide that you (and this generally means "your company") are efficient, responsible, sympathetic, or whatever else it is your purpose to convey to the reader. In fact, the best test of how well you achieve your purpose is to ask yourself how successfully they gain agreement from readers. The successful sales message should get agreement from the reader that a product or service is worth buying; the collection letter should convince the debtor that payment of his bill is the wisest policy; the application letter attempts to win agreement from the prospective employer that the applicant is well qualified for the job.

In fact, it is not too difficult to list the general purposes for which all the letters of the modern business world are written. They fall into three categories:

1.   To get action (e.g., paying a bill)
2.   To build good will (e.g., granting or refusing a request)

3. To supply information or reasoning (e.g., giving facts about your products or about a situation; or providing the reasoning when you have to say "no")

These three purposes are, of course, interrelated in many letters: when you use facts or reasons to explain why you must say "no," you will try to do it in such a way as to build good will. But within these three primary purposes is set all the material which we label by types—for example, sales, application, collection, credit, and adjustment.

THE WRITER'S RESPONSIBILITY

As we have seen, every kind of writing must be preceded by thought and analysis. Far too much correspondence in modern business is essentially thoughtless, and, therefore, a great deal of it is stereotyped and unoriginal. The letters of many correspondents are almost automatic, like the response of a muscle to a nerve impulse. This failure to think about the fundamental purposes of a letter situation *before* starting to write results inevitably in muddled expression or vague and inadequate phraseology. Such thought-lessness also results in wasted time and money, since the automatic response usually leaves questions unanswered, fails to supply sufficient information, or makes the reader feel that he is receiving routine treatment.

Think before you write: this is your first responsibility as a letter writer. Specifically, you must think about the answers to two questions:

1. What am I trying to accomplish in this letter?
2. How can I best accomplish this purpose with my reader?

Consider the following two letters, dealing with the same situation. Which message gives evidence of careful thought? Which writer has made up his mind about what he wants his letter to accomplish?

Dear Sir:

We are sorry that we cannot fill your order of November 5 for 12 dozen men's shirts to retail at $5.75 because we are no longer manufacturing them. We have gone into the production of more expensive shirts for men. In the event that you need any of these, we will be glad to serve you.

Yours truly,

Dear Mr. Wiley:

We regret that we cannot fill your order of November 5 for 12 dozen men's shirts to retail at $5.75.

We have found that men are demanding a shirt that will wear longer and look better than those that can be made to sell at $5.75.

In order to meet this demand, we have designed "The Monitor," a genuine broadcloth, preshrunk shirt to sell at $8.50. These shirts will give you, the dealer, a larger margin of profit; they will enable you to take advantage of our national advertising campaign which features "The Monitor"; they will help to convince your customers that your store carries quality merchandise.

The enclosed postcard lists the wholesale prices for "The Monitor." If you will sign and mail it today, a supply of these high-quality shirts will reach you within a week to bring you added profit and satisfied customers.

Sincerely yours,

The fundamental difference between these two letters lies in the thought and analysis by the correspondent before putting a word on paper. The first writer shows not the slightest indication of thinking in advance about what his letter ought to do. His is the automatic, the thought-less response. A routine brain working in routine fashion simply stops with the refusal of the order. The second writer has analyzed what he wants his letter to do. For him it is not enough merely to refuse the order for $5.75 shirts; he has considered the question "What am I trying to do in this letter?" very specifically. His letter's task is to sell higher-priced shirts, and everything in it after the first paragraph is directed toward that purpose. Its success comes from thought and analysis.

Having determined what he wants his letter to do, the writer's next problem is how best to do it. What technique or characteristics will make the letter most effective as a message to influence its reader to do what the writer wants him to do? Certainly, qualities like courtesy, friendliness, and helpfulness are the minimum essentials of any effective letter, if only because these characteristics help us to persuade others to do what we want them to do. This is putting a low premium indeed upon these personal traits, but where such qualities are naturally a part of the correspondent's personality, he will need no conscious effort to inject them into his letters.

But the real answer to our second question—"How can I best accomplish this purpose?"—leads us to the reader, since we accomplish our purpose only through him. In the following chapter, therefore, we shall really be talking about what letter writers should know about readers—but we shall discuss this in terms of four basic qualities all business letters should have: the "you attitude," a tone adapted to the reader, a personality which appeals to him, and an opening and closing which are designed for his method of reading the letter.

CHAPTER 5

BASIC QUALITIES OF BUSINESS LETTERS

THE "YOU" ATTITUDE

The past ten or fifteen years have witnessed a more searching analysis than ever before of what takes place when one human being tries to persuade another to do something. We have had mathematical analyses of persuasion, studies of so-called interpersonal communication, research on letters and advertising as "an educational factor in wish-fulfillment," and a broad variety of popular and scholarly books and articles involving the study of language as an aid to understanding human nature. In an era when man can achieve what once was impossible and go to the moon, every additional piece of research about persuasion and communication is vital. It is unfortunate, and all too symptomatic of our times, that many such studies are so specialized or esoteric that they do not communicate very effectively.

So far, no new research study has contradicted the old principle of *I–you* communication: if *I* want to persuade *you* to do something, the best way is for me to show you how and why you benefit from doing it. This principle, which we have purposely expressed in the simplest words, offers the best possible guide for writing the business letter. Nothing related to business correspondence is more important than this point of view, known for many years as the *you attitude:* we can most readily persuade others to do what we want them to do by demonstrating that it is to their advantage to do it.

At this point, mental reservations burst out into accusations — usually from students who rate hypocrisy as the one unforgivable sin. "It's just a way of manipulating people." "It's insincere and dishonest because it says the end justifies the means." "It's a phony way to sell stuff."

In Chapter 2, we mentioned the fact that language can be deliberately used for unclear or misleading purposes; now, with the you attitude, we face one aspect of the ethics of business communication as exemplified by the accusations in the preceding paragraph. There is obviously a real danger that some inexperienced correspondents will think of the concept of the you attitude as a pose or a "gimmick" which offers a short cut to achieving their purpose of manipulating people. We have to admit that many business writers will use any means to achieve an end — and the you attitude can be misused as that means. (To provide opportunity for class discussion and/or written response concerning these highly important ethical problems, Problem 5 in the exercises at the conclusion of this chapter presents ample room for divergent viewpoints.)

This book reflects the belief that in the term *you attitude*, the emphasis should be placed on *attitude*, something which reflects our feelings, moods, or convictions. What then are the attitudes which we ought to reflect in our relations with others? Sincerity, truthfulness, and integrity should rank high on the list — and those are the qualities which the you attitude *ought* to reflect. Cynics will comment that the reason is "because it's good business to be sincere, truthful, and honest." So be it then. But one additional fact should be noted — readers of letters are quicker to detect insincerity than any other quality. For that reason, only arrogant and intellectually condescending people will dispute the fact that the essence of good human relations in correspondence is to avoid superficial cordiality, exaggerated claims, and cleverness in the form of distortions of the truth. Properly used, the you attitude should tell the reader honestly, truthfully, and tactfully about the benefits he obtains from an action or attitude implicit in the letter's purpose.

All of us are tempted to write about what we ourselves are doing or hope to do. We delude ourselves by thinking that everyone is interested in *our* problems, *our* wishes, *our* products. In letter writing it is a good principle to forget yourself and to go back to one of the fundamentals of all communication — remember your reader. Here are some examples of how the you attitude can improve letters:

> Dear Sir:
>
> I need a lot of information on the way in which businessmen react to the current crises in our colleges, and I selected you and some others to send this questionnaire to because your names were mentioned in the newspapers.

> I have to have this information within two weeks, because my term paper is due then, and I hope you will help me by returning the questionnaire promptly.
>
> Sincerely yours,

> Dear Mr. Jones:
>
> You and several other prominent businessmen were recently quoted in *The Record* concerning the present crises in our colleges—and your comments so interested me that I decided to write my term paper on "Business's View of Today's Colleges."
>
> Your answers to the enclosed questionnaire—all you need do is to check *yes* or *no*—will be kept completely confidential. If you wish, I will send you a summary of the results based on my survey of 50 prominent businessmen in this area.
>
> You will recognize that I am attempting, in a small way, to open communication between education and business by means of a realistic survey. You can help by checking the answers and returning the questionnaire in the enclosed, self-addressed envelope.
>
> Sincerely yours,

These letters have identical purposes—to get a questionnaire filled out and returned. But notice how the first writer talks only of *my* need, *my* deadline, and *my* hope; by contrast, the second writer stresses how easily *you* can do this, why *you* will recognize its importance, and how *you* can benefit by participating through getting a summary of results.

Here are other examples of the difference when writers focus their attention on their readers' viewpoints:

> We are enclosing an order blank and a booklet containing illustrations and prices of the various items we carry for hi-fi equipment. We hope you understand how much we are looking forward to your order and to being of service.
>
> After you have looked through the enclosed booklet you will know how inexpensive these quality hi-fi components are. And when you send us your order, you will be on the way to the finest sound you have ever heard.

> I happened to see your advertisement for a technical writer in this morning's paper and I should like to have you consider me. In the first place, I am very much interested in working for you because your offices are close to a rural area where I can ski and fish. And in the second place, I have heard of the liberal attitude you have toward employees.
>
> My four years of undergraduate study in Physics at the University of Michigan and a master's degree in English from Columbia should qualify me for the position in technical writing which you advertised.

One of the situations where the you attitude seems ill adapted is collecting past-due accounts; nevertheless, thousands of collection letters are sent out daily whose chief effectiveness lies in their argument that it is to the debtor's own advantage to pay his bills. The following paragraph from one such letter shows how this may be done:

As a businessman, you certainly realize that your most valuable asset is your credit reputation. Without it, you cannot long remain in business. We know that you would not willingly lose this priceless possession for a mere $158.92, the amount of our bill. By placing your check in the mail today, you will help to keep your business on that firmest of foundations—a sound credit rating.

You need only glance through the advertising pages of any magazine to see the reader's viewpoint underscored by pointing out concrete advantages in the form of economy, utility, profit, pleasure, appearance, or enjoyment:

Along the shore are stretches of pink-tinted beach and hidden coves, ideal for you to sunbathe or swim or have picnics. An ocean of clear-blue water invites you to come on in or just to look. Take a horse-drawn carriage or a motorbike or a quaint old-fashioned car for a leisurely look at a historic land.

This little battery-charger will save you time, money, and effort. You won't have to go dashing out for batteries for that flashlight that suddenly went dark, and you'll save the cost of the charger in six months. From then on, it's all charged to your savings account.

A car is to go out with your girl in.

Your family is safer on these tires than ever before, and that's the best car insurance you can buy.

You're a man, not a mannequin—and that's why Custom Tailors were born.

You can pay off your mortgage . . . but could your family do so?

Analyze the purpose in these statements by professionals and notice the appeals by which they attempt to reach readers through the use of the you attitude.

A TONE ADAPTED TO THE READER

In Part One we emphasized the importance of "talking the reader's language" and of writing to him as if he were a human being instead of a depersonalized name. Here, for instance, is a horrible example of what not to do:

Dear Mr. Blane:

Surrender of the policy is permissible only within the days attendant the grace period on compliance with the citation relevant options accruing to the policy so we are estopped from acquiescing to a surrender prior to the policy's anniversary date. We are confident that an investigation relevant to the incorporation of this feature will substantiate that the policy is not at variance with policies of other companies.

Yours truly,

This is how the policy holder replied to that letter:

> Dear Mister:
> I am sorry but I don't understand your letter. If you will explain what you mean, I will try to do what you ask.
>
> Yours truly,
> Henry Blane

The use of such highly specialized language or of supposedly "impressive" terminology is one of the worst faults of business correspondence.

Admittedly, we cannot always know what kind of person our reader is, but we can make a good start by deciding that we're not going to talk over his head or talk down to him. When President Johnson and William McChesney Martin, Jr., Chairman of the Federal Reserve Board, were in disagreement over increasing the rediscount rate, J. A. Livingston, who writes a syndicated column on economic problems, attempted to write an explanation of the economic implications of raising the rediscount rate. As a result of his column, he received the following letter:

> You are interesting, J. A. L., and often informative, but please dumb down to the mutt mind and don't use the money-boys' jabber.

> What has this flap between Martin and Johnson got to do with the price of pork and our loss of gold? Come on, J. A. L., give it to us good—real plain words, short sentences, and no jargon.

Letter writers will do well not to "dumb down" or "dress up" their language but instead to keep it clear, simple, and sincere. When you are answering a letter, you do have certain clues from the correspondence itself; you should then try to form a mental image of your reader from such facts as:

> The type of business he is in, if any
> His position
> His reason for writing
> What he wants to know
> The kind of language he uses
> Information in the letter itself

But even when you have no correspondence to guide you, you can keep in mind the moral pointed up in the following excellent letter from Yeck and Yeck of Dayton, Ohio, and written by John and Bill Yeck:

QUEEN VICTORIA
WAS A TOUGH CUSTOMER:

If you think Congress doesn't like the President because he vetoes some of their bills, you should have talked to Prime Minister W. E. Gladstone back in Queen Victoria's day.

Every time he went in to see her on a matter of State he came out looking vetoed. He didn't seem able to convince her of anything. She was proud and haughty and dignified. She loved to say "no."

Now, when Disraeli was Prime Minister, things were different.

"The Queen was pleased"; "The Queen agreed"; "The Queen commended." Everything was peaches and cream for Dizzy.

One day someone asked the Queen, "Why?"

She thought a moment, pushed her crown back on her head, cleared the room and her throat, and said softly, "It's this way . . ."

"When Mr. Gladstone talks to us, he talks as though we were a public meeting; but when Mr. Disraeli talks to us, he talks as though we were a woman."

The Queen had something there.

When *you* want conviction, remember Queen Victoria of Great Britain and of her possessions beyond the seas, and Empress, if you please, of India . . . it paid to talk to her "man to man"—like a human being.

Yes, in advertising, in public relations . . . it helps to be human. Writing that is friendly, interesting, pleasant, is writing

                    to a Queen's taste.

                                        John r Bill

                                        Yeck and Yeck

What this classic letter has is the remarkable—and indefinable—quality we call personality. Contrary to the opinion of many letter writers—an opinion all too glaringly reflected in their letters—personality does not mean peculiarity or freakishness. The best letters are those which reflect a tone of friendly interest and warmth, as the following:

Dear Mr. Jarden:

The Chinese have a proverb which seems to me to contain a great piece of advice concerning letter writing:

In the midst of joy do not promise to give a man anything; in the midst of great anger do not answer a man's letter.

We're neither joyful nor angry but we are puzzled as to why we haven't had an order from you in more than six months.

If we haven't served you in the way you expect, we hope you'll let us know so that we can correct any lapses on our part. But most of all, we hope you'll drop in to see us as an old friend.

                    Sincerely yours,

While these aren't business letters, note how well personality and humor come through in this interchange between Sir James M. Barrie and A. E. Housman:

> Dear Professor Houseman,
>
> I am sorry about last night, when I sat next to you and did not say a word. You must have thought I was a very rude man; I am really a very shy man.
>
> Sincerely yours,
>
> *J. M. Barrie*

Professor Housman replied:

> Dear Sir James Barrie,
>
> I am sorry about last night, when I sat next to you and did not say a word. You must have thought I was a very rude man; I am really a very shy man.
>
> Sincerely yours,
>
> *A. E. Housman*
>
> P.S. And now you've made it worse for you have spelt my name wrong.

Even a brief business letter can convey a tone of friendliness and warmth in expressing a desire to be of service:

> Dear Mr. and Mrs. Edwards:
>
> Although the telephone book calls us landscape architects, we much prefer to be known simply as people who for over eighty years have been helping folks with THEIR ideas and THEIR schemes in making their grounds more useful and attractive.
>
> If you will visualize a capable friend working with you, that's mostly what it's like . . . and that's somewhat the manner in which we should like to be of assistance to you.
>
> I wonder whether you feel that we could be of service.
>
> Sincerely yours,

BEGINNING AND ENDING LETTERS

Because of the way letters are read and because they are usually short, two parts of the letter need particular emphasis—the first and the last paragraphs.

While every letter writer likes to think that his message will completely absorb his reader's attention, he cannot write from that assumption. As we indicated before, we do not know enough about "how writing is read," but certain inferences about how the business letter is read seem justifiable in view of the following conditions:

1. Many businessmen have numerous claims on their attention and other letters than ours to read.

2.   The vast increase in the number of letters in the mail probably means that less attention is given by the reader to each letter received.

3.   The phenomenon of "junk mail" has made letter readers increasingly skeptical, more likely to toss letters aside after a quick glance.

4.   As a practical, functional form of communication, the business letter carries with it a general expectation that it will be direct, concise, and—as we say—businesslike.

We can reason, then, that the business letter will generally be read by someone who is busy and wants the message to get to the point, who first asks the question "What's this all about?"—and wants it answered, and whose attention must be aroused if the letter isn't to go in the wastepaper basket. Therefore, for this busy or skeptical or mildly interested reader, the letter *must* get off to a running start by saying something from the first word and come to a neat stop by ending without boring repetition or vapid cliches.

The First Paragraph

Ideally, the first paragraph of the business letter should aim at performing some of these four functions:

1.   It should get favorable attention.
2.   It should indicate what the letter is about.
3.   It should set a friendly and courteous tone for the whole letter.
4.   It should link up with previous correspondence by a reference to date or subject.

If the opening paragraph is direct and interesting, the whole letter may be read with care; if it is not, the rest of the message may be skimmed or skipped entirely. To be effective, the first paragraph of a business letter should observe two principles:

1.   It must be short.
2.   It must say something.

A short first paragraph in a letter leads the reader on to the rest of the message. Regard your first paragraph as a kind of headline which will attract your reader to move to succeeding paragraphs. As a general rule, never put more than two or three sentences in your first paragraph; if you can use fewer, so much the better.

That the opening paragraph should say something seems sufficiently evident. Yet many letters in modern business tell the reader nothing he does not already know. Two things should appear in the first paragraph:

1. A reference to the date of the letter being answered or to similar details which will give continuity to the correspondence.

2. A statement of what this letter is about, unless it is a sales letter in which the first paragraph is designed primarily to attract attention.

The reference to the date of earlier letters or to similar details should always be subordinated. A surprising number of correspondents begin their letters with some such sentences as:

> This is to answer yours of October 14.
> We have received your letter of October 14.
> Referring to yours of October 14. (An incomplete thought.)

The fact that a specific letter is being answered should be taken as sufficient evidence that it has been received; why waste the most important part of the letter—the equivalent of a newspaper headline—merely to tell a reader that his letter has been received or that it was dated October 14? The important task of the first paragraph is to announce what this letter is about in order to arouse the reader's interest; all else should be subordinate. Notice the effectiveness of the second method of writing each of the following opening paragraphs:

Weak and ineffective, because the first 10 words tell the reader nothing he doesn't already know:	Replying to yours of May 10, we can say that our research staff has been working for a long time on the problem that you mentioned and has finally succeeded in solving it.
Direct and effective:	Our research staff has successfully solved the problem of insulating old homes about which you inquired in your letter of May 10.
Weak and full of business jargon:	In reply to yours of July 16, we wish to state that we regret the error made in your last order.
More effective:	Thank you for your letter of July 16 calling attention to our mistake in filling your last order.
Incomplete sentence:	Acknowledging receipt of your letter of February 15 in which you asked for a copy of "Better Homes for Small Incomes." We are glad to send you a copy of this booklet.
Better:	We gladly enclose "Better Homes for Small Incomes," which you requested on February 15. In it you will find the answers to your questions about design, construction costs, and financing of your new home.
Trite and ineffective:	Yours of January 15 received and contents duly noted. We wish to say that we are referring your question to our sales department.

More concise and direct: Our sales department is assembling material which should prove helpful in answering your inquiry of January 15.

Good writers never begin a letter with a participial expression. Almost invariably such a beginning indicates that the writer has not thought out what he wants to say and is merely stalling for time until an idea strikes him. Furthermore, there is a strong possibility that this beginning will turn out to be ungrammatical. (See the Reference Section.) Don't warm up with inane expressions: "Referring to your letter of January 27"; don't rehash what your reader already knows: "Your order of March 12 has been received." Avoid all unnecessary preliminaries in your first sentence and get into your message fast. Here are some good beginnings.

You need not pay a cent to examine this new book at your leisure.
Thank you for your request for information about our reproductions of antiques.
The catalogue you requested on May 27 was mailed today.
You can help me greatly by sending a copy of your article on "Executive Training."
Here is the bulletin you asked us to send.
Thank you for your helpful suggestions about our sales conference.
Congratulations on the fine progress your annual report reveals.
We are pleased to send you the material you requested.
We're sorry that we can't comply with your request of November 19.
The material on page 16 of the enclosed brochure will answer the questions in your letter of June 16.
Just as soon as we received your letter, we wired our New York office to ship your fishing tackle.
The tires which complete your order LL-138 were shipped today.

Because the first paragraph is so important, here are ways of classifying the kinds of examples we have been citing:

1. What's the letter about?—Your order for hi-fi components was shipped by Railway Express on January 15.

2. A direct question—When may we expect to receive the 27 copies of *Looking Backward* which we ordered on August 14?

3. A statement of appreciation—You were thoughtful to send the copy of your company's annual report and I do appreciate it.

4. A mention of a name—Professor J. Ashmore Burington has suggested that I write you about (a job, some information needed, a speaking engagement, or whatever). (This beginning is no better than the significance of the name used to the reader—and courtesy and common sense dictate that you request permission to use the name.)

5. A significant time or date—Our New Year celebration we share with customers. . . . July 10 means a great deal to both of us; you started business that day, and we received our first order from you.

6. A statement of regret—We're genuinely sorry that the merchandise which you wrote about on April 19 somehow got delivered to the wrong address. . . . We certainly agree with you that our dictating equipment should give service for many years, and we are sorry that yours did not measure up to the standards which we set and which you quite properly expect.

7. A polite request or courteous command—May I have two minutes of your time to save you hundreds of hours in the future? . . . May I ask a favor that will help both of us? Don't make one more investment until you have read this book! (The test of how effective these openings are is simple: Does the rest of the letter follow through with the implied promise? If not, the opening has merely enhanced readers' cynicism for the future.)

8. A clever or startling or unusually phrased statement—It's quite possible you owe your life to us, and it's time you let us know how you feel about what was done. (Sent as a fund drive for a hospital to previous patients, many of whom thought it too blunt.) . . . Our Aquagirls wear Swimtex—or nothing. (Sales letter from a resort hotel that had a tie-in with a swimsuit manufacturer.) People who pray together, save together. (Sales letter to church groups offering savings on group travel.) You don't owe us a cent . . . but you will after you've seen the bargains in this catalog. (These openings are effective *only* if the rest of the letter lives up to the first paragraph.)

9. A statement of fact—We serve more than half the homeowners in Garden Town. . . . Your laundry was delayed last week because we moved to our new facilities, which are built so that it won't happen again.

10. An appropriate quotation—An old Norwegian proverb says "On the path between the homes of friends, no grass grows." . . . Did you know that the reason the Chinese have a saying "One picture is worth a thousand words" is that it would take a month to write those thousand words in Chinese?

The Last Paragraph

Like today's railroads, a lot of letter writers have inadequate terminal facilities, and despite the customary advice to "end letters with a bang" they trail off into a whimper. If you've ever had guests who say "good night" and then sit down to tell one more story or experience, repeating the process a few more times, you know how annoying the technique can be. Unlike the weary host, the reader whom you weary with repetition and platitudes can—and does—quit reading. One principle governs your conduct in writing final paragraphs: *Stop when your message is complete.*

The function of the last paragraph of every letter is to make it as easy as possible for the reader to take an action or to accept a point of view that the writer wants him to take. If the you attitude is properly employed, the final paragraph will show the reader how easily he may do this thing that will benefit him. Hence, when a department store wants to get a customer to return some piece of merchandise which has been replaced, the last paragraph of the letter should not read:

> We hope that you will return this dress for credit as soon as possible.

It should offer some such incentive to the customer as:

> Just as soon as you return this dress, we shall gladly credit your account with $11.75.

By enclosing self-addressed envelopes or postcards and referring specifically to these enclosures in their final paragraphs, many correspondents stimulate action by making it very easy. Especially effective are such closing paragraphs as the following, which make definite suggestions and offer an easy means of taking action:

> Just sign and mail the enclosed postcard and you will receive all the news in concise, readable form for the next 52 weeks.

> Your check in the enclosed envelope will enable you to maintain that high credit reputation you have always enjoyed.

> A call—collect, of course—to our sales department will bring a trained member of our staff to give you an estimate, at no obligation to you.

A direct question constitutes a good close because it gives the reader a specific query to consider and to answer.

> May I have an interview with you at your convenience? You can reach me at my home address or 213–4289.

> Are you willing to give Blanco Fuel a 10-day trial to let it demonstrate in your home its efficiency and economy? Your signature on the enclosed card will bring you a 10-day supply without cost. May I have ten minutes in which to substantiate these statements?

> Would you jeopardize your credit rating for so small an amount?

The most ineffective of all closes is the participial ending. It is weak, hackneyed, and incomplete in its thought, and it offers no incentive to action because it eliminates the possibility of taking the you attitude. "Thanking you in advance" and "Trusting we shall have your cooperation in this matter" are the products of the same type of mind as that which begins the letter with the incomplete "Referring to yours of October 15." Such closes can always be changed into direct statements, as "We shall hope to hear from you soon" or "We appreciate your cooperation in this matter." By use of the you attitude, these closes can be transformed into direct incentives to action or builders of good will such as the following:

If we can help you in any way, please let us know.

Mail us your check today and your order will arrive on Thursday.

Just sign your name at the bottom of this letter and return it in the enclosed postage-free envelope.

Will you let us know by April 14 so that we can place your order promptly?

We think this brochure will answer your questions, but if you need more information, please let us know.

Just fill in the card and we'll gladly send a representative to help you.

You can think of the various ways of ending a letter as generally falling into one or another of the following categories:

1. A friendly or personal expression of good will—All of us wish you every success with the opening of your new shop. . . . I do hope you will find all of the arrangements that we have made for you at the convention comfortable and convenient.

2. A polite question (usually requiring no question mark)—May we join all your other business friends in wishing you continued prosperity. . . . Would you like more information? If so, please let us know and we'll furnish it promptly.

3. A courteous command—Remember, the sooner you send in the card, the sooner your subscription starts. . . . Write us as soon as possible, please, and we'll get the information for you.

4. A statement of appreciation—Thanks so much for your cooperation. . . . We do appreciate your understanding of our problem.

5. An apology or expression of regret (if you have not included one previously in the letter)—We're truly sorry that this error occurred. . . . You will understand our chagrin that a mistake like this happened with an old customer like you.

6. A statement to cut off further correspondence (use it *very* sparingly)—You will agree that we have now furnished you with all the information that can be reasonably expected. . . . Since we have exhausted every possibility, you will undoubtedly want to consult someone else.

Whichever ending is appropriate, remember the two principles:

Your purpose is to induce the action or attitude you want.

When your message is complete, *stop.*

EXERCISES

1. In each of the following situations, show how you would use the you attitude as described in this chapter, to persuade your reader to take the action or attitude you want him to:

   a. You need 30 copies of a report, "The Principles of Today's Businessman" by Management Consultants, Inc., to distribute to members of your class in business communications as the basis for a class discussion you are to lead. The report was advertised in the *Wall Street Journal* with the words "available in single copies to those who write on company stationery."

   b. As class secretary, you are responsible for collecting funds for "The Living Memorial of the Class of 197_," a scholarship for "a talented but needy student who has demonstrated intellectual ability in high school." Assuming that it is now five years after graduation, persuade your classmates at your institution to give generously for this purpose.

   c. You work in the office of alumni affairs. Following Commencement, at which 117 graduating seniors walked out when an honorary degree of Doctor of Laws was presented to a prominent member of the Defense Department, you receive 35 letters of protest from prominent alumni. It is your responsibility to keep these alumni interested in the university both because they have considerable influence and because they have generously contributed to the Alumni Fund in the past.

   d. You manufacture musical instruments, of which the bestseller is an authentic reproduction of an Elizabethan recorder. Within the past two weeks, you have received angry letters from four widely scattered dealers saying that customers have returned the recorders in large numbers because of a flaw in tone. As one dealer wrote, "People who pay $29.95 for one of these instruments expect it to be right — and they know when it isn't. I'm tired of these returns, and I'll shift to another company if you don't do something fast." You find that a basic flaw in manufacture has produced the wrong tone; you have corrected the flaw, and you are now prepared to replace all the defective instruments. Write the letter to your four dealers persuading them to stay with your company.

2. How would you respond to the following situations?

   a. A friend has asked you to criticize his application for a job in a summer camp:

   > Dear Mr. Seltzer:
   >
   > I'm awfully anxious to get a job as counselor at Tiwanda this summer because my fiancee will hold a similar position at the camp for girls across the lake.
   >
   > I'm athletic, like kids, am a sophomore at the university, and I promise to do my very best to make a good counselor. I know such jobs don't usually pay much, but that doesn't bother me.
   >
   > Will you let me know?
   >
   > > Very truly yours,

   b. After an investigation which shows that the customer's meter is accurate and the bills are correct, you are to answer the following:

Gentlemen:

I can't understand why my gas bill is always so high. My gas furnace has been checked over carefully by my son who is a sophomore in an engineering college, and he says it is very efficient. Yet, regardless of the weather, my bills are always too high.

Utility companies like yours take advantage of the public and put in meters that always read the same. I get tired of you big companies squeezing us small customers. I want some action and smaller bills.

Yours truly,

c. You have received a letter saying that one of the saleswomen in your department store has been rude to a customer. Upon investigation, you find that while the woman who complained has been a good customer for seven years, she has a reputation with your sales clerks of being impossible to please. The incident involving her specific complaint arose when she monopolized almost three-quarters of an hour of your saleswoman's time, bought nothing, and took offense when the saleswoman politely told her that other customers required her attention. How would you answer the letter?

3. You work in the office which handles the Student Revolving Loan Fund for your institution. The fund grants interest-free loans of up to $1,000 annually to needy students during their undergraduate years. After graduation, annual interest of 6% (compared with the commercial rate of 7½%) is charged on the unpaid balance. Payments and interest are put back into the fund to be used for other needy undergraduates.

Outline the major points you would make in order to get repayments and interest from each of the following:

a. A graduate who borrowed $1,200 to get him through his senior year, now owes $1,317.04, and after two years has made no response to eight letters sent quarterly.

b. A graduate of five years ago who borrowed the full amount of $4,800, has made no payments, but wrote last year, "I will start repaying the loan and the interest just as soon as I finish graduate school this June." He now owes $6,422.98.

c. A woman who did not graduate but borrowed $1,800 during her first three years — at which point she left because of the death of her father. Two years later, in response to one of your letters, she wrote, "I realize that I owe this money but I have no income and my husband refuses to assume any debts incurred before my marriage. He also believes that any educational donations should be made to the college where *he* was educated, since it enables him to earn an income for both of us."

d. A man who owes $5,393.28 after two years on the $4,800 he borrowed, but who wrote saying "I've been in military service in Viet Nam, but I'll pay that money back as soon as I can because it gave me the best investment I ever made — my education — and I want some other young man to have the same chance you gave me."

e. A personality with whom you have had endless disputes during his undergraduate years as to why he couldn't get the loan in cash instead of having it applied to his bills, and why he couldn't have the whole loan at once instead of half each semester, owes $2,400. He graduated second in his class, and three months after graduation wrote to you: "I regard this not as a loan but as an obligation which society owes the intellectual elite. I have no intention of 'repaying,' as you so naively describe it in your notice, something which I don't owe."

4. Of the undergraduates who receive the loans described in the previous problem, 97 percent repay the entire loan and the accrued interest within three years after graduation. Outline what you think you might appropriately say on behalf of the university when you acknowledge the final payment of such loans.

5. Use your own attitude and the viewpoint about the you attitude expressed in this chapter to deal with the following situation:

The Advertising Club of your city has for several weeks run a campaign in the newspapers asking readers to send in examples of "fraudulent, distasteful, overexaggerated, or dishonest advertising. We believe the advertising profession renders a great and necessary service to the American economy, and we want the public to tell us about the few instances where advertising fails to meet our standards of integrity."

Since you hope to make a career in advertising, you are greatly interested in this campaign. This morning, your English instructor made the following comments in a discussion of realism in writing:

Writing that is full of superlatives tends to be dishonest writing, because the real world doesn't contain many "bests," "worsts," "most beautifuls," and "finests." If you have integrity and want to write it like it really is, you'll avoid such untruths.

That night you go through all the ads in a national magazine and locate the following:

Now is the best time to buy it.
The longest-mileage high-performance highway tire ever put on wheels.
Floats fat off your body—while you sleep!
Takes "impossible" pictures.
The happiest holiday spot in the whole world.
Gives you the most protection of any oil.
Life's riches are yours when you rub the Aladdin's lamp of your dynamic mind.
The best-looking shirt a man ever wore.
America's most distinguished car.
Lowest in tars.
We move the world (furniture moving).
With this wizardry, you can live to be a hundred.

How would you answer the following questions?

a. Are these the kinds of examples you might write about to the Advertising Club? Which ones would you include if you wrote to them? What would you write?

b. Is the point made by the English instructor a valid one? Suppose you have disagreed with him on the basis that good advertising has to attract attention and is therefore different from a short story or novel and he has told you to write him a paper defending your point of view. What would you write?

c. If you were the secretary of the Advertising Club and received a letter protesting any or all of the above phrases and claims (you choose which ones to include), how would you respond? Write the secretary's reply.

6. If you were to attempt to persuade readers who might be interested in the following services, what specific means would you use to accomplish your purpose?

a. Each spring, the Rent-A-Wedding Shoppe sends out sales letters in time for June weddings offering to rent all the dresses for bride and bridesmaids and formal attire for bridegroom and ushers at prices ranging from $100 to $1,500 depending on the requirements. The Shoppe will also take over all the arrangements for wedding receptions, banquets, flowers, church services, and anything else connected with the wedding. Its slogan for clothes rental is "Why buy it when you wear it only once?" and for other arrangements, "When it's once-in-a-lifetime, you want it to be right."

b. Your company has a new life insurance policy for people under 20; the premium triples at age 30 "when your earnings will be substantial." Policy cost now is $10 per $1,000 of coverage for your college classmates. How would you persuade them to buy?

c. You have organized a service which will prepare well-organized, neatly prepared resumés for college seniors to use in their search for employment at a cost of $20 for 15 resumés. What approach would you use to get college seniors to purchase such resumés?

7. You are greatly interested in getting a course in oil painting started at the local community center. An artist has volunteered to conduct such a class for 10 weeks if you can get 20 people interested. A notice which appeared previously in the local paper elicited mild or enthusiastic response from 31 people of all ages, and you are planning to send them a letter aimed at persuading at least 20 of them to sign up for the courses. Which of the following would you choose?

Come on now—don't be uptight about this.

We're starting a course in oil painting. So maybe you can't even draw a straight line. So what? You can have fun, maybe learn a little, and all for $25 for ten lessons.

Write out a check, put it in the enclosed envelope, and come to the first session. I'll tell you when after I get the check.

Cordially yours,

At one time or another, all of us have had a secret desire to find out whether we could paint—and now you have that chance.

If we can get 20 people enrolled, John Smith, the prominent local artist, has agreed to conduct ten sessions. The cost is only $25 for a lot of education and a lot of fun, too.

Won't you put your check in the enclosed envelope? If we get 20 interested people, I'll notify you when the class starts; if we don't, I'll return your check.

Sincerely yours,

Write your own attempt if neither of these seems effective.

8. Which of the following statements would be most effective to end a letter in which you seek to get an appointment with a prospective employer? Give reasons.

   a. When can I see you?

   b. If possible, I should like to see you sometime when it would be convenient for you to discuss my qualifications.

   c. Please let me know if I can see you between 2 and 4 on Friday afternoon, May 16.

   d. If you are interested, I should appreciate the opportunity to discuss my education and experience with you. I should like to do this at a time which would be convenient for you if there is any possibility of a vacancy for which I might qualify.

   e. I am certain that I have much to offer your company as an employee. May I call for an appointment?

   f. Thanking you for your courtesy and hoping that you will let me discuss this with you soon.

CHAPTER 6

THE FORM AND MECHANICS OF BUSINESS LETTERS

Since previous chapters have emphasized communication costs and decried wasteful practices, two questions seem appropriate as we begin our discussion of the form and mechanics of letters:

1. Why aren't business letters designed to be more efficient?
2. Why do we continue such meaningless forms as *Dear* ____: and *Yours truly?*

To answer these questions, let's suppose that we have decided to make efficiency the criterion of everything connected with the letter. As we design what we will grandiosely call "a letter for the space age," we ask two experts from our cost analysis department to give us their advice. They tell us to keep two facts in mind:

1. Salary and labor costs are by all odds the prime reason for the high cost of letters. The salaries of the dictator and secretary/stenographer account for 70 to 80 percent of the total cost.
2. Good-quality supplies (stationery, envelopes, carbons, etc.) account for less than 3 percent of the cost. (Remaining costs go for overhead and mailing.)

The cost analysis people tell us that the logical way to proceed is to determine the indispensable requirements for a letter to perform its function, so we come up with the following:

1. To identify a source and a destination, it must carry the name and address of both sender and receiver.
2. To ensure that someone is responsible, it must have the sender's signature.
3. For reference now and in the future, it must have a date.
4. It must carry a message—hopefully, concise, clear, and complete—arranged in simple form for the reader.

Now we go to work with our design. We agree to eliminate all salutations (*Dear Mr. Smith:* or *Gentlemen:*) and all complimentary closes (*Yours very truly, Sincerely yours*). We decide that it is useless duplication to put the reader's name and address on both the envelope and on the message, so we agree to put these on the message only and to use a see-through envelope.

Out of a feeling—and it's exactly that, since we can't find objective evidence to prove it—that large sheets of paper encourage writers to fill up the page, we decide to reduce the size of stationery drastically. We start with see-through envelopes size $3\frac{1}{2} \times 6\frac{1}{2}$ as our functional unit. Hence, we replace all $8\frac{1}{2} \times 11$ stationery with units based upon 3 x 6, so that we have one unfolded size 3 x 6; one 6 x 6 that will be folded once with a carbon between, permitting the reader to use this "courtesy carbon" to write his answer on and still retain a copy of the message; and finally one 6 x 9 folded twice, but to discourage wordiness this will be issued only for special messages. The writer's name and company and address will, of course, be printed at the top of each piece of stationery.

Furthermore, we have agreed that the sensible way to send the message to our reader is the way the Post Office reads it; therefore all addresses will feature zone number first, then state, city, street, number, and lastly the name, as follows:

> 12740
> Ohio, Cleveland
> Euclid Avenue, 10900
> Jones, E. M.

(There was some debate about why we didn't have just the zip code number, without the state, to avoid needless duplication.) Finally, since a member of the sales department complained that his correspondents had great difficulty and wasted considerable time in deciding whether women they wrote to were single or married, it was agreed that all letters to women would use "Ms.," which would replace both Miss and Mrs. (At this point a member of the personnel section said that his people had constant difficulty in issuing statements like "every employee of the company is to bring in his/her/their insurance policy for replacement"; to take care of such awkwardness in a company with equal numbers of male and female employees he wanted a new word *hizurher*, but this was voted down as pertaining to content rather than the form of the message.)

As the result of all this discussion, the following sample letter emerged on a 3 x 6 piece of stationery designed to go in a see-through envelope:

```
From - The Blank Mfg. Co. R. M. Smith Vice-president
       49201, Michigan, Jackson, 27 Wildwood Avenue

June 10, 1971

           To - 40124
                Ohio, Cleveland
                Union Commerce Bldg. 1313
                Ms. A. E. Staley

Thank you so much for sending us the information
concerning what you want done with your policy.

We shall make these changes as you wanted them
and will let you know as soon as possible how
much the new premium will be.

                    R. M. Smith

                R. M. Smith
```

At the next discussion, this form was approved enthusiastically. "Now, let's go to work on that message," a young engineer said. "It should read:

Info re your policy here. Expect changed premium costs soonest.

Now we're really saving money!"

There is no doubt that "we" are. But the relevant question is how far and how fast ought we to proceed with such changes? The answer really lies in how rapidly readers will accept changes from the more conventional letter forms to which they have become accustomed by long usage. You can test this by imagining that you received a message in the form we have designed. Would you resent it as too impersonal in an already impersonal society? Or would you applaud it as meritorious attempt to streamline communications?

Do you, for instance, associate see-through envelopes with bills? Efficiency with coldness and impersonality? Does the abruptness of this message make you long for the conventional greeting and farewell of the traditional letter? If so, we may have saved money but antagonized readers.

No one can say authoritatively that one specific form for the letter is *the* correct form. But before we fly in the face of custom, we do well to fall back on what is generally considered as acceptable usage and to expect a *gradual* change. For instance, the past decade has seen growing acceptance by readers and correspondents of a semiformal style which accomplishes some of the things we mentioned in our "efficiency study" but retains more warmth and personality through replacing inside address and salutation with a mention of the recipient's name in the first line or paragraph (see the illustration on page 117).

One way of studying how fast letter form can be changed is for students and correspondents to try out the several modes in which they can clothe their message and to select the most appropriate form. In many instances, this choice will be governed by the practice of the company they work for. That practice will undoubtedly be based on one of the forms discussed next.

LETTER FORMS

The Block Form

This is probably the most widely used form today (see the illustration on page 118). With its two variants—the semiblock and the complete block— it seems to have more reader acceptance than any other format. The block form takes its name from the fact that the inside address, the salutation, and the paragraphs of the letter are arranged in blocks without indention. Divisions between the inside address and the salutation, between the salutation and the body of the letter, and between the paragraphs in the body of the letter are indicated by spacing, with double spaces *between* the units (i.e., between the inside address, the salutation, and the body of the letter) and single spacing *within* the units (i.e., within the inside address and the individual paragraphs). The open form of punctuation should always accompany the block form (see the illustration on page 118).

The block form offers two definite advantages: it saves stenographic time because each part of the letter except the date, the complimentary close, and the signature is aligned with the left margin so that no time is consumed by indention, and, second, its wide acceptance at the present time offers assurance that the letter arranged in block form is correct and modern.

JENNINGS & JENNINGS
MANAGEMENT CONSULTANTS
116 EAST BOULEVARD
TOLEDO, OHIO 43614

October 15, 1970

Thank you, Mr. Jones . . .

. . . for your interest in why we use this form for our letters.

Actually, we adopted it five years ago because we wanted our letters to look modern but not freakish and because we felt that other letter forms contained a great deal of excess baggage like stereotyped salutations and closes.

Our clients like it too because it gets off to a direct start; they learn to use the broken construction of the first sentence very quickly and it can be arranged in a wide variety of ways, but always with the reader's name mentioned.

Finally, this form forces the correspondent to stop without the conventional "gobbledygook" of complimentary endings. In short, we think this form reflects the modern, efficient approach to management problems we use every day.

George C. Demarest

George C. Demarest
Vice-President

Mr. Chauncy E. Jones
3876 Sunset Drive
Long Beach, California 90805

JOHNSON & JOHNSON SECRETARIAL SERVICE

1111 EAST STREET

TARRYTOWN, NEW YORK 10591

March 5, 1971

Mr. J. C. Cummings
347 East Oak Street
Council Bluffs, Iowa 51501

Dear Mr. Cummings:

This letter illustrates the block form of letter dress, which
has become one of the most widely used methods of arranging
letters.

It takes its name from the fact that the inside address, the
salutation, and the paragraphs of the letter itself are
arranged in blocks without indention. The block form offers two
distinct advantages: it saves stenographic time and reduces
the number of margins. Its wide acceptance at the present
time offers assurance that the letter arranged in block form
is correct and modern.

If you desire your letters to be attractive in appearance,
modern, and economical with regard to stenographic time, I
heartily recommend the block form as the most suitable for
the needs of your office.

Sincerely yours,

Geraldine A. Fisher

Geraldine A. Fisher
Correspondence Supervisor

GAF:GWC

The Semiblock Form

This form is exactly like the block form except for the indention of paragraphs, which appeals to those who are accustomed to seeing paragraphs indented in type and print. Most general practice is to indent 10 spaces (see illustration on page 120), which, of course, produces neat symmetry with the 10-space salutation *Gentlemen:*. Many typists let the salutation govern the spaces in the indention, hence *Dear Mrs. Hepplewight:* would require a 22-space indention for paragraphs; others adhere always to the same number of spaces regardless of the salutation.

The Complete-block Form

Another variation of the block form is the complete or full block (see the illustration on page 121). The basic principle of this letter consists of bringing all the elements of the letter out to the left-hand margin. Hence no changes of margin are required of the typist, and the basic premises of the block form can be said to be carried out to their logical conclusion in this form. It is worth noting that some correspondents and readers object to it because it appears to be unbalanced and heavy on the left side.

The Simplified Letter

The simplified letter, originally advocated by the National Office Management Association, is being increasingly used in all kinds of variants for the very logical reasons which we discussed at the beginning of this chapter. It is efficient; it reduces typing time and consequent costs. The chief characteristics of this form (see the illustration on page 122) are the complete elimination of the salutation and complimentary close and the left-hand block format, which is in general like that of the complete-block form already discussed. Each reader can best test his own decision about using this letter form in terms of his own reaction to it. If it seems too unusual, too different, perhaps his readers will react the same way; if it seems to reflect an efficient and modern approach to correspondence, then readers may conclude that it symbolizes an efficient, modern organization.

The Hanging-indention Form

This form has not come into wide acceptance except in sales letters (see illustration on page 123). The block form with open punctuation is used in the

C. L. DREW & CO.

STENOGRAPHERS · TYPISTS · DUPLICATING

100 BROADWAY

NEW YORK, N.Y. 10005

March 5, 1971

Mr. Robert C. Vanderlyn
2202 Middlebury Road
Winchester, Maine 21873

Dear Mr. Vanderlyn:

I appreciate your interest in my reasons for recommending the type of letter arrangement which our company uses in its correspondence.

After careful consideration, I recommended the semiblock form as the most effective for our company. This recommendation was based on my belief that this form combined most of the advantages of the block and the indented forms.

The block arrangement of the inside address appeals to me as symmetrical and economical of secretarial time; furthermore, open punctuation is modern and efficient. Perhaps it is no more than a whim on my part, but I prefer to have the paragraphs of the actual message indented as they are in books, newspapers, and magazines.

The semiblock form meets all these requirements; it has proved effective and is well liked by our staff of correspondents and secretaries after six years of use.

Sincerely yours,

John H. Porter

John H. Porter
Correspondence Supervisor

JHP:CPA

BAUMGARTNER & JONES

MANAGEMENT CONSULTANTS
4 RIVER STREET
CHICAGO, ILL. 60656

March 5, 1971

Mr. Donald E. Woodbury
3126 Westview Road
Seattle, Washington 98119

Dear Mr. Woodbury:

Your comments about the form of our letters interested me
greatly. As you pointed out, letters do reflect the personality
of the firm which sends them, and that fact played a large part
in our decision to adopt the complete or, as it is sometimes
called, the full-block form.

As management consultants, we felt that our letters should
exemplify the same standards of efficiency and the modern
methods we advocate in industry. For that reason, we saw no
sound reason for retaining a letter form which requires changes
of margins and unnecessary stenographic time.

The salient features of the full-block form are illustrated
in this letter. You will be interested to know that we have
received a number of favorable comments about our letter form and
that our Stenographic Department likes it very much.

Sincerely yours.

E. J. Baumgartner

E. J. Baumgartner,
Partner

EJB:mo

FRY'S OFFICE HELPERS

490 175TH PLACE

WESTBERRY. N.Y. 10603

March 5, 1971

Miss Office Secretary
Better Business Letters, Inc.
1 Main Street
Busytown, U.S.A.

HAD YOU HEARD?

There's a new movement under way to take some of the monotony
out of letters given you to type. The movement is
symbolized by the Simplified Letter being sponsored by NOMA.

What is it? You're reading a sample.

Notice the left block format and the general positioning of the
letter. We didn't write "Dear Miss _____," nor will we
write "Yours truly" or "Sincerely yours." Are they really
important? We feel just as friendly to you without them.

Notice the following points:

1 Date location
2 The address
3 The subject
4 The name of the writer

Now take a look at the Suggestions prepared for you. Talk them
over with your boss. But don't form a final opinion until you've
really tried out The Letter. That's what our Secretary did.
As a matter of fact, she finally wrote most of the Suggestions
herself.

She says she's sold—and hopes you'll have good luck with better
(Simplified) letters.

Vaughn Fry

VAUGHN FRY

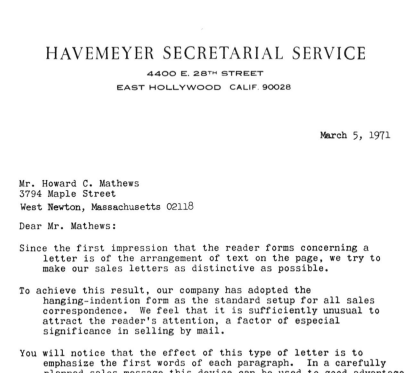

HAVEMEYER SECRETARIAL SERVICE

4400 E. 28TH STREET
EAST HOLLYWOOD CALIF. 90028

March 5, 1971

Mr. Howard C. Mathews
3794 Maple Street
West Newton, Massachusetts 02118

Dear Mr. Mathews:

Since the first impression that the reader forms concerning a
     letter is of the arrangement of text on the page, we try to
     make our sales letters as distinctive as possible.

To achieve this result, our company has adopted the
     hanging-indention form as the standard setup for all sales
     correspondence. We feel that it is sufficiently unusual to
     attract the reader's attention, a factor of especial
     significance in selling by mail.

You will notice that the effect of this type of letter is to
     emphasize the first words of each paragraph. In a carefully
     planned sales message this device can be used to good advantage
     by headlining the salient facts concerning the product sold.

                    Very truly yours,

                    Edward H. DuBois

                    Edward H. DuBois
                    Sales Manager

EHD:ELM

inside address; within the body of the letter, the first line of each paragraph is brought out to the left margin, but every other line in each paragraph is indented five spaces.

This form is effective in attracting attention because it differs from the more common letter arrangements, but that very difference is a disadvantage for those who want to adopt the more widely accepted forms of letter dress. Furthermore, because of its numerous indentions, the hanging-indention arrangement requires more stenographic time.

MECHANICS OF THE BUSINESS LETTER

While the physical setup of the letter is usually the primary responsibility of typists and secretaries, many companies have general policies, set forth sometimes in letter-writing manuals, which govern the mechanical or routine aspects of the letter. Speaking generally, it is desirable for all letters emanating from a company to be uniform both in form (block, semiblock, etc.) and in the arrangement of parts within the letter itself. Since these practices vary from company to company, students should familiarize themselves with the different methods which may be used in setting up the letter and in handling such parts as the salutation or the complimentary close. This section on letter mechanics is intended as a guide to today's widely used practices, but students should remember that change affects all aspects of the letter and that, therefore, these practices are not permenent or rigid.

1. Arrange and center the letter on the page for symmetry and balanced appearance.

Whichever letter form is used, the correspondent should remember that the first impression of a letter results from the arrangement of text on the page. The arrangement is the most noticeable feature of the letter and can interest or prejudice the reader at a glance. A letter's first appeal is to the reader's eye by means of attractive display, balance, and proportion. Lopsided letters, top-heavy letters, or letters running off the bottoms of pages indicate inefficiency and carelessness which reflect unfavorably on the sender. The text should be centered on the page with wide margins on both sides and top and bottom. The usual procedure is to leave a margin of 20 spaces at the left. If the message is very brief, double spacing may be used. The letter should be symmetrical and balanced in appearance; if it is unattractively arranged, it should be retyped, unless the correspondent is willing to have his reader conclude that he is careless and inefficient.

2. Select letterhead and stationery on the basis of simplicity of design and quality.

Businessmen are becoming increasingly conscious of stationery and letterheads, partly because manufacturers have educated them to appraise other companies by their letterheads and stationery. Whether rightly or wrongly, a snap judgment may be passed on a company as the result of the impression made by its letterhead and stationery. Those who use cheap stationery run the risk of being judged parsimonious and careless. While undue importance should not be placed on the letter's physical appearance, an attractive letterhead certainly possesses great value. Like a well-tailored suit, it makes a good impression; and since the cost of this "suit" is a very minor part of letter costs, it should be custom tailored to your needs.

A standard size and good quality of stationery is, therefore, a good investment. Although there has been a trend to various colors of stationery, white or some conservative color is preferable to anything that might give an impression of gaudiness.

The letterhead should be as simple as possible, but it may be considered inadequate unless it answers the following questions:

1. Does it tell who you are?
2. Does it tell what you do? When the company name is not sufficiently descriptive of the type of business, a line should be added to do this.
3. Does it tell where you are located and how you may be reached by telephone, cable, or both?
4. Can it be read easily at a glance?
5. Does it represent your company in a dignified and effective way?

Any symbol or emblem associated with a business may be included as a part of the letterhead. Many companies include the date of their founding and names of company officials, but long lists of agencies, products, or personnel ought never to be a part of the letterhead because they give the whole letter a cluttered appearance. In fact, a recent survey shows that the worst fault of most letterheads is the attempt to pack too much information in them, with a resulting complexity and cluttered appearance. If simplicity of design and quality are the criteria used in selecting the letterhead and stationery, the result will be in good taste.

3. In the salutation and complimentary close capitalize only the first letter of the first word, except for proper names and titles.

A. Except for proper names and titles (President, Mr., Sir, Dr., etc.), capitalize only the first letter of the first word of the salutation.

> Dear Mr. Davidson:
> My dear Mr. Davidson:
> My dear Sir:

B. Capitalize only the first letter of the first word of the complimentary close.

> Yours very truly,
> Very truly yours,
> Sincerely yours,
> Cordially yours,

C. When no salutation or complimentary close is used, as in the more informal or simplified letter forms, the first paragraph with its mention of the recipient's name may be arranged in a variety of ways:

> You know, Mrs. McCleod, that we are having our spring sale this week.
>
> Did you remember, Mr. Jones . . .
> . . . that your premium was due last week?
>
> Thank you so much, Miss Smith, for calling this matter to our attention.

Since these letter forms call for no complimentary close, only a signature above the typed name (and title, if appropriate) is needed:

> We do appreciate your cooperation in this matter.
>
> *James C. Jones*
>
> James C. Jones
> Vice-president

The typed name is usually three spaces below the last line.

4. The salutation and the complimentary close should agree in tone.

As we have seen, much of the verbiage of business letters is now somewhat meaningless as the result of outworn tradition; however, certain degrees of formality or acquaintanceship can be expressed in the choice of the salutation and the complimentary close. These two parts should agree in tone since it is obviously inconsistent to begin with a highly formal salutation and to close in an informal or even friendly fashion. The following groups show the various salutations and closes that may appropriately be used together:

Rather Formal

My dear Mr. Smith: Yours very truly,
My dear Sir: Very sincerely yours,

Less Formal

Dear Sir: Sincerely yours,
Dear Mr. Smith: Sincerely,
Gentlemen: Yours truly,

Cordially yours usually implies acquaintanceship or long business relationship; *Respectfully yours* is generally used in letters to those older or of higher rank than the letter writer. *Dear Sirs* as a salutation is practically obsolete.

5. Punctuate the salutation with a colon and complimentary close with a comma.

Usage in punctuating the business letter has not completely crystallized. The general tendency to reduce punctuation has affected the letter as well as other forms of writing; a number of companies, for example, no longer use the colon after the salutation and the comma after the complimentary close. Letter writers, therefore, have to choose how far they want to go toward an absolute minimum in punctuating the major parts of the letter; if they follow the most widespread practice now used, the date, salutation, and complimentary close will be punctuated as shown in these examples.

Mr. John McDowell
15 East Main Street
Ann Arbor, Michigan 48103

Dear Mr. McDowell:

                                                     Sincerely yours,

The Eastside Corporation
2900 Amsterdam Avenue
New York, N.Y. 10047

Gentlemen:

                                                     Yours truly,

Within the letter itself, the accepted rules of punctuation should, of course, be followed. See the appropriate pages of the reference section for the major rules of punctuation.

6. Company policy should determine the signature.

The signature of the letter should be several spaces directly below the complimentary close; the stenographer customarily leaves sufficient space between the complimentary close (or, if there is none, the last line of the letter) and the typed name and title of the writer for his actual signature, as in the following example:

Sincerely yours,

James Adams

James Adams
Sales Manager
The Green Company

Company policy will determine whether the typed name, title, and company name should follow the pattern of the preceding example or whether the company name comes first, as in the following example:

Sincerely yours,
THE GREEN COMPANY

James Adams

Sales Manager

There is no hard and fast rule on whether the individual's signature or the typed company name is the better practice. A survey by *Printers' Ink* indicates that the use of the company name is somewhat affected by the subject of the letter. Where the message tends to be more personal in tone or is addressed to an individual known to the writer, the great majority of letters surveyed carried the personal signature followed by the typed name and title. On the other hand, when the subject is more general or the correspondents do not know one another, the company name is likely to be used as part of the signature. Recent interpretations of the legal implications of these signature arrangements indicate no difference in legal liability in the two arrangements. This interpretation stems from the obvious fact that when a man signs his name, with his title appearing immediately beneath it, he is speaking for the company or corporation whose name appears on the letterhead.

Another guide as to whether the company or individual form of signature should be used is whether the letter is written in terms of "I" or "we." The use of "we" exclusively in such expressions as "We have looked into the record" and "We want to extend our best wishes for a prosperous year" often gives the letter a rather pompous air. On the other hand, frequent shifts from "I" to "we" within one letter are likely to confuse the reader. Here again practice is not fixed; many companies set up their own policies governing this phase of letter style.

7. A woman should sign her full name and indicate her marital status.

If the correspondent is a woman, that fact and her marital status should be clearly indicated. With the increased number of women in business, the need for a standard technique for their signatures is evident, as anyone will realize who has addressed a letter to "Mr. A. Winters" and found later that his correspondent is Agatha Winters. Such situations can be readily eliminated by having women sign their first names in full instead of using initials. But where initials are used, "Miss" in parentheses should be included. A married woman signs her full name with her married name below it in parentheses:

> Alberta Potter Webb
> (Mrs. Robert J. Webb)

8. Signatures should be legible.

The widespread use of the typewriter has fortunately decreased the need for handwriting. This boon to the business world has not altered the fact that too many correspondents still sign their names in indecipherable scrawls and too many typists fail to type the correspondent's name beneath his signature. Particularly in companies that deal with handwritten letters from the general public the cry is still heard, "Why on earth don't you sign your name so I can read it?" People who have received such letters will enjoy the opinions expressed by Thomas Bailey Aldrich in the following letter to Professor Edward S. Morse:

> It was very pleasant to me to get a letter from you the other day. Perhaps I should have found it pleasanter if I had been able to decipher it.
>
> I don't think I have mastered anything beyond the date (which I knew) and the signature (which I guessed at). There's a singular and a perpetual charm in a letter of yours; it never grows old, it never loses its novelty.
>
> Other letters are read and thrown away and forgotten, but yours are kept forever—unread. One of them will last a reasonable man a lifetime.

Since the signature is an integral and important part of the business letter, it should be legible, placed correctly in the space provided for it, and put on an even keel. Many correspondents erroneously think that a distinctive touch is added by slanting the signature or, what is worse, by writing over the typed name.

9. The date is usually written in the upper right-hand section.

Unless the letterhead is of a design that makes a different place preferable or unless the simplified letter form is used with the date on the left-hand margin, the date should be placed in the upper right-hand section of the letter and at least two spaces above the first line of the inside address. The day of the month should always be set off from the year by a comma:

February 24, 1971
December 5, 1970

Such abbreviations as 6/7/71 should be avoided because they cause confusion; there is no necessity for writing *th*, *nd*, *rd* after numerals in the date (September 15th, May 2nd, July 3rd). Write September 15, May 2, July 3. Military usage requires that dates be written 20 August 1970. While some business writers have adopted this usage, there seems to be little justification for changing from the traditional order of month, day, year—August 20, 1970.

10.   Use the address shown on the letterhead.

The correct address to use in writing to any company or individual is exactly that which the company or individual uses on its stationery or advertising. When street names using numerals, such as Fifth Avenue, East 116th Street, Second Avenue, are part of the address, the best procedure is to write them out if they are numbers from one to ten or if they can be expressed in one word; if they are more complex, use numerals:

79 Fifth Avenue
2719 East 116th Street
3019 102nd Street

With the establishment of the ZIP code (for Zone Improvement Plan), it is probably only a matter of time before all big mailers will be using addresses such as:

Mr. Robert Sterling
291 Middle Street
45202

when they want speedy delivery to Cincinnati, Ohio. The system divides the country into areas east to west (there are exceptions), starting with 00601 (Puerto Rico) and ending with 99929 (Wrangell, Alaska). The first digit identifies one of ten basic geographical areas; the next two mark a major city or sectional center; the last two focus on specific mailing areas. Contrary to general opinion, the real savings of the Zone Improvement Plan result from the fact that large mailings of so-called "promotional" materials and the like are sorted according to zip numbers before being taken to the post office. (An indispensable reference for all businesses is the *National ZIP Code Directory*, which contains the zip codes for every mailing address in the United States and its territories. It may be ordered from the Superintendent of Documents, U.S. Government Printing Office, Washington, D.C. 20402, for $10.50 a copy.)

In using the zip code, correspondents should remember the following:

1. Always use a zip number, if you know it.

2. If you are certain of the number, you need use no state or city identification, as in the example for Mr. Sterling.

3. If you use city, state, *and* zip number, the best practice is to use no punctuation between the state name and the zip number other than punctuation required for the state abbreviation:

> Bloomington, Ill. 61701
> Bloomington, Illinois 61701

4. The zip number is customarily placed on the same line as the city and state names, but with short addresses it is sometimes placed on the last line by itself:

> Mr. James Jones
> Acra, New York
> 12740

Company policy and your own judgment must determine when it is appropriate to make the change to your reader in Bloomington by dropping city and state completely:

> Mr. Jon Smith
> 517 Oak Street
> 61701

11. The salutation should agree with the first line of the inside address.

The most widely used salutations are *Gentlemen* (for companies or organizations) and *Dear Mr. Smith* (for an individual). *Gentlemen* has largely supplanted the former use of *Dear Sirs*. Careful writers feel that mentioning the individual by name in the salutation—as *Dear Mr. Doe*—gives more warmth and a more personal touch to the letter; for that reason *Dear Sir* has come to be considered as too impersonal.

The salutation should always agree with the first line of the inside address; if that line is plural (a partnership, a company, a firm name), the salutation should be plural. If the first line is feminine (a firm composed entirely of women), the salutation should be feminine. Even though the letter is directed to the attention of an individual, if the first line of the address is the company name, the salutation should be plural. The following examples illustrate these points:

> Williams, Clement, Constant, and Williams, Inc.
> 1410 Broadway Building
> Cleveland, Ohio 44106
>
> Gentlemen:

Most American correspondents gag a bit over using *Mesdames;* consequently, *Dear Ladies* or the following can be used:

> The Three Sisters Dress Shop
> 3914 East Third Street
> Seattle, Washington 93071
>
> Ladies:

Note the difference in the salutation when the *Attention* device is used:

> Mr. Arnold Lehman, Sales Manager
> The Viking Air Conditioning Company
> 3133 Constitution Avenue
> Omaha, Nebraska 69717
>
> Dear Mr. Lehman:

but

> The Viking Air Conditioning Company
> 3133 Constitution Avenue
> Omaha, Nebraska 69717
>
> Attention: Mr. Arnold Lehman, Sales Manager
>
> Gentlemen:

When addressing a post-office box, a newspaper number, or a reader whose identity is unknown, use *Gentlemen* as the proper salutation:

> B14978, *The New York Times*
> Times Square
> New York, New York 10036
>
> Gentlemen:

In the reference section, you will find a handy checklist of proper salutations for members of the clergy, the military, governmental officials, etc.

12.   To direct the letter to the attention of an individual within the company, add an "Attention" line two spaces below the inside address.

Frequently it is desirable to direct letters which concern the business of a whole firm or corporation to the attention of an individual within the company with whom one has had previous correspondence or who is familiar with the specific problem at hand. The word *of* after *Attention* has come to be regarded as superfluous, and practice varies as to using the colon after *Attention*. The *Attention* line should be placed two spaces directly below the last line of the inside address and with the same margin. The earlier practice of centering the *Attention* line is no longer followed, because that space is customarily used to indicate the subject of the letter.

> The Black Company
> 1419 Broad Street
> Winchester, Massachusetts 01890
>
> Attention Mr. Michael Cunningham
>
> Gentlemen:

Mention of file numbers, policy numbers, or other aids in identifying the business at hand may be made in a similar manner.

> The Worthy and White Company
> 2789 Canal Street
> Kingston, New York 12749
>
> Your file No. 71698
>
> Gentlemen:

In accordance with the principle that salutations should agree with the first line of the inside address, the following are the forms most frequently used:

Inside address	*Salutation*
Mr. John C. Smith	Dear Mr. Smith:
3194 Blank Avenue	
Middletown, Conn. 06547	

The John C. Smith Company   Gentlemen:
4978 Center Street
Centerville, Idaho 83610

The John C. Smith Company   Gentlemen:
4978 Center Street
Centerville, Idaho 83610

Attention Mr. E. D. White

Mr. E. D. White   Dear Mr. White:
The John C. Smith Company
4978 Center Street
Centerville, Idaho 83610

The Lakewood Women's Club   Ladies:
130 Fourth Avenue
Lakewood, New Jersey 08701

**13.   The second page of the letter should not be on letterhead paper and
should be clearly numbered.**

When letters are more than one page in length, the additional pages should be
on stationery to match the first sheet but without the letterhead. These pages
may be headed in any of the following ways, although the first form is most
frequently used because it is most suitable for filing:

Mr. Cunningham   -2-   July 7, 1971

Page 2
Mr. Cunningham

**14.   The initials of the dictator and the stenographer as well as a reference to
any enclosures should be indicated at the bottom of the letter.**

Numerous methods of indicating the initials of the dictator of the letter and the
stenographer are in common use. This information should be placed at the left
margin of the letter and at least two spaces lower on the paper than the last
line of the signature.

FJP/KRS
FLT:CMJ
W:m

Whenever enclosures are to be made, notation of that fact should be made as follows:

FJP:KRS
Encl.

Enclosures should be arranged in back of the letter in the order of their importance or in the sequence in which they are mentioned in the letter. With the exception of checks or drafts, enclosures should never be placed on top of a letter.

15. Envelopes should give the complete address.

The complete address should always be given on the envelope, and if one of the letter forms with an inside address is used, the address on the envelope should be identical with that on the letter. As section 10 indicates, a name, street and number, and zip code are now considered as a "complete" address if company policy permits. While it seems somewhat gratuitous to say so, a number of correspondents have discovered to their chagrin that a great deal of confusion and embarrassment can be avoided by placing the proper letter in the proper envelope!

16. The signer of the letter has final responsibility for it.

Since the finished letter is, in a very real sense, *your* representative, take care to make it correct in every detail. In today's business world, the best letters are those which are the result of careful thought by *both* dictator and transcriber. Ultimately, the final responsibility for every aspect of the letter rests completely on the person who signs it, but the best results occur when the dictator and transcriber work as a team. The transcriber should proofread carefully for errors in spelling, punctuation, grammar, or typing. She should see that all initials, names, dates, and addresses are accurate. The correspondent should then read the letter carefully for the same purposes and to see that it effectively does what it is intended to do. When he signs the letter without reading it—as too many correspondents do—he is shirking his fundamental obligation to see that every letter he writes is as nearly perfect as he and his typist can make it.

A FINAL WORD ABOUT FORM AND MECHANICS

While the detailed emphasis we have placed on form and mechanics in this chapter is helpful to many correspondents, one should not blow up such details out of all proportion. As we said at the outset, these practices are not permanent or rigid; furthermore, once you get on the job many of these decisions will be settled by company policy, often in the form of a letter-writing manual to ensure uniformity. In the final analysis, good taste and general usage should decide which of the various forms and styles is most appropriate.

Nonetheless, as we look ahead to the decade of the seventies, we can make a reasonable guesstimate of changes to come based on the trends of the past decade:

1. Less punctuation will be used. The criterion will be "Does it add to clarity?" Hence the traditional use of colons after saluations and commas after complimentary closes will diminish or disappear.
2. The more informal and simplified letter forms will be used more frequently. Unnecessary formalisms will disappear; courtesy carbons for reply will increasingly be used.
3. Zip numbers will eventually supplant place and state names in addresses.
4. Because of soaring costs, business will increasingly judge all aspects of correspondence by the question "Does this serve a real purpose, or is it merely traditional?"

All of these guesses add up to one central hypothesis which can be ventured with considerable certainty: the message—rather than the formalities surrounding it—will be the central focus; consequently, people with skill in expression will be in greater demand than ever before.

SUMMARY

In Part Two we have been discussing the basic qualities and the fundamental forms and mechanics of business letters; in Part Three we shall analyze the various *types of letters* in terms of the material they contain. But regardless of the type of letter or the sales or collection material it contains, all the qualities and the techniques of writing thus far discussed in Parts One and Two should be made an integral part of the letter.

We have fixed responsibility for effective communication on the writer. When he writes a business letter, he is sending a message in which he attempts to influence his reader to take some desired action or attitude. With this responsibility and this purpose clearly fixed we can briefly summarize the material discussed in Parts One and Two by insisting that the responsible correspondent do the following things:

1. Before writing, analyze what is the purpose of the letter.
2. Use those qualities which will be most effective in influencing the reader to do what the letter writer desires.

    a. Use the you attitude, which takes the reader's point of view by showing him that it is to his advantage to do it.

    b. Adapt the letter to the interests and understanding of the reader.

    c. Give the letter a friendly tone or personality.

3. Select the appropriate letter form and see that all its parts are consistent with the best usage.

4. Make sure that correct grammar, spelling, and punctuation have been used.

5. Avoid jargon and any wordy, trite, or meaningless expressions.

6. Make the letter easy to read.

    a. Keep the paragraphs and sentences short.

    b. Start with a direct and concise opening paragraph.

    c. Stop when everything necessary has been said.

    d. Avoid wordiness by conscientiously using the techniques of readable writing.

    e. Revise the letter wherever it may be improved.

The following rating scale offers a convenient way for you to apply to your own letters the principles discussed in preceding chapters.

A Rating Scale for Letters

Every letter creates a definite impression on the reader. While the factors involved in such an impression cannot be reduced to a mathematical formula, the following rating scale will help correspondents to evaluate their efforts. If they can answer "Yes" to the questions listed, they are on the road to successful letter writing.

Appearance 20%   Does the letter's appearance make a good first impression? Does it comply with correct usage for this letter form? Is it free from erasures, strike-overs? Is it well balanced on the page? Are the paragraphs short enough to invite easy reading? Has it been checked for errors in grammar, punctuation, and spelling?

Thought 20%   Does it reveal careful thought about the fundamental purpose of the letter? Does it achieve that purpose? Does it answer all the necessary questions? Is the material presented in logical order?

Attitude 20%   Does it point out to the reader how he benefits from the action you suggest? Does it build good will? Does it include all the information he needs? Is it written in language your reader will understand?

Style 20%   Is it clear, concise, and readable? Does it avoid jargon and trite, meaningless, or wordy expressions? Are the sentences short and direct? Has it been revised to correct all errors in style?

Tone 20%   Does it sound as if one human being had written it to another? Does it avoid technical language and negative words? Is it friendly, courteous, and tactful? Does it steer clear of exaggerated claims and overstatements? Does it sound sincere?

EXERCISES

1. Correct any errors in form, mechanics, grammar, punctuation, or spelling in the following examples:

a.

April 21, 1970

Jean's Beauty Shoppe
3197—9th St.
Cincinnati, O.—45202
ATT. of Miss Jean Oglethorpe

Dear Miss Oglethorpe,

The shipment of merchandise your ordered was made two weeks ago and should have arrived within 3 days.

We are going to do our best to check this thru and see what happened. In the meantime to accomodate you, we are sending a duplicate shipment since it is liteweight and small in bulk.

We regret any inconvience you may have had. This is not service like we want to give and we are going to change to another trucking company because of this.

Cordially

Peter Emlyn

cc/PE

b.

April 21, 1970

Thank you Mrs Worthington . . . .
for your prompt payment.

We have a sale going on RIGHT NOW for customers like you; it will advantage you to come on down because sales-wise nothing like this has occured in this town for a milenium.

If you'd want to bring some of your friends you'll do them a big favour.

Yours most Sincerely,

John Williams—Manager

JW___pf

2. Arrange the following material in the form of a simplified letter, omitting any unnecessary material and adding necessary punctuation.

> June 22 1970
>
> The C F Thomas Mfg Co East Liverpool Ohio 26831
>
> Attention M F Ely Sales Manager
>
> Gentlemen
>
> We appreciate your thoughtfulness in calling our attention to the article on Air Conditioning in South Africas Largest City in the June 6 issue of Import-Export Magazine. Since we shall be able to use excerpts from the article in a sales letter you have done us a real service for none of the members of our organization had seen the article before you called it to our attention
>
> Sincerely yours   George C Delaney   President

3. A young colleague of yours has submitted to the head of stenographic services a form which, as he describes it, "will save money and put us in the vanguard of those who want to throw out all the obsolete practices connected with letter writing." The form looks like this:

> To-   Date -
>
> From-
>
> Subject-

   It contains a so-called "courtesy carbon" for reply and can be folded so that the address will show through a see-through envelope, both when it is originally sent out and when it is returned.

   The head of stenographic services has said, "It looks too much like an internal memo to me, but I'm willing to be open-minded about it." Assuming (a) that you have been asked to write a memo to her making a recommendation and (b) that letters from your company go to a cross section of people, what would be your response?

4. If you had free choice of all the various forms discussed in this chapter and your company's correspondence went to a reasonable cross section of the public, which form of letter would you select? Why?

5. Would your choice in question 4 be different if you worked for:
   a. An advertising agency
   b. A university
   c. A teen-age boutique
   d. An accounting firm
   If so, why?

6. Using whatever questions of "A Rating Scale for Letters" (page 137) are appropriate, which of the following letters would you consider unacceptable? Why? What changes would you make in those which you find unsatisfactory?

a.

You know, Mr. Smith, . . . that your credit is your most valuable asset.

That's why we hope you won't jeopradize it for a small sum. Won't you send us $67.13 today to clear up your past account? Thank you.

J. P. Love, Credit Manager

b.

Box 2Z 3719   6–7–70

The SUN-PRESS

New York, N.Y. 10047

Dear Sir:

I was reading the advertisements in this morning's Sun-Press and I happened to see your ad. for a secretary.

I am a high school graduate with one year of business college and two years of experience as secretary to the sales manager of the Brown Novelty Corporation, manufacturer of children's toys.

I hope you will consider my qualifications which I am giving in some detail on the enclosed personal record sheet, because I dislike my present position and I want very much to work in New York City.

In the event that you are interested, I shall hope to hear from you.

Sincerely Yours,

Ruth Smith.

c.

The A. B. Bradley Co.   July 17th, '71

241 East One Hundred Sixth Street,

Birmingham, Ala. 29861

Attention: Mr. C. E. Black

My Dear Mr. Black,

We have recieved your request for our booklet "Principles of Selling" which we are glad to send you. This booklet has had excellent affects in aiding numerous companies to increase their sales.

We hope you will find it useful.

Yours Truly

7. For a business-sponsored annual meeting of the Education-Industry Conference, you have been asked to present a ten-minute talk titled "Shall We Change Our Practices in Business Letters?" For this talk, you are to take one of the following as representing your viewpoint and to write out the major points you will make in your speech:

a. Wasted words and outmoded forms mean wasted money.

b. "Be not the first by whom the new is tried
Nor yet the last to lay the old aside."

—Alexander Pope

c. Make haste slowly.
d. In an era of moon voyages and computers, today's business correspondence is defunct as the dodo.

8. You have had a letter of inquiry from Mrs. Elvira Fullerton, Head of Stenographic Services, University Associates, Inc., University Circle, Cleveland, Ohio 44106, asking three questions:
   a. What form of letter does your company use?
   b. Why did you select it?
   c. If you are not now using the simplified letter form, did you consider it seriously? If so, why did you not adopt it?
   Answer Mrs. Fullerton's letter.

9. Set up in proper form the mechanics required for the following letters (date, inside address, salutation, complimentary close, signature, and typist's and dictator's initials). It is not necessary to write the letter, but if you use a form which omits any of the elements listed, write the first and last sentences of your letter. Use a different letter form for each situation.
   a. A letter to Mr. C. A. May, Vice-President in charge of Distribution and Sales, The Han Co., 37954 East Bolingbrook Blvd., New York, N.Y. 10017, in which you enclose two brochures; you dictate to Sarah du Bois McKnight.
   b. A letter to Mrs. C. Blakesley Weatherington, Director of Sales and Services, Coe Co., Box 4700, Greenville, Illinois 60627, dictated to Karla Goodrich and enclosing a check for $7.50 to correct an overpayment made by Mrs. Weatherington.
   c. A letter to a stockholder in your company who signed her letter Ann Winters. She lives at 391 Maple Street, Batesville, Indiana 40961, and the purpose of your letter is to find out the proper form—Miss, Mrs.—to enter on your list of stockholders. You are enclosing a form for her to fill out for your company records.
   d. A letter to John Milton, full professor of English with the A.B., M.A., and Ph.D. degrees, head of the department of English Literature, the Community College of the County of Ulster, Stone Ridge, New York 12639, in which you ask for an English scholarship for next year. You have good reason to believe that Milton is now on leave of absence.
   e. A letter to P.O. Box 9901, San Francisco, California 95009 ordering a special part you have seen advertised in a magazine.

10. Answer the following questions or fill in the blanks in the statements:
    a. The _____ form is probably the most widely used form of letter today.
    b. Is the date placed in the upper right-hand corner in the simplified letter form?
    c. The only part of the complimentary close ever capitalized is _____.
    d. Is the salutation *Gentlemen* always correct for a letter addressed to a company?
    e. Would a date arranged 6/9/71 be correct in writing to a military man?

    f.   Should a woman always sign letters using her first two initials?

    g.   In a letter to a company but to the attention of Mr. Smith, the salutation should be _____.

    h.   When should the date be written Sept. 15th or Dec. 12th?

    i.   When might *Respectfully yours* be used as a complimentary close?

    j.   Should the second page of a letter be numbered?

    k.   At the bottom left margin should be placed the initials of _____.

    l.   Is anything else other than these initials ever placed there?

    m.   Letters written in the informal style do not use _____ but in the first sentence they include _____.

    n.   Letters are almost always single-spaced, except when _____.

    o.   Is *Dear Sirs* appropriate as a salutation for a consulting partnership composed of men and women?

    p.   Is it true that letterheads and stationery cost so much that they should be designed very carefully?

    q.   To be effective, a letterhead should contain the following information: _____ _____.

    r.   Increasingly, zip numbers are used on envelopes to replace _____.

    s.   Hanging indention in a letter can be used to good effect for _____ (type of letter).

    t.   When can *Dictated but not read* be used appropriately?

    u.   Is the advantage of the full block form the fact that it appeals to those who are used to seeing paragraphs indented?

    v.   Is there a standard number of spaces that letters in the semiblock form should use for paragraph indention?

    w.   Is it true that whether the individual or the company name appears first in the signature of a letter depends on whichever arrangement gives a better appearance to the letter?

    x.   The proper way to address letters to those who write to you is _____.

    y.   The final responsibility for sending out a letter which is correct in all aspects rests on _____.

11.   Using the rules on punctuation in the reference section, punctuate the following sentences from business letters:

    a.   Our records show that on January 3 1971 he ordered the following models No 25 $126 No 27 $139 No 29 $152

    b.   The cost of the repairs on your machine is slight however we must have your approval before we can proceed

    c.   The camera has been dropped or damaged in some way and its lens must be replaced

    d.   This model which is our best seller at present will give you the dealer a 20 percent margin of profit

    e.   This catalogue was not written for the public it was designed especially for executives like you

    f.   Since you have made no reply to our letters of December 15 January 2 and January

15 we must conclude that you do not wish to assume the responsibility which you must realize is yours

g. We shall be forced therefore to turn this bill over to our attorney we are of course reluctant to do this

h. The letter which closes with a specific request for action is better than the one with a vague indefinite or participial ending

i. Our graduates have their choice of three different fields production sales or research

j. Does this interest you you can double your profits within three weeks if you will devote your spare time to our proposal

k. Before signing an important letter you should read it over very carefully and ask yourself how would this sound in court if suit were brought

l. Our representative Mr. Gray has told you of this newest model of ours which has broken all sales records within the first six months of 1970

m. Make your letters sound like you then you need never worry about their impersonality

n. We are grateful to you for telling us of your experience with our heater in your letter of February 12 but we believe that the fuel not the heater is causing your difficulty

o. When you buy Blank products you know you are getting the best

p. At the directors meeting on June 28 1970 Mr. Jones Annual Report to the stockholders was approved and the yearly dividend was increased

q. A refrigerator such as yours that has given ten years of service should have a thorough reconditioning

r. During these many months of material shortages weve had to write so many letters refusing orders that it is a pleasure to tell you that we can now fill your order in 30 days

s. When we extended credit to you we expected that you would meet your obligations promptly however we are forced to the conclusion that we were wrong

t. The applicant is a man of fine character and good habits and I am sure that upon investigation you will find he possesses the qualifications which are necessary for the position he seeks

u. This product which resulted from three years work in our research laboratory will be on the market in three weeks

v. According to authoritative reports from the coat and suit industry there will be a shortage of mens suits and childrens clothes which will last until August 1971

w. This plan a product of our intense market research will give you greater information wider choice of markets and increased protection against price fluctuation

x. Our credit arrangements with the company which you mentioned in your letter have proved rather unsatisfactory however with the greater demand for childrens books they may show some improvement in the future

y. Thank you for your interest in our sales methods we are delighted naturally that you have selected us for inclusion in your report

12. In Exercises 10 and 11, 50 examples concerning form, mechanics, and punctuation of

letters were given. If you could not handle at least 40 of these examples correctly, you ought now to select one of the following reasons (or alibis) and write out in clear, correct, concise English your justification for your selection:

a. All these details are of no importance; it's what you *say* in the letter that counts.

b. I'll have a secretary and she'll take care of all the details. It's none of my responsibility anyway.

c. I don't care about common usage. I know what looks right and I'll get along fine.

d. I know a man whose letters are so bad they fracture all the rules—but he's making $75,000 a year, and that's more than a lot of so-called communication experts are making.

e. Maybe I'd better go back and learn present usage, because even if I have a secretary, I ought to know myself whether what we're doing is right since I'm the one who's going to be responsible.

PART THREE

SPECIFIC TYPES OF BUSINESS LETTERS

We are now going to consider in specific terms the first of the major forms of business communication—the business letter—and the methods, principles, and problems which relate to it. Our earlier definition of the letter in the introduction to Part Two is a useful one to keep in mind: *The business letter is a message that attempts to influence its reader to take some action or attitude desired by its writer.* Similarly important is our earlier discussion of the basic qualities all letters should have—the you attitude, appropriate tone, personality, and correctness in language, form, and mechanics.

The various types of business letters can be classified in a number of different ways. Some textbooks classify them by viewpoint—the persuasive and the disappointing, the acceptance or the turn-down, the routine and the non-routine, those that say "yes" or "no." Far more important than such classifications, however, are the principles and purposes governing the effective ways to write them.

One professional after 27 years of experience says:

I classify every letter I write under one of four headings in my mind—but the important factor is not what I *call* it but what I do with it.

The first two headings are usually easy because it's easy to do what the reader wants you to:

1. Letters that say *yes* -"We're glad to grant your request" (or send the information, or do what you wanted).
2. Letters that say *yes but* or *yes if* - "We'll send it to you, but first we must have signed authorization" or "If we receive it in time, we can do what you requested."

The last two are hard. I call them "salvage operations" because these letters turn someone down in terms of what he wants. I then have to get him to accept some different solution and keep his good will. In any event, I'm trying to salvage something—tangible or intangible.

3. Letters that say *no, unless* or *no, until* - "We're sorry we can't grant credit unless you send us more detailed information" or "We don't accept applications until our recruiters have had personal interviews."
4. Letters that say *no* - "You will understand that we can't divulge this information because our employees have requested us to keep it confidential."

We could probably use this method of organizing the chapters that follow. Or we could divide letters into the routine messages and those that don't fall into any obvious pattern.

It seems more practical, however, to organize our discussion of letters in terms of their precise purpose and to separate them into the functional categories used by most large corporations. Since the business executive tends to think of each letter in terms of purpose—and often to think in organizational patterns performing that purpose—his language classifies it as a collection letter if its aim is the collection of a bill (by the collection department), an adjustment letter if it adjusts a claim (claims department or claims and adjustment section), and so on. This is helpful terminology for the student to learn—but if he intends to become a professional, in the sense we have been describing, he should be wary of jumping to the erroneous conclusion that all letters fall neatly into one or another pat classification. They do not; no textbook, therefore, can do better than to adopt one of several convenient means of classifying letters for the purpose of intelligent discussion. As a matter of fact, once he gets on the job, the student will undoubtedly hear some experienced correspondent say, "When in doubt, think of every letter as a sales letter"—and that is good advice too, because, in effect, it means that every letter should incorporate the qualities of communication we have discussed in Parts One and Two.

Because we now start dealing with the specific problems of specific types of letters, we will in the next three chapters include a *Letter Problem*. (The name is used simply to distinguish it from the Exercises.) The intent is to make the letter problem a specific application of the principles discussed in the chapter and to set up a topic for classroom discussion. Each letter problem has been deliberately selected to require imagination, originality, and skill in expression *in a difficult situation*. In two chapters, alternate solutions to the letter problem are given for the students' evaluation; in Chapter 7, only the letter problem is given, so that students will not be influenced by other solutions.

INQUIRIES, ANSWERS TO INQUIRIES, ORDERS

Among the routine types of letters most frequently written to business firms is the letter of inquiry. This letter seeks information on a broad variety of matters such as the operation of machinery, the price of certain products, the construction of various models or the uses to which they may be put, or any one of an infinite number of similar subjects. The simplest way to classify these letters is:

1. *The solicited letter of inquiry*, which is usually a response to an advertisement inviting the reader to write in for further information to a certain department or division.
2. *The unsolicited letter of inquiry*, in which the writer takes the initiative in asking for information.

While these two types usually emanate from the individual (rather than from the individual as a representative of his company or corporation), it is important to know about them for two reasons: first, every person at one time or another writes such a letter and, second, the response of any business enterprise to such inquiries is a sensitive barometer of its efficiency and atittudes.

149

THE SOLICITED INQUIRY

Resulting as it does from a specific suggestion, the solicited inquiry presents no difficulties. It should be very brief, usually no longer than one or two sentences, and should state definitely what is wanted. Usually, a mention of the advertising medium in which the suggestion to write appeared is appropriate. The following examples are typical:

The Equitable Life Assurance Society
1285 Avenue of the Americas
New York, N.Y. 10019

Gentlemen:

Please send me the prospectus on Individual Annuity Contracts which was mentioned in your ad in *Time* last week.

Incidentally—and perhaps this is just idle curiosity on my part—would you please tell me why your company uses "Assurance" in its name rather than the more normal "Insurance"?

Sincerely yours,
Howard J. Bender
27 Pine Street
Columbia, South Carolina 29202

Pitney-Bowes, Inc.
1350 Pacific Street
Stamford, Connecticut 06902

Gentlemen:

Please send me information about the features and cost of the desk model postage meter which you advertised in *Nation's Business* for July, 1970.

Yours truly,
Robert Black

F. W. Dodge Corporation
119 West Fortieth Street
New York, N.Y. 10018

Gentlemen:

In accordance with your offer in *Business Week* for July 13, 1970, please send a copy of your *How to Improve Sales Effectiveness in the New Construction Market* to me at 2719 Park Street, Seattle, Washington 98114

Sincerely yours,
Esther A. Marshall
(Mrs. Robert Marshall)

Writers of inquiry letters should remember two things that make a satisfactory reply possible:

1. Be as specific as possible about what you want.
2. Include your address if you use paper without a letterhead. Advertisers and business-men testify unanimously to the large number of inquiries they can't answer because writers forgot to include their addresses.

THE UNSOLICITED INQUIRY

The unsolicited inquiry letter is more complex and much more detailed. Since the writer is asking a favor, he should strive beyond all else *to make his inquiry easy to answer.* This can best be done by making the question as direct and specific as possible or, if the inquiry is lengthy, by tabulating the questions or by using an arrangement in which they may be answered by "yes" or "no" or by checking. No writer of an unsolicited letter of inquiry should expect a complete stranger to spend several hours answering questions of a general nature; instead, he must phrase his queries so carefully that answering them will require the shortest possible time. Courtesy demands that a stamp or a self-addressed, stamped envelope be enclosed if the inquiry is addressed to an individual or to a small firm; if it is sent to a large company with its own mailing department, the stamp should not be included because it will probably interfere with the regular mailing routine.

To give the reader sufficient information to enable him to answer intelligently and easily, the well-planned unsolicited inquiry usually contains:

1. A clear statement of the information desired or of the problem involved. This should include:
   a. What is wanted
   b. Who wants it
   c. Why it is wanted
2. A tabulation of questions or a reference to an enclosed questionnaire.
3. An expression of appreciation.

To ensure getting the maximum amount of information from his letter, the writer of an unsolicited inquiry should:

1. Ask as few questions as possible.
2. Phrase them so that they are clear, direct, and easy to answer.
3. Where confidential information is requested, promise to keep it confidential.
4. Try to send the inquiry at those seasons when the pressure of business is least heavy.
5. If possible, stress the way in which the recipient will benefit by answering the questions.

The following examples show how unsolicited letters of inquiry may be used to obtain information:

Gentlemen:

We are trying to improve our communication practices and have been referred to you as a company with considerable experience in this vital function. Would you please give us your help in answering these questions:

1. How many automatic typewriters have you installed?

2. What is the reaction of your typists and secretaries to the use of these machines?

3. What savings have resulted from their use?

The answers to these questions would be of great benefit to us. We shall be very grateful for any help you can give.

Sincerely yours,

Gentlemen:

Have you any information concerning what hours your employees like to begin and end their work? Because of the heavy traffic peaking at the hours of 9 A.M. and 5 P.M., a number of our employees have requested a change.

To do so, we are first undertaking a survey of the practices of a number of other companies within the greater Boston area. You can help us with this survey, which goes only to companies employing more than 2,000 people, by answering these questions:

1. What are your company's present working hours:

    8–4 _____

    8:30–4:30 _____

    9–5 _____

    Other _____

2. Have your employees indicated any wish to change?

    Yes _____   No _____

    If yes, to what hours _____

3. Would you think it desirable for the 20 largest companies in our geographical area to work out a cooperative system of staggered working hours?

    Yes _____   No _____

    If yes, what would be the best means to achieve this end?

4. Since it is obvious that if all of the companies decide to change, we may end up where we started, would your company be willing to participate in a program where starting hours are allocated to individual companies for the greatest convenience of all?

    Yes _____   No _____

You can help yourself and all of the other companies in our congested traffic area by supplying this information promptly. Once the information is tabulated, I shall send you a copy of the results which will, of course, include *your* ideas about what we ought to do.

Sincerely yours,

Progressive companies often use the inquiry letter for a variety of purposes such as sales, keeping mailing lists up to date, and maintaining contact with customers, as in the following examples:

Gentlemen:

We'd like to mail our publication *Market Trends in the Seventies* to a limited number of sophisticated investors.

Our research staff spent long hours studying the implications of today's high interest rates along with the various restraints that the government may choose to exercise.

The result is a brochure filled with rather specialized information invaluable for the mature and experienced investor, a category into which you doubtless fit.

By jotting your name and address on the enclosed postage-free postcard, you can receive this immediately after its date of publication on September 2.

Sincerely yours,

Dear Mr. Grantwood:

You have been on the list of our numerous customers who receive our little monthly folder *Handy Hints to Photographers*.

We hope this has been helpful to you. And now we ask *your* help.

Only a minute of your time is necessary to answer the questions listed below, but by doing so you assist us in making *Handy Hints* more useful to you.

A stamped, addressed envelope is enclosed for your convenience. Thank you for your help.

Very truly yours,

1. In which of the following are you most interested:
   Color _____   Black and white _____
   Slides _____   Snapshots _____   Other _____
2. Which section of *Helpful Hints* has proved most useful to you:
   New equipment _____   Taking better pictures _____
   Enlarging and developing _____   Other _____
3. Would you be interested in a contest for the best picture taken by a local photographer each month?
   Yes _____   No _____
4. Is the address to which *Helpful Hints* has been sent correct? If not, please list the correct address here:

ANSWERS-TO-INQUIRY LETTERS

The time has long since gone when businessmen regarded letters of inquiry as a nuisance or, at best, as trivial matters. A few inexperienced correspondents are still sending out the essentially thought-less responses characterized by "Here's the catalog you asked for and we hope it's useful." But the majority of businessmen now realize that the inquiry—solicited or unsolicited—represents an opportunity to turn requests for information into orders and good will.

One factor should be predominant in answering inquiries—you are writing to a reader who has already expressed an interest in a product, a bit of information, or something else. Your answer is therefore important to him since he has taken the initiative to ask for it. As one expert has said, "A letter to the company is a personal act of the writer. . . . When a woman takes up her pen to write a letter, she is . . . entering into a personal relationship with a company. . . . She hopes that she is writing to another human being like herself."

Suppose for the moment that you are Mr. Bender, whose letter to the insurance company appears on p. 150. What would be your reaction if you received the prospectus you requested along with a form letter but no answer to your question about why the word *Assurance* is used instead of *Insurance?* "Another big impersonal corporation geared to treat my letter just like everybody else's," you growl. "It wasn't really important—the question I asked—but still I'd like to know. . . ." Despite his denial, it *was* important and should have been treated accordingly.

Fortunately, in the instance of Mr. Bender's request, The Equitable Life Assurance Society *did* answer and very effectively. After a "thank you" for the request and a mention of the prospectus enclosed, the letter continued:

> Your question about the use of the term "assurance" in our company's name rather than the term "insurance" is a good one which we frequently receive.
>
> Words such as "ensurance," "assurance," and "insurance" have been, at various times, synonymous, and their usage has overlapped. In 1697, for example, Daniel De Foe spoke of "ensuring of life," in the monetary sense. In 1762, a group of Englishmen founded "The Society for Equitable Assurances of Lives and Survivorships," known since, familiarly, as "The Equitable Society of London" and "The Old Equitable." (Significantly, this company was formed on the basis of "mutual contribution," a concept that is considered the very foundation of mutual life insurance.)
>
> The term "insurance" as part of a company title vied with "assurance" in company titles at least as early as 1799, so Henry B. Hyde had a choice of words when in 1859, at the age of 25, he founded a mutual life insurance company and named it The Equitable Life Assurance Society of the United States. Our historical records do not indicate why he chose the word "assurance."

The explicitness and care taken in this letter from Assistant Vice-President Bruce L. Roberts stand in welcome contrast to the ironic fact that many companies, after soliciting inquiries, do not answer them or answer them inefficiently.

Perhaps computerized responses will correct this situation, but almost every survey—classes in written communication frequently do this by writing, for instance, to every company inviting inquiries in one issue of a magazine—shows tardiness, sloppiness, and error-ridden answers to inquiries. Misspelled names, wrong addresses, delay in writing, and failure to answer at all are surprisingly revealed in such surveys and point up four principles:

1.   Answer all inquiries promptly.
2.   Take special care in addressing, posting, and enclosing material.
3.   Make certain that you have answered all the inquirer's questions in clear understandable language.
4.   Refer specifically in your letter to any catalogues or brochures enclosed or sent separately.

Granting a Request

The simplest way to discuss answers to inquiries is to group them in two categories: those granting requests and those refusing requests. As we have said before, the letter that says "yes" is always easier to write; however, it should go beyond a mere "yes" if it is to build sales or good will. Since someone has already expressed interest in your company's products, methods, or operations, the letter granting a request has already passed the first hurdle of many sales situations—gaining the reader's interest—and the letter should capitalize on that fact.

Frequently, such letters involve the sending of catalogues, brochures, pamphlets, or reprints as part of answering the request. Ideally, on the basis of considerable experience, the best results are obtained when the letter and the supplementary material are sent together as one piece of mail; in actual practice, however, this has to be modified by such practical factors as mailing costs, the size and weight of the material, and the urgency of the situation. Even worse than the outmoded "Here is your catalogue and we hope it is useful" letter mentioned earlier, is the letter which says "The answers to your questions are on page 197 of the catalogue we are sending you," leaving the inquirer's frustration to build while he waits two weeks for the catalogue to arrive. If the answering letter and supplemental materials must be sent separately, tell your reader so, tell him *when* you are mailing the supplemental material (preferably "today," the same day as the letter), and give him an approximation of when he should receive it—"within a few days," "next week," or whatever seems realistic. (The simplest way to handle this is to put a first-class letter on the package of third- or fourth-class material.)

Correspondents answering requests with enclosures will do well to write at least three paragraphs that will be organized around these functions:

1. State the action taken.
2. Refer specifically to the enclosure.
3. Motivate action or build good will.

Notice how this is done in the following example and in the letter displayed on page 157.

> Dear Mr. Slobody:
>
> We are pleased to send you a copy of our pamphlet "Greater Efficiency in Office Layout," which you requested.
>
> You will be interested in the diagrams of typical office layouts on pages 14–19. Surveys by our architects and engineers show that these arrangements effect savings of 50 percent by utilizing space efficiently. And because our lightweight Acme Partitions are tailored to individual needs, more privacy and greater efficiency result, as shown in the five typical installations on pages 26–30.
>
> Our agent, Mr. John J. Pratt, will call on you within the next three days to demonstrate how Acme Partitions can make your office a more efficient, comfortable, and economical place to work.
>
> > Very truly yours,

The tone of these letters and their references to specific pages of the requested booklets make them effective sales emissaries. Their writers properly use an answer to a letter of inquiry as the first step in making a sale.

In situations where answers to inquiries do not directly involve sales, the correspondent should aim at building good will. Above all else, these letters should convey a tone of helpfulness and should contain sufficient information to answer the inquirer's questions. Here is an effective example:

> Dear Mr. Fife:
>
> Your letter asking about our program for executive development interested me greatly. I am glad to have an opportunity of telling you about our policies.
>
> The answer to both of your questions is "yes." We do have a definite program for developing potential executives, and we feel that it has been very worthwhile. I am enclosing a program showing the topics which have been discussed during the past year.
>
> We believe that the success of such a program depends largely on the method of selection by which men are admitted to it. For that reason, we developed a very elaborate personnel appraisal sheet by which candidates for the program are rated by their superiors and their co-workers. The enclosed blank will show you the personal qualities we are concerned with. If we can help you in any way, please let us know.
>
> > Sincerely yours,

This letter avoids the two main pitfalls which characterize many answers to inquiries: giving the reader a sense that he is receiving a perfunctory treatment

HOME BUILDERS SUPPLY COMPANY
271 LAKE AVENUE
ALLENTOWN, PENNSYLVANIA 18104

May 10, 1970

Mr. Ronald E. Thompson
76 Maple Street
Scranton, Pennsylvania 18519

Dear Mr. Thompson:

We are sending you our booklet "Modern Insulation for Older Homes,"
which you requested on May 8.

As the owner of a home which was not originally insulated, you
will be particularly interested in the description on pages 23
and 24 of the simple technique by which Blanktex Insulation can
make older homes as snug and warm as those with original
insulation. You will want to read on pages 37 to 41 the
unsolicited statements by satisfied users of Blanktex Insulation
proving that as much as 20 per cent of the annual heating cost
can be saved by our modern methods.

After you have read this booklet, which has won us thousands of
warm friends, you will undoubtedly have questions pertaining
specifically to the insulation of your home. Our heating expert
in your territory is Mr. Robert Vaughan, 69 Main Street,
Scranton, Pennsylvania 18505 (Phone Diamond 381-3109)

As a graduate engineer, Mr. Vaughan can give you exact figures
on costs, fuel savings, and similar facts regarding your home—
all without obligation on your part. A card or phone call to
Mr. Vaughan can make this winter the warmest you have spent
in your home.

Yours truly,

Allan Whitlock
Sales Manager

AW:MR

or a brush-off and conveying an impression of answering questions grudgingly or in such general terms that the result is meaningless.

Refusing a Request

The refusal of a request is one of the more difficult types of letters. Great tact and courtesy must be used if the reader is not to be antagonized. Many of the requests or inquiries that are made of businessmen are inconsiderate or unreasonable, but the answers to these requests should never be brusque, even when the request is refused. A harsh refusal may antagonize a potential customer or develop a source of ill will toward a company. Regardless of how thoughtless the request may seem, the intelligent technique is to refuse it tactfully. By doing this, good correspondents have learned that they can say "no" and still retain the reader's good will.

The refusal of an inquiry usually follows this pattern:

1. A statement of appreciation to the inquirer for his interest.
2. A refusal of his request without hedging and without apology.
3. If it is convenient, an explanation of why the request must be refused. Wherever possible, avoid vague terms like *company policy* or similar generalities.
4. If possible, a constructive suggestion or offer in the closing paragraph to be of service in the future.

The individual circumstances of each request and the person who makes it will, of course, govern the amount of detail included in the refusal. In many instances there need be no elaborate explanation of the reason for refusal; in others no constructive suggestion can be included. But whatever the details of the situation, the tone of the letter should be tactful and helpful. This is especially necessary when the request comes from a friend, an acquaintance, or a good customer; the refusal of a request from such a source would follow *in detail* the outline above. To illustrate the application of this outline, let us assume that Mr. Lawrence Miller, a customer of yours, is opening a new business which is similar to yours but will not compete with you in any way. Mr. Miller has written to you asking for information concerning the basis on which you pay your salesmen and you must refuse his request. What is the best way to refuse Mr. Miller? Notice the contrast in the point of view of the following letters:

Dear Sir:

I have your letter of April 12 asking about the basis on which we pay our salesmen.

I regret that I cannot let you have this information because confidential reports have a way of getting out. I might say that our system of remuneration has been very successful and our salesmen are completely satisfied with it.

It is my hope that you will not consider this refusal an uncooperative act on our part and that our pleasant business relationship may continue in the future.

Very truly yours,

Dear Mr. Miller:

Thank you for the interest expressed in your letter of April 12 concerning the way in which we pay our salesmen. We are flattered that so successful a businessman should ask our advice.

We regret that we cannot divulge this information. Since each of our salesmen works under an individual contract, we would be violating the confidence of our employees if the terms of these contracts were given out. Because our employees themselves have requested this secrecy, you will understand why we cannot comply with your request.

You undoubtedly are already familiar with E. J. Smith's booklet entitled "Setting Up a Sales Organization"; we have found it invaluable in its practical suggestions for dealing with specific problems. It might prove very useful to you at the present time.

If we may be of assistance to you in some other way, please feel free to write us. We want to offer our best wishes for success in your new venture, along with the hope that our pleasant business relationship with you may continue.

Sincerely yours,

The first letter is completely negative with its wrong emphasis, such as hoping "you will not consider this refusal an uncooperative act"; it is almost insulting in its thoughtless suggestion that the reader cannot be trusted—"confidential reports have a way of getting out"; it is irritating in its teasing tone of "our system of remuneration has been very successful"—*but* we can't divulge it. The second letter, by contrast, is tactful, sincere, and as constructive as possible. Its reader cannot help feeling that the explanation is honest.

USING INQUIRIES AND ORDERS FOR SALES-PROMOTION LETTERS

Alert businessmen make use of all occasions for writing letters to promote business, and high on the list of these occasions is the receipt of inquiries or of first orders. Letters acknowledging other orders tend to be rather routine, but even so, a letter of thanks at appropriate times is an excellent sales promotion device.

When a first order is received, good will can be fostered by a letter of acknowledgment; the sequence of parts can be varied, of course, but such a letter usually contains:

1. A reference to the order and a statement of how it is being shipped
2. A statement of appreciation
3. A brief sales message on the quality of service you expect to render or an expression of interest in the customer's needs.

The following letter illustrates how this outline may be applied:

> Dear Mr. Havens:
>
> We were delighted to learn from your order of May 15 that you are planning to feature our line of Spring Weave men's suits in your store.
>
> You will be pleased, we know, with the way these suits sell. Spring Weave is a name that men know because of our ten-year national advertising campaign.
>
> Your order is being shipped by express today. With it, we are sending you a set of displays, keyed to our advertising campaign, which you will want to use in your shop windows.
>
> Thank you very much for your order. We are looking forward to a mutually profitable relationship, and if there is anything we can do to help you with the promotion of Spring Weave suits, please let us know.
>
> Sincerely yours,

When a new purchasing agent is appointed in a company with which a Chicago firm does business, the following excellent letter is sent to acknowledge an order and to build good will with the new man:

> Dear Mr. Jenks:
>
> Thank you for the fine order that came in this morning. Naturally, we always appreciate orders, but this one makes us especially happy because it represents our first dealing with you.
>
> We've done business with your firm for a number of years and have always enjoyed a friendly relationship. You may be sure that we will do our best to keep it that way.
>
> Congratulations on your new position. If we can make your job easier or help you in any way where our products are concerned, we want to do so. Please call on us—any time.
>
> Sincerely yours,

There is plenty of room for originality, sincerity, and occasional humor in such letters, as demonstrated in this classic exchange between a tongue-in-cheek customer and a correspondent with a sense of humor:

> Gents:
>
> Please send me one of them gasoline engines you show on page 785 and if it's any good I'll send you a check for it.

To which the company replied:

> Dear Sir:
>
> Please send us the check, and if it's any good, we'll send you the engine.

Notice how graciously this original letter performs its function of welcoming a customer's first order:

> Gentlemen:
>
> I walked past a bookstore yesterday. It had a "going out of business" poster on the door, and in the window a sign which said
>
> > Words Failed Us
>
> We're not going to let words fail us in acknowledging your first order. We hope we succeed in expressing our reaction when we say
>
> > We are grateful.
>
> But even those words don't say everything we mean, which is
>
> > We want our service to deserve your business; if it doesn't live up to your expectations
>
> > We want to hear from you.
>
> > > > Sincerely yours,

LETTER PROBLEM 1: *Response to an Order*

You work for a highly exclusive men's wear and sporting goods shop whose name is associated with absolute reliability and prestige. In a recent advertising campaign, you have featured the opportunity to try your custom-made shirts, which are usually sold (with a minimum of three in an order) at $14.95 each, by ordering just one at $12.95. "Once you have worn this one shirt, you will be our customer for life."

Implicit in your advertisement was your intention to get *new* customers to come in and be measured for one custom-made shirt so that with their measurements permanently on file they would continue to order shirts in lots of three at $14.95 each.

To the bewilderment of everyone at Dalrymple & Dalrymple, 497 Fifth Avenue, New York, N.Y. 10019, the following letter addressed personally to Henry C. Stimple, salesman in your Hunting and Fishing Supplies section, arrives three days after the advertisement appears:

> Dear Hank:
>
> Saw that ad of D & D's in yesterday's paper and decided I ought to try one of those custom shirts of yours. Send me one and a bill. I need the shirt for a wedding 10 days from now.
>
> I'll be down this spring because we're going to need a lot of equipment.
>
> > > Yours,
> >
> > > *Amos*
> >
> > > Amos Amy
> > > The Green Lodge
> > > Lew Ridge, New York 12831

At an informal council of war, Henry Stimple says, "He's one of our very best customers. Twice a year he comes to the city and orders thousands of dollars of hunting and fishing tackle for his guests at the Lodge. I don't know whether he knows what a custom-made shirt is or whether he's pulling my leg—but I know one thing: we don't want to antagonize him and lose his business."

Someone else says, "It's a gag. He knows he can't buy custom-made shirts without being fitted and he's just having fun at our expense." Another salesman says, "If you try explaining custom-made shirts to him, he's just going to decide that we're a bunch of city slickers looking down our noses at a country bumpkin. I know because I was brought up in the country myself. If you sound patronizing or snooty, you'll never get another order from him."

Taking all of this background into careful consideration, write the letter you would send to Mr. Amy.

Curiously, most businesses spend more time and effort welcoming new accounts than they devote to their old customers. This is natural, partly because human nature tends to take for granted what it already possesses, and partly because business measures success in terms of new and added sales. Progressive companies realize, however, that the steady customer is the bedrock upon which business success is built, and they write letters expressing their appreciation for his patronage. This type of letter is usually called a *business-promotion letter*. While it is often closely associated with the acknowledgment of an order, it can be effectively used on anniversaries, at year's end, on holidays, or on any other appropriate occasion.

The essence of the business-promotion letter is a statement of appreciation to the customer for his business, his cooperation, his interest, or his promptness. Highly relevant to the spirit of this type of letter is a story about Rudyard Kipling when he was at the height of his career. A group of Oxford undergraduates, upon reading that Kipling was to be paid 10 shillings a word for an article, wired him 10 shillings with the request, "Please send us one of your best words." Back came Kipling's answer, "Thanks." Correspondents who learn to use "thanks" as one of their best words will find its value beyond price. The writers of such letters certainly reap a harvest of good will from a very small investment by letting old customers know that their orders and patronage merit thanks. Here are some excellent examples of the way in which correspondents use letters which are basically acknowledgments of orders or inquiries as a method of promoting sales and good will.

Dear Mr. Bradley:

With Father's Day approaching, you may enjoy the story of the college student who sent Dad a cheap pair of cufflinks with the message:

This isn't much, but it's all you can afford.

This letter isn't much either in terms of expressing our genuine thanks for the confidence you've shown by your increased orders and prompt payments during the past year.

But we did want you to know that your continued patronage affords us the opportunity to say one very important word—THANKS.

Cordially yours,

The next letter faces up frankly to the fact that established customers are too often forgotten:

Dear Mr. Byers:

BEFORE a man marries—
He'll send the girl flowers and take her to the theater in a taxi.

AFTER—the only "flour" she gets is Gold Medal. And she has to lug it home from the Cash and Carry in a 24-pound sack.

Business is a lot like that.

Firms spend much to make a man a customer. And then the best he gets is an invoice.

We believe a firm should tell a customer that his trade is appreciated. And that's why we are writing you this letter to tell you how much we appreciate the steady flow of orders you've sent us during the past year.

Not to sell you—but to tell you—it's always a real pleasure to serve you.

Cordially yours,

Increasingly, a large number of business enterprises are using inquiries to rebuild sales among customers who have not used their charge accounts for a period usually from three to six months; one sends out an actual bill showing a balance due of $0.00 with these words typed on the bill:

We're sorry about "nothing"!

Your account is paid in full, and we're concerned because you haven't bought anything from us lately. On the back of this bill, you'll find three questions about the service we've tried to render. You can help us by checking the answers and returning them in the enclosed envelope.

Better still, stop in and visit one of our convenient suburban branches, where we're featuring Spring sales of ladies' coats.

The following inquiry letter with a penny attached has been highly successful in reactivating accounts:

Dear Mr. Jones:

A PENNY FOR YOUR THOUGHTS—
. . . and here's cash in advance . . .

We are still trying to find out why you have not used your charge account at Rosenfield's recently, and yet we do not wish to annoy an old friend by being too persistent. But we do want to know if anything has happened to displease you in the slightest.

It will take just a minute for you to tell us the reason, in the space below, and to let us know if you would like us to continue sending you your current credit card each month.

We have thousands of customers who find their charge account a great convenience in getting the things they want at Rosenfield's and we sincerely hope you will use your account again. This letter is just to find out your wishes, so that we may serve you as you want to be served.

There's a postage-paid envelope enclosed which will bring your reply to my desk. And thank you very much.

Sincerely yours,

The Joseph M. Stern Company of Cleveland has had great success getting orders with what it calls a "Miniature Message for Busy Buyers":

Dear Friend:

We have some grass mats for which we need orders.

Perhaps you have some orders for which you need grass mats.

If so, we should get together. Right? Write!

Concisely yours,
The Joseph M. Stern Co.

P.S. We may be short on words but we are long on QUALITY and SERVICE. All orders for standard-size grass mats are shipped on the same day received.

In an era when the servicing of a great variety of mechanical, electrical, and electronic devices has become a necessity to the housewife, one highly reputable dealer selling TV sets actually used poor service (caused by a work stoppage by builders of his new repair shop) to win back customers with this letter:

Dear Mrs. Northrup:

Someone told us about the daughter who couldn't spell and wrote her mother:

Please send me my genes.

Her mother replied:

If you don't have them now, there's nothing I can do about it.

Back in September, we decided there *was* something we could do about it—and we started a new repair shop. We were delayed, our service wasn't what we wanted it to be; but now we have the most modern and efficient TV service in the city.

Like the daughter, we say please send us your set. You'll find that there's something we can do about it quickly, honestly, and satisfactorily.

Just put the enclosed sticker with our telephone number on the back of your set to remind you where to call.

Sincerely yours,

The letter displayed on page 166 illustrates an effective acknowledgment of an order from an old customer. It expresses gratitude and builds a sound relationship for future sales.

Many a sermon has been preached on the text, "If a man ask you to go with him a mile, go with him twain." The text is applicable to the whole subject of letter writing. The letter which goes beyond routine, which goes "the second mile" where others stop with the routine "first mile," is the really effective message. For that reason, these letters succeed; they reflect a policy which is designed not only to win new friends but to keep old ones.

EXERCISES

Chapters 5 and 6 of this book present the general principles pertaining to all types of effective letters. In the exercises in this chapter and those following, the student should learn to apply these principles to the specialized problems described. Before attempting to write the letters dealing with these specialized situations, *the student should prepare a brief outline or notation of the points he wishes to make in each letter;* this will ensure a careful analysis of what he wants his letter to do before he actually starts to write.

1. Select any specific advertisement from a nationally circulated magazine in which statements such as "Send for a free propectus" or "For further information write to" are included. Write the letter requesting the prospectus or information.

2. Write a letter to the superintendent of the high school from which you graduated asking for information about what he would suggest you do to prepare yourself for a teaching career in high school in whatever subject interests you most.

3. You have read an advertisement for an investment counseling company which accepts accounts only in amounts above $50,000. The ad has said "Write on your company letterhead for our brochure *Counseling the Busy Executive on his Investments.*" You badly need this brochure for your class in money and banking in which you are to make a 50-minute report on "The Spectrum of Investment Counseling." Write to The Securities Investment Counseling Service, Inc. 409 Broadway, Los Angeles, California, 90024, to get 20 copies of the brochure for use in your class.

4. For a study of the costs of the business letter, you are trying to establish a relationship between the size of the company in terms of the number of its employees and average letter costs. Write the letter of inquiry, with specific questions, which you would send to ten companies with fewer than 500 employees, ten with 500–1,500 employees, and ten with more than 1,500 employees.

5. As secretary of your chamber of commerce, you have received the following inquiry. Write your answer.

> Gentlemen:
> I have read with a great deal of interest your advertising that (your city or locality) is "a good place for industry to locate."

THE GENERAL STEEL MFG. CO.

4156 EASTERN AVENUE
PITTSBURGH, PA. 15215

MYRON WOODRUFF
VICE-PRESIDENT

November 5, 1970

Mr. Charles E. Goodwin
Tool Producers Company
771 West Avenue
Milwaukee, Wisconsin 53404

Dear Mr. Goodwin:

When a friend helps us on with a coat, we smile and say "Thank
you." If we drop something and someone picks it up for us, we
practically burst with gratitude.

Strange? Not at all.

But it is strange that when we get into business, we take so
many things for granted that we forget to say "Thank you."
Take old customers like you, for instance.

You did something pretty important for us—important because
we think so much of your business that it gives us a great
deal of pleasure to see it grow.

I just wanted to write you personally, telling you how much we
appreciate your order, and saying "Thank you" for your confidence
in us.

                              Very truly yours,

                              Myron Woodruff

                              Myron Woodruff, Vice-President

MW:RT

Our company, which manufactures speedometers for one of the largest automobile manufacturers, is considering expanding its facilities and is thinking of your area as a possible site for this expansion.

We should like to know, therefore, about the advantages your city might have for an enterprise such as ours. Our proposed expansion would involve a plant employing approximately 1,000 workers, many of whom would have to be recruited in the place where we decide to locate.

Will you please reply as soon as possible?

> Sincerely yours,
> Henry G. Smith
> Vice-President

6. The students and faculty at your college have for some time expressed considerable dissatisfaction with the academic schedule, based on the two-semester system with classes starting in mid-September and first-semester final exams beginning in mid-January. The second semester begins around February 1 and continues to mid-June. The total number of weeks of classroom instruction has been 32, 16 in each semester. Among the alternatives suggested are:

(1) A quarter system, which would divide the calendar year into four quarters of 12 weeks each, with the student attending three quarters each year or graduating in three years if he attends four quarters each year.

(2) A trimester system, which would divide the calendar year into three 16-week parts, with the student attending two parts or graduating in three years by attending all parts every year.

(3) A so-called 4-1-4 system, which would end the first semester at Christmas; provide a one-month "reading and personal project" period in January, when no classes would be held, but students would be expected to write a comprehensive report on their individual project; and provide a four-month period ending June 1.

(You may add any other scheduling systems you wish to devise.) You are now to write a letter and questionnaire which will be helpful to the student-faculty committee on scheduling. It will go to the registrars of 20 institutions similar in size and character to yours, and its responses will be used as the basis for committee action.

7. A sophomore in the high school from which you graduated has written to you saying, "I want to do what you did and prepare for a career in business. What do you think I should study for the next two years in high school? I have two electives in each of the next four semesters."

Write your answer to this inquiry.

8. Criticize the following answer to a letter of inquiry:

Dear Mr. Parker:

In compliance with your request of November 1, we send enclosed our brochure entitled "Selecting a Piano for the Home" with the hope that it may prove useful to you.

In the event that you are interested in purchasing a Belltone Piano, we would suggest that you consult Mr. J. C. Wiggers, 232 West Street, in your city.

It is entirely possible that he may be of assistance to you.

Hoping that you will see fit to discuss this matter with Mr. Wiggers.

Very truly yours,

9. In your company's advertising, a repeated slogan has been "It costs more, but it's worth it." You may choose any product or service with which you are familiar to answer an inquiry letter from a customer whose general attitude can be expressed in his statement: "I agree that it's good, but now that I've used it I don't really know why it should cost more." Write your answer.

10. The Communication Services Co. has written to you asking if they might publish, in their monthly bulletin to clients, a series of sales letters which your company has used with excellent results. "We will of course make acknowledgment in any form you wish for the use of these letters, and we believe that giving them a wider audience will build a great deal of good will and prestige for your company" is the way they phrased their request to reprint your letters. Write to the company refusing their request because you have decided that reprinting the letters would destroy their originality and prevent your using them in the future.

11. Your travel agency, specializing in a See-America-First sales campaign, has developed a series of outstanding slides dealing with places of historical interest in the United States. Along with the presentation of the slides, a member of your agency always delivers an explanatory talk, ending with a brief comment that a visit to any of these scenes and places can be arranged, at comparatively low prices, through conducted bus tours sold by your travel agency.

   The superintendent of the Home for Senior Citizens in a nearby community has heard one of these presentations and has written asking you to "donate a complete set of slides to the Home where they will be shown over and over again to the delight of our residents." Your staff has unanimously decided (a) that, worthy as this home for senior citizens is, a gift to one such agency may precipitate many similar requests; (b) that the cost of such a gift ($796 for the entire set of slides) is in any case prohibitive; (c) that no business would emanate from the home for senior citizens. Using any of these facts which you consider appropriate, write refusing the superintendent's request.

12. The Citizens for Disarmament of the Earth and Other Planets are having their national convention in your city and have written your company for a contribution of $1,000, so that they may list you as a patron in their program supplement. Because the purpose of this organization is to bring pressure on legislators to achieve its aims and because your company maintains a strict policy of no contributions for direct or indirect political influence, you must refuse the request. Write your letter to James E. Johns, Vice-Chairman of the organization.

13. Mrs. James S. Knox, 76 State Street, Worthington, Pennsylvania 16262 has sent you $12.95 for a pressure cooker which your company advertised in a national magazine. Since your company sells only through dealers, write Mrs. Knox that you are forwarding her order to The Home Appliance Shop, 1970 Broadway, Worthington, and suggest that she go there to select the exact style of pressure cooker she desires.

14. Along with an order blank for $997.12 worth of spring garden supplies from the Garden Shop, Higgs Road, Glenwood, Missouri 63541 came a scrawled note from Vito Angelloni, the owner, saying, "Remember when I was afraid to ask you for $200 credit ten years ago when I sent my first order? And now we're the biggest in town." Write Mr. Angelloni an appropriate letter of acknowledgment.

15. Use a holiday, anniversary, or any other suitable occasion for a sales promotion letter to customers who have purchased merchandise from you for more than five years and who have paid their bills promptly.

16. Evaluate the following inquiry letter, the purpose of which is to inquire why good customers have made no purchases in the past six months:

> You, know, Mrs. Smith, that there's an old saying:
>
>   Life is neither a spectacle, nor a feast; life is a predicament.
>
> We're in a predicament too . . .
>   because we haven't had an order in more than 6 months
>   because our service may not have pleased you
>   because we keep guessing about the reason.
>
> Want to help us out—of the predicament, that is? Please do.
>
>   *C. J. Smith* Manager
>   The Retail Store, Inc.

17. Your organization has decided that this year, instead of spending a social budget of $2,400 for dances, receptions, and parties, the money and energy of your group will be devoted to "worthy causes, with the specific exception that there be no political or religious affiliation." On behalf of your 42 members, who will donate one-half day a week in addition to the money, write a letter of inquiry with a questionnaire to five organizations which you have had recommended to you as meeting all the conditions described.

18. As the student manager of your school's speakers bureau, write a letter of inquiry, with tabulated questions, to be sent to 150 clubs, church groups, and other organizations. Your speakers bureau supplies student speakers for various occasions and is intended to give the students actual experience in talking before groups. There is no charge for this service; last year, members of the speakers bureau presented programs before 42 groups. You are now planning your program for the next school year, and your letter is intended to ascertain how many groups might be interested, what topics they wish discussed, how large an audience might be expected, and whether such facilities as projectors and amplifiers would be available.

CHAPTER 8

CLAIM AND ADJUSTMENT LETTERS

"To err is human," according to Alexander Pope, and the number of errors committed in the routine transactions of business attest the truth of Pope's words. Orders may be filled improperly or incompletely; goods may be damaged or unsatisfactory; misunderstandings may arise over discounts, bills, credit terms, and exchanges. Or, as the lead in *The Wall Street Journal* (June 26, 1969) describes the situation more dramatically:

> Roofs leak. Shirts shrink. Toys maim. Toasters don't toast. Mowers don't mow. Kites don't fly. Radios emit no sounds, and television sets and cameras yield no pictures.

The letters written to bring these errors to the attention of those who must take the responsibility for them are known as *claim letters;* those written to take action on such claims are called *adjustment letters.*

To anyone acquainted with the complexities of modern business, the important fact is not that errors do occur but that the percentage of error is actually very small. The surest indication of the amateur in business is a willingness, at the one extreme, to promise that mistakes will *never* occur or, at the other, to become angry and threatening as soon as such errors are made.

Before the novice in business sends an angry or threatening adjustment letter, he should heed the advice in the following piece of anonymous doggerel:

Lives of great men all remind us
As we o'er their pages turn
That we too may leave behind us
Letters that we ought to burn.

The experienced businessman develops a rather tolerant attitude toward the errors made by his own associates and by others; this is not to say that he is complacent about mistakes made by his own organization or ready to continue doing business indefinitely with those whose blunders are too numerous. But from experience, he has learned that there is an irreducible minimum of mistakes made in business, and this knowledge prevents him from losing his temper over the mistakes of others or from promising that he will never again let such an error occur in his own company.

THE CLAIM LETTER

The tolerant attitude just described is the correct viewpoint from which the claim letter should be written. Claim letters lacking this tone usually originate with those unfamiliar with business. A letter like the following is all too typical:

Dear Sir:

That television set your store sold me last week is a disgrace. The picture is distorted and flops around so that we can't look at it. You've sent your repairman out twice and each time the set is worse after he tinkers with it. I think you knew it was no good when you sold it to me and hoped I wouldn't have sense enough to complain. This is the last time I'll ever buy anything from your store.

Yours truly,

The first and natural reaction to stupid mistakes and unreasonable blunders is anger, but, on second thought, we realize that *we* make mistakes too. Good manners alone should prevent such explosive reactions. To write such an angry and accusing letter is simple to let one's emotions run away with his reason. In fact, the worst attitude for the claim writer is nicely summed up in an old ditty:

In controversial moments
My perception's very fine;
I always see both points of view,
The one that's wrong—and mine!

A little thought before writing a claim letter will show that *it is to the writer's own advantage to be tolerant and even-tempered in his claim letter.* Is it likely that the dealer who receives the vindictive letter about the television set will try to be as scrupulously fair as he might otherwise be if this situation had been called to his attention without malice? Obviously not. If for no other reason than that one stands a greater chance of getting a reasonable adjustment by being fair, the claim letter should avoid anger, sarcasm, and accusations. In its phrasing, the claimant should shun such accusing terms as *complaint, disgusted, dishonest, false, unfair, untrue, worthless,* and *no good.*

An analysis of the claim letter shows that four elements are usually present:

1. An explanation of what is wrong. This explanation should give exact dates, amounts, model numbers, sizes, colors, or any other specific information that will make a recheck easier for the reader.
2. A statement of the inconvenience or loss that has resulted from this error.
3. An attempt to motivate action by appealing to the reader's sense of fair play, his honesty, or his pride. Don't threaten him with loss of business at the first error.
4. A statement of what adjustment is considered fair; if the writer doesn't know what adjustment is equitable, he should try to stimulate prompt investigation and action.

This analysis puts a premium upon specific facts rather than emotions in the claim letter. It is predicated on the assumption that the overwhelming majority of businessmen want to do the fair thing, if only because it is good business to do so; hence, an appeal to fairness or honesty is the best possible motivation. With regard to the actual adjustment, the claimant may not know exactly what he wants or what would constitute a fair settlement of the claim. In that event, *it is generally best to let the adjuster suggest a satisfactory settlement.* Several surveys of department stores and retail establishments have shown that when the customer has a reasonable claim and has left its settlement completely up to the store, the adjuster will usually grant more than the customer would ask. This technique will not appeal to those who believe that all business is conducted on the plane of "beat the customer before he beats you." But for those with a realistic background of experience in business such a technique is the best method of writing claims, because it stems from a belief on which American business is founded—that honesty in business is the best policy.

Contrast the tone of the following letters with the first one presented in this chapter.

Gentlemen:

On your bill for February, I was charged $22.75 for a fishing rod and reel which I purchased in your sporting goods department on December 18.

This bill was paid on January 14 by my check on the Guaranty National Bank. This canceled check was returned with the bank statement which I received on February 2. The next day I received your bill showing this amount still unpaid.

Will you please see that my payment is credited to my account so that I am not billed again?

Sincerely yours,

John H. Middleton

Gentlemen:

The 6.50—15 Rubbertex tire which I purchased on July 23 from The Standard Supply Company, 237 Broadway, Colton, New York 12746 has proved defective after 8,000 miles of use.

Since I bought this tire while I was on a business trip in the East, I am unable to take it to the dealer from whom I purchased it. I have, therefore, asked your local representative, Mr. John Ostrander, 5 Park Street, Galesburg, Illinois 61401 to replace it. He has suggested that I write to you about the matter.

As a user of your tires for the past ten years, I have learned at first hand about their long mileage and safety. This past experience makes me curious to know just why this Rubbertex tire should wear out so rapidly.

In view of the fact that I have come to expect 24,000 miles from Rubbertex tires and that I have been caused considerable inconvenience, I feel certain that you will give me a new tire at a 66 percent discount as figured on the mileage basis.

Very truly yours,

Alvin C. Harding

Gentlemen:

On September 15 we ordered 50 maple kneehole desks to be shipped on September 28 for delivery here on September 30 in time for the opening of our new dormitory.

When this shipment arrived on September 28, we found that it contained 25 desks, which we had ordered, and 25 maple tables. I attempted to get the cartage company, which delivered the furniture from the freight station, to leave the desks and return the tables to the station. They insisted they had no authority to do this and that we would have to accept the whole shipment or return all of it.

When I attempted to call you long distance, I could locate no one who knew anything about this situation. This has caused us considerable inconvenience since we were forced to open our dormitory for inspection before it was completely furnished.

We are, therefore, asking you to send the 25 desks immediately and to arrange to have the tables removed from our dormitory locker room as soon as possible because we urgently need this space for trunks and luggage.

Sincerely yours,

Henry Green

Business Manager

THE ADJUSTMENT LETTER

Typical of the proper attitude of modern businessmen toward handling complaints are the following comments:

> It has been our invariable policy to let people know we appreciate hearing from them if they are dissatisfied in any way. We have always recognized the customer's right to expect our products to fulfill any claim we made for them in our advertising. (H. F. Jones, Vice-President, Campbell Soup Company)

> I make it a rule to answer every letter of complaint that I can personally handle. If a busy schedule prevents me from doing this, an associate takes care of the letter for me; but the point is—every letter is answered. (John C. Whitaker, President, R. J. Reynolds Tobacco Company)

> I think that to fail to answer an intelligent letter about one's product, flattering or the other kind, is to lose an opportunity . . . (G. H. Coppers, President, National Biscuit Company)

> I certainly do welcome flattering letters . . . but I also welcome the other kind because they give me a check on what's happening from indignant sources. It's a standing rule here that each letter addressed to me, in which the writer has a gripe, comes to me personally . . . and is acknowledged at once by me. (L. A. Van Bomel, President, National Dairy Products Corporation)

These and similar comments by business and industrial leaders show that alert businessmen welcome comments from their customers. Actually, claim and adjustment letters offer an excellent check on the quality of service or merchandise, and many companies keep a continuous record of these letters as a control mechanism for their products and service. Furthermore, progressive businessmen realize that there is nothing more detrimental to good public relations than the discontented or dissatisfied customer who goes around telling all his friends and acquaintances that "the Blank Company is a poor place to do business." If he can be persuaded to write directly to the company and thus get his troubles "off his chest," the company has an opportunity to convert a potential liability into a booster who tells his friends, "The Blank Company is reliable; if they make an error or their merchandise isn't satisfactory, they'll make good every time." Of such elements is the intangible quality called *good will* composed—and as we have seen, *progressive* businessmen recognize its importance.

Unfortunately, this progressive attitude is not universal, as shown in a comprehensive roundup titled "Caveat Emptor" by the staff of *The Wall Street Journal* (June 26, 1969). After ascribing a rising tide of complaints about inferior products and service to poor quality control and increased competition, the article ends with a story which should remind all businessmen to handle complaints effectively. An Iowa grandfather, angry at a national chain store which installed a leaky roof on his house years ago, now ends all his letters to his grandchildren with these words:

Love, and don't buy anything from Blank's.

Unadjusted complaints apparently leave their mark "even unto the third generation."

Even worse is the situation described by Lee Kanner, writing in the financial pages of the *New York Times* (November 12, 1967):*

The age of the non-hero and the hippie freak-out has a new addition—the non-response of business, particularly in the retail industry.

The non-response has many variations. In its most elemental form, it is non-response to a letter of complaint. It is non-response that arrives weeks, sometimes months, after a letter is written, but says little or nothing, and is not acted upon.

After citing numerous specific examples of non-response to complaints, the article ends with these ominous words:

Is there a solution to the non-response problem? The stores say time and better training will overcome all difficulties. The facts say no. The non-personalized numbers game of the computers inevitably will more and more de-humanize relations between retail establishments and their customers. Apparently customers —or former customers—will all have to learn to live with this depressing fact of life.

Despite Mr. Kanner's pessimism, another solution seems possible—using the adjustment letter intelligently as a vital element in building good will. Here are four principles which govern its intelligent use:

1. Every complaint or claim, no matter how trivial it seems, is important to the person who makes it.
2. It therefore requires a prompt answer or acknowledgment.
3. The answer should be factual, courteous, and fair.
4. Above all else, it should not argue or take a critical attitude. Remember, instead, an old Italian proverb: One good word quenches more heat than a bucket of water.

Naturally, the adjustment letter will reflect the company's attitude toward claims. In general, there are three policies in effect concerning the granting of claims:

* © 1967 by The New York Times Company. Reprinted by permission.

1. *The customer is always right;* therefore, all claims are granted. This policy is used by only a few firms at present who deal in expensive merchandise for an extremely reputable clientele.

2. *Grant adjustments wherever the claim seems fair.* This is by far the most widely used policy toward claims. It offers the advantage of letting each case be decided on its merits, and it avoids committing the company to a single policy regarding adjustments.

3. *Caveat emptor—Let the buyer beware!* He bought the goods and he can assume the responsibility; therefore, no claims are granted. No reputable firm can afford to adopt such an unfair policy.

Unless there are peculiar problems connected with the particular business, the second policy outlined above is the most effective one.

But regardless of what the policy is, correspondents have a special obligation in handling adjustments to make the policy clear, to apply it to the situation at hand, and to emphasize its fairness and consistency. For that reason, vague statements like "company policy prevents our doing this" should be replaced by specific explanations against the broad background of a company policy which is applied impartially. A company which operates from principle rather than expediency, from policy rather than partiality, has gone a long way toward winning customer acceptance of its fairness.

The writer of the adjustment letter should always realize that he is handling a delicate situation. The customer is disgruntled and probably believes sincerely that he has a very real grievance, whether he has or not. The aim of the adjuster should be to make the reader see that he is trying to be fair; yet he must steer a straight course between the two extremes of sympathizing too much with the claimant and thus making him believe that his grievance is indeed greater than he originally thought and, on the other hand, of seeming to argue or to accuse the customer of making an unjust claim.

More than any other quality, the adjustment writer needs a sensitivity not only to the meanings of words but also to their connotations and overtones. The little boy who wrote home from summer camp to say "I'm glad I'm not homesick like all the boys who have dogs are" was too young to recognize that language carries unstated meanings and unspoken implications. Actually, claim letters used to be called "complaint letters," which they are, but the connotation of "complaint" is too harsh to be used in the reply. Similarly, the writer of adjustment letters ought to avoid such phraseology as *you state* or *you claim* or *we cannot understand*, because such phrases antagonize the reader; nor should he use such words as *failure, breakdown,* or *poor results,* because they add extra weight to the reader's belief that the product is inferior. Instead of saying, "You claim that our heater is no good," the trained adjuster will write, "Thank you for telling us of your experience with our heater."

Test your own reaction to the following negative letter:

> Dear Mr. Sinclair:
>
> We cannot comply with your claim for an adjustment on the radio you purchased from us.
>
> In rejecting your request, we want to emphasize that we never make adjustments on merchandise after the customer has kept it three days. You state that the radio was marred when it reached you, but our final inspection showed it was in good condition when we sent it. Unfortunately our policy prohibits our making any adjustment in this case.
>
> > Sincerely yours,

Instead of this negative approach, this letter should explain in a matter-of-fact way the facts of the situation. In short, it should be expository rather than argumentative in tone.

Granting the Adjustment

Because it says "yes," the letter granting an adjustment is usually easy to write. Its ultimate purpose, however, is not just to grant the adjustment but to retain the good will and the business of a disgruntled customer. Any or all of the following elements—arranged in a sequence appropriate to the specific situation—may be included:

An expression of regret for the inconvenience suffered

An explanation of the cause of the error

A statement of what adjustment is to be made

An attempt to build good will

Skilled adjustment correspondents disagree both as to the way in which these elements should be arranged and as to which should be included. In comparatively routine situations, many follow this pattern:

1. Grant the adjustment.
2. Make any necessary explanation.
3. Resell the product, the service, and/or the company.

The justification for this sequence is a desire to accentuate the positive by eliminating the apologies and regrets; furthermore, it adapts neatly to the reader's first question, "What are you going to do?" by stating the adjustment at the outset.

On the other hand—and particularly in situations where considerable inconvenience has resulted—other correspondents write from the premise that "whenever we make a mistake, we should say that we're sorry for it, and we owe the customer a reasonably complete explanation of what happened." The sequence here is the same as that in the four elements as listed above.

Which is better? Students should regard this as an interesting challenge to their knowledge of human nature, involving answers to such questions as: When mistakes are made, are apologies and reasonably complete explanations expected? Or does the reply "speak for itself" in the form of the granted adjustment? As you read the letters which follow, try to judge their effectiveness in terms of these questions.

Dear Mr. Middlefield:

We're sorry that the radio you purchased from us was unsatisfactory. You have every right to expect merchandise from this store to be in perfect condition, and we appreciate your telling us of this experience.

Our shipping department makes every effort to see that every piece of merchandise is thoroughly inspected before it is sent out. Unfortunately, your radio was not inspected because of the negligence of one of our temporary employees.

We expect to receive another shipment of Finetone Radios tomorrow, and on Thursday we shall send you a new radio to replace the one you have.

Your patronage of our store during the past six years has been greatly appreciated. We want you to know that we value your friendship highly, and, for that reason, we wish to make each transaction satisfactory to you. If it is not, we hope you will inform us, as you did this time, so that we may make an equitable adjustment.

Yours very truly,

Here's another adjuster's handling of the same situation:

Dear Mr. Middlefield:

You're quite right in expecting merchandise from this store to be in perfect condition, and that's why we are sending you a brand new replacement for your Finetone Radio on Thursday.

Apparently some slip-up in inspection caused the problem and you did us a favor in calling it to our attention.

For six years, you've patronized our store. We want you to continue because your judgment that the radio wasn't perfect coincides with our desire to make every transaction satisfactory to the customer. If not, we'll make it right as you now know.

Yours very truly,

By frankly admitting that a mistake has been made, the letter on page 179 carries an air of sincerity which renders it effective.

Refusal of Adjustment

Much more difficult is the refusal of an adjustment, which may be defined as any letter that does not grant the original claim. A partial adjustment

THE CONTINENTAL BANK
WINCHESTER, MASSACHUSETTS 01890

January 8, 1971

Mr. Eugene Gaston
76 Pond Road
Woburn, Massachusetts 01801

Dear Mr. Gaston:

I certainly appreciate your writing me about the fact that
your last two bank statements have been sent to you in
envelopes which were unsealed.

If there is one thing the Continental Bank insists on, it is
having our employees take every precaution to see that the
financial affairs of our depositors are kept absolutely
confidential. I am, therefore, grateful to you for calling
this matter to our attention and for your fairness concerning
a situation which must have annoyed you greatly.

We have taken every precaution to see that this mistake does
not occur again. And we want you to know that we are especially
sorry that this happened to one of our oldest depositors.

Sincerely yours,

Seth L. Everett

Seth L. Everett
Cashier

SLE:CLR

may be made, but if it does not comply with the request, from the customer's viewpoint, it is still a refusal of adjustment. The correspondent who is frequently called upon to refuse claims might well take as his text the Biblical injunction that "a soft answer turneth away wrath"; there is no better advice for the refusal of adjustment. If a "soft answer" is the tone to be given such a letter, its contents will usually be as follows:

1. An attempt to get on common ground with the reader by agreeing with him in some way
2. A clear explanation of the situation from the adjuster's point of view
3. A complete refusal of adjustment or a statement of a partial adjustment
4. An attempt to get the reader to accept the adjuster's analysis of the situation

For example, the claim letter on page 173 requesting a new tire might be answered as follows:

Dear Mr. Harding:

We agree that you should expect more than 8,000 miles of service from the 6.50—15 Rubbertex tire that you wrote us about on September 3. As you know from previous experience, Rubbertex tires are built to give 25,000 miles of trouble-free service under normal conditions.

Our service department has carefully examined your tire, which was sent on to us by your local dealer, Mr. John Ostrander. They find that your tire was driven when seriously underinflated; this caused the side walls to crack. To make this as clear as possible, we enclose a booklet which, you will notice from the illustration, shows a tire injured in the same way yours was. By following the suggestions given in the part we have marked with red pencil, you will have no further difficulty of this kind, and you will be greatly pleased with the increased mileage you will receive.

Looking at this situation from your point of view, we can appreciate how you feel. Our guarantee of "at least 20,000 miles for Rubbertex tires under normal conditions" still holds. But your tire, probably without your even knowing it, was subjected to abnormal strain, which no tire could stand; it, therefore, does not fall within the scope of this guarantee.

Because we want you to know the miles of carefree service that Rubbertex tires can give, we are willing to bear a portion of your loss by offering you a new 6.50—15 Rubbertex tire at a 20 percent discount. Just take this letter to your local dealer, and he will mount your new Rubbertex on your rim—ready to protect you from dangerous skids and blowouts.

Sincerely yours,
The Rubbertex Tire Company
C. J. Cowan, Adjuster

Notice how tactfully the letter on page 181 fixes the responsibility for the breakdown of a washing machine without accusing the customer.

HOUSEHOLD APPLIANCES, INC,

4928 ROANOKE STREET
LOS ANGELES . CAL. 90048

September 10, 1970

Mrs. Patrick C. Kelley
397 Constitution Street
Los Angeles, California 90063

Dear Mrs. Kelley:

We certainly agree with you that it's inconvenient to run a home
without a Supreme Washer. For that reason, we have lost no time
in investigating the source of the trouble in your machine.

The report from our repair department indicates that your washing
machine has a burned-out bearing which was caused by the fact
that it has not been oiled. Although we guarantee the Supreme
for three years against all defects in workmanship or materials,
we cannot assume responsibility for repairs necessitated by
improper care. You will understand, therefore, that we cannot
grant your request to repair your machine without charge.

We shall, however, be glad to put your Supreme in brand-new
condition at the actual cost of the parts, $3.67. When your
machine is returned to you, it will be completely oiled and ready
to operate. Then, if you will follow the directions for oiling,
which are given on page 3 of your instruction book, you will get
years of trouble-free service from your washer.

Just mail the enclosed post card today, authorizing us to proceed
with the repairs, and we'll return your Supreme on Saturday in
plenty of time to banish those washerless Monday blues.

Sincerely yours,

HOUSEHOLD APPLIANCES, INC.

Ralph T Adams

Service Manager

ROA:MS

One of the most difficult situations requiring a refusal of adjustment occurs when customers take unjustified discounts on their bills. Suppose, for example, that your firm has a policy of granting a 2 percent discount for bills paid within 10 days. One of your customers has paid a $600 bill three weeks later but has taken a $12 discount and has protested angrily when you billed him for the $12. Obviously, in this situation it is not the amount, but the principle, which should count. Here is the way one correspondent handled this delicate situation:

> Dear Mr. Leavengood:
>
> Thank you for your letter of November 12. I appreciate your giving us an opportunity to explain a situation which might lead to a misunderstanding if you had not written.
>
> As you know, we have had a long-standing policy of permitting a 2 percent discount to customers who pay their bills within 10 days of the date of their bills. We maintain this policy because it enables us to effect similar savings by paying our own bills promptly. Actually, then, we pass these savings on to our own customers as a reward for their promptness.
>
> Since we make no savings when our customers do not pay within the prescribed time, we must adhere rigidly to our principle. Actually, the amount of $12 is in itself a trivial matter; but in fairness to all our customers, we maintain a consistent policy. I think you would rightly object if we granted certain terms to other customers and different ones to you.
>
> Now that you have the facts in this situation, I am sure that you will see the fairness of our bill for $12. We want you and all our other customers to take advantage of our discount policy, but we want to treat everybody fairly and consistently. To do so, we have to follow our principle, and I am sure you will agree that this is the only just and equitable method of operating.
>
> I am grateful to you for writing to me because I realize that only by frank discussion can our companies work together for their mutual benefit.
>
>   Sincerely yours,

No exact formula will solve the problem of writing effective adjustments. Whether the claim is granted entirely, partially, or not at all, the correspondent must seek to:

1. Convince the reader that he is being treated fairly
2. Gain his confidence in the products, services, or policies of the company
3. Regain his good will

It may be helpful, at this point, to review the entire process of granting or refusing a claim. We can do this best by posing another Letter Problem to which we offer specific solutions for classroom discussion. Remember, as you read the problem, that generally the policy of the company for which the correspondent works will determine whether claims are granted or refused; in this instance, so that we may illustrate both types of letters, we are assuming that company policy is sufficiently flexible so that we can say either "yes" or "no" to the claim.

LETTER PROBLEM 2: Adjusting a Claim

You are one of three adjusters for the Bleakowen Department Store, and you have received the following letter:

> Gentlemen:
>
> On March 26, I purchased a size 14 tweed coat for my daughter in your Junior Miss Department. For this coat, which my daughter wanted for Easter, I paid $42.75.
>
> One week after Easter, you advertised this same coat on sale in the *Morning Chronicle* for $29.95. It seems to me that it is outrageous for you to charge almost thirteen dollars more for a coat just because it is purchased ten days before your sale, which I couldn't have known anything about. And anyway, we needed the coat for Easter.
>
> I expect you to send me a credit slip for the difference in price; otherwise I'll never do business with your store again.
>
> > Sincerely yours
> > Amanda E. Lewis
> > (Mrs. J. E. Lewis)

In the past, the store has been quite careful to avoid adjustments on merchandise purchased prior to major holidays such as Christmas and Easter, which have always been followed by major sales.

After checking on Mrs. Lewis's record, you find that she has been a good customer for nine years, has bought substantial amounts from Bleakowen's, and has paid her bills promptly.

You discuss Mrs. Lewis's letter with two other people in your department and it becomes apparent that there is disagreement about two main points:

1. Whether to grant or refuse her request
2. How the letter should be organized to do either of these things

Here are the pros and cons of these two points as they emerge in the discussion:

1. Whether to grant or refuse the request:
   "Why should Bleakowen's risk losing a good customer for a mere $12.80, which is actually what Mrs. Lewis wants?"
   "A lot of other customers just as good as Mrs. Lewis bought coats before Easter. Just because they didn't ask for a refund, are we going to ignore them?"

"Mrs. Lewis is just one customer. What difference does it make if we keep her happy for a mere $12.80. Tell her we've made an exception in her case, but that we'll never do it again."

"This sets a dangerous precedent. If you grant Mrs. Lewis's request, she's going to tell all her friends her daughter got a new Easter coat at sale prices."

2. How to organize the letter:

"When someone like Mrs. Lewis writes in to us, the first thing she wants in an answer is a direct reply to her question 'What are you going to do?'—and the letter should inform her of our decision in the first paragraph without beating about the bush."

"The way to get her to accept a decision is to give reasons first and then the decision."

(This analysis is intended to provide insight into the variety of factors and methods which can have some bearing on just one letter-writing situation. Actually, most of these questions would be answered by well-established policy.)

Your department head then tells all three of you to write the best letter possible to grant or refuse Mrs. Lewis's request.

Here are the results:

Granting Her Request

Dear Mrs. Lewis:

Your letter concerning the price of your daughter's Easter coat certainly struck a responsive note with us. You see we disliked the price change almost as much as you did . . . but for a different reason.

Our Easter coats were such an outstanding value in quality and workmanship that they were worth every cent of the pre-Easter price, but because we needed space so badly, we had to sell them fast. Hence the lower price a week later.

As you said, "we needed the coat for Easter," and Bleakowen's is pleased that you had it. But since we want all of our customers to know that our reputation has been built on fair dealing, we are crediting your account with $12.80, as you requested.

For your past patronage, we are truly grateful.

Sincerely yours,

Refusing Her Request (A matter-of-fact solution)

Dear Mrs. Lewis:

Your reaction at reading about the reduced price on your daughter's Easter coat was certainly natural. But may we explain?

Bleakowen's always offers sales after holidays such as Christmas and Easter—and always will. But customers like you who buy before the holidays have the advantage of far wider selection and of enjoying their purchase for the holiday itself. For these privileges, they pay a little more—but for your daughter to have the coat for Easter, the difference was certainly worth it.

We're sorry we can't grant your request for credit on the difference in price. To do so would be inconsistent with our policy of treating every one of our customers alike.

We hope you will feel we have been fair. May we continue to serve you?

Sincerely yours,

Refusing Her Request (A more original approach)

Remember last Christmas, Mrs. Lewis? It's funny, but that's what I thought of when I read your letter about the Easter coat.

I got to thinking about how we all go out and buy a tree for four of five or even ten dollars from some corner lot . . . and the day after Christmas the leftover trees aren't worth a cent.

But it was worth four or five dollars, wasn't it, to have that tree for Christmas Eve and Christmas Day. And I think it was the same way with your daughter's Easter coat. Don't you?

We hope so, because we want to keep you as the good customer you are . . . and we want to keep the hundreds of other customers who enjoyed their Easter coats at Easter . . . by treating all of you alike.

Fair? We try to be. Won't you see it that way too?

Sincerely yours,

Which of these letters seems to you most appropriate to achieve its purpose? On what basis would you decide that an adjustment should (should not) be made in Mrs. Lewis's case? Write the letter you would send to grant or refuse her claim.

In concluding this problem, it is fair to point out that neither of the last two letters of refusal may convince Mrs. Lewis. At best, they are what we have called "salvage operations." But they do represent honest attempts to persuade a reader in a difficult situation.

Admittedly, much of the writing procedure in handling claims and adjustments is more or less routine; but it would be a mistake to conclude that the treatment of such situations must necessarily be stereotyped. We have constantly stressed the fact that writing in business offers opportunity for originality, creativity, and humor. As an example of how these qualities can help in situations which otherwise might become tense, we close this chapter with a classic interchange between Harry Bannister of radio station WWJ Detroit and L. E. Kaffer, then on the staff of the Palmer House. If there were the equivalent of a Hall of Fame for letters, these two would be in it. The situation occurred years ago; shortly after Mr. Bannister had stayed overnight at the

Palmer House, he received a letter from Mr. Kaffer telling him that "two woolen blankets, replacement value of $8 each, were missing from the room you occupied" and asking Mr. Bannister to look through his luggage when unpacking since "guests frequently, we find, in their haste inadvertently place such items in their effects and, of course, return same when discovered." Instead of losing his temper, Mr. Bannister used his sense of humor as the basis for the following rather devastating reply:

My dear Mr. Kaffer:

I am desolated to learn, after reading your very tactful letter of September 1, that you actually have guests at your hostelry who are so absent-minded as to check out and include such slight tokens of your esteem as wool blankets (replacement value of $8.00 each) when repacking the other necktie and the soiled shirt.

By the same token, I suppose that passengers on some of our leading railroads are apt to carry off a locomotive or a few hundred feet of rails when disembarking from the choo-choo on reaching their destinations. Or, a visitor to a big city zoo might conceivably take away an elephant or a rhinoceros, concealing same in a sack of peanuts—after removing the nuts (replacedment value of $.05).

In this particular case I may be of slight assistance to you in running down the recalcitrant blankets. As I had a lot of baggage with me, I needed all the drawer space you so thoughtfully provide in each room. The blankets in question occupied the bottom drawer of the dresser, and I wanted to place some white shirts (replacement value of $3.50 each) in that drawer, so I lifted said blankets and placed them on a chair. Later, the maid came in and I handed the blankets (same blankets and same replacement value) to her, telling her in nice, gentlemanly language to get them the hell out of there.

If you'll count all the blankets in your esteemed establishment, you'll find that all are present or accounted for—unless other absent-minded guests have been accommodated at your emporium in the meanwhile. That's the best I can do.

Very truly yours,

Harry Bannister

P.S. Have you counted your elevators lately?

To this, Mr. Kaffer replied as follows:

Dear Mr. Bannister:

I wish to thank you for one of the most delightful letters it has been my pleasure to read in my entire business career. It would take a radio executive to compose a letter that would cause Damon Runyon, Mark Hellinger, and a lot of other writers radio might hire, to blush with futile envy. My sincere congratulations to you.

Yes, Mr. Bannister, we do a lot of counting around here. I've counted the elevators— and they're right where they should be, and operating, every one of them. What I want to count now is more important to me. I want to continue counting you as a friend of the Palmer House.

You, in your executive capacity, must of necessity supervise countless counts of so-called "listening audiences,""program polls," and all the bothersome promotions that annoy countless people in the middle of their dinner, or get them out of bed on cold nights to answer telephone queries. I shall assume, therefore, that you have naturally realized that you were most unfortunately a victim of a machine-like routine made necessary by the very vastness of an organization so well managed as the Palmer House.

There are a lot of folk in this merry world that would, as you so naively put it, "carry off locomotives, hundreds of feet of rails, and pack away an elephant or a rhinoceros." Just put a few ash trays, towels, blankets, pillows, glassware, and silverware in your public studios and reception rooms and see what happens.

Twenty-five thousand dollars' worth of silverware (actual auditors' "replacement value") is carried away annually by our "absent-minded" guests. A similar total (in "replacement value") is cherished annually by sentimental guests who like our linens as a memento of their visit to the Palmer House. They even go religious on us and take along the Gideon Bibles to the number of several thousand yearly. Nothing is sacred it would seem.

And so it goes. We are sorry, Mr. Bannister, that you were bothered as a result of a maid's mistake. Her lapse of memory started a giant wheel of routine. I am, in a way, happy the incident happened, because it gave me a chance to read your letter. It was a swell missive.

As the song says, and WWJ has no doubt played it "countless" times, "Let's Call the Whole Thing Off." And there's another song you also use, "Can't We Be Friends?"

Very sincerely yours,

L. E. Kaffer

So long as letters such as these can be written within the province of claims and adjustments, there is no need for further refutation of the charge that business letters must necessarily be dull and routine. Originality, humor, and cleverness can play an important role in any letter. In closing, we might well adopt Mr. Kaffer's idea of the theme song; for claims and adjustments, our theme should certainly be, "A soft answer turneth away wrath."

EXERCISES

1. Which of the following claim letters do you consider most effective? Why?

    a. Gentlemen:

    You keep sending me a bill for $39.76 for a mattress which I purchased on Feb. 6 and which I paid for on March 3 by a check drawn on the First National Bank.

    Since that time, I have had two bills. Will you please see that the proper credit is given so that I will receive no more bills? Thank you.

    Sincerely,

    John Denman

b.

Dear Sirs:

You certainly did a fine job of doing everything wrong on my order for a day bed. Personally, I don't see how an outfit like yours can stay in business.

I probably shouldn't expect you to remember anything I told you, but I gave you specific instructions to send that bed to my summer camp. Instead of that, you tried to deliver it to my home—so the neighbors told me—while I was on my vacation. I wanted it particularly because we were entertaining extra guests during my vacation and your careless disregard of my instructions spoiled everything—but you don't care about that.

I'd like to know what you intend to do about this. After this experience I'm through doing business with your store.

Yours truly,

Joseph Witherspoon

c.

Gentlemen:

Every time I get an electric light bill from you it is higher than the one for the month before. My December bill was $6.71, which is the highest I have ever had, and I am getting sick and tired of paying such exorbitant bills. You big utility companies take advantage of small customers like me, and it's no wonder you make the huge profits that I see reported in the papers. I want someone to come out and examine my meter because I know I'm being overcharged.

Sincerely yours,

John J. Fallon

2. What adjustments would you make in the situations described in (*b*) and (*c*) in the previous problem, assuming that in (*b*) the facts are as stated in Mr. Witherspoon's letter, and then in (*c*) the meter is working properly?

3. Assume that you are James Jones and that the president of your company has sent the following complaint to your department head with a note: "Let's see what Jones can do in answering this letter, but make him submit a draft to you first." Write out an answer which you think will win approval:

Mr. Farley Auchincloss
President
Uniflex Steel Corporation
511 Daly Street
Scranton, Pa. 18513

Dear Mr. Auchincloss:

I believe you will be interested in knowing the impression made upon me by the enclosed letter of reprimand from one of your company correspondents, James Jones.

This condescending letter extremely annoyed me for many reasons. I am an adult and expect to be so treated by responsible companies with whom I do business.

I have been a customer of your company for a number of years, and it seems to me that your people could have treated the first oversight in this period in the payment of a bill in a more personal way. A well-worded letter, calling the fact to my attention, would have been understood. I believe our relationship should be a mutual one, with definite obligations, including courtesy, on each side. I do not believe that either you or I would be interested in buying something from a company who dealt with its good customers in the fashion represented by the enclosed letter.

I am not presuming to tell you how to run your business, but I do know from my own personal experience that courteous service goes a long way toward getting customers and toward keeping their business and good will. May I have your opinion on this?

Very truly yours,

H. T. Feeley

Harold T. Feeley
President

4. The carpeting for your living and dining rooms, which you ordered from samples submitted by Mr. John Hawkins, salesman for The Elite Home Furnishing Company, does not match the sample which Mr. Hawkins showed you at the time you purchased your carpeting from him. Since your drapes and furniture were ordered to blend with the sample of carpeting, your whole decorative scheme is ruined. Write a claim letter to The Elite Home Furnishing Company, 27 East 55th Street, Chardon, Ohio 44024.

5. As adjuster for the Elite Home Furnishing Company, you have received the claim letter mentioned in Exercise 4. Your salesman has apparently neglected to tell the customer that no two dyes of carpeting are exactly the same and that samples and the delivered carpet do not match exactly. Since the carpeting is already cut to the dimensions of the customer's rooms, you face a considerable loss if the customer does not accept it. Write, offering her a discount of 20 percent and endeavoring to get her to accept this adjustment.

6. What changes would you make in the tone and wording of the following claim letter?

Kast Iron Mfg. Co.
Minneapolis, Minn. 55433

Dear Sirs:

I bought one of your steam irons which you advertise for $13.95 at Kousin Kenneth's Discount Store for $8.99. When I got it home and ironed my best dress with it, it leaked water all over the material and ruined my dress.

You sell your inferior merchandise to these discount stores and then they won't give me a replacement or pay me my money back. So I'm writing to you, and I want a new iron fast.

Sincerely yours,
Jane Smithers

7. As adjuster for the Kast Iron Mfg. Co., what reply would you make when your company policy is that individual stores have responsibility for replacements or refunds?

8. You operate an agency which specializes in taking over all the details of payrolls for small companies. Last Monday, your mail and phone were flooded with protests that

the previous Friday's payroll checks were sent out unsealed, apparently because of a technical breakdown in one of your mailing machines. Among other protests, you have received the following from the vice-president of a large grocery chain in a nearby small town:

> This situation really burned me up. Not only did my own check arrive so that the amount of my salary was clearly visible to anyone in the post office, but most of our workers also received similar treatment.
>
> We have used your service for the past five years—and if you recall, I am the one who recommended our using it because of your promise to keep every one of our payroll details completely confidential.
>
> I now consider that promise broken, and unless I receive satisfactory assurance, I shall recommend terminating our contract with you when it expires next month.
>
> Sincerely,

Write to Mr. E. C. Gannet, Vice-President, Economy Grocery Stores, Middleville, Wyoming 82329 doing your best to keep him from terminating the contract but offering him no kind of price concession on the present or future contract. You may consider whether it is appropriate to mention that because of inflation, all future contracts for your services will increase costs by 10 percent.

9. Miss Amanda Godfrey, Head Librarian, Abbeyville County Library System, Abbeyville, Kentucky 41097 had booked a tour of seven countries in 21 days through your agency, The Abbeyville Travel Service. At the time of booking she told you, "I want to be able to skip the last two days in Paris so that I can go to Dublin, because I've had a lifelong interest in seeing *The Book of Kells*, which is in Trinity College Library there. I'll pay whatever extra is needed to make this trip, and I'll rejoin the flight on Sunday evening at Shannon Airport." Her request resulted in an extra charge of $97.50 for her stay in Dublin, and when she paid it, Miss Godfrey told you "This is the greatest bargain of my life—to see *The Book of Kells* for less than a hundred dollars, just imagine!"

Two days after her return to Abbeyville, you receive the following note from her:

> Never again will I recommend your agency to anyone. It would seem to me that if you really knew what you are doing, you would know that the Trinity College Library has not been open on Saturday afternoon for the past century. Yet you booked me to arrive in Dublin at 1:30 on Saturday afternoon, knowing how much I wanted to see *The Book of Kells*. From now on, my travel arrangements will be made by professionals, not amateurs.

Miss Godfrey's reaction is very serious, because in her post at the library she has been able to refer hundreds of clients to your agency and to use posters you supplied in her section of travel books. Answer her letter, using whichever of the following assumptions your instructor assigns:

a. You can refund her $97.50.

b. You can offer her a 20 percent discount on an 11-day tour of Ireland, with three days in Dublin, which your agency will conduct six months from now.

    c. You can send her a very elaborate volume reproducing *The Book of Kells* as a personal gift. It costs $37.50, and the library already has a copy.

    d. You can make no offer of compensation of any kind but merely take the attitude that, because she is a professional librarian, you naturally assumed she would know all about Trinity College Library.

Finally, disregarding if necessary the assumptions which we have listed, if you had an absolutely free hand in answering Miss Godfrey's complaint, what would *you* consider to be a fair adjustment?

10. Mrs. T. Kelvin Whiteweather has made her first purchase from your exclusive dress shop for the Annual Ball of the Country Club on New Year's Eve. On January 3 she mails it back to you with a note, "I never should have bought this because I don't really like it and I don't think it fits, so please give me credit for $98.75." The dress has obviously been worn—in fact the proprietor of your shop saw Mrs. Whiteweather wearing it at the Annual Ball. Write, refusing her request.

11. Use the situation in the previous problem but now assume that your dress shop has promised Mrs. Whiteweather that your dresses are "one of a kind, and no one at the ball can possibly have one like it." But a guest from New York wore an identical dress bought at a different shop, and Mrs. Whiteweather demands full credit because of that fact. Decide what adjustment you consider to be fair under these circumstances and offer that adjustment in a letter to Mrs. Whiteweather.

12. You have been receiving the kind of non-response treatment described in the previous chapter from the Blankville Sports Shop, where six months ago you bought $115 of fishing tackle. You paid by check the following month but received four bills in succession; finally you talked to the manager, who told you that no more bills would be sent and that you owed nothing.

On the spur of the moment, your wife and you decide to go skiing, and since you have seen an exhibit of all kinds of skis in the Sports Shop window, you take her there, and she selects a complete outfit amounting to $295. This entails a check by the salesman of your credit, and after almost half an hour he returns to tell you that "because of the delinquent account, credit cannot be granted for the skiing outfit." The manager is on vacation, so you and your wife stamp out of the store. Write the letter you would send to the manager.

13. What changes would you make in the following letter?

> Truecolor Television Mfg. Co.
> Indianapolis, Ind. 44164
>
> Gentlemen:
>
> I bought one of your DeLuxe console models last Christmas and in the 8 months since we had it, we've had nothing but trouble.
>
> The Scotch Appliance Co. from whom we bought it says there is nothing more they can do—and that's why I'm writing to you. The longest we've gone without service is four weeks. When you turn the set on, it sounds like the buzzer at a basketball game and the picture is just like when you're in a movie and it flips up and down. And besides it's always blurred.

I paid $1,200 for it and the people at Scotch Appliance refuse to replace it. If I don't get some settlement soon, I'm going to hire a lawyer and sue. This whole thing burns me up because it was a Christmas present.

> Yours,
> Mrs. Evan E. Brown

14. You work as adjustment correspondent for Truecolor Television, and your inquiry to your dealer—the Scotch Appliance Company—reveals the following:

They have made thirteen service calls for Mrs. Brown's set in eight months.

The buzzing noise and the flipping picture have now been corrected.

Mrs. Brown bought the set on credit and still owes the Scotch Appliance Company $594.13.

There is something basically defective in the picture tube which servicemen have not been able to correct, and a replacement (wholesale cost $137.50) is needed. Scotch Appliance will not bear this cost unless Truecolor Television will reimburse them.

Mrs. Brown's lawyer has called Scotch Appliance but was not given any detailed information.

The head of Scotch Appliance has told you, "Be sure to *write* outlining what can be done. She seems to misinterpret every phone call I make to her, and now she says she won't pay any more installments until she hears from you."

The warranty on defective picture tubes is six months; on all other parts a year.

Like all Truecolor dealers, Scotch Appliance offers a $100-a-year complete service and replacement policy on its expensive console models. This Mrs. Brown refused when she bought the set.

Select any of this information which you consider appropriate to include in a letter to Mrs. Brown in which you offer to replace her picture tube free under two conditions: (*a*) that she will take out a one-year service policy for $100 and (*b*) that she will make the two payments of $64.13 each to bring her account with Scotch Appliance up to date. Write the letter to Mrs. Brown.

15. Mrs. George R. Gartstone, 395 Wilshire Blvd., Naples, Florida 33940 has written your company the following letter:

> Gentlemen:
>
> I bought one of your window air conditioners on May 15 from the Big Miami Appliance Store. I selected it chiefly because your national advertising always says "It's whisper soft" and stresses that its solid construction makes it "the quietest air conditioner on the market."
>
> Now that it is installed we find that it makes strange noises loud enough to wake us at night. The Big Miami Appliance Store's service man has been here three times, but he seems unable to quiet it. In fact, last night it seemed noisier than ever.
>
> Can you possibly do something? My husband is very sensitive to noise and we cannot really use your machine in its present state. It's your model R-x283; we've had it a month; and we paid $215.95 for it. We'll both be very grateful for any help you can give us.
>
> Sincerely yours,
> Ruth Gartstone (Mrs. G. R. Gartstone)

What is your evaluation of Mrs. Gartstone's letter on the basis of how effective it is in getting the result she wants? If you were the adjustment correspondent for the Kool-air Company, which manufactured the air conditioner, what would you include in a letter to Mrs. Gartstone if the only feasible solution is to send a factory representative to fix her appliance, and he cannot get there before three weeks at the earliest? Write the letter.

16.　As claims correspondent for Security Insurance Co., you have received a filled-in form from The Community Hospital of your city claiming $798.11 for the hospital expenses of Mrs. Caroly Esteban of your city. The amount includes $79.23 for drugs, which are not included in the medical policy Mrs. Esteban took out with Security Insurance Co.

Unfortunately, when Mrs. Esteban was hospitalized six months previously, a bill for $63.42 worth of drugs was inadvertently paid and the error not discovered until four weeks later. When this finally came to light, your supervisor said, "Let it go. It's just too late to try to recover the $63.42. We'll just keep quiet about it and not let Mrs. Esteban know. But there will be no 'next time' for drugs for her. Our local agent tried to include drug costs when he sold her the policy, but she said she had a friend in a pharmacy who could get drugs for her at cost."

In analyzing all the aspects of this situation, you recognize that Mrs. Esteban is going to be very irate at paying for drugs which she, at least, thinks she could have bought more cheaply elsewhere. And quite properly, she can argue "You paid last time and you ought to pay this time. At least, you should have told me about the mistake last time."

Before you write anything, consider these questions:

1.　Should you wait until the hospital notifies her that the drug bill has not been paid? (You can control this timing to a certain extent by deciding when to send your company's check to the hospital.) Or would it be better if Mrs. Esteban gets your letter of explanation before the hospital calls her to say she owes $79.23?

2.　To what purpose will you use the mistake in paying the first drug bill? Will you ignore it completely? Say, "You were not entitled under your policy to the $63.42 payment during your first hospital stay"? Admit that the company made a serious blunder? Or what?

3.　What use, if any, will you make of the fact that her local agent tried to get her to include the clause for payment of drugs? Or that she should have been in touch with her friend in the pharmacy during her hospitalization?

4.　In explaining the matter to Mrs. Esteban, which details of the situation would you concentrate on? How the mistake occurred? What your supervisor said? Why you are being "inconsistent"—as Mrs. Esteban will say—paying one claim and not another?

Write the letter to Mrs. Esteban using either of the following assumptions about timing, depending on your decision in (4) above:

(a)　She has had a call from the hospital requesting $79.23 and has written you an angry letter of protest.

(b)　Your letter will be her first intimation that her drug bill has not been paid.

CHAPTER 9

CREDIT LETTERS

Someone has said that "credit" is an abstract word—until you have to borrow money. Certainly this word, which derives from the Latin *credo*, "I believe," has many different connotations for economists, businessmen, and average citizens. Businessmen used to speak of the "three C's of credit—character, capacity, and character;" J. P. Morgan remarked that "credit is 99 percent character; " and Alexandre Dumas humorously referred to it as "using other people's money."

Such comments and definitions are interesting, but if we are to get a useful idea of what credit means, as applied to correspondence, we should think of it in simpler terms:

1. To the user of credit it is a means by which he may have something now and pay for it later.
2. To the grantor of credit, it is an estimate of someone's ability and willingness to pay later.

These definitions, oversimplified as they may be, underscore the two salient factors relevant to credit letters—the primary importance of a sound credit reputation and the necessity of rating someone's ability to pay.

Students tend to regard the whole process of granting or refusing credit as being remote from their own lives. To drive home the immediate importance of credit, we suggest thinking for a moment about the answers to these questions:

How much of your college education are you and/or your parents paying for? How is the rest paid for?

Do you now own a car? Or do you want to own one in the future? How much of a down payment can you make on it? Where does the remainder of the money come from?

What is your attitude toward borrowing? Is it a "good" or a "bad" thing to do? What has determined this attitude?

The last questions are particularly pertinent because all of us have value judgments about going into or staying out of debt.

Regardless of our personal judgments, however, it is no exaggeration to say that credit has become a major element in the American economic way of life. Without it, our economic system cannot survive. One essential element must be added to this discussion of the "have now, pay later" concept—*the ability to obtain information as the basis on which credit will be granted or refused*. Note this startling description in *Time* (December 20, 1968).*

For practical purposes, the more than 2,500 credit bureaus in the U.S. exist to protect their clients against the 4% of consumers who are "slow pays" and the 1% who try to "skip" without paying at all. As such, they are essential in a country that lives on credit. More than 60% of an average American's net income is spent on credit obligations of one sort or another. Each month in the U.S. some $8 billion worth of credit is extended, and the current total of outstanding consumer bills is estimated to be $105 billion—or 12% of the annual gross national product.

Hearsay and Fact. It is hardly surprising that the credit bureaus themselves have become big business. Operating on a membership-and-fee basis—a flat rate of $10 to $50 per year, plus anywhere from 75¢ to $50 for a credit analysis—they provide creditors with data on an individual's working, purchasing and paying habits. The Associated Credit Bureaus Inc., a sort of cooperative that represents 2,400 local bureaus that have files on about 160 million Americans is computerizing its nationwide operation. By 1973, credit information on a shopper from Rochester, N.Y., will be instantly available to a storekeeper in Redlands, Calif.

That information may be startlingly complete. The first time a man applies for credit of any sort, the facts of his life are collected and fed to the computer; forever after, his file grows and grows. In addition to such basics as his name, address, bank references, marital status and bill-paying habits, credit bureaus keep track of his employment record, living accommodations and bank balance. They record his debts and how he pays them, and his legal involvements. They

---

*Reprinted by permission from TIME. The Weekly Newsmagazine, Copyright Time Inc., 1968.

scour newspapers and public records for data on births, deaths, divorces, business failures, tax liens and court actions. They may even dispatch a field agent to interrogate an individual's acquaintances, friends and foes.

The remarkable fact that less than 1 percent of credit granted is written off as a loss attests to the efficiency of this information system. While it is not within the province of this book to discuss the big-brother-is-watching-you aspects of credit investigation, resentment is growing at what many consider invasions of privacy. The response to such critics is that because you wanted credit, you yourself started this whole process when you filled out your first charge-account application; and that first application is a good point at which to start our explanation of what happens in the credit process.

Let's assume that you have asked for credit in a department store where you have filled out a form with questions about your income, employment, rent or ownership of a home, and bank references. The store will supplement all this with information from one of the credit bureaus mentioned in the *Time* article. (Normally, such bureaus do not *rate* your credit potential but merely supply background on which the store's credit manager makes a judgment.) If there are no blots on your credit escutcheon, you will be given one of three basic types of credit accounts (the terminology varies from store to store and from place to place):

1. The Regular or 30-day Account. You will get statements monthly on which payment without finance charges is due within 10 to 30 days after billing.

2. The 90-day or Budget Account. Payable in equal installments, i.e. three equal installments in 90 days. No financing charge if paid within 90 days, unless there is a default in any payment. A variant is the Revolving Account, which spreads out payments and new purchases over additional months with interest charges assessed on unpaid balances.

3. Long-term Installment Accounts. The term usually runs 6 months in department stores, 30 months with car dealers. Essentially, this is for major purchases where payments (including finance charges) can be spread over a long period.

There are so many variations of these basic types—and so many different names for them—that we will confuse a very complex situation by going into more detail.

Nonetheless, one can fairly say that within the past few years, the attitudes of credit and collection men have become somewhat ambivalent, to use an overworked word. The reason is that the granting of credit and the charging of interest is a very lucrative business, and some shrewd judgments have to be passed on whether it may be better to let outstanding accounts run on while finance charges mount, *provided*, of course, that payment will be made eventually. The spate of offers of easy credit and credit cards within recent years indicates the potential profitability of credit; it also signals the need for the closest possible relationship between granting credit and collecting bills, which in today's world is a far cry from yesterday's attempt to get as many bills paid in the fastest possible time.

As a result of the Truth in Lending Act passed in 1969, Wallachs, a well-known New York retail chain, took an admirably forthright advertisement in the *New York Times* (July 6, 1969) to explain credit terms on its three basic forms of accounts: 30-day with no finance charge; 90-day with no finance charge, unless a payment is defaulted; 6-month with finance charge paid monthly, unless the entire balance is paid in the first month. Here is the statement about finance charges:

> Where applicable, the finance charge is computed at a periodic rate of 1½% per month, which is an annual percentage rate of 18% applied to the first $500, and at a periodic rate of 1% per month, which is an annual percentage rate of 12% applied to any excess over $500, of the previous balance shown on your monthly statement, after deducting payments and credits.
>
> We have had these terms for a long time. We consider them very competitive. If you agree and would like to open a Wallachs account, you may do so quickly and easily at any of our stores.*

Now—to return to our specific example—let's assume that you have been granted credit up to $450 on a 90-day account and have bought a coat costing $300. You make your first $100 payment on time, but default on your second and third payments. What happens? Here's a credit manager's answer:

> A store will give every possible consideration when a legitimate reason is given for missing a payment. But if we're not notified that the check is not forthcoming, she'll get another bill next month, on the assumption that she forgot, coupled with a reminder letter; the next month the reminder note or letter becomes more insistent. If the bill is not paid the fourth month, the case leaves the routine stage and goes to the store's credit man. Here procedures differ among stores—some use phone calls, more write personal letters demanding payment. By this stage most outstanding bills have been collected—or at least a start has been made on payment—and we rarely have to follow through on threats to take legal action.

To put this into perspective, we will discuss the letters in the credit and collection process (in Chapter 10) as two sides of the same coin. Another element, however, must be noted—the effect of credit and collection upon sales. Customers who owe money usually don't reorder; sales often depend on how easy it is for people to buy, which means a credit account; and finally, the customer to whom credit has been properly granted and by whom bills have been

*Reprinted by permission.

regularly paid represents the best potential for enhancing sales. Credit, collection, and sales together form the base upon which business is built; hence, letters associated with these functions are of the utmost importance.

Increasingly, credit bureaus have obviated the need for certain letters which were formerly integral parts of the credit process and which might include the following:

1. A letter acknowledging the customer's order or his application for credit and requesting that he send credit references
2. Letters to the references furnished requesting credit information
3. Letters from these references giving the credit information
4. The final letter to the customer
    a. Granting him credit and explaining the terms
    b. Refusing him credit

Of these four types, the first and the last are by all odds the most important, but since letters to and from credit references are still used occasionally, we shall discuss them briefly.

ACKNOWLEDGING APPLICATIONS FOR CREDIT

These acknowledgments respond to two situations: (1) When a letter requesting credit is received or (2) when an order is received from someone who has not yet established credit. In either event, the letter of acknowledgment is primarily a sales promotion letter with heavy stress on sincere appreciation of the request for credit and on the kind of service you hope to render. Since the situation and specific company policy determine whether you get credit information direct from the customer, acknowledgments may include most or all of the following elements:

1. A statement welcoming the new customer or expressing appreciation for his first order.
2. An explanation of the firm's policy with regard to credit and payment of bills.
3. (If information is not obtained from a credit bureau) A request that credit references be sent or that an enclosed credit blank be filled out.
4. (If you have requested credit information from him) An incentive to action emphasizing that the sooner the credit information is received, the sooner he may receive the order.
5. (If you have received satisfactory information from a credit bureau) A sales statement about service, quality of merchandise, or your future mutual relationship.

Here's a letter which requests credit information but also fills the first order:

Dear Mr. Weldon:

We certainly appreciate the opportunity you have given us in your first order to do business with your firm. Your expression of confidence in us is most gratifying, and we will do everything in our power to live up to it.

Since you probably need this merchandise as soon as possible we are shipping your order by express tomorrow. So that we can handle your future needs without delay, we'd appreciate your sending us your financial statement. Or if you prefer, just fill out and return the enclosed credit form.

This credit information will, of course, be kept absolutely confidential. We are looking forward to having you as a regular customer. May we have your credit information soon?

Sincerely yours,

Dear Mr. Barrett:

We greatly appreciate the order for $237.21 worth of canned goods which you placed with Mr. White, our representative in your territory.

Since this is our first transaction with you, we must ask you to fill out and return the enclosed blank from our credit department. This is part of our regular routine in handling all new accounts; the information you send us will, of course, be held in the strictest confidence.

Your account will be opened and your order will be shipped as soon as this information reaches us. It is our hope that this is the beginning of a long business relationship. We shall do our best to make it a pleasant and profitable one for you.

Sincerely yours,

Acknowledgments of credit applications offer no serious problems. In dealing with the general public rather than with businessmen, the credit department will lay even greater stress upon the usualness of its request for information, since retail customers, not conditioned to fiscal requirements, may resent the request as being "out of line."

REQUESTING CREDIT INFORMATION

Basically, a request for credit information is a letter of inquiry, which has been discussed in Chapter 7. Above all else, it should be easy to answer. The question asked should be specific rather than general. The customary procedure is to enclose a credit blank to be filled out. Where less detailed information is required, such a form as the following, with the credit applicant's name typed in, is used:

Gentlemen:

The _____ Company of _____ (address) _____

has given us your name as a credit reference.

We will appreciate your giving us the benefit of your experience with this company.

If you will answer the questions listed on the form below and return this letter in the enclosed stamped envelope, we shall be very grateful. Your reply will, of course, be kept in strict confidence.

Sincerely yours,

How long has this company dealt with you?. . . . .
The terms were. . . . .
Amount now owing is $ . . . .
Highest credit you will extend is $. . . . .
Date of the last transaction. . . . .
Remarks. . . . .
. . . .
. . . .
(Signed) . . . .
(Date . . . .

GIVING CREDIT INFORMATION

The letter giving credit information varies considerably, depending upon whether the correspondent speaks favorably or unfavorably of the credit applicant. Where a favorable reply can be given, the letter is frank in answering any necessary questions, as in the following instance:

Gentlemen:

Mr. Allen Eaton, 27 Broadway, Hurley, Indiana 47033 about whom you asked us on July 26, has always had a good credit rating with us. He has been a customer of ours for seven and a half years, and he has usually paid his bills on the first of the month following purchase. His credit limit with us has been $500.

Sincerely yours,
The Taft Brothers

Where the information is unfavorable to the applicant, the letter should be much more guarded and careful in its language because of the legal implications involved in expressing an unfavorable opinion of someone's credit reputation. It is customary to avoid using any names in letters reporting unfavorably on the applicant's credit reputation, as in the following example:

Gentlemen:

The individual about whom you inquired on July 3 has a poor credit record with us. He has been a customer of ours for less than a year, and we are already having great difficulty in collecting from him. His credit limit with us was $250, but at present we are making shipments to him only on a strictly cash basis.

Sincerely yours,

THE FINAL LETTER, GRANTING OR REFUSING CREDIT

Thus far, the letters we have discussed offer no very serious problems. But in his final letter, the credit man must express, however indirectly, his estimate of the customer's willingness and capacity to pay later. If the opinion is favorable, the letter is comparatively easy to compose; but if the opinion is unfavorable and credit is refused, the most difficult of all business letters must be written. Because of the resulting difference in technique, each of these types is discussed separately.

The Letter Granting Credit

The letter granting credit is not merely a statement of terms and conditions; it is also a sales letter which tells the customer of the quality of the merchandise and of the excellence of the service the firm tries to give. It may be compared in its general tone to a note of welcome to a friend who has just arrived in the writer's city; it should welcome him and express the hope that his "visit" will be enjoyable and that he will take advantage of the many facilities the "city" offers. The general tone of welcome, of interest in the customer's welfare, and of willingness to serve him is invaluable at the beginning of the credit man hopes will be a long and pleasant business relationship. Consider the difference in the cordiality of the following letters:

Dear Mr. Jones:

In accordance with your request of May 11, we are granting you credit with a top limit of $500. Our bills are sent on the 28th of each month and are payable by the 10th of the next month. If you don't pay your balance by the 10th of each month, we charge 1½% interest. We hope you will enjoy shopping in our store.

Sincerely yours,

Dear Mr. Jones:

We are happy, indeed, to grant your request of May 11 for a credit account with us. Bills, payable by the 10th of each month, are mailed on the 28th of the month and include all charges up to the 25th. Unpaid balances are subject to a finance charge of 1½% each month.

Formerly, it was possible for the Blank Company to welcome each of its new customers personally. The size of our company and the number of our customers now prevent that, but our growth has come, and will continue to come, from our interest in serving all of our customers in the friendly manner that has become a tradition at Portland's most modern store.

As part of our service to charge customers, you will be given opportunity in advance to shop at all our sales before advertisements reach the general public. You will want to take advantage of our shopping service, which enables you to shop by phone to avoid the tiresome trip downtown. A call to Miss Parker will give you this efficient service and, of course, at no extra charge. All you need say now is, "Just charge it to my account."

The enclosed booklet will tell you of the hundreds of services offered for your convenience. We want you to use them because they will save you time and money. For our part, we hope that we may express our appreciation by serving you efficiently for many years to come.

Sincerely yours,

The second letter and the one displayed on page 203 are far more deft than the first in expressing the hope that this new business relationship will be mutually profitable. By indicating a determination to make it so, they go far toward building good will at the very start of a business relationship. Usually the letter granting credit contains:

1. A granting of credit
2. A statement of terms
3. A sales talk on the type of service the company hopes to render
4. An expression of appreciation

Although the order of these parts may vary, all of them are generally present. The personality of the letter is as important as its contents; if the granting of the credit is friendly, cordial, and helpful in tone, the letter will be effective.

The Letter Refusing Credit

Correspondents customarily believe that the letter they are engaged in writing at any given time is the most difficult of all types of letters. The immediate problem before us always seems the most perplexing, but if we objectively considered what is the most difficult of all the usual types of business letters, there is little doubt that we would select the letter refusing credit. The mere refusal of the credit is not so difficult, although the implication that the applicant represents a poor risk is hardly a pleasant one. The problem in refusing credit arises from the intelligent writer's desire to make his letter something more than just a refusal. Far too many businessmen are content with a routine form letter starting with the unimaginative words, "This is to inform you that we are unable at this time to extend credit," and ending with a pious hope that things may be different at some indefinite time in the future.

What else should the writer try to do? The applicant has been judged so poor a risk that no credit can be granted. Why not let the whole matter end with a vague or indefinite refusal? That is obviously the easiest way out for the

STANDARD EQUIPMENT COMPANY

THE STANDARD BUILDING
75 NEWELL SQUARE, OMAHA, NEBRASKA 68124

March 25, 1970

Mr. Owen L. Conover
Complete Office Supplies, **Inc.**
79 Broadway
Centerville, Nebraska 68724

Dear Mr. Conover:

Thank you very much for sending us your financial statement so
promptly. You are to be congratulated on the fine credit
record your company has established.

We have shipped your order of March 21 by express today, and
you should receive this merchandise by the first of next week.
As you know, we will bill you on the 10th of each month for
goods purchased the previous month. Payments within ten days
of the date of our invoice entitle you to a two per cent discount.

We hope that you will like doing business with us. For our part,
we want to do everything we can to deserve the confidence you
have placed in us. We regard every order as an opportunity for
prompt and efficient service.

Yours sincerely,

Maurice A. Nesbitt

Maurice A. Nesbitt
Credit Manager

MAN:CEL

credit man, but it is not the intelligent way. If the writer has thought out what he is trying to do in this letter, he is not refusing credit so much as *he is trying to get the applicant's business on a cash basis.*

There are perfectly sound arguments which can be used to convince the customer that cash buying is to his own advantage. The credit man can advance such incentives as a discount for cash, savings on interest charges, or the advantages of buying in small quantities for cash and thus keeping up-to-date merchandise in stock, or the pleasures of end-of-the-month freedom from bills, or the fact that cash buying over a period of time will establish his reputation so that credit may be granted in the future. Perhaps the applicant won't accept these suggestions; perhaps he can get credit from another source. But the alternatives for the writer of this type of letter are to refuse him and stop there or to try to do something constructive. The intelligent correspondent will not be content to be negative; he will try to prevail upon the customer to buy for cash.

In its structure, the refusal-of-credit letter, then, should accomplish two tasks: it should tactfully refuse credit and it should attempt to get a cash order. The anomalous character of the refusal-of-credit letter comes from the fact that although it constitutes an unflattering comment on the applicant's financial standing, its language must not reflect this at all. Notice how tactless and inept the following letter is:

> Dear Mr. Haley:
>
> Thank you for your order of February 16. We regret to state that our investigation of your credit standing shows that your firm is not a good credit risk.
>
> We hope that you will understand our position in this matter as we want your business, but we operate on so small a margin of profit that we dare not risk any credit losses.
>
> You stated that 2,100 of our No. 14 cardboard containers would fill your needs for the next three months. In that case, we think we would be placing no hardship on you if we ask you to order C.O.D.
>
> If you still want to place an order with us, we shall be glad to take care of it. As you know, our workmanship is better and our prices are lower than any of our competitors'.
>
> Yours truly,

The entire tone of this letter antagonizes the reader unnecessarily with phrases like "not a good credit risk" or "you stated" and negative language like "we would be placing no hardship on you." However true such statements may be, skilled credit correspondents do not say "you are a poor credit risk" or "your credit references were unsatisfactory." Instead, such facts should be glossed over and expressed in less harsh terms. Effective writers of refusal-of-credit letters attempt to achieve their purposes as follows:

1. Refuse credit by
    a. Referring indirectly to credit information or acknowledging the credit references that have been sent.
    b. Analyzing the situation by beginning with its more favorable aspects but ending with a clear statement of refusal of credit.
2. Attempt to get an order on a cash basis by
    a. Making some practical offer to cooperate (for example, cutting down the size of the order and paying part cash and the balance on specified terms)
        or by
    b. Advancing arguments to show that the customer himself benefits by cash buying, such as

    (1) An offer of cash discount, usually 2 percent
    (2) A suggestion that cash buying in smaller quantities will give a wider selection and more up-to-date stock
    (3) An inducement to establish credit within a short period by buying for six months or a year on a cash basis

Notice how effectively one credit man handles a difficult refusal, making no mention of the probable fact that Mr. Travis is a very poor credit risk:

> Dear Mr. Travis:
>
> Thank you for your promptness in sending us the credit information we requested. We are glad to report that all of your credit references spoke favorably of you as a business-man.
>
> The new store which you are opening in Bellport should eventually prosper, since yours is a thriving community. But its location within 20 miles of New York City forces you to compete with the larger stocks and lower prices of the metropolitan department stores, so readily accessible to commuters from Bellport and similar communities. Because your resources do not indicate that you can meet such competition by starting with a large indebtedness, we must refuse your credit application.
>
> We would suggest, therefore, that you cut your order in half and pay cash for it. This will entitle you to our 2 per cent cash discount, a saving which you may pass on to your customers. By ordering frequently in small quantities, you can best meet the competition of the New York stores through keeping up-to-date merchandise on your shelves. Thus, through cash buying you will establish your business on a sound basis that will entitle you to an excellent credit reputation.
>
> The enclosed duplicate of your order will assist you in making your selection. Just check the items you wish and sign the order. Your merchandise will arrive C.O.D. within two days after our receipt of the order—in plenty of time for your opening sale.
>
> Sincerely yours,

This credit man takes the very realistic point of view that half an order is better than none. To get it, he uses all the arguments he can muster. A comparison of the tone of this letter with that on page 204 will show how ineptly or how deftly credit can be refused, depending entirely on the technique used.

The following letters also reveal a tactful technique of refusing credit in such a way that the prospect will not take offense:

Dear Mr. Doe:

Thank you for your order for 50,000 tags. We are glad to have it.

Unfortunately, however, we now find that the credit information we have in our files is not complete enough to enable us to accept your order on open account. We realize that a thorough credit investigation would probably show that your organization is in good shape financially, but elaborate investigations cost quite a bit and usually require several weeks to complete.

Since you probably need the tags as soon as possible, I thought you might like to send us your check for $79 to avoid the delay that would be caused by our making a credit investigation. Or, if more convenient, send $40 and we will ship them "balance due C.O.D."

We will enter your order as soon as we receive your check—or, if you prefer, send us a list of two or three credit references and your latest financial statement.

Sincerely yours,

Gentlemen:

Thank you for your order given to Mr. Burton on June 11 for Safeway heaters. As is the usual custom before a new account is opened, we have tried to obtain information that would serve as a basis for extending credit. Such information as we have thus far obtained does not permit us to form a definite conclusion, and for the present, therefore, we are not warranted in opening the account.

We realize that misunderstandings sometimes occur through trifling matters, which, if particulars were known, would have little or no bearing on the consideration of one's credit standing. If you feel that our action is not justified, we shall be glad to have you call at our office or write us so that we can arrive at a better understanding.

Please feel sure that we are anxious to serve you; and, after all, credit is a convenience and not a necessity.

Possibly in the future, conditions may change so as to allow us to open an account for you. Meanwhile, we hope you will instruct us to send this merchandise to you collect. We assure you that we will furnish you with the best of merchandise and give you the best prices and the friendly services offered by the Magnolia Heater Company.

Yours very truly,

LETTER PROBLEM 3: *Credit*

You have received the following letter from Dr. John C. Cash, Professor of Ethics, Blank University, Blankville, Anystate, 99999:

Gentlemen:

My daughter, Mrs. John C. Smith, has recently settled in your city because her husband has a position as Research Fellow at your City University.

At her behest—and because I wanted to help them get settled—I sent her $350 as a down payment on a stove, refrigerator, and various other appliances including a television set which she purchased from your organization.

Yesterday I received her letter of thanks for my gift. In it, my daughter makes the comment, "Now we will be able to pay off the balance of $497.31 in the next year and at a charge of only 1½ percent a month on our unpaid balance. Without your check, we couldn't possibly have made the necessary down payment."

I must confess that I was shocked—and that is my reason for writing. In the first place, I have paid cash for everything I ever bought because I was brought up to believe that going into debt was almost sinful. In the second place, your interest charges appalled me since they amount to 18 percent. On $497.31 for a year that amounts to almost $90. And in the third place, I read the story in *Time* and I regard the snooping that goes into credit investigations as an invasion of privacy.

Since my life has been devoted to examining all sides of ethical questions, you will do me a great favor by supplying me with your viewpoint on what I consider to be excessive interest charges and unethical prying into other peoples' affairs.

Sincerely yours,

Your answer is, of course, an answer-to-an-inquiry letter in form; in content, it should reflect your knowledge of the credit process.

Before you write, be sure you have answered these questions:

1. Are there any errors of fact in Dr. Cash's letter?
2. What is the best persuasive reason you can offer to justify the interest charges and the methods associated with getting credit information?
3. What use can you make of Dr. Cash's statement "I have paid cash for everything I ever bought"?
4. Is there any reason to believe that the best solution is the no-response treatment discussed in Chapter 8?

Several different answers to this letter from Dr. Cash are presented before the Exercises in this chapter on pages 211–213. Before you consult them, write your own answer and then compare it with those in this book. Remember that the ones included here are intended to represent both effective and ineffective solutions and should be used as the basis for class discussion.

USING CREDIT SITUATIONS FOR BUSINESS-PROMOTION LETTERS

As we have seen in inquiries and acknowledgments of orders, modern business uses any opportunity from birthdays to New Year's greetings as the occasion to stimulate business or good will. These business-promotion letters can be effectively used as adjuncts to the whole process of granting credit in three situations:

1. Offering credit privileges to those who have not as yet set up credit terms
2. Attempting to revive credit accounts which for one reason or another have become inactive
3. Expressing thanks to customers who have fulfilled their credit obligations promptly or over a long period of time

There is room for originality, humor, and sincerity in these letters, which attempt to create new customers or cement relationships with old ones. Their pattern is comparatively simple:

1. The use of some occasion such as a holiday, a sale, or a span of time as the reason for offering credit, reviving its use, or acknowledging that it has been used with integrity
2. An explanation of the advantages of credit from the users' standpoint
3. A convenient method by which credit may be established or used or an expression of appreciation for using it well

Here are two effective letters offering credit privileges:

Dear Mrs. Greenspan:

You've been busy, we know, since the process of moving from one city to another is generally a hectic one.

The next time you have a minute, we think we can save you a lot of minutes in getting settled. The enclosed card is your passport to the Wonderful World of Wundermans Department Store. We've served Middleburg people for 88 years from a complete stock of the modern merchandise you'd expect in the city's biggest department store.

Just sign and mail the card today. From there on you can do all your shopping by telephone, conveniently and quickly.

Sincerely yours,

Dear Mrs. Blake:

Miss Rita Conway, the head of our book department, has told me of your interest in our spring book sale and has suggested that you might be interested in opening a charge account with us.

You will find such an account of the greatest convenience, for it will enable you to call Miss Conway at any time and order the books you want without the inconvenience of making long trips downtown. In this way you will be able to keep up with the latest books and still have the benefit of Miss Conway's expert advice.

With a charge account, these same privileges are available in all the 51 departments of our store. Just call any one of the departments listed in the enclosed folder, order what you wish, and say, "Charge it"; or if you are undecided about gifts for friends, our Personal Shopping Service is available without cost to charge customers. Furthermore, you will receive advance notice of our many sales in the various departments of the store.

Just sign and mail the enclosed card, which offers you carefree and convenient shopping.

Sincerely yours,

Since businessmen spend considerable time, money, and effort in putting new customers on their books, common sense dictates that they do what they can to keep these accounts active. Letters to revive such accounts are frequently sent in series over a period of months; ostensibly they are letters of inquiry, but actually they promote sales by making the customer feel that he has been missed and that his business is important.

Dear Mr. Dart:

We've just heard about a husky restaurant patron who left his expensive hat with a note:

It belongs to the heavyweight champion and I'm coming right back.

When he returned, the hat was gone and had been replaced by this note:

Taken by the world's champion long-distance runner—and I'm not coming back.

We've wondered why *you* haven't been back since you took out that charge account four months ago. You'll find us champions of service whose major concern is keeping customers like you.

Come right back for our Spring Sale, with savings in every department—even hats.

Sincerely yours,

Dear Mr. Alexander:

Old friends are the best friends. . . .

That's the way we feel about the old friends we've made in our 22 years of business. And when you don't see an old friend for a long time, you're naturally concerned.

That's why we're writing you. Because we're concerned that we have unintentionally done something you didn't like. If so, we want to know about it and remedy the matter.

We have valued the confidence you've placed in us for many years now. A lot of new customers have been entered on our accounts during that time, but the old friends are those we treasure most. Because we've missed you, may we hear from you soon?

Cordially yours,

An amusing indication of the nature of our modern computerized business world was supplied in response to a Texas bank's inquiry as to why a certain customer had closed her bank account. The answer:

I married Account Number 621–30157.

WILLIAMS TOYS AND NOVELTIES COMPANY

4726 SIXTH STREET
CINCINNATI, OHIO 45203

November 12, 1970

Mr. Eldon E. Hightower
The Children's Shop
76 West Avenue
Middletown, Ohio 45042

Dear Mr. Hightower:

We've missed you . . . .

And we're wondering if we haven't somehow slipped up without
realizing it.

Your account and your friendship are important to us, because
we like to think that we continue to deserve the confidence
and the good will of customers like you. For that reason, if
we have not rendered the kind of service you should receive,
we'd appreciate your telling us so that we can do whatever we
can to correct the situation.

We realize, of course, that you may not have needed any of our
products in the past few months. But with the holidays approaching,
we have many novelties and children's toys which will be attractive
to your customers and profitable to you.

Because we've counted it a privilege to serve you in the past,
we are looking forward to hearing from you soon.

Sincerely,

James E. Williams

James E. Williams, President

JEW:RLS

Finally, letters of thanks to customers who have fulfilled their credit obligations present a fine way of maintaining good customers:

Dear Mr. Wynkoop:

Every year we start anew by singing "Should old acquaintance be forgot and never brought to mind . . ."

We don't want old acquaintances like you to be forgot, particularly because it has been brought to our mind that you have provided us with a lot of business in twelve months and have lived up to your credit obligations promptly.

We're grateful to you. May our old acquaintance continue for years to come.

Sincerely yours,

Dear Mr. Kilroy:

A credit manager is usually up to his neck in misery and frowns, but it's companies like yours that give us a chance to smile once in a while.

In checking over our accounts, I was impressed with the prompt record of payment you have established with us over the years. It is really appropriate for me to say that you build up a credit man's morale!

So before I get back to my dunning and frowning, I wanted you to know how much I appreciate your account. And my thanks, of course, go for our entire staff.

Sincerely,

Dear Mr. Franklin:

With a new year just around the corner, we want you to know how much we have appreciated your cooperation during the past year.

Your account has been paid promptly, and we hope that you have enjoyed doing business with us as much as we have with you.

That's why we want to say "thank you" and to wish you a happy and prosperous New Year.

Cordially yours,

These letters demonstrate that situations associated with credit can be used effectively to promote good relations with customers. One danger to be avoided is that of sounding "gushy" or insincere; but properly used, these business-promotion letters allied to the credit function offer countless opportunities for creating favorable impressions, cementing established relationships, and maintaining customers' good will.

SOLUTIONS TO LETTER PROBLEM 3: *Credit*

These answers to Dr. Cash's letter include both effective and inadequate examples. They are intended to be used as a basis for classroom discussion of the problem rather than as models to be followed.

1.

Dear Dr. Cash:

Your letter evoked a certain nostalgia about my own college days. I only wish that I could return to the theoretical academic discussions to which, somehow, a dollar sign never needed to be attached.

As I've found, business is different. Money is a commodity, just like potatoes, books, or a car. Your daughter is using *our* money for the next 12 months, and just as if she were using *our* car for a year, she has to pay for it at going rates.

And in just the same way that you wouldn't let somebody have your car for a year without knowing anything about him, so we can't let people have our money without investigation. That's why credit bureaus exist; without their services, your daughter could not have the appliances she now has in her home.

We hope you will understand our viewpoint. For our part, we're grateful that you wrote.

Sincerely yours,

2.

Dear Dr. Cash:

Along with a lot of other people, we envy your ability to pay cash for everything you've bought. By doing so, you certainly saved a lot of money.

In the process, however, you had to wait a long time for things you wanted. Aren't you delighted then to know that your daughter can enjoy the appliances she wants and needs without waiting? That's what credit accomplishes—and that's what she's paying the $1\frac{1}{2}$ percent for.

Maybe we're insensitive to ethics, but we don't see anything wrong with credit investigations. We can't extend credit to people we don't know anything about any more than your university can admit students they don't know about.

Your letter raised some interesting points. That we disagree with them is unimportant. What is important is for you to understand that we have sound reasons for our method of doing business.

Sincerely yours,

3.

Dear Dr. Cash:

The real answer to the ethical questions you raised in your letter is right in your family—your daughter!

She wants appliances now—and she has them. Before she could have them, we had to know whether she could pay for them. Thanks to your gift *and* our credit investigation, we were able to meet her needs.

We think it's a great system by which millions of daughters and sons can enjoy what they want and pay for it as they enjoy it. We hope you'll think so too. Next time you visit your daughter ask her opinion; it will undoubtedly change your mind.

Sincerely yours,

P.S. We don't want to argue with professors, but you've figured the interest wrong. If she maintains payments, your daughter will pay far less than $90 interest for the privilege of having the appliances to use every day.

4.

Dear Dr. Cash:

As one who has devoted his life to education, you must take real satisfaction in knowing that a lot of students who can't afford it are getting a good education today.

How? Credit in the form of loans.

How do you select them? On the basis of some kind of investigation.

Isn't this similar to your daughter and the appliances? We think it is. We don't believe there is anything ethically wrong with it. And we hope you agree.

Sincerely yours,

5.

Dear Dr. Cash:

Frankly, we were troubled by your letter because its overtones say that we are involved in unethical activities.

Actually our interest charges—which you miscalculated—are the same as anyone else's. We make the same credit investigation that everyone else makes. And since we are following the same practices that everyone else in business uses, we simply have to disagree with the viewpoint of your letter.

We're sorry you feel the way you do, and we hope you'll change your mind.

Sincerely yours,

EXERCISES

1. What changes would you make in the following letters granting credit to new customers:

a.

Mrs. Charles W. Mill
3516 Lee Avenue
Chattanooga, Tennessee 37401

Dear Mrs. Mill:

We've opened a charge account in your name, as you requested, and we've placed an upper limit of $500 on the credit we can give you.

The terms of these credit arrangements are that you must pay the bill by the 10th of the month after the purchase, or we will have to charge you interest at the rate of $1\frac{1}{2}$ percent a month on any unpaid balance.

We hope you understand these terms clearly. If you do not, please call me immediately.

Sincerely,
John Scanlon
Credit Manager

b.

You know, Mrs. Mill, we were delighted that you opened a credit account with us. For you it will mean convenient shopping and complete information *in advance* concerning our sales.

Our terms are the usual ones—payment by the 10th of the month following purchase or a finance charge of 1½ percent each month on the unpaid balance.

You'll enjoy the ease and efficiency of shopping with your credit account, we know. If you have any questions at all, please call me.

                                        John Scanlon
                                        Credit Manager

c.

Dear Mrs. Mill:

At your request, we have opened a credit account in your name—terms 1½ percent a month if you don't pay your bill by the 10th of the month following purchase.

Since the new Truth in Lending Act has as its purpose "to assure a meaningful disclosure of credit terms so that the consumer will be able to compare more readily the various credit terms available to him and avoid the uninformed use of credit," we feel compelled to say that in a credit account you pay for convenience. If you want economy, you should pay cash.

I hope this information will prove helpful to you.

                                        Sincerely yours,
                                        John Scanlon
                                        Credit Manager.

2. Write the letter which you think should be sent to Mrs. Mill by Mr. Scanlon.

3. The County Hardware Store, E. C. Denman, Proprietor, Minnehaha Corners, Minnesota 55406 has purchased a great deal of merchandise from Wholesale Hardware, Inc., for three and a half years, but for the last three months no orders have been received and their account has a trivial unpaid balance of $7.13, which resulted from their ordering four hoes two days after they sent their last check. With the main purpose of reactivating this good account, what would you write in a letter to the County Hardware Store? How would you handle the unpaid balance of $7.13? Write the letter.

4. Rewrite the following letters offering, granting, and refusing credit:

a.

Dear Mrs. Hoag:

We have noticed that you have purchased various items from us on a cash basis during the past year.

We wondered if perhaps you did not find this inconvenient and if, like many of our other customers, you would not prefer to have a charge account, which offers many advantages. That way you can simply call us up, order whatever you want, and just say, "Charge it."

If you do prefer to open a charge account with us, simply fill in the enclosed card. We want to take this opportunity to express our deep appreciation for your past patronage and to hope that we may continue to merit your approval.

> Yours truly,

b.

Gentlemen:

We are glad to grant you the credit which you recently asked for. We want you to understand clearly that your account with us will carry a top limit of $400 and that our bills sent on the last day of each month are payable by the 20th of the following month. We hope you will enjoy the privileges of your credit with us.

> Sincerely yours,

c.

Gentlemen:

In answer to your request of February 2, we must say that we cannot grant the credit which you asked for.

You probably realize that new enterprises such as yours have very heavy risks, and if things do not go well with you, we would incur a big loss. We have had so much experience with new businesses that we just do not dare take a chance, much as we would like to.

In the meantime, we hope you will see your way clear to buy from us on a cash basis because we are really interested in expanding our new accounts.

> Sincerely yours,

5. What is your reaction to this letter sent to a mailing list of people under 25 known to be interested in travel:

> Hi, there, Johns and Janes . . .
>> we've got a GREAT THING going.
>
> Ever wonder whether you'd have to be old and gray, tired and tiresome, before you got to see the world? Well . . . WONDER NO MORE!
>
> We've got a passport to travel by which you GO NOW, pay later. It's our Wonderful World of Travel Credit Card which lets you pay 20 percent when you leave and budget the rest over as long as 18 months. You pay it easily in equal installments including a finance charge of 1½ percent a month on the unpaid balance.
>
> An inexpensive way to see this WONDERFUL WORLD? Of course it is. Just sign and mail the enclosed card for your Wonderful World of Travel Credit Card . . . and start planning where you want to go.
>
>> The Universal Travel Agency

6. As credit correspondent for the Universal Travel Agency in the previous problem, you have received an application for a credit card from Mr. and Mrs. Thomas Jones, 411

Middle Road, Centerville, Kansas 66014. Your check with the credit bureau discloses that they are buying a home and appliances on installments and cannot afford to assume any new obligations. Keeping in mind the letter which the agency sent, write refusing credit to Mr. and Mrs. Jones.

7. Your company is celebrating its twenty-fifth anniversary in the sporting-goods business. It started as a partnership when the two founders opened a shop producing carved gun-stocks and special trout flies. It has since expanded as The Sporting Goods Corporation, which now supplies a complete line of sports equipment. Your credit manager has compiled a list of 156 dealers who have purchased supplies from you for more than twenty years. All of them originally paid cash for small orders, but they, too, have grown in size and now order substantial quantities for which they pay promptly. Write an appropriate letter to these dealers.

8. Write an answer to the following letter you have received from Mrs. Phillip Sidney, Apt. 201, The Soaring Towers, Wilmington, California 90744.

Dear Sir:

When I first came into the Modern Dress Shop, it seemed almost unbelievable that I could take any of your beautiful clothes home and pay for them later on my Revolving Charge Account.

After a year—and I've been a good customer—I sat down and began figuring. I'm not good at arithmetic, but isn't it true that "1½ percent a month" means 18 percent a year? It seems terrible when I think that if I don't pay for a $100 dress for a year, it costs me $118—and the dress is a year older too.

My husband thinks I ought to stop paying such charges and close out my account, but if I want it, he'll let me keep it. He laughed when I told him I was going to write to your shop, but I'm doing it anyway. Will you *please* suggest what I should do?

Sincerely,

Ann Sidney

9. Two years ago when a public-relations-minded executive took over as new president of The National Bank, he started a policy that each of the 41 officers of the bank would make a personal call once a year on individuals (not companies, firms, partnerships, or business organizations) who maintained an *average* balance of $5,000 a year in their personal checking accounts. "I don't know why they do it" the president said, "but by leaving us the use of $5,000, we can earn a lot of money—and we owe them an acknowledgment in the form of a personal visit."

This year, because of business pressures, it has been decided that the visit will be replaced by a letter, with each officer writing to the people he has visited for the past two years. Of the 21 persons you visited, 14 have still maintained average balances over $5,000, and as official policy your bank has devised a Golden Credit Card "which entitles the owner to $1,000 in cash wherever he presents it as guaranteed by the National Bank of Centreville, U.S.A." Write the letter you might send to the 14 persons whom you have visited twice and to whom you now send Golden Credit Cards.

10. As a consequence of a letter you sent to Jasper C. Conrad offering him a Golden Credit Card (see Problem 9), you have received an indignant letter from Mr. Conrad's next door neighbor, Mrs. E. C. Windrow, asking why she did not receive one. Mrs. Windrow has a top-flight credit reputation, is a very shrewd investor in local real estate, but maintains an average balance in your bank of less than $1,000. Which of these facts and what method would you use to explain why Mrs. Windrow did not receive a Golden Credit Card? Write the letter.

11. In a mix-up of names, your firm has granted a regular 30-day credit account with an upper limit of $2,000 to John C. Hansen because the credit bureau mistakenly sent you background on John C. Hensen, who has a top credit rating. Hansen, on the other hand, is notoriously slow in payment and has been through bankruptcy. Hansen has already purchased $157.61 worth of goods with his new charge account. You have also learned that Hensen has bought goods from your firm but has always paid cash for his purchases.

    Write letters that you consider appropriate in view of these facts to both John C. Hansen and John C. Hensen.

12. Mr. C. I. Lee has ordered $450 worth of men's suits from your wholesale clothing firm and has asked for credit. Mr. Lee has had no previous business experience and is opening a new clothing store with the financial backing of his father. Write, suggesting that he pay $150 down and $100 on the first of each succeeding month until the account is paid. There will be a finance charge of 1½ percent a month on the unpaid balance.

CHAPTER 10

COLLECTION LETTERS

As pointed out in the previous chapter, the relationship between the granting of credit and the collecting of debts is a close one; when credit has been expertly managed, the work of the collection department becomes much simpler. Equally important is the relationship between the collection and sales departments. The customer who has owed money for a period of time ceases to be a customer, for if he needs additional merchandise, he may turn to competitors of the firm that has carried him on its books.

Many collection men face up quite candidly to the fact that debtors aren't buyers in letters like the following:

> Dear Mr. Johnson:
>
> Last night the children were shrieking and pounding upstairs until I finally asked my wife, "How on earth do you stand all that noise?"
>
> "It's when I don't hear anything that I really get worried," she said.
>
> And that's why we're worried . . .
>
>   . . . because we haven't heard anything about that $178.42 you owe us
>
>   . . . because you probably won't order anything else from us until you've paid it.
>
> This silence means that you lose sales and profits and we lose your business. Why not make a noise with that check of yours? We'll both benefit.
>
>   Yours truly,

Dear Mr. McMaster:

We send you this not just to collect the $47.52 you owe us but also *because we want you to buy from us again.*

Sincerely yours,

Another firm sends out this letter showing the amount due in very large figures in a drawing of a magnifying glass:

Dear Mr. Locke:

Little things sometimes get magnified out of all proportion.

Maybe your outstanding balance doesn't seem a "little thing" to you—but we don't want it magnified so that it affects our relations. We appreciate all the business you have given us in the past and we want it to continue.

Won't you send us your check—in full, if you can—or a substantial payment? After all this time, you must need a number of our products . . . and we, of course, want you to have them.

Sincerely yours,

Unfortunately, the letters of many companies sound as if their collection correspondents and their sales correspondents were not speaking to one another. While the salesmen have been dealing with the customer under the theme of "how to win friends and influence people," the collection department all too often takes over with a rough, offensive tone more than likely to nullify all the sales effort. This situation—a little like the contrast between the sweetness and light of fraternity rushing and the grim reality of the pledge period—can be corrected only through the closest cooperation between sales and collection policies. To do this, correspondents must remember the twofold object in collecting a past-due account—to get the money and to retain the customer's good will and patronage. The language and the tone of the collection letter should be carefully scutinized on the principle that a collection letter which retains the customer's good will stands a better chance of collecting the amount due than one which irritates or antagonizes him. Try your own reaction to the following letter sent out by a company that spends a considerable amount for advertising and sales-promotion efforts:

Dear Mr. White:

We cannot understand your failure to reply to our previous reminders about your delinquent account amounting to $47.43.

By ignoring our letters, you leave us little choice but to decide we were wrong in extending your credit. After all, you must realize that the expense of sending repeated reminders makes this a very unsatisfactory experience for us.

You can prove we are not wrong in our judgment by sending us your check, now.

Yours truly,

The needless negative emphasis of such words as *cannot understand, your failure, delinquent, ignore, wrong, unsatisfactory* certainly cancels a lot of sales-promotion effort; and without appearing soft, the correspondent can collect and still keep good will by being persuasive and constructive. Notice the difference in point of view and general tone of the following letter dealing with the same situation:

> Dear Mr. White:
>
> We have sent you several reminders about your past-due account for $47.43, without a response from you.
>
> In fairness to yourself, we hope you'll consider how important an asset your credit standing is. Certainly, you would place a far higher value on it than the amount you owe us.
>
> To protect this asset, you can write us frankly as to when you will make payment—or better still, send us your check now. By doing so, you'll get this off your mind. Use the envelope we are enclosing for your convenience—and mail it today, please.
>
> Yours truly,

As we said in Part One, large companies can now computerize their entire collection procedures so that bills and letters are automatically handled at the proper time. In these cases it is more important than ever for notices and letters to avoid giving an impression of machine-like dullness. The dangers of impersonality and dehumanization are nicely illustrated by the following note from a customer to her bank:

> Dear Machine:
>
> You have misspelled my name again and failed to correct last month's wrong balance. If you don't make these corrections next month, I shall bend your card.
>
> Yours truly,

Regardless of whether the mechanics involve a computer, an automatic typewriter producing "personalized" letters endlessly, or simple pen and ink, the collection letter is a message from one human being to another. Its central purpose is *to persuade the debtor that it is to his own advantage to pay*. Its strongest appeal, therefore, is to the reader's self-interest and sense of fair play. It proceeds from the assumption—and actual statistics show it to be a sound one—that most people want to pay their debts, that persuasion and perseverance are the best ways of getting them to do so, and that curtness, sarcasm, or righteous indignation merely antagonize debtors. In fact, collection letters have taken on many of the characteristics of sales letters with attention-arousing devices, humorous stories, and clever wording; while this approach should not be overdone, collection correspondents have discovered that if they can use an unusual or humorous approach, the chances of payment increase.

Naturally, the technique of collection varies greatly with the individual debtor, who will probably be classified in one of the three general groups of good, fair, or poor credit risks, or *prompt pay*, *slow pay*, and *poor or uncertain pay*, as they are sometimes called. If a utopian situation prevailed, all the customers would belong to the good or fair categories where they could be easily entertained, amused, or cajoled into payment, but since the poor are always with us, the collection man must deal with this group of customers on the theory that they will pay if they are made to pay—and with this group his letters take on a sterner tone. Without completely disregarding all the different situations and debtors involved, can we determine the basic structure of collection letters? When properly considered as sales messages, collection letters usually contain the following elements:

1. The opening paragraph states the business at hand—i.e., the amount due, dates of letters or orders, and mention of specific merchandise where necessary—unless the first paragraph is an attention-arousing device.
2. The next two paragraphs present the argument for payment.
3. The closing paragraph motivates action.

THE COLLECTION SERIES

Actually, there is no such thing as *the* collection letter; like troubles, collection letters "come not singly but in battalions," known as *the collection series*. This series of letters is a practical expression of the fundamental belief behind all collection procedures—*that the customer will pay if he is reminded regularly and with increasing insistence that payment is due*. The frequency of the reminders and the degree of insistence will depend entirely upon the type of credit risk the customer is and what upper limit has been placed upon the credit extended to him. But regardless of these factors, successful collection always results from a carefully thought-out plan, which starts with gentle reminders in the form of bills or brief notices that payment is due and, if payment is not made, goes through to its most insistent point of threatening to take drastic action (legal action, garnisheeing of wages, repossessing merchandise) to collect. Perhaps because ours is an affluent society, perhaps because of credit and collection efficiency, the final stages are reached less and less frequently. As one credit executive of a big New York store commented, "We've gone out of the repossession business completely. We'd rather get some money."

How to "get some money" through a series of bills, notices, and letters is best explained by examining the assumptions which underlie them and the manner in which each assumption contributes to the increasing insistence of the series as a whole.

1. The assumption that the customer wishes to be reminded that payment is due

This reminder may be a very brief letter or simply a statement. If a letter is sent, it is very routine, as in the following:

> Dear Mr. Davis:
>
> Just a friendly reminder of our terms, which are full payment monthly. Our account will be off your mind if you send us your check for $13.48 in the enclosed envelope.
>
> > Very truly yours,

> Dear Mr. Brady:
>
> We thought you'd appreciate a reminder that your account is past due. If you have sent us your check, please accept our thanks and disregard this notice.
>
> > Sincerely yours,

2. The assumption that the customer has forgotten to pay

Sometimes called the *follow-up reminder*, this is most often a bill or statement stamped with some such notation as "Second Notice" and sent usually to good credit risks. Many stores and companies do not use these follow-up notices or letters on the theory that one reminder is enough.

> Dear Mr. Graham:
>
> We previously reminded you that your account, as shown on this statement, is past due. Since we have not yet received your payment, may we again ask that you send us your check as soon as possible?
>
> > Sincerely yours,

> Dear Mr. Jewitt:
>
> An executive whose garage delivers his car to him every day found a card on the front seat one December morning:
>
> > Merry Christmas from the boys in the garage.
>
> Despite good intentions, he delayed doing anything about it, so the next week he found another card:
>
> > Merry Christmas, Second Notice.
>
> This is our second notice about that $65.37 bill. Will you please send us your check to-day?
>
> > Very truly,

> Dear Mr. Franklin:
>
> Perhaps you overlooked it—
> Possibly you forgot—

At any rate, we haven't received the monthly payment of $. . . . . . requested in our recent statement. We want to explain that Club Plan Accounts are opened with the understanding that the installments shown on the contract are to be paid each month when due.

A stamped, addressed envelope is enclosed for your convenience in remitting.

Yours truly,

3. The assumption that something is wrong with the goods, the service, or the records of the transaction

This letter is actually an offer of adjustment, and to the inexperienced it seems out of place in a collection series. But by suggesting that perhaps the customer hasn't responded because of an error in billing or dissatisfaction with service, the letter performs two important functions in the collection series:

a. It forestalls the possible alibi later that "I didn't understand the credit terms" or "I haven't paid your bill because I didn't like the service."

b. It provides an opportunity for a response from the most difficult of all debtors, the *silent customer.* Skilled collection men work on the general principle that any response is better than none. If the debtor can be persuaded to reply, a solution to the problem may be worked out. The theory is that this offer of adjustment combined with a sales message about the kind of service you want to render may dent the silence of such a customer.

The following are good examples of this type of letter:

Dear Mr. Robertson:

This is not a dunning letter. We want the $219.17 you owe us—but we also want to keep your friendship.

You have always paid your bills with us promptly in the past. Therefore, we know there must be some special reason for nonpayment in this instance.

We try our best to render the most efficient service possible, but we are aware that errors occur occasionally. If there has been any tardiness in delivery or any mistake in our records, we want you to tell us about it.

Or, if you will write us frankly, we can perhaps work out some plan whereby you can take care of the past-due balance without imposing too heavy a burden on yourself while, at the same time, we can continue to make shipment to meet your immediate needs. The enclosed self-addressed envelope is for your convenience in replying.

Yours very truly,

Gentlemen:

DID WE OVERLOOK SOMETHING?

Is it because of some omission on our part that we have not received your check? If so, may we please have an explanation? We'll do our part toward making any necessary adjustment.

On the other hand—if we've performed our part of the sales contract, won't you now complete yours? Your check will do the trick. And, by the way, if you need any more cups, include your order.

                                                    Cordially yours,
                                                    Universal Paper Products Co.

Gentlemen:

A long time ago one Greek said to another, "So now you've invented a zero—and what do you have? Nothing!"

That's what we've had in response to our previous notices and letters.

If our service wasn't what you expected, tell us. If we've made any mistakes in your bill, let us know.

We'll gladly make any fair adjustment. But if there are no corrections to be made, please use the envelope enclosed to send us your check for $167.31.

                                                    Sincerely yours,

4.   The assumption that the ideas of all the previous letters were erroneous

This letter marks a transition in the total collection process—a transition into greater insistence that the bill be paid. Oftentimes, it sums up the record of bills and notices sent; at other times the writer assumes an air of being puzzled by the lack of response. Its general theme can be described as, "We delivered the goods or services; we've notified you of the amount; we've even offered an adjustment if something went wrong—and still you remain silent. Is that fair?"

Dear Mr. Drake:

Let's take a look at the record!

   . . . We delivered $279.10 worth of our products in February.

   . . . We mailed your first bill on March 1.

   . . . We've sent you three reminders and a letter asking you to tell us if anything was wrong with the goods, the service, or our records.

   . . . And still we have no reply from you.

Maybe you'd like to put something else on the record. Frankly, we hope that "something else" will be your check for $279.10; but at the very least, we hope you'll let us know if we can work out some satisfactory method of settling this account.

We're asking you to go on record by sending us your check or an explanation of why we have had no response to our previous letters.

                                                    Sincerely yours,

At this stage of the collection procedure, one company shatters all the principles of summing up and seeming to be puzzled by sending out what is probably the most concise collection letter ever written:

Gentlemen:

When?

Sincerely yours,

The next two letters are more conventional in their approach:

Dear Mr. Whitcomb:

In our letters of June 17, July 2, and July 16, we tried unsuccessfully to obtain payment of your past-due account of $84.02 or to gain some explanation from you.

We are sorry that you have made no reply because we want to help our customers whenever possible. We filled your order promptly and in a manner that must have been satisfactory to you since you have made no reply to our offer of an adjustment.

As you know, our credit terms call for payment within 30 days. You have not complied with these terms nor given us the facts by which we might arrive at a solution.

Won't you use the enclosed envelope to send us your check or an explanation of why your payment is so long overdue?

Very truly yours,

Dear Mr. Smith:

Frankly, we're puzzled. . . . Did we judge you wrong?

After three notices and a letter reminding you of your unpaid balance of $142.77, we have heard nothing from you—and meantime the interest on this amount grows.

Why not be fair to yourself and to us and send us a total of $149.31 to end further interest charges and to start us off on a clean slate for the future? The enclosed envelope will deliver your check to us promptly.

Sincerely yours,

5.   The assumption that the customer is not taking his proper responsibility

This letter places the burden of responsibility squarely on the shoulders of the debtor. There is no longer any talk of reminders, adjustment, or similar reasons for the delinquency. This letter points out that the customer is not fulfilling his responsibility. It appeals to his sense of pride, or his honor, or best of all, his self-interest. No time is wasted on sales talk about merchandise or service at this stage; the sales message of this letter concerns the value of a sound credit reputation. It points out that credit is the very lifeblood of business; that no businessman can long survive without a sound credit reputation; that by paying this bill he preserves his most valuable asset—thus, it is *to his own interest* to see that the delinquent account is settled. Otherwise, there will be unpleasant action. Notice the strong emphasis on a sound credit reputation in the following letters and the one displayed on page 226:

MARSHALL AND SMITH, INC.

4317 SOUTH DEARBORN STREET
CHICAGO ILLINOIS 60609

January 7, 1970

Mr. George N. Miller
437 Green Avenue
Elkhart, Indiana 46514

Dear Mr. Miller:

Up along the west coast of Canada lies one of the greatest
aids to ships and commerce—the world-famous Inside Passage.
Its reef of rocks several miles out from the mainland acts as
a barrier against the wild north Pacific and the Bering Sea.

Outside that reef, the storms lash the ocean into a fury,
while ships move safely and easily in the Inside Passage.
Without that channel, commerce between America and Alaska
would be seriously curtailed.

A sound credit rating is like that Inside Passage, Mr. Miller,
and because of it, your "ship" of business can move smoothly
and easily. The barrier which protects that rating is the
promptness with which you meet your obligations.

You can form a protective reef for yourself by sending in your
check for $91.79   Why not take care of it today?

                        Sincerely yours,

                        MARSHALL AND SMITH, INC.

                        Louis M. Ross

                        Collection Department

ROT:LMF

Dear Mr. Meyer:

From school days on, we learn the importance of "good marks."

In business, for example, we all know the value of silver marked "sterling," of jewelry by Tiffany, of cars by Cadillac.

Your "mark" is your credit standing. To keep it high requires constant vigilance. We're sure that you don't want your past-due account for $113.43 marked "Delinquent."

For your own sake, don't neglect this account another day. We expect your check by return mail.

Yours very truly,

Dear Mr. Martin:

As a businessman you certainly realize the value of a good credit reputation. You know that it is probably your most valuable asset.

Yet you are jeopardizing your credit rating for $89.26, the balance of your account with us. Surely you are being unfair to yourself to place so low an estimate on your most valuable asset.

Prompt attention to your obligations is the one way to maintain your credit reputation. Otherwise, we shall have to report your account as delinquent to the local credit bureau. Your check will make it unnecessary for us to make such a report.

Sincerely yours,

6. The assumption that the customer will pay only if he is made to pay

In this final stage, letters often become adjuncts to other methods in modern collection practice. To impress debtors with the urgency of the situation, phone calls, telegrams, and personal interviews are being used increasingly. When letters complement these methods, they are frequently sent by registered mail or over the signature of a top executive. The motivating force here is that unless payment is received, or other terms worked out by a specific date—usually within five or ten days—action will follow in one of various forms: reporting to the credit bureau, turning the account over to lawyers or professional collecting agencies, garnisheeing a percentage of salaries or wages (in states where that can be done), or repossessing merchandise. Where letters are used, their tone reflects a genuine reluctance to resort to this action and their content suggests that the debtor has a far more pleasant solution, but no doubt is left that the creditor intends to go through with the action necessary. Here are examples whose effectiveness readers can test by imagining that they themselves have received such messages:

Dear Mr. Jones:

Our records show that we have received no payments on your $233.11 pastdue account for merchandise we shipped to you on August 7.

Since we have not had any reply to our previous correspondence, there seems to be no alternative for us except to place this matter in the hands of our attorneys.

For you, there is still one alternative—send us your payment in full within five days. Otherwise we shall be forced to take an action which, frankly, we dislike.

Yours truly,

Dear Mr. Bender:

Frankly, we are reluctant to report your delinquent account to our credit bureau and out collection agency. After all, without the ability to obtain credit, you simply cannot operate a business in today's world.

We are, therefore, giving you a final chance to avoid such actions.

But you must do your part. Your check for $150 and assurance that you will pay the remaining balance within two months are what we consider your part. Within the next five days, it's your move.

Sincerely yours,

The following are samples of telegrams used in the final stage of collection:

WE HAVE BEEN VERY PATIENT. PLEASE REMIT. URGENT.

VERY IMPORTANT YOUR CHECK REACH US BY MARCH 15. SEND TODAY.

UNWILLING TO WAIT LONGER. YOUR ACCOUNT MUST BE PAID WITHIN FIVE DAYS.

WILL TAKE ACTION UNLESS CHECK OR MONEY ORDER IS MAILED TODAY.

YOUR LAST CHANCE TO MAKE GOOD. WIRE REMITTANCE TODAY.

WILL TAKE IMMEDIATE ACTION UNLESS REMITTANCE IS RECEIVED AT ONCE.

In summary, the collection series should be viewed as a logical *but flexible* method to be adapted to different debtors (the good, fair, or poor risk), to changing economic conditions (at the moment this is being written, interest rates are at the highest point in history, described as "the money crunch"), and to different company policies. Furthermore, if debtors respond by telling of expenses caused by illness or other contingencies, reputable companies are willing to temper the wind to the shorn lamb. What all this adds up to is that a *system* of collection should never make us forget that debtors are individuals, and, regardless of how we group them, they remain individual human beings.

The following suggested procedure for timing a collection series should therefore be considered as tentative and subject to change. It is based on the procedure of a retail firm which considers it as a guide, rather than a fixed time table. Assuming that a purchase has been made in December, the normal collection procedure for three classes of debtors would follow these schedules:

Poor risk

January 1	A statement
January 15	An offer to make any necessary adjustment

February 1	A letter explaining that the collection department is puzzled by the debtor's silence and appealing to his sense of fairness
February 15	An expression of the collector's feeling that the debtor is not assuming proper responsibility, and a sales talk on sound credit
March 1	A demand that payment be made by March 10 or the account will be turned over to an attorney for action

Fair risk

January 1	A statement
February 1	A statement
March 1	A note assuming that the customer wishes to be reminded that payment is due
March 15	A brief letter assuming that failure to pay is the result of an oversight
April 1	An offer of any necessary adjustment
April 15	All previous assumptions were wrong; the collection man is puzzled. Appeal to the customer's sense of fairness
May 1	An urgent expression of the collector's feeling that the customer is not taking the proper responsibility, together with a sales talk on sound credit
May 15	A demand that payment be made by May 25 or the account will be turned over to an attorney for action

Good risk

January 1	A statement
February 1	A statement
March 1	A statement
April 1	A note assuming that the customer wishes to be reminded that payment is due
April 15	A brief letter assuming that failure to pay is the result of an oversight
May 1	An offer of any necessary adjustment
May 15	All previous assumptions were wrong; the collection man is puzzled. Appeal to the customer's sense of fairness
June 1	An urgent expression of the collector's feeling that the customer is not taking the proper responsibility, together with a sales talk on sound credit
June 15	A demand that payment be made by July 1 or the account will be turned over to an attorney for action

ORIGINALITY AND HUMOR IN COLLECTION LETTERS

It was mentioned earlier that many types of letters that were formerly handled in routine fashion have now become clever or humorous messages strong on getting attention. Such letters have been used to good effect in collecting small accounts, usually in the early stages of the collection series. An almost endless variety of devices, gadgets, and novelties are used by collection correspondents to point up the basic message, *please pay*. Typical are letters in small type (we're whispering about your bill), letters with strings attached (as a reminder to pay), or messages with bars of music across the top (we have the blues about your account). Such stunts and the use of gadgets can be carried too far, but their basic purpose of attracting the reader's attention is important. The following letters demonstrate how originality, cleverness, and humor can be used to get results:

Dear Mr. Rose:

A friend of ours vactioning in Miami sent a postcard to his psychiatrist:

Dear Doc,

Having a wonderful time. *Why?*

Why not send us $13.50 in the enclosed envelope so we can try having a wonderful time?

Sincerely,

Dear Mr. Miller:

The public utility in our area had to notify a bride: "Please pay the amount. You have been paying the date."

May we make it clear that *your* amount is $17.40, and just date the check today, please.

Very truly,

Dear Mr. Fernwood:

Someone defined a pessimist as "an optimist—after taxes."

Want to help with our definition—"an optimist is a pessimist after all his bills have been collected"? It takes a mere $9.50 and we'll both feel better.

Yours truly,

dear mr. meyer:

we don't want to make a big fuss and we know you don't want us to—so could you please send us that check for $21.49 today? thanks

sincerely yours,

Gentlemen:

After winning an important case a lawyer wired his client:

JUSTICE HAS TRIUMPHED!

Back came the answer

APPEAL AT ONCE!

May we appeal for justice? Just $24.13 *today*.

Sincerely,

Say, Mr. Cornwall,

Are you still carrying that check for $10.50 around in your pocket?

Yours truly,

Dear Mr. Richards:

We assigned your account to a new clerk and she wrote this opening sentence:

You have been one of our best customers for many years and I think this is due to an oversight.

On second thought, maybe she's right. You *have* been a good customer. Now will you correct that oversight by putting your check for $39.56 in the enclosed envelope? Thank you.

Sincerely yours,

The letters which follow have, in a sense, become classics. They are probably too well known to be used with any freshness, but they are included because they illustrate what originality and humor can accomplish and because users of this book in previous editions have requested that they be included:

Dear Mr. Engel:

An effective collection letter should be:

1. Short

2. Courteous

3. Successful

This letter is short; we hope you think it's courteous. The rest is up to you.

Sincerely,

Dear Mr. Dowling:

Said Mark Twain: "Always do right. This will gratify some people—and astonish the rest."

We won't be astonished, but we'll certainly be gratified if you'll do right by your account for $87.12.

Yours truly,

Dear Mr. Eaton:

We've done our best to follow an old Chinese saying

"Man who wants pretty nurse must be patient."

Now . . . we've been pretty patient nursing your account along . . . and we'd like to see our patience rewarded.

Sincerely yours,

The City Club of Cleveland used this to dust off delinquencies:

Dear Member:

> Man is made of dust.
>
> Dust settles.
>
> Be a man!
>
> Your Treasurer

Dear Mr. Millet:

A shy secretary didn't want to tell her boss the reason for her resignation, so she asked her husband to explain. He sent the following note:

"My wife's reason for leaving will soon be apparent—and so will I."

It's just as apparent to us that there must be an explanation as to why we haven't heard from you. Won't you write and explain—or better still, send us your check for $23.49?

> Sincerely,

Dear Mr. Richardson:

> How do you do?
>
> Some pay when due.
>
> Some pay when overdue.
>
> A few never do.
>
> How do you do?
>
> Your balance is $ . . . . . .
>
> Very truly yours,

Gentlemen:

I have a hobby—it is looking up word sources. One day I checked on the word "dun."

It comes orginally from the Old English word *dunnen*, which means making a loud noise. Now some folks would call this a dunnen letter—but I assure you there's nothing explosive about it.

It's just a request for the $21.67 which is past due on your account. All we ask is a fair effort on your part to meet this indebtedness, or a word of explanation.

> Yours truly,

Such letters as well as the one on page 233 reflect creativity and original-ity, but the real test is whether they get results. The writer of collection letters cannot lose sight of the fact that his purpose is not entertainment but collecting bills; there is no substitute for the basic principle we have discussed in the col-lection series—*the best way to collect money is to keep constantly pressing delinquent accounts with a gradually increasing insistence culminating in ac-tion.* Perhaps this insistence may result in a reply such as the following re-ceived by a Georgia firm in answer to a long series of collection letters:

SMITH AND SON

4719 JEFFERSON AVENUE
CENTERVILLE, VIRGINIA 22020

April 5, 1971

Mr. Walter E. Baker
5 Park Street
Conway, Maryland 20627

Dear Mr. Baker:

We've just heard about a Vassar girl who had had several dates
with a Yale senior and then heard nothing from him for four
weeks.

"DEAD, DELAYED, OR DISINTERESTED?" she wired.

"HUNTING, FISHING, OR TRAPPING?" was his reply.

We hope that nothing like this has happened to you, but we
do want you to know that we've been hunting and fishing for
your past-due check for $37.19. And while we aren't setting
any traps, we are making a date for April 22 when we'll
expect your check or an explanation.

Sincerely yours,

Charles Smith Jr.

Charles Smith, Jr.

CS,Jr:AC

Dear Sir:

Here is your money and you won't be one bit gladder to git it than I am to send it. Please don't send me no receipt for I don't want to hear from you no more.

Yours truly,

But at least the debt *was* collected.

EXERCISES

1. Mrs. C. Worthy Bridge, 211 Canal Street, Oceanville, Connecticut 06372 has purchased carpeting for the first floor of her home from The Home Furnishing Store, Broadway and 21st Street, Hartford, Connecticut 06374. Information from the credit bureau justified opening a long-term installment account in which finance charges and payments would be spread equally over 6 months at $197.41 a month. The first three payments have arrived promptly, but two weeks after the fourth payment was due, you have heard nothing. Write an appropriate letter to Mrs. Bridge from The Home Furnishing Store.

2. Rewrite the following collection letters:

    a.

    Dear Mr. DeHavens:

    Your account is now three months past due and we have sent you numerous reminders and letters to call your attention to the $56.19 you owe us.

    Will you bring this up to date immediately or we shall be forced to take steps to protect our interest.

    Thank you.

    Sincerely yours,

    b.

    Dear Mr. Albright:

    When we permitted you to have the privilege of a 90-day account with us it was with the definite understanding that you were to pay all bills in three equal installments over a three-month period.

    Now we find that you have paid only the first month's portion on that new refrigerator and that the interest at $1\frac{1}{2}$ percent per month is piling up on your balance, which is now $320.64 but will be larger a month from now.

    To help you with dividing, you owe us $160.32 this month and again next month *if* you send us a check right now. If you don't, we will reluctantly keep adding interest charges. Why not pay now?

    Very truly yours,

    c.

    You knew, Mr. Pendleton, that you would have to pay promptly in order to justify our giving you a 30-day charge account.

These accounts are the bread-and-butter of all business since that's the way we get capital to operate on. We give them only to customers who pay their bills within 15 days after we render them. And we thought you were in that category.

Now we're uncertain. But your check for $119.71 will improve our opinion of you. Why not send it today, Mr. Pendleton?

The Middleburg Service Shop

d.

Dear Miss Smathers:

We know you have the wherewithal to pay that overdue bill of $76.41 for LP records and tape cassettes. And we know that you know you owe us because we've sent you two reminders.

So why not get with it and send us your check today? Or better still, bring the money in and we'll let you buy some more music.

Very truly yours,

e.

Gentlemen:

Of all the people who take out billions in credit each year, 95 out of 100 pay promptly, 4 pay slowly, and 1 doesn't pay at all.

Since we've been reminding and billing you for that $219.43 for a long time with no results, we are thinking of demoting you from the 4 percent slow payers to the 1 percent nonpayers.

Shall we do it—or would you rather send us a check now?

Sincerely,

3. Clinton & Associates is a newly formed management consulting firm whose services next year will include advice to clients about communication in business. To prepare for this service, E. C. Clinton has ordered 8 subscriptions to your Personalized Letter and Report Service which sends bulletins monthly along with examples of good and poor letters and reports, and also returns corrected and improved versions of the clients' own letters. Your normal charge for this service is $150 annually per client, but because of the 8 subscriptions taken out by Clinton & Associates, your total charge for a year is $1,000, payable in equal quarterly installments. The first two installments were paid promptly but it is now one month after the third installment is due. Write, first, a letter assuming that something is perhaps wrong with your service; second, a letter expressing the view that Clinton & Associates is not taking proper responsibility; and third, a letter assuming that they will pay only if made to pay.

4. Using your background and knowledge of your own school, college, or university, write a letter which you think would collect money in each of the following circumstances:

   a. Alpha Roger Omega, a social organization, has held a weekend retreat at the annex of Ye Olde Inn in rural Middlefield under a contract promising to "pay for any and all damage beyond normal wear and tear." As manager of Ye Olde Inn, you find that damage and items missing amount to a total of $295. Write the letter to the president of Alpha Roger Omega, who signed the contract.

b. As class chairman for the fund drive for the new Alumni Memorial Building, it is necessary for you to write to 30 of your classmates who have not paid their pledges made during the campaign. Write an appropriate letter, using the fact that the fund drive ends in one month as the occasion for writing. If these 30 make their contributions, your class will have 100 percent of its membership contributing and, in all probability, will top the record for all classes.

c. Because of a metal shortage, your firm, Intercollegiate Jewelers, specializing in "personalized jewelry for college women," has been unable to deliver various rings, sorority emblems, pins, and earrings before the end of the school year. The women who ordered paid 40 percent down at the time of the order, but it was your intention and their understanding that the balance would be paid when you made personal delivery to them. Write a suitable collection letter, with a blank for filling in the amounts due; these range from $12 to $120 and are to be paid before you will mail the jewelry.

d. Write an appropriate collection letter to an alumnus who borrowed $600 from the school's loan fund while he was in school. Up until the time of his graduation, there was no interest charge on this amount. After graduation, the interest is computed at 6 percent a year; in this instance, the total amount now due is $630.

e. Tau Roger Tau fraternity ordered $5,617 worth of house furnishings from your store and were given credit because their Alumni Corporation, comprising several prominent businessmen, guaranteed the payment of the bill, the terms being $650 a month for 10 months starting in September and running through June. A campus riot in February led by several Tau Roger Tau members so alienated their Alumni Corporation that three members told you they "no longer wanted any part of the organization." In March, no $650 payment was sent.

Write the letter you would send on March 15 to the president of Tau Roger Tau.

Write the letter you would send on April 15, when no payments have been received, to Mr. E. Whitfield McCoy, chairman of the Alumni Corporation of Tau Roger Tau and alumnus of your institution, class of 1928.

5. Write a collection letter using one of the following as the opening paragraph:

a. The Chinese certainly deserve credit! Every year, just before New Year's Day, they pay a visit to all their creditors to square up their bills so as to start the new year with a clean slate.

b. We heard of the president of a tiny railroad who sent a pass to the president of one of our largest railroads with the request that the favor be returned. When his request was refused, he wrote, "My railroad may not be as long as yours, but it's just as broad." Our credit arrangements with you are as broad as they are long.

c. A credit manager's job is no bed of roses. From the time he accepts an order until the time payment is due, he keeps wondering what percentage of his accounts will be paid on time.

d. "Give him credit for what he's done"—those are the words in which we pay tribute to past performance. And when we gave *you* credit, we were doing exactly that.

    e. What would *you* think if we had been four months late in delivering those suits you needed so badly in April?

6. Under what circumstances, if at all, and for what kinds of business and customer would you use the following collection letter:

> Ah, there Mr. Jones:
>
> > Your wallet bulges
> > Fat and hard
> > With various kinds
> > of credit card.
>
> And when we sent it to you, we thought:
>
> > But ours is new,
> > And when the bill
> > To him comes due,
> > Pay it he will, he will. He will?
>
> Why don't you? It's only $14.95.

7. Ben Lonstein, owner of the Reliable Pharmacy, Center Square, Patauquet, Rhode Island 02871, has been a consistent purchaser from your Wholesale Drugs Inc. for three years, but he also belongs among the 4 percent who are slow to pay. Nonetheless, his business is profitable to you, with terms of 1 percent on all unpaid bills each month. At present, he has owed you $971.17 for three months, with no response to your bills and reminders, and with interest mounting each month. Nor has he ordered anything in the past three months. Write, as the correspondent for Wholesale Drugs Inc., the three collection letters you would send to Mr. Lonstein in the next month with the purpose of (1) collecting the bill and (2) keeping him as a customer.

8. Your store has a policy of "working some kind of an arrangement out" when customers respond to bills and reminders. As collection correspondent, you have received the following letter:

> Dear Sirs:
>
> I got your bills and I know we owe you $317.81.
>
> We've had sickness in the family and have had to move from the house on Canal Street to Johnson's Trailer Park, where the rent is lower. I know our bill with you gets larger every month because of the finance charge, and we're going to pay it just as soon as we can.
>
> Next month, when my husband will be able to go back to work, I'll try to send you $50. Will that be all right?
>
> > Yours truly,
> > Alice Gardner

Write an answer to Mrs. Gardner "working out an arrangement" which you consider fair, but which will over a period of time collect the debt. The finance charge is 1½% a month.

9.   Do you consider the following collection letters to be effective? Why? If not, why not?

a.

Dear Mr. Barton:

I know that it has long been the custom for collection men to pretend that bills aren't paid because they have been "overlooked" or that the customer needs to be "reminded."

In this instance, I'm going to come right out and say that I think the reason you ignored our last letter and the previous statements is that you didn't have the money at that time. Am I wrong in this assumption?

If the situation were reversed and we owed you money, I know that you would certainly expect at least a reply from us. I am, therefore, appealing to your sense of fair play in asking you to send us a check for $69.76 to settle your account. Were the situation reversed, you would expect the same consideration from us.

We are awaiting your remittance in the envelope enclosed for your convenience.

                                                  Very truly yours,

b.

Gentlemen:

We should appreciate very much your sending us your check for $61.25 to cover your past-due account.

We confess that we have done everything possible to collect this amount during the past three and a half months and that we are puzzled as to just what we should do next. Perhaps we should turn your account over to our attorney for collection, but we dislike taking such drastic action.

Won't you help us solve this dilemma by sending in your remittance as soon as possible?

                                                  Sincerely yours,

c.

All we ask from you, Mr. Stevens, is fair play.

We delivered the merchandise you ordered, we sent you bills, reminders—even the reasons why credit is absolutely vital to your business.

No answer. Is that fair? We think not, but you can change our thinking by sending us $131.87 today.

                                       The Homewood Wholesale Store

10.   As the result of some technical quirk, your computerized collection system has sent a bill for $10,237.50 to John J. Blue, proprietor of Blue's Music Shop, Coeur D'Aline, Idaho 83814. Actually, Mr. Blue has owed $237.50 for four months. He has sent back the wrong bill with a handwritten comment "I knew inflation was here, but I didn't think it was quite this bad." But with his comment came no payment. Write an appropriate collection letter to Mr. Blue.

CHAPTER 11

SALES LETTERS

Why use letters as a medium when selling goods or services? The debate about the merits of direct mail selling compared with magazine, newspaper, radio, or TV advertising has been going on for years. Advocates of each medium present "conclusive" evidence that theirs is the most productive or inexpensive or widest in coverage or hardest-hitting of all media.

One fact is certain—the volume of sales letters has increased tremendously over the past five years, and this increase is likely to continue during the seventies. By somewhat circular reasoning, one can conclude that if the sales letter is used increasingly, it must be effective. Anyone within reach of the post office can name several very profitable concerns whose business has been built up by direct mail exclusively. Of course, ample evidence is also available to show the efficacy of magazines, newspapers, radio, and television in building sales. But since a discussion of the relative advantages of various advertising media does not fall within the scope of this book, we should concern ourselves with two interrelated questions relative to the sales letter:

1. Why is it used so widely?
2. When is it most effective?

In a sense the answer to both questions is the fact that *the sales letter is the most selective of all advertising media*. It can reach almost any age group, financial class, professional group, geographical area, or occupation that may be potentially interested in a given product or service.

The reason for this selectivity is the mailing list, which sorts people into endless — and sometimes amazing — categories. (The compiling and renting or selling of mailing lists is a big business in itself; one firm employs almost 10,000 people and is said to have lists of more than 150 million names.)

To the uninitiated, a glance through a catalogue of mailing lists is an eye-opening experience in terms of the way it divides humans into "all sorts and conditions of men." You are offered a range of choice from 28,000 owners of parakeets to 16 manufacturers of celery salt; from thousands of people who practice self-hypnosis to more thousands who buy baby chickens. You can select lists of those who want to quit smoking or those who like to make home brew, wines, and liqueurs. Literally, the lists proceed from birth to death: you can have monthly lists of babies born in all the states of the Union or of any more precise geographical subdivision, such as a county; as for death, you have your choice under "Cemeteries" of such lists as "Names of superintendents of," "Largest," "National," Divided by states," and even "Cemeteries for pets."

The rifle-shot selectivity of such lists as these makes the sales letter the least expensive form of sales *per potential customer*, because if the list is up to date, little or no money is wasted on uninterested readers. A second advantage claimed for the sales letter is that its reader has no other items competing for his attention when he reads it — as does the magazine reader, for example, who probably has pictures or a story before him along with the advertising. This second advantage may indeed be theoretical, since we do not know enough about how readers peruse their mail — in front of a TV set, for instance, or when they first get home and are hurrying to do something else, or at leisure giving it their full attention. Finally, sales letters will carry a heavier percentage of advertising than other media; they can concentrate on material bearing directly on the product or service being sold without wasting time or space on irrelevant entertainment or attention-arousing pictures.

These advantages may be somewhat offset by what appears to be growing resistance to "junk mail" — a term which raises hackles among direct-mail practitioners. Whether this resistance is real or confined to a highly vocal minority is debatable: the Direct Mail Advertising Association sponsored a study in the mid-sixties showing that eight out of ten people surveyed have no general dislike for direct mail. On the other hand, numerous newspaper and magazine articles cite rising resentment. Finally, to conclude with a controversial aspect of sales letters, a number of citizens regard the selling of names — as compiled for instance from registration of automobiles — as an invasion of privacy. (As we suggested earlier in connection with compiling of credit information, such ethical questions offer an excellent subject for candid class discussions.)

The sensible viewpoint is to agree that when sales letters are cheap, mass-mailed, corny appeals to join this or that "exclusive" club or to take advantage of some "once-in-a-lifetime" offer, they truly deserve to be called "junk mail." (It is fair to say that our era also has "junk" magazines, books, movies, products, and newspapers.) But one should not abandon perspective. A great many sales letters are honest and sincere; others are original and humorous; and many render a useful service. These are the types we will discuss from this point forward.

The advantages of the sales letter—selectivity, concentrated attention, and high percentage of sales message—must be considered in terms of specific products, services, or merchandise. In answer to our question of *when* it is most effective, we find that it is best adapted to selling products or services of specialized appeal, of fairly expensive items, or those belonging within the class of "novelties." By contrast, it is abundantly clear that manufacturers of toothpastes, groceries, tires, spark plugs, cameras and films, drugs, and tobaccos select other media (namely, those reaching the greatest numbers) because these products are used by almost everybody. With its selectivity, the sales letter should be used where potential buyers can be picked out from many uninterested ones. Its success, in the last analysis, will depend on three factors:

1. The product or service which is being sold
2. The prospect or list of prospects to which the material is sent
3. The sales letter itself

When the product or service is attractive, the list of prospects is carefully selected, and the sales letter is effectively written, direct-mail selling is a highly profitable medium. Progressive businessmen, recognizing its flexibility and selectivity, use the sales letter for the following purposes:

1. To make direct sales
2. To obtain inquiries about services and products and to locate leads for salesmen
3. To announce and test the reaction to new services and products
4. To reach out-of-the-way prospects and to build up weak territories
5. To reinforce dealers' sales efforts and to secure new dealers
6. To build good will

Such enumerations oversimplify the very complicated phenomena which more properly belong in the sphere of behavioral scientists or motivational analysts.

Nevertheless, to writers of sales letters one question is of salient importance: *Why do people buy what they buy?* Thus stated, the question seems deceptively simple; yet its answer is very complex, only dimly understood, and fraught with too many imponderables to be answered satisfactorily by the sales correspondent's criteria that sales by mail require "A fine product, a good mailing list, and an effective sales letter." Certainly, we know that this pragmatic explanation has worked; in fact, we shall proceed on the basis of it during the remainder of this chapter. But before we do, students who may themselves be doing creative sales work during the seventies can profit by examining *their* reasons for buying whatever it is they buy.

Is it because you really need things? Or because you want to keep up with—or ahead of—the Joneses in the student body? Because of vanity, prestige, self-respect? Or pride of ownership? Or a desire to be like others? Or different from them? An honest self-appraisal of such motives will help you to understand why other people buy what they do because, presumably, many others are motivated by the same desires that you have. (A more complete list of reasons why people spend money is given on page 248. A frank class discussion of this topic can be very helpful in revealing a cross-section of the motives for buying.)

As well as illustrating what we have called the "imponderables" associated with these and other motivations, the following factual cases reveal some of the problems and the unexpected relationships inherent in the process of selecting the "right" mailing list:

A men's magazine, traditionally aimed at hunters, fishermen, and outdoor devotees, decided that its potential circulation was limited by its "hairy-chested" image. It decided, therefore, to tone down this aggressively masculine reputation in order to acquire new mail advertising campaign.

The problem was how to pick out lists which would offer maximum potential subscribers for the "new look" in the *Outdoor Magazine* (not its real name).

As might be expected, a list of names rented from a manufacturer of sleeping bags zeroed in with excellent results. But unexpectedly, so did two other lists— of ham radio operators and of door-to-door salesmen.

A list of 200,000 people who sent in for a leather wallet which sported a thick sheaf of plastic windows for credit cards proved to be excellent prospects for books on travel and on business. They also turned out to be just as excellent prospects for corrugated boxes!

Lists made up of people who sent in for a reducing pamphlet proved to include excellent prospects for inspirational magazines; several thousand people who sent in for special pillows and various sleep aids showed an abnormal interest in buying fruit cakes; and people who sent in for a widely advertised, chemically treated cleaning cloth for cars were excellent prospects for mutual funds and theater tickets.

By citing such examples, we are not trying to make sales motivation "a mystery wrapped in an enigma." But students can learn much by thinking about—and discussing—such questions as these:

What is the possible connection between ham radio operators or door-to-door salesmen and outdoor activities like hunting and fishing? Between leather-wallet purchasers and corrugated-box buyers? Or between subscribers to inspirational magazines and buying fruit cakes and aids to sleep? Or between users of car cleaning cloths and prospects for the theater or for mutual funds?

Is it possible that no logical relationship exists between such apparently disparate interests?

Is it perhaps just as well that we don't know the precise answer to these questions? Is it better for us not to know exactly the way to "manipulate" people by understanding why they buy what they buy?

To these and other questions associated with buying motives, no one 'right answer' exists. In order not to compound the confusion further, we had best rely on the pragmatic answer which sums up what we *do* know: a fine product, a good mailing list, and an effective sales letter do produce sales. In the rest of the chapter we will proceed on this assumption.

THE STRUCTURE OF THE SALES LETTER

So basic is the structure of the sales letter that it can be used for almost any letter in which an attempt is made to obtain agreement or favorable action from the reader. To make anyone act or think as we want him to, we must first gain his attention, next create a desire for the product we sell, then convince him of the truth of what we are saying, and finally make it easy for him to act. The structure of the sales letter is designed to arouse these reactions in the reader. Its parts are arranged to:

1. Attract the reader's attention
2. Create a desire for the product or service
3. Convince the reader that the product or service is the best of its kind
4. Motivate action

Frequently, the individual sales letter devotes a paragraph to each of these functions, which for brevity we shall call *attention, desire, conviction,* and *action;* in a series of sales letters, one or more of the letters may be devoted to each of them. But whether a single letter or a long series is used, the basic structure remains the same.

One of the best methods by which the novice can learn the fundamentals of sales-letter structure is through an analysis of printed advertising to see in detail how advertising experts accomplish these four tasks. A careful reading of the advertisements in any magazine will show that the underlying structure is always the same although the details may vary considerably:

Attention   by pictures, catch phrases in large type, questions, commands, or humorous illustrations

Desire   by descriptions of pleasure, profit, utility, or economy of the product or service

Conviction   by statistics, testimonials, samples, tests, or guarantees

Action   by easy-to-follow suggestions such as "Fill in the coupon" or "Send for this pamphlet" or "Go to your neighborhood grocer today"

These four elements in the structure of a sales letter must be adapted to a viewpoint which answers one central question:

Why should my reader(s) do what I am asking him (them) to do? The following pages of the text suggest various methods which may be used to answer this question in the four-part structure of the sales letter.

1.   Attracting attention in the sales letter

As we have indicated, the vast number of sales letters mailed annually has developed a rather heavy armor of sales resistance among readers. To exaggerate this would be pointless; nonetheless, there is little doubt that many readers glance at the first paragraph of the letter and either read the rest of it or toss it aside *depending on what the first paragraph says.* If it attracts the reader's attention, the rest of the letter can capitalize on that fact; but if it does not, the whole sales letter fails. What devices can be used to attract the reader's attention?

One method employed successfully in numerous sales letters is a *pertinent question*, which has the virtue of being direct and of arousing the reader's curiosity to read further in order to discover the answer. Here's an example which at first glance seems a shocker and a *faux pas:*

Why don't you try minding your own business?

Actually this opening comes from a successful sales letter in which the reader is completely won away from his first resentment or surprise when he learns that it is a sales letter to interest readers in a franchise operation in which they would own and operate their own business. After what seems a blunt and brash opening, the reader is disarmed by reading the rest of the message, which he unquestionably will do.

The following questions are intended to develop a similar desire to read on:

Could you ask your boss for a raise today and get it?

Were you born in July?

Did you sleep well the last time you were in New York?

Are you satisfied with the amount of money you save?

You know about "twiggers," don't you?

How many times have you wished that you could find time to read the best sellers that all your friends are discussing?

How about a different vacation this year? Could you enjoy two weeks of riding through sun-dappled forests, splashing through cool gurgling streams, or just sitting among blue mountains?

A *courteous command* is another technique used frequently to open sales correspondence.

Don't waste your time and energy in a sweltering office when you can enjoy the cool comfort of air conditioning!

To invite Romance, be yourself! So say Hollywood beauty experts.

For your family's sake, don't drive on tires that are worn smooth!

Don't read this if you have all your labor troubles solved!

A *"split" beginning* arranged in such a way as to attract maximum attention is widely used. The chief drawback to such an opening is that it gives the reader a feeling of being tricked or let down as in the famous sales letter that begins "Would you like to save a million dollars? Then you'd better open a mint. But we can save you $3.27!" The following illustrates the split beginning:

ARREST—
declining income! Our financial service is designed to do just that.

Millions of people enjoy gum—
but not in their carburetors.
(Letter with stick of gum attached to sell a carburetor cleaner.)

We can't make all the roofing in the world—
so we just make the best of it!

They canceled their order . . .
and we liked it
(The letter goes on to explain that the original order was canceled and replaced by an order for twice as much.)

Don't spend a nickel on fluorescent lighting—
unless you can answer "Yes" to these four questions.

A *statement of a significant fact* or a *quotation from an eminent authority or prominent individual* will arouse interest if the fact is significant or the authority is known to the reader:

You can judge a company by the customers it keeps. Forty-nine percent of our customers have "kept company" with us for more than fifteen years.

One out of three has it! . . . Did you know that one out of every three electric water coolers sold is a G.E.?

Napoleon's $2,500 began a million-dollar business. . . . In 1795, hard pressed to feed his armies far from home, Napoleon offered 12,000 francs (about $2,500) to anyone who could invent a process for preserving foods. Years later, this sum was awarded to Nicolas Appert, who developed a method of sterilizing foods and sealing them hermetically. (Sales message for Dextrose as a preservative in the canning industry.)

Surveys show that the average executive increased his work capacity an hour a day by dictating his data, correspondence, and details to an Edison Voicewriter.

Anecdotes are frequently used to attract attention, and they do get read. Their purpose is not to entertain the reader, however, but to promote sales; therefore, the story should have some connection with the sales message and should not be told just for the story's own sake. Your reader may be an ardent golfer, and an anecdote about golf will doubtless get his attention; but if the rest of the letter sells electric fans or nuts and bolts, which don't interest him, you'd better avoid the opening. Here are two which are relevant to the message which follows them:

Mark Twain once remarked that the most dangerous place to be is in bed, because more people die there than anywhere else. (This is followed by a sales message for home accident policies showing that Twain "had a point.")

A little boy we know wrote Santa at Christmas saying
Dear Santa:
Do you leave presemts for little boys who flunk speling? A freind of mine wants to know.

John

Yes, John, he leaves "presemts" for poor spellers. (Goes on to describe a well-known dictionary as a suitable present for birthdays, graduation, and Christmas.)

The sales letter offers opportunity for all kinds of *devices and stunts* to attract reader's attention. Common is the technique of enclosing checks for the reader's time, stamps, keys, pencils, cigarettes, samples of products, and strange contraptions designed to arouse his curiosity. Sales letters are printed on all shades and all shapes of stationery. The Ralph J. Bishop Co. has had excellent results by designating their best customers "honorary directors," even to the point of declaring 7¢ dividends. Enclosures, unusual letters, and offbeat designs cost money; whether they pay for themselves in terms of added business should be the criterion in deciding whether to use them. The sales letter must, as we have said, attract attention, but if the reader is merely interested in a tricky device or clever opening which does not carry him along into the remainder of the sales message, the correspondent has failed as badly as if his opening aroused no interest at all. To the sales correspondent, the attention-arousing device is a means to an end rather than an end in itself.

2.   Creating desire for the product or service

One of the longest—and most inconclusive—discussions about readers centers on what is the best method of making them desire goods or services. Basically, there is the appeal to emotions or the appeal to reason, or, more frequently, a combination of the two. In a simpler era, it used to be thought that males responded to logic, the distaff side to emotion—but no longer. Perhaps it is an unflattering commentary on mankind's rational power, but a glance through the advertising in most magazines will show how much more widely the emotional appeal is used than any other form. Refrigerators, oils, automobiles, and similar workaday products are sold through advertisements that depict pretty girls or humorous situations or play on our desire to keep up with the Joneses. These are frequently attention-arousing techniques, but often we are made to want some product not on its merits alone but through highly emotional appeals to snobbishness, or fear, or the need to be like (or different from) other people. A lot of insurance, for instance, is sold to supposedly logic-motivated men through an appeal to their emotions ("If you weren't here, could your wife pay off the mortgage?"; "You do want to guarantee your children a college education, don't you?").

Whether to appeal to the reader's logic by expository and rational methods or to his emotions by descriptive techniques will depend on product, kind of reader, and the overall situation. For instance, a sales correspondent for an air conditioning company might choose between a description of "the cool, clean air like a mountain breeze, free of pollen and dust" or an exposition of the way the apparatus works. The deciding factor in this instance would be the type of reader; if the letter is sent to dealers, it will use a logical appeal with emphasis on profits, construction of the equipment, and the way it works; if it is written to the general public, it will probably concentrate on the joys of air-conditioned homes or offices. It is generally thought that a logical appeal is best for necessities and an emotional one for luxuries or novelties, but here again there are so many exceptions that we have to fall back on the old saw of elementary logic: "All generalizations are false—including this one."

Nonetheless, certain human desires are more or less universal, and appeals directed to them will at least reach readers. A few years ago the Direct Mail Advertising Association listed the following 25 reasons why people spend money:

To make money	To gratify curiosity
To save money	To protect family
To save time	To be in style
To avoid effort	For beautiful possessions
For comfort	To satisfy appetite
For cleanliness	To emulate others
For health	For safety in buying
To escape physical pain	To avoid criticism
For praise	To be individual
To be popular	To protect reputation
To attract the opposite sex	To take advantage of
To conserve possessions	opportunities
For enjoyment	To avoid trouble

These are at least reasonably specific, and you can test your own reasons against them. The following excerpts from sales letters show how correspondents use the you attitude in their sales appeals:

You've heard the names all your life—Tahiti, Bora Bora, Moorea—the land of Bali Ha'i, Bali, Rarotonga, and our own Hawaii—home of Waikiki and Diamond Head. Now instead of being names, they'll become real places, places you once dreamed of, shining places in your memories.

You want to keep intelligently informed about the rapidly changing world in which we live. You want to be able to talk confidently about national affairs and foreign affairs, about what is being invented, voted, written, painted, about what is being discovered in medicine and science. You want the news fully, concisely.

We have a book that you will want; your secretary will want it; your mailing department will wonder why they couldn't have had it long ago. It is a concise encyclopedia of authoritative postal knowledge compiled with the cooperation of the Postmaster General.

Wouldn't you like to have the most successful collection men in the country explain their methods to you, show you the actual letters they use, and tell you how economically they have solved their collection problems?

At sunset, the haze over the Catskills is a soft purple. You remember, of course, how much you enjoyed vacationing here in Rip Van Winkle Land last year—and it's just as peaceful and lovely this year.

3. Convincing the reader of the merits of the products or service

Thus far, our analysis has revealed the technique of the sales letter to be chiefly descriptive, expository, or narrative. The function of the third section is to marshal support to show that the claims made for the product are true. This is the technique of argument, which may be defined as *the art of influencing others to accept our beliefs by an appeal to their reason.* Previous claims and statements must here be supported by fact or logic; otherwise, the reader will correctly assume that the claims are grandiose and the statements untrue. In general, three types of logical support may be used in sales:

Expert Testimony. This consists of statements by qualified experts concerning the product sold. Through the widespread use of testimonials from people in no way qualified to speak about various products, the average reader has become rather skeptical of this sort of support. But if the person quoted is really qualified by education or experience to speak about the product, his endorsement constitutes a very sound sales argument.

Facts. Since the statements in the first part of the sales letter belong in the category of opinion (e.g., "The Colderator is the most economical refrigerator on the market today"), their truth is best shown in the third section by a solid basis of fact. Tests made by independent experts, statements about the number of sales made within a specified period, actual cost of operation of the product, mention of the number of satisfied customers, and specific data about the product under actual working conditions—all these give an objective, factual support to the claims made for the product.

Use of Logic. Since our logical faculty uses both facts and expert testimony on which to base its conclusions, this final division is somewhat arbitrary. In the sales letter, however, logic may be used to appeal favorably to the reader's reasoning or to get him to draw his own conclusions. A trial offer of the product may be made with the purpose of getting the reader to conclude, "If they are willing to let me try it out, it must be pretty good." Samples and guarantees are similarly effective. A correspondence school may use analogy to show that a student has taken a given course and has gone on to great success. The conclusion, "What he has done, you can do!" is inaccurate logic, but it seems to create sales. Widely used are causal relationships, such as "Because Pan-American coffee is packed in air-tight tins, it reaches you as fresh as the day it was roasted."

Whichever of these three types of logical support he employs, the sales correspondent should make sure that his statements do rest on a solid foundation and that his conclusions are logical. The following examples show specific applications of how these methods may be used to win conviction:

Sixty years is a long time, isn't it? And that's how long we've been serving companies like yours with the technical skill that comes only from experience.

Just to substantiate these statements, I am enclosing a circular which contains the names of over a thousand graduates of our secretarial course who have voluntarily reported salary increases within the past year. Perhaps you may know, or know of, some of these people. Their record shows in dollars and cents the value of the Blank Secretarial Course.

Our company has paid off its insurance claims through four wars and a half-dozen depressions. Our eighty years' experience is your guarantee that your policy is secure in spite of unsettled conditions.

As a person who has shown interest in conservation, you should join the 35,000 subscribers to a magazine which is dedicated to conservation. For two decades, we've informed readers when natural resources were being despoiled, told them what to do, and urged them to do it. We need your subscription to be more effective; but you need us to become a member of a group which knows what's new in conversation—and *does* something about it.

Because more than 50,000 Europeans used it, we imported it. Because our own tests showed its quality, we guaranteed it against defects in material or workmanship for one year. It costs a little more, but it's worth it. If you don't agree, you can return it after a two-week trial.

4.   Motivating action

The final paragraph of the sales letter should do two things; offer a specific suggestion concerning the action the reader should take, and point out how he will benefit by taking this action. The easier it is for the reader to take this action, the more effective the sales message will be; hence, stamped and addressed envelopes or the more economical business-reply permit envelopes, which do not require the payment of postage unless used, are frequently enclosed, or the reader is told to call by telephone or to wire collect. Whether these devices are economically feasible depends largely upon the product being sold. But the most inexpensive sales letter must perform these functions; otherwise, the sales correspondent has failed in what is the acid test for his letter—how many of his readers do take the suggested course of action? The following closing paragraphs show various methods to motivate action:

You have nothing to lose—and perhaps much to gain—by using the enclosed card.

Which models would you like to see on approval? Just check them on our order blank.

Won't you use the enclosed card to tell us when our representative may call at your convenience and with absolutely no obligation to you?

The enclosed card requires only your signature to bring you 52 issues full of entertainment, information, and enjoyment.

Wouldn't you like to see the way this new machine might aid you to reduce overhead? Just sign and mail this postcard for a demonstration.

The coupon below will bring you a copy—without obligation. Won't you sign and mail it *today?*

Take a moment *right now* to check the items that interest you. We'll gladly send you a sample of each.

Your subscription expires with the next issue. Act now! Sign the enclosed blank and you won't miss a single issue.

Send for this booklet today. Just use the coupon we are enclosing.

You'll find our new savings plan intensely interesting. JUST FILL IN THE EN-CLOSED CARD for our interesting booklet. No salesman will call.

EXAMPLES OF SALES LETTERS

The sales letter can be used effectively both as an individual message—for instance, to announce a sale for individual customers before public announcement is made—or as part of a series. Such series frequently consist of an original message and three or four follow-up letters; other series, such as those sent to dealers, are never-ending.

The following sales letters show the various ways in which devices to stimulate attention, desire, conviction, and action can be incorporated into unified and coherent messages. Try to decide what motivation they appeal to, and judge their effectiveness in terms of how well they would stimulate action by the reader.

Dear Mrs. Johnson:

"The world is a book of which those who remain always at home read only one page."

Whoever wrote those words knew what travel can do to broaden mental horizons and to free us from the narrow routine of daily living.

For 27 years, we've helped thousands of people travel near and far . . . cruises to the Caribbean, escorted tours to our National Parks, group and go-it-alone trips to Europe. . . . Whatever you choose, we can make your arrangements for you, by land or sea or air.

The enclosed folder lists the various ways you can read the many pages of this book we call the world. Just check the trips that interest you and mail it back to us postage paid. We'll call you then and tell you about costs, alternate arrangements, and financing. The world is literally waiting. Don't let it wait one more day.

Sincerely yours,

Dear Mr. Peters:

We'd like to BLOW YOU UP!

Don't call the police. We just want you to send us any black or white picture and we'll blow it up to poster size.—2 x 3 feet costs $3.50, 3 x 4 costs $7.50. We'll return your photo and the poster in a sturdy mailing tube.

Send your check in the enclosed envelope and in a week you'll have a perfect example of pop art, a genuine conversation piece, and a unique decorative ornament for your home.

                                              Very truly yours,

Dear Mr. Myers:

Early this morning the white mists were lifting their curtains to reveal the blue-green Catskills in the distance.

Your summer home is at its loveliest now. Haven't you longed for those blueberries that line the winding paths around the hotel? Or for that view of the soft haze around High Point? Your four weeks at the Mountain View last summer must hold a cherished place in your memory.

Why not store up more memories to gladden your future? You'll go back to work more fit, more efficient, if you get away from it all for a while.

Mountain View offers you the same rates as last year, and if you want us to, we'll reserve the same room. Why not wire your reservation to us today?

                                              Sincerely yours,

*Do you know how much your
Social Security is worth
under the law now in
effect?*

The Social Security Act has been changed repeatedly, and for some people the changes made will mean increased benefits.

But do you know what you personally may expect to receive?

At no cost to you, we will be glad to give you an estimate of your benefits, based on your own Social Security taxes and the number of your dependents who might become eligible to receive Social Security payments. This service has been very popular because most people like to know how their benefits have been affected by the changes.

In a day or two I will call and make this information available. The estimate of your benefits can, with your cooperation, be made in a few minutes.

                                         Sincerely yours,
                                         (From a representative of an
                                         insurance company)

Dear Mr. Ellender:

                                         Sincerely yours,

P.S. We have an idea that's too good for words. May we stop in and tell you about it at your convenience?

Dear Mr. Cole:

Someone has said that "brevity is the art of speaking volumes without writing them" . . . and so we'll be brief.

We've been in business for 23 years . . .

   . . . supplying commercial photographs

   . . . to more than 30,000 customers

   . . . for catalogues, house organs, sales brochures
     and presentations of all kinds.

May we discuss your photo problems with you? There's no obligation. Just mail the enclosed card and I'll call at your convenience.

                                            Sincerely yours,

HOW MANY
SQUARES IN THIS
FIGURE?

You have to watch yourself with the word "square". You can buy a □-deal from a □-shooter, but you'll have trouble if you refer to him as a □-head, or even lately as a plain, unvarnished □.

There's no trouble at all, though, if you get yourself □ed-around to ordering your advertising printing from □-shooting A & A. We keep our production □ed-away to handle your toughest problems, and every piece of artwork that goes through our shop is carefully checked with a T-□ to be sure everything lines up as it should.

Extra care might cost just a bit more, but our customers know they get □ treatment from A & A, on prices and delivery, too. It's these little extras that mean more effective promotions, greater returns—and more □ meals for our customers from the extra dollars that good advertising creates.

Let's get □ed-away. Fill in and mail the enclosed reply card, or give us a call at 241-2510 to have one of our account men call and tell you more about our services. Do it today!

                                      Best regards,
                                      Advertising & Addressing, Inc.

DID YOU GET
THE RIGHT COUNT?

We've had so many comments on these □s that we thought you'd like to know the answer.

The number of squares is 30: 16 singles, 9 doubles, 4 triples and one over-all.

Take a look again—and then get □ed away.

CONWAY, GREEN, AND MILTON
CONSULTANTS TO MANAGEMENT
FIDELITY-PHILADELPHIA BUILDING
PHILADELPHIA PA 19118

February 3, 1971

Mr. William O. Zentgraf, President
The Chemical-Industrial Corporation
The Dupont Building
Wilmington, Delaware 28032

Dear Mr. Zentgraf:

"Sculpture is very easy," said a famous sculptor. "All you do
is take a block of marble and chisel off all the stone you
don't want."

That's a good description of the way we can serve you as
management consultants. For fifteen years, we've been aiding
industry by cutting off the inefficiency and red tape that
management doesn't want.

The enclosed brochure describes the many ways we can serve
you—from expert time and motion studies to personnel
evaluation plans. You'll be interested in the comments from
our clients on pages 24-26.

Your signature on the enclosed card is all that's needed for
you to arrange an interview at your convenience and, of course,
at no obligation.

Sincerely yours,

Charles E. Conway

Charles E. Conway
Partner

CEC:MEG

And while you're ☐ing things up on all sides, remember to get your mailing and promotion problems ☐ed away, too. Call A & A to give you a ☐ deal on your printing and mailing requirements. Or fill in and mail the enclosed card. We'll be out to help you right away.

Cordially,

Dear Mr. Palen:
ThisisthewayourstorelooksforthreeweeksbeforeChristmas.
And   this   is   the   way   it   looks   now.
Why not do your shopping while you have a bit of r o o m?

Sincerely,

One conclusion to be drawn from these examples of sales letters is that it is generally more effective to use a variety of appeals than to harp constantly upon one theme. This was nicely demonstrated when an appliance dealer sent out a sales series concentrating on savings, the last of which ended with "you can save enough on your food bills to pay for this new food freezer in a few years." One harried housewife responded as follows:

Dear Sir:
We are paying for the car on the carfare we save, we're paying for the washing machine on the laundry bills we save, and we're paying for the storm windows on the fuel bills we save. Frankly, we just can't afford to save any more money at the present time.

EXERCISES

1. Write a sales letter which might be used for each of the following purposes:
    a. To attract teenagers to a sale of records and hi-fi equipment at a 15 percent discount.
    b. To get people to subscribe to your favorite magazine of general interest.
    c. To send to lists of people who are known to have an interest in the more or less specialized magazines such as *Dress Design, Fishing and Hunting, The Stamp Collector*, or any other you want to suggest.
    d. To attract new investors to a Forum on "How to Invest in Stocks" sponsored by a brokerage house.
    e. To get wealthy citizens to come in to your very exclusive and expensive Dress Shop or Men's Clothing Store for a showing of new spring models.

2. Your company has just taken over all the assets of the bankrupt Fishing Tackle Co., in whose warehouse you find 20,000 obsolete fishing creels made of wicker with a leather handle. They are of excellent construction, but a bit too heavy for today's fishermen. A woman in your office saw one of them and said, "They'd make wonderful handbags for teenagers. You know how young girls are always starting fads of carrying cart-

ridge cases and lunch boxes and all kinds of stuff. We ought to start a fad for these creels." Write a letter which will go to 1,000 teen-age girls to start the fad.

3. Here is a sales letter which generated considerable controversy in the sales department:

> Our business, Mrs. Jones, is alarming people.
>
> Yes—we make burglar alarms. And like all other citizens, we think you should be alarmed at the rising crime rate, the danger of civil disorders, and beyond all else, the fact that no home is safe from burglars unless it has some form of protection.
>
> We have mechanical devices, electronic detecting machines, and a variety of locks and safes to protect your home.
>
> We want to alarm you. You will sleep better nights if you just sign the enclosed card instructing us to send a qualified expert to discuss our products with you.
>
> Can we alarm you? We hope so.
>
> Detect-Protect Devices, Inc.

Several people in sales said "We have no right to scare people the way that letter does"; others thought it "a great selling letter." What is your reaction? How would you rewrite it?

4. Your purpose in each of the following situations is to persuade readers to fill out a card requesting one of your representatives to make a personal call at the reader's residence. Write the letter you would use if your ultimate goal is:
   a. To sell insurance on the lives of children while guaranteeing them enough money to get a college education.
   b. To sell a monthly investment plan in a Mutual Fund for ten years to people expecting to retire at the end of that period of time.
   c. To sell housewives beauty aids and cosmetics which are not sold in any store.
   d. To sell an encyclopedia to families with children in the elementary grades.
   e. To interest parents in sending children to eight-week sessions of your summer camp.

5. Hank's Discount Store has prospered greatly in selling "everything for the home" on a strictly cash basis. Its newspaper advertising has maintained a humorous, bantering tone with slogans like "Owe the bank, not Hank" and cartoons showing a couple dropping a newly bought TV set on Hank's parking lot as the wife says, "Isn't it wonderful that Hank gave us a savings of 20 percent?"

   Now a new management has decided to offer charge accounts with a finance charge of 1½ percent a month for any unpaid balance. A survey has shown that 60 percent of the purchasing at Hank's has been by people who have been married from 1 to 10 years. Write the letter you might send to a list of such customers persuading them to apply for the new charge accounts.

6. The Help-for-Children Committee, of which you are a member, has a goal of sending 2,200 children to Camp Sunshine for two weeks to get them out of the slums and ghettoes of the city. Cost per child per two-week stay is $42, and all financial support must be donated by individual citizens in response to a sales letter.

Your committee prides itself on the fact that every cent raised goes for the support of children and that every facet of the activity, from raising the funds to running the camp, is a volunteer effort. Against the background of this philanthropic effort, you are to assume that you as a committee member are charged with responsibility for the following:

a. A letter to college students to persuade them to serve as counselors at Camp Sunshine.

b. A letter to three local bus companies to get them to transport four busloads of children to Camp Sunshine every two weeks.

c. A letter to 219 doctors in your city asking them to serve as Medical Director of the camp for one week each.

d. An accountant on your committee has written the following draft of a letter which he believes will get financial support for Camp Sunshine:

> Dear _____:
>
> Again this year we seek your support for Camp Sunshine, where not a cent goes for anything but underprivileged children.
>
> For just $42, a child can have 14 nights, 42 meals, and medical attention and supervised recreation. Last year, the camp had 1,987 children and operated with such financial efficiency that our audit showed a loss of exactly $37.12 on the entire operation.
>
> We promise you the same efficiency this year. Won't you send your donation in the enclosed envelope?
>
> > Truly yours,

You are to submit your criticism of this letter to the committee in writing along with a different letter you have written based on your statement that "the letter to raise money for camp ought to have a strong emotional appeal."

7. An offbeat friend of yours has developed something called a ZERO Box, so named because, as he says, "It does nothing. It just sits there." He wants you to draft a sales letter to be sent to a list of 1,500 names of people who have expressed an interest in similar oddities. "It costs me 70 cents to make but I want to sell it for $4.75 because I believe that people like to pay good money for a laugh," he says. Draft the letter to comply with his wishes.

8. Write a sales letter to members of the freshman class at your school telling them that you have been appointed the campus agent for Acme Portable Typewriters. Among other advantages of your product, stress the fact that it may be obtained with mathematical symbols on the keyboard and that this will be most useful in the two years of mathematics required at your school.

9. Futuro Realty Company has developed the land around what used to be called Dumbbell Lake—now Paradise Lake—because it consists of two lakes connected by a narrow channel shaped like a dumbbell. The Upper Lake has been laid out for summer homes with lot sizes 125 by 400 with homes in the $37,500 to $65,000 class; the Lower Lake's lot sizes are 40 x 60, with homes costing $9,500 to $12,500. A high wire fence across the channel separates the two developments, each of which has its own roadway and entrance.

As sales correspondent for Futuro Realty, your task is to persuade as many prospects as possible to visit the model homes and recreation facilities at Paradise Lake. On the basis of the following assumptions, answer the questions below:

By income you can separate people interested in Upper and Lower Paradise Lakes.
Potential customers for Upper Paradise properties will be taken by private car for the 95-mile drive; customers for Lower Paradise properties go by bus on Thursdays, Saturdays, and Sundays.
A month's experience shows that prospects for Upper Paradise are older, have married children, and prefer quiet and solitude; prospects for Lower Paradise have been married 10–15 years, have two or three children, are interested in community recreation facilities and get-togethers, and want a place to spend week-ends.

Before you write your promotional letters for Futuro Realty, answer the following questions:

a. Should the same letter be written to prospects for both Upper and Lower Paradise?
b. Will there be any common elements in the letters even if different ones are sent to different prospects?
c. What appeal is best—snobbishness, exclusiveness, a sound investment for Upper Paradise? Fun, togetherness, an escape from the city for Lower? Or the opposite, togetherness with grandchildren for Upper Paradise and "a place in the country is always a good investment" for Lower Paradise?

Having answered these questions, write the letter(s) you would send to prospects interested in buying property at Upper and Lower Paradise.

10. You and two other graduates of your school have just organized the Complete Business Writing Service. Your service will prepare letters, reports, charts, booklets for any kind of business. Write a sales letter to be sent to a selected list of executives.

11. Give reasons why you would find any of the following unacceptable for the first paragraph of a sales letter:
a. We have reserved a membership in this exclusive group of subscribers, but you must hurry because the number is limited. (Sales letter for magazine.)
b. How would you like to LIVE OFF THE FAT OF THE LAND? (Sales letter to sell franchises in a reducing salon.)
c. Here is the greatest money-saving offer you have ever received. (Letter selling complete home repair services for an annual fee.)
d. Don't you get sick and tired of working harder and knowing more than your boss? (Letter from an employment agency for executives.)
e. Don't just sit there, Mr. Smith. DO SOMETHING! (Letter to recruit people to work in a campaign to aid the needy.)

12. Write a letter to *housewives* in your community, where husbands commute to the metropolis, offering them quick, dependable service on the family car and rental car for $6 a day while repairs or service are being done.

13. Write the sales letter for which these are the first paragraphs:
a. If you could have pictures, sound recordings, and a complete official account of

Columbus landing in the New World, you'd jump at the chance. That's what our $5.95 packet *Man's First Step on the Moon* does to record an equally important event.

b. For your reading pleasure, we'll send you the new *Science Fiction Anthology*, 1,131 pages of suspenseful, action-packed reading by the greatest writers of science fiction.

c. Now that you've bought that lovely new home, you are going to become interested in the shrubbery, the lawn, and the landscaping that form its setting. For 25 years we have been aiding homeowners in this community with just such problems.

d. Ever forget an appointment?
You *can't* with the new Blank Memopad on your desk!

e. Don't just say "Charge it"—DO IT with our efficient little battery charger, which will save you ten times its cost of $5.95 by recharging batteries.

14. What changes would you make in the following letter from a service which supplies office help as replacements for vacationing personnel or when an abnormal volume of work occurs:

> You know, Mr. Lindstad, a typist has been called a girl that you teach to spell while she looks around for a husband.
>
> Maybe. We'd suggest that you do a little looking around yourself to see whether your office is keeping up with the current workload, to find out if the typing of letters and reports reflects the high standards you want.
>
> Then give us a call for temporary help. Our girls can spell, take dictation swiftly, and turn out the best letters and reports you ever saw. And they won't spend your time looking around for a husband.
>
> Temporary Office Help, Inc.

15. A survey shows that while farmers are decreasing in total numbers, their income is rising, they have a high level of education, and they constitute a potential market which is genuinely interested in the mail received. Assuming that you have a carefully selected list of farmers with above-average income, write a sales letter for one of the following:

a. A package travel plan including four nights in New York City, three shows, tours of Radio City and Wall Street, a trip around Manhattan Island, and all meals and air transportation, for $197.50 a person.

b. A book entitled "The One Hundred Greatest Paintings of the Western World and Why They Were Selected," with 100 color reproductions of the paintings, for $13.95.

c. An album of seven 11-inch LP recordings of "Country Music" for $19.95

d. A utilitarian product such as seeds, fertilizer, household equipment, or lawn and garden supplies.

16. For the following novelty or specialty items write imaginative or unusual sales letters on the assumptions that (1) they are sold *only* by mail, and (2) you have up-to-date mailing lists of interested customers:

a. A series called "Great Documents of American History" reproduced on parchment. There are twelve documents (you are to name them), with three button-back frames so that they can be displayed and changed, postage-paid cost $9.95.

b. An imitation stone historical marker which bears a plaque reading "On this spot in 1620 absolutely nothing happened." The "rock," which looks like a small boulder, is made of plastic, can be filled with sand to make it heavy, and will withstand all kinds of weather. Cost is $22.95, but the buyer must pay express charges on delivery.

c. The "Animal-a-Month Service." This caters to the thousands of people who collect statues of various animals like dogs, cats, rabbits, deer, elephants, and horses. For a fee of $42.50 payable in advance, the Service will send each month for a year "a reproduction of your favorite animal which is truly an objet d'art." Customers have their choice of getting 12 dogs, for instance, or 12 of any one animal, or the Variety Collection, which offers one reproduction of 12 different animals.

d. The "Five Most Difficult Jig-Saw Puzzles in the World." These consist of more than 1,000 separate pieces each, require at least 8 hours to assemble, and represent five abstract or nonobjective paintings by well-known artists. Cost of the puzzles is $27.50 postpaid.

17. Criticize the following letter and rewrite it if you think it is not effective:

a.

A bore, Mrs. Jones, is a person who is here today . . . and here tomorrow.

But tomorrow, you can be a different person by subscribing to *Facts Illustrated*, the magazine for people who know.

Your conversation will be brighter, your understanding of events deeper, and your interest in life greater, if you spend two hours each week reading this tautly edited, brilliantly illustrated magazine for the cognoscenti.

Just sign the enclosed card. We'll bill you for $11.95. And you'll be off and running with all the facts and all the background you need.

Facts Illustrated, Inc.

18. On what basis would you decide whether to send out the following sales series in which each letter is sent within two or three days of the preceding one:

Dear Mr. Brown:
I do good printing.

Sincerely yours,

Dave Schonberg

Dave Schonberg

Dear Mr. Brown:
I deliver good printing on time.

Sincerely yours,

Dave Schonberg

Dave Schonberg

Dear Mr. Brown:

I don't charge much.

Sincerely yours,

Dave Schonberg

Dave Schonberg

Dear Mr. Brown:

I said I don't charge much for good printing delivered on time.

Sincerely yours,

Dave Schonberg

Dave Schonberg

19. Using your experience and background with faculty members, select some service, product, or activity which you think they might be interested in, then write the sales letter which you would consider effective for this group.

CHAPTER 12

THE APPLICATION LETTER

"It is now the employers, not the young men and women who have their hats in their hands," said John W. Gardner, former Secretary of Health, Education, and Welfare to describe "the great hunt for educated talent" of the late 1960s. Yet, as the seventies began, the situation had reversed, and the hat *was* in the hands of educated applicants for jobs. Such ups and downs of the economic cycle dramatically illustrate one fact: every individual ought to possess the ability to apply in writing for a new or different job. Whether he may ever have to use this ability is beside the point; he should regard it as good insurance against stormy economic weather as well as an effective means of improving his own position. For these reasons, no writing the individual will ever do has greater potential for affecting his own life than the writing connected with the process of application for a job. And it is worth noting that employers often attach as much importance to the *way* in which job credentials are presented to them as to the experience or education contained in those credentials.

THE PROPER POINT OF VIEW

Throughout this text, we have stressed the theme, "Think before you write." The process of applying for a job is one situation in which careful thought can pay handsome dividends. An indispensable ingredient of successful job seeking is *objective self-analysis;* and since the gift of seeing ourselves as others see us has not been universally conferred upon humans, self-appraisal is not easy. Here are some questions you ought to think about before you put anything on paper:

> What are my best qualifications for employment?
> Education?
> Experience?
> Some specific skill?
> Personality traits?
>
> Am I seeking a specific position (i.e. secretary, salesman, accountant, engineer, typist, receptionist etc.) or general employment?
>
> What is it that I really want in a job—salary, opportunity for advancement, challenge, commitment, the opportunity to serve others, or what?
>
> What organizations offer the best opportunity for me to find what I want?

Unless you are the casual I-just-want-a-job type, you need a detached and searching look-at-yourself-in-the-mirror answer to these questions.

Later, you can check up on how well you've passed this self-examination by asking a classmate or a teacher to go over what you write about yourself in your application. But the self-analysis must come first.

After this emphasis on "I" you will have to translate the results of your thinking into a prospective employer's viewpoint and write in terms that appeal to him. It's all too easy for applicants to write about "how much *I* would like to work for your company" or "how much *I* dislike my present job" or "how badly *I* need work"; but after the objective I-analysis we have described, the results must be transformed to answer a reader's question: "What does the applicant offer which will prove useful or profitable to me?"

THE PURPOSE AND METHODS OF APPLYING FOR A JOB

The purpose of writing application letters is not, as many think, "to get a job" but more normally *to get an interview.* The positions which educated applicants seek are almost never given without an interview; the goal of getting one, therefore, is primary in the application process.

Although we are discussing *written* techniques only, it may prove helpful to examine briefly the other ways of seeking an interview. Why not go in person and ask for one? Or why not use the phone to arrange an interview? In other words, why *write?* The answer actually will depend on timing, distance, and various other circumstances, all adding up to the conclusion that there is no one "best" way. But if you make a personal visit unannounced, you may not see the person you want to, and if you do, you may interrupt a busy schedule. By phoning, you may not get through to the right person, and you'll be told to come in for the interview before you've had a chance to supply your background. The advantages of these two methods are, of course, that they are quick and direct and reflect your interest and willingness to get a job promptly. While the written process of application is slower, it has these advantages:

1. It gives the person responsible an opportunity to analyze your qualifications and the company's needs at his convenience.
2. It provides background for a constructive interview.
3. It can be put on permanent record against the time when a suitable position is available.

A final aspect is worth mentioning: whether you phone or call in person, you will usually have to write anyway, since most companies have forms or questionnaires to be filled out. By using the steps in the process which are explained in the next pages, you have the chance to present your credentials in a form that *you* have chosen as the best way to present them.

THE STEPS IN APPLYING FOR A JOB IN WRITING

The following are the most widely accepted steps in writing to apply for a job:
1. A comparatively brief letter, usually three or four paragraphs, featuring the applicant's best qualifications and ending with a courteous request for an interview. In the middle paragraph(s) of this letter, an indirect reference is made to the résumé which is enclosed.
2. A résumé which gives all necessary details about the applicant's background under such headings as Education, Experience, Personal, and References.
3. A follow-up letter after the interview or (in very rare instances) a follow-up letter when there has been no response to an application letter and résumé sent earlier. Since these letters depend heavily on varying circumstances, we shall discuss them briefly at chapter's end.

The letter of application and the résumé are, of course, the two most important steps in this process.

The advantages of the combination of letter and résumé are fourfold. First, it enables the applicant to feature, in a letter short enough to be readable, those qualities which best fit him for the specific position for which he is applying. Second, he can convey a far greater amount of information about himself in a readable form in this combination of letter and résumé. Third, this form of application is adaptable and sufficiently flexible so that it can be used in a variety of situations. Regardless of whether he sees immediate need for it or not, every young educated person should have a résumé readily available, because once it is drawn up, it can be used over and over again; the letter to accompany it can be varied to meet the specific employment situation. Fourth, the résumé presents in a concise form, which can be filed easily, all the details about an applicant and how he may be reached. Hence, it remains as a ready reminder of the job seeker's qualifications and availability if a vacancy does occur. These advantages suffice to make the combination of letter and résumé the most effective technique of seeking employment by mail; the applicant who wishes to make the best presentation of himself will certainly use it.

All of this discussion is, of course, based upon the assumption that the job seekers possess the essential qualifications to fill the position for which they apply. It should not be necessary to say that even the best letter will not get a job for an unqualified applicant; yet a surprisingly large number of persons seem to believe that by a lucky break they can get jobs for which they are not trained. All cynical jokes (such as the advertising agency's ad "Room at the top for son of big advertiser") to the contrary, it is education, experience, and ability that successful job applicants must depend upon.

In the following pages, we shall examine in greater detail the specific steps in the application process.

The Letter to Accompany the Résumé

This letter is used as a device to feature the job seeker's best qualifications. It follows the structure of the sales letter, but it leaves the details to be filled in by the personal record sheet. Its contents should include:

1. A direct opening statement of why the applicant's training or education or experience may be profitable to the prospective employer
2. A short paragraph amplifying this opening statement or stressing other qualifcations that might appeal to the reader's interests
3. A reference to the fact that complete details about the applicant are contained in the enclosed résumé
4. A request for an interview

The Opening Paragraph. Beginning the application letter is probably the most difficult part of the whole technique, as the hundreds of thousands can testify who have told their teachers, "If I could only get this letter started, the rest would be easy." Ideally, the opening paragraph should be direct; it should have the you attitude; it should feature the applicant's best quality. One of the simplest ways of attaining these qualities is by a summary beginning:

This is to request your consideration of my qualifications for a position with your company.

My seven years in the credit department of the Blank Company qualify me for a position as your credit manager.

Two years at Blank Business School have given me a training in business administration which should be useful to you.

Because of my three years' experience as a salesman for the White Company, I feel that I can qualify for the sales position which you advertised in this morning's *Boston Herald*.

My five years' experience in the collection department of the Black Company makes me confident that I can solve your collection problems as you want them solved.

Four years of college at the University of Michigan plus two summers of work with the Brown and Brown Company have given me a knowledge of the theory and practical application of engineering problems.

Although such beginnings are not too original, they will arouse the interest of an employer who is seeking applicants. From the writer's standpoint, these summary beginnings make the transition to the second paragraph very simple because it logically should give further details about the education or experience referred to in the opening paragraph. Furthermore, the summary beginning avoids the possibility of using such negative, colorless, or completely useless openings as:

No you attitude, trite, colorless	I should like to be considered as an applicant for a position as clerk with your firm.
Don't bother telling him such trivial details	I happened to be reading the *Washington Star* and saw your advertisement for a secretary.
Don't tell him what is really his own business	Now that business is again aggressively pushing sales, you are undoubtedly adding to your staff. I should like you to consider my qualifications.

Applicants are usually much too concerned with the introductory section of their letters and, consequently, spend so much time in introducing themselves that they lose the reader's interest before the preliminaries are concluded. A good test of an introductory paragraph is to read the letter without it; if something important is omitted from the letter with such a reading, the opening paragraph is important and says something direct; the three opening paragraphs above, like the various pests in Gilbert and Sullivan, "never would be missed."

Another effective way to begin, if you have the person's permission, is the *name beginning*, which mentions some business associate, friend, or customer of the prospective employer.

> Mr. James Johnson of your advertising department has told me that you will soon need another secretary. My college education and three years as a private secretary in a legal firm should merit your consideration.

> Mr. J. J. Moore has suggested that I might be well qualified for sales work in your International Division because of my command of four languages and my background of travel abroad.

The ultimate value of such beginnings depends almost entirely on the name used; but the fact that a friend, business associate, or customer is mentioned will invariably win consideration for this type of letter.

A third method of opening is by a question intended to challenge the reader's attention. While this type of beginning sounds rather abrupt, it has the desirable effect of forcing the applicant to plunge into the middle of his most salable qualities without any preliminaries or introduction.

> Can your sales force write letters which get a minimum of 5 percent returns? I have done that consistently and with a more highly specialized product than yours.

> Can your stenographers take dictation at the rate of 120 words a minute? I can—and I am eager to prove that such speed does not lessen my accuracy.

> Could you use a general utility infielder? A man who could fill in at any of the positions on your staff and relieve you of the worries and delays caused by absences of personnel?

The applicant who uses this question beginning should first be absolutely certain that his qualifications *do* answer the question which he himself raises; otherwise, his letter accomplishes nothing.

The Middle Paragraph(s). Depending upon whether the letter is a three- or four-paragraph application, the one or two middle paragraph(s) generally amplify or highlight the features you want to stress. Somewhere in this part of the letter should be a reference to the enclosed résumé, but this reference should always be indirect. Sophisticated readers of application letters don't need to be told, "Enclosed please find a résumé of my education and experience" as if they would have to hunt for it. Make such references indirect and casual, as follows:

> As you will see on my résumé, I am fortunate in having my military service behind me.

My previous education, which is listed on my résumé, has motivated me to seek a position where I will be able to do part-time graduate study.

My major interest is people, as the section on extracurricular activities in my résumé shows.

The best way to regard the function of the middle paragraphs is to think of them as your chance to emphasize or select from the factual and rather impersonally presented material on the résumé those qualities or experiences you want to stress for a specific job. Here are some examples:

You may consider it important that I earned more than 80 percent of my college expenses doing sales during summer vacations. As my résumé shows, I have done door-to-door selling, worked in a booth at the Centennial Exposition exhibiting merchandise, and served as a promotion agent for a summer camp.

My interest in communications has increased steadily. As my résumé shows, the courses I selected and the activities I tried out for centered on learning how to express my ideas in speech and writing.

Perhaps my hope of participating in your research activities is best revealed by my preference for things rather than people. The highlights of my undergraduate years involved serving as assistant in the biology laboratory and participating in the Physics Symposium, both of which are described in detail on my résumé.

What I offer, actually, is a very good education combined with a limited experience in summer jobs shown on my résumé. But this combination makes me very eager to apply what I have learned to actual business problems. My enthusiasm to "get going" may well prove to be most useful to you.

As you will see on my résumé, I have always moved to a position with greater responsibility and higher salary. A broad variety of experiences with middle management has prepared me for the abilities and responsibilities required at the top level of managment.

My skills, which are detailed on my résumé, include the usual ones required of a secretary. But the intangibles are hard to put down on paper the way I can quantify how many words a minute I type or take dictation—and those intangibles include the ability to work with others, to run an office which is gracious but efficient, and to relieve my boss of unnecessary detail.

One very good clue to the effectiveness of these middle paragraphs is to judge them from the reader's viewpoint—do they give an insight into the kind of person writing the letter? And reversing the perspective, the applicant can judge how well they represent him by asking: "Is this a clear statement of my best qualifications?" These criteria ought to be supplemented by applying the principles of unity and coherence to the middle paragraph(s); trite as it is to say so, the application letter has a beginning, middle, and ending. Thus, the choice of the opening paragraph drastically affects the middle paragraph(s);

if that beginning is a summary paragraph (My four years at Blank University qualify me . . .), then the middle paragraph(s) should supply details; if the beginning uses a name (Professor Blank has suggested that I apply . . .), then the middle paragraphs ought to supply reasons why you and Professor Blank think you have the requisite training or experience; and finally, if you begin with a challenging statement or question (Could you use a general utility infielder?), your next paragraph had better supply an answer focused on the reader's question, "What makes him think he can be 'a utility infielder'?"

The Closing Paragraph.   The closing paragraph has just one function—to ask for an interview. On the theory that the application letter, like the sales letter, ought to make action easy for the reader, many applicants formerly enclosed self-addressed postcards on which the prospective employer could fill in the date and time when he could conveniently see the applicant; others ended by suggesting that "You may call me at 231-2897." Such closings ought to be avoided, because any intelligent reader can locate your phone number and address on your résumé and would prefer to use his own means of getting in touch with you *if* he is interested. The following closes are effective:

> When may I see you?

> May I have an interview?

> May I show you examples of the kind of work I have done?

> Although my résumé contains considerable detail, you doubtless have questions you want answered. May I come in for an interview at your convenience?

Notice how much more direct the preceding examples are than the following timid or colorless endings, which should be avoided:

> I trust that you will grant me an interview.

> I shall hope to hear from you soon.

> If you feel that I may be of use to your organization, please let me come in for an interview.

How should the letter close when the prospective employer is at considerable distance from the applicant? This situation is always a difficult one to which there seems no completely correct solution. The job seeker cannot very gracefully suggest that he come 600 miles to be interviewed by the prospective employer. A few employers would welcome so tangible an expression of interest in their company, but the great majority feel that it places too much responsibility on them. They fear that the applicant is likely to conclude that since he is not deterred from coming, he certainly must have excellent prospects of getting a job. The ideal way is for the applicant to be invited for an interview or, barring that, to suggest a means by which the interview can be arranged without too much difficulty. The following closes may suggest methods of handling such a situation:

> I shall be in New York from December 22 to January 3. Would it be convenient to talk to any of your staff there concerning the possibility of employment?
> (This is obviously a student making good use of his Christmas vacation.)

> Is it possible that you or some member of your staff will be in this vicinity within the next month? A telegram to me, collect, will bring me to see you at your convenience.

> I shall be in Wilmington on May 4 and 5. May I see you on one of those days?

> (It is altogether possible that the applicant's sole reason for being in Wilmington is the chance of getting this job, but it is usually better not to tell the employer this. Many an applicant has obtained a job through being willing to take a five- or six-hundred-mile trip to "Wilmington" on his own responsibility.)

> You or your associates will undoubtedly be in _____ (name of the nearest large city) during the next few months. When you are there, may I have the opportunity of seeing you?

> Does a representative of your company plan to visit this school? If so, I should be grateful for an opportunity to talk with him.

If none of the above can be adapted to the applicant's needs, he can always close by saying:

> I hope that my qualifications will merit your consideration.

This would ordinarily be a very weak conclusion when an interview is desired or when the company is within easy reach. But when the applicant and prospective employer are hundreds or even thousands of miles apart, such a close may prove effective because it leaves the next move up to the employer. If he is indeed interested in the writer's qualifications, he can probably make some specific suggestion as to how they may meet.

The following letters show how some of these suggestions may be incorporated into complete applications accompanied by personal record sheets:

> Mr. D. J. Wright, President
> The William C. Bryan Company
> 3190 West Canal Street
> Boston, Massachusetts 02126
>
> Dear Mr. Wright:
>
> Could you use a dependable secretary?
>
> During the past two years I have been with Jennings and Sessions, Inc., of this city. Because our office was small, I performed many different duties; this gave me an excellent understanding of the routine of an office.

I can take shorthand, operate a switchboard, type rapidly and accurately, act as a receptionist, and write letters dealing with routine situations. The enclosed résumé will give you complete details about my education and personal qualifications.

May I come in to see you at your convenience?

Sincerely yours,

Dear Mr. Stevens:

My ten years' experience as a salesman for the Green Wholesale Grocery Company should qualify me for a position as sales manager with your company.

I have traveled in western Massachusetts for the past six years, and my wide acquaintance among grocers and food buyers in that section should be valuable to you in marketing the new line of Premex Foods which you are introducing. My record as a salesman has been excellent, as my references will show; as a sales manager, I could use my own experience in training personnel rapidly but efficiently.

As the enclosed résumé indicates, I am a college graduate and have taken several graduate courses in Marketing and Sales Organization. I am widely known among businessmen in this city, since I have been active in many civic and fraternal organizations.

May I have an interview to substantiate these statements and to answer your questions? You may reach me at 106-4137.

Sincerely yours,

Since it is helpful to see how people actually handle the letter of application, here are two rather offbeat examples. Reaction to their unusual approach has tended to be strong—either very favorable or very unsympathetic. How do you react?

Edward Blank

Sincerely yours,

me at 317-1004 at Blank, Ohio.

I am sure that we can arrive at a satisfactory arrangement if you will write or telephone life, and I believe that I shall continue to do so. This is the only way to get ahead.

Well, as you can see, I am not afraid to start at the bottom. I have done this all through the bottom, to become a sales representative for your firm.

You state that you have a position open for a young man, who isn't afraid to start at January 14.

I am writing this letter in response to your advertisement in the New York Times of Gentlemen:

New York 10010, New York
2471 Park Avenue
Blank Sales Company

January 19, 1970
Blank, Ohio 44444
747 Miami Street

Dear Mr. Smith:

You have the job that I want . . . in ten or twenty years.

As president of your company, you've established a great record . . . and I think I can do the same.

This may sound like the job applicant who said, "During the five years I worked for IBM the company doubled its sales and profits" . . . but if you'll look at my résumé, you'll find I'm more realistic.

Interested? Then I hope you'll see me. Will you?

                                                        Sincerely,

A Special Word to Students

Before going on to our detailed discussion of the résumé, we should appropriately address a few words of advice to students, whose usual concern is their lack of working experience. Quite obviously, then, they should stress their education, avoiding the two extremes of apologizing for their lack of experience or of assuming that the world is the college graduate's oyster.

When you feature your education in both your application letter and your résumé, you should attempt to answer such questions as the following for the prospective employer:

1. What specific courses have you had which might be of value in the work for which you are applying? (But don't give the impression that you now know all the answers!)
2. How did you get along with your fellow students? (Don't express your own opinion on this subject; if you've been elected to offices or membership in organizations, the personnel man can draw his own conclusions.)
3. How were your grades? (Mention the third of your class you were in or what scholastic honorary societies you belonged to. If you were in the lowest third of your class, a golden silence is probably the best policy!) If your scholastic record is good, stress that fact. If your grades are merely average, discuss major subjects or specific courses which are relevant to the kind of job you seek.
4. What activities did you participate in? (In recent years most industry recruiters on college campuses have stressed grades rather than activities. But participation in activities is still regarded as evidence of the ability to get along with others as well as potential leadership qualities.)
5. Did you earn any part of your school expenses?
6. Did you work during your summer vacations? If so, this may be listed under "Experience" on your résumé. Be sure to include a description of the type of work you did.

These questions should suggest the way in which the detailed presentation of your educational experience should be approached. On pages 270 to 278, examples of résumés and an accompanying letter are shown. The résumé of

Robert C. Cartwright on pages 275 to 278 is designed primarily as a guide for school and college students who must stress their educational preparation rather than their working experience.

The Résumé

The greatest advantage of the résumé is that it can be adapted to any individual's needs or experience. Certain characteristics are, however, invariably the same. Centered at the top of the sheet are the name and address of the applicant with the phone number in the upper left-hand corner and the date in the upper right-hand corner. This arrangement makes for easy visibility of the information when the sheet is filed. The conventional headings for listing other information are Education, Experience, Personal Details, and References. Thus the fixed parts of such a résumé look like this:

| Telephone
607-213-1246 | John Smith
12 Main Street
Elmira, New York 14901 | August 22, 1970 |

Education

Experience

Personal Details

References

No pains should be spared to make this personal record sheet pleasing in appearance by keeping it well-balanced and uncrowded. The headings may be made to stand out by capitalizing all the letters or by underlining in either black or red type. The order of parts should be arranged to fit the applicant. If his accompanying letter stresses his experience, that should be placed first on the personal record. Many job seekers list their business experience in reverse order on the sound theory that a prospective employer is chiefly interested in what the applicant has done most recently. When reverse order is used for one part, such as Experience, it is a good idea to use it for other parts, such as Education. Since the material on the résumé sheet need not be expressed in complete sentences, there is room for great detail and for attractive spacing. Dates of educational, military, and business experience ought always to be given, and wherever possible no gaps in the applicant's record should be left unaccounted for. The following sample shows the way the material under education and experience might be arranged.

Education

| 1960–63 | Cleveland Heights High School; graduated June, 1963. |
| 1963–67 | Oberlin College; Bachelor of Arts degree, June, 1967. |

Experience

January, 1970 to present	Employed as copywriter for the Blank Company. My duties include writing copy for electrical appliances and soliciting new accounts.
June, 1968, to January, 1970	Employed as reporter on the *Cleveland Heights Journal;* this was a temporary position which I took for the journalistic experience it offered. I acted as proofreader and general news reporter during the leave of absence of a regular member of the staff.
June, 1967, to June, 1968	Employed as proofreader in my father's print shop. This job offered the chance to learn general problems of the printing business. My duties consisted of helping out in any department where extra help was needed; this gave me the opportunity to see all the operations of the printing business in some perspective.

As in the above example, it is best under Experience to tell not merely the title of the job but to specify as exactly as possible what its duties were. Don't merely say clerk, salesman, or chemical engineer, but describe what the specific duties of these positions were.

The section labeled Personal or Personal Details is difficult to categorize, since personnel men are not in any agreement as to just what should be included. Furthermore, laws affecting fair employment practices vary from state to state, but customarily no mention of race or creed should be included. The Personal section of the résumé can be regarded as a miscellany containing what is not classifiable under the other headings. Normally, it will include statements concerning the applicant's age, height, weight, state of health, marital status, number and ages of children, if any, nationality, and a description of any major interests or hobbies. Some applicants use the Personal section for forthright statements about why they want to change jobs; others use it to give clues to their personality traits, as "My interest in people led me to serve as a volunteer at Memorial Hospital," although generally speaking, such subjective comments can be better included in the letter rather than the résumé. Personal material may be arranged in almost any fashion to suit the individual's needs. He may save space by arranging it as follows:

Personal Details

Age, 25; height, 6 feet, 1 inch; weight, 185 pounds; health, excellent; unmarried; American; veteran, USNR; hobbies—photography and stamp collecting; sports—tennis and golf.

Or if the personal record sheet seems to have too little material on it, the personal details may be listed this way:

Personal Details

Age	 25	Nationality	. . . . American
Height	. . . . 6 ft. 1 in.	Veteran	. . . . USNR
Weight	. . . . 185 lbs.	Hobbies	. . . . Photography,
Health	. . . . Excellent		stamp collecting
Marital Status	. . . . Unmarried	Sports	. . . . Tennis, golf

Under References are placed the names and addresses of at least three people who can testify to the applicant's business experience, education, or character. Common courtesy requires that the consent of the individual used as a reference should be obtained *in advance* of the actual application. The full title and complete address of each reference ought always to be given; where the references are local, their telephone numbers may also be listed like this:

References

The following men have agreed to act as my references:

Mr. James Dwyer, President
The Blank Company
2034 Market Street
Newark, New Jersey   07107   Telephone: 112-3267

Professor Arthur Wright
Department of Physics
Rutgers University
New Brunswick, New Jersey 08903   Telephone: 112–0200

Mr. Arthur Smith, Attorney
326 Main Street
East Orange, New Jersey 07208   Telephone: 112–6913

The example on page 276 shows how a well-organized personal record sheet looks and what material it may include.

The following personal record sheet and accompanying letter are a guide for students who must stress their education, emphasizing specific courses and school activities.

Robert C. Cartwright
271 College Street
Lafayette, Indiana 46207

112–3926   May 15, 1971
EDUCATION
1961–65   George Washington High School, Eastport, New York.
                 Graduated, June, 1965.

312-0392   Chester C. Parsons
                                  6710 Parkwood Place
                               St. Louis, Missouri 63141   November 6, 1971

EDUCATION
  1961-65   Beaumont High School;
                         graduated June, 1965

  1965-67   Central Business Institute
                         Business Administration Course;
                         graduated June, 1967

EXPERIENCE
  January, 1969,   Employed as an assistant to the chief engineer of
  to present   the American Food Corporation, St. Louis, Missouri.
                         My duties included compiling reports for the chief
                         engineer on production in the various departments.
                         I also made time-study analyses of production methods.

  June, 1967, to   Worked as a traffic rate clerk for the Continental
  January 1, 1969   Engineering Company of Pittsburgh, Pennsylvania.
                         In this position I started as an assistant in the
                         traffic department and later prepared and filed
                         claims for overcharges.

PERSONAL DETAILS   Age, 24; height, 5 feet, 9 inches; weight, 165 pounds;
                         health, excellent; married, no children; American;
                         hobbies, photography, amateur radio, stamp collecting;
                         sports, tennis, bowling, and swimming.

REFERENCES   Mr. Ernest G. Blankenburg
                         Central Business Institute
                         St. Louis, Missouri 63108

                         Mr. H. L. Judson, Personnel Manager
                         Continental Engineering Company
                         3926 Seventh Avenue
                         Pittsburgh, Pennsylvania 15215

                         Mr. H. C. Williams, Chief Engineer
                         American Food Corporation
                         2241 Euclid Avenue
                         St. Louis, Missouri 63121

| 1967–71 | Purdue University. I expect to receive my degree of Bachelor of Science in Metallurgical Engineering in June, 1971. |

Major Courses Studied:
Fundamentals of Metallurgy
Metallurgy of Iron and Steel
Ferrous Alloys
Nonferrous Alloys

Other Courses that Would Prove Useful in this Position:
Fundamentals of Writing
Creative Writing
The History of Science
Psychology

Activities in College:
Glee Club—three years
Student paper—three years
Speakers Bureau—two years
Member of Tau Beta Pi and Blue Key

Scholastic Record
For 3½ years I have been in the upper third of my class scholastically; during my first two years I earned approximately half of my college expenses working in the bookstore and library.

EXPERIENCE

1965–1967
I served for 21 months in the U.S. Army, 13 months in Viet Nam, and was honorably discharged in July, 1967 with the rank of Technical Specialist, 4th class.

1970
June to September—During my summer vacation, I worked as a counselor at the Lakeside Boys' Camp, Clifton, Michigan, where I had the chief responsibility for 24 boys, ages 12–15.

PERSONAL DETAILS

Age, 26; height, 6 feet, 1 inch; weight, 185 pounds; health, excellent; unmarried; hobbies—singing, writing, and photography. I am particularly interested in combining full-time work with the opportunity of going to graduate school to obtain a master's and eventually a doctor's degree.

REFERENCES

Professor Kenneth H. Dewitt
Head of the Department of Metallurgy
Purdue University
Lafayette, Indiana 46207

Dr. James C. Struthers, Director
Lakeside Boys' Camp
Clifton, Michigan 49235

Mr. William E. Knight, Principal
George Washington High School
Eastport, New York 13056

To accompany this résumé, the following letter with a name beginning and closing request for an interview would prove effective:

Dear Mr. Bateson:

Professor Kenneth H. Dewitt, head of the Department of Metallurgy, has informed me that your agency is looking for an engineering graduate with the ability to write about technical subjects for nontechnical readers.

My four years at Purdue have given me a thorough foundation in such fundamental sciences as physics, mathematics, and chemistry, in addition to specialized courses in metallurgy. I have also taken as many courses in English and psychology as possible with the expectation that I would enter the field of technical sales or editing following my graduation this June.

Fortunately, as my résumé shows, my military experience is behind me, and I now have a mature interest in finding a satisfying job.

May I come in for an interview at your convenience?

Sincerely yours,

Robert C. Cartwright

Robert C. Cartwright

MISTAKES TO AVOID IN THE CAMPAIGN FOR A JOB

Because of inexperience or ignorance of the job-seeking technique, writers frequently do their cause more harm than good by the appeals that they make in their letters. The following list of "don'ts" for application letters should help you avoid such pitfalls.

Don't appeal to the employer's sympathy. Even if a position is obtained by such a method—and that rarely happens—the conditions of employment will probably be highly unsatisfactory since the employer will always feel that he is doing the applicant a favor by granting employment. Don't say, "I need this job very badly because I must support my family"; try to get the position because you can be useful, not because you are to be pitied.

Don't discuss salary in the application letter; leave that for the interview. Advertisements often use the unfair technique of demanding that the applicant "state the salary desired"; the best answer is to suggest that salary be discussed in the interview, unless you are willing to be hired as a bargain because you will work for less than any of the other applicants.

Don't be afraid to use the pronoun "I" in your application. Since the letter is personal, "I" will be used rather more frequently than in other kinds of letters; don't try to avoid it by using "the writer," "the undersigned," or similar circumlocutions. What should be avoided is a conceited and aggressive air in the letter; a quiet tone of confidence in one's own ability is the ideal.

Don't stress dissatisfaction with your present position. If a change is desirable because no chance of advancement is offered, that is a legitimate reason which will be borne out by references. But personal dislikes or grievances should not be put into writing; if necessary, they can be explained in the interview. Employers are afraid of the "drifter" who goes from one job to another because of imagined grievances.

Don't express a lot of opinions in the application letter; particularly avoid expressing opinions about yourself. The facts of the applicant's career should speak for themselves in the letter; let the references give the opinions.

Don't waste time telling the employer a great many things he already knows. The best part of the application letter is wasted when the applicant begins with such statements as:

> Because you are an advertising man, you certainly realize the value of a broad background of education. You must know, too, that a knowledge of the principles of correct English is invaluable in writing copy.

Don't apologize for applying for work. Every employer respects your honest attempt to find the position for which you are suited. No apology is expected, and none should be made because it weakens the whole letter.

Finally, *don't* send out anything less than the most nearly perfect letter and résumé of which you are capable. Quite properly, employers expect educated applicants to write clearly, correctly in every detail; when your writing does not meet these standards, adverse judgments are passed on you even before you get an interview.

ONE LETTER MORE

Let us suppose that the job seeker is in that blissful state of having worked long and well over his letter and résumé and that his labors have had their reward in an interview. Is there anything he can do but sit and wait?

The answer is *yes:* he can write a follow-up letter *if* his best judgment based on his experience in the interview suggests that he will help his cause by writing such a letter. If, for instance, the interview terminated with anything like "Don't get in touch with us; we'll get in touch with you," no such letter should follow. If the applicant has the slightest suspicion that any further move on his part would be considered overly aggressive, he should not write. But if in your best judgment an occasion for the follow-up letter emerges *naturally* from the interview, use it. Why? Because it will set you apart from other applicants (nine out of ten won't use it), because it will recall you and the interview to the employer's mind, and because it will give you the satisfaction of knowing that you have done everything possible to get the job you want.

Such a follow-up letter may express thanks for the interview; it may refer to your attitude about the firm or company or job now that you know more about it; it may mention something that took place during the interview; or it may supply new information that now seems appropriate because of the interview. Frequently, during the interview, brochures, annual reports, or similar company publications are handed to applicants, and a natural response can be made after you have read them. The letter should always be brief and modest in tone and generally should be sent a day or two after the interview. Here are two examples:

Dear Mr. Moore:

I appreciate your kindness in granting me an interview yesterday. Your explanation of the problems faced by the automotive industry was very helpful to me. I hope that my past experience may entitle me to favorable consideration because the problems which you mentioned aroused my interest and I should like to aid in solving them.

Sincerely yours,

Dear Mr. Minard:

I have now read the pamphlet you gave me on "Educational Opportunities with Blank Industries." Because my most urgent wish is to continue my growth through education, I was truly impressed by the wide range of educational opportunites which are available to your employees.

Thank you for your courtesy. I do hope that my educational background will merit favorable consideration by Blank Industries.

Very truly yours,

One other form of follow-up letter is occasioned when the application letter and résumé have been sent and no acknowledgment has been received. Discretion here dictates that (1) sufficient time has elapsed for the reply to have been made and (2) the applicant has reason to believe that his qualifications fit the employer's needs. Actually, any application—or indeed any letter of any kind—deserves acknowledgment, but some companies do disregard far-out or off-beat or totally unqualified job letters. Because there is always the possibility that mails are delayed or misdelivered or that the original application reached the wrong person, a follow-up letter may properly be sent. It should be regarded strictly as a letter of inquiry; it should not repeat or duplicate the information sent earlier; it should refer courteously to the job sought, the date of application, and any other items which will identify the original application. And its tone should be polite, neutral, factual. Above all else it should avoid any suggestion of being pushy or accusatory ("I sent you an application on May 19 and you never answered it.")

EXERCISES

The exercises which follow are in a sense "academic," since there is just one exercise that readers of the preceding chapter should indulge in—the preparation of an individual résumé and letter(s) to accompany it for various situations. The purpose of these exercises is, therefore, somewhat different from that of other sets; in doing them, the student should constantly keep two questions in mind: (a) What would I do if this were a situation for which my background would qualify me? and (b) What would my reaction be if I were the recipient of this letter?

1. Assume that you have your résumé prepared and that the following advertisements ask for just one qualification—the background that you have. How would you vary the letter to accompany your résumé in each instance?

   a. A position which calls for at least four days of travel each week.

   b. An advertisement which insists that "applicants apply by mail only; those who apply will be judged on the originality of their letters and their statements about what salary is required."

   c. A position with an international oil company which requires that you spend two 2-year periods in a foreign country with a 6-month leave at home at full salary after each 2-year stint abroad.

   d. An ad by an executive who says, "I'm tough; I expect results; but if you qualify, you will receive top salary and an assured future. Write to Box 9781, *The Times*."

   e. You are most interested in finding employment in California because of any of these reasons: the climate; the opportunity for some year-round sports; your fiancé or fiancée lives there; you want to get away from home. The nearest branch office of the company to which you apply is in New York City, 750 miles from your home. You must, therefore, write to the central office in Los Angeles with the purpose of being interviewed in New York City.

2. After reading each of the following letters from the viewpoint of the employer, would you grant the writer's request for an interview? Give reasons.

   a.

   > You know, Mr. Jones, I read one of your company publications and I decided, "That's the place for me."
   >
   > Your location, your type of business, and your educational opportunities all mesh with what I've been doing and what I hope to do, as my résumé shows.
   >
   > May I come to see you? I'll call your secretary for an interview at your convenience.
   >
   > *Evan C. Evans*
   > Evan C. Evans

b.

Gentlemen:

I know that this is the time of year when a lot of graduates hope to see you.

But I hope you'll grant me the chance because my educational background (shown on my résumé) exactly fits what I think are your needs.

It will take only 15 minutes of your time to find out. Will you let me know when it will be convenient? Thank you very much.

Sincerely yours,

c.

Dear Mr. Glore:

Ever hear the gag about the student who asked his English teacher, "When you want to get ahead in the world is it what you know or who you know?" and she answered, "It's neither—it's whom you know."

A different way of beginning an application letter, isn't it? And it's intentional—because I'm a different kind of person from the ordinary run of jobseekers.

If you'll spend a minute or two looking at my résumé, you'll see that I've had a lot of good experience for a position in your sales department. I work well with other people and I can produce results.

Is it worth a few minutes of your time to find out about me in an interview? It may be of mutual benefit to both of us.

Very truly yours,

d.

Dear Sir:

I should like very much to have you consider me for a position in your advertising department which a friend of mine who works for your company has told me will be available next month.

Although I have not had much experience in advertising, I have taken such courses in college as would best prepare me to do work along these lines. My major in college was English and I have also taken a lot of psychology, which some people think should be useful.

Although I realize that advertising men such as you do not regard work on college papers as very valuable, the writer has spent three years on the business staff of our paper and was elected business manager in the senior year. The details of my record are enclosed.

I shall hope to hear from you in the event there is an opening with your company.

Sincerely yours,

e.

Dear Mr. Ellis:

I think you'll agree that I'm unusual because:

   I completed a four-year college course in three years.

   I had three short stories published in national magazines while I was an undergraduate.

   My major interest was in dramatics and I was president of the Thespian Society.

Now, I'm interested in working for your advertising agency because:

I like to write.
Meeting people is my forte.
I know that you can use original ideas, and I have them.

You'll find all the details on the enclosed résumé. May I have an interview?

Sincerely yours,

3.   Yesterday you had an interview with Mr. F. E. Hammer, Personnel Director, The Blanco Manufacturing Company, in a city where you want to work. In fact, everything about the company, the city, and the educational opportunities available at the City University has made you decide that "This is the job for me." Unfortunately, in the course of your interview, Mr. Hammer said, "We were really looking for a person with a little more actual business experience than you have had."

Write the follow-up letter you would use in these circumstances.

4.   What changes would you make in these follow-up letters:

a.

Dear Mr. Grimm:

I've read the brochure about your company, and I found it very interesting indeed. Do you think it would be possible for me to come back and talk to you about it? I hope so, because I have several questions I want answered.

Sincerely,

b.

Dear Mr. Grimm:

Our brief talk yesterday left me in a daze.

I finally have found the company I want to work for! All the girls in the secretarial section and Mrs. Orange who supervises it were *so* courteous to me.

It was good of you to see me. When will I know about the job?

Cordially yours,

c.

Dear Mr. Grimm:

I'm very grateful to you for giving me the chance to talk with you yesterday, and I want you to know that I was most favorably impressed by the two-day Forum the officers of your company put on for the group of potential employees from various colleges. I have decided that if Blankco offers me a job, I will accept it—and that decision is probably the most sincere evidence I can offer of my appreciation for what you did for me.

Sincerely yours,

d.

Dear Mr. Grimm:

I've read the brochure you gave me about the company and I liked it very much. As you said, "It's just a little thing we prepared," but it really helps.

Thanks for seeing me—and I hope I'll be seeing you again soon.

Yours,

e.

> Dear Mr. Grimm:
>
> As I sat in your office during our interview yesterday, I certainly realized what a busy man you are. It seemed to me that the whole organization revolved around you because so many people were waiting to see you and your telephone rang so often.
>
> That's why I hope you will give favorable consideration to my application for a position as your secretary because I thrive on hard work, and I like to be where there are lots of people and plenty of activity.
>
> Sincerely yours,

5. Criticize these opening paragraphs from application letters:
   a. You state in your ad in this morning's *News* that you need a salesman familiar with electrical appliances. Without question, I am the man you've been looking for.
   b. I regret taking up your time this way because I know that you are a very busy man. The fact is that I need work badly, and I've been hoping that you might help me.
   c. As a personnel man, you certainly know how hard it is to find good sales correspondents. You must have learned that years are required to develop an employee who can write letters which bring results. That's why I want you to look over my qualifications.
   d. If you happen to be adding any new men to your college training group, I would appreciate it greatly if you would be so kind as to consider my qualifications.
   e. I saw your advertisement for a young business-school graduate in this morning's *News*, and, as I read it, I realized that I had many of the qualifications you want. And so I am making this application for the position.

6. What changes would you recommend in these closing paragraphs from application letters?
   a. I must apologize for having taken so much of your time with this letter, but you probably know how difficult it is for inexperienced young people to get started in business. And, of course, the only way for us to get started is by writing letters. I hope you will write me and tell me to come in to see you.
   b. After looking over my qualifications, I am sure that you will want to talk to me. I can come in any time you say. Thanking you in advance for the interview, I am
   c. If you are hiring new men now, I do hope you will let me talk to you. Or if you don't need anyone now, would you please keep my letter on file in the event that you may need someone in the future?
   d. In this letter, I've outlined the reasons why I need work so badly. If you will give me a chance to talk with you, I can tell you about these reasons in greater detail. May I have an interview?
   e. Thanking you in advance for the consideration that you have given in reading this letter, the writer hopes to hear from you soon.

7. Would you be willing to use the equivalent (adapted to your qualifications) of the following letters? Or are they ineffective and unsuitable as application letters?

a.

Gentlemen:

I've read all the textbooks about

Send a letter and a résumé
Follow it up a few days after the interview
Put your best foot forward
Tell the company what you have to offer

Well, I'm not doing any of these things . . . no polite letter . . . no résumé . . . no sales talk.

Instead, I believe you and I should talk. You're smart enough to know whether you want to hire me when you see me . . . and I hope I'm smart enough to know whether I want to work for you.

Seems fair enough, doesn't it? If you think so, just let me know when I can see you and I'll be there.

Yours,

b.

Dear Mr. Smith:

Are you looking for a person

. . . who has had college courses in business correspondence, English, mathematics, French, German, biology, shorthand, and typing?

. . . who has a secretarial background supplemented by considerable practice in industrial dictation, transcribing and filing?

. . . who is interested in fostering good morale among associates by trying to see things from their point of view?

. . . who has initiative and enthusiasm and will carry an assignment through to completion?

. . . who has supplemented her knowledge of a subject by further study when beginning a new position?

If these are questions you have been thinking about, you may find the answers on the next page, which gives my complete record and references.

Will you please write me at 2021 Blank Street, Centerville, 44106 or call me at 315-3129 at my expense, giving the time I may talk with you about how I may assist you? So that you may be the judge, I shall welcome an opportunity to demonstrate my qualifications.

Yours very truly,

8. You have been offered positions in two different companies—A and B—and have finally made up your mind to accept the offer of company A, because it gives you the opportunity to take a special six-month training course. Yet there is a possibility that some time in the future you may wish to seek employment with company B, which is engaged in the same general line of business. Write a tactful letter declining company B's offer.

PART FOUR

THE REPORT AND MEMORANDUM

If you are planning a career in business or industry, six words—or their equivalent—are an inevitable part of your future: "Give me a report on that." The report has become an essential means of business communication; even the facetious statement that "It takes a ton of paper to produce a ton of product in today's business" is an acknowledgment of the importance of reports.

The report-writing function of business will unquestionably increase in importance. As companies grow larger and employ more people, the number of reports required to maintain communication increases not in an arithmetical progression of 1, 2, 3, 4, but more nearly in a geometrical progression of 2, 4, 8, 16. Added to increasing size is increasing distance, resulting from the trend toward widely separated plants and agencies and creating an attendant need for better communication through reports. Businessmen even estimate an employee's status in the organization by saying "He reports directly to the vice-president" or "He reports to the sales manager."

The ability to write effective reports is, therefore, one of the most useful skills you can acquire for a career in business. In Part 1 we discussed business writing as a demonstration of your ability. To a large degree, you will be judged solely on the basis of the reports you write, often by key personnel who have no other contact with you. Whether you view report-writing assignments as an opportunity or an ordeal will depend largely on how well you can learn the techniques of report writing, for we like to do the things we do well. That is why most of the complaints about the need to write reports in business come from employees who can't write them effectively. Business badly needs people who can write clear, concise, accurate, and readable reports, and if you can fill this need, you'll go far. It is no exaggeration to say that in modern business a man is known by the reports he writes.

Or course, how successful you are in demonstrating your ability depends on how well you perceive and serve the needs of your readers. In the next chapter we will discuss the reader's purposes in requesting a report, and the succeeding chapters will deal with how to serve those purposes. This introduction will tell you, in general terms, what you should know about reports.

What is a report? This is a surprisingly difficult question to answer. Etymologically, we can derive the word from its Latin sources: *portare*, "to carry" (as in *portable*, *transport*, and *export*), and the prefix *re*, "back" or "again." Thus, a report is something which carries information back or again, although this definition is none too precise. We might also define it by example, citing such types of reports as progress reports, research reports, periodic reports, and a host of others. If time were our criterion, we could list weekly, monthly, quarterly, and annual reports; or, if we give our readers top billing, we would name reports to stockholders, directors, and management. All this terminology may seem confusing, but it merely reflects the actual usage of the word *report* in modern business. In fact, one basic thing to remember about the word, as you will hear it used in your business career, is that it means a great many things to a great many people.

More often than not, the terminology of business and industry stems more from local usage and company practice than from any overall and consistent system of classification; the Sales Report of one company, for example, may be the Performance Analysis Report of another. When you are asked to write a report, you will, therefore, have to apply a very loosely used word to a particular purpose, business, and reader. Your supervisor may say "Give me a report on that by tomorrow," and mean what is often called a memorandum. In fact, we might informally define a report as a memo in full dress, for the line of demarcation between the long memorandum and the report is very thin. If, on the other hand, he says "I wish you'd spend the next week at the Bartlesville substation and give me a report on why production fell off there last month," you ought to know that he expects something more comprehensive than he wanted in the first instruction. And, just as obviously, your report on the Bartlesville situation will differ from the report made after three years' study by 52 engineers on "The Water Needs of Blank City for the Next Twenty-five Years." The trend in business, however, is to use short report forms more frequently and to make them less formal; this brevity and informality have been achieved by limiting the scope of reports to a single definite subject and by breaking complex or broad subjects into clearly defined reportable elements.

Probably the best way to define a report is in terms of what it *does*. Its purpose, generally, is to provide managers with information on the basis of which they can decide or act. Professor C. A. Brown, chairman of the English department of the General Motors Institute, defined a report in this way:

> We say it as simply as we possibly can, and that is, that a report is a communication from someone who has information to someone who wants to use that information. The report may be elaborately formal, it may be a letter, or in a great many organizations it is simply a memorandum, but it is always planned for use.

The usefulness of your reports is what you must constantly keep in mind. Whether a report is good or bad generally boils down to how useful it is to its readers. Suppose the sales manager of a manufacturing company is considering adding a new product to his line. He wants to know how well it would sell and how it should be priced. He asks his salesmen, or perhaps a market research staff, for reports that will help him answer these questions. He needs to know the cost of production and whether the company has the necessary manufacturing facilities. He asks production people for reports which answer these questions. The decision as to whether to manufacture and sell the product will be based on the reports. When production begins, reports will tell the sales and production managers whether the costs are within the expectations and whether the quantity and quality are satisfactory. Reports will tell the sales manager whether sales are up to expectations, whether competition has appeared unexpectedly, whether anticipated prices can be maintained. On the basis of these later reports, plans may be changed, new research undertaken, or production or sales methods changed. A great many reports will have been written, probably by many people. Each report will have had a specific purpose or set of purposes to serve; each will have been expected to enable its readers to do or to decide something. Whether or not a particular report was successful will have depended largely on how well the writer understood the use his readers expected to make of it.

At this point you may still wonder what is unique about a report, what makes it differ from a letter or memorandum. The answer will vary from company to company and even from businessman to businessman. But it is probably safe to say that, in general, a report, as "a communication from someone who has information to someone who wants to use that information," is marked by three characteristics:

1. It is preceded by considerable investigation or research.
2. It tends to be longer, more complex, and more detailed than the letter or memo.
3. Its scope requires more careful analysis and organization than the shorter forms of business communications.

The thoughtful reader may properly ask why reports, like letters, cannot be divided into types. After all, we have analyzed letters by types: *credit, inquiry, application,* and *sales.* Why not a similar analysis of business reports? The answer is that actual business practice makes such an analysis unrealistic. Our analysis of letters parallels actual business organization, which, if it is of considerable size, divides its functions into such units as a credit department, a sales department, and a personnel department, to mention a few. Each of these units has a reasonably precise function in letter writing.

In report writing, the function tends either to be spread around so that "everybody writes reports or memos" or to be so specialized that time would be wasted discussing it. For example, a prime function of business is getting out an annual report to shareholders, a function, incidentally, in which business has shown a remarkable degree of improvement over the past ten years. How are such reports "written"? Normally, everybody gets into the act. Each department, division, or unit submits a report on its annual activities. Within each department, each section head has probably written a report about his section's activities. His reports, based on reports from individuals in his section, are incorporated into the department's report; the departmental reports go up the line to the division heads, the executive staff members, or the vice-presidents. They then go to the president or the chairman of the board, who presumably "writes" the report for the stockholders. All along the line, material has been compressed, condensed, or deleted. This is a reasonably accurate account of the way reports ascend the business pyramid, with the important additional statement that at some point all this mass of information will generally be turned over to a specialist—to a committee, to the public relations office, to one person, or to an advertising agency—for *writing*.

The report function of modern business, then, is both so diffused and so specialized that it would be totally unrealistic to approach it from the same basis as the function of correspondence, which is reasonably clear-cut. Your business career will unquestionably involve a myriad of reporting situations; you will write reports directly to one other person, reports to groups, reports that are passed up or down through several levels of authority, reports for other people to sign, reports written with other people, reports concisely digesting other reports, and so on, ad infinitum. In this welter of types, kinds, and occasions, the only realistic preparation you can make is to learn the problems and principles of good report writing and apply them to the specific on-the-job situations which you encounter.

In preparing to do this, you should heed the importance which business executives almost unanimously attach to the ability to write effective reports. Equally significant is their increasing complaint that "too many of our recent college graduates come to us from college with no ability to express themselves logically. They have never been taught to size up a situation or a problem and to direct their report to a concise discussion of the problem, their results, and their conclusions in a readable form." As one executive has said, "The ability to write clear memos and reports lies at the foundation of all other management skills. And this ability becomes more important as one advances to more responsible managerial activities. In an age of rapidly advancing technology and increased specialization, preparation in writing reports is certainly one of the most basic aspects of education."

CHAPTER 13

THE REPORT-WRITING PROCESS — A SPECIFIC EXAMPLE

Because the process of preparing a report or a long memorandum involves several steps in gathering, organizing, and presenting pertinent material, we are going to use this chapter for a preliminary view of the entire procedure. Naturally, individual memos and reports must be adapted to such specific conditions as, for example, whether the writer initiates the report or memo or responds to a request, or whether reports are regularly circulated to groups or are read only by the individual chiefly concerned with the problem. Such on-the-job conditions affect the form, the organization, and even the style of reports and long memos. At the outset, however, the important fact to remember is that once you understand the basic principles governing effective reports and memos, you can readily adapt these principles to differing requirements and conditions.

To that end, we will follow a report-writing situation through its various stages—from the moment a problem first materializes to the gathering of necessary information and finally to the writing of the report incorporating solutions to the problem. Each of these steps in report writing will be discussed in greater detail in subsequent chapters; our central purpose here is to show *by specific example* how you can respond effectively to the challenge labeled ". . . So you have to write a report." The topic we have selected is one that most college students are familiar with.

From now on, you are to identify yourself as Jupiter Doe, a member of the student council of Quidnunc College, with an enrollment of 1,000 students equally divided between males and females. Each of the 1,000 full-time students takes five courses; and 750 students in Quidnunc's Evening Divisions each take one course. You and the ten other students elected to the student council are, in the council's charter, "responsible for bringing student problems and possible solutions to the attention of the college administration so that action may be taken promptly whenever it is warranted in the judgment of the appropriate member of the administration."

The council's first meeting of the second semester occurs on February 24, one and a half weeks after classes have started. The president opens the meeting by saying, "We have had a lot of complaints from students because their grades for the first semester were late. The seniors particularly are upset because they need their transcripts to apply to graduate schools or for job interviews." A rambling, unorganized discussion ensues; the following excerpts may or may not be relevant to the president's opening comments:

"I hear that the real reason grades are always late is that the Dean and the Registrar don't like each other and they won't cooperate on anything."

"What difference does it make whether we get grades two weeks after exams end? I don't think it's important."

"Who's responsible for getting grades out?" (To this the "answers" include the Dean of Students, the Dean of the Faculty, and the President.)

"The real cause of the trouble is that they scheduled all the English exams on the last three days of the exam period. Somebody goofed, because those exams take longer to grade than any others."

"I heard the real reason is that a lot of the profs take off for Florida right after their last exam and mail their grades in."

"What do these people who are complaining mean by "late"? The last day of exams was January 31 and I got my grades at home on February 10. I don't think that's bad." (An informal poll of the council on this point shows that grades were received from 9 to 15 days after the end of the examination period.)

"There's no excuse for such lateness. They have only 5,750 grades to record, and they should be able to get them processed and mailed two days after the student takes his last exam."

"The trouble probably is that they do Evening Division grades first. Full-time undergraduates always come last at Quidnunc."

"I heard it was because they don't hire enough help. They've got five girls in the office and they spend most of their time talking to students they know."

"My brother's at Quidproquo University, where they use a computer for grades. Last semester he got his grades at home three days after he took his last exam. The only trouble was that his roommate got 27 grade cards, none of which belonged to him, and he had to pay 27 cents extra postage on the envelope they sent him. Our system at Quidnunc may be slower but it's better."

"We ought to find out what other colleges do about grades. Maybe Quidnunc should go to a computer."

"The real headache from getting grades late is that a lot of us couldn't plan our second-semester courses until we knew whether we flunked something the first semester. I found out just this week that I flunked calculus and have to repeat it, so my whole schedule had to be changed."

"I heard that the Registrar won't send out a single grade card until he sends them out to all students."

The council president finally terminates the discussion by saying, "It looks as if we have a problem on which the student council should act. I'm therefore appointing Jupiter Doe to find out what causes it and to prepare a report or memo with recommendations we can send on to the college president. Let's have the written report for our meeting on April 10."

In your role of Jupiter Doe, you make the traditional response to all report-writing assignments by groaning; nevertheless, this being the first such assignment you've ever done, you decide that you're going to learn as much as you can from the experience. To do so, you write across the top of the first page of your notebook THINGS TO REMEMBER ABOUT WRITING A REPORT.

PREPARING TO WRITE THE REPORT

Since you took no notes at the council meeting, forgot the exact words of the president's assignment, and had to ask the secretary and several other council members to reconstruct what had been said, you make your first entry in your notebook the next day:

TAKE ADEQUATE NOTES

You look over the reconstructed notes about the meeting, searching for clues as to the best method of getting material for your report. Wisely you decide that you will discard anything which doesn't relate to the purpose of your report—in this instance, (1) to find out whether grades were late, and if so, why; and (2) to recommend ways in which lateness of grade reporting can be avoided in the future. You make your second entry in your notebook:

DECIDE ON THE PURPOSE OF YOUR REPORT AS SOON AS POSSIBLE

As you look at your own statement of purpose, it occurs to you that the word "late" was tossed around rather loosely in the council meeting. What exactly does it mean in the context of this problem? Some students were apparently completely satisfied with the timing of their grade reports; others considered them "late" or "very late." Into your notebook, because of the elusive word, goes another admonition:

DEFINE IMPORTANT WORDS OR TERMS

Finally, in glancing through the excerpts from the council meeting, you find comments like:

I heard the real reason grades are late is that the Dean and Registrar hate each other . . .

. . . the reason is a lot of profs take off for Florida after their last exam and mail their grades in.

. . . the trouble is they scheduled all the English exams on the last three days, and they take longer to grade than any other subject.

Who's responsible for getting the grades out?

You realize that the first statement belongs in the realm of opinion, hearsay, conjecture, assumption; the last three can be verified by investigation. *Were* all exams in English scheduled on the last three days? *Who* actually has final responsibility for getting grades out? One more injunction goes into your notebook:

SEPARATE FACT FROM OPINION, VERIFIABLE ASSUMPTIONS FROM SHEER
CONJECTURE

Now, with these four bits of learning behind you, you start examining what you have thus far, what you need to find out, and how you will find out. You jot down the results:

Forget all rumors about the Dean and the Registrar disliking each other; about English profs in Florida; about girls in office gossiping with students; about "my brother at Quidproquo."

Find out these things:
1. Do other schools get grades out faster? How?
2. Has Quidnunc ever considered using computerized grade reports? If so, why aren't they used?
3. Does the scheduling by subject matter (i.e., English exams) affect the speed of reporting grades?

All of this, of course, adds up to one action—you must interview the official who is responsible for reporting grades and collect relevant facts from other sources.

GATHERING THE INFORMATION

Before you interview the Registrar, who *is* responsible for recording, transmitting, and maintaining all academic records at Quidnunc, you use what you learned in an Elementary Logic course: in your subject for investigation you have a known *effect* (lateness of grade reporting) and you must reason your way back to the *causes(s)* which produced it. You list all the causes you can possibly think of:

> Lateness of reporting grades could be caused by:
>> Insufficient help in the Recorder's Office
>> Faculty not reporting grades on time
>> Obsolete methods—replace by computer?
>> Inefficient scheduling of final exams—English exam last?
>> Grades for Evening Division interfere with efficient reporting of undergraduate grades?
>> Any other causes?

You write each of these at the top of a 3 x 5 card and go off for your interview with the Registrar prepared to take notes on what he says about these possible causes. You also carry another card on which you have written, "What do we mean by 'late'?" You wonder whether, because of his job, the Registrar may not be a bit defensive and, perhaps, a rather prejudiced source of information; you write yourself one more admonition:

MAKE SURE SOURCES OF INFORMATION ARE UNBIASED

The Registrar seems to be a model of an efficient administrator; his desk holds a four-foot shelf of black loose-leaf notebooks, carefully labeled, into which he seems to dive for answers to your questions. When you tell him about the council's investigation and the possibility that seniors will send a petition about late grades to the President, he merely laughs and says, "My name has always been Mudd"—which, incredibly, it is. From Mr. Mudd, you get the following information recorded on your cards:

> This year grades were mailed on Feb. 9; records going back to 1945 show the average time between the end of the examination period and mailing is eight days. This time interval is checked by Mr. Mudd, who inserts cards to 25 people, including himself, all of whom report when they receive them.

> Mr. Mudd thinks the help in his office is adequate; this year, because two of his regular girls were ill, he brought in three temporary replacements.

> Grades for Evening Division students are sent out one week after all undergraduate grades have been mailed.

An article in *the Bulletin* of the Association of University Registrars for February, 1968 shows that "the average time for reporting grades in colleges of approximately 1,000 is seven days between the end of the examination period and the student receiving his grades."

This year English examinations *were* scheduled in the last three days, but this was done at the request of the head of the English department who wanted to attend a meeting during the early part of the examination period. "If I had my way, I would never do it again," Mr. Mudd says. "But under college rules, I have to comply with the faculty's wishes wherever I can." Members of the English department were one day late in getting their grades to the Registrar's office.

Grades for students who fail one or more courses are sent by faculty members directly to the office of Dr. Leonard E. Holcomb, Dean of the Faculty, so that a letter can be addressed to the student asking him to come in for an interview at a specific time. The names and grades of these students are then sent from the Dean's office to the Registrar's office. "It delays us about two days," Mr. Mudd says, "because normally about 125 or 130 students fail one or more courses."

Among the opinions expressed by Mr. Mudd were the following:

"As long as I'm registrar, we'll never use computerized grades. They're too impersonal for a college this size, and I've read somewhere that they are too costly for use in colleges where the enrollment is under 5,000 students.

"I believe all students should have their grades mailed at the same time. I don't favor putting senior examinations in the first five days and then mailing their grades out first. All they would do is go home the minute their last exam is finished. Furthermore, it's more efficient for my office to handle all grades at the same time. And the only fair way to treat students is for all freshmen, sophomores, juniors, and seniors to get grades simultaneously."

From your interview with Mr. Mudd, you go on to the office of Dr. Holcomb, the Dean of the Faculty, where you talk with Euclid Fourier, a teaching assistant in the mathematics department who spends half of his time assisting Dr. Holcomb with interviews. He tells you that neither Dr. Holcomb nor Mr. Mudd takes the student council's investigation of grade reporting very seriously because they believe that it reflects the views of only a small minority of students. He also tells you that no friction exists between the Dean's and the Registrar's offices, although Dean Holcomb would prefer to have senior grades sent first, grades of failures next (with a letter setting up an interview with the Dean), and then grades of freshmen, sophomores, and juniors in that order. "Thus far the Dean has deferred to Mr. Mudd's belief that it's faster and fairer to send out all grades at the same time," says Fourier. "The Dean believes the Registrar's office should use the sole criterion of efficiency, and for that reason he didn't approve of the English department having its exams placed last this year. Dr. Holcomb will give Mudd all the power he needs to schedule exams any way he wants to as long as it gets grades out more promptly."

The major fact you learn from Fourier is that there is a definite possibility that the mathematics department will obtain shared time on a computer next year "if a governmental agency acts favorably upon one of the department's research proposals." According to Fourier, this time on the computer could be used for grade recording and reporting "at what would be a reasonable cost."

With this mixture of fact, opinion, and authoritative evidence, you can at least eliminate such conjectures as "slowness in reporting grades is caused by inefficient help in the Registrar's office" or by "friction between the Dean and the Registrar." Now you must decide how to find answers to two nagging questions:

1. Do most students really believe that there is a problem of "late reporting" of grades, or do complaints to the student council represent a small minority, as Dean Holcomb and Mr. Mudd believe?

2. What criterion or definition for "late" can be used? Shall it be the seven-day average from the end of exams to students receiving grades, reported in the bulletin of the Association of University Registrars? Quidnunc's average of eight days from the end of exams to the grades being mailed? Or something different?

Wisely, you decide that if Quidnunc students think there is a problem, that very fact attests to the existence of a problem—although you realize that it may be a problem of a different nature, such as bad communication in informing students of the problems of reporting grades. The way to proceed, therefore, is to find out how many students think there is a problem and what most of them would consider "lateness" in reporting grades. To that end, you prepare a questionnaire to go to all Quidnunc students (see Chapter 7, Letters of Inquiry) which contains these four parts:

1. My class is (check one)

Freshman	_____
Sophomore	_____
Junior	_____
Senior	_____

2. Taking into account the practical necessities of recording grades, which of the following number of days *after the final day of examinations* would you reasonably expect to get your grades at your home address:

4–6 days	_____
6–8 days	_____
8–10 days	_____
10–12 days	_____
12–14 days	_____

3. Would you have any opinion or reaction if Quidnunc were to send you your grades on computerized cards:

No opinion _____

Favorable _____

Unfavorable _____

4. If you have had any inconvenience or any problems because of what you considered slowness in grade recording and reporting, state what it was in the space below:

When the returns are in and tabulated, you have these results:

Percent of Class Answering		When Grades Are Expected	Computerized Grades
Fresh.	87	4–6 days (56% of those answering)	Favorable (90% of answers)
Soph.	46	10–12 days (60% of those answering)	No opinion (62% of answers)
Juniors	54	6–8 days (72% of those answering)	Favorable (60% of answers)
Seniors	92	6–8 days (90% of those answering)	Favorable (90% of answers)

Your fourth question asking them to state inconvenience because of slowness in grade reporting was apparently a poor one, because it brought forth a number of snide attempts at humor: "I suffered considerable inconvenience when my parents heard I'd flunked two subjects" and "My grades got there *too* fast— before I got home my parents had read them." Only seniors responded directly: 85 percent of them classified the inconvenience as needing transcripts for graduate school or for getting a job.

With this information you do three things for your report:

1. "Late" means for the majority of students receiving grades at home more than 8 days after the final day of examinations. This year they were *mailed* 9 days after that day.
2. The focus of the problem seems to be the senior class, where seniors need grades for a practical reason: to get records for admittance to graduate school or for a job. Freshmen are eager to know grades but lack the practical need other than to satisfy their curiosity.
3. A computerized grade system is overwhelmingly favored, but the response, you now realize, is probably wishful thinking, because your question was not accurately phrased. Students apparently jumped to the conclusion that computerization would speed up the grade process, which is a possibility but not necessarily a fact. Suppose computerization were slower or about the same as the present system? On the basis of your experience with questions 3 and 4 of your questionnaire you add another admonition to yourself:

MAKE CERTAIN THAT ALL QUESTIONS ARE ACCURATELY PHRASED TO ASSURE A RELEVANT RESPONSE

ORGANIZING THE MATERIAL

The time has now come to take stock of the material you have, to start organizing it, and to prepare to write the report, which is due one week from now on April 10. You get a bit panicky at the deadline and add the warning that every report writer knows:

NEXT TIME, ALLOW MORE TIME FOR ORGANIZING AND WRITING

As if to avoid noticing that big 10 which you have circled on the calendar for April, your mind drifts off to what might have been: I shouldn't have wasted so much time on that questionnaire. . . . Maybe I should have polled the faculty. . . . I ought to have gotten a lot more information. . . . I should have read a couple of books on how to do a report. . . . I should have told the student council at the March meeting that there isn't a problem. . . . I should have taken a lot more time. . . .

Abruptly, you say farewell to such wishful thinking about what-might-have-been, and you decide two things:

1. I've spent nearly six weeks on this subject, so I must know more about it than the other council members.
2. I'll have to use the material I've got, because a report has to be written, and I can't go on forever accumulating more information.

Then you go to work by writing out three questions:

1. Is there or is there not a problem of grades being reported late?
2. What causes the problem (if indeed it exists)?
3. What is the best way to solve it?

As you look back over your research and leaf through your notes, the answers to these questions *seem* to be:

1. There is a problem, but it's a different one from what the council thought. It's confined chiefly to seniors and freshmen, and because those two groups *think* there is a problem, it requires solving.
2. The problem is caused by any or all of the following: (Here you decide to list every possibility you can think of and mark them "yes," "no," or "maybe" on the basis of what you have found out.)

    The Dean and the Registrar dislike each other and won't cooperate on getting grades out. (*No*)

    A lot of professors go off to Florida, and that's why grades are late. (*No*)

All English exams were scheduled on the last three days. (*Yes*)

Insufficient help to record grades. (*Maybe*)

Methods are obsolete. (*Maybe*)

Replacement by computerized grades. (*Maybe*)

Delay in Dean Holcomb's office because he wants to have appointments with those who fail courses. (*Maybe*, but it affects only a minority of students.)

Mr. Mudd's insistence that all grades be mailed at exactly the same time. (*Maybe*)

Quidnunc's failure to use methods of other colleges. (*Maybe*, but the report of the Association of College Registrars doesn't show that Quidnunc is very much slower than others.)

Evening Division grades slow down reporting of undergraduate grades. (*No*)

3.   Here are all the solutions you can think of to anything marked "yes" or "maybe":

Schedule English exams first.

Get more help, temporary or otherwise, to record grades.

So far as you know, Mr. Mudd's methods are reasonably efficient, although he is prejudiced against the use of a computer and says he won't use one. Nevertheless, the possibility of using the new computer to be acquired by the math department should be thoroughly investigated.

Dean Holcomb's office could just as well use carbon copies of flunkers' grades while the originals go direct from the Registrar's office.

Find out what other colleges of similar size and character to Quidnunc are doing.

You now have what you consider a reasonable method of arranging your material into three parts:

An *Introduction:* What the Problem Is

A *Body:* Causes of the Problem

A *Conclusion:* Recommended Solutions for the Problem

On these three pegs, you think you will be able to hang the various materials you have gathered.

WRITING THE REPORT

Mistakenly, you try to put your material into its final form at once. To your chagrin, you soon learn that you can't do an effective job of arranging all your material in logical sequence while you try at the same time to polish the way you express it. You give up on this attempt to do too many things at once and add this note to your list:

DON'T TRY TO WRITE THE FINAL VERSION OF THE REPORT IN YOUR FIRST ATTEMPT

Next day, you simply put down all the facts, reasoning, explanations, and definitions in appropriate and logical sequence, paying minimum attention to the way they are expressed. Your sole purpose is *to get your ideas, facts, and conclusions down on paper* so that you can check to establish logical relationships among them. On the hunch—and it's a good one—that it will be easier to delete material rather than to add it during revisions, you include material whenever you are in doubt about it.

The following day you work on form and style, reading your first draft as if you had never seen it before. You find a paragraph or two which are so illogical in sequence that you wonder how you could have arranged them that way the day before. You find that by linking ideas and paragraphs you make your report more readable; and you realize what English teachers have told you for years, that the paragraphing is the basic method of presenting information in readable units. When each paragraph develops your thought in a logical way and is linked to the paragraph preceding it or following it, smooth and readable writing results.

By this process of waiting, at least overnight, to do your revising, you find that it is much easier to identify and correct the errors in the rough draft. You have learned two things by this process:

WRITE A FIRST DRAFT AND LET IT AGE AT LEAST OVERNIGHT

REVISE IT BY READING IT AS IF YOU, LIKE THE READER, HAVE NEVER SEEN IT BEFORE

THE REPORT

Here is "your" report, which you decide is not as good as you had hoped it would be—but that's a reaction all report writers share. Nonetheless, it does seem to you to be sufficiently factual and logical that the Quidnunc administration can take action on it, once the student council sends copies to the appropriate administrators. For you, therefore, the report has achieved its purpose.

(At the end of this chapter, the usual exercises have been supplemented by questions about the effectiveness of this report. Students should, therefore, read the report carefully to determine what changes they might make in it and whether the President and Dean Holcomb and Mr. Mudd, who are the responsible administrators, should act favorably on its recommendations after it is transmitted to them by the student council.)

A Report

on

The Reporting of Grades for Courses at Quidnunc College

Prepared

for

The Student Council

by

Jupiter G. Doe

April 10, 1971

Background

At its meeting on February 24, 1971, the Student Council authorized a study of the procedures and practices related to the recording and sending out of semester grades. It instructed Jupiter G. Doe to report on the results of the study he was to make as the Council's representative in accordance with the Council's authorization to "bring student
problems and possible solutions to the attention of the college administration. . . ."

The report which follows is based upon discussions with students, a questionnaire to
all full-time students, and interviews with the Registrar and representatives of the office
of the Dean of the Faculty. (A copy of the questionnaire with the returns tabulated on
it is attached to this report.) In every instance, the Council's representative received
complete cooperation and interest from the representatives of the Administration, all
of whom were helpful in solving the problem under study.

Statement of the Problem

From the beginning of the investigation for this report, it has become very clear that
considerable confusion exists among undergraduates at Quidnunc College as to the following questions:

Who is responsible for sending out final grades?
Does the system of reporting grades at Quidnunc operate as efficiently as that at other
colleges?
Does the administration contemplate using a system of computerized grade report-
ing?
Are grades reported late?

Student answers to the first three of these questions seem to be based on rumor and
hearsay, rather than fact. For that reason, a very important by-product of this report
could be to have administrative officials provide factual answers to these questions in
The Quidnunc Student. The Council makes this suggestion out of a conviction that a
well-informed student body is a student body with high morale.

The final question, "Are grades reported late?" which is the focus of this study, requires definition. What is meant by "late"? According to the results of the questionnaire,

grades are late when students do not receive them at their homes within 8 days after the close of final examinations. Here are the "expectations" of each of the four classes:

Freshmen	56% of 87%	answering expect grades in			4–6 days
Sophomores	60% of 46%	"	"	"	" 10–12 days
Juniors	72% of 54%	"	"	"	" 6–8 days
Seniors	90% of 92%	"	"	"	" 6–8 days

Since records provided by Mr. Mudd show that this semester's grades were *put in the mail* 9 days after the last examination on January 31, it may be concluded that the great majority of Quidnunc students other than sophomores considered their grades late in arriving. This fact is underscored by the undergraduates who are presumably most mature in their judgment and experience—the Juniors and Seniors—who expect grades within 8 days.

The Council considers it very important to record its belief that *if students think they have a problem, then a very real problem exists—and should be solved.* On that basis it believes that prompt action should be taken by appropriate administrative officials to ensure semester grades arriving at students' homes within 8 days after the close of examinations.

To maintain the long record of constructive approaches to student problems by both the Administration and the Council, we urge that serious consideration be given to the next two sections of this report, which deal with the causes and solutions of the problem of lateness in reporting final grades.

Causes

Relevant to our earlier statement that student opinions are based on hearsay and rumor is our finding that many students ascribe lateness in reporting grades to such factors as:

Lack of cooperation between various segments of the college administration
Absenteeism among the faculty at grade-reporting time
Necessity of reporting Evening Division grades at the same time as undergraduates'
Inefficiency of employees in the Registrar's office

Fortunately, our investigation shows that there is little or no basis for any of these so-called reasons.

A careful analysis does show, however, that one or more of the following causes may account for lateness in reporting grades:

1. Ineffective scheduling of such final exams as English, which require the longest time to grade. In the examinations for the last semester, all examinations for courses in English were held in the last three days. Certain members of the English department were therefore a day late in getting their grades to the Registrar.

2. Grades of approximately 150 students were delayed because they had to be sent from the Registrar's office to the Dean of the Faculty so that appointments could be made for those failing courses.

3. A prevailing policy of sending out all the grades of all students (except the 150 who fail) at the same time. This policy stems from a belief that it is "more fair to send all grades at the same time."

4. An unwillingness to consider computerized grades despite the fact that the mathematics department will soon have a computer and has three graduate students anxious to work on a system of accelerating the dissemination of grades.

It is significant to note that one or more of these causes is responsible for the fact that although a report by the American Association of College Registrars shows the average time for grades in students' hands is 7 days, Quidnunc's time is 9 days between the end of the examination period and the *mailing* of the grades.

We respectfully urge that the Administration give serious consideration to putting into effect the actions which have Student Council endorsement and which are discussed in the final section of this report.

Recommendations

On the basis of this study, the Student Council of Quidnunc College recommends that the following actions be taken, as soon as feasible, to speed up the recording and transmitting of course grades:

1. Schedule examinations on the basis of which require the longest time for grading. For example, examinations in English, History, Economics should be scheduled early; Mathematics, Statistics, Physics later.

2. Send carbon copies of grades of students failing courses to the Dean of the Faculty's office so that originals may be sent directly from the Registrar.

3. Establish a priority to replace the present policy of sending all grades of all students at the same time. This priority might well be as follows:

   a. Seniors, because they need semester grades for transcripts for graduate school and for job applications.

   b. Freshmen, who are receiving their first course grades at Quidnunc and are particularly eager to know how well they are doing in their first experience with the academic standards of the college.

   c. Sophomores and Juniors.

   This priority should be incorporated in the examination schedule so that all senior exams are included in the first five days and all freshman exams in the first seven days, with sophomore and junior examinations being spread over the entire two weeks.

   As soon as the examination schedule is completed by each of these classes, the Registrar should start sending out grades.

4. Investigate the possibility of using a computer for grade reporting, using the knowledge and the facilities of the mathematics department to determine the effectiveness of this method.

The Student Council believes that these four recommendations, if put into effect, will clear up much of the confusion and tardiness which characterize the present method of reporting grades.

EXERCISES

1. The following questions concerning Jupiter Doe's report are intended for classroom discussion or for written critiques of the report.
   a. Would this report be more effective in achieving its purpose if it were arranged with its recommendations placed first and the supporting material for the recommendations placed after them?
   b. From interviews and other sources in the investigation it seems reasonable to assume that Dean Holcomb will, in general, approve the recommendations in the report and Registrar Mudd will oppose some of them. Is the material in the report presented with sufficient persuasiveness to get serious consideration from Mr. Mudd, or will it alienate him? If the latter, what changes would you make in tone, phraseology, or organization to make the report more persuasive insofar as Mr. Mudd is concerned?
   c. After reading this report will Dean Holcomb and Mr. Mudd still think, "This complaint about grades is not to be taken very seriously," as Euclid Fourier told you? What changes would you incorporate in the report to make its subject seem more important to the administrators?
   d. Does the definition of "lateness" used in the report seem to be a reasonable one? If not, how would you define it for use in the report?
   e. Are the recommendations contained in the report sufficient to produce the desired effect of prompt reporting of grades? What additional information would you need if you were to write a sequel to this report urging that a computer be used for reporting grades?
2. Using what you have learned from the report-writing process discussed in this chapter, write a report on a parallel situation selecting from the following material whatever is appropriate for your purpose.

   You have been asked to submit a report on behalf of the Study Commission on the Academic Calendar at your institution. This commission, after four months of study, is proposing that the present academic calendar at your college or university should be revised. Its specific proposal, which eventually must be approved by a majority vote of the faculty and of the student council, is as follows:

   It is proposed that the present academic year calendar be revised to provide two fifteen-week semesters (4 months each) and one four-week (one-month) session. The first semester would be completed, including final examinations, before Christmas recess; the four-week session would be held in the month of January; the second fifteen-week semester would begin on or about the first of February. The first semester will be designated the Fall semester; the four-week session in January will be called the Intersession: the semester starting on or about February 1 will be called the Spring semester.

Academic credits for courses taken in the Fall and Spring semesters will remain the same as at present; no academic credit for the Intersession will be given, but each undergraduate must participate in at least two Intersessions during his four years of college and receive at least two grades of Pass since all Intersession activities are on a Pass/Fail basis. Tuition for Intersession activities is included as part of the year-long flat fee.

This proposal is known as the "4-1-4 Plan." You are to use any of the following material, supplemented by information from your own educational experience, to prepare a report whose purpose is to get this plan adopted. (If you disagree with it as educationally undesirable, you may write a "minority report" urging its rejection.) The material which follows ranges from fact to sheer speculation, from relevant arguments to highly prejudiced opinions. You are to select the relevant and the factual to persuade your readers that the 4-1-4 Plan would— or would not—have definite educational advantages over your present academic calendar.

Under the 4-1-4 Plan, the Fall semester must start early in September, before Labor Day in some years.

The use of time in January under the present system is inefficient.

The insertion of a short Intersession between semesters provides an opportunity for innovative, exciting, or frankly experimental learning experiences.

Shortcomings of the present system are all too apparent. After Thanksgiving vacation come two and a half weeks of instruction, followed by two weeks of Christmas vacation; then, with only two and a half weeks of classes after Christmas vacation, come final examinations. Thus education is chopped into bits and pieces with no continuity and little coherence.

"Final exams before Christmas? I use that vacation to write all my term papers that are due at the end of the semester in January."

"The Fall semester under 4-1-4 will be a horrible monotonous grind—fifteen weeks with just one two-day break at Thanksgiving."

The Study Commission on the Academic Calendar believes that the short Intersession provides great potential for a new kind of learning experience. Only a few of its potentials are:

a. An opportunity for the faculty to experiment with new courses, course content, or teaching methodology to find out, on a "pilot" basis, whether such experiments would work.

b. A chance to develop special topics from current events in seminars dealing with, for example, black power, pollution, urban decay.

c. An ideal time for remedial courses such as speed reading, or in-depth courses in languages to meet requirements for graduate study.

d. An opportunity for independent study in the laboratory or the library.

"This whole plan is merely part of the general permissiveness of our society designed to give students and faculty time off from the rigors of regular class-work."

The 4-1-4 Plan will enable sufficient time for the various activities of January, which are now conducted in hectic haste, to be carried on thoughtfully and thoroughly. The activities which would benefit are the grading of examinations and reporting of grades, registering for the Spring semester, and the counseling of students.

The student newspaper has editorialized, "The 4-1-4 Plan is a step in the right direction of freeing up academic requirements and of giving students a broader choice of courses in the Intersession. This newspaper warmly endorses the plan."

A letter to the editor of the student newspaper: "We pay very high tuition to be *taught*. The 4-1-4 Plan is an abdication of faculty responsibility for teaching; it permits students and faculty literally to do nothing from the end of Christmas vacation until February 1. It asks students to pay for something which they do not get."

A survey of five colleges or universities similar to yours who have used the 4-1-4 Plan for a year shows no conclusive results in terms of whether the plan is educationally an improvement.

An eminent educator has said: "Education consists of discipline, of repetition, of accumulating knowledge through a day-to-day regimen. Anything that breaks this discipline destroys the cumulative effect of learning."

The 4-1-4 Plan meets educational needs better than any other academic schedule. It maintains the formal semester-long courses and also provides the flexibility of short seminars, intensive independent study, and experimental, less institutionalized curricula.

Twenty-seven faculty members out of thirty polled informally objected to the plan; these twenty-seven strenuously objected to having to return to college before, or shortly after, Labor Day.

"You will have a wholesale exodus of all the students not participating in the Intersession right after Christmas, and we won't see them again until February," said the Dean of Students. "How can anyone object to the Christmas vacation 'interrupting' studies when this new plan interrupts them for six weeks?"

Professor J. X. Smith, who has just won the Best Teacher of the Year Award, commented, "Anything that breaks the present academic lockstep of requirements and credits is a step in the right direction. This Intersession will provide me with an opportunity to take 8 or 10 students to the Caribbean to study marine life at first hand."

An informal poll by the Interfraternity Council shows that 91 percent of the 700 students answering preferred the 4-1-4 Plan. Some of the reasons given were: it will give me a chance to goof off; I can earn money for six weeks; the whole house can go to Florida; I can look for a summer job; for once I'll have a chance to do some reading that isn't assigned; I can stay home and sleep; I believe in the Intersession because learning takes place outside the classroom for most students.

The chairman of the Study Commission on Academic Calendar discussing the Intersession in an interview with the editor of the school paper said, "Our students are mature enough to judge this new calendar solely on its educational merits. And when they do, they will endorse it almost unanimously."

The disadvantage of starting classes early in September under the 4-1-4 Plan is more than offset by the fact that all academic activities for the Fall semester are completed by Christmas vacation.

The amount of student interest at various universities in such things as "teach-ins," "experimental colleges," and "free universities" shows the need for incorporating some such device as the Intersession into the academic schedule.

The following comparison of how the present two-semester calendar and the 4-1-4 Plan would work in a typical year was distributed to members of the Study Commission on the Academic Calendar:

Two-Semester Plan	*4-1-4 Plan*
Fall Semester	
(Labor Day, Mon. Sept. 4)	
Registration, Sept. 15–17	Sept. 4–6
Classes begin Sept. 19	Sept. 7
Mid-term Grades Nov. 10	Oct. 27
Thanksgiving Nov. 23–26	Nov. 23–26
Start Final Exams Jan. 17	Dec. 14
Finish Final Exams Jan. 25	Dec. 22
(Christmas Recess Dec. 23–Jan. 3)	

Intersession, Jan. 4–31

Spring Semester

The academic schedule would be the same under both plans with Registration on Feb. 2–5, classes beginning Feb. 6, Spring recess April 1–8, final exams beginning on May 22 and ending May 31, with Commencement on June 5.

Here are the "ground rules" for the 4-1-4 Plan as agreed upon by the Study Commission on the Academic Calendar:

a. Each student and faculty member shall participate in the Intersession once every two years.

b. Course offerings will be planned jointly by students and faculty with the initiative for a course or program of independent study arising with either the faculty member or the students.

   c.   In each Intersession, there will be a limit of one course or.study program for each student and for each faculty member.

   d.   There will be minimum reliance on the mechanics of education such as regular times for courses to meet, regularly scheduled length and number of meetings, and formal papers and examinations. The intent of the Intersession is to place the student on his own responsibility but to make faculty guidance available when he needs it.

   e.   Tuition for the Intersession is not required, since it is included in the annual flat fee.

CHAPTER 14

PLANNING THE REPORT

In the preceding chapter we followed the entire process of producing a report by using a specific example. Implicit in Jupiter Doe's first attempt at report writing was a considerable waste of time and effort; his inexperience resulted in a search of several blind alleys and unnecessary waste motion because he did not decide what to do in the early stages of preparing the report.

As a matter of fact, students should recognize that no more disastrous "education" for report writing can be found than the way in which many students respond to assignments for term papers and long reports in college. All too often the customary procedure involves waiting until the night before the long paper is due and then, in a kind of frenzy matched by a last-minute Christmas shopper's desperation, attempting to transform scattered notes, miscellaneous clippings, and superficial "background material" into a report. This planless process results in thousands of words which fail to convey a single thought. Unfortunately, this same pattern of putting-off-to-the-last-minute prevails in the business as well as in the academic community—but here it becomes not only a wasteful but also a very expensive process.

The true professional in any human activity—whether it be playing football, investing money, or building a home—knows that at the outset *he must have a plan*. Similarly, the experienced writer confronted with a report-writing situation knows that his first step is to plan his time, his method, and his purpose before he does anything else. As his first step in writing a report, he should think his way through to the answers to four questions:

1. What is the purpose of this report?
2. How shall I define the problem?
3. How will I keep track of the material I collect for my report?
4. Who will read the report, and what use will he make of it?

We shall discuss each of these aspects of planning a report in the rest of this chapter.

PURPOSE IN REPORT WRITING

Time and time again, businessmen complain that the reports they receive do not tell them what they need to be told. Sometimes the fault lies with the reader himself: He has either given misleading instructions or has simply failed to indicate what purpose he expects the report to serve. Generally, however, it is the writer's fault. If he did not receive clear enough instructions, he should have gone back for more. Before he began work on his report, he should have been absolutely clear about what the reader expected from it. In the next few pages we will discuss three purposes which readers often expect reports to serve.

1. Recommendation

Your reader may be expecting you to make a specific recommendation for a course of action. Let us take a situation where a company's sales manager has asked you for a report making a recommendation on whether or not to cut the price of a product. The sales manager, first of all, wants a specific recommendation. You must come up with a yes-or-no answer, and, presumably, if you come up with a yes answer you must indicate the specific amount by which the price should be reduced.

This is only a beginning, however. What sort of reasoning or justification of your conclusion does the sales manager expect you to give? If you are experienced in your job and he trusts your judgment, it may be that he will not expect much justification. On the other hand, if you are relatively inexperienced, and particularly if the sales manager has not yet begun to rely on you, he may require considerable justification of your conclusion. Even if you are experienced and the sales manager trusts your judgment, he may still want detailed reasoning and justification. He may be passing on your recommendation, and your reasons for it, to a higher official of the company. Or he may know that if the decision turns out to be a poor one, he will be asked to produce the reasoning that led to it. Hence he may want you to provide him now with your reasoning. And you, for your own purposes, may wish to have on record the reasons for your conclusion, in case it is criticized or reviewed later.

Suppose you have determined, then, that the sales manager wants not only your conclusion but your reasoning. It may still be important to know just why. If he is not prepared to accept your recommendation without your reasoning, he probably wants the reasoning included in the main body of the report. If he wants your reasoning only as justification in case the decision is later criticized, he may expect you to present the reasoning as a sort of appendix or attachment to your report. Before you can decide exactly what kind of report the sales manager expects, you will have to decide not only whether he wants your reasoning, but, if he does want it, why he wants it and in what form he wants it presented.

The reader of a report may, however, not be expecting a recommendation at all. He may be expecting you to present alternative courses of action in a report containing the significant data and reasoning which might lead to a choice, but leaving it up to him to make the final decision. It is important to know whether the reader expects you to make the decision or expects you to leave this to him. It is frustrating to a reader who expected a concrete recommendation to find only a series of possibilities, leaving the choice or decision to him.

If your report is to serve as the basis for someone else's decision, you are going to have to include a good deal of data and reasoning. Just how much you should include will depend on whether your reader expects you to work with the data and reduce the choice to a simple weighing of pros and cons, or whether he wants to go through the data himself. The more precisely you can pin such factors down, the better your report will serve its reader's needs. If he wants a concise presentation of the major factors, he will not be pleased with a lengthy report that presents only masses of raw data. On the other hand, if he likes to work with raw data and draw his own conclusions, he will not be pleased with a concise summary of the significant factors and no mention of the data that went into them.

2.   Information

Your reader may simply ask for information, a deceptively simple request. Why does he want the information? This is a crucial question, because the amount of information which you present and the form in which you present it must be tied to the use that is to be made of it.

Suppose, for example, that the same sales manager asks for sales information on a particular product. He may want the information in order to decide whether the price should be cut and, if so, by how much. He may want the information in order to project future sales for the product and so establish production schedules or inventory levels. He may want the information in order to pass it on to a superior who is endeavoring to establish the profitability of various company products. Obviously, the kinds of information wanted and the way in which the information should be presented are not the same for each of these purposes. If you work on the assumption that the sales manager wants your information in order to plan inventory levels, and it turns out that he really wanted it in order to determine whether the product is profitable, he is likely to be dissatisfied with your report.

3. Display of Ability

Your reader may be quite frankly asking for an indication of your own ability when he asks for a report. This is particularly true when he asks you for a progress report. What he is looking for is evidence of what you have accomplished. It may even be that he is asking for a progress report which he will pass on to his superior as evidence of what he and his staff are accomplishing. In the first case, you will be demonstrating your own ability and accomplishment to your immediate superior; in the second case, you are enabling him to demonstrate his abilities and accomplishments to his superior and indirectly displaying your own abilities. Again, it is essential to be quite clear about the purpose before you begin to write.

Here are a few questions that may help you to establish the purposes of a written communication. These questions may not always be appropriate, and you may have to think of others yourself. They will, however, give you a start.

a. To whom am I addressing my communication? Who else may read it? (We will discuss this question in greater detail later in the chapter.)

b. If the communication was requested by the reader, has he told me specifically what he wants? Should I ask for clarification? Are there any unstated purposes my reader probably wants the communication to serve—purposes he is not likely to tell me about? If others may read the communication, what purposes will they expect it to serve?

c. If I am writing not in response to a request but on my own initiative, do I know exactly what I am trying to accomplish? What do I want the reader to do? to say? to believe?

d. Am I trying to persuade my reader? Am I attempting to change or strengthen his convictions, or is he undecided? Am I sure what his convictions are? Do I know why he holds them?

e. How important will my communication be to my reader? Will he be impatient with a long, detailed discussion? Will he think I have done a careless, skimpy job if I am brief?

DEFINING THE PROBLEM

A particular aspect of the purpose of a report is to define the problem. In fact, one of the most useful questions you can ask yourself as you first plan your report, while you are doing your research, and finally when you write is to constantly repeat: "What is the problem?" In asking this question you should maintain a flexible attitude, because your definition of the problem may change as you do your research. In this respect, it is worth noting that Jupiter Doe's "problem" of defining "lateness" could shift from deciding on a precise number of days to an attitude that "if students *think* there is a problem, there is one"; thus, the real problem was, in part, a communication problem to which his report pays little or no attention.

Suppose you work for a factory manager who is plagued with complaints that special orders—orders for unusual, custom-made products—are not being completed on time. He says to you: "Find out why we can't keep track of these orders and get them out on time, and give me a report telling me what to do about it." At its broadest, your purpose or problem is clear: The manager wants to know how to get special orders out on time. But let's move on to a more specific, narrower definition of the problem. The manager implies that delay is due to a failure to keep track of special orders. Is this failure the real problem? You may not be so sure. There is little doubt that special orders are not being finished on time, but the reasons are not so clear. Could the real problem be faulty scheduling, poor judgment in promising deliveries too soon, or a system of priorities that always puts special orders after regular production? Until you investigate a little, it is probably unwise to select any of these, or the manager's suggestion, as *the* problem.

Suppose after some research you find the real source of delay is faulty scheduling. Too much time is allowed for some production operations, not enough is allowed for others. The result is that orders are sometimes set aside after an operation has been completed and yet are often not ready when another operation is supposed to begin. You now want to refine your definition of the problem even further. Why is the scheduling at fault? Is the problem carelessness among those responsible for scheduling? Are these people following a set policy that should be changed? Do they understand what operations must be performed and how much time is required to perform them? Or do they fail to take regular production into account and, therefore, fail to plan so that special orders can fit into the regular production schedule?

Again, investigation should reveal which of these is *the* problem. Eventually you should be able to determine the exact source of the trouble. You will have defined the problem as narrowly and specifically as possible, and you can get on with a solution.

In the example above we began with an obvious problem, in the form of an undesirable result, and then proceeded to trace this result to its source in an effort to reach a more specific definition of the problem. Sometimes the reverse is called for.

Suppose you work for the vice-president in charge of production in a shoe manufacturing company which produces both handmade and machine-made shoes. Demand for its products has led to a need for expansion. The vice-president, who views skilled hand workers as a very important part of his labor force, asks you for a report recommending a new plant location where the company will be assured of an adequate supply of skilled hand workers. As you try to formulate the problem you have been given to solve, you realize that adequacy of the supply of skilled hand workers is only a part of a larger problem: the number of hand workers needed. And this, in turn, is part of the larger problems of how big the new plant is to be and how much of its output will be handmade. And these questions lead back to the problems of how fast the company wishes to grow and what balance of hand- and machine-made shoes should be planned. Such problems may be beyond your jurisdiction. Some of them may be for the vice-president to solve, some for the president or board of directors. But until you have answers to these questions, you cannot solve the narrow problem you have been given. The best you can do is to assume certain solutions to the larger problems and solve your problem on the basis of these assumptions.

We can summarize our observations on problem definition by saying that you must first understand the magnitude of the problem you are setting out to solve: you must be satisfied that you are not beginning with what is only part of a more fundamental problem and failing to deal with the fundamental problem itself. You must then identify the reasons for the existence of your problem; you must narrow down the definition of the problem until you reach the ultimate cause and can devise a solution.

KEEPING TRACK OF YOUR MATERIALS*

The bane of the report writer is the lost fact—"I've got a note on that somewhere, but I can't put my finger on it." In anything but the simplest or briefest

* The material in this section is from *Business Research and Report Writing* by Robert L. Shurter, J. Peter Williamson, and Wayne Broehl. Copyright © by McGraw-Hill, Inc., 1965. Used with the permission of McGraw-Hill Book Company.

report, the method you use to assemble your material will determine the accuracy and effectiveness of your final product. As bad as the lost fact is the fact inadequately or inaccurately recorded.

While the gathering of material will be discussed in the next chapter of this book, you should at the very outset of your planning decide on the *method* you will use to record information. Most likely the major part of your research can be recorded simply—in a notebook (journal) or on note cards. (As you do further research, though, you will soon become acquainted with more sophisticated techniques—punch card, electronic tape, etc.) If you choose to keep your information in a notebook or journal, you will be entering your material in a chronological or serial fashion. This has the advantage of keeping the information together in prearranged order, and you need not fear losing one item.

Though the journal has its devotees (Edward Gibbon, the famous historian was one), the use of a note card is far more widely used. Here a piece of information is entered on the card or sheet of paper (many researchers advocate only one item per card), and the cards are then sorted into a scheme of classification.

In either method, though, the bywords are *system* and *consistency*. Use the top of your card or the margin of your journal for key words and phrases that allow you to classify and find information quickly. Date each piece if you use separate cards—probably at the top of the card. Be certain that you have accurate documentation. And do all these things consistently—*always* use the key words in the same way, *always* enter the date in the same place.

Treat each piece of information to the famous reportorial questions "Who? When? Where? How? Why?" Be precise and accurate, even though the material you will use in business research is often not like the "hard facts" of the exact sciences. If you are interviewing a fellow worker, be certain you quote his words accurately. Be precise on his name—it would be dangerous to attribute a statement you read to "Professor Rostow," for your reader will not have you there to ask whether it was Eugene Rostow of Yale or W. W. Rostow of Texas (or perhaps another Rostow altogether). The time—and embarrassment—that you will save by being careful and exact in your gathering of facts will pay off handsomely for you. Contrariwise, slipshod research is worse than no research at all, for it dignifies inaccuracy and misinformation.

If you plan it correctly, your process of keeping track of materials will soon become almost automatic. As you gain experience, you will develop certain refinements that will make your technique even more efficient. But only by starting with a plan—and sticking to it consistently—can you record what you need in the proper fashion, with no last-minute doubts about its accuracy. Any worthwhile report requires such planning.

KEEPING THE READER IN MIND

As we have said, a report is written for a purpose. It is also written for a person. Generally speaking, report writers have the advantage of knowing more about the person for whom they write than do letter writers. In addition, they often have the further advantage of going back to the person requesting the report so that the assignment can be clarified. When both the purpose and the person are known well, the business report can be a creative instrument for business accomplishment. Fortunate indeed, therefore, is the report writer who knows the precise answers to these questions:

Who will read my report?
What use will my reader make of it?
What questions does he want answered?
How much information does he need?
What is the best way to present the information?

Ideally, in the interpersonal relationships of a business enterprise, effective reports stem from an understanding not only of the boss but of the boss's problems.

The size and complexity of today's corporate organizations, however, tend to place insulating layers between superior and subordinate, between writer and reader. Furthermore, reports written for one reader are frequently transmitted to others or get included in the larger package of the boss's report to his boss. Certainly a lot of wasted effort and unnecessary expense could be eliminated if forthright attempts were made to reduce the muffling, insulating barriers between those who ask for reports and those who read them. Even so, many situations would still prevail in which the writer has little to guide him as to his reader's needs and preferences. What to do then?

An excellent booklet called *So You Have to Write a Report*, prepared by Arthur D. Little, Inc., offers this perceptive advice for report writers in such situations:*

> In short, remember that the reader is a human being, not a corporation. He is not omniscient; if he were, he wouldn't have asked for your help. Remember also that he doesn't want to devote his whole career to deciphering what you have to say. The project you're reporting on is undoubtedly only one of many that require his attention. Your report should provide answers, not create more problems.

An enlightening guide to other aspects of what readers want, even though they

---

*Reprinted by permission of Arthur D. Little, Inc.

are unknown, can be found in these comments from representatives of top management:

> My people who write reports always talk about the trouble they have writing the beginning of the report. They say that once they get started they can go along fine. My chief comment is that these same people, once they get started, don't seem to know how to stop.

> Why can't they learn to highlight the main ideas or the chief points of their reports? I take a lot of reports home in my briefcase every weekend and I find myself wading through page after page looking for the main points. They waste their time and mine burying the very things I read for in a mass of unimportant details.

> I'm always suspicious of sheer length, and most of our reports are far too long. After all, the navy commander who sent the message "Sighted sub, sank same" gave a pretty fair report of the essential facts of a situation. I keep telling my staff that I'm not impressed with sheer bulk, but they still keep on trying to "impress" me with the detail and the thoroughness of their investigations.

> Too many of our reports sound as if no human ever had any part in writing them. In a day when magazines like *Fortune* know how to present facts vividly and accurately, why can't we adapt a few of these techniques to reports? Give them a little punch and some originality, and report readers won't have to pinch themselves to stay awake.

> We employ hundreds of engineers, accountants, and research workers, and the chief basis on which we judge their activities and progress is the reports they send us. In too many instances, this is a disastrous judgment as far as their careers are concerned. The engineers send us elaborate accounts subtitled "apparatus," "calculations," "data," "procedure," "computations"; the accountants give us page after page of "financial exhibits" and explanatory (?) footnotes; and both of them write as if they had learned a special version of the English language. Isn't there some way these people can learn to write normal English? I think it was Boss Kettering who once said, "I've never seen a report that was too simple." Neither have I, but I've seen too many that are too complicated and specialized.

One final word needs to be said about keeping your reader in mind:

> A report is always developed backwards.

This means that by the time you are ready to write, you generally know more about the subject than your reader knows—otherwise you wouldn't be writing the report. You must, therefore, plan to lead him into the report easily by asking yourself, "What does he need to know to understand this subject?" One means of doing this well is *to remember what you as a report writer knew when you began your investigation and to start your reader there.* In this respect, you are like the novelist who knows the conclusion of his tale but by exposition, description, and step-by-step narration leads his reader to the climax.

Thus, by the time you are ready to write (the presentation) you have already accumulated your facts and information (the research), and you should have thought your way through to the conclusions or recommendations you will present before you put a word on paper. Let's use an analogy from the process of building a skyscraper to make this plain. You will start with your foundation—*the research*; erect your structure's steel framework—*the organization*; and then finish your skyscraper—*the presentation*—from the top (the introduction) down to the first floor (the conclusion)—as some skyscrapers have actually been built—or you can start with conclusions and work the other way, letting your reader "in on the first floor," so to speak, as many reports do. You will also want your structure to be functional (i.e., readable); economical (i.e., clear and concise); and in keeping with the best architectural standards (i.e., the rules of good writing). You will have, of course, a choice of many good architectural styles, of which you can always select the best by considering the preferences of your skyscraper-dwellers and the use to which they will put your edifice.

In succeeding chapters, we will discuss the three phases which are always involved in report writing:

1. Research: getting the facts and information (Chapter 15)
2. Organization: imposing a pattern on your material (Chapter 16)
3. Presentation: writing, using graphic methods or statistics to get your material across to your reader (Chapters 17 and 18)

But before we start our detailed discussion of these three phases of report writing, we cannot overemphasize the fact that for writers of reports, the process of digging for facts is a far more rewarding form of intellectual exercise than the process of jumping to conclusions. For the report cannot stand on its rhetoric; it generally conveys opinions, recommendations, and conclusions from someone who has information and expert knowledge to someone who will have to act or decide. The report writer carries, therefore, a responsibility for seeing that his facts and information are accurate and that his conclusions and recommendations rest solidly upon them.

EXERCISES

1. You work as assistant to the executive vice-president of the Zanetown Widget & Gadget Company, which maintains a Research Division kept completely independent of

other company activities so that it may follow research wherever it seems promising. Whenever research leads to a new product, it is your boss's job to report on it to three other executives:

1. The technical director, who has always disliked the organizational arrangement, in which the Research Division reports to someone other than himself.
2. The marketing director, who last year forecast sales of 125,000 for a product developed two years ago; actual sales were 19,117.
3. The production manager, who has capably directed Zanetown's manufacturing facilities for 19 years but has just sent in a report saying that "our production facilities are at present taxed to the limit. If new products come along, we shall desperately need more space, more skilled employees, and two new assistants to the manager."

Assume that the Research Division of Zanetown Widget & Gadget Company has developed a plastic toy which the executive vice-president believes should be put into production as soon as feasible because it has real sales potential. He has asked you to prepare drafts of a report or reports which he will send to the three other executives.

a. Would you send the same report to all three or three reports emphasizing different aspects to take into account the different attitudes and interests of the three men?
b. What would be your central purpose if you sent just one report to all three? How would you change this purpose if you sent three different reports?
c. Which different aspects would you emphasize—giving careful consideration to his areas of interest, his background, and his probable education—in separate reports to the technical director and to the marketing director?
d. Write a one-sentence statement of your central purpose as the report writer in this situation.

2. Define what you consider to be the basic problem in the following situation and then, assuming that you have the responsibility for writing an action-getting report, write a one-paragraph statement of what purpose your report would serve.

Your institution maintains a cooperative bookstore which carries a complete line of supplies used by students. In the past three years, the Co-op has been able to refund an average of 12 percent to students at the end of the academic year.

Recently, however, merchants in town have been raising serious complaints about "a tax-free institution providing services which compete with and undercut tax-paying private enterprises." These charges have now been brought formally before the president of your institution by several members of the board of trustees.

This situation has been worsened by these statements:

Mr. Rouncival Roe, Manager of the Co-op: "Why don't the local merchants cut their exorbitant charges so they can compete with The Co-op? If they were as efficient as we are, they wouldn't spend so much time complaining."

An editorial in the student paper: "Students are lucky to have a Co-op which helps cut the cost of their education. What right have local establishments to grow rich at students' expense?"

An influential member of the board of trustees: "This educational institution was founded by believers in private enterprise. It has had consistent financial support from private enterprise. And I do not intend to see that it impinges on private enterprise. The college's business is teaching and research; it has no business selling books and supplies."

The president of the college: "We want to be good neighbors, to maintain harmony between town and gown."

Your report will go to the president of the college, the president of the local Chamber of Commerce, and the chairman of the board of trustees, and it will be printed in the student newspaper.

3. On the morning of Monday, February 15, 1971, David Martin, head of the Plastic Dinnerware Section of the Randall Chemical Company, received this note from his department head, William Taylor.

> February 15, 1971
>
> Dear Dave:
>
> News of your problem with R-60 has reached Mr. Maxwell and he has asked me for a report on the dispute with Wilson and a statement as to what you propose to do about it. I don't know exactly how much Mr. Maxwell knows about this, or from whom he learned what he does know.
>
> Would you please let me have a report by Monday, the 18th, to pass on to Mr. Maxwell.
>
> Bill

Stanley Maxwell was a vice-president of the company, reporting directly to its president. He was in charge of the Consumer Products Division, which included Mr. Taylor's department, the Household Products Department. Mr. Taylor reported directly to him, and David Martin reported directly to Mr. Taylor. A partial organization chart shows these relationships:

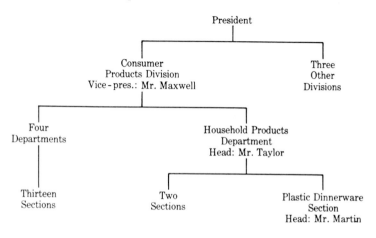

The problem to which Mr. Taylor's memorandum referred could be traced back to 1966, when the company's research laboratory came up with an idea for a new kind of thermosetting plastic, one that would be cheaper to make than existing plastics and better adapted to a wide variety of uses.

The laboratory offered the idea to the Thermosetting Plastic Materials (TPM) section, whose head was Tom Wilson. The TPM section was part of the Plastics Sales Department, which was, in turn, part of the Plastics Division. The following is an organization chart for this part of the company:

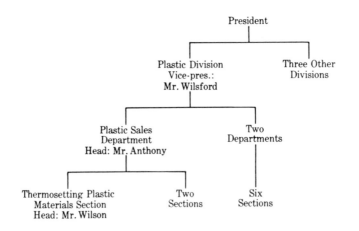

The TPM section was very busy in 1966, and Mr. Wilson was skeptical about the new idea. He decided not to commit his section to the time and expense that would be needed to turn the theory into a commercial product.

The laboratory then offered the idea to Mr. Martin. The Plastic Dinnerware Section used thermosetting plastics for three-quarters of the 200 items it manufactured. About half of these plastics were purchased from the TPM section and half were manufactured in the dinnerware section itself. Mr. Martin and his staff were enthusiastic about the new idea and agreed to take on the development job.

Almost five years went into development, and over this period the dinnerware section spend $300,000 on the project. This expense had been included in the section's profit-and-loss statements for these years. The result was more than Mr. Martin had hoped for. The new material cost only half as much to make as other plastics the section was using, it performed much better in most products, and it offered the prospect of making new plastic products.

Mr. Martin began to plan how to use the new plastic, called R-60, keeping in mind its importance to all the manufacturing sections of the company. He realized that all should be able to use it. At the same time, he wanted to protect his own section against its many competitors outside the company. He knew Mr. Taylor was enthusiastic about the advantages of the material to the whole Household Products Department. A good performance by the dinnerware section would reflect credit on Mr. Martin, Mr. Taylor, and Mr. Maxwell.

Personal responsibility for the success or failure of a section, department, or division had become especially important during the preceding year. Until 1970, the company had been organized on functional lines. There had been four divisions—production, marketing, finance, and accounting—each with its own vice-president. These divisions, with their departments and sections, had cut across product lines.

In 1970, the company decided its organization was inefficient, and a decentralized organization, based on product lines, was introduced. This is the organization depicted in the two charts above. Along with the new organization went a new concept of responsibility: The vice-presidents were responsible to the president for the performance of their respective divisions and had the authority to make policy decisions within those divisions. The vice-presidents, in turn, held the department heads responsible for department performance, and the department heads held the section heads responsible for section performance.

The president of the company had stated that the objective of the new organization was that "authority, accountability, and responsibility for making and carrying out decisions be placed as close as possible to the level of operations affected." He had said further that he would like to see section heads acting as much as possible like presidents of their own small businesses. Each section head was to be specifically responsible for policies and practices related to new product development, production facilities, and processes.

The president hoped that all managers would keep the welfare of the whole company uppermost in their thinking, but he also expressed the hope that competition among divisions, departments, and sections would foster efficiency and progress. Some limitations were placed on this competition. Each section was assigned responsibility for a particular type of product, and only this section was permitted to sell the product outside the company. But a section was free to make any product for its own use or for sale within the company.

The division and department heads realized that competition at the section level could be beneficial, but also that it would pose some serious problems. They were agreed that the new organization would test the capabilities of the section heads and that the section heads should be encouraged to resolve their problems for themselves.

Before Mr. Martin had made any definite plans for the production and use of R-60, he received a visit from Mr. Wilson, head of the TPM section. Mr. Wilson congratulated Mr. Martin on his success and asked when R-60 would be turned over to the TPM section. Mr. Martin replied that he intended to keep R-60 for his own section. Mr. Wilson pointed out that only the TPM section would be permitted to sell R-60 outside the company and that this section was better equipped to produce R-60 than was the dinnerware section.

The two men failed to agree and had two more meetings. At these meetings Mr. Martin insisted that R-60, which was patented, should be kept within the company and not sold to competitors for at least a few years. He also insisted that his section derive some financial benefits from the very low cost of manufacture of R-60. He pointed out that his section had risked $300,000 and should receive credit for the profits resulting from the new material.

Mr. Wilson felt that his section was the only one that should make R-60, that R-60 should be sold to competitors in order to bring in profits for the company as quickly as possible, and that the $300,000 spent by the dinnerware section was not important— it was company money no matter which section spent it.

Mr. Martin felt that he was right and Mr. Wilson wrong, but he was not so sure what the department heads and vice-presidents would think. Although he was convinced that the interests of the company as a whole would best be served by keeping R-60 away from competitors for a few years, he realized that eventually sales to competitors would be advisable and that only the TPM section could make these sales. He thought he could probably settle the matter satisfactorily with Mr. Wilson without appeal to a higher authority, but he was not sure.

Question: What purposes should Mr. Martin have in mind in answering his department head's request for a report? Precisely what feelings should he try to arouse in Mr. Taylor and Mr. Maxwell, and which should he try to avoid?

CHAPTER 15

RESEARCH, DATA, AND REASONING

Today's business world is a world of research—and tomorrow's will be even more research-oriented. You do not need to be a scientist working in the company's laboratory to find yourself called upon to do research. Throughout the firm—in marketing, in finance, in production, in personnel administration—research forms the basis for manangement decision making. Old-time methods of operating by rule of thumb are practically extinct.

Clearly, therefore, you will need certain skills in research methods. Some of these can be learned only after close association and experience with the particular field of business you choose. But there are certain requirements common to all business research, and while this book is not intended to present a comprehensive treatment of all forms of research, we will cover the basic principles and methods applicable to report writing. It is worth noting, however, that the infinite variety of report-writing situations in business makes it impossible to provide specific instructions covering even a small fraction of report-writing activities that involve research.

FINDING THE FACTS

A common mistake of inexperienced report writers is failing to take advantage of what is already known. It is true that much of the research required for reports in business involves material you get firsthand from the source — your own activities and experiences, questionnaires, work papers, and other materials from the company files or from conferences, interviews, and discussions with fellow employees. We will say more about these in a moment. But first, you should make certain that you do not needlessly repeat research that is already done. Certain important business publications, directories, and indexes of publications serve as excellent starting points. The following are useful:

Overall Guides

A helpful place to begin is the comprehensive guide or bibliography of business sources such as these:

DARTMOUTH COLLEGE: AMOS TUCK SCHOOL OF BUSINESS ADMINISTRATION. *A Reading List on Business Administration*, 7th rev., Hanover, N.H., 1958.

HARVARD UNIVERSITY: GRADUATE SCHOOL OF BUSINESS ADMINISTRATION, BAKER LIBRARY. *Selected Reference Sources*, Boston, 1963.

JOHNSON, H. W. AND MC FARLAND, S. W. *How to Use the Business Library, with Sources of Business Information*, 2d ed, Cincinnati, South-Western Publishing Company, 1957.

MANLEY, MARIAN C. *Business Information: How to Find and Use It*, New York, Harper & Row, Publishers, Incorporated, 1955.

MURPHEY, ROBERT W. *How and Where to Look It Up*, New York, McGraw-Hill Book Company, 1958.

WASSERMAN, PAUL. *Information for Administrators*, A Guide to Publications and Services for Management in Business and Government, Ithaca, N.Y., Cornell University Press, 1956.

Indexes

There are many excellent indexes in the business field. The following are widely used:

a. Periodical Indexes

Business Periodicals Index, New York, The H. W. Wilson Company (monthly, with periodic cumulations).

Note: See *Industrial Arts Index* for articles prior to 1958.

Public Affairs Information Service, New York, Public Affairs Information Service, Inc. (weekly, with periodic cumulations).

Readers' Guide to Periodical Literature, New York, The H. W. Wilson Company (semimonthly, with periodic cumulations).

b. Newspaper Indexes

New York Times Index (semimonthly, cumulated annually).

Wall Street Journal Index (monthly with annual cumulations).

Financial and Industrial Directories

These three general directories are widely used in business research:

DUN AND BRADSTREET. *Million Dollar Directory* (annual, with supplements). Identifies officers, products, annual sales, and numbers of employees for over 23,000 United States companies with a net worth of $1 million or more.

Poor's Register of Corporations, Directors, and Executives of the United States and Canada (annual, with quarterly cumulated supplements). Similar information as the above for about 29,000 corporations and for about 75,000 executives and directors.

Thomas' Register of American Manufacturers (5 volumes, annual). The first three volumes list manufacturers by product, the fourth is an alphabetical directory of companies, and the fifth a "product-finding guide."

Business and Financial Periodicals

A variety of periodicals are available in specialized business fields. These are also widely read for their general business information:

Barron's; National Business and Financial Weekly (weekly)

Business Week (weekly)

Commercial and Financial Chronicle (semiweekly)

Dun's Review and Modern Industry (monthly)

Fortune (monthly)

Harvard Business Review (bimonthly)

U.S. Board of Governors of the Federal Reserve System. *Federal Reserve Bulletin* (monthly)

U.S. Bureau of Labor Statistics. *Monthly Labor Review* (monthly)

U.S. Department of Commerce. *Survey of Current Business* (monthly)

Statistical Compendiums

The following contain statistics for business as a whole:

Economic Almanac. National Industrial Conference Board (annual).

Handbook of Basic Economic Statistics . . . A Manual of Basic Economic Data on Industry, Commerce, Labor, and Agriculture in the United States. Economic Statistics Bureau of Washington, D.C. (monthly, quarterly, and annually).

United Nations, Statistical Office. *Statistical Yearbook* (annual).

U.S. Bureau of the Census. *Historical Statistics of the United States.*

U.S. Bureau of the Census. *Statistical Abstract of the United States* (annual).

GATHERING FIRSTHAND INFORMATION

A large part of the research required for reports in business involves, not published material from secondary sources, but primary material you gather from your own sources. In school or college, you came much closer to the actual kind of research used in business reports if you made an investigation of such subjects as "What Students at Blank College Think about the Peace Corps" or "The Salaries and Kinds of Jobs of Last Year's Senior Class" or "A Survey of the Cost of Room and Board in Our 23 Fraternities" or "What the Student Council Should Do about Representation on the Faculty's Student Affairs Committee." To report on these subjects you needed *primary sources*, materials that were directly available on your own campus; and while you may possibly have used secondary source materials in the library—for instance, you might have compared a senior class's jobs and salaries with those of other colleges' seniors—most of your investigation should have come from facts or opinions or ideas you got firsthand. What you did if you assembled the data, information, and calculations for a laboratory report probably came closest of all in technique to the research and investigation needed for business reports, though it was probably not so polished a job as you now are expected to do.

Research that involves something other than the facilities of a library we can call *field research*. It presents some difficulties you do not encounter in *library research*. The card catalog in a library, provided you know how to use it, plus an assortment of bibliographies and indexes, will lead you to everything the library has to offer on your topic. There is no handy catalog for field research. You have to decide such things as: What information must I have? What would I like to have? What is probably available? Where? How do I go about getting it? How much will this cost? How much time will it take? How valuable will it be? And how can I implement the information—put it to work in solving my problem?

Suppose you work for the owner of a small company that is about to market a new child's toy—a small cart made to look like an automobile, in which a child can sit and propel himself by pushing pedals. The owner asks you for a report on how many carts the company can plan to sell, who will buy them, and through what distribution channels they should be sold and at what price.

As you begin to think over your problem, you may conclude that you have to know what parents would be willing to pay for the cart. It might occur to you that you would like to interview every parent within 250 miles of the company to find out. The time and expense involved would clearly be prohibitive. But suppose you took a sample of opinion. You might mail a questionnaire to a list of parents. Or you might ring some doorbells in your own city or town. Or perhaps it would be enough to ask some toy-shop owners or buyers for large stores. Or, easiest of all, you could just drop in at a toy shop or two and see what the prices are for similar products.

In order to see whether children like the toy, you might try a form of experiment—you could take two or three experimental models of the go-cart to a group of children to test their reactions as they actually drive them. The cost of this experiment might be much higher than the cost of some of the simple methods suggested earlier for obtaining price information. You might obtain some useful information from the children, but the expense incurred in gaining it might not be justified.

Which course of action you adopt will depend on how you evaluate the reliability of each course, how badly you need reliable information, how much time and money each course would involve, and how much you have to spend. It might occur to you to find out if there is a trade association for toy makers, a magazine, or a journal that possibly has data available on toy prices and consumer behavior. You may be able to obtain detailed information at little cost.

But, however you decide to get the information, you are going to be constantly concerned with these three criteria:

1. Is the information *valid*—are the facts the information gives accurate?
2. Is the information *reliable*—would I get the same facts if I repeated the process again at a later date?
3. Is the information applicable to my research—does it tell me something *I need to know?*

These three cardinal criteria—validity, reliability, and applicability—go far in determining what information you will choose to use in your research.

FACT AND OPINION

Facts and opinions are the primary products of business research. It should be obvious that your facts should be relevant to your problem and that they should be complete. And, of course, your facts should be facts. High school students tend to believe that anything in print is a fact. It is to be hoped that you are beyond this. We will deal with the distinctions between facts, inferences, and assumptions after we have discussed opinions.

Opinions present more difficulty than facts do. In evaluating the usefulness of an opinion you must consider its validity—that is, whether the source is *reliable* and *qualified.* You must ask why the source of an opinion might not be reliable. Has he a reputation for exaggeration or falsehood? Even if he is generally reliable, has he a personal interest he may be defending in the particular opinion he gave you? You could hardly expect the most honest sales manager to give you an unbiased opinion on whether the position of sales manager should be eliminated. You must also consider the education, experience, and general knowledge of your source in judging how well he is qualified to give an opinion. Here you may be relying on one man's opinion of the qualifications of another, and you must evaluate the first opinion to be able to evaluate the second. Of course, all such judgments are relative. There is no such thing as a perfect opinion, but some are more valid than others. You must be satisfied as to the degree of validity you need in your particular research and the degree you actually have in the opinions you have collected.

Be careful not to ignore *conflicting opinion*. It is easy to say: "I believe we can sell our product at $18.95, and six highly qualified department-store buyers agree with me," omitting the opinion of three equally qualified buyers that $14.95 is the most you should charge.

We have spoken so far of satisfying yourself of the validity of an opinion. But you must also consider whether your reader will accept your judgment, or whether you will have to offer evidence of reliability and qualification. Finally, you must be sure that your source will let you use his opinion. A lot of irritation has been engendered by writers who reported the opinions of other employees without first letting them know.

REASONING

How you reach a conclusion based on your primary product—the facts and opinions you have collected—can be described as part of a reasoning process. The four elements of this process are inference, analogy, assumption, and logic.

Inference

Suppose you observe the sales of two products, A and B, identical in all respects except name and price. Product A, which is priced below B, outsells B. In fact, in one day 10 units of A are sold for each 1 of B. So far we have discussed only facts: the nature of the products, their names, their prices, and their sales. Suppose you now conclude that A outsells B because it is cheaper. This is an inference. It is not a fact. It may be true or untrue; but until it is established as a fact or falsehood, it is an inference. Suppose that you have interviewed 600 purchasers of A and can present as a *fact* that 500 say they bought A because it was cheaper and 100 because they didn't notice B. (Notice that the reasons given are not facts, but opinions, although the *giving* of the opinions is a fact.) This information would strengthen your inference. It becomes stronger as you find more facts or opinions to support it and as you investigate and prove groundless the objections to it. But it is still not as strong as a fact.

Inferences are important, at least as important as facts, but they must be evaluated. Facts can usually, although not always, be proved without much difficulty. You can ascertain that the price of product A is $14.95, and that is that. You may be very certain of your inference that A outsells B because of its lower price, you may be fairly certain, or you may not be certain at all.

When you are trying to decide whether to recommend to the manufacturer of product B that he reduce his price to increase sales, the degree of your certainty becomes important. First, you must decide whether the inference is strong enough to justify a conclusion that the price should be reduced, and second, you must explain in your report how certain you are. If your inference is little better than a guess, but you can't do any better, you should say so. Don't pretend that you are sure. Make clear to the reader of your report which conclusions you are sure of and which you are not so sure of. When he decides what to do, he will have a basis on which to evaluate the risks involved and cannot blame you for misleading him.

Many writers of business reports fail to appreciate the varying quality of inferences, and some are rather vague about the difference between fact, opinion, and inference. The result is that their analysis of a business problem is muddled and their reports do not make clear what can be relied on and what cannot, what is almost certain and what is only probable.

Here is an example of a test in which statements are classified as fact or inference, a "critical inference test." (Two tests for you to work on are included in the exercises at the end of this chapter.) The example consists of a story followed by a series of statements based on the story. Each statement is to be classified as factually true or false, or as a strong or a weak opinion or inference. The classification is given in parentheses.

> The firm of New Toys, Inc., owned by Carlton Wellman, manufactured the "Tot Walker," a device invented by Mr. Wellman to help babies learn to walk. During its first year the company sold 500 units to a large mail-order house at $3 each. The mail-order house offered them to the public at $4.50. Mr. Wellman believed the public would pay more than $4.50. He was confident that he could reduce his own price below $3 when his company began large-scale production.

1. *The "Tot Walker" was invented by Mr. Wellman.* (This is factually true, as stated in the story.)
2. *The "Tot Walker" was unique.* (This is not a fact, but an inference. The story does not say whether the device was unique. We know Mr. Wellman invented it, but others may have done the same. Whether you regard the inference as trustworthy or not will depend on whether you trust Mr. Wellman to have investigated to make sure there were no similar products available.)
3. *The public will pay more than $4.50 for the device.* (This is an opinion. We are in no position to evaluate it because the story tells us nothing about Mr. Wellman's reliability or about his qualifications for judging what the public will pay for his device.)
4. *New Toys, Inc., will be able to reduce its price below $3 per unit.* (This is opinion, and not a complete opinion at that. Mr. Wellman said he could reduce the price when his company began large-scale production. If you are willing to infer that the company will begin large-scale production, then you can treat this statement as Mr. Wellman's opin-

ion. We still have no way of judging his reliability, but he has some qualifications which lend support to this opinion. He owns the company that has been manufacturing the "Tot Walker" and he invented the product, so he could be expected to have some expert knowledge of the cost of production.)

5. *The public will pay at least $4.50 for the "Tot Walker" because 500 were sold at this price.* (This is an inference. New Toys, Inc., sold 500 to a mail-order house. We do not know how many were resold and have no way of inferring the number. There is some support for the inference that the public will pay $4.50, because it is a fact that the buyer for the mail-order house, who is presumably an expert at this sort of thing, thought they would. In other words, this inference rests on an opinion that is not expressed in the story but which we can presume.)

Analogy

Analogy is a common method of reasoning. It consists of noting that two situations are similar in several respects and concluding that the similarity will hold for other respects.

Suppose you have observed that a much-advertised brand of fresh milk sold in grocery stores consistently sells at a higher price than a less advertised brand. You reason, therefore, that an advertising campaign could enable a sugar refiner to sell its sugar for more than its competitors, who do little advertising.

The first question to ask is whether the two situations are really analogous. You have a sound analogy only if the two situations have a sufficient number of *essential characteristics in common within the area of comparison* and if there are *no essential differences* within this area.

Several similarities are evident here: Both sugar and milk are grocery items, probably purchased by the same sort of person; both are staples; both are sold in large quantities at a fairly low price per unit. These similarities are certainly within the area of comparison—importance of price. Both are white, too, but this characteristic is irrelevant. We must next ask if there is any essential difference. One such difference will probably be enough to demolish the analogy. Most people would concede that sugar is sugar; there are no noticeable differences in quality. But milk may differ in freshness and in butterfat content, within legal limits, and purchasers may detect or think they detect quality differences. If customers consider quality differences in the case of milk but not in the case of sugar, then your analogy breaks down. No matter how many similarities you can find, that one essential difference prevents you from using the results of the milk case to decide the sugar case. This doesn't prove that advertising won't enable a sugar refiner to charge more than its competitors, but it means that your milk case does not support a conclusion that it will.

Analogies, like inferences, are rarely true or false. They range from poor or weak to good or strong. And, as in the case of inferences, you must evaluate them both for yourself and for your reader.

An analogy can be dangerous if it is not tested analytically. An article in *Fortune*, entitled "The Language of Business," describes how the owners of a consumer-goods corporation, who were entranced with the analogy between football and business and convinced, therefore, that building a good team was the key to success, spent all their time recruiting and training talent while their competitors developed a new product and took away the market.

Assumption

An assumption differs from an inference. An inference is based on specific data—facts or opinions. In the example discussed above, we knew that product A outsold B, we knew A was cheaper, and we knew of no other reason why purchasers would prefer A. We inferred that product A outsold product B because of its lower price. Our conclusion that purchasers would prefer a low price to a high price, however, was an *assumption*. It seemed reasonable, but we had no data to justify it. Therefore, it was not an inference. It was based on general knowledge, on experience, on what most people would call "common sense." But it was a supposition, a taking for granted, and should be recognized as such. There are instances where this particular assumption does not hold. Purchasers of jewelry, for example, or perfume, often prefer a high price to a low price because, even though they cannot perceive differences in quality, they believe that a high price in some way gives assurance of high quality.

There is nothing wrong with assumptions. We have to make them when factual data are not available and when no inferences can be drawn. In fact, we have to make assumptions about inferences. Frequently we have to assume that an inference is valid even though we are not really sure, in order to get on with research or a report. In order to discuss how large a cut in the price of product B would increase its sales to a profitable level, for example, we have to assume the validity of our inference that product A outsells it because of price. We can't set out to verify every inference as we go along. When a final conclusion is reached, however, we may want to review the inferences on which it is based and decide whether some should be verified before action is taken.

It is important not to use assumptions when data are available and inferences can be drawn. When you know the price of A is \$14.95 and the price of B is \$16.95, it is foolish to assume a price difference of \$3. And if you have actually interviewed purchasers and found they chose A over B because of the price difference, it is not necessary to assume that some purchasers chose A because of its lower price. A conclusion that *most* purchasers will behave this way, however, may involve an assumption that your interviews are a satisfactory measure of general purchaser opinion.

It is common for a business researcher to assume that his company wants to grow as fast as possible, that a new product will add to the company's profits, or that a reduction in price will increase sales, without bothering to use data he has at hand that might lead to quite opposite inferences. It is, unfortunately, always easier to assume than to work with data and infer.

Assumptions, like inferences and analogies, must be evaluated. An assumption must be consistent with the available data; it must have a reasonable possibility of being true. You can't assume no one will buy product B at a price of $16.95 when you know perfectly well that people are buying it.

It is especially important to label your assumptions. Be honest enough with the reader of your reports to tell him when you have no data and are relying on assumption, or when you are not certain of the validity of an inference but will assume it is valid for purposes of further discussion. Your reader may disagree with your assumptions: he may feel his experience and general knowledge are a better guide than yours. At the same time, he may respect your inferences as being based on a familiarity with the data greater than his own. Give him the opportunity to sort out the assumptions from the inferences.

When you have completed a research project and reached a conclusion, it is important to review the inferences, analogies, and assumptions that went into it. You must judge the *importance* and the *validity* of each one. And, in the case of the inference, this involves judging the validity of data—facts and opinions. If an inference, analogy, or assumption is important, then you must be concerned about its validity. If you have inferred that an investment will earn 10 percent and you know that any return under 10 percent is not acceptable to your company, then you had better be sure of your inference before you recommend the investment. On the other hand, if the inference, analogy, or assumption is not very important, then you may not have to worry much about its validity. If you have assumed that a bank loan will cost 6 percent interest, but your conclusion would be no different even if the rate were 10 percent, probably you won't worry much about whether your assumption is a sound one.

When you write your report, perform the same service for your reader. That is, identify the important inferences, analogies, and assumptions. Assure him of their relative validity, which means also warning him of unavoidable weaknesses. And point out which are unimportant, so he won't expect detailed evaluation of these.

Logic

There should be no need to stress the importance of logic in business research and business writing. Yet business reports all too frequently reveal the writer's failure to test his statements on logical grounds.

An example is quoted below. It is taken from a report on the subsidizing of scholarly books published by a university press. Subsidized books are not expected to sell well enough to reimburse the publisher for their cost. Sometimes the publisher expects to lose money on a book, and hence to subsidize it; sometimes other institutions—educational foundations or councils—will provide the funds (a collateral subsidy) to make publication possible. It is often argued that if a foundation provides the money to subsidize a scholarly book which later proves to be profitable, the university press should refund the subsidy. The following paragraph from the report deals with this argument.

It is occasionally suggested that a collateral subsidy should be "returnable" that is, that when the Press has recovered all its costs of publication, further proceeds, if any, should be applied to the reduction of the investment of the institution which provided the collateral subsidy. At first sight, this suggestion may seem to have merit, but in practice serious flaws appear. First, it will be noted that such a grant is not a genuine subsidy, but simply the provision of working capital, which may or may not be needed. Secondly, if the Press does not recover from sales its costs of publication above the amount of the collateral subsidy, its funds will be depleted—it is therefore risking an indefinite sum on its publishing judgment, and it should not speculate with the Subsidizing Fund on the basis that it will either be depleted or exactly reimbursed. Thirdly, the administrative cost of recording, computing, and returning proceeds in very small amounts is disproportionately high, and could even exceed possible returns. The situation is quite different if the institution providing the subsidy underwrites the entire cost; it is then assuming the whole publishing risk, and is entitled to all proceeds over and above the actual cost of handling sales.

Let us look at the three "serious flaws." The first argument is that if a grant is repaid it is not a genuine subsidy. This is not a logical argument; it is a play on words. *Subsidy* is defined in Webster's dictionary as "any gift by way of financial aid." If the gift is returned, it is perhaps no longer a gift. But it really makes no difference to the foundation whether this money is called a gift, subsidy, or refundable advance.

We can break the second argument down into three parts. First, the writer says that if the press does not recover its own costs of publication over the amount of the subsidy, its funds will be depleted. But this argument is fallacious, since the writer has already stated at the beginning of his paragraph that the suggestion he is disputing is that the collateral subsidy be repaid only after the press has recovered all its costs of publication.

The second portion of the second argument is that the press would be risking an indefinite sum on its publishing judgment if it returned a gift from another institution once a book had recovered its cost. It is hard to tell what the writer had in mind here. The risk was run when the book was published, when no one knew whether it would sell enough copies to repay its cost. Returning the gift after the book proved profitable could not increase this risk. Even so, the risk was never an indefinite one. The press knew how much money it was putting up to publish the book, and it knew that at most it could lose this amount.

The third portion of the second argument is that the press should not speculate with the funds available for subsidizing books in the expectation that these funds will either be depleted or exactly reimbursed. In other words, subsidizing funds should be used only when there is also a possibility of making money on a scholarly book. But the original suggestion seemed to be that a foundation's subsidy be returned to it only *after* the press had recovered all its costs and that *only* the subsidy be returned, so that profit would be kept by the press. Thus the statement that the result could only be depletion of funds or exact reimbursement is false. (It may be that the writer meant to discuss a suggestion that profits would go to the foundation; the first sentence in the paragraph quoted is ambiguous.)

The third argument may have some merit, but the amount of bookkeeping involved would probably be no greater than is always necessary in order to compute an author's royalty.

The quoted example is an interesting one because, on superficial reading, it appears to make sense. You have to subject each of the writer's arguments to rather close scrutiny to discover that, on a logical basis, it falls apart.

This chapter cannot offer you a course in logic. But we have already discussed the use and misuse of inferences, analogies, and assumptions, and we will deal briefly with two classes of fallacious reasoning because they are so common in business reports. These are *begging the question* and the *non sequitur.*

Begging the question

When a writer begs the question, he assumes what has yet to be proved and, therefore, simply substitutes one question for another. Here is an example:

I have no hesitation in recommending this investment, because the return on it will be more than satisfactory.

In this sentence, the writer is *assuming* a satisfactory return in order to support a recommendation for investment. Whether the return will be satisfactory is the key question, the one that must be answered affirmatively before the recommendation can be justified. In other words, the question "Should I invest?" is not very different from "Will the return be satisfactory?" and you cannot logically answer the first by assuming an answer to the second. What the example above really says is, "I assume the investment should be made because I assume the return will be more than satisfactory." The recommendation is now shown for what it really is: a pure assumption, not a logical inference.

The Non Sequitur

Non sequitur, which means "it does not follow," is perhaps the most common fallacy in business reports. In a strict sense, every inference that is not justified by the data from which it is drawn is a *non sequitur.* The *non sequiturs* with which we are particularly concerned are conclusions drawn from irrelevant or quite insufficient data. For example:

There are several communities within a 50-mile radius of our plant where we do not have stores. Most of our business is done with local customers; therefore, I believe that any stores opened in these towns would increase customers and sales.

The fact that most business is done with local as opposed to nonlocal customers does not justify the stated conclusion. The writer may have had some reason to think his premise was relevant to his conclusion, but he has not given it to us. Here is another example:

We are just breaking even at our present sales volume. Because of competition we cannot raise our prices; therefore, the only other way to make a profit is to lower costs.

The writer is concluding that there are only two ways to make a profit—raise prices or lower costs. And he deduces this, or appears to, from the fact that the company is breaking even. The conclusion simply does not follow. Why, for example, is an increase in sales volume not a way to make a profit?

If our discussion of reasoning and logic points to one thing, it is the need for care—for a study of every inference, analogy, assumption, and conclusion, to make sure that it makes sense logically. The ease with which an absurdity can slip by when thinking and reading are quick and superficial is shown by this gem from a book called *Sex and the Adolescent:*

> There are plenty of statistics which suggest how early is too early. Different studies come up with slightly varying figures but the conclusions drawn are quite similar. They indicate that about 60 per cent of the husbands who were married between the ages of twenty-eight and thirty are happily adjusted whereas almost two-fifths of the boys who marry under twenty-one make poor marital adjustments.

We have covered a variety of topics in this chapter, and you may find the following summary helpful in remembering and applying them. The questions under each topic are designed to remind you of the discussion and give you a specific guide for testing your own research and reasoning.

1. *Defining the Problem.* Have I isolated the fundamental problem facing me, or am I dealing with a problem that cannot be solved until others have been solved? Have I narrowed down the scope of my problem so that I know exactly what are its causes?

2. *Research.* What information is necessary or desirable? Where can I obtain it? How difficult will this be? Will the information be worth its cost?

3. *Fact and Opinion.* Have I clearly differentiated between what is fact and what is opinion? Have I judged the reliability and qualifications of the sources of opinions I am relying on? Can I convince my reader of the value of these opinions?

4. *Inference.* What is the basis for the inferences I have drawn? How reliable are these inferences? How important are they to my conclusions? Have I made both their reliability and their importance clear to my reader?

5. *Analogy.* When I draw an analogy, am I comparing things that are essentially the same? Have I overlooked any essential difference?

6. *Assumption.* Are my assumptions necessary? Have I exhausted my resources of fact and inference? How reliable are my assumptions? How important are they? Have I clearly identified for my reader the assumptions I have made, and have I shown him their reliability and importance?

7. *Begging the Question.* Have I pretended to reach a conclusion by logic when, really, I have simply assumed the conclusion?

8. *Non Sequitur.* Do my conclusions really follow from my reasoning? When I describe or imply a cause-and-effect relationship, does this relationship really exist?

EXERCISES

1. Identify the type of reasoning in each of the following, and in each case say why you believe the statement would or would not achieve its purpose:

   a. From a report to convince a large industry that it should move into the field of mass-produced prefabricated housing:

   > For more than fifty years, American industry has been producing millions of cars by mass production techniques. Through these techniques, we are able to deliver the lowest-priced models to the customer for around $2,000. For this price, he gets what is essentially a room which has mobility. Is there not reason to believe, then, that by using the same techniques we can produce a five-room mass-produced, prefabricated house for $10,000?

   b. From a report whose purpose was to convince college administrators that the retirement age of 65 should be waived and left at the option of individual professors:

   > Many colleagues on the faculty are at the peak of their creative powers at age 65, and it is a waste of talent and experience to force their retirement at age 65.
   >
   > Cervantes wrote the second part of Don Quixote when he was 68; Goethe wrote Faust, Part I, at 59 and Part II at 83; in 1944, during World War II, Secretary of War Henry Stimson was 77, General Douglas MacArthur was 65, Chief of Staff George C. Marshall was 65, Admiral Leahy was 69, and Admiral Hepburn was 67. Konrad Adenauer was very active as the strong man of German government during his seventies and eighties, and Winston Churchill began a four-year term as Prime Minister of Great Britain at the age of 77.
   >
   > These facts show that most of our very useful citizens do their best work after the time when business, industry, and the academic world retire them.

   c. From a statement designed to convince potential investors to participate in short selling:

   > Some investors erroneously get nervous about short selling. They do so because, as they say, "the seller is selling something that he doesn't even own." But the contractor who "sells" you a house doesn't even own the materials from which he expects to build it. In fact, that is the way the contractor makes money. Similarly, by wise use of short sales, you can make money too.

   d. From a report urging Giant Enterprises Inc. to acquire by merger a small firm called Electronic Protective Devices, Inc., 95 percent of whose business and profit derives from an electronic device which sets off a loud siren whenever the doors of residences are tampered with:

The increase of crime throughout the nation shows that there is a tremendous potential market for protective devices for the home. And with the crime rate increasing annually, there is every reason to believe that this market will continue to increase in the foreseeable future.

Since the real problem of Electronic Devices, Inc. in the past has been its small size, Giant Enterprises Inc. will be able to supply the production facilities and the marketing staff which Electronic Devices has lacked in the past.

This merger is, therefore, a natural one in which Giant's size and staff complement Electronic's need for broader sales coverage and enhanced production.

e. A report to the head of a college recruiting department in industry with the purpose of developing better methods of employing college graduates:

College students don't emerge after four years with a natural hostility to business and industry. They have acquired this attitude from professors who make fun of the free-enterprise system and go out of their way to deride businessmen.

The first step, then, should be for this company to stop making financial contributions to any college where such hostile attitudes are encouraged. Second, we should bring these professors to this company for seminars which would educate them to the true nature and the real service of this company. Third, we should tell the students at every opportunity that professors who deride business don't know what they are talking about.

When these three recommendations are put into effect, the difficulties of recruiting good college graduates will disappear. That is why these recommendations are the only solution to our inability to attract college graduates at present.

f. From a report forecasting sales of a new product:

Since our new washer sells for about half the cost of General Cleaners' product and 20 percent below the cost of Central Washers Inc., we should certainly be able to take almost half of General Cleaners' market and 20 percent of Central Washers'. Since General last year sold 120,000 washing machines and Central sold 200,000, this means that we have a market of approximately 100,000 practically assured for our new washing machine.

2. A college daily newspaper is anxious to obtain more advertising revenue from local merchants, especially department-store owners. With what reasons might the newspaper persuade these merchants to place advertisements? What data would be necessary to support the reasoning? How should the newspaper go about obtaining the data? How much would it probably cost, and how long would it take to gather?

3. What sources of information and what methods of obtaining data would you use if you were asked to write the following reports:

a. A report to the vice-president in charge of employee relations on the attitudes and morale of 1,500 employees in your company.

b. A report to a publisher of fiction on the changing reading habits of Americans as revealed by best-selling books of the past twenty-five years.

c. A report to the president of a company manufacturing a new plastic tile (which homeowners themselves can install in kitchens and bathrooms) on the comparative advantages of advertising on radio, on television, or in newspapers.

d. A report to your interfraternity council on cooperative buying practices among fraternities at 10 institutions similar to yours.

e. A report for a large construction company on the need for a new supermarket, motel, or gas station in your community.

4. If you were the executive reading the reports in which the following statements are made, what would you properly expect by way of supporting evidence or reasoning?

a. *It is apparent, therefore, that the majority of our employees are satisfied with their working conditions and remuneration. It is equally apparent that we must continue to improve both our working conditions and our salaries if we are to maintain our position of leadership in our industry.*

b. *Because the demands on managerial skills will be greater in the next five years, the need for better-trained managers will increase. For that reason, we must both broaden and intensify our training programs for young men entering our management. I therefore recommend that our education and training budget be doubled for the next year and that we use this increased amount to start recent graduates on an intensive course in management skills.*

c. *Our sales letters appear to achieve little in terms of actual sales. It is my conviction that sales result almost entirely from personal calls by salesmen. Letters are too slow, too impersonal, and they don't get results. I would urge that we eliminate them, transfer our two sales correspondents to another department, and add two salesmen to our sales force. I am convinced that this idea is the only way to increase sales within our present budget and that we have no other alternative than to stop our direct-mail effort.*

d. *It has been my personal observation that our policy of placing recent college graduates as individuals in various departments should be changed. They should be kept together as a group for group training and orientation; then they could exchange ideas and information with people of their own age and background. While I don't know the exact number of these graduates we have lost to other companies in recent years, it does seem to be a rather large number, and the reason is our policy of assigning them to different departments as soon as they join the company. I believe that a number of other companies have changed this policy and that we should follow their example.*

5.* Wilbur Morrissey is president of a machine tool company employing about 400 men. He was called one morning by Harry Willis, the president of the union local to which

* Based on the case "Durbin Implement Co." in Austin Grimshaw and John Hennessey, *Organizational Behavior: Cases and Readings*, McGraw-Hill Book Company, New York, 1960, and used with permission.

most of the men belonged. Willis announced that a maintenance man, Carl Neely, had been fired by the maintenance foreman the night before and that, unless Morrissey ordered his reinstatement, there would be a strike that afternoon.

Morrissey called the maintenance foreman, Herb West, and asked him what had happened. West said that shortly after he had come to work the evening before, he had learned that some important shipments were expected at 7:00 A.M. the following day and that falling snow was blocking the company's loading platforms. He said that Neely was the only maintenance man on the night shift and that no laborers were available; he therefore ordered Neely to shovel the platforms clear. Neely refused, according to West, replying that he was not a laborer. West then told him he was fired. "Neely had it coming to him," said West. "He's been nothing but trouble ever since he lost the union president election two years ago."

Morrissey recalled that Neely had been president of the union for five or six years until Willis had defeated him in the last election. After that, Neely had become difficult to handle and had worked on several jobs before becoming night shift maintenance man. Morrissey had had a good deal of trouble with the union while Neely was president, but very little since Willis had taken over.

Morrissey next called Willis back and told him that Neely had been fired for disobeying orders. Willis answered that Neely had told him he had no warm clothing with him when he was told to shovel snow; that was why he had refused. Morrissey called West back, and West said that Neely had not mentioned warm clothing the night before. "Anyway," West added, "if he'd worked at the shoveling, he'd have kept warm enough."

Classify the following statements as factually true, factually false, inference, opinion, or assumption. Evaluate the inferences, opinions, and assumptions as well as you can.

a. Carl Neely is a maintenance man on the night shift.

b. The employees of the company will go on strike if Neely is not given his job back.

c. Neely had been night maintenance man for several years when he was fired.

d. Herb West had no right to order Neely to shovel snow.

e. Harry Willis admitted that West did have the right to order Neely to shovel snow, but only if Neely had proper clothing.

f. Neely is a troublemaker, and the company will be better off without him.

g. Neely refused to shovel because he did not have the proper clothing.

h. Neely has been difficult to handle during the past two years because he resented losing the office of union president.

i. Willis will not fight hard for Neely if Morrissey absolutely refuses to reinstate him.

j. It will be more difficult for West to maintain discipline if Neely is reinstated.

6. Bob Allen, a student in a graduate school of business administration, received a letter from his mother's sister, Mrs. Wilcox, in which she told him of a proposal made to her

by William Owen, a real-estate broker in her city, regarding an apartment building she owned.

Mrs. Wilcox is a widow, about fifty years old. Her husband had died ten years before, leaving her an estate that consisted almost entirely of the building. She had no children of her own, and her will provided that all her property would pass to her brother and two sisters, or, if they did not survive her, to their children.

According to her letter, Mrs. Wilcox had been asked by Mr. Owen to sell the building to a client of his for a price of $555,900. She would be paid $255,000 in cash and would receive a note for $300,900, payable in ten years at 8 percent interest and secured by a mortgage on the building. Mrs. Wilcox mentioned in her letter that, if she kept the building, she would soon have to spend $10,000 on new stoves and refrigerators. She concluded by saying that she had turned down an offer of $595,000 cash for the building a few months earlier on the advice of her lawyer, who managed the building for her, but would like Bob's opinion on the new offer.

Classify the following statements as in Exercise 5.

a. Bob Allen had no personal financial interest in Mrs. Wilcox's decision as to whether or not to sell her building.

b. Mrs. Wilcox had no dependents.

c. Mrs. Wilcox wanted as large an income, consistent with safety, as possible.

d. Bob Allen would be better off if Mrs. Wilcox were to invest her money in property that would grow in value instead of in income-producing property.

e. Mrs. Wilcox's building was worth more than $595,000.

f. The offer of $555,900 was not as attractive as the offer of $595,000 which Mrs. Wilcox had turned down.

g. Mrs. Wilcox had shown that she trusted Bob Allen's judgment.

h. Mrs. Wilcox's lawyer would certainly advise her not to accept the offer of $555,900, but she would have more faith in her nephew's judgment than in her lawyer's.

i. If Mrs. Wilcox were going to sell her building, it would be advantageous to her to sell it quickly.

j. Mr. Owen would raise his offering price if Mrs. Wilcox told him $555,900 was too little.

7. The Occupational Planning Committee of a civic welfare association in a large Eastern city made a study "to determine why qualified workers for certain occupations and professions are always in short supply." They gathered statistics from 1,221 male and 1,083 female students in schools in the area to determine whether the social prestige of some occupations is so low as to affect the number of students going into that occupation or profession. The table on page 346 shows the preferences of more than half the student population of the area, ranking occupations and professions by prestige and social status. Read the table *before* the rest of this problem.

Occupational Prestige Ranking of 30 Male Occupations by 12th-grade Males

Occupational Prestige Ranking of 30 Female Occupations by 12th-grade Females

OCCUPATION	RANK	OCCUPATION	RANK
Doctor	1	Nurse	1
Attorney	2	Teacher (high school)	2
Banker	3	Teacher (elementary school)	3
Engineer (civil, electrical, mechanical, etc.)	4	Airline hostess	4
		Laboratory technician	5
Teacher	5	Secretary (takes dictation and types)	6
Electrician	6	Social worker	7
Pilot	7	Dietician	8
Insurance salesman	8	Employment mgr. (hires and supervises)	9
Foreman (in a factory)	9		
Policeman	10	Reporter	10
Professional entertainer	11	Bookkeeper	11
Carpenter	12	Buyer (for a department store)	12
Soldier	13	Artist	13
Salesman (sells to factories and stores)	14	Librarian	14
		Telephone operator	15
Machinist (die maker, tool maker, pattern maker, etc.)	15	Beautician	16
Farmer	16	General office worker (types, files, records)	17
Social worker	17		
Auto mechanic	18	Professional entertainer	18
General office worker (does typing, filing, recording, etc.)	19	Office machine operator (runs mimeograph, multigraph, etc.)	19
Barber	20	Hostess (in a restaurant)	20
Plumber	21	Inspector (checks goods in a store or factory)	21
Factory machine operator (runs, e.g., drill press, punch press, lathe)	22	Sales person (sells dresses, millinery, etc.)	22
Grocer	23	Cook or chef	23
Sales clerk (in a retail store)	24	Sales clerk (in a drugstore, grocery, notions, etc.)	24
Truck driver	25		
Cleaner, presser	26	Factory machine operator (runs, e.g., drill press, punch press)	25
Filling-station attendant	27		
Waiter	28	Factory sewing machine operator (in a clothing factory)	26
Elevator operator	29		
Janitor	30	Waitress	27
		Elevator operator	28
		Maid	29
		Laundry worker	30

Further studies of representative schools in the area added the following facts:

There was little difference in these prestige ratings between the schools in the better suburbs and in the poorer districts of the city.

A subsequent study of students in the tenth grade and of the same students two years later in the twelfth grade showed only a few significant changes—airline hostess had dropped from first to fourth place, auto mechanic had dropped from tenth to eighteenth place.

Sons rated the occupations of their fathers higher than the average rating of the entire group of students. The only exceptions were the occupations of janitor and filling-station attendant.

If you had to write a report based on these actual facts, what conclusion or conclusions would you draw?

a. The results are inconclusive, and the prestige of occupations and professions is haphazard.

b. To recruit students for the various professions and occupations, find out what the fathers are doing and then try to interest their sons.

c. Students prefer occupations requiring mental rather than manual skills.

d. Students are idealistic and, therefore, rate highest those occupations which serve humanity.

e. Students are materialistic and, therefore, rate occupations on the basis of income.

f. Radio, television, and the movies have made medicine, law, nursing, and teaching the "glamour" occupations and this has affected the students' ratings.

g. Recruiters for various occupations and professions should start working with high school sophomores instead of seniors.

h. Specialized occupations requiring college educations have the highest prestige in today's society.

i. Intensive publicity about shortages of teachers, nurses, and engineers explains the high ratings of these occupations.

j. Every individual makes up his own mind what he wants to do or what he is fitted for, and prestige and "social status" have nothing to do with his choice.

k. The students may rank certain occupations high in prestige, but that rating has nothing to do with whether the students will try to enter these occupations.

If you were the secretary of the local engineering, nursing, medical, banking, or any other society interested in attracting young people into that occupation or profession, how would you use the facts in the study in a report on "How We Can Attract Young Men or Women into Our Profession or Occupation"?

8. What is wrong with the following:

a. Mr. Sutton's final course of action will depend on the answers to these three questions. I have chosen these three questions because this is the most logical way for Mr. Sutton to determine a course of action.

b. The Reynolds management must answer this critical question: Can they maintain their present policies and continue to expand the business? When they have answered this question, they must decide *how* to make the business grow. On the basis of this appraisal, they should build a new plant at Dover.

c. You will find it is better to advertise in magazines with large circulation because these magazines have more readers.

d. City dwellers spend more time watching television than rural people do, because during the last decade technological advances have given people much more leisure time.

e. Every reduction in price, if quality is not reduced, often results in greater sales.

f. Our salesmen displayed energy and initiative that our competitors could not match, and our share of the market rose from 10 to 25 percent, proving that ours is a superior product.

CHAPTER 16

ORGANIZING THE MATERIAL

Now that you have collected the material for your report, you face the most difficult task of the report writer—organizing it so that your reader will easily follow the structure you have selected. The absence of such organization is detected by almost any reader, although he may not be aware of precisely what is wrong. When a businessman complains that the reports he receives are badly written, yet he cannot explain exactly what is wrong, the chances are that they are poorly organized.

Organization involves imposing a pattern upon your material so that your reader can follow it easily and logically and so that it serves the purpose to which he will put your report. This task will be made much easier if your research methods follow our recommendation in Chapter 14 (*Keeping Track of Your Materials*, page 317) to use a consistent method of recording your research, because your cards can now be sorted into a skeleton outline for your report. In this process, you will have to eliminate extraneous ideas or irrelevant materials by using the criterion of whether they serve the reader's purpose. Particularly, you must avoid the temptation of inexperienced report writers to say: "I've done a lot of hard work to get this material, and I'm going to use it all even though some of it doesn't quite apply." This mental attitude will inevitably result in a report which confuses and overwhelms its reader with a mass of undigested facts. Remember that your job is to serve the reader's purpose, not to impress him with the amount of hard work you have done. If you have worked hard at both the research and the organization, the results will impress him without your being obvious about it.

Fundamentally—and we are speaking now in the broadest terms—there are three patterns by which material can be organized for reports. Each of them has innumerable adaptations and modifications depending upon purposes and readers, but a knowledge of these patterns is essential as you think about how to organize your report:

1. *The inductive pattern*, which proceeds from *specific* facts, statements, and examples to *general* conclusions, recommendations, or results based on them.
2. *The deductive pattern*, which starts with *general* material—conclusions, results, recommendations, effects—and moves on to *specific* information, i.e. facts, statistics, causes, opinions which support the general material.
3. *The step-by-step* or *time sequence pattern*, which proceeds in the same order of events or the same sequence of time as the situation covered in the report.

You should keep these overall patterns clearly in mind not only because they are helpful to you but because you will want to *tell your reader how you have organized your material*. To do so is like providing signs along the highway—making it easy for people to follow their route to a destination. We shall discuss these three patterns in more detail in the following pages.

THE INDUCTIVE PATTERN

One of the oldest patterns of presenting thought can be paraphrased by saying, "Tell him what you are going to do. Do it. Then sum up what you've done." In fact, this is so old that if we trace it back across the centuries we find ourselves back to Aristotle, who pointed out that "a whole is that which has a beginning, a middle, and an end." In the inductive report pattern these three parts are:

1. An introductory section in which you tell your reader what you are going to do and how you're going to do it
2. A central portion in which you report on what you have done in the way you said you would do it
3. A conclusion (or summary or recommendations or results) summing up what you have done (or indicating what should be done next)

It will be helpful for you to arrange reports in this inductive pattern if you raise the following questions:

Why was this work done?
What work was done?
What were the results?
What do the results mean?
What action should be taken because of these results?

This report goes from specific—facts, figures, material of research—to general—conclusions, summary, recommendations. Along with this, it uses the well-tested method of starting with introductory material and progressing through factual support to conclusions.

Psychologically this pattern of organization is particularly adapted to one type of reader and to one situation. The reader who likes to examine all the evidence, who wants to look the whole situation over carefully before he makes up his mind, will usually welcome reports in this pattern. The situation in which it is psychologically sound to use this pattern occurs when the report writer knows that his reader may be hostile to or even surprised by his conclusions. The psychological effect of leading him through this orderly presentation takes him gently toward the unpleasant or surprising answer and prepares him along the way. Generally it will arouse less antagonism than if he were confronted with what he considers disagreeable, unusual, or "unfounded" conclusions and recommendations at the outset of the report.

THE DEDUCTIVE PATTERN

This is by far the most widely used form of report organization in today's business world. It is often called the *executive* report, the *management* report, or the *action-getting* report. Whereas the inductive report can be thought of in terms of

Reason or reasons
therefore
Conclusion or conclusions

The deductive pattern follows this pattern:

Conclusion or conclusions
supported by
Reason or reasons

As he turns the pages of a report in the deductive pattern, the reader goes from the general to the specific, the more important to the less important. It tends to become more detailed or more specialized in its last pages because it is designed for a reader whose fundamental question is "What do I need to know to act or to decide?" and who wants the answer at the outset.

For such a reader, you must lead from your main point (or points); if it's a recommendation, you present that first and follow it with an analysis of the factors that led you to make the recommendation; if it's a summary, you start there, indicating that it is based on the factual or statistical information presented later in the report. Your reader wants to be told concisely what the facts are, what ought to be done, how it should be done, and if we do it that way, what the results will be.

In the deductive pattern, therefore, you have a special obligation to *think your way through to the central issue or main point;* that is where you have to start, and, in effect, you retrace your own thinking with your reader, starting from that central point as you go into successive pages of the report. Actually, your process here is close to the newspaper reporter's; he knows his whole story when he starts writing. But into his "lead" paragraph he puts the major ideas, facts, or statements so that the reader can get a general idea of what it's all about; successive paragraphs give more and more details and specific information so that these may be lopped off in later editions without serious loss to the reader's understanding.

The deductive pattern imposes one obligation on the writer—*to start on common ground with the reader.* Before you state your conclusions or recommendations, you must orient him by answering his natural question: "What is this about?" As a matter of fact, the chief complaint voiced by executives about deductive reports is that they seem to start in the middle without adequate explanation. Therefore, while your conclusions and recommendations say to your reader "Here's the story in a nutshell," you must always introduce him to this story by saying "Here's what you must know to understand the story." You can do this by considering such questions as the following and providing answers to those which are relevant in a brief paragraph preceding the conclusions or recommendations:

What is the report about?

What relation does this report have to other problems, policies, research in the company?

How is it organized? (Unless report forms are so standardized as to require no explanation.)

How was the investigation done?

How long did it take?

What procedures, techniques, or materials were used?

What persons were involved?

Who authorized or requested the report? If it isn't authorized, why are you writing it?

What is the reader supposed to do with it? Read it? Read it and route it to others? Keep it as part of a permanent record?

THE STEP-BY-STEP AND TIME-SEQUENCE PATTERNS

Too many reports follow one or the other of these patterns because their writers are too lazy or too unaccustomed to think about their material. These patterns offer writers an easy way out by merely following the pattern the material itself offers—a sequence of time, a narration of steps involved, or a blow-by-blow description of how it all happened. This is effective when you aim at building to a climax, but the result is usually heavy on detail and light on emphasis. Furthermore, events or steps in an operation frequently follow one another in point of time, but they do not necessarily come to a conclusion or an end. The responsible report writer ought to look for causal relationships and logical developments in his material instead of merely recording chronological episodes.

Since the thesis of this book has been that by thinking you should impose an order on your material for your reader, we can hardly endorse a method which frequently avoids thought and allows the writer to say, "It happened in that order, and that's the way I'm going to tell it." Executives who read a lot of reports agree that this sequence-of-events pattern is used far too frequently. Young report writers will do well to use this pattern only when:

1. Time or the sequence of events are the most important factors in transmitting the facts of the report.
2. Readers express a definite preference for these patterns of organizing material.

Using the first of these criteria, you will generally find that a step-by-step pattern is well adapted to reports of manufacturing operations where a step-by-step analysis is essential; it is useful for reports about methods and procedures where you must follow through the responsibilities of individuals or departments so that a new procedure may be developed or an old one improved. Occasionally, this pattern is well suited to progress reports covering only a short period of time. Finally, some very specialized forms of report have to follow this pattern—for instance, claim reports on industrial accidents.

As to the second criterion, certain readers do prefer an analysis based upon a sequence of time or events. Often this preference is based upon an erroneous notion that such a pattern is the best way to present "all the background information." Such readers tend to be distrustful of attempts to summarize or to present the facts in brief. They prefer to have all the details, relevant or not, and occasionally they tend to lose sight of the forest because of all the trees. But if your readers prefer the blow-by-blow analysis, the step-by-step procedure, your reports should be patterned to these preferences.

The old cliché "first things first" does not really hold as a guide for writers, because the first event in time may not be the first in importance. To sort the inconsequential from the significant, the important from the trivial is the real function of effective report writing. To fall back on "it happened this way and I'm reporting it this way" is therefore an abdication of responsibility in most report-writing situations.

Nonetheless, there are situations in which the writer properly falls back upon the nature of the material he transmits and upon his own purpose to ascertain the best organizational pattern. For example, a report might be aimed at obtaining quick approval of a research project for which additional funding is needed. Tactically and psychologically the writer would err by beginning his report with a blunt request for funds. Psychology and the content itself dictate that the request be garbed in an inductive pattern starting with the importance of the project, the possible benefits accruing, and similar matters before the request for money is made. Similarly, a report intended to recommend change in an involved manufacturing process is best broken into a step-by-step analysis of components so that the reader is not forced to comprehend it in totality.

MAKING ASSUMPTIONS ABOUT READERS
AND PURPOSES

So far we have emphasized situations where readers and purposes are known. Unfortunately, this knowledge is not available in an increasing number of report-writing situations in today's business world. Complexity of organization often imposes layers of authority between executives requesting reports and those who write them. Frequently—with the best of intentions—intervening ranks try to "interpret" what is wanted; equally often, these interpretations are misleading or erroneous. Furthermore, since most large companies have facilities in different locations, sheer distance blurs what was formerly firsthand knowledge of readers' preferences and purposes. This lack of rapport is wasteful and costly, but it will doubtless persist until the specific cost of reports can be ascertained to reveal this inefficiency in terms of dollars and cents.

In such situations, the writer's only recourse is to make the best assumptions he can and proceed to organize and write his report on these assumptions. We can make this clear by showing how such assumptions will affect an actual report-writing situation. Suppose you get a request for a report from the Director of Office Services, whose office is located 500 miles from yours, saying, "I want to know whether we could save money on all our large mailings by typing the recipient's address on the envelope only, thus eliminating the duplication of an address on the letter itself."

The principal purpose of your report seems fairly clear: you assume that a decision must be made, and you collect the data necessary to make it. When you come to the writing of the report, however, you have to think through its purposes in more detail.

Let us look at one way in which you might organize your report:

Statement of Problem
Method of Getting the Information
1. You have sent out a questionnaire to 1,000 companies.
2. Here is how they were selected.
3. Here is the questionnaire sent.

Results of the Study
1. You have received replies from 490 companies, divided by size as follows:
    a. 79 replies from companies with fewer than 50 employees
    b. 153 from companies with 50 to 500 employees
    c. 81 from companies with more than 500 employees
    d. 177 from companies among the 1,000 largest in the United States

Conclusions
The study shows that:
1. A majority in all categories, except companies with fewer than 50 employees, pass mail on to individuals with the envelope unopened.
2. Even when the envelope is opened in the mail room or by other employees, the envelope is attached to the contents.
3. Of all firms answering, 87 percent—and, significantly, 95 percent of the largest companies, where mail could be misdirected more easily—either pass the mail on unopened or attach the envelopes to the contents.

You can, therefore, conclude that:
1. Your company need not go to the extra expense of double-addressing its direct mail.
2. However, it will have an added obligation to have the outside envelope in the most presentable form, since the great majority of recipients actually see it.

Notice the assumptions you have had to make in this situation. You are assuming that the Director of Office Services wants a recommendation, not merely information. You are assuming that he wants a systematic, fairly detailed presentation. If he wants only conclusions, your assumption was wrong, and he will find your report tedious. If he wants conclusions first, reasoning second, and the details supporting the reasoning last, you have made another wrong assumption, because you have probably organized your report backwards for him. Finally, you are assuming that he will want to read the questionnaire and the list of companies. If he doesn't, then this information should have been attached as an exhibit (or in an appendix) to indicate that it is optional reading.

Only one person—The Director of Office Services—can say which of these assumptions are right and which are wrong. But speaking generally, we can guess with reasonable certainty that the report writer was correct in his assumption about purpose and a systematic, detailed presentation but that he was wrong in not presenting conclusions first and in not using an exhibit or appendix for the details.

EXERCISES

(You may find it helpful to read Chapter 17 before beginning these exercises.)

1. You work as assistant to the director of personnel for Danny's Discount Stores, a chain of eleven retail outlets in strategic locations throughout a large metropolitan area. Recently, absenteeism among employees has curtailed sales because customers have been unable to get prompt service from salespeople and cashiers.

    Store hours at Danny's are 10 A.M. to 9 P.M. Monday through Friday and 9 A.M. to 9 P.M. on Saturday. These hours and the salaries at Danny's are comparable to similar stores in the area. One policy differentiates Danny's from other retail establishments: its stores always have separate geographical locations, i.e. Danny's will not build or lease in large urban shopping centers where it must compete with a number of other stores in close proximity. This long-established policy stems from management's conviction that by separating themselves from direct competition in their location, Danny's can sell more to each customer. This policy seems to be confirmed by seven years of profitable operations, in which the outlets expanded from one to eleven.

    As the first phase of your investigation of absenteeism, you have spent a week at Danny's Westwood branch, which is typical of the ten other outlets. It has 54 "permanent" employees, who work 8 hours a day on salary and commission; they are augmented by 36 "temporaries," who work at least 4 hours a day. Usually, the temporary help consists of high school students working after school and mothers who work during the time their children are in school.

    Absenteeism during the week from November 30 to December 6 when you were at the store was as follows:

	54 *permanent*	36 *temporary*
Absent on:		
Monday	13	14
Tuesday	9	7
Wednesday	11	5
Thursday	7	12
Friday	9	10
Saturday	6	16

The director of personnel has told you, "We'd like to aim at no more than 10 percent absenteeism for all permanent employees and 15 percent for temporary help. I don't know whether these figures are realistic or not, but I want you to find out. I also know that when pay day rolls around on Saturday, absenteeism drops for the permanent employees, but the temporary help don't seem to care."

Using all of the material in the last three chapters, outline how you would go about investigating (a) the causes, (b) the costs, and (c) the ways to control absenteeism in this situation. How would you organize this material for a report to the director of personnel, who has told you, "We need fast action to reduce absenteeism"? If your research shows that the isolated location of Danny's outlets is a cause of absenteeism (because employees can't go to restaurants nearby for lunch, because they can't see friends in other stores, etc.), would you recommend changing the policy of isolated locations? Give your reasons.

2. As background for this problem, you are to assume that your institution has been plagued by sit-ins which stopped class instruction, violent dissension about whether campus speakers should be screened and whether the campus newspaper should be controlled by the administration, and widespread discussions of how students can obtain a broader voice in such things as faculty appointments, the curriculum, student cheating, and extracurricular activities.

As a result of these events and disagreements, a group known as the Moderates has been formed with the slogan "Come let us reason together." Its purpose is to produce change through evolution rather than revolution, and it proposes to convince the 30 members of the board of trustees, in whom ultimate responsibility for the instituion is vested, that certain changes should be made.

Here is the composition of the board of trustees, to whom you must address written reports on behalf of the Moderates:

Average age in the fifties; more than a third over 60.

All well-educated; average income above $30,000.

Majority occupy "prestige occupations" in law, medicine, and business. One dean from another institution is the only representative of education.

Twenty-six males; four females. Twenty-nine white, one black.

In response to a formal request from the student publication, the trustees have submitted their answers to the following questions with their answers broken down as shown:

		Agree	Disagree
1.	Do faculty members have the right to free expression of opinion?	21	9
2.	Should campus speakers be screened by the administration?	22	8
3.	Should the administration control the contents of the student newspaper?	12	18
4.	Should students have an equal voice with the faculty in adding or deleting courses?	20	10
5.	Should students deal with cheating problems?	9	21
6.	Should students punished by local authorities for off-campus matters be disciplined by the college?	15	15

7.	Should students participate in appointments to the administration and to the faculty?	6	24
8.	Should scholastic aptitude be the most important factor in admission to college?	27	3
9.	Should the socially disadvantaged be admitted even though they do not meet normal requirements?	20	10
10.	Should students make the rules pertaining to student housing?	14	16

With this group as your readers, how would you go about doing the research, organizing the material, and presenting a written report whose purpose on behalf of the Moderates is to persuade and convince the trustees of each of the following:

a. Membership on the board of trustees should be increased to 40 by the addition of 10 student members.

b. The Curriculum Committee of the faculty, which has final jurisdiction on adding or deleting courses, should be increased from its present 7 members to 15 by the addition of 7 students and one alumnus.

c. All speakers on campus should be screened in advance by a committee composed of three faculty members, three representatives of the administration, and three students.

d. The student editor should have complete control over the student publication with no intervention by the faculty or administration.

e. The college should take no action in cases where students are involved in legal violations off the campus.

f. No student should be granted admission to the college unless he meets the normal entrance requirements.

g. Students should have an equal voice with the faculty in making new appointments and promotions to the faculty.

3. The following is a report written in April, 1970, by a telephone company employee, in answer to his supervisor's request for an analysis of the usefulness of tuition-aid plans and for a recommended course of action. A tuition-aid plan involves company payment of tuition fees of employees who attend school in their free time. The writer of the report was a graduate of a well-respected college who had been with the company for less than a year. X and Y have been substituted for the company names in the original report.

Make an outline of the topics dealt with in this report, and rearrange them into a logical sequence. Explain why your order is an improvement over the original. Rewrite the report to follow your outline.

Report on a Tuition-aid Plan

The problem facing the Employment Division of the X telephone company is the need to find a recruiting inducement capable of attracting greater numbers of qualified full-time personnel.

The local employment outlook is quite serious in an ever-tightening labor market. Expanded industries and general business growth are making huge demands on the labor market, and it is expected that these demands will increase still further in the future. Even without these pressures, every year, due to marriage, retirement on pensions and other reasons, a certain number of employees leave and must be replaced.

The sources being tapped for qualified labor are normal recruiting media such as newspaper, radio, and television advertising, public displays, and, more selectively, through high school, college and employee recruiting. However, these recruiting measures, although proven most satisfactory, have failed to produce the required number of applicants.

It is my opinion that the company has not achieved a good competitive position with other companies vying for the labor market supply because they do not offer enough to attract employees.

For example, the beginning wage for all first-level positions is $89 per week, in an area where $92–$105 can be obtained. However, because it is a public utility, a wage hike is difficult to obtain unless the Department of Public Utilities finds it satisfactory and so recommends it. Even if the Department of Public Utilities were to recommend it, the contention is that the company's stiffest competition, banks and insurance companies, await a telephone company wage increase and raise their beginning wage a few dollars higher. So a wage increase would appear to be of little competitive value.

In order to counteract the effects of the low beginning wage, discounted telephone service is advanced as a most desirable fringe benefit. After six months of service an employee is eligible for half rates on residence telephone service, applying only to exchange service and toll calls to points within the territory. However, one must have attained twenty years' service before becoming eligible for residence service without charge, including a "reasonable" amount of toll calls.

In addition to a low beginning wage, Blue Cross and Blue Shield are not paid by the company. This fringe benefit appears among those offered by many of the other companies in the area. When inquiry was made here, it was admitted that this definitely needed attention and was scheduled for a May revision.

The company's policy of first-level starting assignments may have a detrimental effect upon many applicants. For example, there are ambitious college or postgraduate people who feel that a first-level position, which they qualify for without their additional education, can be greatly improved upon elsewhere.

This problem of the need to improve company benefits to prospective employees is recognized by the Employment Division. In an effort to provide more of a stimulus for taking a position in the company, the Employment Manager and Recruiting Head formulated a tuition-aid plan for adoption by the telephone company.

My first step in gathering and evaluating data on the advisability of adopting this tuition-aid proposal would be a consideration of the financial structure of the company. I think it would be essential to determine the amount of money the company has available to spend. This should be obtained from the comptroller's office. This appears requisite to any further consideration due to the company's past financial record—one of the last among telephone companies until this present year, when the "belt was tightened" and they moved up close to the top.

Can this loosening of the financial belt be expected not to exceed $120,000 per year? This is the figure I have been given by a financial officer as the probable cost of a tuition-aid plan. And further, is this a valid cost figure to assume for the telephone company? The basis for this figure is derived from a proportion taken on the Y telephone company's tuition-aid data. (See exhibit below.)

The total payroll for that company is 38,986, compared to this company's 24,000, and the former's yearly expense is $180,000. By a simple proportion, which was used to obtain this $120,000, it does not work out to that figure, but $110,000. How is the additional $10,000 obtained? And why is only a mathematical assumption used when there are variable factors also needed? For example, differences in the two areas' educational opportunities, educational desires of employees, and wage variations all play a part in this cost figure.

Also playing a part in this cost figure is the Department of Public Utilities. Just how much control is exercised by them on company expenditures of this nature? Also, will there be any increase in rates, requiring Board approval, to finance such a proposition, or can this be absorbed by normal business operations?

After the financial data has been evaluated to determine the cost to the company of such a program, I would then try to ascertain the value of such a measure in performing the desired recruiting aim. Will this be of any discernible benefit to employee recruiting? Has it been to any other telephone company of those who presently have it?

Since the Y company's tuition-aid program has been in effect for three years, have they found a rise in applicants through the introduction of this fringe benefit? If so, how was this measured, and to what degree? If not, how do they justify the $180,000 expense per year?

If this program does not satisfy the need for a recruiting inducement, then it should be dropped at this point, and another alternative selected.

However, if after satisfying myself that implementation of a tuition-aid program would be beneficial for this company, I would then develop a program, using other programs in other companies for reference.

The benefits accruing to the company through such a program would be the attraction of more qualified personnel eager to improve themselves through education. The education thus gained can make an employee a more qualified, well-rounded member of the company. And in becoming a more well-rounded and efficient employee, he improves his chances of advancing in the company, thus obtaining not only intangible, but tangible, benefit from tuition-aid.

Exhibit
Proportion Obtained for Cost of Tuition-aid Plan
38,986 — No. of employees on payroll of Y company
24,000 — No. of employees on payroll of this company
$180,000 — Yearly tuition-aid program cost to Y company

$$\frac{38,986}{\$180,000} : \frac{24,000}{x}$$

$$38,986x = \$4,320,000$$
$$x = \$110,000$$

4. Among the proposals placed in the suggestion boxes of your company is one from Jack C. Hildreth. He has said, in part:

> *The most rewarding study that could be made to reduce costs would be an examination of reports in the company. Supervisors don't tell report writers precisely what is wanted in reports, and as a result, reports frequently have to be rewritten two or three times. Assignments of reports often filter down through two or three levels of management, each of which adds its own interpretation to the original assignment, so that the report writer is uncertain about the original request. I suggest that all 621 supervisory employees hold a meeting to discuss this situation in the interest of economy and better communication.*

Assume that you are a member of the committee on employee suggestions, which passes judgment on all suggestions and gives cash awards for meritorious ones. The committee believes that Mr. Hildreth's suggestion has merit but also feels that the meeting he recommends would be ineffective and cumbersome. You have been asked by the committee "to prepare a report which will make specific suggestions as to how Mr. Hildreth's ideas can be put into effect." How would you go about getting information for your report? How would you organize it? What methods would you suggest to achieve the results Mr. Hildreth wants?

5. Use an actual lecture, meeting, or conference you have attended as the subject matter for a report you have been asked to write for a person who was unable to attend. What changes would you make in the pattern of organization and writing if this report were to be prepared for persons who gave you the following statements of the purpose of such a report:

   a. "I want to know whether the time and money spent on the meeting was worth while."

   b. "I intend to use your report as part of my effort to have more such meetings next year."

   c. "Give me a synopsis of the high points to include in my annual report."

   d. "Let me know how this meeting relates to other things we have done this year."

   e. "Give me a frank appraisal of who benefited from the meeting and why."

6. For the past eight years, the General Merchandising Corporation, for which you work, has sent gift turkeys at Thanksgiving and Christmas to all its retired employees on pensions. With 431 such pensioners now on the company records, Mr. Manual C. Yates, in charge of employee relations, has asked you to give him a report on whether this policy should be abandoned, whether it should be continued, or whether some other form of gift should be substituted. The original purpose of this gift plan was to make older employees on pensions feel that they are remembered and that they are still part of the company, but in the past three years conditions appear to have changed. In the first place, 161 of the pensioners now live in Florida or California, and the problems of packing and refrigerating turkeys sent from Virginia have increased costs appreciably. In the second place, about 10 percent of the retired employees have registered complaints rather than gratitude at this policy. Typical of this reaction are such comments as, "We live alone now and, while we like being remembered, we don't know what to do with a

15-pound turkey," and "We live with our son and his wife and four children and we never quite know whether we ought to buy another turkey or not."

Your investigation reveals the following:

> The actual cost of the turkeys, which average 14 to 16 pounds, is $7.50, so that the company spends annually around $6,000 for the two holidays.
>
> Added to this cost is the fact that two company trucks are used for two days preceding Thanksgiving and Christmas delivering turkeys to the 271 employees still living in the general vicinity of the company. This cost has never been added to the charges for this gift plan on the company records.
>
> Two older employees in the employee relations department have made this gift plan almost a personal perquisite by spending the two days before the holidays riding along with the truck drivers and visiting with the retired employees. In many instances these two men have strongly hinted that if it weren't for their urging, the company would abandon the gifts.
>
> A quick check of five other companies in the area indicates that two follow the same policy as General Merchandising, one has never given such gifts to retired employees, and two are now sending checks for $10 with a turkey or a Christmas tree imprinted on them. These two companies are completely satisfied with their policy of sending these checks along with an appropriate letter of greeting from the president.

Using these facts, how would you organize a report making a specific recommendation to Mr. Yates? What criteria would you stress to support your recommendation—good employee relations, financial considerations, saving of employee time, or what?

7. As a member of the student governing board of your college, you are confronted each year with the vexing problem of how to allocate funds from the students' activities fees to various organizations and activities. Each year, representatives of the publications, athletics, musical, debating, and other organizations come before the board asking for more money for their budgets for the next year. At present, the $35 fee paid by all students is allocated as follows: $10 to athletics, entitling the student to admission to all home games; $12 to publications— $7 for the yearbook and $5 to the weekly newspaper; $5 for membership in the Student Union; $4 to the musical clubs; and the remaining $4 divided among the remaining organizations and activities.

The only official statement concerning the activities fund is contained in the catalogue: "The moneys obtained from the students' activities fees shall be administered by the student governing board and shall be so allocated as to foster school spirit, encourage extracurricular activities, and promote the best interests of the students and the college." But because of an outbreak of complaints on the present year's allocation of funds, the board has decided to attempt to write a more clear-cut and specific statement of policy. Furthermore, it has decided to make a complete study of how funds can be allocated most equitably because of protests in the columns of the weekly newspaper, which wants a larger budget to increase its size from six to eight pages weekly. An editorial has raised such questions as:

Why should all students contribute to debating when only 11 actively participate in forensics?

Why doesn't the Governing Board use the number of students participating in each activity as the basis for allocating funds?

Why should those who aren't interested in athletics be, in effect, forced to support them financially?

An athlete "answered" the last question by writing a letter to the editor saying: "I know that many students don't read the paper. Why should they pay for it? And how can you prove that you are really printing what students want? Maybe the board should take a readership survey; it might show that the paper's budget could be cut."

Assume that the board has assigned to you the task of preparing a report which will cover three central points:

1. A method of evaluating the contribution each of the activities or organizations makes to campus life.
2. An equitable basis of distributing funds
3. A statement of policy to replace the existing statement

How would you go about getting information for your report? How would you organize it? Write the report, adapting it to specific conditions or activities at your college.

CHAPTER 17

WRITING THE REPORT

When you have done your research and imposed a pattern on your material—
and only then—you are ready to write. At this point, you may yearn to imi-
tate the procedure of John Ruskin, the English essayist, to ensure the privacy
you will need for your task. He sent out cards reading: "Mr. J. Ruskin is about
to begin a work of great importance and therefore begs that in reference to
calls and correspondence you will consider him dead for the next two months."
You probably won't need such drastic measures, but at least you can try to
find times when you will be uninterrupted.

STEPS IN WRITING THE REPORT

Here is a suggested sequence of steps in writing a report. They will help you to
improve all aspects of your reports, but especially your organization.

1. *Plan your time* so that you are not forced to write your report at the last minute. Don't
   put off till today the report that is due tomorrow.
2. *Prepare an outline,* based on the structure you've selected and the notes you have arranged in groups, which shows your main points and the way the subpoints or subordinate detailed material relates to these main points. This will not only ensure that the

discussion follows a logical sequence, but will keep you from inadvertently omitting points as you write.

3. *From your outline, write an entire first draft.* At this stage, you are attempting to get the whole report down on paper. Don't aim at perfection; it is hard enough to get down what you have to say without trying to say it perfectly.

4. *Put the completed rough draft away at least overnight and preferably for several days.* This aging step is important. When your subject is fresh in your mind, you cannot read your report as a stranger would. Your mind fills in the gaps in your exposition and you are not aware of them. You are so sure of what you meant that you don't notice the points at which a reader may be confused.

5. *Then, come back to it and revise thoroughly.* At this point, you will have gained perspective, a more objective attitude toward your first draft. Generally speaking, it's always easier to edit someone else's writing. The lapse of time will help you to attain more of that impersonality which is invaluable when you revise. Now you can look at the proportion of your whole presentation to see that you've given adequate space and treatment to your central ideas. You can insert transitions where you had left gaps. You can polish your writing—and you'll doubtless find that some of the phrases you thought highly of the day before aren't quite up to standard. And, beyond all else, you can read your report from the point of view of your reader, using the criterion of whether it serves its purpose. Many writers find it useful to have someone who is not familiar with the subject of the report read it, to pass judgment on it.

Don't be afraid, or too lazy, to tear your first draft apart. If your organization seems faulty, use scissors and paste to change it. Test each paragraph by asking, *How does this paragraph move the reader ahead toward my conclusion?* If the answer is that it doesn't, then delete or rewrite the paragraph.

Eliminate irrelevancies. No one likes to do a lot of research and get no recognition for it, and no one likes to cut well-written paragraphs out of his reports. But if it turns out that the research results and the fine-sounding paragraphs are not essential, cut them out. They won't earn you any praise from a reader who recognizes their irrelevance.

You can't apply these judgments until you have something concrete before you—that's why you need a first draft. You can't judge effectively while you are preparing the first draft, because you're too involved in the writing, too close to your material; that's why you should back off and let a little time elapse. Later, with your draft before you, you can apply your most rigorous standards, aim at perfection.

Is this procedure too cumbersome? too involved? Not at all. Even the greatest writers—poets, novelists, essayists, and journalists—have had to go through a similar process. We see only the final product and tend to forget the hard work, the rigid discipline of change and revision, that produced it. Except in the rarest instances, polished performance stems only from the grind of constant rehearsal, of endless attention to detail.

In the last analysis, the quality of your reports will depend on the standards you set for them. There will be times and occasions when you may not be able to follow through all the steps we have suggested, but your reports will show that you haven't. If you are convinced that the ability to write clear, accurate reports is of inestimable importance to your career—and all the evidence indicates that it is—you'll have to develop the capacity for taking pains which this procedure involves. The experience of others has proved that you'll save time and write better reports by doing them this way instead of trying to turn out the final product in one frantic rush before the deadline. In the rest of this chapter, we will discuss the more specific aspects involved in the five-step process of writing a report.

PREPARING AN OUTLINE

An outline is to a final report what a preliminary sketch is to a completed painting. It takes time, effort, and thought, but without it your report will lack coherence and logic. Just as when you outline your reading to understand it completely, you outline your report material to help your reader grasp it in its final form. An outline helps in three ways: it enables you to spot gaps in your report, to test the relationships between parts of the report, and to see how the assertions, recommendations, or conclusions are validated. In summary, the process of outlining forces you to put your own thoughts in order so that you can put them before your reader in orderly fashion.

For many students, outlining has been made to seem too formidable a task because of overfussy instruction in the mechanics of outlining. The important fact for report writers is that it doesn't matter what type of outline you use so long as it helps you. For short reports, a few major points jotted down in logical sequence will serve as a sufficient guide. Effective speakers learn this technique early, always noting their main points in relation to their thesis or their recommendation. Here's the way a brief report—oral or written —on metered mail might be arranged in what is called "jotted form," the simplest method of outlining:

Thesis: Our company should install postage meters
for all departments

1.   Use of stamps is wasteful, inefficient
        Have to be licked
        Require frequent trips to post office
        Employees frequently appropriate them for personal mail
        Costly because frequently two 6¢ stamps are available and used for 10¢ air mail

2. Metered postage is more businesslike
   Letters are dated, canceled, and postmarked be-
     fore they go to post office; hence, they get
     through post office faster
   Provides place for small ad for business
   Always gives right postage for letters and pack-
     ages
   No waiting in line at post office
   Provides better appearance for letters

The great advantage of even such a simple outline is that it schedules the writer's ideas so that he is sure of his direction, certain of the relationship of parts.

Probably the most useful form of outline for report writers is the topic outline, which expresses each point in single words or brief phrases or clauses and arranges material into heads and subheads, each rank in parallel phrasing. The heads and subheads are marked by alternating numbers and letters in the following sequence: Roman numeral I, capital letter A, arabic 1, lowercase a, and finally (1) and (a). The mechanics are not important in themselves, but they are significant in revealing relationships, as for instance that A, B, and C are much more important then (1) and (2), and that A and B as well as (1) and (2) have the same *relative* importance. To illustrate the topic outline, let's assume that you have been commissioned to do a report on all forms of communication within your company and to recommend how economies can be effected. You have decided that a number of publications, reports, bulletins, and procedure manuals must be eliminated, but your first task is to show the large number and the diversity of readers prevailing at present. Here's how a topical outline of such material would look.

*Thesis: Only by eliminating some of the large number
of publications at Blankco can economy be achieved*

I. Publications classified by readers:
   A. For stockholders
      1. Quarterly reports accompanying dividends
      2. The Annual Report in June
   B. For the general public
      1. "Research at Blankco—a Service to So-
         ciety"
      2. "Free Enterprise"
   C. For Blankco employees
      1. To all employees
         a. Blankco Magazine
         b. "Your Pension Plan"

    2.   To members of management only
       a. Six-month forecast
       b. Various manuals
          (1) Parts manuals for the repair de-
              partment
          (2) The service manual for dealers

II.   Criteria for judging these publications:
    A. _____
       1.   _____ etc.

By making your headings grammatically parallel (i.e. using all nouns or all verbs for parallel topics instead of mixing phrases, nouns, sentences), you will underscore the relationships you are trying to develop in writing the report.

But the really important aspect of outlining is not such conventions and mechanics, *but what works for you.* You will develop your own efficient techniques with practice. Can you write a report without an outline? Perhaps—but unless you are very experienced, the odds are against you. Actually, the best argument for outlining is that it saves time—one experienced writer estimates that every minute spent on outlining saves him a half hour in writing.

BEGINNING THE REPORT

If you follow the method we recommend—writing a first draft and putting it aside for revision—the sometimes painful process of beginning the report is greatly simplified. At this stage, the important goal is to *start writing:* you will waste time waiting for the perfect beginning to leap into your mind. There are several approaches that may be helpful when you start to write.

Many writers recommend, if you cannot think of the right beginning for your first draft, that you skip it and go on to something else. Start with some specific description or analysis. You will probably think of an appropriate beginning later—perhaps by the time you have written a paragraph or two, perhaps not until you have finished the whole report. It is usually much better to write up the material you feel able to handle and set the harder parts aside. It is easier to fill in the gaps than to struggle to produce a perfect document the first time through.

If you don't like leaving gaps, then simply write any sort of beginning, no matter how poor, and get on with the rest of the writing. You can then come back and think of a better beginning later. As a matter of fact, you are quite likely to find that you come up with an excellent beginning in the second, third, or fourth paragraph, or even later, and that all you have to do is transpose the material or discard your first paragraph or two.

Another way to get started is to imagine that the person you are writing to is sitting across from your desk. How would you begin a conversation about your topic? Use this as the beginning of your report.

There are at least three elements that may be called for in a beginning. One is a simple statement of what the communication is all about. For example, just as you might begin a letter by saying: "You have requested a list of the distributors of our product in eastern New Jersey. The list follows," you might start a report by saying: "This report analyzes the profitability of our product X and deals with the question of whether we should reduce its price." This kind of statement tells the reader what he is going to read about. It is useful to the writer, too. He can check back on it once in a while to see if he is really talking about what he promised to discuss.

The second element is a statement of the writer's proposition, thesis, or conclusion. For example, your letter might begin: "Our distributor located nearest to your business is the X Company. I am sure you will find the people there helpful and courteous." Your report might begin: "Our product X is currently not as profitable as it could be, and its price should be lowered 50 cents per unit." This kind of statement tells the reader right away what the point of your communication is. Again, it serves as a useful guide to the writer, who can ask himself, as he goes on with his writing, whether he is sticking to the point.

The third element is a statement to catch the reader's interest, to persuade him that what you have to say is important and that he should take the trouble to read it. For example, your letter might begin: "You will find that our distributors can help you to make money." Or your report might begin: "Our product X is currently unprofitable, and unless we reduce its price it can lead the company into serious trouble."

Any particular piece of writing may require, in its beginning, one, two, or all of these three elements. It may require none of them, although this is unlikely. Sometimes you may feel that your reader already knows what your report is about, especially if he asked for it, and that there is no need to tell him in your introduction. But before you come to this conclusion, there are a few possibilities you should consider. It may well be that by the time he receives your report, he will have forgotten his request. Or he may have forgotten exactly what he requested. This is especially possible if the request was made much earlier or if he has requested many reports. In many cases, even when the reader remembers exactly what it was he asked for, he may be interested in knowing whether you understood him. He may expect to find, at the beginning of your communication, an assurance that you are going to give him exactly what he asked for. If there is any doubt in your mind as to whether your reader needs or wants this information, you had better put it in.

There is an important advantage in this first element of a beginning. It is usually very easy to write. All you have to do is decide what the content of your report is, and then describe it in a sentence. We will soon discuss some reasons why this may not be the most effective first sentence of a report, but if you cannot think of any other way to start off, you can always fall back on a simple statement of what the report is all about.

Here is an opening paragraph restricted entirely to this first element. It is from a report replying to a request for an analysis and appraisal of a company's situation.

(1) As you have requested, I have analyzed the current situation of the company. My analysis will be presented in three sections: first a group of general comments, then a discussion of specific strengths and weaknesses in the company's position, and finally a conclusion based upon them.

The second element, a statement of the writer's recommendation or conclusion, is useful in that it gives the reader something to focus his attention on. It tells him why you have written the kind of report that you have. You may have written an analysis or appraisal in response to a request. But this, alone, does not explain the kind of analysis you have written. Once the reader knows what your recommendation is, he can relate everything you say to that recommendation, and what you say becomes that much more meaningful. At times, you may not want to state your recommendation at the beginning of your written communication. For one thing, you may be afraid that it will produce an unfavorable reaction. In such a situation, you may want to lead up to your conclusion gradually. Or you may simply feel you cannot express your recommendation or conclusion in one sentence, or even in one short paragraph. In this case, you are perhaps only wasting your reader's time if you try to describe your conclusion concisely. Here is an example from another report written in response to the same request.

(2) We are faced with current liabilities of more than one million dollars and the necessity of meeting an annual sinking fund payment plus interest of about $100,000, while we possess only $800,000 in cash. For these reasons, this company must take immediate action to increase sales if it is to stay in business.

This beginning tells us immediately what the writer's conclusion is—immediate action to increase sales. He has not spelled out his recommendation—that is, he has not said *how* to increase sales—but he has shown us that increasing sales is his theme.

The third element, the statement designed to attract the reader's interest, is much less important in report writing than in almost any other kind of writing. Except in special situations—when you are writing sales literature, for example, or an article for a business journal—you can assume your reader's interest. The writer of an essay or a short story cannot make this assumption. He must awaken interest at the start and persuade the reader to go on. Still, if you are in any doubt as to whether the subject matter of your communication will seem important to your reader—and this is likely when you are writing on your own initative and not in response to a request—it may be worthwhile to begin with a statement that will convince the reader of the importance of what he is going to read. Here is a third beginning for the report we have been discussing.

> (3) This company is in very serious trouble. The drain on cash caused by unanticipated capital expenditures, the drastic sales decline, and the consequent operating loss have put the company close to bankruptcy. Therefore, the most pressing problem is increasing sales to a profitable level.

Compare this with example (2). The first sentence, especially, is designed to catch the reader's attention and hold it. The writer of example (3) then goes on to state his theme or proposition. Observe, however, that the writer of (2) has given us specific information. We can see more clearly what is wrong with the company from example (2). While both include an indication of the writer's proposition as well as a statement designed to attract interest, the writer of (2) has stressed the former, while the writer of (3) has stressed the latter. Neither has shown any concern for the first element—describing what the report is all about—as the writer of example (1) did.

You may feel that example (1) is not as interesting or informative as it might be. You may also feel that (2) and (3) begin too abruptly, and that there should be some introduction stating what the report is all about. Here is another example, offering within itself an interesting contrast between the two ways of beginning.

> (4) The purpose of this report is to analyze this company's current position. On the basis of this analysis, the concluding section of the report will present the major issue to which the company must devote immediate attention.
>
> The most striking characteristic of the company is a serious decline in sales which, unless corrected, could lead to bankruptcy in a short time. [The paragraph then went on to document this statement and draw a conclusion.]

The first paragraph of example (4) is very similar to example (1). The first sentence of the second paragraph is very similar to example (3), and somewhat similar to example (2). Some writers would simply strike out the first paragraph of example (4) and begin with the statement of the writer's proposition. A compromise between this and leaving example (4) as it stands might be to greatly abbreviate the first paragraph, leaving some explanation of what the report is all about, but moving very quickly to an attention-getting statement of the writer's proposition. Suppose we simply delete the second sentence of the first paragraph and move the first sentence of the second paragraph up:

> The purpose of this report is to analyze the company's current position. The most striking characteristic of this position is a serious decline in sales which, unless corrected, could lead to bankruptcy in a short time.

Now we have a beginning that incorporates all three of the elements we have discussed.

No one has ever contended that a business report will make the best-seller list or, indeed, will reach any but a limited group of readers. But there is no reason to conclude, therefore, that devices to make reports interesting are prohibited. Since the beginning and the concluding sections of reports are the parts which will most surely be read, a beginning that whets the reader's interest can alleviate the general air of dullness characterizing the majority of business reports. Students can learn many useful techniques by becoming conscious of the way professional journalists begin their stories in the business press such as the *Wall Street Journal* and *U.S. News and World Reports.*

Regardless of the specifics of the beginning, we are led back to our original theme—that *purpose* is all-important and that you must put yourself in your reader's place and ask yourself, "What would I want or need in an introduction to this report?" We have suggested some wants and needs, and some purposes, that are likely to be applicable. But only by thinking through the particular report you are about to write can you arrive at an appropriate beginning.

PARAGRAPHING THE REPORT

During the process of actual writing, the best way for the writer to view a report is as a number of paragraphs linked by logical relationships. For the paragraph is the basic unit in the organizing and writing of a report. It serves to break the text into readable units; it groups sentences around a central idea or subject; it presents information in easily assimilated units because it clusters sentences around one central thought. This central thought is generally expressed in the *topic sentence*, and the accompanying sentences within the paragraph should expand, explain, define, contrast, exemplify, or support it. If you think of the topic sentence as providing a general label as to the contents of the paragraph, you can then make sure that the paragraph contains no extraneous or irrelevant sentences which cannot be classified under that label.

The ways of organizing and developing paragraphs are myriad. Because of the special functions and reading habits involved in reports, beginners will find it helpful to place the topic sentence either at the beginning or the end of the paragraph. Later on you will learn other methods of placing the topic sentence. But in your first reports, try to begin with a sentence which introduces the subject of the paragraph or to end with a sentence which summarizes its whole thought. By doing so, you learn to judge whether all the material in the paragraph is relevant to the topic sentence; you also help the reader who wants only your main ideas as well as the reader who prefers to be led through the detail.

You can generally support the statement in the topic sentence in three ways:

1. By giving reasons or facts
2. By providing examples or details which explain or clarify
3. By following a sequence of events or the steps in a process

Later, you can learn other methods to vary your paragraph organization; you can then use comparison, contrast, definition, restatement, and building to a climax.

No one can give dogmatic rules for developing paragraphs, but you will come very close to the essence of effective paragraphs if you ask two questions:

1. What is the central idea or main point in this paragraph?
2. What must I tell my reader to support or explain or clarify it?

We can illustrate this relationship between the topic sentence and the reader's expectation by a few examples of topic sentences from reports.

This policy of retaining canceled checks for six years needs revision.

Here the reader's natural question is, "*Why* does the policy need revision?" and the writer has an obligation to give reasons in the rest of the paragraph.

Several occurrences during the first quarter confirmed this opinion.

The reader logically expects specific instances which confirm the opinion.

The modern manager ought to be a teacher too.

The reader expects an explanation to answer his question, "Why?"

Using the last topic sentence, we can show the difference between an organized, integrated, and logically developed paragraph and one which is thoughtless:

> The modern manager ought to be a teacher too. While college professors frequently lack business experience, they have had experience in teaching. Managers in business, however, do not normally think of themselves as teachers, but they are. Many a young man starting his career wishes that his first supervisor had been a better teacher. His whole career might have been different if only the supervisor had learned to train him properly. In fact, business wastes time, money, and future potential by not learning to teach.

(Notice the irrelevant comments on college professors, the shift in viewpoint to the opinions of young men in business, the jump to the last sentence.)

> The modern manager ought to be a teacher too. In reality, he has two major functions—training an understudy for his job and helping young employees to start their careers effectively. In both these functions he is essentially a teacher. By learning to instruct those he supervises, he can save time for himself and money for the company. In training an adequate understudy for himself, he is actually preparing himself for greater responsibilities in the future; in helping young men to start their careers properly, he is developing the potential human resources of the company.

(Notice the consistency of viewpoint, the logical analysis of the two functions of the manager, and the subsequent development of each of these functions.)

Vary the length of your paragraphs. When they appear too long and too unwieldy, break them up. Long paragraphs usually indicate that the thought expressed in your topic sentence is too complex or too inclusive; try breaking it down into smaller and simpler components. Test your paragraphs by these criteria:

1.   What is the central idea or topic?
2.   What does the reader need to support it or explain it?
3.   Is there anything which does not relate to that idea or topic?
4.   Are the sentences in logical sequence to explain or support the topic sentence?

LINKING THE PARAGRAPHS OF A REPORT

In the previous section we have urged you to consider the paragraph as the basic unit or building block of the report. In this section we will discuss how paragraphs and sentences can be used to give unity to your report by linking one part to another with a device which makes your reports readable—the transitional paragraph or sentence.

Now, take a careful look at the paragraph you have just read. It is called a *transitional paragraph*; it makes a transition between the material preceding it and the material which follows. The function of such a paragraph is to help the reader as he moves along from one phase of the presentation to the next. It prods him to look back to where he has been and to look ahead to where he is going. Here is how the paragraph bridges the gap as we move into a new phase:

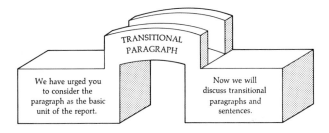

Since many reports are long, complex documents, you should be particularly careful to insert such paragraphs of transition between the sections. You can place them either at the end of one section or, as we have done, at the beginning of the next one. The technique is simple—tell the reader briefly of the major points you have covered, or remind him of your earlier announcement of the overall plan of your report and point out what you are going to do next.

In linking your ideas as you go from paragraph to paragraph, you can employ this same technique, but here you will use transitional sentences instead of paragraphs. To do this skillfully, you must become aware that certain words and phrases make your reader look back and others make him look ahead. As your writing becomes more effective, you can do both in the same sentence. Notice how the underlined words in the following illustrations perform one or both of these functions:

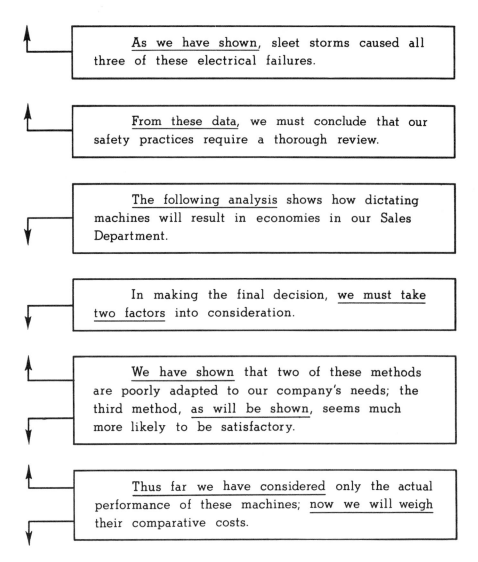

By using such sentences, you can make your reports easy to follow because these transitions show your reader what material is coming next and how it relates to what he has already read. This is the mortar that holds chunks of ideas together. Make frequent use of words like *since, as a result, because of this* to show causal relationship; show purpose by *to* (*to do this*), *so that, with a view to*. Underscore added ideas by *also, in addition, furthermore*. Emphasize contrast by *and yet, on the other hand, in contrast to*. Give your reader a guide to the steps in your story by using *next, in the second place, the third step,* and *finally*.

USING HEADINGS

Some writers prefer to insert headings at the time of final revision; others find them useful guides for the rough draft. Regardless of the timing, headings are among the most useful devices in reports: they tell the reader what is coming next; they break the text into readable units; and for business readers who are frequently interrupted when they read, they supply a convenient peg for emphasizing the section where the interruption occurred. Furthermore, headings clearly show the main divisions, subdivisions, and sub-subdivisions of your report, so that he can see your outline at a glance and can easily locate the sections which are of special interest to him.

But don't rely on headings as a substitute for good organization. Many writers of business reports seem to think that any writing becomes adequately organized when headings are inserted. If your organization is bad, headings will either emphasize this or be inaccurate. In either case, your reader will not be pleased.

The kinds of headings

In a long, complex report, the position of the heading and the use of capitals or of underscoring help your reader to see the importance of the material as well as the subordinate relationship of the supporting material within the report. The best current practice is to indicate these headings and subheadings as follows:

1.

TITLES or MAJOR DIVISIONS

(Center on the page; all capital letters; underscore each word.)

2.

MAIN HEADINGS

(Center on the page; all capital letters.)

3.

Subheadings

(Center on the page; begin each word with a capital letter;
underscore entire subheading.)

4. Marginal Headings
   (Begin at the margin on a separate line with double space above and below; begin each important word with a capital letter; underscore each word.)

5. Paragraph Headings   (Place these headings at the usual five-space paragraph indention; begin each important word with a capital letter; underscore each word. The entire heading is followed by a period, two spaces after which occurs the first word of the paragraph.)

You will probably use all of these headings and subheadings only in your longest reports, term papers, or theses. Shorter pieces of writing would require an adaptation of these headings to make them suitable to the material and useful to the reader. For instance, you would probably use only the marginal headings for short pieces of writing such as two- or three-page reports. Your use of headings will require judgment on your part, since it is impossible to lay down any basic system of headings which will cover all kinds of reports; but remember that most reports use too few headings and present their material in large eye-repelling chunks. By using headings judiciously, you can help your reader to locate the significant parts of your report and to see the relationship of one part to another.

You can also help him by the mechanical setup of the pages of your report. Since many reports are bound, you should take special care to see that the margins are wide, that the pages are numbered clearly—the most convenient place is the upper right-hand corner—and that you have left plenty of white space to let daylight into your copy. These are mechanical details, but they directly affect the impression your report makes.

THE STYLE OF THE REPORT

The way in which you express your thoughts and information is your style. When we come to the style of business reports, we run headlong into a convention or tradition which has straitjacketed the writing of generations of business writers. This tradition insists that the style of all reports should be impersonal, formal—and deadly dull reading. In grammatical terms, this convention insists on reports written in the third person, passive voice; it leads to such blurred pomposities as: "In the case of the fourth experiment, however, a problem is presented which is very difficult," instead of "The fourth experiment, however, presents a difficult problem."

Here, for instance, is a statement from a book on report writing which was written about two decades ago and was used by many of today's business readers for their instruction in report writing:

> Good style is slightly formal; impersonality is the rule. Instead of "We completed the experiment," the preferable form is "The experiment was completed." All pronouns of the first and second person, colloquialisms such as "a lot of," and contractions such as "don't" are to be avoided. Yet, despite the professional tone, a successful report reflects its writer's personality.

The thoughtful reader of these instructions might well be a bit puzzled; he should also be a bit skeptical and ask *why* reports clothed in such style are effective and *how* "a successful report reflects its writer's personality" when these instructions can only lead to formality and impersonality.

In all fairness, we should point out that such rules governing the style of reports have grown up from many writers' laudable desire to be modest and to avoid injecting themselves into their reports. Commenting on this awkward style, *Fortune*, in an excellent article called "The Language of Business," examined the flaws of written and spoken English in today's business world:

> First, the written variety—and that infamous jargon, which for want of a better term, we'll call businessese. Almost invariably, "businessese" is marked by the heavy use of the passive construction. Nobody ever *does* anything. Things *happen*—and the author of the action is only barely implied. Thus, one does not refer to something, reference is made to; similarly, while prices may rise, nobody raises them.*

By now you have probably decided that in choosing a style for your reports you are between the devil and the deep blue sea. We have been saying that the style of a report follows a convention of being formal and impersonal —and we have been poking fun at the results. What's the answer for the person who wants to write reports in a style which is both effective and acceptable in business?

As always, the answer lies with the report reader. If he is of the older, more conservative school who learned the conventions of report writing from a textbook similar to the one we quoted, he will probably prefer a formalized, impersonal style. The number of such report readers will certainly diminish in the seventies if only because ours is an era which strips aside artificial and conventional barriers to communication. For that reason, we can conclude that personalizing, simplicity and directness in language, and use of the active voice will increasingly characterize business reports. Here then are a few suggestions for transmitting your ideas in a clear readable style for the majority of business readers, who are not so much concerned about a "special style" for report writing as they are about getting results from reports.

Make every word count

Wordiness is without doubt the worst fault of all report-writing style; it results in needless expense and waste. The investment that business, industrial, and research organizations put annually into reports is impossible to calculate, but it is unquestionably a huge sum. To make your reports a sound

---

*Reprinted, by special permission, from *Fortune's* Communication Series, *Is Anybody Listening?* Copyright 1950 by Time, Inc.

investment, you will have to get rid of certain preconceived notions that have plagued report writers in business and industry. We can sum up the best ways to eliminate wordiness in reports by offering three suggestions: First, you will have to forget the concept of the formalized conventional style we have discussed. Second, you will have to get over the idea that a long report is somehow better or more impressive than a short one. Third, you must be willing to revise.

Keep your sentences short

One of the barriers to good reports is the long, rambling, unorganized sentence, which we have already discussed in Chapters 2 and 3. We need only emphasize the general principle here—when you write reports, keep in mind that the short sentence is generally better than the long one. As you look over your first draft of your report, watch out for sentences that run on and on. Break up these long sentences into shorter ones.

In your preference for short sentences, you should avoid extremes; a series of short, choppy, uniform sentences can be as annoying to your reader as very long ones. Ideally, you should aim for variety in both the length and structure of your sentences. Here is an example of the writing of a student who thought that all he had to do to write well was to write short sentences. "There are two parts to the process. The first is the preparation of the sample. The second part is the actual test. The preparation of the sample requires three steps. The first step is the washing of the sample in dilute acid. The acid should be handled carefully." Such a series leaves your reader with a feeling that he is running in place; you can avoid this effect by tying your ideas together and varying your sentence patterns.

Avoid these word traps

We cannot make a comprehensive list of all the faults of report-writing style, since every writer has his own devices when he starts to pad. Certain forms of wordiness are, however, common to many reports, partly because writers are trying to be impersonal and partly because they pick up these "fuzzy" expressions from other reports. Notice how clear thinking cuts down the wordiness in the following sentences from actual reports:

> This appears to be particularly difficult in view of the fact that much of the detailed information required is not presently available until March of the following year.

By linking this causally, we can say: "Since much of the detailed information is not available until the following March, this will be difficult."

Will you please get in touch with me at your earliest convenience in order that we can review this audit. We would also like to review with you at that time your final conclusions with respect to this situation.

When this concluding sentence of a report was discussed in a class of young businessmen, they agreed that "If it's the boss writing, he should use two words—*See me!*" If the relationship is the other way 'round, say "I'd like to review this audit with you, particularly the conclusions, whenever it's convenient."

An extremely undesirable condition in the mismailing of invoices to customers is reported by our Accounts Receivable Department. This type of condition must not exist if we are to maintain satisfactory customer relationships. (*33 words*)

By tying ideas together: "To maintain satisfactory relationships with our customers, we must correct the mismailing of invoices which our Accounts Receivable Department has reported." (*21 words*)

Another advantage of the prepunched form is that by reducing the time required to process a credit transaction, the next customer to be served will not be kept waiting as long as he normally would be. (*36 words*)

By eliminating unnecessary words: "The prepunched form will also reduce the time required to process a credit transaction so that the next customer can be served faster." (*23 words*)

Bills were paid promptly thereby enabling us to take full advantage of any discounts which were offered to us by vendors. (*21 words*)

By making this direct and active: "By paying bills promptly, we took full advantage of vendors' discounts." (*11 words*)

We do not anticipate any difficulty in meeting the due date which we established, which is April 30 for this project. (*21 words*)

By eliminating the unnecessary clauses: "We expect no difficulty in meeting the established due date of April 30 for this project." (*16 words*)

Each of these men has instituted several changes during the last four weeks which have contributed toward the excellent operation of that section despite the

temporary handicap due to the loss of a Control Clerk and a Supervisor as reported in last month's Summary of Operations. (*One sentence—46 words*)

By breaking it into separate sentences: "Both these men have made several changes which contributed to the section's excellent operation. They accomplished this despite the loss of a Control Clerk and a Supervisor which
was reported in last month's Summary of Operations." (*Two sentences—
36 words*)

It is therefore necessary that a varitype production schedule be set up and maintained if this job is to be completed and in Minneapolis by April 30th. (*27 words*)

By cutting out the waste: "We must set up and maintain a production
schedule to get this job completed and in Minneapolis by April 30." (*20 words*)
The mere counting of words saved by recasting these sentences is not
primarily important except to demonstrate what can be accomplished. What
is significant is the waste produced when such writing is multiplied throughout a long report—a waste of time in writing, in transcribing, and in reading.
And, more important, these sentences *obscure* the line of communication by
forcing the reader to wade through vague, indefinite expressions to figure out
relationships which the writer ought to point up for him. Such writers simply
duck responsibility and, in effect, say to their readers. "Here it is—you figure
it out and get to the essence. I'm too lazy, too tired, too busy, or too vague to
think and to revise."

One last word about your style

In the final analysis, you should aim at a readable, unobtrusive style
adapted to your reader. But get rid of any notions that you have to be pompous or dull. You can persuade or convince your reader more easily by being
interesting than by being routine. Keep in mind the fact that the reports you
write in business may be passed up, or down, or across the organization to
salesmen, lawyers, accountants or personnel men and to representatives of
advertising, operating, methods and procedures, or purchasing departments.
The one quality all these people have in common—other than working for the
same organization—is that they are all human beings. As one topflight executive said, "I don't care about anything else in reports as long as they are
accurate, concise, and sound as if they had been written by one human being
for another, which most of our reports don't!"

ENDING THE REPORT

Endings

Concluding paragraphs are generally easier to write than beginning paragraphs. When you reach your concluding paragraph, you know what your report is all about; you know what conclusions you have reached, which are important and which less important; you know which will be most useful to the reader, and which less useful; which he will probably be pleased to read about and which he may not like so much. You are in a position to sum up what you have to say.

With the inductive pattern, a strong ending is easy because the whole structure builds from specific to general. With time or step sequence, you also have an order which often leads naturally to climax and effective conclusion. Even when you use the deductive pattern, don't just trail off into trivia the way some people let their voices drop off at the end of their sentences. Remember that different people may read different parts of your report for different purposes—and that you should end your detail section by a brief summary of its highlights. In this characteristic, the deductive report may well have both an overall summary at the beginning for the management reader and a concluding statement at the end of the more detailed section for the technical reader. This arrangement may deny the old Danish proverb that "Everything has an end, except a sausage, which has two"—but it is nevertheless functional for the two types of reader. The really important instruction for ending a report is to stop when you've said what is necessary to your reader's understanding.

A helpful way to think about concluding paragraphs is in terms of their three basic functions—to give the reader a sense of completeness, to emphasize the things you want emphasized, and to indicate what the reader should be thinking about and what course of action he may follow.

In using the final paragraph for the first function, you should let your reader know that you have said all you need to say.

Consider the following example. It is the last paragraph of a report written in response to a request for an analysis and appraisal of a company's situation, with a recommendation for action.

(5) The President of the Company is in a state of poor health and there is some question as to the length of time that he will be able to remain as an active manager of the company. In early 1971, he was forced to retire from the active role of President for several months for reasons of poor health.

This paragraph gives the impression that the writer simply ran out of time, paper, or perhaps words, if he felt he had a word limit. We expect something more: some explanation of the importance of his conclusion and some recommendation for action. Here is a similar example:

> (6) The credit terms given by this company may be too tight, since there have been no major bad debt losses for a long time. Tight credit, when the industry trend is toward very liberal credit, could harm sales, as could a shortening of the discount period.

Again, we are led to expect that a topic will be discussed more fully, but the writer simply stops. Contrast examples (5) and (6) with the following:

> (7) I feel that this plan will enable your company to grow at a satisfactory rate. You may someday take your place as a national distributor, but you must grow into this stage gradually. I hope I have been of help in establishing the direction that you and your company should take in the future.

A second function of the concluding paragraph is to emphasize the things that you want to emphasize. You want to focus your reader's attention on the important matters and leave him with the proper perspective. Here is an example, again from a reply to a request for an analysis and appraisal and recommendations for action:

> (8) The President's selection of executives is further questioned, since he obviously has no one on his staff who can initiate ideas for new products, increased sales, or decreased costs. A vice-president maintains strict credit policies, whereas a more lenient policy might result in more dealers and increased sales.

This conclusion rounds out the report somewhat better than examples (5) and (6), although the second sentence seems to start a new train of thought. But example (8) does not provide any emphasis. It does not single out any particular problem or course of action with which the reader should be left.

Here is another example, one that appears to be better:

> (9) The company's basic difficulties lie in a lack of planning and a superficial analysis of their management, marketing, and production problems. Management concern should be centered on the company's overall strategy and its implementation in these general areas.

This paragraph is rather deceptive. It appears to be emphasizing the problem the writer feels is most important and suggesting the most important course of action to be followed. But if you read it closely, you will realize that it says very little. In extremely vague and general language, the writer directs the reader's attention to what looks like a major problem but turns out to be little more than a conclusion that the company should be better managed. Example (7) was much better, although more subtle: it quietly emphasized the need for *gradual* growth.

Finally, a concluding paragraph should provide a sense of direction. It should indicate what the reader ought to be thinking about and what course of action it is most important for him to follow. In some respects, this third function is not too different from the second. Consider this example:

(10) The company's problems are many and complex, but related, and one cannot be satisfactorily solved without depending upon the solution of another. The present condition of the company and the intensity of competition imply that continuance of the present management policy will make survival of the company increasingly difficult.

What is the reader supposed to do now?

Here is an even more extreme case:

(11) As a whole, your company has more bad points than good points.

Example (7) did a fairly good job of indicating direction. Here is a more specific example:

(12) The purpose of this study was to investigate and make recommendations. Because little useful data were available, I have concentrated on identification of the information you need to control your operation. I have then attempted to show what analyses should be made with this information. The data are not easy to obtain and the analyses are not easy to make. Both require time and money. I feel the expenditure of both is necessary to maintain control over a rapidly expanding organization. I have tried to indicate exactly where and why money might be saved, and I believe the savings will more than offset the expenditures.

Notice how the writer has rounded out his report and given a sense of completeness. He has indicated clearly and specifically what he wishes to emphasize, and he has established, as specifically as he could within the limits of a single paragraph, just what the reader should do next. This is the kind of concluding paragraph that tells the reader that the writer knows what he is talking about.

EXERCISES

1. What changes, if any, would you make in the following opening paragraphs of reports?

    a. In attempting to decide what you would want in this report on a change in our personnel procedures, I decided to keep it as brief as possible. This decision was based on my assumption that you would probably talk to a lot of other people about the problem. It, therefore, seemed that a lot of wasted effort would be involved in doing a comprehensive and detailed study.

    b. Like a woman's skirt, this report is long enough to cover the subject, short enough to be interesting. So let's get to the main points: *Why* are costs increasing in our mailing department? and *what* should we do about it?

    c. One can hardly discuss methods of increasing sales without first discussing the qualifications of our sales force. This report begins with an analysis of the educational background of every member of our sales staff based on the questionnaire exhibited on page 3. It then presents a list of educational courses which would reduce the educational deficiencies shown in our survey. Finally, it suggests a few tentative methods by which sales might be increased.

    d. To meet your goal of a 50 percent increase in the business of the Acme Travel Service in 1972, we recommend first, a greater emphasis on group travel rather than tours for individuals; second, heavy advertising of short cruises to the Caribbean; and third, a shift from direct-mail advertising to radio and newspaper ads. Our reasons for each of these recommendations are detailed in the pages of this report, and a specific statement of how each of these recommendations should be put into effect is presented on page 14.

    e. The research for the report which follows occupied almost five weeks of the writer's time. Whether this was a wise investment is left to the reader to judge. Suffice it to say that although no specific recommendations could be evolved, this study does shed considerable light on the intangible factors affecting the problem which you asked me to investigate.

2. Adams Industries, Inc., is a small electronics company founded by Mr. James Adams in 1968. Mr. Adams had proved himself an outstanding designer of transistors, and he set up Adams Industries to design, develop, and manufacture a new transistor. He also set up a machinery division within the company, to develop and manufacture machinery for the production and handling of transistors. He expected that this division would be profitable from the start and would help provide the funds necessary to sustain the transistor research. By the summer of 1969, the research was far from finished. And the machinery division, instead of contributing profits, had consistently lost money. In 1970, Mr. Adams asked some management consultants for advice. Reproduced below are the first and last paragraphs of three consultants' reports, addressed to Mr. Adams. If you were Mr. Adams, which report would you be most likely to read in its entirety, after reading the beginnings and endings? What do you like or dislike about these beginnings and endings? What changes would you suggest?

    a. To determine the best course of action for Adams Industries at the present time in view of the problems that now face the company, I have found it advantageous first to examine the transistor industry itself, and the prospects for a small company in that industry, and second to assess the specific strengths and weaknesses of Adams Industries.

. . . .

These suggestions all constitute an attempt to ensure profitable operations once the immediate cash bind is passed. Along with the recommendations presented earlier in the report, they represent an overall attempt to promote the eventual success of Adams Industries in the transistor industry.

b. There are probably several courses of action open to your company, and each of them has certain attractive features. But before discussing these alternatives, I would like to present what I believe to be your present position, operationally and financially, and your future prospects at present levels of operation, since my recommendations are dependent upon this analysis.

. . . .

In summation, unless you find that you are able to improve the situation in the machinery division in the very near future, I see no alternative to discontinuing production. I have tried to present any additional alternatives as fully as possible so that you may examine the feasibility and desirability of each and determine which is best for your situation.

c. The material that has been presented to me, I find, may sorely misrepresent the present and future operating position of the Machinery Division of Adams. I think you, as officers of the company, may have been misled by control and accounting concepts that do not fairly indicate the profitability of this division. Before I can suggest steps to be taken in the immediate future, it is necessary for me to explain how I view your present position. I think you will then agree that the situation may not be as desperate as it currently appears and the need for drastic action might not be quite as urgent.

. . . .

In conclusion, I feel I have covered the major areas of concern. I have tried to provide you with what seems to me to be the only available means of pulling out of your present hole. I have done this under the most optimistic assumptions. In view of this, I have tried to cover myself at every step, for I feel that there are any number of statements or estimates that could be wrong or go wrong. However, I do feel there is a definite path for you to follow at any juncture, and I think that in the long run, if this transistor is as good as you say, you will eventually see your way clear.

3. In 1970, a shoe manufacturing company in Springfield found its manufacturing facilities inadequate and decided to move its line of hand-sewn shoes into new quarters. The choice of a new plant site had been narrowed to three cities: Crandall, Manchester, and Springfield. The executive vice-president of the company asked consultants for reports to help him choose one of the three sites. The following are the final paragraphs from four reports. What is good or bad about them? How would you improve them?

a. If you were able to obtain the services of hand sewers in Crandall, your decision could be based largely on cost considerations. It would be necessary to calculate the probability of return on investment in all areas under consideration, with intangible factors such as flexibility playing a more important role. In this instance, I would estimate that Crandall would stand up quite well on any basis of comparison (providing undesirable consequences did not result from the tax situation). Otherwise, Manchester provides the only logical site.

b. My above arguments convince me that you should choose the Springfield site.

c. If your efforts to find an ideal location fail, you may find it necessary to consider the advisability of discontinuing your hand-sewn line of shoes. In the long run, it may prove more profitable to shift production to other lines which can be manufactured in favorable locations such as Crandall.

d. As for remaining at Springfield, I think there is sufficient reason to move if a suitable place can be found. I think the site available in Springfield is suitable. The only other alternative is some out-of-state location.

4. How would you improve the way in which the following paragraphs are written?

a. This led us to our recommendation to emphasize short cruises to the Caribbean. Incidentally, a similar boom market exists for cruises to the Mediterranean, but most people use airplanes to go there. But the real advantage of a cruise to the Caribbean is that the passengers can unpack just once and their cabin thus serves as their hotel room regardless of what port they are in. Furthermore, a cruise to the Caribbean is short enough so that it can be within the budget of almost anyone. Our 10 percent commission on such sales can, therefore, be obtained from a broader market. It is well known that every prospective traveler wants to begin by seeing the Caribbean.

b. To give students a voice in faculty appointments is an absolute must if this university is to attain excellence. What do faculty members care about student opinion at present? All of us know faculty members who don't even go to football games. This shows the present indifference. And how can excellence result from indifference? Since the students are the ones who benefit most if they get a good education or suffer most if they don't, they should be a part of the process when new faculty are appointed.

c. It seemed futile for us to spend much time investigating new methods of reimbursing our sales representatives. After all, there have been so many studies made of this subject. It was decided, therefore, that we could save your time and ours by making a geographical analysis of the areas of highest and lowest sales. While this does not do exactly what was wanted, it was thought that this analysis could be even more useful than finding out whether new methods of paying salesmen might result in higher sales.

d. These facts add up to one conclusion: We must install new labor-saving devices in the Collection Department. We can't survive with horse-and-buggy methods in the age of the throughway. Look at what happened to the Edsel. Each year the volume of mail going through the post office increases and the complaints about slowness of the mails multiply. All of these factors have a direct effect upon our Mailing Department and prove that modern devices must be installed there at once.

5. How would you improve the style of the following excerpts from actual reports?

a. There is a tendency in making such a study to overemphasize one of three things, costs, design, and date of completion. It should be pointed out that the relative emphasis which is to be placed on these factors is dependent upon the specific situation which is to be studied. For that reason, it is of the highest order of importance that the client's wishes be clearly ascertained at the earliest possible moment. To make this specific, it should be determined whether the crucial factor in his mind is when the construction can be completed or how much it will cost or what architectural features he wants. Once this is clearly known, it is possible to proceed with expedition.

b. The thing which bugs our salesmen is that they lack security for the future. Our present so-called fringe benefits are a joke. To get with it in today's competition, we're forced to offer hospitalization, better pensions, and a piece of the action by. way of stock participation plans. If we don't, we're done.

c. As is customary under our normal procedure, the sponsoring department is requested to obtain one or more bids from sources which are outside the company in order to assure that the costs are realistic and compatible with the general practice of the industry. Once this procedure has been followed and the appropriate comparison of costs has been made, it is possible to proceed with the finalizing of the actual cost commitment.

6. You have been employed for a special report-writing project by a real-estate syndicate which has purchased more than 1,000 acres of very desirable land located near Ashtabula, Ohio, on the south shore of Lake Erie. Mr. Lawrence Rubin, head of the syndicate, has told you that he selected you because he believes you can write. "If you can turn out the kind of report we want, this will be the most lucrative time you have ever spent because we will pay a handsome sum for the right kind of presentation. Furthermole, we'll get you any kind of expert assistance you need to provide maps, graphs, charts, topographic surveys, or anything else."

The purpose of this report is to interest various industries in buying the land the syndicate owns. The report will go to 15 companies who intend to expand their manufacturing plants by locating in new sections of the country. Mr. Rubin has discussed the desirability of the Ashtabula area with officials of all 15 companies, has promised them the report which you are now commissioned to write, and has learned that each company is considering competing sites in other sections of the country. "I want to go back to them in a month and leave them a report which will really sell them on the Ashtabula area so they have something tangible to discuss with their boards of directors," Mr. Rubin tells you. "Here's the complete information our engineers, surveyors, employment analysts, and Chambers of Commerce have gathered. When you read it, you'll know everything except the price of the land which I'll discuss with them personally. Now write me a report that is a sales document and let me know what kind of graphic aids you want to use to supplement your writing."

Write the report, using any of the following facts you have been given, and list the specific aspects of the report for which you want graphic aids. (You may, of course, use material applicable to some other community or geographical area if it is available.)

Ashtabula, Indian word for "River-of-Many-Fish," is a city of 26,000 located 60 miles east of Cleveland on the south shore of Lake Erie.

The lands owned by the syndicate are 2 miles west of Ashtabula; some parcels are on the lake front, others ½ mile south of the lake.

Ashtabula is an important lake port and manufacturing center. Millions of tons of iron ore and limestone pass over Ashtabula's docks annually, and 8,000 feet of new dock space will soon be completed.

The main east-west lines of the Penn Central and Nickel Plate Railroads pass through Ashtabula and north-south connections are provided by the New York Central and Pennsylvania Railroads.

Recent new plants in the area include chemicals (Electro-Metallurgical Division of Union Carbide and Carbon, Hooker-Detrex, National Distillers, Archer-Daniels-Midland) and metals (Timken-Detroit Axle, Ashtabula Bow Socket, and Nelson Machine and Manufacturing).

Ashtabula is on U.S. Route I-90, and Ohio Turnpike Number 2, linking northeast Ohio to Cincinnati in the southwest, passes 5 miles south of Ashtabula.

The land owned by the syndicate is within 30 minutes' driving distance, in moderately heavy traffic, of 77,500 people. Of these, 15,700 men and 17,200 women are in the 20 to 45 age group. By 1970, estimates show 17,900 men and 19,500 women in this age group, and by 1975, 21,300 men and 23,200 women in the 20 to 45 age group out of an estimated total population of 105,000 people.

At present, 85 million people, three-fifths of the nation's effective buying power, two-thirds of the nation's wholesale capacity, and three-fourths of all U.S. manufacturing are within a 500-mile radius of the Ashtabula area.

More than 100 truck lines serve the area, and the St. Lawrence Seaway, completed in 1959, opens world markets to shipping.

In the Cleveland-Ashtabula-northeast Ohio area, plants turn out 3,500 different manufactured products.

The entire northeast Ohio area's more than two million people include a labor force of 765,000 persons.

The area has been nationally advertised by the Cleveland Electric Illuminating Company as "The Best Location in the Nation."

In 1969, Ashtabula had a $64.6 million tax duplicate, yet its debt was only $1.8 million, equal to 2.75 percent of the tax duplicate although the legal limit is 5 percent.

Utility services are readily available for the syndicate's lands. The Ashtabula Water Works Company has a pumping capacity of 20 million gallons of Lake Erie water daily, and average daily use is 5 million gallons. Low-cost electric power is available from a 33,000-volt line from the Cleveland Electric Illuminating Company; the Lake Shore Gas Company will extend natural gas lines into the syndicate's lands for new customers.

A 1970 report of the Ohio State Employment Service on "Labor Market Information" in the area surrounding the syndicate's lands shows an estimated 1,000 persons (400 women) could be hired at current wage rates. One-tenth of these persons are skilled, three-tenths semiskilled, and the rest unskilled. Hourly wage *rates usually paid in 1970 in the area are as follows: Men: unskilled, $2.25 to $2.80; semiskilled, $2.35 to $2.90; skilled, $3.50 to $4.20. Women: unskilled $1.50 to $2.05; semiskilled, $1.85 to $2.60; skilled, $2.00 to $3.70.*

Ashtabula is a unique city-manager community with the world's only elected city manager. Three of the seven city councilmen are elected at large.

Lands owned by the syndicate are unzoned and hence available for all kinds of industrial use. All these lands, in parcels of 40-acre units to the largest unit of 125 acres, lie between Lake Erie and the main line of the Penn Central, 2 miles inland.

The syndicate has every intention of disposing of all its land within the next year and has already received offers for specific parcels from four nationally known companies.

Schools and churches are adequate at present. Recreational facilities—swimming, fishing, boating, golfing—are excellent.

A survey of workers in the area indicates strong dissatisfaction when they have to drive more than 30 minutes to get to their places of employment.

Since the area around Ashtabula is predominantly rural, many industrial workers maintain small farms in addition to their jobs.

CHAPTER 18

CONVEYING INFORMATION GRAPHICALLY*

Charts and graphs offer a very useful adjunct to the written word for conveying information in reports. You should learn to use them where and when they are appropriate.

The test to apply in deciding when to use charts and other graphs is simple: Ask yourself whether your reader will understand the information better or more easily if it is presented graphically.

Graphic presentation has three major virtues—it is concise, dramatic, and revealing. Graphs condense a large amount of information into a small space; when well designed they are forceful and convincing; and they can be extremely effective in explaining and clarifying the information you wish to convey.

There are three principal forms of graphic presentation that are effective for business reports: charts, maps, and diagrams. Charts answer the question "how much," maps show "where," and diagrams show "how."

In executive reports, graphic presentation usually consists of charts. Maps or diagrams are sometimes called for, but not often. Of course, a report concerned with how something is distributed geographically may use only map

* This material on charts and graphs has been prepared by Kenneth W. Haemer, formerly Manager, Presentation Research, American Telephone and Telegraph Company.

illustrations; a report discussing the organizational make-up of a company or the flow of money or goods might rely on diagrams. But in general the kind of information contained in reports can be conveyed best in chart form; for that reason, the following discussion of graphic presentation is centered on charts.

In most charts used in management and administrative reports the graphic part is geometrical rather than pictorial, making use of devices like circles and bars and lines rather than pictures. One reason for this is that many important kinds of comparisons cannot be shown effectively in pictorial form. Another is that pictorial presentation is slower, is more costly, and generally requires much more space for presenting a given amount of information. Nevertheless, pictorial charts have their place. They are valuable for their popular appeal and are especially useful for presenting simple comparisons to audiences who are not familiar with conventional charts or who simply will not read them. Their field of use is in reports to customers, to employees, and to the general public; they are seldom appropriate in reports to management or administrative reports from management.

Charts used in business reports divide into two main groups: those using only one scale of measurement and those using two. (There are charts that make use of more than two scales, but they are specialized technical tools that are of no interest here.) In general, one-scale charts are much simpler and more limited than two-scale charts. However, you will find plenty of use for both types.

ONE-SCALE CHARTS

One-scale charts take two main forms: pie charts and bar charts.

A *pie chart* is a circle divided into wedge-shaped slices. Its purpose is to show how component parts add up to make a total. It is a good form for showing this sort of information because it so obviously adds up to 100 percent, and it has the additional virtue of looking simple and nontechnical. Figure 1 is an effective use of this type of presentation: notice particularly how the two parts of the major component are held together by using the same shading pattern for both.

But pie charts can be used for showing only the components that make up a whole. They are of little or no use for comparing changes from time to time or for comparing a series of totals of different size. In general, pie charts have a very limited usefulness and are awkward to handle. You will soon find that most of the amount comparisons you want to put into graphic form are not quite simple enough for a pie chart and that even when they are, another type of chart will usually do the job better.

Bar charts are made up of horizontal oblongs, placed one above the

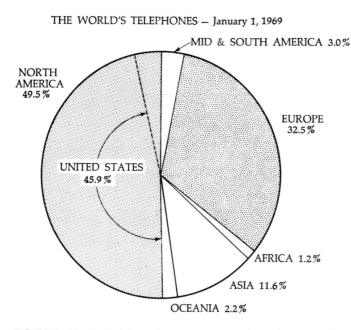

THE WORLD'S TELEPHONES — January 1, 1969

FIGURE 1   The pie chart shows the component parts that make up a total.

other. In this form of chart the length of each bar shows the size or amount of some item under study. Thus a bar chart is a means of comparing the magnitude of a series of items. In Figure 2, the portion of the labor force unemployed is quickly seen and compared for each of several Michigan cities.

Remember that this type of chart has only one scale and that it measures horizontally: the vertical dimension is used only to list the items. The order of items is flexible and may be varied in many useful ways. For example, items can be listed alphabetically, in order of size, importance, or in some arbitrary but established order, such as men, women, children, or shareholders, employees, customers.

There are several subtypes of bar chart, each of which can be used to bring out a different aspect of the information that is under study.

As shown in Figure 3, the bars can be subdivided to show the component parts of each item. This chart provides the same information as a series of pie charts, but in a more manageable and compact form. Subdivided bars can be handled in two ways: the components of each bar can add up to a total amount in dollars, carloads, customers, or some other absolute measure; or they can add up to 100 percent. In the 100 percent form, the bars are, of course, all the same length and show the *proportion* of the total that each component part contributes.

Figures 4 and 5 show two other useful variations of a simple bar chart:

both are the result of adding a second set of information. The first goes by the name of *bar-and-symbol chart*. This is merely a simple bar chart with additional amounts showing such information as results for an earlier period, goals or standards, or results before or after some sort of adjustment. The other type brings two simple bar charts together for comparison. Shading the most important set of bars to set them off from the others makes this chart easier to understand.

TWO-SCALE CHARTS

The identifying feature of this large family of charts is two scales placed at right angles, one measuring vertically, one horizontally. Thus each point drawn on the chart has a value on the vertical scale and a value on the horizontal, in the same way that the location of the New York Public Library has a value of 42 on the north and south (street) scale and a value of 5 on the east and west (avenue) scale. This two-scale arrangement permits you to picture all sorts of useful relationships that would be difficult to see in any other way.

Two-scale charts separate into three distinct yet related groups: line charts, surface charts, and column charts. Many of the varieties within each of these groups are matched by a corresponding variety in the other two groups. In fact, the same general kind of information can be shown in either line-chart, surface-chart, or column-chart form. However, these three forms aren't exact substitutes: as you will see, each provides a different emphasis,

PERCENT OF LABOR FORCE UNEMPLOYED — 1968

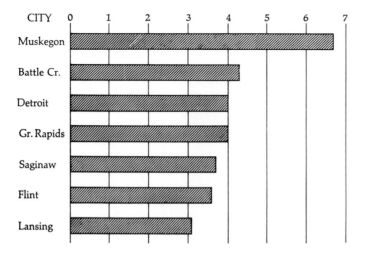

FIGURE 2   The simple bar chart compares different things at the same time.

EMPLOYMENT — Major Occupational Groups

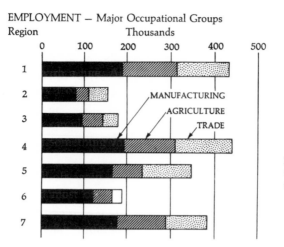

FIGURE 3 Subdivided bars show the component parts of several totals.

VALUE OF RESIDENTIAL CONSTRUCTION CONTRACTS

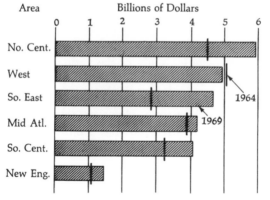

FIGURE 4 Bars and symbols compare results with earlier results.

INDIVIDUALS OWNING STOCK
in 5 Large Corporations

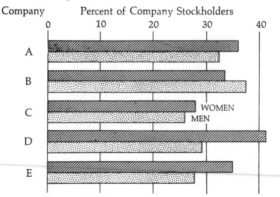

FIGURE 5 Grouped bars compare two different but related sets of data.

and usually one type is clearly more appropriate—for a specific set of data—
than either of the others.

A *line chart* is well described by its name. It is made by joining a series
of points with a line. Although this line is called a *curve* in chart language,
it may vary from extremely smooth to extremely jagged, depending on the
behavior of the data presented.

The example below, Figure 6, is a simple line chart showing how the
quantity of something varied from one time to the next. It gives a clear, direct
picture of how production dropped in the first few years and then increased
rapidly, fell off again, then increased somewhat more slowly. In this type of
chart—and most of the others that follow—the horizontal scale is used to
measure *time*, the vertical scale to measure *number or quantity*.

Figure 7 is a somewhat more analytical chart: it shows a three-year span
of data cut into yearly pieces and superimposed on a one-year chart. This form
is especially useful for comparing each month this year with the same month
in earlier years. It is widely used for such business data as production, sales,
expenses, and earnings.

The next two illustrations are also examples of typical line charts. Figure
8 compares the behavior of three measures of business activity, showing clearly
that the leather and coal industries are not following the pattern of industrial
activity in general. The type of chart illustrated by Figure 9 is somewhat more
complex, but is still clear and informative. This example is adapted from a
chart used in the Department of Defense to show progress and plans for purchases of a certain type of defense equipment.

ANNUAL PRODUCTION – ROCKET X14A2

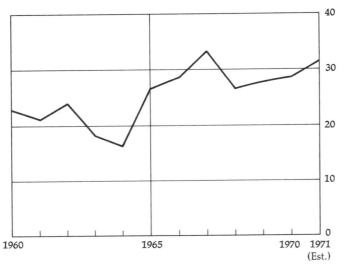

FIGURE 6   The simple curve chart shows successive changes over a span of time.

There are many other kinds of line charts, each useful for a specific purpose. In fact, this basic type of chart is so versatile that it is used more than
any other in the internal administration and operation of all businesses, whether private or government.

A *surface chart* looks like a shaded line chart, and in its simplest form it
is exactly that. If you shade a simple line chart between the curve and the base
you get a simple surface chart; and the two are identical in meaning. The only
difference is that the surface form is more striking. But shading other types of
line chart changes their meaning. The reason is that in surface charts it is the
distance *between* curves that is important; not the distance from each curve
to the base.

The following examples illustrate the three most useful types of surface
chart. The first two show the component parts of a total and how they change
over a span of time. Figure 10 shows absolute amounts, such as dollars, tons,
or employees; Figure 11 shows relative amounts, i.e., each component as a percentage of the total. The 100 percent version is especially valuable because it
clearly shows changes in the *relative* distribution of the parts of a total—
changes that are easily overlooked when the total is growing rapidly.

Notice that in both cases the bottom layer is the only one that can be
measured directly from the scale. The reader may, therefore, find it difficult
to gauge the other layers with even approximate accuracy. Another weakness,
from the reader's point of view, is that all surface charts are subject to an occupational disease—optical illusion. An irregular layer—one that moves up and
down—makes all layers above it seem to move up and down also. The way to
avoid this is to put irregular layers on top, if the order can be changed to do so.
Another illusion occurs because a layer that moves along at the same level,
then suddenly shoots up—or down—seems to be much thinner where it
changes level than it really is.

To a moderate degree, the chart shown in Figure 12 lets you have your
cake and eat it too. It measures the volume of "ins" and "outs" and also shows,
by means of contrasting shadings, when and by how much one exceeds the
other. This sort of presentation is effective for picturing such information as
imports and exports, revenues and expenses, orders received and orders
shipped.

The next four illustrations show a family of charts that are related to line
charts but look like bar charts turned on end. These charts, called *column
charts*, provide an entirely different kind of comparison than bar charts. Instead of comparing a number of different items at a given time, they compare
a given item at different times, in the same general way that line or surface
charts do.

Column charts are, in fact, first cousins to surface charts and are useful
for the same general purposes. But usually the nature of the information to be

MONTHLY OUTPUT – PLANT #7

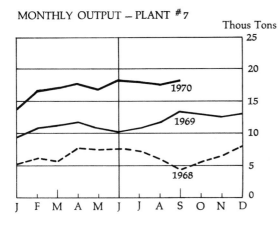

FIGURE 7 The repeated time scale compares changes during comparable periods of time.

LAGGING INDUSTRIES
in a Growing Economy

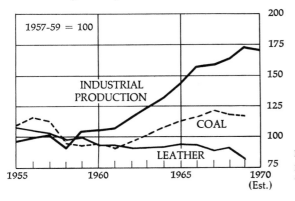

FIGURE 8 Multiple curves compare changes in two or more series of data.

RADAR SET SC _ _ _ _

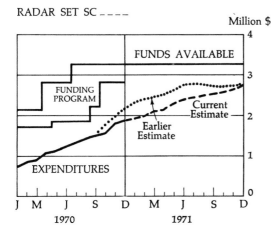

FIGURE 9 A combination of step curves and slope curves compares data that change abruptly and those that change gradually.

EMPLOYEES — BY TERM OF SERVICE

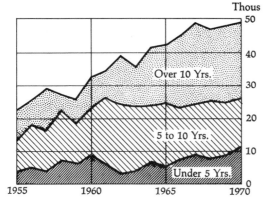

FIGURE 10 Subdivided surface shows the changes in the component parts of a total.

PERCENTAGE DISTRIBUTION OF EMPLOYEES
By Term of Service

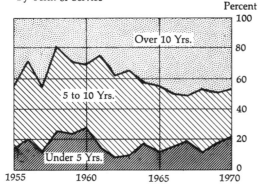

FIGURE 11 The 100 per cent surface chart shows changes in the relative size of the components.

SALES ACTIVITY — Meton Corp.

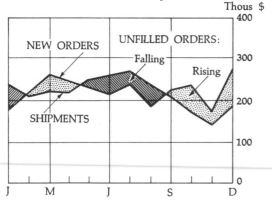

FIGURE 12 The income-outgo chart compares inward and outward movement, and emphasizes net differences.

presented will suggest which to use. Surface charts are better when there are a large number of time periods to be shown, when the data do not move up and down very sharply, and when the nature of the information suggests a carry-over from one period to the next (for example, average number of acres under cultivation each year). Column charts are better when only a few time periods are shown on the chart, when the data change level sharply, and when the information suggests a fresh start for each period (for example, number of acres added each year).

Figure 13 is a simple column chart showing the money spent for new construction by a large and growing company. It tells the story directly and forcefully, the separated columns emphasizing the size of each year's expenditures. Figure 14 is the same kind of component-parts presentation that is used on the bar chart in Figure 3. Note that the columns are divided into four segments in this example. The use of more than four segments in such a chart is generally unwise, because the reader is given too many things to keep track of. Usually you can avoid too many divisions by combining some: by either using fewer but broader components, or by lumping several small components under "all other."

The next two examples show the result of combining two simple column charts and of presenting differences instead of totals. Figure 15 presents a picture of gradually increasing farm income in a forceful way. You can easily see that this form is much better than a line chart would be for so few amounts.

EXPENDITURES FOR NEW CONSTRUCTION
West Coast Aluminum Corp.

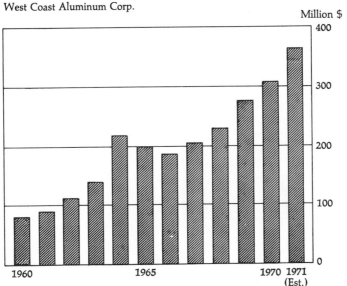

FIGURE 13   The simple column chart compares the same things at different times.

MAJOR ISSUES
Causing Work Stoppages

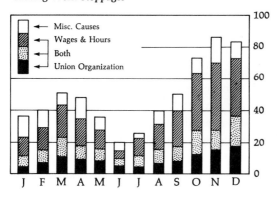

FIGURE 14 Subdivided columns show the component parts of a total at different times.

FARMERS' CASH RECEIPTS — Michigan

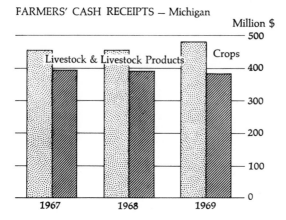

FIGURE 15 Grouped columns compare two related series of data over a span of time.

INVENTORY CHANGES —
Selected Industries

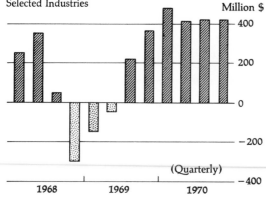

FIGURE 16 Net-gain-or-loss columns measure the differences between total income and outgo.

Figure 16 stresses the net gain or loss resulting from an "income" and an "out-go," in this case the difference between quantities put in and taken out of stock. (Compare this closeup of net results with Figure 12, which measures the income and outgo but shows the differences only indirectly.)

There are other families of two-scale charts, but most of these are too technical for management reports. Only one needs to be mentioned here: this is the so-called frequency chart. Frequency charts use a different set of scales than time-series charts. Instead of amount, the vertical scale measures frequency of occurrence; instead of time, the horizontal scale classifies size. A chart showing the number of employees (frequency measure) in each of several wage groups (size measure) is a typical frequency chart. In appearance they take the form of simple curve or column charts.

As you can readily see, there is a wide variety of charts to choose from, each useful in its own way. Before deciding which kind to use, be sure you have a clear understanding of what the data mean and precisely what aspect of the data the picture is to focus on. No two types of chart serve exactly the same purpose, and so the type chosen should be the one that conveys information most clearly, accurately, and forcefully. Be sure to avoid these two extremes: don't rely on one or two favorite types regardless of whether they suit the purpose or not; don't invent types that are so special and complex that no one else will understand them.

In designing charts, the most important thing is the choice of scale. As shown by the examples in Figure 17, the same information can be scaled to give widely different impressions. There is no rule for proper scaling: the correct scale is the one that produces the appropriate effect. What is appropriate will depend on the purpose of the report, the subject matter, the circumstances under which it is being studied, and your estimate of how important the changes or differences really are. For example, a million-dollar increase in the national debt is scarcely worth mentioning; a million-dollar increase in a manufacturing company's debt is quite a different matter.

Although charts are valuable mainly because they are graphic, note that they are meaningless without words and figures to explain and measure. How

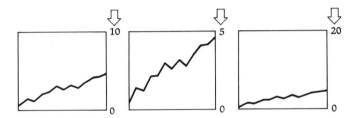

FIGURE 17 The importance of scale selection: the same data plotted on different amount scales.

these words and figures are handled is just as important as how the graphic part of the chart is designed. In general, the same principles that apply to clear, informative writing apply equally to chart titles, labels, and captions, but with even more force. A single inept, foggy, or long-winded sentence may escape notice, but a poor chart title will not.

Chart titling is especially important because of the growing use of statement, or "narrative," titles. Instead of merely identifying the subject matter of the chart, this type of title tells what the chart shows. Sometimes it even goes a step further and explains the causes behind the results or the conclusions they lead to. As you can see from the example in Figure 18, this method is effective. It helps the reader to understand the chart more quickly and to remember its message more easily.

Although graphic presentation is excellent when it is appropriate, there are several cautions about using it:

1. *Don't use so many charts that they overwhelm the rest of the report.* The reader will either ignore everything else, or—if he doesn't like charts—ignore the entire report.

2. *Use charts to explain or support the major points in the report.* The fewer charts you use, the more attention each gets; so if you use only one or two it is doubly important that they relate to the main facts you are trying to convey.

3. *Don't try to convey too much information on one chart.* If you do, it will be cluttered and hard to understand. It's better to put the information in two simple charts than to crowd it into one complex one.

4. *Design the chart to focus on the meaning you are trying to convey.* Don't merely convert figures into graphic form and expect this to tell the reader what you want him to know.

5. *Keep it simple.* Leave out all unnecessary frills and trimmings. Don't add technical notes and other details that are not needed to *understand* the chart.

6. *Tie it in with your written presentation* by referring to it in the written text and by placing it as close as possible to the section of the text where you discuss it. This will spare your reader the annoyance of holding his thumb on page 4 when you refer him to a chart on page 45.

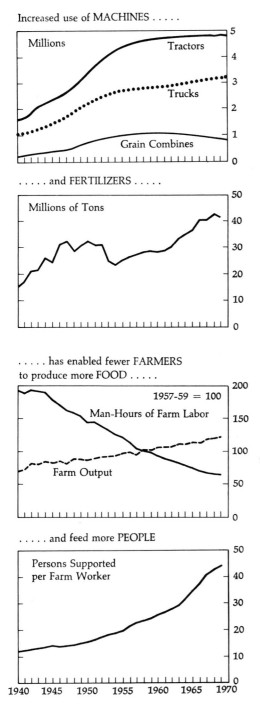

Increased use of MACHINES . . . . .

Millions

Tractors

Trucks

Grain Combines

. . . . . and FERTILIZERS . . . . .

Millions of Tons

. . . . . has enabled fewer FARMERS
to produce more FOOD . . . . .

1957-59 = 100

Man-Hours of Farm Labor

Farm Output

. . . . . and feed more PEOPLE

Persons Supported
per Farm Worker

1940   1945   1950   1955   1960   1965   1970

FIGURE 18 "Narrative" charts: related
charts connected by titles that state the
meaning of the data. This method of titling can be used also for single charts.

CHAPTER 19

THE FORMAL REPORT AND
THE MEMORANDUM

In Part 1 of this book, we called attention to the fact that many details of form and style in business writing vary from company to company and can only be learned on the job. This is particularly true of formal reports and memorandums for which many companies have worked out detailed forms, and if you go to work for one of these companies you will have to learn its forms. Yet it is possible to generalize about memos and formal reports so that general principles can be applied to specific on-the-job requirements.

THE MEMORANDUM

As we indicated in the introduction to Part 4, the line between the short report and the memorandum is thin. We can come close to the function and definition of a memorandum by thinking of it as an *internal letter*, as contrasted with letters going outside the organization, and as shorter and less formal than the average report. In fact, some companies call memorandums *interoffice letters* or *intraorganization reports*. Generally speaking, the memorandum performs three functions:

1. It maintains a flow of information *across* the levels or ranks of an organization, as when an employee in one department sends a memorandum to his counterpart in another department or office.

2. It conveys information and policy procedures both *up* and *down* within the organization, as when a subordinate writes a memorandum to a superior or when a vice-president notifies his staff of a policy change or sends information on to his subordinates.

3. It serves as a reminder and maintains a permanent record of discussions, meetings, activities, changes, procedures, or policies. Said Lewis Carroll in *Through the Looking Glass:*

> "The horror of that moment," the King went on, "I shall never, never forget!"
>
> "You will, though," the Queen said, "if you don't make a memorandum of it."

The memorandum is generally written under pressure of time. The great majority of memos are undoubtedly written under conditions that add up to instructions to "do this right away." The department head, the section chief, or the top executive usually couches his directions in such terms as, "Send out a reminder of that meeting tomorrow," or "Give me a memo on last month's employment figures so that I can have them for today's conference," or "Let me have a summary of the meeting I missed before we discuss it tomorrow." As a matter of fact, it is precisely because the memo is so well adapted to such urgent conditions that businessmen have made it their most frequently used medium of exchange *within the organization.*

That there are other reasons than sheer adaptability for the proliferation of memos is neatly shown by Theodore Irwin's satirical "Memo on Memos (Six Copies, Please)" in the *New York Times Magazine* (November 17, 1963)*:

> Consider, particularly, the Memo. How to succeed in business through memos is preoccupying the get-ahead-fast organization man. In the classic ploy, "You spend half your time doing your job and half your time telling your boss how good a job you're doing." Thus, as management consultants observe him, the chronic memo-writer falls into two main categories:
>
> (1) The reputation-builder. The more memos he pours out, the more executives will hear about him.
>
> (2) The alibi-fixer. Generally he produces defensive memos to protect himself and prove he is right if anyone should question him. ("You see I didn't want to do it, he forced me to.")

Mr. Irwin concludes his article by describing a humorous method of disposing of the mountains of memos produced in business:

---

* © 1963 by The New York Times Company. Reprinted by permission.

Today, despite the herculean efforts of systems-and-procedures doctors, American businessmen continue to battle their paperwork with a ferocity akin to Don Quixote's tilting at windmills—and with pretty much the same result. One possible answer may have been discovered in the Lake Maracaibo, Venezuela, branch office of a New York oil company. There the staff was being plagued by wild goats in the area.

"When we receive a memo from New York," the branch manager complained, "before we get a chance to read it, a goat sticks his head through the window and eats it."

Perhaps what the U.S. economy needs is more goats.

Nonetheless, the memo is the workhorse of written communications inside the organization because it provides a medium for quick response when information, recommendations, or background are needed. It provides no time generally for "fancy" writing or prolonged revision. These factors place a heavy premium on the memo writer's ability to analyze a situation quickly and to state it concisely. In this process he must do three things:

1. Decide on the central idea or main purpose of the memorandum.
2. Subordinate every fact or idea to this central idea or main purpose and show how these facts or ideas are related logically to the central theme.
3. Reject any material which is superfluous, irrelevant, or unnecessary for the reader's understanding of the central idea.

In many memos, he will not have to lead his reader into the subject by telling him what it's about—the time interval may be short, and the form of the memorandum takes care of this. But regardless of the circumstances, the process of preparing a memorandum follows the same steps we have analyzed for the more complex report—getting the facts, imposing a pattern on them, and writing to serve a reader's purpose.

We can illustrate this process best by a specific example which occurs frequently in business. Suppose that your superior has sent you to New York to attend a three-day meeting on the problems of modern management and has asked you to send him a memo about the meetings when you return. You could conceivably begin your memorandum this way:

As you requested, I attended the three-day meeting in New York on "The Problems of Modern Management."

After a rather a rather rough flight which got me there 45 minutes late, I tried to get a room at the hotel where the meetings were held but there was apparently a mix-up in reservations. I then had to spend another hour locating a room and finally arrived at the meeting at the end of the president's address of welcome. Incidentally, a friend told me later that I hadn't missed anything.

On Monday morning, I heard talks on "The Obligations of Modern Management" and "Changing Concepts of Today's Executive." That afternoon, I heard an excellent presentation by Mr. Fred W. Becker on a specific program for "Evaluating and Preparing Tomorrow's Executive" which the Blank Company has carried on during the past year. This program consists of . . .

Ridiculous? Not at all; this memorandum typifies too much memo writing with its irrelevant detail and rambling style. Above all else, it illustrates the worst faults of the step-by-step pattern of organization discussed in a previous chapter of this book. The result is a tiresome, detailed, blow-by-blow account which irks the reader and makes him lose patience.

Suppose, instead, that the writer of the memo, once he had his material assembled, had asked himself two questions:

1. What does my supervisor want to learn from my visit to the meetings?
2. How can I best tell him?

From such thinking, he could probably draw two conclusions—the supervisor wants to know what the writer learned that might be useful to his company and wants him to sort out all the information so that it will be presented in readable form to stress only the essentials. Elementary as it seems, this is the essence of good organization. The result might be a memorandum which starts this way:

This memorandum summarizes those meetings on "The Problems of Modern Management" which I thought were especially applicable to our own problems. Of all the discussions listed on the attached program, the following three seemed worth consideration since they concern problems which we have been thinking about:

1. Mr. Fred W. Becker of the Blank Company described his company's experience with a one-year training program to select and prepare personnel for executive responsibilities. This company has spent almost two years developing a method of evaluating management personnel; they now have an elaborate rating sheet by which every member of management is rated by (a) his immediate superior, (b) two members of the executive staff, and (c) five subordinates. At my request, Mr. Becker will send you a copy of this rating sheet, which I think might help us to develop one of our own.

Notice what has been accomplished in about the same number of words as the first example used for mere rambling. This writer tells his reader the following things:

1. What the memo concerns (a report on the meetings)

2. The method of selection (information most applicable to the organization's problems)

3. The method of rejection (the attached program gives all the unimportant details)

4. The organization (three meetings are described in detail because they are most useful to the reader)

Most companies have developed specific printed forms for their memos in an attempt to reduce all details to a standard pattern. The ultimate purpose of any such form should be to help the writer get on with his message as soon as possible and to place at the top of the first page, where it is readily accessible in the files, all the information about who wrote it, to whom it was sent, when it was written, and what was its subject. These topics should be arranged for maximum efficiency in typing and easy reading, as in the following typical example:

THE BLANK ELECTRIC COMPANY

MEMORANDUM   PAGE NO. 1

TO Members of   FROM C. W. Black DATE May 17, 1970
Management   PHONE 757
Committee   SUBJECT Advanced Management Program

The individual elements of such a form will, of course, depend on the size, diversity, and location of the business. Companies with plants or buildings in various places usually have *Location* or *Plant* or *Building* in place of the phone extension. Businesses with a large number of offices in the same building frequently include *Room* or *Office* or *Department* under *To* and *From* so that internal mail can be delivered easily. Small concerns often reduce the elements to *To, From, Subject,* and *Date.* Practice varies considerably on whether titles are used, either as part of the printed form or the typed information; for example, the use of such titles as

TO: Mr. Florent E. Virden, Director of Personnel

FROM: Mr. Charles W. Black, Manager of Personnel
      Evaluation

should be cut to a minimum unless a very good reason exists for their use. Generally speaking, the larger the company, the more information is needed; but even here, every element on the memo form should be carefully scrutinized to see whether it is absolutely necessary. In an attempt to take care of every contingency, some companies have developed such cumbersome memo forms that they defeat the main purpose of having such forms printed—namely, to reduce details to a standardized form, easily typed, read, and filed. The classic four W's, which a good newspaper reporter should answer in his lead, still constitute the best guide for material to be included on a memo form — Who? What? When? Where?

EXAMPLES OF SHORT MEMORANDUMS

Memorandum Giving Information

This will remind you that we agreed in our last management meeting to extend our discussions for three additional sessions. We have now scheduled these as follows:

March 27 — Speaker: Professor Ernest Dale, Columbia University
        Subject: "Organization"
April   24 — Speaker: Mr. Arch Potter, Reed, Barton, and Stow, Inc.
        Subject: "Management Compensation"
May   21 — Speaker: Mr. Karl Rudolph, Doane and Smith
        Subject: "Financial Structure and Interpretation"

All sessions will start at 9:30 A.M. in Conference Room C. If you *cannot* attend any of these meetings, please let me know before March 20.

Memorandum Giving Policy and Procedure

As you know, the Company has designated certain organizations in which we will pay one-half the membership fees. To assure uniform procedure in all departments, we request that you follow these instructions:

1. Each employee wishing to join or renew membership in such an organization .should first obtain the approval of his department head.
2. The employee will then make his own arrangements for joining, pay the full amount of the fees, and obtain a receipt showing the amount and the period covered.
3. He will then prepare a petty-expense voucher, Form H-3, for one-half the amount of the fees.
4. His department head will then sign the voucher, which the employee may take to the Cashier's Office, Room 107, to receive his check for reimbursement.

If you have any questions about our policy or procedure in this matter, I will be glad to discuss them with you. We, of course, want to be as generous as possible in helping employees with these memberships; at the same time, I urge you to scrutinize each application carefully to see that it will be of practical benefit to the Company.

Memorandum Asking for Recommendations

During the last two months, we have had approximately 3,000 requests for the pamphlet "A Giant Conserves His Resources," which we issued for our twenty-fifth anniversary. I should like your recommendation as to whether we should reissue this pamphlet, which is out of print.

Factors to Consider

Mr. C. M. Eckman has reported the following facts, which I hope you will consider carefully in your recommendation:

1. The cost of reprinting 5,000 copies is approximately $3,250.
2. An analysis of the requests we now have shows that 1,731 came from high-school and college students, 339 from other industries, and 891 from individuals.
3. Our previous printing of 10,000 copies was sent to all shareholders, employees, and key industrial and educational leaders in the area we serve.
4. Pages 12 to 15 of the pamphlet should probably be revised, since we now have more up-to-date sales figures and more accurate analyses of costs.

Recommendations

Since I am sending this request to 47 members of management, I will greatly appreciate your making your recommendation in the form of answers to the following questions so that we may tabulate the results easily:

1. Do you think we should reprint 5,000 copies of the pamphlet?
2. What, in your opinion, was the chief value of this publication?
3. Could it be improved in any way to get across our message that modern industry is interested in conserving natural resources?

May I have your answers by May 21?

Example of a Long Memorandum

This memo covers the general characteristics our company should aim at in our audit reports. It results from a two-week survey by the procedures group at the request of Mr. C. F. Smith, Controller.

Importance and Scope of Audit Reports

Since our audit reports are the principal means of recording our work, they greatly influence the judgments made about our activities and our personnel. Furthermore, they go to people who have many demands on their time and who are primarily interested in results.

For these readers, audit reports should be short, concise, and factual. Usually they should include the following:

1. What was covered in the audit
2. What was revealed that should be called to the manager's attention
3. What is the effect of the variance, if there is one
4. What you recommend to correct the situation

While we do not want reports which follow a rigid pattern, we can reduce both writing and reading time by following these topics.

General Arrangement and Organization

Audit reports should generally include:

1. A letter of transmittal which serves as a guide to tell the reader what really significant information the report contains.
2. The main section of the report covering the scope, findings, and recommendations.
3. The schedules and exhibits which present documentary evidence to support a finding or a recommendation. In the Quarterly Audit Reports, this should be labeled "Exhibit Section" with the exhibits clearly separated into three classifications:

    a. Information furnished the previous month to all managers who will read the report.
    b. Material previously furnished to some, but not all, district supervisors
    c. Material which the auditor creates and which does not duplicate previous monthly reports.

As a general rule, we should limit material to what is necessary for a complete understanding of the audit, being careful always to include enough to avoid any possible misinterpretation.

Review with Local Management Personnel

Wherever possible, discuss your findings with the local management *before* you prepare the final report. This review is intended to do three things:

1. Assure the examining auditor that his data and opinions are correct and factual.

2. Minimize any feeling in the local office that the audit is an undercover operation.

3. Provide the local manager with advance information on the report so that he can take corrective action immediately or recommend changes which lie outside his authority.

Analysis of Present Reports

Our survey covering the entire Auditing Division showed that we can improve reports by:

1. Putting all facts in a general context. For instance, if the auditor says, "Ten errors were discovered," it is difficult for the reader to evaluate the situation. How many items were examined? What was the ratio of errors? Is this ratio within our generally accepted standards or is it too high?

2. Making all statements clear-cut and forthright. Many comments in our present reports seem to hedge. They force the reader to read between the lines. Where an honest difference of opinion exists between the auditor and local manager, say so clearly. If possible, give the reasons for both opinions so that the reader can pass factual judgment rather than guessing.

3. Ending with a definite conclusion. When everything reviewed complies with established policies, say so. If you believe policies should be changed, say so, giving your reasons and the benefits which may result from the change.

Conclusion

Our sole aim is to make our audit reports effective instruments for telling management whether action is needed, and, if so, what action should be taken. Remember that you write for readers who dislike technical terms, detailed analyses, and repetitious statements. Give them adequate information for making judgments; present your recommendations clearly; revise your report thoroughly. By doing so, you can help us make our reports an effective management tool.

THE FORMAL REPORT

Some day you may be asked to write what is called a *formal report*, although less use is being made of this form in today's business. (These reports are generally written by people who through years of experience have acquired an expert knowledge of some field and are asked to apply that knowledge to solving a complex problem.) Nevertheless, you ought to know the components of a formal report and, if possible, get some actual practice in writing one. These reports usually contain the following elements:

1. A *title page*, which includes the title of the report, the name of the author (or authors)

with his title, company affiliation, and address, and the date when the report is submitted.

2. A *letter of transmittal*, discussed later in this section.

3. A *table of contents*, designed to make it easy to refer to and to give an outline of the main topics in the report.

4. A *synopsis*, or *summary*, which gives the reader the most significant information contained in the report without his having to read the entire document.

5. The *body of the report*, which is, of course, the main part of the report, telling what you did, how you did it, what you found, and what conclusions or recommendations you have drawn.

6. The *appendix*, which might be called the department of miscellaneous, but very essential, information. Its purpose is to keep the rest of your report unencumbered by a lot of detail. Here you can put tabulations, data sheets, work papers, calculations, samples of forms, questionnaires, records, and anything else that is relevant to the text of your report. If it isn't relevant, perform a partial appendectomy.

7. An *index*, which provides easy reference to specific information in the report. This is generally needed only in long and highly complex reports.

8. A *bibliography*, listing books or articles cited in the report or relevant to it, is particularly useful in technical or highly specialized formal reports.

The order of these elements may be changed by local conventions and the reader's preference—for instance, the letter of transmittal sometimes follows the table of contents. But the basic principles of investigation and organization which we have discussed apply just as much—and probably more so—to the formal report as to any other report form.

The new element in the formal report is the letter of transmittal, and since you may be asked to include such a letter with even your shortest reports—certain companies insist on this—you should know its pattern. While practice varies considerably, this letter usually contains the following information:

1. A reference to the person or agency who authorized the report

2. A general statement of the purpose and scope of the report

3. A reference to the time spent in the investigation

4. Any appropriate statements of appreciation or acknowledgment of assistance

The letter of transmittal, like the answer to an inquiry accompanying printed material, may also refer to specific parts of the report without duplicating them. However, if the material is included in a foreword, the letter of transmittal is not needed. The following is a good example of a letter of transmittal:

Gentlemen:

Our study of possible reorganization plans, which your Board of Directors authorized on February 16, has been completed.

Mr. E. C. Jacobs, Mr. J. W. Greene, and Mr. C. E. Wilcox spent six months visiting your seven production plants and thirteen distributing centers and interviewing all members of your management. Their information was then analyzed by our planning Committee.

Since your instructions were to find the best plan for centralizing authority, we have incorporated this policy in the charts shown on pages 11 and 12. Our central purpose in the report and the charts is to adapt to the actual conditions and personalities the best method of organization.

I want to express our appreciation for the frankness and cooperation of all your employees whom we interviewed, and particularly to Mr. C. W. Winne, who was of invaluable assistance as a liaison man. I shall, of course, be glad to go over any parts of the report with you in detail or to answer any questions you may have.

Respectfully yours,

EXERCISES

1. In your company, which has 543 supervisory employees, the appointment of James Roe as vice-president of general services has just been made. As yet, this appointment is known only to six members of the executive committee. Since Mr. Roe joins your organization from another company, the announcement will disappoint at least three candidates who are veterans with your company and will be an important factor in the careers of many other supervisory employees.

   a. In this situation, Jonathan Jones, chairman of the executive committee, has told you to "give me a memo on the best way to get the news of Mr. Roe's appointment out to all our supervisory employees." You have the choice of the following:

      A memo to all supervisory employees

      A letter over Mr. Jones's signature to all of them

      A meeting of all 543 employees

      Meetings with individual departments

      Calling 45 department heads by phone and requesting them to transmit the information to members of their departments

      Coverage of the story in the company magazine, which will appear in the next two weeks

      Write the memo to Mr. Jones, giving the reasons for your choice.

   b. Assuming that Mr. Jones has decided that a memo sent to all supervisory employees is the method that he prefers, write the memo making the announcement of Mr. Roe's appointment. (You may supply whatever background information on Mr. Roe that you consider appropriate.)

2. Use any of the following information to write a long well-organized memo recommending that your company should (not) initiate a policy of sending letters to all 1,583 employees who are classified as "nonsupervisory." The purpose of the letters would be to

increase employee morale; the decision as to whether they should be used and how they will be used will be made by a three-man company who will use your recommendations to guide them.

Nonsupervisory letters provide a quick means of getting information to all employees at once. They offer a method of emphasizing important information; they invite interest of the wife and the family when the letters are sent to the home; they give an official company version of news and policy; they make a permanent record; they give the boss one of his few opportunities to personalize his message. Reply cards, signed or unsigned, provide feedback from employees.

Usual topics of such letters include any current items of interest to all employees such as company policies, operations, problems. Some companies have found that discussions of bargaining, employee benefits, and political affairs arouse the ire of many employees.

Letters are usually ghostwritten for the president's signature by another employee, but they should reflect the president's style and personality. They can be sent either first-class mail to the home or included with the employee's pay envelope.

Practice varies among companies using letters to nonsupervisory employees: some issue them regularly once a month, others use them only when an important piece of information occurs.

Costs for mailing, processing, and preparing one letter to go to all your 1,583 employees are estimated at $750, or between $9,000 and $10,000 annually if a letter were sent each month.

A few company presidents who have used these letters have found them ineffective. One says, "They're a poor substitute for good human relations on a day-to-day basis"; another said, "They just give dissatisfied workers a chance to pop off in their replies"; another stated, "We snow our employees under with paper. These letters accomplish nothing which a good Suggestions Plan and alert employee relations can't do better."

When the writer doesn't have a clear-cut understanding of employees' problems and attitudes, such letters should not be used, according to a survey of ten companies using them.

A survey of a company close to yours in location and character showed that 40 percent of the employees receiving the letters classified them as "more brainwashing from management."

Several companies sending such letters on a regular once-a-month basis regret their decision to do so because they often do not include an important timely message. They would retain the use of the letter but send it only when important information occurs.

Make certain that your memo to the three-man committee presents a balanced view of the pros and cons of nonsupervisory letters as well as specific recommendations about contents, frequency, and other pertinent matters affecting your central recommendation.

3. Prepare a memorandum to go over your supervisor's signature to all employees calling attention to the policy that "All company personnel are expected to be at work promptly at 9:00 A.M. Habitual tardiness will result in discharge." This memorandum is intended to serve as a warning to members of the sales department, where there has been increasing tardiness within the past week. While you yourself prefer a personalized style, you know your supervisor will not accept anything but a very impersonal method of writing.

4. Because of a last-minute emergency, all your office employees must be called on to work on Memorial Day. Factory employees, on the other hand, will have a holiday since the production of goods is running far ahead of the office records, and the management of the company is using Memorial Day as a means of reducing this lag. Company policy, as set forth in the "Procedures Manual," does not permit overtime pay for office workers. Write a memorandum, which will be issued over the signature of the director of personnel, explaining this situation and informing all office workers that if the lag in office work is corrected by July 4, they will be given a two-day holiday at that time.

5. Prepare a memorandum for your boss, who told you, "I'm getting worried about the amount of time our people are spending in the 'coffee hour.' It seems to me that this thing is getting out of hand. Send me a memo telling me what you think we should do."

6. Using material that is familiar to you, write a brief memorandum for each of the following purposes:
    a. To announce a meeting
    b. To explain a course of action
    c. To explain a problem and to offer possible solutions which may be considered in a meeting
    d. To announce the appointment of a man from outside your organization to an important job within your company
    e. To report to your supervisor on a meeting you have attended
    f. To remind someone that an action must be taken before a deadline
    g. To survey the opinions of a group concerning a policy or action
    h. To report your business or educational activities for one week
    i. To recommend that a specific action or policy should be changed
    j. To sum up the merits or faults of a book on which your supervisor has asked for a one-page memo

7. Your employer has assigned you to analyze all the carbon copies of correspondence sent out by your company during one week. You have analyzed this correspondence very carefully and found four major faults: excessive wordiness, a large number of trite expressions, slovenly typing with crowded margins and careless spelling, and a variety of letter forms. You now believe that a training program for typists and dictators is needed and, above all, that the company letterhead, listing the 46 branch offices, should be changed to improve the appearance of the company's letters. In giving you this assignment, your boss said, "I looked over a lot of our letters last week, and they

seemed pretty good to me. But I'd like to know if you'd make any changes, so give me your recommendations."

8. The Radical Club on your campus has assumed leadership in several demonstrations and sit-ins, and on one occasion its members used violence to break in the door of the Dean of Students' office. Now they propose that all classes be canceled "to honor the publication date of Karl Marx's *Das Kapital* by having speakers, seminars, and demonstrations to underscore the significance of this date." There have been many heated discussions of how to handle this and similar problems on campus. Finally, the Dean of Students has requested each member of the Council to submit a personal memo "stating his views and recommendations on how to respond to this request and to provide, if possible, an overall policy for dealing with demonstrations, sit-ins, and similar actions in the future." Write the memo to the Dean.

9. Your company provides full tuition for employees taking courses in the evening division of local colleges and universities "so long as such courses are successfully completed and so long as they are of direct benefit to the employee's work with the company." Write appropriate memos to deal with the following situations:

   a. A woman employee requests full tuition for a class in ballet dancing because it "will provide poise and charm needed in her job as receptionist."

   b. A male employee claims that he is entitled to the full-tuition refund even though he failed a course in Computer Programming. His instructor has notified you that he missed class on eight consecutive Wednesday nights because he went bowling. As a result, his department won the company bowling league's championship.

10. Taking any situation which you believe needs changing in your institution, write a memo to the responsible person stating why the change should occur and how you would suggest improving the situation.

PART FIVE
SELF-DEVELOPMENT ON THE JOB

If you could poll top management of American business, you would discover one problem all executives share—how to find people with the capacity for growth. To develop growth among employees, business and industry annually spend billions on on-the-job training, on advanced management courses, and on tuition-refund programs. These educational programs are means to an end, but they do not necessarily ensure growth.

In the last analysis, most executives agree on a widely used phrase— "You don't develop people; people only develop themselves." As an employee who may rely heavily on the skills of communication, it is important, therefore, that you use every opportunity for self-development in communication. "We have many employees who know their specific jobs thoroughly," comments one executive, "and yet they are not reaching the top-level jobs, principally because they show no capacity for growth in communication skills."

The main purpose of this part of this book is to suggest certain skills which aid you, directly or indirectly, in developing yourself as a writer. In Chapter 20, we will discuss dictation, a skill which will make you more efficient in communication because mastery of its techniques enables you to get more done in a shorter time. In Chapter 21, we will analyze some of the special problems of on-the-job writing and two skills which are invaluable to writers— vocabulary building and using the dictionary. In Chapter 22 we will stress the importance of reading, explain the techniques of increasing speed and comprehension in reading, and suggest a list of books for future reading.

In developing yourself as a writer, there is no royal road to learning; instead, you must follow the hard path of working constantly at improving yourself and of learning from experience. The chapters which follow are intended to help you on that path, but, in the last analysis, self-development depends on you and on your willingness to spend the time and effort necessary to improve yourself on the job.

CHAPTER 20

DICTATION

If you have the opportunity to practice dictation, either to a stenographer or to a machine, by all means take advantage of this timesaving method. A surprisingly large number of people in business still avoid dictation because they have never learned the technique. Skill and confidence are required for effective dictation, and you should learn the skill as soon as possible. In your career in business you will use dictation for just one reason—to produce better results more quickly and economically. Anyone who persists in ignoring this efficient method is wasting his company's money and hampering his own career. You will, of course, have occasions when you want to "write it all out in longhand" —that way you can see what you write and, therefore, revise easily, although you can do essentially the same thing with a dictated rough draft. But the important thing is to learn the skill of dictation and to use it when circumstances permit. This chapter is intended to help you with the essentials of dictation and to indicate some of the problems involved in the process.

In dictation, two people are working as a team to get a job done quickly. Since this relationship between the dictator and transcriber vitally affects the process of dictation, it is worth analyzing at the outset. Whether the transcriber is a secretary who actually takes the dictation directly or a typist in a stenographic department working from a machine, certain ground rules should be clearly established and understood at the outset:

1. The person who signs the letter or whose name is on the memo or report is finally and irrevocably responsible for everything connected with it.

2. It is his responsibility—or occasionally that of the head of the stenographic department—to make absolutely clear to the transcriber what company policy is regarding dictated material. This involves all matters affecting the form of letters, memos, and reports and anything else relevant to the reproduction of typed materials. If there is no company policy governing these matters, he should clearly state his own preferences. The sooner all these details are reduced to routine, the more efficient is the dictation.

In an effective relationship between dictator and transcriber, there cannot be two bosses. But this does not mean that certain responsibilities cannot be delegated, for delegation of authority simply means that the person who delegates it is still *responsible* for having done so. When and how far should such delegation be permitted in dictation? No pat answer will suffice, because this question really involves the degree of confidence the dictator has in the secretary or transcriber, and confidence arises only from experience in working together. Sound human relations, the essence of good business, consists of using every individual's abilities to the fullest extent which experience shows he or she is capable of. If this spirit characterized all dictation, typists and secretaries could supply a great deal of assistance to the men they work for. In the first place, women are usually more conscious of correctness of phrasing, of propriety of punctuation, of exactness of meaning than men are. In the second place they usually read more, and because they liked English in school or college they generally have a better command of language. Dictators can capitalize on these feminine powers by encouraging secretaries and typists to make suggestions. This close cooperation also imposes certain obligations on the secretarial half of the team—not to be officious, to make suggestions tactfully, and to follow the ground rules as they have been set up.

Assuming, then, that the dictator and transcriber work as a team, we can analyze the whole process of dictation in four phases:

1. Preparing to dictate
2. Dictating
3. Transcribing
4. Signing of the materials dictated

Admittedly, this functional analysis may appear to make a comparatively simple process unnecessarily complex, but by following it through step by step, we can analyze the problems which arise in dictation.

PREPARING TO DICTATE

To the long list of signs and slogans—THINK, Do it TODAY, and Better Service at Lower Cost—which adorn the desks and offices of businessmen, we might profitably borrow from the Boy Scouts a special admonition for dictators, *Be Prepared*. Without question, the worst qualities of most dictated material are a rambling, disorganized style and unnecessary repetition; both stem from the dictator's failure to take time and thought before he dictates. In earlier chapters of this book we have stressed the importance of thinking before you write—and this applies especially to dictation. Until correspondents abandon the foolish idea that they can "dash off" a dictated answer to a letter or memo, there is little hope for improving business communications. In fact, if secretaries appeared for the dictation session as ill-prepared as many of their bosses are, they would arrive without notebook, pencil, and knowledge of shorthand. Here's the way unprepared dictators sound:

> Take a letter, Miss Jones, to the-uh . . . oh yes, the Brown Swidget Company . . . you've got the address somewhere . . . I sorta remember writing to them the first of the year or maybe it was last year . . . make it to the attention of E. Z. or something Brown . . . get the initials from your correspondence files . . . Dear Mr. Brown . . . no, change that to Gentlemen . . . We are-uh in receipt of your letter of the fifteenth in which you inquired about . . . now what was it he wanted to know? Oh, here it is . . . whether in the event you send us your remittance in 10 days after the invoice our terms don't permit a cash discount of 2 percent for payment within 10 days . . . Certainly, I wanted you to take that down, Miss Jones. On second thought, maybe that sentence is too long. Let's start all over. Dear Mr. Brown . . . I mean, Gentlemen.

This costs money because it occupies the time of two people. Let's see how we can cut the high overhead of such dictation. In a few minutes of advance preparation, the dictator should:

1. Assemble all the materials he needs for dictation. This includes copies of letters or memos to answer as well as any previous correspondence or information relevant to his needs.
2. Read over carefully the letters to be answered, checking important points or questions.
3. Make a mental note or write marginal notes on the actual correspondence or the material he wants to cover.
4. Decide on what is the most important function of his letter or memo and organize his material to achieve that function.
5. Select as the starting point something which is close to the reader's interest by answering a question he has raised, by telling him what the letter is about, by agreeing with

him, or by any of the other methods which have been discussed as appropriate for letters, reports, and memorandums in the previous chapters of this book.

When you dictate, try to visualize your reader so that *you can talk directly to him* instead of merely uttering words to be transcribed on paper.
Montgomery Ward, for example, instructs its correspondents to imagine they
have a television set before them and to talk their messages to the image on the
screen. Artificial? Perhaps—but not nearly so artificial as the letter dictated
without any mental picture of the reader. If you have this picture, you'll ask
yourself before you dictate:

What does he want to know?
Have I enough information to answer his questions, to convince him, or to interest
him?
What is the best way to approach him?
What do I want him to do or to think?

And if you follow the steps we have outlined in preparation for dictation,
keeping your reader always in mind, you're bound to be prepared.

DICTATING

The legend of American business is heavy with the "howlers," the "boners,"
and the hilarious mistakes which occur in the process of transcribing sounds
into typed words. An enterprising graduate student or author may some day
produce a side-splitting collection of these true and apocryphal stories as a
commentary on business mores; his research will early show the conventional
pattern that mistakes arising from dictation are *always* the typist's or secretary's error.

Among these classics is the tale of the insurance agent, a native of Ala-
bama, who dictated to his Iowa-born secretary, "We are gravely concerned by
the report about Mr. Blank's heart murmur" and got back a typed version of
concern about "Mr. Blank's hot mama." Another one concerns the district
manager's memo in the central office that "Miss Brown has asked us to do
something about the bare inner office," which emerged as Miss Brown's startling request to do something about "the bear in her office."

These footnotes to the folklore of modern business underscore the prime
function of dictation—to produce in type the exact words of the dictator. In
this process, the dictator is completely responsible for getting his words across
to the transcriber exactly as he utters them; the transcriber is equally obligated
to ask questions if there are things she doesn't understand or if the meaning

seems confused. Most of the difficulties of dictation can be eliminated if dictators will follow five simple principles:

1. Relax and dictate in a clear, natural tone of voice.
2. Enuniciate clearly.
3. Spell out any names or words that sound similar to other names or words.
4. Dictate only periods, paragraphs, and unusual punctuation. Leave normal punctuation to the transcriber.
5. Ask the transcriber to read back—or if it is machine dictation, play back—any parts of the message which may not be clear.

An analysis of each of these principles may be helpful to start youthful dictators on the road to good dictation or to guide "experienced" dictators back to the shortest path.

Relax and Dictate Clearly, Naturally

You doubtless remember the pompous, classic poses assumed by the political dictators of the twentieth century—Hitler, strutting and prancing; Mussolini, with jutting jaw and arm raised in Fascist salute; Stalin, cold and expressionless in a pose he must have considered appropriate for a man of steel. Many dictators in business unconsciously assume similar pompous poses in the dictation period. Some become orators, making the walls of the office—and their secretary's ears—ring with their words. Others affect a special form of speech, an expressionless monotone which seems to arise from a feeling that any expression will hinder the transcriber's ability to get the words down. Still others belong on the raceways, since they cover 10 paces for each word uttered. Some day, the Society for the Prevention of Cruelty to Secretaries will draw up bills of indictment against these offenders with the appropriate punishment that they be forced to listen to or watch themselves in action. When you dictate, relax. Think of yourself as *talking* directly to your reader, and do it in a natural tone of voice without affectation, without posing. This concept of *talking* to your reader in dictation is vitally important, because the pompous affectations we have described are almost invariably accompanied by pompous, stilted, artificial language. Regard your dictation session as simple, natural talk and you'll go far toward unaffected, direct language in your letters, reports, and memos. If you freeze up, as many dictators do, you'll cover up by using mannerisms which really aren't you at all. Listen to yourself occasionally when you dictate, or, better still, listen to a recording of your dictation. If you want to profit from good human relations, ask your secretary or transcriber how you are doing occasionally. After all, you are missing a chance to improve if you don't find out how the signals are getting across to the other half of the team.

Enunciate Clearly

Among the notable charactertics of the English language is the fact that words which sound alike can be poles apart in meaning; some of these words are listed under the next point to be discussed. In certain instances, the only recourse is to spell out the word. But speaking generally, your best assurance for getting an accurate transcription is to enunciate clearly when you dictate. The difference between words like *receive* and *received*, between the sound of *m* and *n*, and *f* and *v* is often hard to get by ear, unless considerable emphasis is placed on their pronunciation. If you slur your speech, "this sort of machine" can sound very much like "the sorter machine" or "this order machine."

You can check your own enunciation quite easily. If people have difficulty understanding you in conversation and, particularly, on the telephone, you're probably not enunciating clearly. Here, too, listening to a playback of your dictation will prove helpful. Most important of all, become conscious of the way you enunciate; listen to find out whether you have a tendency to slur your words together, to drop syllables in saying "incidently" instead of *incidentally* or "finely" instead of *finally*, to ignore the final *g* in "writin' new copy," which can emerge as "write a new copy." Slovenly speech is frequently just one indication of a lot of other sloppy habits; avoid it in dictation and then let your good practices there carry over into all your speech.

Spell Out Words and Names That May Be Strange or Confusing

Even the most precise enunciation will not clear up confusion where words have identical sounds. For instance, *cite, sight, site; know, no; coarse, course; through, threw;* and a host of other words are identical. Here, of course, a transcriber's intelligent appraisal of the context will help, although a realtor, for example, can just as logically be describing a beautiful sight as a beautiful site and examples can be both cited and sighted. In such instances, the dictator should remember that whatever admirable traits his secretary has, being a mind reader is not among them. He should spell out technical terms, unfamiliar words, strange names; if he doesn't she should ask—and then, like Ko-Ko, the Lord High Executioner in *The Mikado,* she should keep "a little list" of these terms, words, and names so that she will know them the next time they occur. Here is another little list of words which cause confusion:

accede, exceed	forth, fourth
accept, except	incidence, incidents
access, excess	its, it's
addition, edition	legislator, legislature
affect, effect	loose, lose
allusion, illusion	maybe, may be
already, all ready	miner, minor
altogether, all together	no, know
anyone, any one	new, knew
assistance, assistants	ordinance, ordnance
bare, bear	passed, past
brake, break	personal, personnel
capital, capitol	practical, practicable
cease, seize	precedence, precedents
coarse, course	principal, principle
cite, sight, site	residence, residents
complement, compliment	respectfully, respectively
correspondence, correspondents	rite, right, write
council, counsel, consul	some one, someone
decent, descent, dissent	stationary, stationery
deference, difference	their, there, they're
disapprove, disprove	therefore, therefor
eligible, illegible	through, threw
era, error	waive, wave
everyone, every one	whose, who's
finally, finely	your, you're
formally, formerly	

Dictators should take particular care to see that names are properly spelled. The most efficient way is to give the secretary the letter or memo which is being answered at the end of the dictation pertaining to it; she can then check names, addresses, and dates carefully with the written information before her when she transcribes. Since people are most sensitive to the spelling of their own names, special care should be taken by both dictator and transcriber to see that names like Stewart or Stuart, O'Neill or O'Neal, Schwartz or Swarts are accurately typed. The same care should, of course, prevail with names of companies, partnerships, titles, or anything else where errors may occur.

Dictate Only the Major or Unusual Marks of Punctuation

One of the most annoying habits a dictator can develop is to include every mark of punctuation in his dictation. Not only does this interrupt his own thinking, which should be focused on the content rather than the mechanics of his material, but it also distracts the secretary or transcriber from her main task of getting his words down exactly. This habit implies that you don't trust the transcriber to punctuate properly and that you know more about it than she does. Perhaps you do, but the best way to find out and to maintain the teamwork we have advocated is to let her try. If you're not satisfied with the results, maybe you need a new secretary—or maybe, since this habit reflects considerable ego, you should take a course in shorthand so that you can be dictator, secretary, punctuator, and transcriber, all in one.

Basically, only three situations require punctuation by the dictator:

1. Punctuation at the end of the sentence—say "period," "question mark," exclamation point."

2. The end of a paragraph—say "new paragraph." Your transcriber can help you a great deal with paragraphing if you let her make suggestions. Even the most experienced dictators occasionally lose sight of how much material or how many sentences they incorporate in a paragraph.

3. Unusual punctuation marks—a dash for emphasis, an exclamation point, or quotation marks.

The only other mechanical aspects of the letter, memo, or report that should concern you in dictation are the number of carbon copies to be made, to whom they must go, and what enclosures or attachments are to go with the dictated material. Occasionally, you should tell the transcriber how you want material set up in special situations; for instance, where you have dictated a list of comments numbered 1, 2, 3, 4 which are to be indented within the margin of the text of a letter, you can help her at the end of the list by saying, "This goes back to the original margin." But remember that you and your typist, secretary, or transcriber are both specialists—and give her as much freedom in her specialty as experience warrants. After all, you still hold a veto power which you can exercise when the time comes to sign the letter, memo, or report.

Reading or Playing the Material Back

Even the best-prepared dictator will want to make changes in wording or phraseology during dictation. By having the secretary read back or the machine play back your dictation, you are doing exactly what you do when you revise your written material. The sole difference is that you can't pencil in the changes yourself; for that reason, your instructions for changing dictated material must be unusually explicit and clear. Say, "Let's change that 'arbitrary decision' in the second sentence to 'final opinion'" or "Omit the 'very' before 'delighted' in the last paragraph." Be sure that your transcriber understands the changes you want.

One aspect of dictation which worries the inexperienced is how fast to go. Generally, this is likely to be more a mental than an actual problem. In the early stages, you will be wise to slow down your normal rate of speech a bit until experience guides you as to the speed of your transcriber. Then you can go at a pace which produces the best results, under the principle that in this division of labor, it is her responsibility to keep up with you rather than yours to slow your words down to her shorthand or typing.

At the beginning of this chapter, we stressed dictation as a tool to produce better results more quickly and economically. Like every tool, it has its merits and limitations. Dictation is most useful for writing a large number of short letters or memos; unless you are very unusual, you should not try to dictate the final draft of a long report or a complex memo. If you do, you will find that you are merely pouring words into the microphone or the secretary's notebook and wasting two people's time in the process.

TRANSCRIBING

From the transcriber, the dictator should expect one result—an exact transcript of his words, set up in appropriate form, and without errors in typing, division of words, spelling, or punctuation. If the transcriber finds errors in grammar in the dictation, she should always suggest a correction, on the general principle that the company doesn't want such mistakes recorded permanently in type.

SIGNING THE MATERIALS DICTATED

Read over all dictated material before you sign your name because your signature means that you are assuming final responsibility for everything in the letter, memo, or report. For that reason, the humor or annoyance that many dictators express about "my secretary's carelessness in making that error" only reflects their own carelessness in not catching the error when they signed the material. By insisting on accuracy and excellence at the time you sign, you are also establishing the high standards of performance you expect from your transcriber.

MACHINE DICTATION

To increase efficiency in producing written communications, more and more companies are installing dictation machines. The greatest advantage of machine dictation is its saving in time, since it eliminates the necessity for tying up the dictator and the transcriber at the same time. The machine is always there for the dictator to use at his convenience and to fit his dictation into his schedule. Furthermore, modern electronic and mechanical dictating equipment is so flexible and adaptable that all of the objections which used to be raised about the difficulties of making changes in dictated materials have been removed. The actual fact is that almost all of the failures of machine dictation arise from the human element rather than the machine. Because of their reluctance to change, to adopt new and efficient methods, many executives are handicapped by their inability or lack of familiarity in using dictating equipment.

Everything that we have said about dictation to a secretary applies in even greater degree to machine dictation. Because the transcriber cannot ask questions directly, machine dictation makes even greater demands for preparation, clarity, and enunciation on the part of the dictator. One of the greatest faults of the novice at machine dictation is a tendency to shout. The sensitivity of modern equipment is so great that this tendency merely distorts the message. Another fault of the novice is to hesitate and to leave long pauses in his dictation. This fault stems partly from lack of preparation, partly from a mild form of microphone fright or fear of the unfamiliar. Anyone who wants to learn to dictate efficiently to a machine should follow these guiding principles:

1. *Hold the microphone or speaking tube in the position recommended by the manufacturer. Don't* wave it around, don't shift it from one position to another.

2. *Speak in a normal conversational tone. Don't* shout and don't drop your voice.

3. *Talk steadily and at a little slower rate than normal,* unless you are a very slow speaker. *Don't* fluctuate by rushing occasional phrases or by hesitating for long intervals.

4. *Take special care to enunciate clearly,* to speak distinctly, and to pronounce unusual words with unusual care. If there is any doubt, always spell such words out. *Don't* mumble.

5. *Dictate paragraphs and uncommon punctuation:* semicolons, colons, dashes, parentheses. Voice inflections as in normal conversation will indicate commas and other conventional punctuation.

6. *Dictate figures by digits.* Spell names and unusual words unless they appear in the correspondence which you send on to the transcriber.

7. *Make all corrections carefully* in accordance with the directions for the type of equipment you are using. Many a transcriber confronted with a dictator who either neglects to indicate corrections, or indicates them on a following cylinder or record when they force her to retype material, might give vent to her feelings in the famous words from the *Rubáiyát* of Omar Khayyám:

> *The moving finger writes; and, having writ,*
> *Moves on; nor all your piety or wit*
> *Shall lure it back to cancel half a line*
> *Nor all your tears wash out a word of it.*

Don't force the transcriber to guess at corrections or to retype material because the corrections are not clearly indicated at the appropriate place.

8. *Attach all necessary forms,* guide sheets, cards, or all other information to the cylinder or records. *Don't* force the transcriber to call you or to ask you for additional information which you should have sent.

9. *Start the machine before you begin dictating and stop it after you have finished. Don't* clip your words at the beginning or chop off the end of your dictation.

The best test of the effectiveness of your techniques of machine dictation is the transcriber herself. For that reason, many companies ask transcribers to analyze the effectiveness of individual dictators at regular intervals. Such an analysis is recommended as a practical device for securing good teamwork between dictators and transcribers of machine dictation.

The following is a simple illustration of the actual procedure used in dictating, with the instructions to the transcriber italicized, the dictation to be transcribed in regular type.

Operator this is to be a letter with two carbons Indicate that one carbon copy *goes to Edward C Borton our dealer in Middletown* Letter to Charles M *as in Mary* Kohn *K as in kick* o-h-n *as in November* 2739 Broadway Middletown New York 12760 Dear Mr Kohn We appreciate your telling us of your interest in our air *hyphen* conditioning units as advertised in Life *Operator underline Life Paragraph* Our dealer Mr Edward C Barton *correction* Borton will call on you to discuss the various Breezie units in which you expressed an interest Since we regard every installation as an individual engineering project we want you to have the opportunity to discuss your needs with Mr Borton so that he can work out the best and most economical solution *Paragraph* You will be interested I know in reading the three brochures I am enclosing *colon   Operator please indent and list the following items* 1 What Breezie Air Conditioners Can Do 2 A Survey of the Effects of Air Conditioning on Retail Sales by Professor R. O. Fidel *F as in Frank i as in island d as in door e as in eat l as in lot* and 3 We Cite *Operator that's c-i-t-e* These Results with Pride *Operator return to the original margin* Thank you for giving us the opportunity to discuss our units with you I know that one of our units will suit your needs and that air conditioning will mean better business for you *Operator underline you* Sincerely yours *Mark the letter for three enclosures and pick up the brochures listed from Miss Gompert at the reception desk   That's all*

SOME OTHER SUGGESTIONS

Now that we have analyzed the process of dictation from pre-dictation preparation through to the signing of materials, here are a few other suggestions to help you when you get into business and dictate frequently:

1. If possible, set up a regular period for dictation. Try to arrange your dictation schedule so that you can take care of answering an average day's mail the same day it comes in.

2. Without being officious or pompous about it, let it be known that you don't want to be interrupted when you are dictating. There will, of course, be important exceptions to this, but you'll do your best work if you can arrange to concentrate on your dictation and go straight through from beginning to end. Many companies insist on this in the interests of efficiency and set up specific dictation periods when, by mutual agreement, all telephone calls between departments stop and outside calls are handled by one person in each department.

3. Your relations with your transcriber will improve—and so will your typed material—if you'll avoid the frictions generated by the following situations:

    a. Don't habitually locate "one more important letter" that has to be dictated at 5 P.M. and mailed that day. Remember that she has a life of her own to lead.

    b. Don't mark up typing which she can easily correct or draw ink lines across a whole letter because one word is misspelled. Indicate changes by light pencil checks or by telling her what you want corrected.

But since no mere male can see dictators as their secretaries see them, here is a qualified opinion in the form of a satire by a secretary. It should be required reading for every dictator, present or potential:

SO YOU CAN DICTATE?

Most men imagine that they are splendid dictators. About one man in twenty-five *is* a good dictator.

I've devised a simple test below. If you aren't mentioned in this list of the commonest types of Bad Dictators, perhaps you *are* that rare exception—a man who dictates well.

The staring dictator

If you're this type, you can cure yourself with lots of will power. The staring dictator is the one who keeps staring at the shorthand pad. He usually means well—he wants to be sure he isn't going too fast, or otherwise he's helplessly fascinated by the sight of shorthand. The results of staring can be serious. The stenographer feels that she's got to take the whole thing down in shorthand, instead of writing every other word out. Some shorthand symbols can look mighty funny when it's time to transcribe them. So look away, boys. Stare out of the window that the office manual says the stenographer shouldn't stare out of and get your letters back the way you like them.

The vicarious stenographer

This man is a born stenographer himself; in his subconscious mind he's itching to change jobs with the stenographer. He wants to do *all* the work. He's the one who says: "In reply to your letter comma I believe comma when you have seen all the simply splendid features of our newest Dolly Dimple Dandee-Didies comma you will want comma definitely comma to reduce your order just received comma for the old-type comma Super De Luxe Dandee-Didies period and paragraph."

The stenographer can be in a comma—I mean coma—and still take and transcribe this man's dictation. If she does too much of it, her mind decays. No self-respecting stenographer will stay with this type of dictator very long.

The monster

This man is the reverse of the Born Stenographer. He buzzes for a girl and says "Take a letter to Mr. Alan Trout." The letter will have to be retyped later because he doesn't bother to spell "Alan." Whey should he have to SPELL for the stenographer? After all, she takes shorthand, doesn't she? He never hands her any previous correspondence so she can check any of the names or terms. She's a STENOGRAPHER, isn't she? And he doesn't give her the time or opportunity to ask any questions. She took a COURSE and applied for a JOB, didn't she?

In the middle of a letter he picks up a paper on his desk which contains some technical information to be incorporated in the letter. This he rattles off as fast as he can read. It never occurs to him that if the stenographer were fast enough to be a court reporter, she'd be making a mighty nice SALARY and be far removed from HIM.

Enough of him. You can't be that bad. You won't be if you will remember that shorthand makes a stenographer and not a swami. If the stenographer is new, don't be too sure that she won't be just as fast and competent in time as Miss Crow, who has been with you now for 15 years. After she's been with you a week or two, her efficiency and speed should increase by leaps and pothooks. For instance, she'll probably write Dolly Dimple De Luxe Dandee-Didies in longhand the first time you let her have it. The second time she'll probably try it in shorthand just for the hell of it. The third time she'll probably be all set with a quick symbol, and after that you'll be able to throw didies at her at a great rate.

The stillborn dictator

This is the man who sends stenographers straight into sanitariums. He has no idea as yet, when he buzzes or bellows for a stenographer at 9:10 prompt, just what it is that he wants to say. He thinks that another living shape in the room with him, with a pad and pencil in its hand, will tidy up his fuzzy mind for him. He is the one who says: "Take a letter to Crump & Crump . . . (minutes go by) . . . Gentlemen . . . (one minute) . . . No, better address it to Mr. Slaughter at Crump & Crump I think his first name is Axel . . . (paper shuffling) . . . I can't find the letter . . . better address it to the company and make it to Mr. Slaughter's attention . . . (satisfied throat clearing) . . . Gentlemen . . . Thank you for your recent letter addressed to our Mr. Dumm . . . make a copy of this for Mr. Dumm . . . who has turned your letter over to me for attention scratch that . . . since our Mr. Sam Strangle . . . of our sales staff scratch that . . . make a copy for Strangle too will you . . . will be in your territory the early part of next week or not later than Friday . . . make it not later than *next* Friday I am instructing him scratch that . . . asking him to call on you and give you or say and *show* you . . ."

After an hour of this the stenographer begins to feel light in the head. When she looks at her notebook, she has the feeling that something is not what it could be isn't something wrong what could it be is amiss somewhere somehow it isn't quite right or am I just hungry oh it's all wrong.

The trouble with this dictator—of course he may be misplaced in the didies business in the first place—is that he thinks of himself as someone who has to "write a letter" instead of thinking of himself as having something to communicate (which he hasn't).

The mumbler

This man has an inferiority complex, and it's an infectious one. After the stenographer has said "Pardon me?" . . . "I'm sorry, I didn't hear?" . . . "What was that name?" five or six times in one hour, she begins to think that she is losing her hearing. She doesn't want the man to know that she is almost stone deaf, so she gives up interrupting him every few minutes and writes down the approximate sounds that he is mumbling. Sometimes she can figure out what these approximate sounds represent. But as days go by, she has a harder and harder time with her notes. She has lost all confidence in herself. A hunted look appears in her eyes—and the mumbler hunts in vain, in her letters, for what he actually mumbled. One day she hands him a weird-sounding letter that she has just transcribed all about a "Burlis Station." He blows up and fires the stenographer. If he had only spoken up, instead of mumbling, she would have known he was talking about a *berler* station.*

In this chapter we have outlined the four aspects of dictation, all of which contribute to the final result. While it is impossible to assign accurate equivalents to each phase of dictation, the checklist following arbitrarily rates each phase of dictation as equally important. If you can answer "yes" to these questions, you are indeed a good dictator.

---

*Reprinted by permission of *Printers' Ink*, from "A Steno's View of Dictators," October 25, 1946.

A CHECKLIST FOR DICTATION

Preparing

Do you have all the previous correspondence and other information you need
to dictate efficiently? . . . .
Have you read through the material you are answering and made notes of the
points you want to cover? . . . .
Have you decided on the main point of your letter or memo and how best to
get it across to your reader? . . . .
Do you visualize the kind of reader you are dictating to and how you can ap-
proach him?   25

Dictating

Do you have a mental picture of your reader as an actual human being to whom
you are talking when you dictate? . . . .
Are you dictating naturally without affectation? . . . .
Are you enunciating clearly? . . . .
Do you spell out names or words that may be strange or confusing to your tran-
scriber? . . . .
Are you dictating only the major and unusual marks of punctuation? . . . .
Are you revising by having the secretary read back or the machine play back,
and are you indicating your revisions clearly? . . . .
Are you dictating at a rate which is efficient for both you and the transcriber? . .   25

Transcribing

Is the material transcribed in a form you approve? . . . .
Have you been consulted about any changes? . . . .
Is it accurate and without errors in spelling, punctuation, and grammar? . . . . . .
When your transcriber generally does a good job, have you told her so occa-
sionally?   25

Signing

Have you read over the transcript carefully before you signed? . . . .
If it does not meet the standards set up under "Transcribing," do you insist that it
be corrected or done over? . . . .
Do you habitually establish high standards of performance which you expect
from your transcriber?   25

                                                                                                           100

EXERCISES

Most colleges and universities today provide facilities for students in their business communication courses to practice dictation. Ideally, such students should have the opportunity to dictate to a machine as well as to a secretary. On the principle that in learning a new or unfamiliar technique the student should start with simple examples, the following exercises are rather elementary so far as their content is concerned, their main object being to give the student confidence in and the opportunity to concentrate on his dictation.

Subject, of course, to the discretion of the instructor, these exercises will probably produce the best results if the specific assignment is made a short time before the student actually dictates. The student should use this time to prepare a few brief notes for his answer. (Do not write out the entire answer and read it to the transcriber or voice recorder; if you do, you will lose the benefit of a valuable experience.)

1. Dictate an answer to a letter from Mr. Marion V. Willson, 971 Ferth Street, Cincinnati, Ohio. Mr. Willson, a customer of yours for seven years, has mildly complained that "the fifty 7-inch I-beams I ordered on May 27 haven't arrived yet, and I'm finally writing to you to find out when they will get here." Your information shows that delivery of this merchandise, shipped May 29, was delayed because of a holiday, Decoration Day, and a wildcat strike which tied up all freight shipments from Pittsburgh on May 31 and June 1. The merchandise left Pittsburgh on June 2 and should have arrived there before today, June 5, when you are answering Mr. Willson's letter of June 3.

2. Using the material in this chapter, dictate an answer to the following inquiry:

> Gentlemen:
>
> Our class in Business Correspondence is making a survey of the various factors which affect dictation. I have been asked to get answers from your company to these questions:
>
> 1. What are the five most important instructions you would give dictators to produce good results?
> 2. What are the responsibilities of the secretary in turning out an accurate and well-formulated letter?
>
> We are going to tabulate the results of this questionnaire, and I'll be glad to send you a summary if you want one. Thank you for your cooperation.
>
> Sincerely yours,
>
> Jonathon O'Conner
> 111 First Avenue
> Albuquerque, New Mexico

3. Dictate an improved final draft of a letter which your instructor has recently handed back to you, incorporating his suggestions for improvement in your dictated draft.

4. Dictate an appropriate letter to the Blank Department Stores, Inc., Quiston Street, Schenectady, New York, explaining that you ordered a silver tray costing $22.95 on December 1 to be sent gift-wrapped as an anniversary gift to your parents at Greshems-

ville, New York 12746. When you arrived in Greshemsville on December 6, the anniversary date, the gift had not arrived, nor has it yet come on December 8, when you are writing this letter from Greshemsville. The clerk in the Blank Department Stores, Inc. gave you every assurance that the gift would arrive in plenty of time for the anniversary. You now want the charge of $22.95 canceled by the store where you have had an account for six years.

5. Dictate a letter of appreciation and congratulation to a former teacher, whose personal counsel and classroom instruction have been especially helpful to you. You have read in the latest issue of your alumni magazine that he is retiring after 35 years' service in the teaching profession "to spend his years in pursuing his favorite hobbies."

6. Dictate an answer to a young friend who was two years behind you in preparatory school and who has written asking you how you like your present institution. He especially wants to know whether you can give him any information about the course in business administration—or any other subject with which you are familiar—at your college or university.

7. Dictate a sales letter in answer to an inquiry from Ernest C. Greene, 2917 Whitside Avenue, Los Angeles 90053, about a product or service with which you are familiar. Mr. Greene has written to you as the local agent for this product or service.

8. Dictate an answer to a request from Earle N. Milvertun, 47 Munn Street, Chattanooga, Tennessee 37401, for a pamphlet your company published—"Consider Our Location for Future Business." This promotional pamphlet, intended to attract new business to your area, is out of print. Your letter should, therefore, sum up the advantages your area has which would induce new businesses to consider it as a site for possible expansion.

9. Dictate a memorandum to be sent to 17 members of your company's stenographic department setting down the general rules which should apply to the *form* of all letters they type.

10. Your supervisor has asked you to "put in writing" your request to attend a certain two-day meeting which will, of course, mean that you will be absent from work those days. He has told you that he will have to pass judgment on your request by applying the company policy which says "employees are encouraged to attend those meetings which can be shown to be of practical assistance to them on their jobs." Dictate the memo.

SPECIAL PROBLEMS AND SKILLS FOR THE WRITER

The main purpose of this chapter is to suggest answers to a few of the special problems you may encounter in writing when you get on the job, and to offer some suggestions for your own self-development as a writer. Most of your writing in business will, of course, consist of the types discussed in previous chapters—letters, reports, and memorandums. Increasingly, however, business is calling on its younger personnel to assist in a wide variety of communications problems and techniques. It does so because junior staff members have new ideas; because they have educational backgrounds which prepared them well for writing in business, college courses in business communications being a comparatively recent development; and, to be realistic, because older personnel sometimes prefer to avoid these assignments, which involve writing for or with other people and thinking about overall communications. You *may* never get such an assignment; but if you do, you ought to regard it as an opportunity for you to learn something about writing.

Let's look first at three problems in communication which you may encounter and then analyze certain methods which will help you to develop yourself as a writer.

WRITING FOR OTHER PEOPLE'S SIGNATURE

In this book, we have stressed three basic elements of communication—the writer, the reader, and the purpose for which the material is to be used. To these three, in certain situations, we must add another —an individual who will sign memos, letters, and reports which you may be asked to write for him. You will find that this practice is quite general, especially in large companies and in certain organizations like banks and financial firms in which only designated officials are authorized to sign letters and memos. Still other companies adopt this practice on the theory that better customer relations will result from letters apparently from John Johnson, vice-president, than from John Jones, a young employee without benefit of title, who actually wrote them. And, finally, executives with numerous responsibilities frequently delegate part of their writing to others but reserve the power of signing as a means of checking what goes out.

The introduction of this fourth element in communications, however necessary it may be, is vexatious at best. For whom and in what style shall you write? The vexation arises because you may not be sure which "reader" you write for—your boss or the ultimate consumer—and in what style—your own or the way you think your signer would say it. Ideally, "style is the man," and writing should therefore be as personal as possible; actually, however, numerous employees in today's business find themselves obliged to assume a kind of artificial Dr. Jekyll-and-Mr. Hyde method of expression which precludes the naturalness always present in good writing.

In the last analysis, the only solution to such a situation is for both the writer and the signer to arrive at a clear-cut understanding of two things:

1. That the reader to whom the letter or report goes is always the most important element in communication.

2. That there are often different, and equally effective, ways of expressing ideas.

This requires tolerance on both parts: on the signer's, because it is after all the reader's reaction and not his own whims that should count; on the writer's, because his supervisor has had more experience and knows how to deal with certain situations which require written communications. Perhaps it is heresy, but in the long run you will make a mistake if you are satisfied merely to kowtow completely to your signer's preferences; the result is bound to be both artificial and superficial. The most difficult relationship occurs when the signer prefers an impersonal style and the writer wants to express himself personally and directly; the gnashing of these signers and the wailing of their writers can be heard throughout business, and the net effect is waste in rewriting.

But it would be equally heretical for any young writer to insist brashly that his own form of expression is superior to any other. Stubborn pride of authorship can be even more dangerous than servile imitation. If wisdom and tolerance are to prevail, the young writer must take due cognizance of the fact that his signer is his boss, without being slavishly parrotlike; and if the signer is wise, he will remember that the final reader is *his boss* and that young writers sometimes express themselves differently but none the less well. When such wisdom and tolerance can't be attained, you will simply have to forget your own style and become a ghost—a role calculated to inhibit your spirit. But since this is a role you may have to play in certain circumstances, you will do well to learn the technique of writing in different styles, particularly both personal and impersonal, to prepare yourself for such contingencies.

WRITING WITH OTHER PEOPLE

The teamwork which properly characterizes many of the functions of modern business finds expression in numerous clichés adopted from the sporting world, such as "Members of the Blankco team," "We're going to have to pull together to score a touchdown at year's end," and "Let's hit the line hard on this campaign." Admirable and efficient as such concepts may be in production and sales efforts, they have unfortunately been carried over into the production of written communications. Committees and small groups in business are told: "Come up with a statement of policy on this problem" or "Let's have this group prepare a consensus on that." In fulfilling these assignments, too many cooks tend not only to spoil the broth but to transform it into hash.

This team technique in communication is often called *democratic* since everyone has the opportunity to add his ideas, attitudes, opinions to the general fund—and as far as this aspect of contributing and exchanging ideas is concerned, the technique produces excellent human relations. But when it comes to *writing* the actual communication, these joint efforts are usually wasteful of time, weak in expression, and watered down in content. Since good writing stems from a highly personal sense of responsibility, these cumbersome "committee efforts" too often defeat the purpose for which they are intended. Even in creative writing, the teams of collaborators are few—Beaumont and Fletcher, Addison and Steele, and a few moderns—and such group documents as the Declaration of Independence were first drafted by one writer. Yet there is a strong possibility that you will be a collaborator on reports, policy statements, and similar materials; and you'll wisely decide that you want to be "a good team member," to use the current cliché, though it seems only fair to comment that even good team members need a quarterback to coordinate their efforts.

How to proceed then becomes the question. In the first place, you can re-member that as a general rule, no communication that is long or involved can be *written* effectively by a group or committee. The best procedure is to fix responsibility for the actual writing on one or two members of the group and to do this at the *beginning* of the assignment or the meeting so that they can take adequate notes. Another procedure is to assign responsibility for writing various parts of the communication to the individuals best qualified or most concerned, a technique which is especially good for complex reports. Once this responsibility is fixed, the person or persons responsible for the writing should be informed of the time when the deadline is set or when the group will meet again; these writers should be instructed to prepare copies of their drafts for circulation to the members at least a day before the deadline or the time of the meeting. This precludes the wasteful haggling and bickering which always re-sult when a group is handed copies of a draft in an actual meeting; it forestalls the inevitable comment that "Of course, this is the first chance I've had to see the draft"; and it presents the opportunity to make changes or corrections in in advance. With this procedure, you are following essentially the same tech-nique we have suggested for reports—writing the draft and then using the group's thinking for revision and editing. It, therefore, combines the best re-sults from individual and group effort. When you work with one or two other people to prepare a communication, you should be certain that:

1.   Each knows the part he is responsible for.
2.   Each sees the section written by the others.

Only by doing this can you be sure that:

1.   Transitions are clearly made.
2.   The style does not shift abruptly.
3.   Conclusions or recommendations are stated in words which everyone agrees with.

By tactfully suggesting that groups or committees merely waste time by *writing,* you are probably going to get the writing assignment yourself, human nature (even in committees) being what it is. When you do, you can find some consolation in knowing that you are conserving other people's time and your own nerves by avoiding the inefficiency and bickering of what George Orwell in *1984* might have called "groupwrite."

IMPROVING YOUR OWN COMMUNICATIONS

In the past ten years, American business has worked hard at the job of improv-ing its communications; through training programs, writing clinics, and the use of outside consultants business has offered its employees many opportunities for learning about the techniques of writing. But even if your company does not offer these opportunities, you can still do several things to improve your writing once you are on the job. Beyond everything else, you must recognize that you have to work constantly at the task of writing; even though you've had excellent preparation in college, don't trade on your previous training too long. For if writing is important to your career, it is continually important, and you should therefore plan a continuous means of improvement.

Some companies encourage department heads to look over all carbons of letters and reports written during a week for the purpose of constructive criticism—and this is a useful device for improvement. In other companies, small groups get together occasionally to discuss one another's communications; this, too, can be very helpful if the participants are tactful and constructive in their comments. Most urban areas provide courses in business writing which you can take, and almost every library contains a number of excellent books for self-study, some of which are listed in the bibliography at the end of Chapter 22.

Best of all, you can use the techniques of the letter-writing clinic on yourself. At regular intervals, get out the carbon copies of your own letters, memos, and reports and read them critically from your reader's point of view. This simple device will improve your writing as much as anything you can do. In this process, you'll undoubtedly notice that some of your letters would have been more effective if you'd started with your second paragraph; that the sentences in several reports were far too long and involved; that a few of the memos might have provided more background for your reader. It's too late to correct these mistakes now; but it's exactly the right time to see that they don't occur again. Like great men, all good writers make mistakes; what distinguishes them is that they don't make the same mistakes over and over again—and that's why this self-criticism of your carbons will help.

BUILDING A VOCABULARY

Throughout this book, we have emphasized the principles of expressing yourself simply, concisely, and in a tone adapted to your reader. Is it inconsistent now to urge you to increase your store of words by adding some which may be unfamiliar to your readers? Certainly you will be inconsistent if you develop a large vocabulary merely to impress your friends and confound your readers.

The real purpose of developing your vocabulary is consistent with what we have said, for words are the basic tools with which you think. You can test this the next time you get to daydreaming; when you return to reality, check back on what you were doing—there may have been a few pictures flashing across your mental screen, but most of your wandering was probably done in words. This concept of words as *the tools of thought* was exactly what your foreign language teacher meant by saying that you would really be learning French or German or Spanish when you began thinking in that language.

In a famous article in the *Atlantic Monthly*, Johnson O'Connor, the director of the Human Engineering Laboratories, summed up his researches on the factors that produce success by saying, "An extensive knowledge of the exact meanings of English words accompanies outstanding success in this country more often than any other single characteristic which the Human Engineering Laboratories have been able to isolate and measure."* Words, therefore, are the mental labels you place on situations, concepts, and ideas; and whether you use them frequently in your speech or your writing doesn't matter—but it does matter that you can think precisely because precise thinking directly affects your writing. And certainly, as an educated person, you don't want your speech dominated by the trite expressions of the dullard—O.K., swell, nice, cute, check, corny, didn't get to first base, and others which have lost their luster or precision by overuse.

If you read widely, you are on the path to a good vocabulary, and you'll find that your excursions in the world of books are more interesting and meaningful if you can develop a consciousness of word meanings. Actually, almost any method you use to increase your vocabulary will prove beneficial if you work at it. Some people try to learn ten new words from their newspaper or magazine reading each week; others concentrate on learning a word a day; still others group families of words in their minds; the *anthropes* family —misanthropy, philanthropy, anthropology; *chronos*—chronology, anachronism, chronometer; *lithos*—monolith, neolithic, lithograph. These are all good methods, and they can be supplemented by other intellectual calisthenics for developing mental muscles:

Take any common word like *fat, thin, rich, stingy, new, glad* and intensify it by putting *very* in front of it. Instead of overworking this tired *very*, think of synonyms which exactly express *very fat, very thin,* etc.

Select common verbs like *said, sent, try* or adjectives like *new, pretty, interesting* and list as many synonyms as you can, using your dictionary to find out how these synonyms differ in their precise meaning and usage.

Think of the various ways you would express the opposite (the antonym) of words like *generous, frank, clever, stupid, out-of-date,* and *sincere.*

Differentiate the precise meanings and usage of word pairs like *practical, practicable; continual, continuous; farther, further; principal, principle; affect, effect; liable, likely.* You'll find a list of such words on page 431.

Learn to find the story behind the word by getting its derivation, its original

*Reprinted by permission of the *Atlantic Monthly.*

and present meaning from your dictionary. Since your *salary* is of more than passing interest to you, you may be surprised to learn that it is closely related to words like *saline* and *salt* because of the Roman custom of paying wages in salt. Here are ten words which have interesting tales to tell: *nasturtium, hocus-pocus, gerrymander, slogan, boycott, bedlam, gregarious, carnival, quixotic,* and *sabotage*.

These—or any other methods you use—will help you develop a consciousness of words which is the only mental climate in which your vocabulary can flourish. In the oldest English epic, *Beowulf,* a picturesque phrase occurs again and again; when one of the characters speaks, the unknown poet describes him as "unlocking his word-hoard." It's a good concept for moderns who first must acquire their "hoard" through constant effort and then in the "unlocking" develop a sense of discrimination and preciseness. But this is one form of hoarding from which both you and your business associates will benefit.

Using a Dictionary

The vocabulary growth we have discussed can be cultivated with the one invaluable implement which most people use for only a fraction of its potential—a *good* dictionary. Fortunately, a number of very excellent dictionaries have appeared in the last decade, and there is no valid reason why every student should not own one.

Don't make the mistake of buying a dictionary just because it is small in size or a "bargain"; you deserve and need the best. For use in college and business, choose one of the following dictionaries:

The American College Dictionary, New York, Random House, Inc., 1963 ($6.75 with thumb index).

The American Heritage Dictionary of the English Language, Boston, Houghton Mifflin Company, 1969 ($8.95 with thumb index).

The Random House Dictionary of the English Language, College Edition, New York, Random House, Inc., 1968 ($7.95 with thumb index).

Webster's Seventh New Collegiate Dictionary, Springfield, Mass., G. & C. Merriam Company, 1963 ($6.95 with thumb index).

Webster's New World Dictionary of the American Language, Cleveland, The World Publishing Company, 1960 ($6.75 with thumb index).

By using any one of these dictionaries, you can make your original investment pay off a thousand times. Here are a few of the questions such an invaluable book will answer about a word:

1. How is it spelled?
2. What part of speech is it?
3. How is it divided into syllables?
4. How is it pronounced?
5. Where did it come from and what other forms does it have?
6. What is its meaning or meanings?
7. What is its "social standing"? Is it slang, obsolete, colloquial, rare, or technical?
8. What are its synonyms?
9. What are its antonyms?
10. What other words come from the same root?

And besides all this, your dictionary provides brief sketches of historical, literary, and other persons; common foreign expressions; and information on all kinds of subjects.

To realize this vast potential, you have to know *first* what a dictionary attempts to do and *second* how to use it. You will be making a mistake if you think of your dictionary as a kind of "last word on words" handed down by higher authority. Actually, a dictionary is a *guide which records as far as possible the best present usage* in such matters as spelling, pronunciation, and meaning. It is *not* an attempt to dictate *what usage should be.* Intelligent use of the dictionary requires following it as a guide and not as a Bible. The *last* word on words will never be written because our language is living and constantly changing; but the *best* word on words is still your dictionary, provided that you know what to expect—and what not to expect—of it.

And now, how to use it; for most people use and understand only about one-tenth of the resources their dictionaries provide. The following entries, which are reprinted from two authoritative desk dictionaries, show how a lot of information is presented in condensed form:

busy*

¹busy \'biz-ē\ *adj* [ME *bisy,* fr. OE *bisig;* akin to MD & MLG *besich* busy] **1 a :** engaged in action **:** OCCUPIED   **b :** being in use ⟨~ telephone⟩   **2 :** full of activity **:** BUSTLING   **3 :** OFFICIOUS, MEDDLING   **4 :** full of distracting detail ⟨a ~ design⟩
   syn INDUSTRIOUS, DILIGENT, ASSIDUOUS, SEDULOUS: BUSY chiefly stresses activity as opposed to idleness or leisure; it may connote purposive activity; INDUSTRIOUS implies characteristic or habitual devotion to work; DILIGENT suggests earnest application to some specific object or pursuit; ASSIDUOUS stresses careful and unremitting application; SEDULOUS implies painstaking and persevering application
²busy *vt* : to make busy : OCCUPY ~ *vi* : BUSTLE

* By permission. From *Webster's Seventh New Collegiate Dictionary,* copyright 1963 by G. & C. Merriam Co., publishers of the Merriam-Webster Dictionaries.

report*

re·port (rĭ pōrt′), n. 1. an account brought back or presented; a statement submitted in reply to inquiry as the result of investigation, or by a person authorized to examine and bring or send information. 2. an account of a speech, debate, meeting, etc., esp. as taken down for publication. 3. a statement of a judicial opinion or decision, or of a case argued and determined in a court of justice. 4. (pl.) Law. a collection of adjudications: New York reports. 5. a statement or announcement. 6. a statement generally circulated; rumor. 7. repute; reputation. 8. a loud noise, as from an explosion. —v.t. 9. to carry and repeat as an answer or message; repeat as what one has heard. 10. to relate as what has been learned by observation or investigation. 11. to give or render a formal account or statement of: to report a deficit. 12. to make a formal report on (a bill, etc., officially referred). 13. to lay a charge against (a person), as to a superior. 14. to make known the presence or whereabouts of (oneself); present (oneself) to a person in authority, as in accordance with requirements. 15. to take down (a speech, etc.) in writing. 16. to write an account of (an event, situation, etc.), as for publication in a newspaper. 17. to relate or tell. —v.i. 18. to make a report; draw up or submit a formal report. 19. to act as a reporter, as for a newspaper. 20. to report oneself, as to one in authority. 21. to present oneself duly, as at a place.
[ME reporte(n), t. OF: m. reporter, g. L reportāre]
—re·port′a·ble, adj.

Notice, in the first definition, that *busy* is in heavy boldface type, divided into syllables, with the accent on the first syllable. Where more than one spelling form is given—and this, of course, does not apply to *busy*—the first is generally preferred. Then comes the pronunciation in parentheses, followed by the part of speech—an adjective—in italics, and the inflectional forms (in this instance the comparative *busier*, and the superlative *busiest*). The etymology in square brackets shows that *busy* comes from Old English *bisig*. Definitions follow and are numbered to indicate different meanings; these definitions are also labeled to show special or technical senses as *Botany* or in this instance to indicate usage in the United States. Notice especially the synonyms for *busy*—all printed in heavy-faced type, and the highly useful discrimination of meanings of this group of words. Then *busy* as a transitive verb and intransitive verb—the symbols are v. t. & i.—is taken up.

Notice that *report* involves eight definitions as a noun, one of them a technical definition pertaining to law; eight as a transitive verb; and four as an intransitive verb. The etymology, within brackets, means that the word comes from Middle English, a modification of which is Old French, *reporter*, both forms going back to the Latin *reportare*. The numerous definitions of *report* illustrate the help you can get from a dictionary in using a word precisely. But because so much information is packed into one entry, you have to read care-

*Reprinted from *The American College Dictionary* (Copyright 1947, © Copyright 1963) by permission of Random House, Inc.

fully; hasty reading can sometimes lead you to erroneous and misleading results.

After all, the best way to learn to use a dictionary is to use it—and in using it, you'll be constantly amazed at the amount of information it contains. Start by reading the "Explanatory Notes" on page xxviii (the page just before the A's of the actual dictionary) if you use *The American College Dictionary* or "Explanatory Notes" on pages 7a to 14a of the *Webster's New Collegiate*. Read these explanations carefully. Then go to work by looking up the answers to such diverse questions as these:

1. What is a *quid pro quo?*
2. How are the plural forms of the following words written: *memorandum, formula, criterion, stimulus, postmaster general, index?*
3. What is a *lettergram? A letter of credit? A letter of advice? A scrivener? The case system?*
4. If you make a report twice a year, is it a *biannual* or a *biennial* report?
5. How did a *secretary bird* get its name?
6. Should you use *boss* in formal writing?
7. What is the origin of *O.K.?*
8. When the first letter of *Mimeograph* or *Multigraph* is capitalized, what is specifically indicated?
9. What is *typescript?*
10. Which form is correct—*never-the-less, never the less, nevertheless?*
11. Which phrase would you prefer in the ad for your new product: *caveat emptor; honi soit qui mal y pense; ne plus ultra?*
12. What is a *surtax? An excise tax?*
13. How should the noun *envelope* be pronounced?
14. Would you prefer to have *disinterested* or *uninterested* evidence?
15. To what would you apply the word *Duodecimo* and how big is it?
16. What is the correct spelling and pronunciation—the *maintainance* department or the *maintenance* department?
17. What is the difference in meaning of the prefixes in *quasi-serious* and *semiserious?*
18. Which syllable should be accented in pronouncing *comparable, admirable, preferable, municipal,* and *precedent* (adjective)?
19. How many sheets of paper are in a *quire?*
20. When the following words come at the end of a line, how would you break the last syllable: *occurrence, predominant, swimming, omission,* and *appreciation?*
21. What is the difference in the effect of the prefix *in* used in the following words: *invaluable* and *invalid?*
22. What is the proofreader's symbol for *delete?*

23. Which of these forms is preferred: *woolen* or *woollen; canceled* or *cancelled; judgement* or *judgment; development* or *developement?*

24. Which form would you use in the following sentences?
    That is not *likely, apt, liable* to happen.
    We think no useful purpose can be served by *farther, further* discussion.
    She left because she could not stand the *constant, continual, continuous* confusion and
    noise of the factory.

25. Who said, *"Après moi le déluge"?*

"I have fair meanings, sir—and fair words to them" wrote the great master of words, William Shakespeare. To find fair words for your meanings, the dictionary is your one indispensable aid.

CHAPTER 22

READING

One of the soundest generalizations that can be made about good writing is that it always stems from a broad background of reading. Almost unconsciously, reading will help you develop techniques of style, of word usage, and of organization which you can carry over into your own writing. But beyond these techniques, reading gives you the inestimable benefit of learning from other people's experience. Notice what C. B. Larrabee has to say in the following editorial from *Printers' Ink* (May 28, 1954, p. 13):

START WHERE THE LAST MAN LEFT OFF

FROM A GENERAL ELECTRIC advertisement, by way of *Mill & Factory News*, this quotation:

"Edison, to explain his incessant and tireless reading of scientific journals . . . said he read to avoid useless repetition of old experiments. 'I start where the last man left off.'"

That seems to me to be the best answer to the man who says, "I don't have time to read."

The "don't-have-time-to-read" people usually want to leave you with the impression that they are so busy gaining practical experience that they can't waste any precious minutes on magazines, newspapers or books. They are the "school of experience" boys, who fail to realize that even their favorite school operates a lot better with a library.

I think it is significant that most of the great leaders in almost every business activity have been students. Oh, yes, I know of cases of the hardbitten self-made man who never got farther than the third grade and eventually became head of a great steel company. The only reading he ever did was supposed to be financial reports.

Somehow when they write the lives of those people, they neglect to point out in almost every case they were surrounded by some pretty smart lads who were not afraid to crack a book—or even look into a business paper.

Civilizations are built on the ability of today's man to start where yesterday's man left off. And there are only two ways to do this. You either work with the other man, or with someone who did, or you read about what he did.

One of the most expensive wastes in business is caused by the unnecessary duplication of effort. Every time a man in a laboratory does as an original experiment something that's been done by somebody before him and written down, he has wasted time. Every time a businessman tries out a plan that has been tried out and failed before, he is wasting time and money.

That is why reading is so essential to the modern businessman. And that is also why you can be pretty sure that the successful businessman who says, "I don't have time to read," is either lying or is surrounded by a lot of people who do have time.

Don't fall back on the worn-out alibis which Mr. Larrabee mentions; what these statements really mean is "I don't want to read" or "I don't know how to read"—and that is exactly where you must start by:

1. Making up your mind that reading will give you the breadth of interests, the personal development, the added experience, and the fun that confirmed readers know it does.

2. Learning how to read so that you can at least use this tool at your highest efficiency.

No one except you can make the first decision. Your college career may already have developed your interest in reading; if so, you should make every effort to continue a good habit. If not—and a college education is no guarantee that you will read—you should consciously make the effort. The best way to begin is by getting a book that interests you; more personal reading programs have been stopped short by dull books than by any other cause. Select your book carefully, and choose one outside your field of business or professional interest; it's always a good measure of a person to learn what he knows *outside* his own field of specialization. Reading is the one key to unlock the doors which will otherwise hold you within the narrow confines of specialization.

But whether you read for general breadth and pleasure or for professional advancement, you can at least learn how to read well. By now, you probably want to protest "Of course I can read. I've been reading ever since

I was in the second grade." But the chances are good that you aren't reading efficiently and that you are plodding along at about the same rate you used in the fifth grade. For studies show that the average adult reads about 250 words a minute; that with normal vision, he can increase this rate by 50 to 100 percent; that in doing so, he will suffer no loss of comprehension, the old saw of "I'm a slow reader but I really remember what I read" having been disproved time and again. Hence, you have the opportunity to acquire a skill which will help you read from one and a half to twice as much material in the same amount of time and with just as much, and probably more, comprehension. How?

Depending on your job and location, you have two possibilities: to get professional guidance or to do it on your own. If you are in a college or university or metropolitan area which offers the facilities of a reading clinic— many business organizations have set up their own—by all means take advantage of this opportunity. In six to twelve sessions you can learn the basic principles and can work with the reading accelerators, tachistoscopes, and reading films which such clinics have.

If this opportunity is not available, you can still accomplish a great deal in improving your reading on your own by following these instructions:

1. *Start by finding out what your present speed is.* You can do this by reading the next pages of this book or anything else you select for exactly three minutes. Read with the purpose of comprehending, since speed alone is useless if you don't know what you've read. At the end of three minutes, determine your rate each minute by getting an average of the number of words a line, multiplying by the number of lines you have read, and dividing by three. This book, for example, averages about 12 words a line, 42 lines a page.

2. *Before reading, take an overall survey of the material to be covered.* This will give you a general idea of what the material contains, what the main ideas and details are. Look for clues in boldface type, headings and subheadings, and the other devices which we have emphasized as helps to your reader when you write.

3. *Keep forcing yourself to move ahead.* The more regressions (moving back) you make, the slower your reading. If passages seem vague or hazy in meaning, move on; they may be clarified later, or you may come back to them at the end after you have the general meaning. When you start this technique, your comprehension will suffer a bit, but when the habit of moving forward constantly is firmly established, you'll gain.

4. *Learn to group words into thought units instead of proceeding word-by-word.* To the word-by-word reader the following sentence goes like this:

The / office / boy / put / the / mail / on / the / desk.

Learn to break it into units of thought like this:

The office boy / put the mail / on the desk.

Your eyes should move along in a definite rhythm, stopping (called a *fixation*) about the same number of times on each line and pausing about the same length of time at each fixation, and swinging back to the next line like the carriage on a typewriter. (Here is where the devices of the reading clinics are especially helpful; but if you want to get a rough check on your eye movements, you can have someone sit across from you and count your eye movements or you can place a mirror on the page opposite from the one you are reading and have the person counting stand behind you.) Usually you should make three or four fixations for each line to read efficiently.

5.   *Postpone looking up the unfamiliar words until you are finished.* Jumping back and forth from dictionary to reading interrupts your comprehension. Check the unfamiliar words and look them up later.

This reading technique involves getting rid of old habits and learning new ones. For that reason, you will have to *practice* it, making periodic checks of your reading speed to ascertain your progress. But no matter how fast you now read, you can still improve if you are willing to work at it; and increased efficiency in reading is important to you and your company. A survey of 200 employees, ranging from supervisor to top management, shows that they averaged four and one-half hours of daily reading. Their average speed was 250 words a minute. By doubling their reading speed, they could save themselves and their companies 450 man-hours a day!

FOR FURTHER READING

"Knowledge is of two kinds," said Samuel Johnson. "We know a subject ourselves, or we know where we can find information upon it." This selected bibliography is intended to help you with the second kind of knowledge. Since there are hundreds of books and articles dealing with the principles and problems of communication, it seems best to focus on a few which are recent, readable, and useful. These books will lead you on to other sources of information. But you should remember that all reading can help you—and novels, biographies, and articles of general interest will help you to become a better writer just as the books on communication do.

The words of Francis Bacon have been repeated so often that we perhaps lose slight of their significance. Nonetheless, it is true that for the twentieth-century citizen whose career is oriented toward business, the words of this seventeenth-century genius hold profound meaning: "Reading maketh a full man, writing an exact man, and conferring [conversation] a ready man." In a technological society which has made inexpensive paperbacks available to every citizen, there is little or no excuse for not broadening one's horizons through reading—no excuse, that is, other than the age-old ones of laziness, indifference, and lack of intellectual curiosity.

As part of your program of self-development as a writer in business, you should become a regular reader of such periodicals as *The Wall Street Journal, Business Week, Fortune, U. S. News & World Report. Direct Marketing,* and *The Saturday Review,* which each month publishes a very useful section on communication. All of these magazines are themselves good examples of communication, and you can learn a great deal by studying the techniques they use to get information across. But you will be wrong if you limit your reading exclusively to books and periodicals dealing with business and communication; in fact, there are business executives who recommend staying away from the specialized subject matter of one's career. Business in the seventies is an activity heavily influenced by, for example, a national report on pollution or a widely read study of crime or a bestseller dealing with the civil rights movement. Read as widely as you can, therefore, because in the interdependent society of the United States almost every social movement or trend directly affects the businessman and his career.

The following books are intended to suggest the wide variety of interesting, provocative, and informative treatments of the topic of communication in its various facets:

BARNLUND, DEAN C. (ed.). *Interpersonal Communication: Survey and Studies,* Boston, Houghton Mifflin Company, 1968.
A useful anthology containing 37 articles about what the social sciences can offer to improve communication.

BERNSTEIN, THEODORE M. *The Careful Writer: A Modern Guide to English Usage,* New York, Atheneum Publishers, 1965.
A well-known editor of the *New York Times* wittily attacks awkward constructions and distortions of language in a book which contains more than 2,000 alphabetically arranged entries.

FLESCH, RUDOLPH. *The Art of Readable Writing,* New York, Harper & Row, Publishers, Incorporated, 1949.
Flesch's book developed one of the first yardsticks of readability in the form of his controversial Readability Formula (pages 213–216), but it also provides sound advice concerning the principles of clear writing.

FOLLETT, WILSON. *Modern American Usage,* New York, Hill & Wang, Inc., 1966.
Edited and completed by Jacques Barzun in collaboration with several distinguished scholars, this authoritative book presents a sensible approach to problems of usage

FOWLER, HENRY WATSON. *A Dictionary of Modern English Usage* (2d ed. revised and edited by Sir Ernest Gowers), New York, Oxford University Press, 1965.
This classic, which first appeared in 1926, has now been revised and updated. A mixture of dictionary, style book, and arbiter of good taste in writing, Fowler's book offers bright and amusing comments on such topics as "Battered Ornaments," "Elegant Variations," and "Hackneyed Phrases."

HANEY, WILLIAM V. *Communication and Organizational Behavior,* Homewood, Ill., Richard D. Irwin, Inc., 1967.
This is one of the increasing number of studies centering on the important relationship between organizational patterns and communication.

HUFF, DARREL. *How to Lie with Statistics,* New York, W. W. Norton & Company, Inc., 1954.
This is a tongue-in-cheek approach to what is usually a formidable subject, but report writers

can learn a great deal from it about "conclusions" drawn from statistics which do not add up to anything.

JOHNSON, H. WEBSTER. *How to Use the Business Library*, 3d ed., Cincinnati, South-Western Publishing Company, Incorporated, 1968.
  A useful reference and guide to the handbooks, directories, business services, government publications, and trade reports which can be found in a library.

LAIRD, CHARLTON. *The Miracle of Language*, Cleveland, The World Publishing Company, 1953.
  This is an exception to the characteristic dullness of books about our language. It achieves its purpose of answering "the most important questions about our language" in a very readable fashion.

MOCKRIDGE, NORTON. *Fractured English*, Garden City, N. Y., Doubleday & Company, Inc., 1966.
  Mockridge takes aim at today's malapropisms and tortured language and uses hilarious examples and illustrations to hit his targets.

REDDING, W. CHARLES, and GEORGE A. SANBORN. *Business and Industrial Communication: A Source Book*, New York, Harper & Row, Publishers, Incorporated, 1964.
  Although it is intended primarily as a college text, this collection of readings makes readily available to businessmen and others 44 important articles dealing with all aspects of business communication.

SHIDLE, NORMAN G. *The Art of Successful Communication*, New York, McGraw-Hill Book Company, 1965.
  An original approach to the subject of business communication, this book contains two chapters which are especially valuable—"Barriers to Communication: In the Writer" and "Barriers to Communication: In the Reader."

STRUNK, WILLARD, and E. B. WHITE. *The Elements of Style*, New York, The Macmillan Company, 1959.
  This brief book is probably the best treatment of style written in the past twenty years.

THAYER, LEE O. *Communication and Communication Systems*, Homewood, Ill., Richard D. Irwin, Inc. 1968.
  Basing his book on the premise that better understanding of communication theory leads to better practice of communication, Thayer offers a mind-stretching analysis of communications concepts.

VARDAMAN, GEORGE T., and CAROLL C. HALTERMAN. *Managerial Control through Communications*, New York, John Wiley & Sons, Inc., 1968.
  A difficult book requiring serious study, but it achieves its authors' aim "to provide the means by which managers can improve personal and organizational operations" and to present "useful theories, concepts, and principles which the manager can translate into action on the job."

WHYTE, WILLIAM H., JR., AND THE EDITORS OF *Fortune. Is Anybody Listening?* New York, Simon and Schuster, 1952.
  This collection of articles, which originally appeared in *Fortune* two decades ago, is still pertinent and provocative in its analysis of how and why business fumbles its communications.

WILLIAMS, FREDERIC. *Reasoning with Statistics: Simplified Examples in Communication Research*, New York, Holt, Rinehart and Winston, Inc., 1968.
  On the assumption that readers have no expertness in statistics, this book fulfills its promise of explaining basic statistical methods in understandable and nonmathematical terms.

The following articles provide considerable information on various aspects of communication; they will also serve as excellent sources for classroom reports and discussions.

ANONYMOUS. "Ask Questions That Get Results," *Nation's Business*, July, 1959, pp. 34–35, 94–96.
A discussion of the guidelines business executives should use to ask questions which provide answers for decision making.

ANONYMOUS. "Caveat Emptor: Many Americans Complain about the Quality of Goods," *The Wall Street Journal*, June 26, 1969, pp. 1, 15.
This survey by the staff of the *Wall Street Journal* provides excellent background on the situations which lead to claim and adjustment letters.

ACKOFF, RUSSEL L. "Management Misinformation Systems," *Journal of the Institute of Management Sciences*, December, 1967, pp. 146–156.
An expert examines some of the ways in which the systems approach to communication may go astray.

ANDREWS, FRANCIS S. "Computer Letters: Newest Wrinkle in Direct Mail," *Direct Mail*, Summer, 1968, pp. 4–9.
A thorough analysis of how and when to use computerized letters for direct mail. Contains excellent suggestions on the pitfalls to be avoided.

BARZUN, JACQUES. "English as She's Not Taught," *Atlantic Monthly*, December, 1953, pp. 25–29.
Professor Barzun, in this controversial article written almost twenty years ago, accuses college graduates of undermining the language by overuse of jargon.

BRITT, STUART HENDERSON, and IRWIN A. SHAPIRO. "Where to Find Marketing Facts," *Harvard Business Review*, September–October, 1962, pp. 44–49.
A useful analysis of sources of information for the marketing and sales aspects of business which provides good background information for sales correspondents.

BROWN, DAVID S. "Shaping the Organization to Fit People," *Management of Personnel Quarterly*, Summer, 1966, pp. 12–16.
A brief look at the increasingly important relationship between the structure of the organization and its communication.

CIARDI, JOHN. "On Writing and Bad Writing," *Saturday Review*, Dec. 15, 1962, pp. 10–12.
The poetry editor of the *Saturday Review* expresses provocative opinions about the causes and consequences of bad writing.

COE, ROBERT K., and IRWIN WEINSTOCK. "Publication Policies of Major Business Journals," *The Southern Journal of Business*, January, 1968, pp. 7–9.
A useful summary of publication practices for those who consider submitting material to business publications.

DAVIS, KEITH. "Management Communication and the Grapevine," *Harvard Business Review*, September, 1953, pp. 43–49.
This study provides a fine starting point for a discussion of the role of the grapevine in business organizations and in their communications. For another aspect of the grapevine as a means of communication, see William H. Whyte's article "The Web of Word of Mouth," *Fortune*, November, 1954.

DRUCKER, PETER F. "How to Be an Employe," *Fortune*, May, 1952, pp. 126–127, 168 ff.
A well-known writer on business and economics gives advice to college students that success in business, government, or military service depends in large measure on the ability to communicate.

FARRELL, THOMAS. "Understanding Improves Communications," *Personnel Journal*, July–August, 1960, pp. 93–97.
A description of three experiments in internal communication involving a group of salesgirls in a department store and two groups of men in middle management.

FITZGERALD, STEPHEN E. "Literature by the Slide Rule," *Saturday Review*, Feb. 14, 1953, pp. 15–16, 53–54.
Written shortly after the formulation of Flesch's Readability Formula and Gunning's Fog Index,

this article protests the principles and techniques of what the author calls "the readability boys and their word-counting machines." It raises excellent questions for discussion of whether readability can be reduced to formulas.

GEHMAN, BETSY HOLLAND. "Junk Mail," *This Week*, March 6, 1966, p. 11.
A humorous account of the various methods "second-class" citizens have used to get their names removed from mailing lists.

GENERAL ELECTRIC COMPANY, Public and Employee Relations Services. "Letters to Employes' Homes; the Techniques of Employe Communication," New York, no date.
A practical discussion of the role of letters in employee communications and how to write them. Sample letters to individuals and groups are included.

GREER, ALLEN. "All You Have to Do Is Get a List," *Direct Mail*, Summer, 1968, pp. 25–27.
Useful background on the general subject of mailing lists, how to test them, and what may reasonably be expected from their use.

GRAY, DWIGHT E. "Making Technical Reports Understandable," and "How Readable Is Your Technical Report?" *Journal of Chemical Engineering*, April, 1948, pp. 226–228, and July, 1949, pp. 374–376.
These two articles supply considerable useful information concerning the unnecessary traditions surrounding technical styles as well as useful checklists for technical writers.

HEIDINGSFIELD, M. S. "How the Computer is Used in Marketing," *Sales Marketing Today*, February, 1969.
Although not directly relevant to the specific problems of written communication, this article provides interesting glimpses of how the computer is—and will be—used for sales analysis, forecasting, marketing, and long-range planning. It can be used for sound background on how such communications as sales letters and planning reports will be affected by computers.

HICKS, TYLER J. "How to Write Reports That Get Read," *Society of Automotive Engineers' Journal*, November, 1960, pp. 75–79.
A helpful discussion of the principles and specific methods by which readable reports are produced.

IRWIN, THEODORE. "About Mailing Lists," *The New York Times Magazine*, March 22, 1964.
A comprehensive view of the methods used in compiling lists, how lists are classified, and what problems are involved in getting a name removed from a mailing list.

JACOBS, HAYES B. "A Word to the Word-Wise," *The New York Times Magazine*, July 26, 1964, p. 18.
A freelance writer takes potshots at contemporary cliches including the bulletin of a church which announced, "The two services will be identical sermon-wise."

KEYES, LANGLEY CARLTON. "Profits in Prose," *Harvard Business Review*, January–February, 1961, pp. 105–112.
An executive in an advertising agency argues convincingly that the great waste of American business lies in "the sprawling, edgeless area of written communication."

LARSON, RICHARD L. "How to Define Administrative Problems," *Harvard Business Review*, January–February, 1962, pp. 68–80.
A mature and thoughtful approach to decision-making which underscores the fact that the first step toward a sound decision is the definition of the problem.

KRUTCH, JOSEPH WOOD. "Who Says It's Proper English?" *Saturday Review*, Oct. 14, 1967, pp. 19–21, 132, ff.
A well-known scholar and writer presents a thoughtful analysis of the age-old problem of "correctness" in language.

LOCKE, EDWIN A., JR. "What Price Verbal Incompetence?" *Harvard Alumni Bulletin*, Feb. 17, 1962, pp. 11–12.

An eloquent plea by a leading corporation executive to eliminate verbal incompetence as "the chronic disease of the American intellect" along with a challenge for American education "to meet this problem head-on."

MERRILL, PAUL W. "The Principles of Poor Writing," *Scientific Monthly*, January, 1947, pp. 72–74.
This article, written by a staff member of Mount Wilson Observatory, has been so widely reprinted as to become a classic. Dr. Merrill starts by asking "Where can you find sound, practical advice on how to write poorly?" By giving that advice, he provides sound counsel on how to write well.

McLEAN, ED. "How to Write a Profitable Letter," *Direct Mail*, Summer, 1968, pp. 37–40.
An executive in a firm of direct mail consultants provides ten practical rules for writing effective sales letters.

MINTZ, HAROLD K. "How to Write Better Memos," *Chemical Engineering*, Jan. 26, 1970, pp. 136–139.
A good concise discussion of the importance, organization, and stylistic qualities of the memorandum in today's business and scientific world.

MORRIS, JOE ALEX. "What Credit Bureaus Know About You," *Reader's Digest*, November, 1967, pp. 85–89.
Useful background on the methods by which information is obtained and exchanged whenever credit is granted.

MORRIS, M. D. "Why Engineers Don't Write," *Engineer*, September–October, 1969, pp. 15–19.
Despite its title, this article applies not only to engineers but to all technical specialists who are struggling to express technical contents in readable English.

PEI, MARIO. "A Loss for Words," *Saturday Review*, Nov. 14, 1964, pp. 82–84.
An eminent linguist takes a look at the debate between "the Advocates of Usage" and "the Custodians of the Language." This is an eminently sensible approach to the heated discussions which followed the publication of Merriam-Webster's *Third International Dictionary* in 1961.

POWERS, RODERICK D. "Measuring Effectiveness of Business Communication," *Personnel Administration*, July–August, 1963, pp. 47–52.
An unusual evaluation of the effectiveness of formal communication inside the company by tracing one specific item from top management down through various levels of employees.

ROSS, BRUCE E., and JOHN WHITE. "The Computer and Direct Mail," *Pharmaceutical Marketing and Media*, May, 1968, unpaged.
Provides specific examples in a very specialized medium of how the computer can team with direct mail to provide new and more sophisticated marketing techniques.

SCOTT, DOUGLAS. "The Inhuman Style," *Technology Review*, February, 1962, pp. 27–29.
An examination of three major causes of dull, clumsy reports.

SESSER, STANFORD N. "How Credit Bureaus Collect and Use Data on Millions of Persons," *The Wall Street Journal*, Feb. 5, 1968, pp. 1, 14.
This feature story presents data and background excellent for credit and collection correspondents and for students who want to find out how the credit system works.

SPENDER, STEPHEN. "The Age of Overwrite and Underthink," *Saturday Review*, March 12, 1966, pp. 21–23, 132–133.
Poet Spender doesn't even mention business writing, but he does present a brilliant analysis of the role of language in the famous controversy about two cultures with his statement "If there truly is a gulf between the literary and the scientific culture, it cannot be bridged by science but only by language."

TOBIN, RICHARD L. "Like Your Cigarette Should," *Saturday Review*, May 14, 1966, pp. 59–60.
The communications editor of *Saturday Review* takes a conservative view of the advertising

for Winston cigarettes, concluding that "talking English and writing English are two different forms of language and that certain colloquialisms acceptable in casual, regional conversation are still unacceptable on the formal printed page." Readers' reactions in subsequent issues of *Saturday Review* make an excellent subject for student reports.

WITKOVICH, CARL. "Neither Rain, Nor Snow, Nor ZIP Code . . ." *The Columbia University Forum*, Spring, 1968, pp. 46–48.
A good account of how and why zip numbers were set up and of some of the idiosyncrasies of the system.

Throughout our discussion of reading, we have stressed the desirability of selecting books and articles which provide a broad background for business or a general knowledge of people. It is interesting to note, for example, that three of the best-selling books of the past dozen years have dealt satirically with one or another aspect of the business community or the business organization—C. Northcote Parkinson's *Parkinson's Law and Other Studies in Administration*, Lawrence J. Peter and Raymond Hull's *The Peter Principle*, which remained on best-seller lists for more than 50 weeks in 1969 and 1970, and Robert Townsend's *Up the Organization*, which bids fair to have equal circulation in the 1970s. Students and those who make careers in business would do well to keep up with all facets of writing concerned with the business community—from Ralph Nader's *Unsafe at Any Speed* (1965) and James Bishop and Henry W. Hubbard's *Let the Seller Beware* (1970) to William Rodgers' *Think: A Biography of the Watsons and I.B.M.* (1969) and William Cahn's *Out of the Cracker Barrel* (1970), a history of the National Biscuit Company. All reading is grist to the writer's mill, and books about business are especially valuable for those who intend to write in business.

Nevertheless, you may want to refer occasionally to books which deal with the specific aspects of writing reports and letters and the other technical aspects of writing in business. To the production of such works there seems no end, but here is a representative sample:

ANONYMOUS. *Writing Reports That Work: A Programmed Instruction Course*, prepared and published by the American Management Association, New York, 1969.

AURNER, ROBERT R., and MORRIS P. WOLF. *Effective Communication in Business*, 5th ed., Cincinnati, South-Western Publishing Company, Incorporated, 1967.

BERLO, DAVID K. *The Process of Communication: An Introduction to Theory and Practice*, New York, Holt, Rinehart and Winston, Inc., 1960.

BLUMENTHAL, LASSOR A. *The Complete Book of Personal Letter Writing and Modern Correspondence*, Garden City, N.Y., Doubleday & Company, Inc., 1969.

BRENNAN, LAWRENCE D. *Modern Communication Effectiveness*, Englewood Cliffs, N.J., Prentice-Hall, Inc., 1963.

BROMAGE, MARY C. *Writing for Business*, Ann Arbor, Mich., The University of Michigan Press, 1965.

BROWN, LELAND. *Effective Business Report Writing*, 2d ed., Englewood Cliffs, N.J., Prentice-Hall, Inc. 1963.

BUCKLEY, EARLE A. *How to Increase Sales with Letters*, New York, McGraw-Hill Book Company, 1961.

CLOKE, MARIJANE, and ROBERT WALLACE. *The Modern Business Letter Writer's Manual*, Garden City, N.Y., Doubleday & Company, Inc., 1969.

COMER, DAVID B., and RALPH SPILLMAN. *Modern Technical and Industrial Reports*, New York, G. P. Putnam's Sons, 1962.

COYLE, WILLIAM. *Research Papers*, New York, The Odyssey Press, Inc., 1964.

DAMERST, WILLIAM A. *Resourceful Business Communication*, New York, Harcourt, Brace & World, Inc., 1966.

DAWE, JESSAMON. *Writing Business and Economic Papers: Theses and Dissertations*, Totowa, N.J., Littlefield, Adams & Co., 1965.

DAWSON, PRESLEY C. *Business Writing: A Situational Approach*, Belmont, Calif., Dickenson Publishing Company, Inc., 1969.

DEVERELL, C. S. *The Techniques of Communication in Business*, London, Gee & Co. Ltd., 1964.

GALLAGHER, WILLIAM J. *Report Writing for Management*, Reading, Mass., Addison-Wesley Publishing Company, Inc., 1969.

GRAVES, H. F., and L. S. S. HOFFMAN. *Report Writing*, 4th ed., Englewood Cliffs, N.J., Prentice-Hall, Inc., 1965.

HAY, ROBERT D. *Written Communication for Business Administration*, New York, Holt, Rinehart and Winston, Inc., 1965.

HICKS, T. G. *Writing for Engineering and Science*, New York, McGraw-Hill Book Company, 1961.

HIMSTREET, WILLIAM C., and WAYNE M. BATY. *Business Communications: Principles and Methods*, 2d ed., Belmont, Calif., Wadsworth Publishing Company, Inc., 1969.

HOOK, J. N. *Hook's Guide to Good Writing*, New York, The Ronald Press Company, 1962.

HOUP, KENNETH W., and THOMAS E. PEARSALL. *Reporting Technical Information*, Beverly Hills, Calif., The Glencoe Press, 1968.

HUFFMAN, HARRY, and SYRELL ROGOVIN. *Programmed College English*, New York, McGraw-Hill Book Company, 1968.

JOHNSON, THOMAS P. Analytical Writing: *A Handbook for Business and Technical Writers*, New York, Harper & Row, Publishers, Incorporated, 1966.

KEITHLY, ERWIN M. and MARGARET H. THOMPSON. *English for Modern Business*, Homewood, Ill., Richard D. Irwin, Inc., 1966.

KREY, ISABELLE A., and BERNADETTE V. METZLER. *Writing for Business*, New York, Harcourt, Brace & World, Inc., 1968.

LAMB, MARION M., and EUGENE H. HUGHES. *Business Letters, Memorandums, and Reports*, New York, Harper & Row, Publishers, Incorporated, 1967.

LAMBUTH, DAVID. *The Golden Book on Writing*, New York, Viking Press, 1964.

LESIKAR, RAYMOND V. *Business Communication: Theory and Application*, Homewood, Ill., Richard D. Irwin, Inc., 1968.

LEWIS, LESLIE LLEWELYN. *The Business-Letter Deskbook*, Chicago, The Dartnell Corporation, 1969.

McCRIMMON, JAMES M. *Writing with a Purpose*, 4th ed., Boston, Houghton Mifflin Company, 1967.

McLUHAN, MARSHAL. *The Medium is the Massage*, New York: Bantam Books, Inc., 1967.

_____. *Understanding Media: The Extensions of Man*, 2d ed., New York, Signet Books, 1966.

MAMBERT, W A. *Presenting Technical Ideas: A Guide to* Audience Communication, New York, John Wiley & Sons, Inc., 1968.

MARKMAN, ROBERT H. and MARIE L. WADDELL. *10 Steps in Writing the Research Paper*, Woodbury, N.Y., Barron's Educational Series, Inc., 1965.

MENNING, J. H. and C. W. WILKINSON. *Communicating through Letters and Reports*, 4th ed. Homewood, Ill., Richard D. Irwin, Inc., 1967.

MENZEL, DONALD H., HOWARD MUMFORD JONES, and LYLE G. BOYD. *Writing a Technical Paper*, New York, McGraw-Hill Book Company, 1961

MILLER, LYLE L. *Increasing Reading Efficiency*, 3d ed., New York, Holt, Rinehart and Winston, Inc., 1970.

MITCHELL, J. *A First Course in Technical Writing*, London, Chapman & Hall, 1967.

MORRIS, RICHARD H. *Credit and Collection Letters: New Techniques to Make Them Work*, Great Neck, N.Y., Channel Press, Inc., 1960.

NEEDLEMAN, MORRISS H. *Handbook for Practical Composition*, New York, McGraw-Hill Book Company, 1968.

New York Times Style Book for Writers and Editors, New York, McGraw-Hill Book Company, 1962.

OTTE, FRANK R. *Complete Book of Extraordinary Collection Letters*, Englewood Cliffs, N.J., Prentice-Hall, Inc., 1965.

PERRIN, PORTER G., GEORGE H. SMITH, and JIM W. CORDER. *Handbook of Current English*, 4th ed., Glenview, Ill., Scott, Foresman and Company, 1969.

PUGH, GRIFFITH T. *Guide to Research Writing*, 3d ed., Boston, Houghton Mifflin Company, 1968.

REID, JAMES M., JR., and ROBERT M. WENDLINGER. *Effective Letters: A Program for Self-instruction*, New York, McGraw-Hill Book Company, 1964.

ROBINSON, DAVID M. *Writing Reports for Management*, Columbus, Ohio, Charles E. Merrill Books, Inc., 1969.

ROODMAN, ZELDA, and HERMAN S. ROODMAN. *Effective Business Communication*, Toronto, McGraw-Hill Company of Canada Limited, 1964.

SHERMAN, THEODORE A. *Modern Technical Writing*, 2d ed., Englewood Cliffs, N.J., Prentice-Hall, Inc. 1966.

SCHMITZ, ROBERT N. *Preparing the Research Paper*, 4th ed., New York, Holt, Rinehart and Winston, Inc., 1957.

SHIDLE, NORMAN G. *The Art of Successful Communication*, New York, McGraw-Hill Book Company, 1965.

SHURTER, ROBERT L. *Effective Letters in Business*, New York, McGraw-Hill Book Company, 1954. [Paperbound edition, 1963.]

––––––. *Handy Grammar Reference*, New York, McGraw-Hill Book Company, 1959. [Paperbound edition.]

–––––– and JOHN R. PIERCE. *Critical Thinking*, New York, McGraw-Hill Book Company, 1966.

–––––– and JAMES M. REID, JR. *A Program for Effective Writing*, New York, Appleton-Century-Crofts, Inc., 1966.

––––––, J. PETER WILLIAMSON, and WAYNE G. BROEHL, JR. *Business Research and Report Writing*, New York, McGraw-Hill Book Company, 1965.

SIGBAND, NORMAN B. *Communication for Management*, Glenview, Ill., Scott, Foresman and Company, 1969.

TICHY, H. J. *Effective Writing: For Engineers, Managers, and Scientists*, New York, John Wiley & Sons, Inc., 1966.

THAYER, LEE O. *Administrative Communication*, Homewood, Ill., Richard D. Irwin, Inc., 1961.

WALTON, THOMAS F. *Technical Manual Writing and Administration*, New York, McGraw-Hill Book Company, 1968.

WARD, RITCHIE R. *Practical Technical Writing*, New York, Alfred A. Knopf, Inc., 1968.

WEEKS, FRANCIS W (ed.). *Readings in Communication from Fortune*, New York, Holt, Rinehart and Winston, Inc., 1961.

WEISMAN, HERMAN M. *Basic Technical Writing*, 2d ed., Columbus, Ohio, Charles E. Merrill Books, Inc., 1968.

WELLS, WALTER. *Communications in Business*, Belmont, Calif., Wadsworth Publishing Company, Inc., 1968.

WILLIAMS, CECIL B. and F. GLENN GRIFFIN. *Effective Business Communication*, 3d ed., New York, The Ronald Press Company, 1966.

WILLIAMS, FREDERICK. *Reasoning with Statistics*, New York, Holt, Rinehart and Winston, 1968.

WYLD, LIONEL D. *Preparing Effective Reports*, New York, The Odyssey Press, Inc., 1967.

YECK, JOHN D., and JOHN T. MAGUIRE. *Planning and Creating Better Direct Mail*, New York, McGraw-Hill Book Company, 1961.

Finally, anyone who becomes deeply involved with business communication should read the invaluable *Journal* of the American Business Communication Association, published four times a year at the University of Illinois, Urbana, Illinois, 61810. Its issues provide one of the best means of keeping up with changing attitudes, methods, and principles in business writing. Similarly, publications and proceedings emerging from the annual institutes on technical and organizational communication at Colorado State University, Fort Collins, Colorado and on technical writing at Rensselaer Polytechnic Institute, Troy New York constitute valuable sources for staying up to date with the experts in communication.

CASES

The cases in the following section are intended to confront you with actual problems of written communication as it occurs in business. They are designed to counteract the erroneous notion that the sole problem of business writing is to produce one letter or one memorandum or report. In reality, communication in modern business frequently involves a specific situation from which a whole series of related and interrelated memos, letters, and reports flow. These communications often encompass different departments within the company, people outside the company, and messages up, down, and across the organizational pattern. They emerge as the result of conferences, committee meetings, and instructions from supervisors and frequently require the preparation of written material for other people's approval or signature.

Each case begins with a general statement of the situation or problem from which the various communications arise. In some instances, this situation or problem changes as the result of the communications or because of the lapse of time—and this, too, is realistic in view of the dynamic rather than static nature of business communication. *It is important, therefore, that you read through the entire case before writing any of the specific letters, memos, or reports involved.*

Because *people*, as readers, as supervisors, as customers, are the essence of communication, their preferences—even their whims or their prejudices— are of salient importance. For that reason, certain cases include oral statements by key people who make assignments, request information, or state policies. These statements should be read carefully as clues to the purpose of the communication and to the best choice of appeal and organization for the specific memo, report, or letter.

The cases are arranged in order of difficulty and complexity with the simpler ones first. At the discretion of your instructor, several of them can be used as the basis for classroom discussion and for roleplaying by students. In certain instances, it will be easy to add other examples of communication to the total case; in others, your instructor may want to select certain problems from those which are suggested within the case. The first cases can be carried out by a single student, while the later ones may be assigned to a team of students, depending, of course, upon the judgment of the instructor.

A COLLEGE SENIOR'S ENGLISH

The senior who won the Albert J. Schlemmer Commencement Award of $500 for "demonstrating outstanding campus citizenship" sent the following letter to Mr. Schlemmer:

Dear Sir,

I want to extend may sincerest thanks for the 1970 Schlimmer Award. As for deserrving it, I am granting to myself the benefit of the doubt; who am I to question.

The award itself came at a time of particular want and will be appreciated a second time in that sense. My only regret is the work of the other fellows which never seems to gain significant recognition, but then they will get their's.

I hope that someday I will be able to thank those responsible in person. In any event

Sincerely,

Peter M. Roberts [signature]

Peter M. Roberts

Mr. Schlemmer has sent an angry note with a copy of Roberts' letter to the Development Office, which persuaded him to set up the prize in the first place with the eventual hope that he would make substantial contributions to the university. Here are excerpts from Mr. Schlemmer's letter:

It seems to me that the one mark of anyone graduating from your college ought to be the ability to speak and write good English. This letter from Roberts is a disgrace. He doesn't know what to say and he doesn't know how to say it. I would like to know how the college can justify letting such a person graduate when he can't spell or write a clear sentence.

Using this situation, you are to write the following:

1. The letter you would write to Mr. Schlemmer if you had won the Schlimmer Award.

2. The letter you would write to answer Mr. Schlemmer's comments on Roberts' letter if you were a member of the staff of the Development Office of the college.

3. After a meeting of the whole staff, the Development Office has decided to use this situation as a way to get Mr. Schlemmer to give an *additional* award next year—The Albert J. Schlemmer Commencement Award of $1,000 for "demonstrated excellence in speaking and writing." Write the letter. (This is not a substitute for question 2.)

THE ETHICS OF COMMUNICATION

You represent your company on the Junior Board, known as the Jaybees, of the local Industrial Council comprising representatives from business and industry. Each year, on behalf of members under 35, the Jaybees hold a meeting at which they are hosts to members over 35. This meeting usually attracts an audience of approximately 400, consisting of the top executive and civic leaders of your area.

This year, the Junior Board has decided to invite Professor J. Aubrey Whitman to speak. Professor Whitman is the author of *How Industry Speaks to America: Communication — the Fatal Flaw?* and numerous other books and articles which have added to his reputation as an interesting and provocative lecturer at a well-known Eastern college. He has consented to speak to the annual meeting of the Jaybees for a fee of $500 and expenses on the topic "A Look at Communication in Actual Practice."

Before the largest audience of the year, including all the top executives of your company, Professor Whitman delivers a scathing attack on communication in business and industry as "dishonest, hypocritical, and self-serving." Here are excerpts from his speech:

> There is no reason why good communication and effective communication should be thought of as synonymous. Good communication implies honesty and forthrightness; but the most effective communication of business usually withholds information or points out that to do something benefits the customer when actually it's the business alone that benefits.
>
> Complete honesty has no real role in effective communication. True honesty in communication can be a terrible weapon. How many of you in this room dare to tell the absolute truth as you see it to your wife, your friends, or your business associates for the next 24 hours? To be that honest would end your marriage, your friendships, and your business relationships.
>
> Who expects his sales correspondents to write letters admitting that his company's products are no better — and no worse — than their competitors'? Can you executives honestly say that those sales correspondents, looking for promotion in your companies, will write letters that honestly disclose all the features of your products? Of course not!
>
> Why does this myth that honest and ethical communication equates with effective communication persist? Because of the textbooks which say so. Because you won't admit that effective business communication involves manipulating information, withholding information, and coloring information as effective means of achieving your goals.
>
> The really successful communicator in today's business knows how to get others to accept the attitude or the action he desires. He knows how to play on emotions; he knows how to mold attitudes and behavior. To say that this has anything to do with honesty is nonsense. What I am saying here today is the real honesty about communication.
>
> When they enter the actual business world, a lot of our students become cynical about the difference between the idealistic communication they have been taught — communication that is clear, complete, accurate — and communication as it is practiced.

To expect communicators to abandon any verbal advantage they may have is to expect them to abandon their self-interest in favor of the general welfare represented by complete and honest communication.

In conclusion, let me leave these questions with members of the audience who think I exaggerate. How many of your department heads could post an honest appraisal of their subordinates on the bulletin board each month and survive? How many of you executives turn in an honest budget, uncolored and unpadded, to your superior?

At the end of Professor Whitman's talk almost 50 members of the audience walk out; these include a half dozen executives from your company. They make no attempt to conceal their irritation and anger, and one executive says in a loud tone of voice, "No wonder college students are antagonistic to business when they hear things like that from their professors."

The question period is very heated, with Professor Whitman blandly defending his attitude toward communication but making no attempt to expand his remarks. Here are a few of the comments and questions from the audience:

An executive: "You make us sound like a bunch of crooks. The fact is that if you professors would teach your students to write and speak clearly, we wouldn't have to worry about effective communication. The trouble isn't that we try to withhold information or twist it to our purposes, but that you in the colleges haven't taught our employees to say what they mean. What you think is distortion is really the result of irresponsible education."

A student who is part of an invited group: "If what you say is true, Professor Whitman, colleges ought to give courses in 'how to use language to influence people' without regard to anything but the results."

A businessman: "I think it's about time we started teaching that the American system of free enterprise is based on honesty and truth."

An executive from a retail establishment: "My firm has been in business for 78 years. Its reputation has been built on absolute honesty. We are scrupulous in seeing that every advertisement, every letter is accurate and truthful. I deny everything you have said here today, and I think it applies to about 2 percent of American business."

The meeting terminates when a thoughtful businessman says, "I think there is another side to this matter of honesty in business communication. Perhaps the Jaybees could render a real service by permitting us to hear the other side at some future meeting. Perhaps they might render an even greater service by providing us with a code of ethics for business communication. At any rate, I want to thank them for an occasion today which has provoked me to considerable thought."

1. Write a brief memorandum to your boss, who has inquired "How can the Jaybees justify presenting such an all-out attack on business as that presented by Professor Whitman?"

2. Write a statement of what you would consider an adequate Code of Ethics for honesty in business communication.

3. Write a memorandum which would be helpful to one of your company's executives who has been selected to "present the other side" at an upcoming meeting of the Jaybees.

4. Write a report to the dean of your college urging that there should (not) be a course in the ethics of business communication included in the curriculum.

(Students and instructors who wish to pursue this topic more fully should consult *The Journal of Business Communication*, October, 1964, in which excellent articles by Bernard Sarachek, O. Hobart Mowrer, and Paul M. Dauten, Jr. discuss it in detail.)

SELECTING THAT SWING IN USAGE?

The Swing Company, where you work, manufactures such unglamorous plastic products as garbage containers, pails, basins, and a wide variety of sizes and shapes of inexpensive plastic packages for use in the home. Its advertising slogan "Swing holds everything in the house" is intended to convey its broad range of products.

All major decisions at the company are made by Robert J. Swing, founder and now chairman of the board. At 63, Mr. Swing believes that dignified language and correct grammar are—as he expresses it—"the surest sign of an educated and logical mind. I will not tolerate abuses or misuses of language in anything that represents the Swing Company."

In a drive for new clients, the Creative Advertising Agency, which has recently opened a branch in your city, has submitted to your company a series of sketches, examples of copy, and plans for TV commercials all based on the theme:

> It don't mean a thing
> It it ain't got that Swing.

"That Swing," in this instance, is a readily identifiable and memorable garbage pail on a swing extolling the virtues of the company's products. Without exception, everyone who has seen the Creative Advertising Agency's presentation calls it "the best advertising this company has ever had." Also without exception, everyone agrees that R. J. Swing will want no part of it.

At a meeting of department heads, the following unrelated comments were made in a discussion centered on how to convince Mr. Swing to endorse the new advertising and its slogan:

"For the past three years our production has just about leveled off. The chief reason is that we haven't been aiming our advertising at the young married people who offer the greatest sales potential."

"With half the American population under a median age of 28, we have to convince Mr. Swing that times have changed and that our ads must change too."

"Why should we antagonize him with that slogan? Everybody here knows that Mr. Swing will never accept it, so let's change it so he will. Let's use

> It doesn't mean a thing
> If it hasn't got that Swing.

That way we can change slogans and get him to approve."

"I think it's hopeless to convince him, so we might as well give up without even showing him the new advertising."

The meeting ends with unanimous agreement that the company should adopt the material submitted by the Creative Advertising Agency and that you should be the one to convince Mr. Swing.

1. To convince Mr. Swing, would you first try to get him to look at the material submitted by the Creative Advertising Agency? Or would you insist that representatives of the agency do that themselves? Or would you first send Mr. Swing a memo describing your colleagues' enthusiasm for the new slogan in an attempt to prepare Mr. Swing to accept it?

2. Would you consider advocating the grammatical change proposed in "It doesn't mean a thing," etc.?

3. How would you use Mr. Swing's attitude toward correctness and dignity in language? Would you ignore it? Agree with it? Try to prove that it is inappropriate in today's society?

4. Write the statement by which you hope to persuade Mr. Swing to use the advertising submitted by the Creative Advertising Agency.

AN EXPLANATION OF A STATEMENT OF POLICY

The following policy statement concerning vacations has been posted on every bulletin board in the offices and production facilities of your Company:

The vacation period shall be from January 1, 1971 to December 31, 1971, and vacations will be granted as follows:

Employees with less than 1 year's service—none
Employees with more than 1 year's service but less than 5—one week
Employees with more than 5 years' service but less than 10—two weeks
Employees with more than 10 years' service but less than 15—three weeks
Employees with more than 15 years' service—one month

All 1971 vacations must be completed by December 31, 1971.

The time which is lost by an employee for a period of at least one payroll week during the vacation period due to the exigency of the company needing to reduce its work personnel, or due to bona fide sickness or accident on the company's premises or injury, or due to leave of absence (granted under the customary terms affecting such leaves of absence) may be applied to any vacation time to which such employee is entitled but with the direct stipulation that it must be at the request of said employee.

It is the intent and purpose and implication of the company vacation plan that all individual employees shall receive the benefit of a relief from work, a relaxation from normal rigid scheduling, and an opportunity for a change of environment or normal activities. However, the employee who is required or given the privilege to work in lieu of seizing the opportunities presented by vacations shall be entitled to receive vacation pay in addition to and over and above his regular pay, providing he has not lost time as described applied to all his vacation time to which he is entitled.

The employee shall take his vacation as scheduled by management and in the amount to which he is entitled as indicated above, provided he has not had time lost as described applied to all vacation time to which he is then entitled. The employee's wishes as to time off or vacation pay insofar as he decides to continue employment rather than to exercise his vacation benefit will be considered, but such scheduling shall, in the final analysis, be based upon and/or decided upon by the operating requirements of the company.

Here are some of the questions that have come in from employees:

"I want to start my two-week vacation on January 1, which is a holiday. Do I get just two weeks or do I get 15 days?"

"This thing says I've got to work on my vacation if you want me to. When am I going to know? I want to plan right now."

"I started work on July 5, 1966 and I want to start my vacation on July 1, 1971. Are you going to tell me I get only one week when, if I wait four days—one of which is a holiday—I'm going to get two weeks?"

"I'm going to work on my new house during my vacation. Is that what the statement means by 'a change of environment'?"

"I took a leave of absence to go to summer school. Does that time get deducted from my length of service?"

"Can I start my vacation the day before Christmas and carry it over into 1971?"

"I'd like to keep on working here during vacation to earn more money. What must I do to be sure I can?"

"I was sick for three months in 1970 but I've been here seven years. How much vacation do I get? Or does that three months wipe out my vacation?"

There has been such confusion about this statement, which was drawn up by a committee representing the management of the company and the company union, that both the union and management recognize the need for clarifying the statement.

Keeping in mind the questions that have been raised, you are now to write out a statement which will (1) answer these questions and (2) meet the need—subscribed to by both management and the union leaders—for "a clear, simple statement which tells employees how much vacation they can have, what it's based on, when they can take it and who makes the decision, and what happens if they want to or have to work during vacation."

Write such a statement.

CHANGING A NAME?

Bookkeepers for Business was founded in the 1870s to serve the bookkeeping needs of small retailing establishments in the Victorian era. As long as the founder, McNulty Hodge, and his son, McNulty Hodge II, were alive, no opportunity of changing the name of the firm was possible, although there has been much talk about the name being "obsolete," "quaint," or "ridiculous" for the twentieth century.

The firm is a partnership, with 68 partners scattered in offices across the country and a main office where McNulty Hodge III is the managing partner.

By the time of its 100th birthday next year, the present McNulty Hodge has promised to make a decision about changing the firm's name, although he is very conscious of his father's and grandfather's wishes in this matter.

From its small beginning, the partnership—known always as Bee & Bee to clients, employees, and members of various communities—has expanded until its activities encompass consultation, guidance, and preparation of taxes, pension plans, record systems, accounting, and employee benefit programs. Hence, the thrust for a change of name stems from the fact that "Bookkeepers for Business" is not descriptive of the functions and highly efficient modern operations carried on. Those who favor a change prefer "Business Services" as a better name.

Nonetheless, many clients and employees have protested the change to a title which they call "neutral and forgettable"; they feel that "Bee & Bee" is memorable and carries the weight of years of tradition behind it, and as one older partner expresses it, "Bookkeepers for Business carries a fine connotation of long-established reliability; it belongs with such fine old names as Adams Express and Wells Fargo and B. F. Goodrich. Those names don't describe *their* business today, but you don't see those companies changing names."

A year before the 100th anniversary of Bookkeepers for Business, McNulty Hodge employs you as a consultant in this matter. "I want you to do three things," he tells you. "First I want a representative cross section of opinion from our employees, from our clients, and from members of the 57 communities where we have offices concerning our present name and whether we should change it. Second, if we decide to change, I want you to recommend the methods we should use to get the new name across. Third, I want you to submit other new names for me to consider besides this 'Business Services,' which seems to me awfully bland and hard to remember."

1. Write a letter to accompany a questionnaire (which you prepare) to representative employees, clients, and citizens.
2. Assuming that the returns from this questionnaire are evenly divided, write a report to Mr. Hodge making your recommendation.
3. Assuming that the name is to be changed, write a report recommending how the new name can be gotten across to the firm's various constituencies.

BUILDING A COMPANY'S IMAGE

You work in the public relations department of a large manufacturing company whose director of engineering, Eric M. Halvorsen, is a very able, very articulate, and very opinionated individual who boasts that he had little formal education. He insists that the only useful function of the public relations department is "to keep my name and the company's name out of the paper when I want it out and to get it on the front page when I want it there."

At a recent Chamber of Commerce panel discussion, Mr. Halvorsen launched into an unexpected attack on today's colleges as being "irrelevant to today's specialized needs and too theoretical." To prove his second point, he cites what he calls "illiterates with B.A.s and graduates with all the letters after their name who can't write a letter."

The following are excerpts from his remarks:

> Just to show you how they preach all this theory and then forget it, I've got a collection of letters from our university here. They're nice and dignified—and they belong back in the nineteenth century.
>
> So I went out and talked to the head of the business communication department and I asked him if he knew how to save money on letters and reports. He did—he knew all about simplified letters; he knew about enclosing what we call a "courtesy carbon" so the reader can just write his answer on the carbon of our letter and send it back to us; he knew about using window envelopes and cutting out all the guff about "Dear Mrs. Smith" and "Yours truly"—but *not one letter from that university reflected what he knew.*
>
> And so, gentlemen, I say to you that if our universities really know about management techniques, about political techniques, and especially about communication techniques, it's time they put their own house in order by using what they know!

That night's paper carries a headline:

LOCAL EXEC FIRES AT COLLEGE HYPOCRISY

Halvorsen is furious both at the headline and because public relations didn't "keep it out of the paper." Professor Wilcox, head of the business communication department at the university, says in an interview that "I was never asked for any advice about the letters and reports that go out from the university." Your boss, John Minshall, head of public relations, says, "This is real trouble. We've got to salvage whatever we possibly can because no modern business can go around attacking education."

From this situation, you are to write any of the following:

1. A statement that supports the viewpoint expressed by Eric M. Halvorsen.
2. A memo which includes a specific set of recommendations to the university concerning its techniques and methods of written communication based on the premise that "they should use what they know."
3. A letter defending the university's conservative attitude toward its own communications.

4. A statement which will fit in with Minshall's attempt to "salvage what we can." (This will involve "translating" Mr. Halvorsen's statement and viewpoint into less blunt language.)

5. A brief report that might be sent to the university concerning its practice in communication with the purpose of "making it as modern as today."

6. A memorandum to Mr. Halvorsen from the public relations department recommending "certain ways in which he can be helpful in projecting the best image for the company in the future."

THE BUSINESS READERS' SERVICE

Two months before your graduation, Professor Howard C. Neal, head of the business administration department of your college, has informed you that there is a position open at Bluestone, Knox, and White, a well-known firm of management consultants who specialize in services to small business. They want a young graduate who knows various forms of business communication, especially reports and letters; who can write well; and who has ambition and imagination.

1. Write an application letter for this position.

As a result of your letter, you are interviewed by Mr. Warren Bluestone, president of the company. When he finally decides to employ you, he says: "Your advancement will depend on how many ideas you can come up with. The field of management consulting is very competitive, and Bluestone, Knox, and White have to stay ahead of the pack. We want you to have ideas about how we can do things better and we want you to be able to sell those ideas to us in writing. The report is the backbone of our business, and we judge our employees on their ability to sell us and to convince us in their reports."

Your first assignment is in the research department, where a librarian, seven other research workers, and four typists work at assembling business statistics, analyzing business trends, and digesting books and articles of interest to key employees of Bluestone, Knox, and White. The library contains a complete collection of books and magazines on business subjects. The annual budget for staff, books, and magazines is $93,500, and the librarian has told you that the three partners in the firm have been looking for some method of reducing the cost of this operation.

One day an idea strikes you—if this work of digesting books and articles, compiling abstracts and bibliographies is useful at Bluestone, Knox, and White, why wouldn't it be helpful to the small businesses who are clients? The firm could get out a 12-page newsletter every month calling their attention to things they ought to read. That way the costs of operating the department could be covered by putting it on a paying basis. In your mind you go over the other reasons for venturing on this project: you've just seen a report showing that the average businessman reads about three and one-half hours a day and he still can't keep up with all the available material; the small businessman usually can't afford to maintain a library or research staff to give him information; the library contains a list of 12,500 companies that could potentially be interested in the other management services of Bluestone, Knox, and White; most of the work necessary for such a newsletter is already being done, and therefore little additional staff will be needed.

You go to Mr. Bluestone with your idea. He is somewhat skeptical but admits that your plan has some possibilities. "We could charge $100 a year for such a service, and if we got 1,000 subscribers, it would carry the costs of the research department. But you'll have to convince Mr. Knox and Mr. White and me—as partners we make all policy decisions. I'm interested in cutting costs; Mr. Knox likes anything that gets our name out before people—he might like this as a method of getting new clients for our other services; Mr. White wants as much diversification in our services as we can get. You think this thing through and then give us a complete report on why Bluestone, Knox, and White should go into it. Or maybe you'd better emphasize what will appeal to each of us in a separate report prepared differently for each partner. I'll leave that to you; you're supposed to know about written communication."

2. Write one report to go to all three partners or three reports angled to the individual interests of each partner. Choose the method you think will be more effective in this situation.

A week later, Mr. Bluestone informs you that your proposal has been tentatively approved. The three partners have agreed that the service must sell for $100 but that an offer can be made to those who subscribe and apply for the service in advance to obtain it for $75; others will be billed for $100 at the end of a three months' trial period. Mr. Bluestone tells you: "Mr. Knox and Mr. White are greatly concerned about the way we sell this service. We've been in business for 21 years, our reputation is excellent, and we want to maintain it. Both my partners and I want you to prepare a sales letter, for our approval, which will be dignified and yet get results."

3. Prepare a sales letter for the partners' approval, assuming that it will go eventually to the 12,500 companies on the list of those who may be potentially interested.

Assume, now, that the project has complete approval and the first issue of

Business Readers' Service will appear in three months. Two problems immediately arise. The librarian, who, of course, will be in charge of all printed and source materials, has expressed some fear that there may be certain books and magazines not now in the library of Bluestone, Knox, and White. "We ought to send out a letter of inquiry asking publishers about their important books in the field of business and making sure that we get all their announcements of new books in the future. I think they ought to see that it is to every publisher's advantage to have his publications represented in our service since we intend to list the publisher's name and the price of the publication with every item we mention."

4.   Write such a letter of inquiry to go to publishers.

The other problem concerns human relations within the company. Rumors of this project hang heavy on the office grapevine; strong feelings have been expressed that this new service is outside the scope of the normal professional activities of management consultants, that the firm will lose professional standing, that "we are going into the publishing business."

5.   Prepare a memorandum for the 16 department heads to use as a basis for discussions with the members of their departments. Explain in the most tactful way you can why the decision has been made and why it will enhance rather than diminish the prestige of Bluestone, Knox, and White.

Business Readers' Service has now sent out its first three issues to 1,107 subscribers—803 of whom paid $75 in advance, the other 304 to be billed for $100 at the end of three months. Since you need every subscriber you can get, Mr. Bluestone has authorized you to send out a letter which will offer to send the next 12 issues of your service to these 304 for $100; in effect, you are, therefore, giving them the first three issues if they pay the $100 fee for the next 12 issues within three weeks.

6.   Write a combination collection-and-sales letter to be sent to the 304 companies which have already received the first three issues.

In the fourth issue, just when you want most to impress readers with your service, through a mistake at the printer's in assembling pages, approximately 400 copies go to subscribers with the same four pages of copy repeated three times. These readers are, therefore, short eight pages that they should have received. Since you don't know which subscribers have received the garbled copies, except for 34 who have written in to complain, you have to reissue the material to all 1,107 subscribers.

7. Write a claim letter to Mr. Morgan C. Newell, The Blank Printing Company, explaining this situation and insisting that he bear the expense of reissuing and mailing complete copies to all your subscribers.

8. Write a letter of explanation to the 34 subscribers who have written in to register complaint.

In the twelfth issue of *Business Readers' Service* you are to include a questionnaire which has two purposes: first, to get reactions from subscribers as to the general usefulness of the service, what they would like included (such as, more complete synopses of books and articles, coverage of specialized areas like accounting, finance, and sales, or carefully selected short lists of the most important books and articles); second, to get statements from subscribers which you can use as testimonials for a sales letter you expect to send out to get new subscribers.

9. Prepare this questionnaire.

The readers' response to the questionnaire shows that they have found *Business Readers' Service* very useful. Among the suggestions they have made for changes are the following:

Pay more attention to articles in the better-known and easily accessible magazines. Our company library does not contain a number of the highly specialized magazines you refer to, so this aspect of *Business Readers' Service* is useless to us.

We wish that you would select *one* important article or book each month and really highlight it. Continue the lists of magazines and books, but add this useful feature.

We'd prefer that you pay more attention to general articles and books on the skills and techniques of management. Some of the specialized articles on accounting, operations analysis, and automation don't fit our needs.

Among the statements from subscribers that you can use as testimonials are the following:

Your service has been invaluable because we have used it as a guide in building up a small collection of carefully selected books and magazines. It has paid for itself many times over.

C. V. Smith, President
The Standard Company

One article, mentioned in *Business Readers' Service*, which we wouldn't have known about under ordinary circumstances, enabled us to save $1,200 on a phase of our operations. You can imagine that we feel we made a good investment when we subscribed.

E. J. Baird, Vice-President
Baird and Jones, Inc.

You've helped me immeasurably. For the first time I feel that I can keep up with developments in our field. I no longer waste time reading a lot of material that is irrelevant and I can concentrate on the most significant published materials.

N. M. Wilson, Superintendent
White and Company

Assume that *Business Readers' Service* will, in its forthcoming issues, incorporate the suggestions made by the readers and that you can use the statements from Mr. Smith, Mr. Baird, and Mr. Wilson.

10.   Write a sales letter to go to potential new subscribers for the service at $100 a year.

COMMUNICATING WITHIN THE COMPANY

(This case is intended for both class discussion and student writing.)

You work as assistant to Edwin C. Stowe, executive vice president of the Secure Insurance Company. Mr. Stowe's attitude toward communication is reasonably well summed up by his response to you when you told him that you had once taken an excellent course called Effective Supervisor-Employee Relations. Said Mr. Stowe: "I came up through the ranks of this company in the days when communication meant doing what the boss told you to do with no questions asked. Maybe if we stopped talking about all this fancy psychology of communication, we'd get some work done."

An essential but routine part of Secure Insurance's operation is the processing of premium notices, which are followed up by form letters emphasizing the importance of maintaining the insurance, and finally by personalized letters indicating various alternatives when the premiums are not paid on time. These notices, forms, and letters are handled by 157 clerks, all women, who sit in a huge room occupying the entire sixth floor of Secure's building. In one corner is the office of J. Edgar Whipple, the department head.

One day, three men appear on this scene, stand for about a half an hour in whispered conversation, and leave with a wave to Mr. Whipple. Five minutes later, Jane Goodnow, the senior employee among the group and a gossip who takes pride in knowing about what goes on in the company, asks Mr. Whipple what the men were doing. His answer is, "I don't know."

Three days later, two members of the maintenance staff arrive with tape measures and make marks on the floor with chalk. Before they leave, Jane Goodnow accosts one of them to find out what they intend to do. "We don't know," one of them says. "The top brass wants to know if we can fit a big machine in here."

"It's a computer," Jane gasps. "We're all going to be replaced by a computer!"

Within the next hour, every woman in the room has found an excuse to leave her desk to join one of the clusters of employees around the water cooler, the coffee machine, or the lockers. Jane Goodnow is now insisting authoritatively that "within two months every girl in this office will be out of a job, except that a few of us with seniority will be shifted to another department."

Production in the department can be accurately measured by the number of pieces of mail produced; in the week in which these events take place it drops off more than 33 percent, and absenteeism increases 15 percent above the normal level. When these figures reach Mr. Stowe, he tells you, "Go down and talk to Mr. Whipple and if necessary interview some of the women in the department. But be sure you get Whipple's permission first. We always follow lines of authority in this company."

Your talks with Mr. Whipple and your interviews with ten of the women, including Jane Goodnow, confirm the facts as we have stated them. The vice-president to whom Mr. Whipple reports has told him only that "there may be some changes coming up but they aren't immediate." This comment emerged from last week's meeting of Secure Insurance Company's administrative council, at which your boss Mr. Stowe had not been present. In this meeting, there had been a discussion of whether Secure Insurance should lease, buy, or rent time on a computer. The president had commented that any such planning would have to be long-range, since high interest rates made financing difficult. "At any rate," he added, "we ought to begin planning where we would house a computer and the functions associated with it, even though we won't do anything specific for about two years."

At this point, the vice-president to whom Mr. Whipple reports had said, "It looks as if the sixth floor is the logical place. Why don't I send a couple of our time-and-motion people and some members of the maintenance department to look the situation over? In the meantime, I'll tell Whipple that we're thinking about some very long-range changes but that nothing is decided." With this comment, the matter was dropped.

You now look back through your notes from the course in effective supervisor-employee relations and find the following principles:

a. Employees are most deeply affected by the immediate working conditions around them, such as the location of a desk, its relationship to desks of others, a change in the immediate supervisor, and, in fact, the daily environment and the people closest to the specific doing of the task involved. Therefore, *any change affecting immediate working conditions should be carefully planned so that communications to employees will inform them in advance, prepare them for the change with the reasons, and keep them informed until the change is effected.*

b. If this meticulous planning of communication is not done, *employees will fall back on the omnipresent "grapevine," where the tendency is for them to exaggerate and overemphasize all of the most pessimistic and ominous aspects of the situation.* Morale can thus be damaged for a long period of time.

c. *The damage thus created* by the failure to plan carefully and to communicate fully at every step *can be corrected only by applying the principle described in a. above.*

Using our description of this situation and the three principles of supervisor-employee relations, answer any or all of the following questions in class discussion or in written form, as your instructor directs:

1. Write a report responding to Mr. Stowe's directive to "Put in writing what you think went wrong here and how it can be corrected right now."

2. The president has asked each member of the administrative council "to get some younger member of their staff to write down what specific steps we should take for a long-range improvement in company communications with employees." Mr. Stowe has assigned this task to you.

3. If your one purpose were to correct the specific situation described and if you were responsible for correcting it, which method would you use:
   a. A meeting in which Mr. Whipple explained the situation to the 157 women in his department?
   b. A notice to be posted on their bulletin board? Signed by whom? What would it contain?
   c. A meeting in which the president and Mr. Stowe talk to all the women with the purpose of building Mr. Whipple's status as a knowledgeable department head?
   d. Some other method to achieve your purpose?

4. To whom should the president talk if the vice-president to whom Mr. Whipple reports insists that he "did just what was agreed on in the administrative council"? Should he meet with this vice-president, Whipple, and a few of the women in the department (i.e. Jane Goodnow) jointly? Should he do nothing? If not, state whom he should talk to about the situation and whether he should interview the key personnel singly or in groups.

5. Assume that your recommendations in (2) have been adopted by the administrative council as a long-range policy of communication. Your task now is to announce this policy to all 1807 employees of the Secure Insurance Company. You have the following choices of medium:

The monthly company magazine (out in 2 weeks)

The meeting of all supervisors and department heads (next week)

Announcements on all company bulletin boards

The annual Christmas party (two weeks from now) at which the president customarily makes a brief speech on "the state of the company."

Meetings of all employees, department by department. They would have to be held in the company's large classroom seating 250 and would have to be scheduled from 8 A.M. to 5 P.M. on one day.

How large a factor should timing be in your choice of one of these methods? How would your choice of a communications method be affected if (a) the gossip and indecision among the women in Mr. Whipple's department are at their peak and (b) if it is three weeks after Mr. Whipple has explained the facts of the specific situation to his employees?

6. In Mr. Stowe's absence on vacation, you have just received an angry letter to him from Jane Goodow resigning after "32 years of service, in which I have been a loyal and competent worker." Obviously, Mr. Stowe will want to talk with her when he returns in two weeks, but Miss Goodnow wants action now. Write the response to her. Should it be signed by you? Or by someone more prestigious in the organization, such as a vice-president or even the president? Would it be appropriate for you to talk to Miss Goodnow or to defer any interview until Mr. Stowe returns?

7. Assuming that the grapevine does what is indicated in the second of the supervisory-employee communication principles, is there any way of making the grapevine a constructive ally of communicating company policies? How? Would it be possible to have communications so effective within the Secure Insurance Company that the grapevine would wither and die? Should a responsible manager ever use the grapevine to accomplish his purposes as, for example, by providing information to employees like Jane Goodnow?

8. What would you write in answer to Mr. Stowe's comment that "maybe if we stopped talking about all this fancy psychology of communication, we'd get some work done"? How much would this comment affect your written communication with him?

9. Do you as an individual agree with the principles of supervisory-employee communications set forth in this case? What changes would you make in them?

10. Now—contrary to everything we have said previously—suppose that the administrative council *has* decided to install a computer but has unanimously agreed that "no employee with more than six weeks employment in the company will lose his/her job as a result but will be given, wherever possible, employment at the same level and at the same salary elsewhere within the company." What method and to what purpose would you use communication to (a) those most affected in Mr. Whipple's department and (b) all the other employees?

FRANCHISING IN HIGHER EDUCATION?

A wealthy friend of yours has long contended that if business methods were applied to higher education, costs could be reduced greatly, the efficacy of education improved, and a profit made. He proposes, therefore, to set up a corporation which will sell franchises to take over the function of business education in existing colleges and universities.

His reasoning is as follows: Highly reputable department stores and other establishments lease departments and sections to concessionaires although the general public believes it is dealing with the store or establishment itself. Similarly, franchises could exist within the college or university so long as the educational quality of the franchise complied with the institution's standards.

"We can pay the sponsoring college or university 50 percent of our profit," he argues. "Look at it this way. Let's assume the average cost for a three-hour semester course is $150—that's low for many colleges. That means that if you have 40 students' you take in $6,000 for a course that meets 30 times during a semester—$200 a meeting. We would hire the best-known teachers of business administration in America, increase the size of their classes to 250 or 300, and take in between $35,000 and $45,000 for one class for a semester. We can pay the best people in the country $10,000 for teaching just one class, one semester, and twice as much for taking on two classes. We pay the sponsoring college or university $5,000 for overhead—use of the lecture room, printing brochures, registration costs etc.—and we have a profit on one class of between $20,000 and $35,000. Half of it we give to the college or university, because the one thing we have to have is their name."

Using your own knowledge of educational costs, standards of education, and the reasons why students seek higher education (for example, to get a better job, to satisfy intellectual curiosity, to prepare for a career, to obtain social status), analyze this proposal to decide whether you would support it as a business project or reject it as an educational experiment.

1. If you oppose it, write a report to your friend stating all the reasons for your opposition.
2. If you would support it as an experiment at one or two colleges to see whether it would work, write the following:
   a. A report to your friend stating why you support the the project on an experimental basis and clearly expressing any limitations or restrictions you would place on the experiment.
   b. A letter to the presidents of five institutions to persuade them to try this franchise plan.
   c. A letter to directors of training and education in local industries urging their support of the plan.

d. A letter to 20 wealthy investors persuading them to invest in the franchise plan.

PROBLEMS IN THE COMMUNICATIONS AND
EDUCATION SECTION

You have just been employed by the personnel department of the New Utility Company and have been assigned to the section called C & E, meaning Communications and Education. The functions of this section, as indicated by the title, are (1) to edit the company's magazine; (2) to run the in-service training programs in what is called the Employees Educational Program, conducted by the company in its own classroom facilities and taught partly by company employees, partly by teachers brought in from outside; and (3) to arrange for company employees to take courses at two local universities, where the company will pay 50 percent of the tuition "provided the education or training can be shown to be directly related to the job the employee is doing within the company."

Mr. Fewsmith, head of the whole personnel department, has talked to you on your first day on the job and told you: "We've been having some problems in the C & E Section, and I hope you'll be able to help us out since you're close to your own education. Mr. Washington, the section head, is going to retire in a few months and he's lost interest in planning next September's educational program. So I'm going to ask you to do some things in which you report directly to me. But there's one thing you have to remember—in the New Utility Company, the C & E section is by definition a service function. That means that we supply the in-service courses or the communication services which are needed, but we don't initiate them. We serve the needs of the various department heads and executives—so, for example, if Mr. Casey as head of the accounting group thinks his people need a course in programming a computer, or writing accounting reports, it's our job to get the best teacher available and to take over all the mechanics of getting the course set up the way Mr. Casey wants it. If it doesn't work out the way Casey expected it to, we hear from him—and fast."

At this point Mr. Fewsmith starts thumbing through a number of reports and memos on his desk. "Well, we might as well get started," he says. "Now I understand that you don't know the forms and methods we use yet, and I can't expect you to. But if you can just put something down in writing about each of these—and I'll tell you who to talk to about them and you can say I told you to get the information—it'll give me a good idea of where we can use you best, and you'll get a good chance to get your feet wet on some of our problems. Now I'll go through each of these memos or letters with you, and you make notes on it about what's to be done when I hand it to you."

Here are brief summaries of the messages, plus the background Mr. Few-smith provides you with, plus what you have found out by your own subsequent investigation and what Mr. Fewsmith wants you to do. For convenience they are divided into (a) the message to be answered, (b) the background provided by Mr. Fewsmith or by your own investigation, and (c) the assignment given you by Mr. Fewsmith.

1. a. A letter from Mr. J. S. True of the accounting department complaining that the New Utility Company pays only 50 percent of employees' tuition at the University, whereas four other local companies pay 100 percent.

   b. "He's wrong. Two of them pay 100 percent, the other two pay 100 percent if the employee gets a grade of A—otherwise it's 50 percent. The theory of our educational committee is that employee education is more meaningful if the employee puts a little of his own stake in it. But the committee would change policy if they saw good reason to do so because they've talked it over several times.

   c. *Write* for Mr. Fewsmith a draft of the message he might send to Mr. True.
      Write what Mr. Fewsmith has described as "a clear-cut presentation for the educational committee stating all the pros and cons of this tuition plan." (Last year 57 employees were enrolled in approved courses at various universities at a cost of $8,500 to the company and an equal amount to the employees.)

2. a. Mrs. Tillie Jones, with 18 years of service on the maintenance staff, writes "I feel that if you would let me take a course in eurhythmic dancing I would be in better condition to perform my duties on the maintenance staff, and I am hereby requesting you pay half my tuition for a year, which will cost the company $150."

   b. "We have to be awfully careful here. Tillie's a good worker, but she sulks and tells her problems to everybody in the place. Besides, if we don't stick to our policy of insisting the course be directly related to the job, we'll have everybody in the place taking all kinds of stuff from basket weaving to stamp collecting. But treat Tillie very carefully."

   c. *Write* the response to Tillie.
      Write to the educational committee telling why you think the policy of job-related courses should be modified and state in specific language the new policy. (You have found that there is some resentment among a number of employees that the policy has been so rigidly enforced.)

3. a. Five members of the in-service course in economic theory complain, "This is nothing but company propaganda telling the services and charges of the company are always right. Why don't they bring in a labor leader, a Communist, and a member of a regulating committee to give different viewpoints so we can hear all sides?"

   b. Mr. Fewsmith groaned when he read this one to you. "We've got a president and several directors who already think we shouldn't be in the education business when our job and our revenue involve providing cheap power. I can imagine what they'd say if they read this request. I'd rather keep what we have as an educational program than run the risk of having the whole thing canceled. Maybe we ought to cancel the economic theory course—it's been a headache every time we offer it." He pauses for a moment. "Incidentally, why does a young fellow like you think we *should* offer our own in-service educational program—or do you think we shouldn't?"

   c.   *Write* an answer to the five members of the course in economic theory.

      Write a formal statement presenting your answer to Mr. Fewsmith's last question, and do it in such a way that he can transmit it to the educational committee without any change.

4. a.   The company magazine committed a horrible blunder in announcing as winners of the company bowling league championship the team of the auditing department rather than the customers' service department, and displaying a picture of the auditing department's team on the front page of last month's issue. "Sometimes I think we should give up this bowling competition. You have no idea of how seriously they take it. We've had about thirty phone calls and notes complaining about that wrong picture."

   b.   You find that the editor of *The Utilitarian* left the front page to the photographer, thinking that he knew which department won the bowling championship, and then an assistant, seeing the cover layout, wrote a long complimentary article congratulating the auditing department.

   c.   *Write* down the steps you would take to correct this error. (The next issue of *The Utilitarian* appears in three weeks.)

      Write recommendations to Mr. Fewsmith to set up a procedure to minimize the possibility of such errors in the future.

      Write what you think *The Utilitarian* should carry concerning this situation in the next issue.

5. a.   Twenty members of the advertising department have signed a request for a course in creative writing to be included in the Employee Educational Program's offerings in September and sent the request directly to Mr. Fewsmith without any approval by John Stark, the department head.

   b.   "I know why," Fewsmith tells you. "Stark won't sign it if they ask him to. He thinks they're all going to write novels and short stories on company time. This puts me right in the middle because I won't authorize anything without departmental-head approval. On the other hand, when we've had that many requests for a course in the past, we've always given it."

   c.   Write out a statement which Mr. Fewsmith can transmit to Mr. Stark, explaining why you think the request for such a course should be rejected (or granted).

      On the assumption that the request was rejected by Stark, *write* a memo which will be sent to the 20 members of the advertising department announcing the reasons for the decision.

6. *a.* Six employees who were urged by their department heads to take a course in business law at the university have, at Mr. Fewsmith's request, submitted an appraisal of the course so that he will have information to give to other department heads for the coming year's offerings. The gist of the six employees' comments is: "It was a waste of my evenings"; "For the most part it was unstructured and disorganized"; "Even though I paid only half my tuition, I wasted my money"; "I should have stayed home and read a good textbook—I would have learned a lot more."

b. The reason underlying these comments is that although business law, taught by Professor Jack Kirksteen, is one of the best courses in the university, during the past year Professor Kirksteen has been doing a great deal of consulting—occasionally for the New Utility Company—and a lot of speechmaking, so that the course was for the most part handled by Kirksteen's graduate students.

   "We have to tread lightly in dealing with this one," Fewsmith says. "Our president's on the university's board of trustees, and we've made generous contributions to support their educational program every year. But if Jack Kirksteen isn't going to teach a course, the catalogue should say so. Instead, he's listed as teaching this course, and that's why the department heads urged our employees to take it.

   "Actually what the university needs is one official who can serve as the liaison man with business and industry. Every time I have any dealings with them, I get shunted from one provost or academic vice-president or dean or director of this-or-that to another, until I decide it's useless. They could use the help of our specialists in management organization for a few weeks."

c. *Write* any of the following on the assumption that you graduated from the university and know its organization and personnel reasonably well:

   (1) A memo to the six employees who took the course in business law. Mr. Fewsmith hopes to send six more employees to take the course next year, if it is taught by Professor Kirksteen.

   (2) A letter to Professor Kirksteen, whom you know, to get his assurance that he will actually teach the course next year.

   (3) A letter to be signed by Mr. Fewsmith suggesting to the provost in charge of education that the university should appoint one person to deal with the educational problems of business and industry.

   (4) A report which Mr. Fewsmith can transmit to the president of your company urging that the university and industry would mutually benefit if the university were to use qualified people from business to advise on problems of organization and to teach some of the courses dealing with management problems.

   (5) A response in writing to this note from Mr. Fewsmith: "The presi-

dent is very much annoyed by the attached editorial from *The Record*, the students' daily newspaper. Give me your best thinking as to how this company should respond to it so that our goal of establishing a partnership between the university and the business community is clearly stated."

The following excerpts are typical of the editorial:

This University's problems are compounded by a kind of false notion that we must serve business and industry, we must do research for the industrial-military complex, and we must forget teaching in favor of consulting, publishing-or-perishing, and being all things to all agencies in society.

Let us now—this minute—start a policy by which every administrator, every faculty member puts first-things-first. And that means that every one in the administration and on the faculty will right now decide that his first obligation is to the students enrolled here and that he will give up every other obligation (however lucrative) in favor of that obligation.

This means no courses for businessmen at night, it means no research for the government agencies, it means that every resource of everyone in this community will be directed toward teaching the full-time students who spend their time and money to benefit from great teaching which they don't get now.

THE THREE ENTREPRENEURS

(This case is intended primarily to provide a basis for students to analyze the role written communications of all types might play in setting up a new business venture. Instead of raising the specific questions typical of other cases, this situation should be analyzed for answers to three basic questions applicable to all communication:

1. At what points in this developing situation will written communication play a vital role?
2. What is its purpose in each instance?
3. What kind of reader will it be addressed to?)

Richard Einstein, a graduate student in mathematics, has asked you, as a communications expert, and John Sloan, a management major, to join him in a business venture to be called Evaluate Your Education, known as EYE. As a result of his research, Einstein has developed a method of programming appropriate information in a computer so that it contains a model of an elementary or secondary school system.

As Einstein describes it, "By this technique, we can build into a computer the characteristics of the very best schools in existence, in fact the 'School for Utopia.' Then other schools, hopefully our clients, can have their characteristics fed into the computer for comparison. That way, school board members and school administrators can evaluate their own school's performance against the best, or the typical, or systems that resemble their own in socioeconomic community traits.

"Best of all" Einstein continues, "EYE enables them to find these and countless other answers without actually doing the work, without committing the school to new policies, and with a small expenditure of money—invested in us, we hope! EYE puts an end to the old question 'How good are our schools?' which is usually answered in irrelevant terms such as how many merit scholars are produced, or how many advanced degrees there are in the faculty, or how much money is spent per pupil. By programming, we can provide factual evidence about how the school compares with others, where the best teaching occurs within the school, where money ought to be spent most advantageously. EYE enables administrators to project enrollments, budgets, space requirements into the future—in fact it can be programmed to provide answers to almost any specific situation involved in how good is the school, how and where can it be improved, and what should be done to improve it."

For the first year after you and Sloan join EYE, the going is very rough financially. You try to persuade various foundations to support it for a one-year trial as a research project. You and Sloan debate endlessly as to whether EYE's sales efforts should be aimed at school administrators or school board members or both. He argues, "If we don't direct our appeals to try EYE to the superintendent, we can't make a sale." You reply that a lot of superintendents won't want their systems evaluated and that the school board member is the one who wants to know how good his school system is. Einstein thinks that the best approach might be to approach all the parents in a given school district to bring pressure on their school board to sign up with EYE.

By now Sloan has figured the basic costs for computer time, for clerks to record data necessary for programming a school system, and for office expenses and overhead as follows:

System-wide Enrollment	Cost
2,000 or less	$5,000
4,000 or less	$6,500
over 4,000	$7,500

"These are the costs for the first year, with absolutely no profit for us," Sloan says. "After the first year, when we get the information fed into the computer, we can carry on the service for $1,000 a year, answering any questions a school system may want answered. It's after the first year, when the model of the school system is built into the computer, that we can make our profit."

Crucial to the survival of EYE at this stage is your ability to get ten school systems to enroll at actual cost on a trial basis so that you can use these systems' experience with EYE as a solid basis for sales to many more systems. Einstein also expresses an important idea. "We ought to get endorsement of the methods and possibilities of EYE *on a theoretical basis* from prominent mathematicians and educators. This would help sales tremendously, I think, and it's all we have to offer until we get ten systems who have actually participated in EYE."

At this point in the development of EYE the following events occur:

> Four levies in local communities were rejected by voters. A newspaper survey of the reasons shows that the majority of the voters believe that "all the schools want is money, and we don't know whether the schools are really good or bad or where the money should be spent to improve them."

> The chairman of the board of a huge corporation has made a speech saying, "Education is America's biggest domestic business. We invest more than $60 billion a year in it, and yet we have no yardstick by which to measure it. If business followed such practices, we would be bankrupt in two years."

> The County Association of School Superintendents, comprising administrators of 34 school systems in your area, has endorsed a resolution "condemning excessive use of mathematical measurements and comparisons of school systems. We disapprove of ranking students in class and comparing one school with another. We believe the individual student and the individual school system are just that— *individual*—and that comparisons and rankings serve only to confuse parents and the general public."

At year's end, EYE has had experience with ten school systems. It has a letter from an educational foundation suggesting that it might now take favorable action on financial support for EYE "provided that you furnish us with adequate information for us to make a judgment." Sloan has also turned up ten investors, each of whom would put $10,000 into EYE in return for a 51 percent portion of the stock to be issued under the terms of their investment. Sloan favors this arrangement; Einstein prefers to wait for foundation support; your attitude is, "I'd like to see the pros and cons of all these alternatives written down in black and white."

At your instructor's discretion, of course, you may write any of the communications that emerge from your analysis of this situation. In addition, you may also write the year-end report making the recommendation which you prefer for EYE's future.

ATTRACTING AND COMPENSATING A COMPETENT
SALES FORCE*

You work for Security Devices, Inc., a large corporation which sells a wide variety of products to protect residences and industry from burglary or theft. The future success of your organization depends upon its sales force, which is nationwide and which calls on dealers organized into 12 geographical territories. The central problem of Security Devices is its inability to attract qualified people to its sales force.

Within Security Devices considerable debate has centered on whether an all-out effort should be made to recruit college graduates for its sales organization. Certain key executives believe that the increasing professionalism of sales work requires more formal education; others speak of the fact that careers in sales lack social prestige, that college students dislike business, and that the commission-only method of remunerating salespeople at Security Devices does not appeal to college graduates accustomed to thinking in terms of secure salaries.

At this point, C. E. Pinkham, vice-president for sales at Security, calls you to his office, explains the problem, and tells you to drop all of your other duties until you complete a report which will "give us accurate information about the compensation methods currently used by business to motivate and retain high-caliber employees recruited from the nation's colleges.

"Your report will be used as the basis for a decision by our top executives and, eventually, our board of directors," Mr. Pinkham tells you. "So give us the broad trends and your recommendations, but don't get involved in what-company-pays-its-salesmen-how-many-dollars-a-month. In the first place, they probably won't divulge that information, and in the second place, we know that we can match the remuneration of other companies. Just think in terms of how Security can attract young college graduates—we need 86 new salesmen by next June—and what our plan of compensation should be."

1. *Write the letter and accompanying questionnaire* that you might send to the 452 members of Security Devices, Inc.'s present sales force.

Among the responses to your letter and questionnaire, the following remarks from members of your present sales force are worth noting:

Commissions are the incentive which keep salesmen working hard. Pay me a salary and I'll do only what is necessary."

*I am indebted to Professors James E. Bell, Jr. and William O. Hancock of the Department of Marketing at Northern Illinois University for permission to use their excellent study "Compensating College Graduates in Field Sales" in *Business Perspectives*, Summer, 1969, for background information for this case.

"A sales job does not require a college education, and Security Devices will have a lot of dissatisfied college graduates on its hands if it starts recruiting them."

"Too often a sales position is viewed as a place for the man who couldn't make top management. Nothing could be further from the truth. I am a college graduate; my career with the sales department at Security has been satisifying, and I've used my college education to great advantage."

"Something should be done to increase the prestige of sales if college graduates are to be recruited successfully. Too bad that Arthur Miller ever wrote about Willy Loman in *Death of a Salesman*. College students think we are all like Willy—poor, broken down, and obsolete. Security Devices will never get top college graduates as long as that image persists."

"My son graduates this June and wants to enter sales. But he dreads the insecurity of commissions while all his classmates work for salaries."

"Security Devices will have to set up an adequate formal training program as an incentive for college students to join our sales force."

A library search for material on methods of compensation for salesmen reveals the following (students are urged to continue this research for more specific information):

"Today's generation is *not* fed up with the world of corporations and profit making." *U. S. News & World Report*, Feb. 19, 1968, pp. 98–100.

John L. Mason, "The Low Prestige of Personal Selling," *Journal of Marketing*, October, 1965, pp. 7–10.

Carl Rieser, "The Salesman Isn't Dead—He's Different," *Fortune*, November, 1962, pp. 124–127.

"In failing to sell itself to college graduates, business has often overlooked its market knowledge and groped blindly." "Sales Force Management," *Sales Management*, Oct. 15, 1967, p. 104.

In a study by Professors James E. Bell, Jr., and William O. Hancock of Northern Illinois University ("Compensating College Graduates in Field Sales," *Business Perspectives*, Summer, 1969, p. 14), respondents were asked to identify trends occurring in the initial compensation and training of new college graduates entering sales. The following results highlight these trends:

a. A larger initial salary is needed to provide security during a training period for the more highly educated new employees entering field sales.

b. There should be a decreasing emphasis on individual sales performance and more on company profits as a basis for added compensation.

c. An attempt should be made to insulate the compensation of sales representatives from effects of economic fluctuations beyond their control.

d. Salary adjustments will have to be increasingly based on an appraisal of individual performance, rather than across-the-board increases in quotas and commissions.

e. In the short run, it is becoming increasingly difficult to objectively appraise individual performance because of the uncertain cause and effect relationship between sales and the efforts of salesmen.

You now decide to supplement this information by conducting a survey of approximately 100 companies to find out what beginning compensation plans they offer, whether a training program is conducted for new employees, whether the method of remuneration is changed after employees complete the training program, and if so how it is changed. To get a list of business organizations currently recruiting college graduates, you write to the Director of Placement, Northern Illinois University, DeKalb, Illinois 60115.

2. *Write the letter*, explaining your purpose and requesting the names and addresses of such business organizations.

3. *Prepare the questionnaire and the letter* to the 100 companies which have been sent to you through the courtesy of the placement office of Northern Illinois University.

4. *Write a letter* expressing your thanks to the director of placement of Northern Illinois University.

5. At this point, you are expected to make a brief report of your progress to Mr. Pinkham. Using memo form, *write the report* summing up what you have done and what you plan to do.

6. *Prepare a letter of appreciation* to be sent to the companies which provided useful replies to your questionnaire. (Out of more than 100, 51 sent helpful replies.)

The firms replying planned to hire more than 5,000 college men for sales; the average firm anticipated hiring 104 college graduates, and the firms you contacted had available job openings ranging from 8 to 981. The following tables show the organizations and job openings and the initial compensation plan and whether it is changed.

TABLE 1 *Organizations and Job Openings*

Number to be Hired	Number of Firms	Total Jobs	Average Firm
0–19	22	170	7.7
20–49	14	401	28.5
50–99	5	433	86.5
100–199	4	672	168.0
200–299	3	600	200.0
300 and over	3	2,943*	981.0
TOTALS	51	5,329	104.4

*Survey findings were affected by one large firm which planned to hire 2,000 new sales representatives.

TABLE 2 *Compensation Plans*

Plan	Initial Firms	Initial Percent	Final Firms	Final Percent
Salary only	32	58.0	7	13.7
Salary plus commission or bonus	21	38.0	36	70.6
Commission only	2	4.0	8	15.7
TOTALS	55*	100.0	51	100.0

*Some firms used more than one initial compensation plan.

7. *Prepare a chart or table* for any of the following additional information from your survey which might appropriately be transmitted in graphic form:

> Thirty-three companies planned to change from the initial plan of compensation after the training period. Twenty companies planned no change from the initial plan of compensation.
>
> The average training period for all companies was 14 months; the range was from 6 to 36 months.
>
> The companies replying could be broken down into eight industry categories. The two descriptions which follow are the categories which most closely fit the activities of Security Devices, Inc.
>
> *Category A* included eleven companies. None of the beginning compensation plans in this group were straight commission. After completion of an initial training period averaging 6 months, the employees of only two

of the eleven companies were on a straight salary plan. All other companies converted to salary-plus-commission plans. The typical company in this category planned to hire 35 new college graduates for its sales force; these new employees would represent about 10 percent of the toal sales force in the organization.

Category B included nine companies, the largest of which anticipated hiring 2,000 new college graduates for sales. Excluding this organization, the typical organization sought to add 40 new college graduates to a sales organization averaging 210 members. Seven of the nine organizations started new employees with a salary-only compensation plan; two used a salary-plus-commission plan. After a one-year average training program two companies continued straight salaries as a method of compensation, four had salary-plus-commission plans, and three reimbursed salesmen on straight commission only.

8. Using any of the information presented in this problem or obtained from your own research, *write the complete report* for Mr. Pinkham.

9. *Write a brief synopsis* of your findings to go to the 51 companies which replied to your questionnaire and to follow through on your promise, at the time you sent your letter with the questionnaire, "to provide a summary of our findings which will certainly prove useful to any company employing college graduates for its sales force."

A REPORT ON EDUCATIONAL NEEDS*

You are to assume that late in the 1960s a group of publishers, industrial leaders, and representatives of education in Pennsylvania met to discuss "Our Needs for Business Education in the Seventies." From this meeting emerged a resolution that "an executive committee be appointed to ascertain whether a formal study of educational needs should be conducted; and, if so, a report shall be prepared to supply specific and factual information to guide us concerning this state's needs for managerial and supervisory education in the 1970s."

The following conditions led the executive committee to decide that such a study should be made:

1. There is a significant increase in managerial positions and a resulting increase in the need for managerial education and training.

---

*The material on this and the following pages is adapted from a report titled "Managerial and Supervisory Educational Needs of Business and Industry in Pennsylvania," by Professors Samuel S. Dubin, Everett Alderman, and H. Leroy Marlow (1967), a study by the Planning Studies Division, Continuing Education Services, Pennsylvania State University, by whose permission it is reprinted here.

2. The rapid growth of managerial knowledge has increased the importance of disseminating such information.

3. The development of increased competence and resourcefulness in keeping with the greater emphasis being placed on leadership and motivation.

4. Management must recognize changes which will affect the company's long-range planning.

5. Companies must operate in increasingly complex and competitive environments.

6. Greater emphasis will be placed on international management.

7. Business growth necessitates keeping up with scientific research and development.

8. Expanding computer operations and data processing require judicious application to decision making.

As the result of these conditions, a research study is authorized by the executive committee, and you are charged with writing the final report, which will be sent first to all members of the original symposium and then be given widespread dissemination to representatives of education, government, industry, and publishing.

Research Findings of the Study

The study shows the educational needs as perceived by 3,620 managers and supervisors in Pennsylvania business and industry. Three separate questionnaires were sent to three levels of management: top managers (senior executives who direct an enterprise as a whole or who head major divisions); middle managers (personnel assigned to executive duties in the area between senior executives and supervisors); and first-line supervisors (personnel who perform activities at the beginning level of the management organization.)

All three levels of management indicated their educational needs on a three-point scale: "Should have," "Could use," and "Don't really need." Top managers and middle managers were also asked to indicate if the course listed in the questionnaire represented a training need of those they supervise. Middle managers and first-line supervisors were asked to provide information on their backgrounds, educational plans, methods of updating used, preferences for various educational media, and company attitudes toward education.

Top Management

The subjects seen as a "should have" need by 50 percent or more of 705 top managers are:

	"Should Have" Percent
Communication in the Organization	59
Management Development	53
Long-Range Planning and Forecasting for Corporate Growth	50
Overall Strategy and Goals	50
Effective Written Communications	50
Effective Speaking	50

Subjects which 50 percent or more of top managers thought represented educational needs of those they supervise are:

	"Subordinates' Needs" Percent
Effective Written Communication	74
Effective Speaking	67
Working Efficiently with Individuals and Groups	66
Communication in the Organization	65
Effective Reading Skills	62
Listening Skills	61
Performance Appraisal and Counseling Techniques	57
Management Development	56
Improving Decision Making of Managers	54
Human Aspect of Management	54

When the educational needs are compared by industrial category, the most needed course is *Communication in the Organization,* with 12 of the 22 industrial categories expressing a "should have" need of 60 percent or more.

While there is a slight variation in needs for continuing education among companies of different size, the needs are generally similar in all sizes of companies.

Middle Management

Thirty-seven percent of the middle managers were 40 years of age or younger, 93 percent had completed high school, and 44 percent had completed the bachelor's degree. Seven percent had the master's degree.

A majority of middle managers reported that they would be willing to enroll in college credit or non-credit courses if they were available locally, the interest in non-credit courses being higher (71 percent as compared to 60 percent for credit courses). Discussion with company personnel is the most frequent method of keeping up to date with new developments. Middle management reported workshops or seminars on managerial subjects as being the most prevalent type of education or training participated in during the last four years.

Two-thirds of the managers reported that their company had an educational assistance plan, and slightly over half of the companies encouraged managers to participate in specific educational activities. However, 54 percent of the managers expressed the opinion that their immediate supervisors were noncommittal toward further education.

The subjects seen as a "should have" need by 50 percent or more of 1,202 middle managers are:

	"Should Have" *Percent*
Management Development	66
Working Efficiently with Individuals	65
Effective Communication in the Organization	64
Supervisory Training and Employee Development	53

	"Subordinates' *Needs"* *Percent*
Working Efficiently with Individuals	62
Supervisory Training and Employee Development	61
Effective Communication in the Organization	56
Listening Skills	50

When the needs for the subjects were compared by industrial category, the course most frequently wanted by 60 percent or more of the middle managers was *Working Efficiently with Individuals*. This level was reached in 18 of the 22 industrial categories.

Comparing needs by company size, demand for a course in *Working Efficiently with Individuals* was 60 percent or more in all eight sizes of companies. Educational needs were remarkably similar in all sizes of companies, although there was a slight tendency for middle managers in the larger companies to express needs for more of the courses than those in the smaller companies.

First-line Supervision

Forty-three percent of the supervisors were 40 years of age or younger; 80 percent were high school graduates, and 20 percent had completed the bachelor's degree. One percent had the master's degree.

A majority of supervisors said they would be willing to enroll in college credit (53 percent) or non-credit (72 percent) courses if they were available locally. Company in-service training was the educational method most frequently participated in during the past four years. Discussion with company personnel was used most often to keep up to date with new developments.

Sixty-one percent said their company had an educational assistance plan, and about half reported that their company encouraged them to participate in educational activities. However, 51 percent of the supervisors believed that their immediate supervisors had a noncommittal attitude toward their continuing education.

The subjects seen as a "should have" need by 50 percent or more of 1,713 first-line supervisors are:

	"Should Have" *Percent*
Fundamentals of the Supervisor's Job	64
Leadership	57
The Tools and Techniques of Effective Supervision	55
Decision Making	54
Human Aspect of Management	53
Communications	51

The course most needed in the largest number (13) of the 22 industrial categories was *Fundamentals of the Supervisor's Job.*

The self-perceived need for further education was slightly greater among supervisors in the larger companies as compared with the other size companies.

Comparison of Background Information of
Middle Management and First-line Supervision

Comparisons were made between middle management and first-line supervision on a series of questions on background information: personal data, methods of updating, and company attitudes toward education.

The major fields of undergraduate study of college graduates who are part of middle management or first-line supervision are the same—engineering (39 percent and 34 percent), business administration (26 percent and 32 percent), and liberal arts (17 percent and 16 percent).

Of the types of training or educational work listed, which did not include formal degree work, the four most frequent types engaged in by middle management and first-line supervision within the last four years are workshops or seminars on managerial topics, attendance at regional or national meetings of professional societies, company in-service training courses, and management development for personnel within the one company.

The three top sources of information for keeping up to date for middle managers and first-line supervisors were the same: discussion with company personnel, informal or formal (65 percent and 57 percent); in-plant reports and bulletins (57 percent and 54 percent); and subordinate-superior discussions or meetings (53 percent and 43 percent).

Using these data, you are to write the following shorter aspects of your final report first:

1. Write an answer to the executive committee's request for a memorandum "providing us with a brief analysis of contrasts and similarities in the educational needs of the three managerial levels."

2. As a matter of policy, the committee has agreed that "the report should contain separate recommendations addressed to various groups and interests of readers." These groups are the following:
   Universities
   Business and industry
   The individual manager and supervisor
   Professional organizations and associations
   Students enrolled in management courses in college
   Write the recommendations in the forms appropriate for the various groups.

3. Write a 150-word abstract summarizing the research findings.

4. Write a 350-word account of this entire project for readers who have a general interest in business news.

5. Write a letter in answer to a request from the newly appointed Dean of the Business School of Blank University in another state who writes: "I know that your report will be published in six months, but we are currently revising our curriculum. Could you tell me how your research findings might affect our planning of courses?"

6. Write an answer to a student in management who says, "I want to be a top executive, so I should take a course in Long-range Planning and Forecasting for Corporate Growth since 50 percent of top management say they need it."

7. Answer a letter from a business executive who comments, "The report shows that education for management should be concentrated in Pennsylvania's colleges and universities, and that industry should stop giving in-service classes within their own four walls."

8. Prepare a brief memo for the executive committee in which you attempt to

account for the reasons for the different educational interests of the three levels of management.

9. Prepare an answer to a reader from Ohio who says, "I don't think the results of your research are very conclusive since they are confined to Pennsylvania. I am certain a similar study in Ohio would bring greatly different results."

10. Write the final report as described in the formal resolution at the original meeting.

REFERENCE SECTION

As the reader is well aware, there is an endless debate between those who are permissive about language usage and those who are restrictive or conservative about rules and "what is correct." On the following pages we attempt to present sensible answers to the specific problems of usage encountered by writers in business. The rules are given as a refresher for those who want to brush up on principles or as a reference section for business writers to consult for guidance on specific problems.

In using these principles, students should remember certain specific conditions that affect business writing. In the first place, as we said in Chapter 6 when we discussed the reasons why change does not occur more rapidly in the form and mechanics of the business letter, the force of tradition is strong in the commuunications of business. In the second place, much business writing reflects not only the writer but the company or organization for which he works. In the third place, probably no other type of writing so directly forms the basis of judgment as to the writer's future career—for promotion, for transfer to new assignments, for assuming new responsibilities. For these reasons, most business writers realistically decide to "play it safe" with a conservative approach to linguistic innovation and a healthy respect for generally accepted standards and rules.

It is worth noting, for example, that a great corporation, the General Electric Company, recently issued thousands of copies of a pamphlet called "Why Study English." Among other things, designed to stress the importance of writing correctly and effectively, the pamphlet says: "Every day in your future you will be called upon to speak and write, and when you open your mouth, or write a letter or report, you will be advertising your progress and your potential worth."

Errors in grammar and spelling call attention to themselves and thus distract the reader's mind from the message. And in that moment of distraction, he will probably make this harsh comment about the writer, "He doesn't know any better."

As a minimum standard for business writing, we can certainly expect correctness in grammar, spelling, and punctuation. Although errors in grammar do not always result in a lack of clarity—for example, so far as clearness is concerned, it makes no difference whether a writer says, "It don't matter to us" or "It doesn't matter to us"—yet students should remember that the grammatical rules of our language generally incorporate the most logical means of expression. Grammar involves not an artificial and arbitrary set of rules but a logical system of expressing our thoughts clearly and exactly. We should follow these rules not—as so many students seem to think—because they are the annoying whims of English teachers, but because good grammar is the easiest, most logical form of construction and because certain usages have become conventional. To the writer in business, a knowledge of correct English usage is a basic and minimum skill. Not only do grammatical errors distract his reader, but ignorance of correct usage interferes constantly with the task of writing. For if the writer has to stop continually to think about whether his verb should be singular or plural or whether his pronouns should be subjective or objective case, he cannot concentrate his whole attention on his message. Effective writers have learned to use correct language in the same way that good drivers instinctively use the mechanical equipment of their cars without stopping to decide whether they should step on the accelerator or the brake.

In using these principles, students should remember that many of them incorporate logical relationships, many reflect mere custom or tradition. The danger in printing such rules is a real one because they appear so final, so dogmatic, whereas serious students of the language now think of several levels of usage or "cultural levels" of language as being appropriate to different uses or functions. Since most business writing tends to be semipermanent and somewhat formal, these principles incorporate the rules of language suitable to these functions and the cultural level of the educated or professional man characterized by precision, good taste, and logic. For such people, certain conventions are important, particularly when they write; these conventions are the essence of the following pages. They are not final and absolute dogma, and many good writers have violated them when the occasion demanded it; but to be realistic, we should also add that the demands of such occasions on young writers in business will be rare.

WRITING CORRECTLY

Attitudes toward correctness in writing run the gamut. At one extreme is the famous comment of Will Rogers: "A lot of people who don't say 'ain't,' ain't eating." At the other are the well-known advertisements with a gentleman pointing an ominous finger and asking: "Do *you* make these mistakes in English—mistakes which can be ruinous to your career?" Between these two extremes we can probably find agreement that correctness is important to business writers if it is not extended to the slavish worship of rules that marks the pedant.

Nonetheless, one has to face up to the fact that the past five or ten years have brought a more profound change in American manners, morals, and methods than any previous era—and certainly our standards of expression have been greatly affected by this rapid evolution. We could quote the ominous words of Ralph Waldo Emerson ("The corruption of man is followed by the corruption of language") to draw some pessimistic conclusions about what has been termed the breakdown of linguistic standards. There are those who believe sincerely that we approach linguistic anarchy if we proceed any farther down the road of denying that there are "right" and "wrong" standards in speech and writing.

At the other extreme are those—and they have a great deal of scholarly support from linguists and lexicographers—who insist that correctness rests on usage and that today's linquistic innovations will be tomorrow's accepted standards endorsed in textbooks and recorded in dictionaries. Unquestionably, much merit rests with the argument that language usage is a dynamic, changing pattern, that flexibility and vigor will be lost if rules become inflexible and restrictive.

The key to this debate rests with the word "usage"—but usage *by whom?* By advertisers with "Me and my Winston, we got a real good thing"? By activists with the four-letter words of the so-called "free speech movement"? By the purist at the switchboard haughtily inquiring, "To whom did you wish to speak?" By the *New York Times*, or the hastily mimeographed underground newspaper? Here we get into the most difficult of human value judgments— *good taste*, a term which is practically undefinable and which, says the Latin adage, "there can be no disputing about."

Fortunately, the answer to these questions of usage and taste is relatively clear for writers in business. Except for those employed in advertising, most skilled business writers adopt a wait-and-see attitude toward rapid linguistic change. Their viewpoint seems to reflect a conviction that fundamental changes in linguistic etiquette benefit from evolution rather than revolution. Since their writing almost invariably represents a company or partnership or corporation, they tend for the most part to be conservative about infractions of "rules" and to make haste quite slowly toward more permissiveness.

One of the curious characteristics of discussions of "good English" and "correct grammar" in business is that such discussions provoke the strongest opinions and emotions from those who, as students, considered grammar "the driest subject I ever studied." Many executives over 40 would rather be caught with no clothes on than use "contact" as a verb, just to cite one example. It would be helpful if we could argue from a premise that correctness is always a method of achieving clarity—but this is not always true. "I ain't got my pay yet" is perfectly clear, but you wouldn't try using it in a letter or report as an effective representative of your company's writing. On the other hand, the incorrect "After eating lunch, the bus went its way" is a logical absurdity. There are two good reasons for avoiding incorrect writing: first, it annoys readers who recognize such mistakes, and, secondly, it presents a poor impression of the company or firm for which you write. For these two reasons, no one planning a career in business should accept sloppy or substandard English, nor should he accept excuses for his own or others' deficiencies in the use of English. Instead, he should subscribe to the viewpoint expressed in this reference section: *Certain standards of usage are generally accepted by the business community in letters, reports, and memos, and competent writers follow these standards.*

The danger here is that in emphasizing standards we become too *prescriptive*, the opposite of the "permissive" attitude toward usage. You can go too far in following rules. This is the mark of the purist, the office pest. He insists on observing rules that are becoming obsolete. Rules follow usage by what used to be called "cultivated people," not the other way around. About six hundred years ago Geoffrey Chaucer quite properly used triple negatives, as in "There was never no man nowhere so virtuous," but subsequent changes in usage have made this form of expression obsolete and ungrammatical. What you should aim at is the standard of best usage in business writing *today*. That usage is being affected enormously by increased casualness and informality, by the diminishing gap between our oral and written expression, and above all else, by the impact of mass media, particularly television. Yesterday's bad grammar may be today's most widely used phrase and tomorrow's archaic or obsolete form in the long perspective of linguistic change. As you read the rest of this section, therefore, you should temper the heavy boldface print of the rules with the wisdom of these five concepts, which have the endorsement of the National Council of Teachers of English:

1.   Language changes constantly.
2.   Change is normal.
3.   Spoken language is *the* language.
4.   Correctness rests on usage.
5.   All usage is relative.

The best policy is to try to stay up to date with regard to current usage, and you can begin to do so by forgetting two "rules" that for some reason seem to be stamped indelibly in the mind of almost everyone who has taken courses in English. The first is that you should try *to never split* an infinitive. The second is nicely stated in the following bit of verse:

> *The grammar has a rule absurb*
> *Which I would call an outworn myth:*
> *A preposition is a word*
> *You mustn't end a sentence with!*

These "rules" have a purpose: to avoid the lack of emphasis in a sentence ending on a minor note, such as a preposition; and to avoid the awkwardness of putting unnecessary words between *to* and the verb form of the infinitive.

But there are times when you'll find it less awkward to end with prepositions and to split infinitives. Said Sir Winston Churchill in an ironic comment on this overprissiness, "This is arrant pedantry up with which I will not put." The late Carl Van Doren, a great teacher and writer, used to tell a story to end all stories about prepositions. A father was asked by his small boy, who was sick in bed upstairs, to read from the boy's favorite book. He selected the wrong book and was greeted by, "What didya bring that book I don't want to be read to out of up for?" You'll have to try very hard to achieve such awkwardness, but try to avoid splitting the infinitive in the following sentence without changing the meaning:

He will try to more than justify the cost of an assistant.

("Try to justify more than the cost" and "try more than to justify the cost" do not convey the meaning of the statement. *More than* must be located so that it clearly refers to *justify*.)

Where split infinitives and concluding prepositions are less awkward, use them; where they can be avoided without unnaturally warping the word order of the sentence, avoid them. There are far more important things to remember in achieving correct English than these minor points, which have somehow attained a significance far beyond their worth.

The rest of this section attempts to do three things to help you meet the generally accepted standards of correctness in business writing:

1. *It states 10 principles which will aid you in avoiding the most frequent and most important errors in business writing.* This will give you a starting point, just as when you begin collecting classical records it is helpful to have a list of "the 10 classical records every music library must have." You may later decide you don't agree with the selection; they may not agree with your standards or with what you consider to be the standards of the business community. But, together with the topics discussed in Chapter 2 and 3, they will get you started.

2. *It attempts to reduce grammatical terminology to a minimum or to translate it, wherever possible, into other terms.* Nonetheless, a certain amount of grammatical shop talk cannot be avoided.

3. *It gives you an opportunity to test your knowledge of correct usage.* On pages 525 to 530 you will find 100 sentences taken from business letters, reports, and memos. If you think this part is not for you, skip over to the test. If you can correct the errors and explain the principles, that is, the reasons why the examples are incorrect, in 85 of them, your skepticism is justified, and you need not start in again right here.

Later in this reference section you will find a more conventional and comprehensive statement of rules, including those given here. It serves three purposes: an instructor may want to refer you to them when you write in college; or, more important, you may want to keep them for reference when you are writing, either in college or in your business career; and, finally, it relieves your author from having to say, "Consult a good handbook of grammar or composition for details." You will be urged frequently to consult a good dictionary, you have already encountered a list of recommended reading on the subject of word choice, and you will find enough grammatical principles in the reference section to solve most of your problems in business writing. You are especially encouraged to read the sections on punctuation, which has not been discussed previously.

TEN MAJOR PRINCIPLES

Subjects and Verbs

Since you express yourself in sentences, and since you can't write a sentence without a *subject* and a *verb*, these words constitute a good place to begin. If you're an adult you don't say "we is," "he are," or "you wasn't," although you may be guilty of "it don't," which means *it do not*. The rule—and it's a hard and fast one—states that *verbs must agree with their subjects in number* ("singular," meaning *one*; "plural," meaning *more than one*) *and person* ("first person," *I, we*; "second person," *you*; "third person," *he, she, it, they*).

The rule is simple. The difficulties arise when you are not sure whether the subject of a verb is plural or singular, or when you aren't sure even what the subject is. Principles 1 through 4 following are designed to help you in these situations.

Principle 1 Words intervening between the subject and verb do not affect the number of the verb.

Correct examples:

The manufacturing *processes*, which are under the direct control of the vice-president in charge of production at the head office, *are* extremely complex.

Particularly when you're dictating, you'll have a natural tendency to forget just what the subject of your sentence was and to think of intervening words— here, *control*, *production*, and *head office*—as affecting the number of the verb. They don't; and you should follow the same advice in handling this construction as the counsel given to speakers: *Keep your mind on the subject.*

Improvements in the annealing and cleaning process *were* a basic factor in this increased efficiency.

Here the subject, *improvements*, is plural; the intervening words are singular; and the businessman who originally wrote it succumbed to a tendency to let the last words affect his verb and used *was*.

Principle 2   **Words linked to the subject by expressions such as** *together with, as well as, along with, including, and not,* **and** *in addition to* **do not affect the number of the verb.**

Here, too, is an easy trap for dictators to fall into because of the tendency to lose sight of the subject.

Correct examples:

The office *manager*, as well as her two assistants and the three supervisors, *writes* concise reports.

This *example*, together with the ones cited in our last three reports, *shows* how important it is to correct this situation.

The *vice-president*, and not his reporting department head, *was* charged with this responsibility in the Procedures Manual.

The *statement* of policy, in addition to its general provisions, clauses, and applications, *is* wordy.

Principle 3   **When the subject is any of the following words or is limited (modified) by them**—*each, everybody, anybody, nobody, every, a person,* **and** *either*—**the verb must be singular. When the subject is** *neither* **or** *none,* **the verb is almost always singular.**

Correct examples:

Each of these men *has* instituted several changes during the last month.
Everybody in this office *is* permitted to take a 15-minute coffee break at 10 o'clock.
Neither of us *wants* that to happen.

Current usage is recognizing plural verbs after *neither*, and you will find constructions using *neither* to link plural nouns. In the latter case, a plural verb is demanded:

Neither the men nor their wives *want* to stay.

A plural verb after *none* is well-accepted in constructions such as this:

None of our employees *are* so incompetent as the men in his department.

You might note, incidentally, that the indefinite *it* always takes a singular verb:

It is the workers who join unions.

Principle 4 **When the subject is a collective noun, a word which by its meaning collects a lot of people or things—such as *committee, staff, company, crowd,* and *group*—the meaning you wish to convey should determine whether the subject is singular or plural.**

When you are thinking of the parts, units, or individuals comprised in the collective, make your verb plural; when you are thinking of the collective as a whole, make your verb singular. You will use the singular more frequently, as:

The *group was* interested in investing in new plant facilities.
The *staff is* holding a monthly meeting to discuss sales forecasts.

Occasionally, you will want to emphasize the individuals, as in:

The executive *staff are* listed on page 42 of the annual report.
The *committee were* evenly divided in supporting the two policies.

Verbs

The verb is a remarkably versatile part of speech: It describes action or situation, tells time (by its *tense*), and provides a general background of assumptions (by its *mood*). It can describe reality (in the *indicative mood*), give commands (in the *imperative*), or express certain assumptions or statements that are not true (in the *subjunctive*). Besides all this, it adapts itself to performing the functions of other parts of speech. When *-ing* is added, the verb can function as a noun (a *gerund*) or remain a verb (a *participle*). This versatility adds importance to the need for knowing just which role the verb is playing.

In the next section, under "Danglers and Squinters," we will take a look at the participle form of verbs. Here we will discuss tenses, an aspect of verbs that often seems to leave business writers tied in knots. Later, under V3a, you will find the major tenses of the verb *prepare*. Look these over and be sure you know what the tenses of a verb look like. Then observe the rule:

Principle 5   **Tenses of verbs in a sentence should accurately indicate the correct sequence of actions; the verb in a subordinate clause should therefore take a tense consistent with the verb in the main clause.**

If your sentence describes actions at different times, you must sort out the proper time sequence, decide what tense you want for the main clause, and then make the other clauses relate logically. For example:

> When the machine *stopped*, the foreman *realized* that no one *had oiled* it.

The main clause is *the foreman realized*, and it is in the past tense. We imply that the stopping came simultaneously with the realizing. (If we wanted to make clear that the stopping came before the realizing, we would use *had stopped* rather than *stopped*, and *after* in place of *when*.) The second subordinate clause *no one had oiled it* describes an action that clearly preceded both the stopping and the realizing. Since we have chosen to put the realizing in the past, we must put the oiling in the past perfect.

Here are two incorrect examples:

> When he *oiled* the machine, it *was ready* for service again. (The main clause is in the past tense, but the oiling had to take place before the machine was ready. The correct form is *had oiled*.)
>
> When he *retires* this month, the foreman *will complete* ten years of work for the company and *will train* over a thousand men during those years.

We have a specific point of time in mind here—the foreman's retirement date. As of that time he will be able to look back on a training job completed: He *will have trained* over a thousand men. As it stands, the clause means he will train the men on his retirement day. We might quibble over *complete*, too, and argue that it should be *will have completed*. Does the foreman complete ten years of work the moment he retires or the moment before? The point doesn't seem important.

Frequently, words like *after* and *before* and even *since, therefore,* and *because* clarify time relationships and eliminate reliance on tense to show sequence. Compare the following examples:

> When he had come, I left.
>
> After he came, I left.
>
> Before he came, I left.
>
> Because he came, I left.

The time sequence is quite clear in each sentence.

Danglers and Squinters

A dangling phrase is one that ought to refer to something in the sentence, but doesn't. Most dangling phrases are participial phrases, hence the common term "dangling particple."

By adding *-ing* (as in writ*ing*) to a verb, or by placing *being* or *having* before it (as in *being seen* or *having done*), we form participles. When such forms function as nouns (as in "*writing* is hard work," or "*having* the work *done* was a source of satisfaction to him"), they are called *gerunds* or *gerundives*. Since participles get heavy use in letters and reports, you should watch them to see that they follow this rule:

Principle 6   When a participle is used in a phrase (such as "*referring* to your letter," or "*reviewing* these results"), there must be something appropriate for the phrase to modify, to cling to or depend on.

Here is an example of a dangling participle:

While watching the Browns on TV recently, an argument broke out.

Even if you change the word order, an argument cannot watch the Browns. This is clearly nonsensical, but you are being equally illogical when you use any of the following constructions in your letters and reports:

Referring to your letter of March 25, the situation is being investigated.

Reviewing the results of the Greenpoint Plant, the same conclusions were reached.

It is only fair to point out that the meaning of these two sentences is probably clear, despite the dangling participles. For this reason, many business writers will defend the sentences as they stand and regard our criticism as characteristic of the "office pest." It may be that dangling participles will come to be accepted where there is no doubt as to what the reader means, but you are on safer ground when you avoid them. And unless you make a habit of avoiding them, you may find yourself using them to create unclear or even humorous statements like the following example from a London newspaper's description of a race won by a horse from the royal stables:

Sired by the Royal Stallion, the Queen could not but feel satisfaction at the result.

Usually the dangling participle results from the use of the passive voice.

One method of correcting the construction is to make the doer of the action in the participle serve as the subject of the sentence (ask yourself *who* is referring to the letter), and eliminate the passive voice:

> Referring to your letter of March 25, *we* are investigating the situation.
> Reviewing the results of the Greenpoint Plant, *the committee* reached the same conclusions.

A second method of correcting the dangling construction is to change the phrase containing the participle to a clause (by giving it a subject and verb) and eliminate the participle.

> *While we were watching the Browns on TV*, an argument broke out.

> *After the committee reviewed the results of the Greenpoint Plant*, the same conclusions were reached.

Sometimes a phrase which refers to something in the sentence, and is therefore not a dangler, is so located that the reader is prevented from seeing the reference clearly. For example:

> The testimonial dinner will be held in the grand ballroom of the hotel *consisting of the regular banquet fare.*

The italicized participial phrase modifies *dinner* and should be placed next to it in accordance with this simple rule:

Principle 7   Modifiers must be located so that it is clear what they modify.

We have already discussed the matter of logical location of the parts of a sentence in Chapter 2, under "Organization of a Sentence," so we won't deal with it any further here except to note the special problem of the "squinter." A squinter is a modifier located so that it might refer to more than one element in the sentence; the reader doesn't know which. For example:

> Even though it will take six years for the machines to pay for themselves, if conditions do not bring about a change in prices, the investment is decidedly attractive over the long run.

Does the *if* clause refer to *it will take six years* or to *the investment is attractive?*

Pronouns

If verbs and nouns play leading roles, pronouns may be called *stand-ins*. They take the place of nouns and serve the highly useful function of giving variety to such monotonous repetitions as this:

Mr. Smith wrote a report in which Mr. Smith summed up the observations Mr. Smith made based on Mr. Smith's six months' stay at the Brookside Plant.

Troublesome as pronouns may be at times, this sentence should make you thankful that you can use them in your cast of characters. And their function as substitutes or stand-ins gives you the clue to why they are troublesome. Basically, your problem is to notify your reader without a shadow of doubt for *whom* or *what* your pronoun is substituting.

When Mr. Smith reported the matter to the proper department head, he told him he would take action.

This is as bad a business sentence as you will ever see, because it fails to do what business communication must do: tell the reader clearly and unmistakably what the actual situation is. Who told whom? Who will take action? The reader doesn't know. Worse than ungrammatical, awkward, and non-standard forms of English—bad as they are—is ambiguous English in business, and a large amount of this ambiguity derives from careless use of pronouns.

Reference of Pronouns

A pronoun stands for a noun; the noun for which it stands is called its *antecedent.* Your prime responsibility when you use *he, she, it, they, who, which, this, that,* and other pronouns is to see that they refer unmistakably to their antecedents. There are certain exceptions. We can use *it,* for example, in an indefinite sense: "it rains," "it becomes more difficult," "it was felt," etc. But then we must be sure we don't create confusion by mixing an indefinite *it* with one intended to refer to something specific.

It (indefinite) is the responsibility of the management to see that *it* (supposed to refer to *management*) gets reports promptly; to do this, *it* (indefinite) is necessary to have *its* (management's?) report writers properly prepared.

The principle to keep in mind is this:

Principle 8 **Pronouns must refer unmistakably to their antecedents, and relative pronouns—such as** *who, which, that*—**must be placed as close as possible to their antencedents.**

Here are some incorrect examples:

We are sending you a check for the defective part which we hope will prove satisfactory. (Not the defective part, we hope, which has already proved unsatisfactory.)

During the second half of the discussion of Mr. Green's report, it was decided that it would be unnecessary to continue it. (Continue the report, the discussion?)

She had already informed the typist that she would be responsible for the general form of letters. (Who is responsible?)

Our economy of operation, achieved through an intensive work-simplification program, has eliminated the former high cost of production. This we can now pass on to our customers. (A new method of losing customers by handing them high costs.)

The supervisor told the young accountant that his statement was incorrect. (Whose statement?)

Selling has always been this young man's major interest, and that is why he is looking for employment as one in your company. (One what?)

We can correct these statements in this way:

We are sending you a check for the defective part, and we hope this adjustment is satisfactory to you.

During the second half of the discussion of Mr. Green's report, the committee decided that he need not continue the report (*or* decided that further discussion of the report was unnecessary).

The supervisor, who was responsible for the general form of letters, had already told the typist of this responsibility.

By getting rid of high production costs through an intensive work-simplification program, we have achieved greater economy of operation. The savings we can now hand on to our customers.

The young accountant's statement was incorrect, the supervisor told him.

Selling has always been this young man's major interest; that is why he wants to be a salesman in your company.

These examples show what you can do to clear up vague pronoun references. Occasionally you will have to repeat words, but repetition is better than ambiguity. Sometimes you will have to recast the whole sentence or break it into two sentences.

Case of Pronouns

In their role as stand-ins for nouns, English pronouns have the troublesome trait of changing their garb when they perform different functions of the same role. If you think you have troubles as an English producer, though, you should be thankful that you aren't in charge of a language production in German or Latin, where four or six such changes are possible, or, to take an extreme, in Finnish, which has no less than fifteen cases! This functional change of garb is called *case*. When English nouns change case, they affect only one minor costume change. You can use *letter* as subject, as in "The letter was written," or as object, as in "He wrote the letter." The word remains the same. The only alteration is in the possessive, as in "The letter's style is objectionable." Your major attention to case, therefore, can be concentrated on certain pronouns. The terms used to describe the three cases illustrate their functions— *subjective, possessive, objective.* Here are the changes of case you ought to keep an eye on:

Subjective	I	you	he	she	it	we	they	who	whoever
Possessive	my	your	his	her	its*	our	their	whose	whosever
Objective	me	you	him	her	it	us	them	whom	whomever

*Not *it's*, which means "it is."

This is not an overwhelming list, and you are well advised to keep it in mind and to place special emphasis on *who, whose,* and *whom,* which particularly plague business writers.

Principle 9   The form (case) of pronouns must suit their function, as follows:

a. *A pronoun as the object of a preposition must always take the objective case.* (Prepositions relate nouns or pronouns to some other word in the sentence. Among the most frequently used prepositions are *at, by, in, for, from, with, to, on, between, except, below, above,* and *under.*)

b. *A pronoun modifying a gerund uses the possessive case.* (A gerund is a verb used as a noun: "*Swimming* is good exercise.")

c. *A pronoun used to explain, to give in detail what is covered by another word* (this is called *apposition*), *takes the same case as the word which it explains.*

Here are examples. You might note that your intuition is especially likely to let you down here and lead you to incorrect constructions.

a.   Between you and *me*, this must remain strictly confidential. (*Me* is object of the preposition *between*.)

This report did not agree with the previous one submitted by Mr. Jones and *her*. (*Her* is object of the preposition *by*.)

Copies were went only to the executive staff and *him* as secretary. (*Him* is object of the preposition *to*.)

He has been a capable employee with *whom* I have worked closely. (*Whom* is object of the preposition *with*.)

No one from our company attended except Mr. Jones and *us*. (*Us* is object of the preposition *except*.)

b.   We appreciated *your* writing us frankly. (*Writing* is a gerund; *your* is possessive.)

We did not learn about *his* being in the city until too late. (*Being* is a gerund; *his* is possessive.)

c.   Only three employees could be located when the accident occurred—Mr. Smith, Mr. Henry, and *I*. (*I* is in apposition with *employees*, which is subjective case.)

There was some question as to whose responsibility it was—*his* or *mine*. (*Whose* is possessive; *his* and *mine* must be in the same case.)

You know that pronouns used as subjects of verbs are subjective case, and objects of verbs are objective case. Here are some situations affecting *who* and *whom* which cause difficulty:

He is one of the people *who*, I think, should be considered for the position. (The difficulty here arises from *I think*, which actually is a parenthetical kind of comment injected into the middle of the sentence. *Who* is the subject of *should be considered* and must be subjective case.)

He is the man *who*, you will remember, was interviewed last year. (This is like the previous sentence, with *you will remember* as the interjected parenthetical comment.)

On November 12, Mr. Smith, our representative, questioned the dealer as to *who* was responsible for this misunderstanding. (This type of involved sentence causes confusion because many writers think they must use *whom* as the object of the preposition *to*. Actually, your primary obligation is to provide a subject for the verb *was responsible*. This situation arises from the fact that an expression such as "the person" or "the individual" is understood, but not expressed, immediately before *who*. By saying this more simply, you can avoid all the confusion: "Mr. Smith questioned the dealer to find out who was responsible for the misunderstanding.")

We would appreciate your letting us know *whom* you addressed your reply to. (This usage shows some signs of breaking down, but in formal communication, like letters and reports, you will do well to stick to the objective *whom* as object of the preposition *to*. The sentence could be improved and the case of *whom* made more obvious by moving the concluding preposition: "We would appreciate your letting us know to whom you addressed your reply.")

Our receptionist is instructed to jot down this information: *Who* called? *Whom* did he ask for? (*Whom* is objective after the preposition *for*. The best method of analyzing grammatical problems in interrogative sentences is either to turn them around: "He did ask for *whom*," or to eliminate the concluding preposition: "For *whom* did he ask?" As in the previous example, this usage is breaking down. In speech we say "Who did he ask for?" but it is just as well to observe the rule in written communication.)

Principle 10   The spelling of all words should be correct; where there is any doubt, a good dictionary should be checked.

Admittedly, in an era of atomic fission and lunar exploration, the ability to spell does not rate as one of our highest skills. Nonetheless, it *is* assumed to be an acquisition of educated citizens who are motivated by a desire to follow accepted usage. You can test these generalities best by noting your own reaction if you were to receive a letter or report in which these errors occurred:

> We recieved your request and it occured to us that you would get prompter delivery if we sent the heaviest items seperately by freight.

Quite properly, the reader concludes that such a writer is either uneducated or contemptuous of correct usage.

Admittedly, too, certain words are difficult to spell. (You can win bets with your friends, most of whom will be unable to spell these five words: desiccate, rarefy, vilify, supersede, inoculate—but they are hardly expressions used frequently in business writing.) The solution to your spelling problems is fairly obvious: learn to spell the words you use frequently, and use a good dictionary to find out the proper spelling for the others. To assist you, we have included in the Reference Section under "Mechanics" first of all a helpful list of the 25 words most frequently misspelled and then a list of 300 words frequently misspelled in business writing. Both lists make an excellent place for you to begin if you want to check your ability to spell correctly.

In this section we have presented 10 principles which should help you to attain correct usage in your letters, reports and memos. By committing them to memory, you can learn to avoid the oft-repeated errors of much business writing. By applying them constantly, you will find that you are improving your efficiency as a writer because through practice you will soon learn to concentrate on *what* you want to say instead of *how* to say it correctly. These 10 principles will not, of course, solve all your problems of correctness in writing; but they will carry you a long way because they are based on an analysis of the actual errors that occur most frequently in business writing. (In the following pages you will find a much more detailed analysis of grammar, punctuation, and spelling.) You can have a little fun in the process of going through the following tongue-in-cheek "instructions" by Marie Longyear, manager of editing services at McGraw-Hill Book Company:

—Subject and verb always has to agree.

—Being bad grammar, the writer will not use dangling participles.

—Parallel construction with coordinate conjunctions is not only an aid to clarity but also is the mark of a good writer.

—Do not use a foreign term when there is an adequate English *quid pro quo.*

—If you must use a foreign term, it is *de rigor* to use it correctly.

—It behooves the writer to avoid archaic expressions.

—Do not use hyperbole; not one writer in a million can use it effectively.

—Avoid clichés like the plague.

—Mixed metaphors are a pain in the neck and ought to be thrown out the window.

—In scholarly writing, don't use contractions.

—A truly good writer is always especially careful to practically eliminate the too-frequent use of adverbs.

—Use a comma before nonrestrictive clauses which are a common source of difficulty.

—Placing a comma between subject and predicate, is not correct.

—Parenthetical words however should be enclosed in commas.

—Consult the dictionary frequently to avoid mispelling.*

A Test of Correctness in Business Writing

In a more serious vein, you can test yourself with the following 100 sentences containing many of the most frequent errors in business writing. A few of the sentences contain more than one error. You ought to be able to correct the error and to state the general principle it violates.

1. Upon reviewing your credit references, a decision to open an account was made.

2. Since our products are only available through dealers, we have asked Mr. Jones to immediately get in touch with you.

*Reprinted by permission of the author.

3. We are making every effort to find out as to whom was responsible for this oversight; in the meantime, we want you to know that we appreciate your calling this matter to our attention.

4. This was one of those errors which is particularly unfortunate when it happens to an old customer like you.

5. These advantages in addition to the clear presentation and simple style makes this a book you will want for your office.

6. The increase in sales as well as economies of operation and recent wage adjustments make an optimistic forecast possible for the next six months.

7. We only use the finest materials and most skilled craftsmen.

8. He had sent one of those letters which is usually better thrown into the wastebasket.

9. Three representatives were asked to be present—Mr. Smith, Mr. Jones, and myself. With the purpose of insisting that all kinds of businesses be represented to give a cross section of Blanktown's industry.

10. When the letter you sent to the Main Office was not forwarded, there was naturally some confusion between their accounting division and I.

11. Neither of these possibilities were explained in your letter to us.

12. These facts are simply background material, and if they are to be included at all should have been condensed into a paragraph or two.

13. Every one of our 48 inspectors have been trained at the factory before they are given a territory.

14. We were pleased to learn that the crowd at your opening were so enthusiastic about the new models.

15. He is one of those people who I suppose we should consider.

16. I own a car that the brakes don't work.

17. I wish I was there when the report was presented.

18. Referring to your request of October 22, the brochure on "How Sales Affect Production" is out of print, and I am very sorry that we cannot send you a copy for that reason.

19. This is a growing company. Their sales have increased steadily in the past and I think they will continue to do so.

20. The personnel policy which had been submitted to all the administrative staff and to the department heads were then issued.

21. Neither of these machines can be used at speeds which are beyond their capacities. Which are listed on the metal tags attached to the base.

22. A consistent policy and not the trivial amounts of these discounts are our first concern.

23. If anyone else was in his place, they would do the same thing.

24. He as well as our thousands of other representatives have learned that selling Blanko Products in spare hours pays big dividends.

25. Among the services we intend to provide is constant supervision of the product and prompt replacement of parts.

26. I certainly agree that I would not expect this mistake to be repeated and if I was in your place, I would expect an adjustment.

27. The dealer who had sent three orders and two requests for window displays were visited by our representative.

28. Neither of these letters contain information about the exact model number or the date when you purchased the equipment.

29. If we do not hear from you in five days, we shall have to turn your account over to our collection agency which, I am sure, neither of us wants.

30. Beginning work on a Monday, he found he was not paid until the following week.

31. This product not only has years of tested experience behind it but also a reputation for efficiency established by those who have used it.

32. We should have asked them to have stayed.

33. The writer of the report and not the three accountants who supplied the facts and cost estimates believe the change is necessary.

34. Each of our representatives have told us of your interest in Blanko Products. A report by which we are highly gratified.

35. In this assortment is contained a wide variety of toys for children of all ages and a set of dolls in authentic historical costumes.

36. To everyone who worked so hard on this sales campaign and to our sales manager especially go our appreciation for a job well done.

37. He notified the new employee that he would see the office manager about his office that day.

38. Her income depends on rents which is less stable than income from bonds.

39. When the machine stopped we realized it had not been oiled and since then we oiled it daily.

40. Enclosed with this letter was a signed affidavit and a carbon copy of his request to our main office.

41. A question has arisen as to whose territory Belleville is—Mr. Smith or me.

42. Neither of us want to see your credit reputation jeopardized by only an amount of $72.19.

43. He has been a conscientious employee who I have enjoyed working with and who I will miss.

44. He presented a great many reasons why he did not approve them going to lunch at the earlier period.

45. Your last order as well as the two previous ones were sent, as you instructed, by truck.

46. This campaign was conducted to reduce the number of accidents at the end of the year which was successful.

47. In my letter of August 4, I said that we would send our technical expert to call as to who was the person to see.

48. Along with this offer goes a money-back guarantee and a six-month supply of detergent to make your wash days easy.

49. A loss of morale could be caused among workers kept underground by officious foremen.

50. Employing such communication media as newspapers, posters and employee meetings, the financial position of the firm was presented.

51. Neither of our field representatives were able to get to the factory on such short notice.

52. I would gladly grant this request if it was possible for me to do so; but we have a policy of keeping such information confidential.

53. This was one of those situations which is unfortunate but which are almost inevitable in sending out large mailings.

54. I don't believe anyone besides the president checks the treasurer's report as carefully as himself.

55. We are hoping to find a man for this job that he gets along well with other people.

56. The departmental staff were planning to attend the local Community Chest Luncheon at which the results of our company giving was to be announced.

57. Your signature as well as those of two members of your Board of Directors are required to complete the document.

58. We must reward every worker to raise our production standards to meet those our competitors who is trying hard.

59. Included in the group invited to attend the sales conference were three dealers—Mr. Smith, you, and me.

60. The group were agreed in inviting you to be the speaker.

61. He is one of those rare people whom I think are never at a loss for words.

62. The Annual Report together with our last two quarterly reports to shareholders are being sent to you by our Public Relations Department.

63. We are sending you this check to compensate you for the loss of time which we hope you will use for something you want.

64. We certainly appreciate you writing us as one of the 15 companies which was selected.

65. I expect that salary increases this year that will please us all.

66. Referring to your letter of April 23, in which you requested information about our Model U Home Air Conditioning Unit.

67. Trends in consumer buying and the individual's preference for one brand name affects the situation.

68. To the best of our knowledge, this company is well known for their excellent working conditions.

69. It is apparent that it was his responsibility to remove the hazard; since he didn't carry it out, he should at least have reported it.

70. He only does what he is told and that is done none too well.

71. Being unaccustomed to long reports, this one has been kept brief.

72. A person like you who pays their bill promptly is the backbone of American business.

73. Every one of his references speak highly of his business abilities; this will, of course, affect his chance of getting a position here.

74. The committee members disagreed and has to meet again.

75. In this invoice is included the charges for the past month.

76. Our sales are falling, but we hope they can be reversed next year.

77. He has sent us this information too late on the sales increase which was unfortunate.

78. The board of directors meets this week and are going to debate the question of whether to expand.

79. Referring to our telephone conversation yesterday, the materials you asked for are enclosed.

80. The accountants give us reports that are in such technical language that we can't understand always.

81. Neither the file copies nor the original, which was sent on March 12, were found; we appreciate your waiting so patiently for this information.

82. Included in our last letter was the statement of terms, a signature card, and an air mail envelope, none of which has yet been received.

83. Concluding that this customer was a poor risk, the question was submitted to the Central Office for decision.

84. This is only one of the many problems which confronts the writer in business and which this service will help you to solve.

85. With our granting of this credit goes our best wishes for continued success in the expansion of your marketing facilities.

86. A smaller staff might be appropriate for handling the regular volume of clerical work but not a larger one.

87. Either of these products are ideally suited for the purpose you mentioned in your letter of February 2.

88. Will you please let us know who you sent your original request to since it apparently was not received at this office.

89. We will try to replace the machinery that the cost of operation is too high, this year.

90. They urged that he was considered for the position.

91. Necessary to complete this agreement is your signature on the contract and three references from firms with whom you have done business.

92. Attached to this letter is an employment form and three sheets which your references should fill out.

93. Everybody in our office want to express their appreciation to you for your thoughtfulness.

94. As analyses such as was requested in your report constitute an important source of executive decision, I will attempt to give you some helpful suggestions.

95. The foreman could help the new employee to increase his output without much difficulty.

96. After taking all the factors into consideration and analyzing the potential sales in your area, your best course seems to us to be buying on a cash basis for the next six months.

97. To make up for the noise and dirt employees who work in the foundry we offer extra pay and shorter hours.

98. If a delay was to occur we can ship by truck but we will never have had to do it yet.

99. The supervisor puts his name on the notice board to humiliate him every time an employee is late.

100. The store in Lee, Massachusetts, is doing very well and its population is only 5,271.

PARTS OF SPEECH

If in our communication we had only to consider words as individual units of thought, writing the English language would be comparatively simple. To be sure, English words change form in what is called *inflection*; but basically, most problems arise from the relationship of words or word groups to one another within the sentence. This branch of grammar is called *syntax*; the branch of grammar devoted to the study of the eight parts of speech and their inflections is known as *morphology*.

But these are academic definitions. What the writer in business usually needs is the answer to such questions as: Should that verb be singular or plural? Should it be *I* or *me*? Should I say *was* or *were*? How do I punctuate that clause? These are questions which businessmen might appropriately label "matters of procedure"; for answers, modern management would ask "What is the policy?" or if there is none, they would formulate one.

Grammatical policy is rather clearly formulated, though it is not nearly as rigid as many college students think. In the following pages, you will find the policy statements which apply to the parts of speech; when you're in doubt about writing procedure, you'll find it good business to consult this policy manual, which is not intended to be complete but to refresh your mind on the major points of syntax. All of this derives from the fundamental principle that all parts of a sentence must fit together or must *agree*, as it is called, in the working relationship of the sentence. Since you cannot write a sentence without a subject and verb, we will start with the verb and then go on to the other parts of speech which make up the sentence:

Nouns and pronouns
Adjectives and adverbs
Prepositions and conjunctions

These are, of course, seven parts of speech, *interjections* (Hello there! Alas! Wonderful! How about that! and similar exclamations), the eighth, present no grammatical problems, so we can ignore them. Following the parts of speech, we will analyze the sentence, modifiers, and problems of logic and consistency in writing.

Verbs

Verbs are the words or word groups used to make an assertion (he *leaves* tomorrow) or to express a state or condition (business *is* good). The properties of verbs are discussed in the rules which follow. Since no complete sentence can be written without a verb, writers in business ought to take special care that their sentences always contain verbs. Verbless sentences, known as *incomplete thoughts*, are discussed in the section on "The Sentence," but they occur so frequently in business writing as to justify emphasis here. Only by making sure that every sentence has a verb can business writers avoid such often repeated errors as the following:

Not: Referring to your letter of August 16, in which you requested our latest catalogue.

But: Thank you for your letter of August 16, in which you requested our latest catalogue.

Not: This being the decision and the final business of the committee.

But: This decision was the final business of the committee.

Not: To accomplish this efficiently and with a minimum of confusion resulting from the transfer of machinery.

But: To accomplish this efficiently and with a minimum of confusion, we must plan the transfer of machinery carefully.

Not: No word as yet as to when the typist will return.

But: We have received no word yet as to when the typist will return.

Agreement of Subject and Verb

V1 *A verb always agrees with its subject in number and person.*

This rule is basic and universal. When we say that a verb *agrees* with its subject, we mean that they have the same *person* (first, second, or third) and *number* (singular or plural). Since English verbs (except *to be*) have just one form for singular and plural and for all persons (except the third person singular—I *write*; he *writes*), this basic rule would seem to be easy to apply. The real difficulty in applying it arises from certain specific situations where the subject is hard to identify or where its number or person may seem confusing. These specific situations are explained in the following rules.

V1a *The number of the verb is not affected by words intervening between the verb*

When business writers dictate their letters or reports, they frequently lose sight of the subject. Because intervening words may be of different number, they tend to "sound" as if they governed the verb. Notice how easily this could happen if you were speaking the following sentences:

Incorrect: The decision to add 11 new salesmen and to conduct intensive advertising campaigns in industrial areas *were made* at the monthly meeting.
Correct: The *decision* to add 11 new salesmen and to conduct intensive advertising campaigns in industrial areas *was made* at the monthly meeting.

Incorrect: One of the new models sent for exhibition purposes *were lost* in transit.
Correct: *One* of the new models sent for exhibition purposes *was lost* in transit.

Incorrect: These improvements in the filter and in the motor *makes* it our outstanding buy.
Correct: *These improvements* in the filter and in the motor *make* it our outstanding buy.

The best time to correct such errors is when you revise reports, when you sign letters or memos. Read them over *carefully* to see that verbs and subjects agree.

V1b *The number of the verb is not affected by such phrases, joined to the subject, as as well as, together with, along with, in addition to, including, and and not.*

Not: The department head together with his three assistants *report* weekly to the head of the division.
But: The *department head* together with his three assistants *reports* weekly to the head of the division.

Not: The clean-cut lines as well as the noiseless operation *makes* this an attractive addition for your kitchen.

But: The *clean-cut lines* as well as the noiseless operation *make* this an attractive addition for your kitchen.

Not: Your promptness in meeting your obligations as well as your unfailing cooperation and courtesy *have made* our relationship a pleasant one.

But: Your *promptness* in meeting your obligations as well as your unfailing cooperation and courtesy *has made* our relationship a pleasant one.

V1c *When any of the following words is the subject of the sentence or modifies the subject, the verb is always singular:* each, everybody, anybody, nobody, every, a person, either, *and* neither.

Not: Everybody in the entire organization *are* responsible.
But: *Everybody* in the entire organization *is* responsible.

Not: Neither of them *were* qualified for that position.
But: *Neither* of them *was* qualified for that position.

Not: Every man and woman in our company *are* factory-trained to service these machines.
But: *Every* man and woman in our company *is* factory-trained to service these machines.

Not: Either of those decisions *are* difficult at best.
But: *Either* of those decisions *is* difficult at best.

Be especially careful to distinguish this use of *either* and *neither* as pronouns from *either . . . or, neither . . . nor* as correlative conjunctions.

V1d *Collective nouns (words like* company, group, staff, committee, crowd, *and certain expressions of money, time, or distance) are singular when they are thought of as a unit; they are plural when the individuals or individual elements are thought of. For the most part, business writing properly treats the great majority of such words as singular in number.*

Correct: The committee *has* sent in *its* report.
             The group *is* in a meeting.
             Twenty-five years *is* a long time for a company to stay in business.
             A thousand dollars *is* a lot of money to save on just one process.
             This company *has* an excellent reputation.

In such sentences as the following, where the individuals or individual elements are stressed, the collective noun can be considered plural:

Correct: The committee *were* unable to agree.

The board *are listed* individually on the inside cover of the Annual Report.

V1e *Subjects joined by* and *require a plural verb.*

Correct: The report and the accompanying letter *are* being sent.

The chief accountant and I *have* been invited.

This is so obvious as to require no special emphasis. Only one situation can cause confusion; when the *and* connects two titles or designations which apply to the same person, the verb is singular:

Correct: Our comptroller and treasurer *is* the person for this assignment.

The vice-president and director of services *informs* us of this.

V1f *When the subject contains singluar and plural words linked by* either . . . or, neither . . . nor, *the verb agrees with the subject closer to it.*

Correct: Either the method used or the *principles* involved in this investigation *were* wrong.

Neither the chief accountants nor the financial *vice-president was* able to attend.

V1g *When the normal order of words in the sentence is shifted so that the subject comes after the verb, the verb agrees with the word which is actually the subject.*

This shift in the normal pattern of sentences is a good device for varying sentence patterns, but don't lose sight of your subject in the shuffle.

Correct: Included in this offer *are* a six months' guarantee, a complete set of instructions, and one free inspection of the equipment. (To locate subjects in this inverted order, find the verb—*is included? are included?*—then ask *what* is included? Here, the subject is *guarantee, set of instructions, free inspection;* hence the verb must be *are included.*)

Among the items on the bill *were* an overcharge of $2.19 and an omission of the credit for my last payment.

To these and to the others who cooperated on this venture *go* our congratulations and best wishes.

V1h *When the sentence begins with* there is *or* there are, *the verb agrees with the subject which follows it.*

Correct: There *is* little time for long-range planning. (Subject is *time*, singular.)

There *are* many reasons for doing this.

There *are* so many communications needed to conduct business today.

V1i *The verb agrees with the subject and not with the predicate complement with which it is sometimes confused.*

Not: His chief concern *are* his many co-workers.
But: His chief concern *is* his many co-workers.
Not: The most important sales feature *are* the three new elements in the design.
But: The most important sales feature *is* the three new elements in the design.

Careful writers will note that even the correct versions of this construction are awkward and can be greatly improved by recasting the sentence.

The welfare of his many co-workers is his chief concern.

The three new elements in the design comprise the most important sales feature.

V1j *Certain nouns though plural in form are singular in meaning and, therefore, take singular verbs.*

Usually singular: *news, economics, ethics, mathematics, whereabouts.*

Correct: The news *is* good.
The ethics of business *prevents* that conduct.
His whereabouts *is* unknown.

Other words with similar form like *tactics, politics, acoustics* are usually plural. The best guide as to whether a specific word is singular or plural is to consult a good dictionary.

Verbs — Mood

V2 *Use the correct mood of the verb to indicate whether the statement is a fact, a command, or a wish or unreality. The English language has three moods, the indicative, the imperative, the subjunctive.*

Indicative is the mood of actuality, reality. This you use about 99 percent of the time.

Imperative is the mood of command. "Bring your textbook to class next time." The "polite imperative" occurs frequently in letters and may be used without a question mark in such expressions as "Will you please let us know if there is anything else we can do."

Subjunctive is the mood of unreality, improbability, and, finally, of high desirability in formal motions or strong necessity or insistence, as in collection letters.

V2a *Use the subjunctive mood in verbs when you make statements that are contrary to fact, highly improbable, or expressive of formal wishes, as in parliamentary procedure, nominating, or electing.*

Since the verb *to be* causes most subjunctive troubles, all you need to remember is that:

a. The present tense uses *were* in all persons.
b. As an auxiliary form (that is, part of other verbs), *be* is used after verbs like *ask, urge, insist, require, vote, move,* etc.

Here are correct uses of the subjunctive as it occurs commonly in business writing:

> If I *were* you, I would call on him again. (Contrary to fact, since I am not you.)
> If that *were* to occur, we would have to cut production in half. (A highly improbable supposition.)
> He moved that the meeting *be adjourned.* (Following a formal expression of wish; note the *be* as auxiliary form.)
> I, therefore, urge that this *be reconsidered.*
> We must insist that this payment *be made* within three days.
> He strongly urged that all violations *be reported* within twenty-four hours.
> If he *were* to do that, we would cancel the contract.
> We are, therefore, requesting that your check *be sent* immediately.
> He insisted that he *be given* one more chance.
> If I *were* in his place, I would take the following action.
> I wish this report *were* more simple and less technical.
> He then ordered that all requisitions *be signed* by department heads.
> I wish it *were* possible to comply with your request.
> Even if that *were* to happen, we have a big backlog of orders.

Verbs — Tense

V3 *Use the correct tense of the verb to express time accurately.*

To express various times and their relationships accurately, the English language has six tenses — present, past, future, present perfect, past perfect, and

future perfect. The keys to forming all these tenses are the *principal parts*—
the present, the past, and the past participle—*employ, employed, employed*.
Employ is a regular verb because it maintains its basic form and adds *-ed, -ed*
to form past tense and participle. Irregular English verbs change these forms—
write, wrote, written; sing, sang, sung; lie, lay, lain. The best guide to whether
a verb is regular or irregular is the dictionary; but note carefully that if the verb
is regular, *only one form is given*, i.e., *employ*, but where it is irregular, all
three forms are given, i.e., *sing, sang, sung*.

Formation of Tenses

V3a *Learn how to form the tenses of regular verbs.*

Here are the major tenses of the verb *prepare*—principal parts, *prepare, prepared, prepared*; infinitive forms, *to prepare, to have prepared, to be prepared,
to have been prepared*; participles, *preparing, having prepared, being prepared*, and *having been prepared*.

INDICATIVE MOOD

Present tense	*Active*	
	I prepare	we prepare
	you prepare	you prepare
	he prepares	they prepare
	Passive	
	I am prepared	we are prepared
	you are prepared	you are prepared
	he is prepared	they are prepared
Past tense	*Active*	
	I prepared	we prepared
	you prepared	you prepared
	he prepared	they prepared
	Passive	
	I was prepared	we were prepared
	you were prepared	you were prepared
	he was prepared	they were prepared
Future tense	*Active*	
	I shall prepare	we shall prepare
	you will prepare	you will prepare
	he will prepare	they will prepare

Passive

I shall be prepared	we shall be prepared
you will be prepared	you will be prepared
he will be prepared	they will be prepared

Present perfect tense

Active

I have prepared	we have prepared
you have prepared	you have prepared
he has prepared	they have prepared

Passive

I have been prepared	we have been prepared
you have been prepared	you have been prepared
he has been prepared	they have been prepared

Past perfect tense

Active

I had prepared	we had prepared
you had prepared	you had prepared
he had prepared	they had prepared

Passive

I had been prepared	we had been prepared
you had been prepared	you had been prepared
he had been prepared	they had been prepared

Future perfect tense

Active

I shall have prepared	we shall have prepared
you will have prepared	you will have prepared
he will have prepared	they will have prepared

Passive

I shall have been prepared	we shall have been prepared
you will have been prepared	you will have been prepared
he will have been prepared	they will have been prepared

As one student once commented, "This is an awe-inspiring mess of tenses." But you need not let it worry you because in actual writing you might have to contrive some highly ingenious time sequences before you used certain of these forms. What you need to know is the basic pattern of how the tenses are formed, the proper sequence of tenses, and the difference between the use of active and passive voice.

V3b *Learn the principal parts of irregular verbs.*

To help you with the formation of tenses of certain irregular verbs which are widely used in business, here are the principal parts of those that cause difficulty:

arise	arose	arisen
begin	began	begun
bid	bid	bid *(to make an offer)*
break	broke	broken
choose	chose	chosen
deal	dealt	dealt
dive	dived	dived
get	got	got or gotten
lay	laid	laid
lead	led	led
lend	lent	lent
lie	lay	lain *(to recline; to be situated)*
lie	lied	lied *(to tell an untruth)*
loose	loosed	loosed
lose	lost	lost
pay	paid	paid
prove	proved	proved
raise	raised	raised *(to cause to rise, as salaries)*
rise	rose	risen *(to get up of its own power)*
set	set	set
sit	sat	sat
write	wrote	written

Proper Sequence of Tenses

V3c *Use each tense to express the time of the action accurately and to show its relationship to other verbs in the sentence.*

1. Use the present tense:
   a. To express present time:

   I interview, I am interviewing, etc.

   b. To express actions which take place habitually or ideas which are permanently true:

   Every day he *opens* the store at 9 o'clock.

   He always *tells* his employees that he believes in them.

   In his speech he emphasized his conviction that honesty *is* the best policy. (Not "honesty *was* the best policy"; presumably, this is a permanent truth.)

   He had been taught that concise writing *is* the best writing.

2. Use the past tense to express action completed in the past.

I *wrote* to him yesterday.

He *told* me in his weekly conference.

The only difficulty here is with irregular verbs, where the second principal part (*the past*) and the third principal part (*the past participle*) are confused. Hence result such illiteracies as:

I *swum* for I *swam*; I *drunk* for I *drank*; I *laid in the hammock* for I *lay in the hammock*.

3.   Use the future tense to indicate that an action or condition will take place in the future.

I *shall write* to him.

You *will be attending* the convention next week.

V3d *In the more formal types of business writing, distinguish between the use of* shall *and* will.

Perhaps no phase of English has been the subject of greater dispute than the distinction between *shall* and *will*. (The only other candidate within recent years would be the famous "This is *me*, Winston Churchill, speaking.") In speech, most of us get around the whole subject easily by saying *I'll*, *we'll*, *they'll*; or we express futurity by *going to* or *about to* as "He is going to do it Tuesday." Many writers still have strong convictions that the only correct way to express simple future in formal writing is:

I shall do it	we shall do it
you will do it	you will do it
he will do it	they will do it

and that is strong determination can only be expressed through:

I will do it	we will do it
you shall do it	you shall do it
he shall do it	they shall do it

There is little question that this distinction is breaking down; many business writers use *shall* and *will* almost interchangeably. The extent of this change is illustrated by a story widely current some twenty years ago. It seems that a group of English professors were walking along a lake when an unusually obtuse freshman shouted from the lake, "I will drown; nobody shall help me!"—and the professors let him drown. Recently, another professor told this story, without explanation, to a group of students, and none saw the point.

Because the lines of distinction between *shall* and *will* have become greatly blurred, you will have to use your common sense in such sentences as:

We *shall* insist on payment. (Would your insistence be stronger with *will*? Probably not.)

Will you make an address at our annual meeting? (This sentence illustrates why the distinction breaks down, because *will* here is in the sense of "are you willing to." Some purists insist that such a question should anticipate the answer ("I shall") and use the same form in the question. This kind of hairsplitting has probably been a major cause of the breakdown in distinguishing between *shall* and *will*.)

We *will* be glad to ship the order as you directed. We *shall* be pleased to follow instructions. I *will* be there next week. I *shall* send the instructions you asked. (The distinction in sentences such as these has largely passed away. Use whichever form seems comfortable and less artificial *unless* you feel better with an absolute rule to follow—then you can follow the conjugation given.)

V3e *Use* should *and* would *carefully.*

Should and *would* similarly have tended to follow patterns of meaning rather than standards of arbitrary usage. *Should* chiefly implies obligation in the sense of "ought to"; *would* expresses a customary action with all three persons.

I *should* urge you to keep this policy. (Ought to)

You *should* do everything possible to protect your credit reputation. (Ought to)

Every day he *would* answer his letters as soon as he finished reading the incoming mail. (Habitual action)

I *would* always advise a careful revision before signing. (Habitual action)

They *would* take a coffee break every morning at 10.

V3f *Use the perfect tenses to express time relationships precisely.*

The perfect tenses, for the most part, are used to indicate time relationships with regard to other times expressed or implied.

By the first of the month, we *will have completed* our quota for the year if the present sales rate continues. (Notice the use of future perfect to look back on something from a point in the future.)

Last month he reported he *had met* his sales quota. (The main verb *reported* is past tense; to indicate action prior to that we use the past perfect.)

The action was taken by the time all the facts *had been assembled.*

By next year, we *will have been* in business a quarter of a century.

Of the three perfect tenses, the present perfect is probably the most frequently misused in business writing. This results from a misunderstanding of the meanings of the three basic ways the English language has of indicating action in the past. A simple way to think of these three methods of expressing past actions is:

Past tense: Action begun and completed in the past. Example: I *wrote* to him yesterday.

Past perfect: Action begun and completed in the past prior to some other stated or implied time. Example: I *had not heard* (past perfect) from him before I *wrote* (past) him yesterday.

Present perfect: Action begun in the past and completed at any moment up to the present. Example: Up until today, I *have written* him every day this month.

Taking the present as the line at the right, the sequence of these tenses in their relationship to one another may be indicated thus:

The Present

Past Perfect   Past   Present Perfect

Hence in correctly using the present perfect tense, business writers should avoid such statements as:

Wrong: So far this month I *sold* 11 refrigerators. (Misuse of past for present perfect.)

Right: So far this month I *have sold* 11 refrigerators.

Inaccurate: He left the first of the month and I since *completed* his assignment. (Notice that there is no discrimination between two past tenses here; actually the completion of the assignment occurred after his leaving, as the sentence indicates.)

More precise: He left the first of the month, and I *have* since *completed* his assignment.

Inaccurate: We read your comments with great interest, but lack of information *prevented* a complete reply until today.

More exact: We read your comments with great interest, but lack of information *has prevented* a complete reply until today.

Inaccurate: The Chicago office *corresponded* with him ever since it happened.
More exact: The Chicago office *has corresponded* with him ever since it happened.

As a general principle, be careful to use the tense that exactly expresses the time you want indicated in the verb, particularly when these verbs show a relationship to other verbs or implied times in the same sentence. Do not shift back and forth from one tense to the other without reason.

V3g *Use the present infinitive to express all times except when the infinitive represents action clearly completed before the time of the main verb.*

One other aspect of tenses plagues business writers—the use of the infinitive. Shall we say:

I hoped *to see* you before the meeting.
I hoped *to have seen* you before the meeting.

We were pleased *to see* you at our quarterly meeting.
We were pleased *to have seen* you at our quarterly meeting.

Use a present infinitive except when the action in the infinitive was clearly completed *before* the action of the main verb. Hence, *seeing* did not precede *hoping* in the first sentence, and the correct form is:

I hoped *to see* you before the meeting.

In the second illustration, the correct form is:

We were pleased *to see* you at our quarterly meeting.

Thus, the following infinitives are correct:

We intended *to be* at the meeting. (Not *to have been* because the action of intending preceded being there.)

He was expected *to report* in Waco by the first of the month.

To have reported this to his superior would have caused him all kinds of trouble. (Note that the *reporting* comes prior to the *causing trouble*, hence the past infinitive.)

Verbs—Voice

Besides tense and mood, verbs have *voice*, a grammatical term which indicates whether the subject of the sentence is performing the action or being acted upon. In the *active voice*, somebody or something does something.

He *wrote* the report.
The typewriter *fell* to the floor.

In the *passive voice*, something is done to or by somebody or something.

The report *was written* by the new employee.
The typewriter *was knocked* off the desk by the secretary.

(The complete conjugation of all tenses of the verb *to prepare* in the passive voice is shown on pages 537 and 538.)

V4 *Use the active voice for direct, personalized expression; the passive for indirect, impersonal expression.*

In this book, we have stressed concise, direct, and personalized writing for business purposes. For achieving such qualities, the active voice is most appropriate. But students should recall that we have also stressed the primary factors of all writing—the purpose for which it is written and the reader. These are the criteria which determine our use of the active or passive voice according to these principles:

Use the active voice when direct and natural expression suits the purpose and the reader.

Use the passive voice when impersonal expression is appropriate to the subject matter and to the reader.

Because so much business writing is couched *unnecessarily* in passive voice, authors of books such as this belabor the construction as if it were incorrect or ungrammatical. It is neither, and it has its uses. When you want to make a suggestion, many readers will accept it as less harsh, less blunt, if you write:

It is suggested that this method be tried by the Marketing Group. (passive)

instead of:

I suggest that you try this method. (active)

You can test your own reaction to the following ways of expressing ideas in active and passive voice:

Passive: It is suggested by the Executive Staff that only one coffee break a day be taken by employees.

Active: We suggest that employees take only one coffee break a day.

Passive: Members of the department are urged to contribute as much as possible to this worthwhile cause.

Active: I urge you to contribute as much as possible to this worthwhile cause.

Passive: When the business day is ended, the totals should be phoned to the Central Office, Extension 6533.

Active: At the close of business, you should phone the totals to the Central Office, Extension 6533.

Many readers—and particularly older ones who were trained to write in an impersonal style—prefer the passive for suggestions, instructions, and recommendations. But don't use the passive merely to avoid the use of *I* or *we;* if you are writing about youself or your company, *I* or *we* is the natural and unaffected method of expression.

Instead of: It is the belief of the undersigned that prices will be increased.

Say: I think prices will increase.

Instead of: It is the opinion of our management that a stock participation plan will be helpful to employee morale.

Say: We think a stock participation plan will help employee morale.

In short, use the active for direct, forthright, personalized—*and concise*—writing; use the passive for impersonal and indirect expression.

V4a *Do not shift unnecessarily from active to passive or from passive to active.*

Indefinite: We began our investigation and the report was written later. (This is accurate if "we" did not write the report or if you want to leave your reader in the dark as to who wrote it.)

More accurate: We began our investigation and later wrote our report.

Unnecessary shift: We have a fine selection of the latest books and records, and a complete stock of sporting goods is being displayed for our customers this week.

More direct: We have a fine selection of the latest books and records, and we feature a complete display of our sporting goods this week.

Awkward: We use adding machines at the tellers' windows; the electronic computers are used by the Central Office.

Improved: We use adding machines at the tellers' windows; the Central Office uses electronic computers.

More concise: We use adding machines at the tellers' windows and electronic computers at the Central Office.

Nouns and Pronouns

In grammatical handbooks, nouns are properly treated as well-behaved parts of speech—and can, therefore, be ignored. Pronouns as the trouble-makers properly receive the major share of attention because they change form, called *case*, as they perform various functions (see the discussion on the following pages). A pronoun is a word which stands in place of a noun; the noun for which it stands is called its *antecedent*.

P1 *A pronoun should agree with its antecedent in number, person, and gender.*

Number means, of course, singular or plural: *I* or *we; he* or *they,* etc.

Person means whether it is first person, *I,* as the speaker; second person, *you,* as the person spoken to; or third person, *he, it, she, they,* as the persons or things spoken about.

Gender means classification by sex—masculine, *he;* feminine, *she;* neuter, *it;* and common, *they.* All changes in grammatical form affecting gender have disappeared in English.

P1a *When a pronoun has as its antecedent such singular words as* every, each, anybody, either, neither, nobody, a person, *etc., use a singular pronoun in the third person. (This is one aspect of modern life which remains a man's world because you use third person masculine* his *when you don't know; feminine readers can find consolation in knowing that ships and colleges are always* her.*)*

Each of these employees should check *his* list of responsibilities. (*Each* is sing-ular; the pronoun referring to it must be singular; gender may be masculine, fem-inine, or common—therefore, *his.*)

Neither one of these men was sure of *his* exact time of arrival.

Everybody in the office should report to *his* supervisor on Monday at 10.

Every department head is requested to sign *his* own requisition slips.

A person who is not sure of *his* writing should study grammar.

Nobody should authorize changes which affect summer employees in *his* de-partment.

Similarly, business writers frequently use such expressions as "one of those situations which," "one of those problems that," "one of those people who." Should these be followed by singular or plural verbs? Your best rule of thumb is to regard the word closer to the pronoun as its antecedent; so "instead of one of those situations which is annoying," you will follow this practice:

> She described one of those situations which *are* annoying to secretaries.

> This is one of those problems that *are* constantly coming up in business.

> He is one of those people who *annoy* everyone in the office.

Case refers to the change in form of nouns and pronouns to show their relation to other words in the sentence. Since English nouns have only one change of form—the *'s* to indicate possession—it is pronouns which cause most difficulty. Here are the changes in the three cases—subjective, possessive, and objective:

Subjective	I	you	he	she	it	we	they	who	whoever
Possessive	my	your	his	her	its	our	their	whose	whosever
Objective	me	you	him	her	it	us	them	whom	whomever

P2 *The case of a pronoun is determined by its function in the sentence.*

Applying the basic principle that the case of the pronoun depends upon its use, we get the following specific rules:

P2a *Use the subjective case of the pronoun as the subject of a verb and as predicate nominative.*

The first part of this rule is so obvious as to call for no explanation; sheer habit should require you to say "We write" not "Us write." After forms of the verb *to be*, formal writing requires the use of the subjective case in what is called a predicate nominative. While "It is *me*" and "That was *him*" are acceptable colloquialisms in speech, business writers use the following subjective cases in letters and reports:

> It was *we* who first sent the report on that subject.
> That was *he* who sent this suggestion.

Notice that these sentences are wordy and awkward and that you can avoid the whole difficulty by more incisive writing: "We first sent the report on that subject" and "He sent this suggestion."

P2b *Use the possessive case of the pronoun to indicate possession and to modify a gerund.*

Again, only the second half of this rule calls for explanation. A gerund is a verb form used as a noun—"*Writing* is fun"; "*Having accomplished* that is a record in itself." Pronouns modifying gerunds should be put in the possessive case. To the person saying, "Do you mind me making a suggestion?" the following response in doggerel is appropriate:

> *Please don't think I'm too aggressive*
> *By suggesting your participle needs possessive*

Not: We appreciated *you* sending this information promptly.
But: We appreciated *your* sending this information promptly.

Not: We must insist on *you* paying this bill.
But: We must insist on *your* paying this bill.

Not: He did not object to *us* collaborating on reports.
But: He did not object to *our* collaborating on reports.

P2c *Use the objective case of the pronoun as the object of a verb, the object of a preposition, and the subject of an infinitive.*

The chief source of trouble here is the pronoun as object of a preposition, and usually it is the pronoun linked to another pronoun by *and* which causes the incorrect construction.

Wrong: We found it impossible for him and *I*.
Right: We found it impossible for him and *me*.

Wrong: Between you and *I*, that is correct.
Right: Between you and *me*, that is correct.

Wrong: Copies had been sent to the members of the executive staff, the secretary of the committee, and *he*.
Right: Copies had been sent to the members of the executive staff, the secretary of the committee, and *him*.

But notice that when the pronoun is subject of an infinitive (*to* plus a *verb*), it is objective case too.

Wrong: He instructed Mr. Smith and *I* to decide that problem.
Right: He instructed Mr. Smith and *me* to decide that problem.

P2d *Pronouns in apposition take the same case as the word with which they are in apposition. (A word in apposition explains or gives in detail whatever is comprised in another word in the sentence.)*

Not: The three sales representatives—Smith, Jones, and *me*—were sent.
But: The three sales representatives—Smith, Jones, and *I*—were sent. (Smith, Jones, and I are in apposition with representatives which is subjective case.)

Not: There was some problem of deciding whose service was better —*him* or *me.*

But: There was some problem of deciding whose service was better—*his* or *mine.*

Not: He informed the three of them—Smith, Jones, and *he*—that they would be transferred to the new plant.

But: He informed the three of them—Smith, Jones, and *him*—that they would be transferred to the new plant.

Not: Among the employees affected, principally Miss Smith, Mrs. Jones, and *she,* the only one to refuse the transfer was Mrs. Jones.

But: Among the employees affected, principally Miss Smith, Mrs. Jones, and *her,* the only one to refuse the transfer was Mrs. Jones.

P2e *In an elliptical clause in which the verb is omitted, the pronoun takes the case which would be required if the verb were expressed.*

> We have been in business longer than *they* [have].
> They have had a better sales volume than *we* [have had].
> Their company makes greater use of mechanical equipment than *we* [do].
> You are as good a student as *she* [is].

While the informalities of speech occasionally make the use of the objective case permissible—careful writers regard pronouns as the subject of the verb understood and, hence, use the subjective case as in the examples given above.

P3 Myself, yourself, himself, ourselves, themselves, *and other reflexive pronouns require as reference a personal pronoun in the same sentence.*

> He hurt *himself.* (Reflexive)
> She washes *herself.* (Reflexive)

This would become a minor grammatical error were it not for the widespread use businessmen make of these *self* words, which are also called *intensive pronouns:*

> I bought *myself* a new coat. (Intensive)
> He will do it *himself.* (Intensive)
> We *ourselves* did not understand the meaning. (Intensive)

You can avoid such frequent misuses as the following by inserting a personal pronoun.

> He and *myself* are members of the committee. (Replace with "I.")
> Mr. Jones and *yourself* are to attend. (Say "you.")
> He addressed his remarks to his own staff and *ourselves.* ("Us")

You can generally get along very well without these *self* words by using the personal pronoun; when you really want to emphasize or intensify your meaning, use the *self* words but only after the appropriate pronoun.

P4 *In using the relative pronouns* who, which, *and* that *in formal writing, remember that* who *refers only to people,* which *refers only to things, and* that *refers to people and things.*

Not: He sent me to the chief correspondent, *which* I finally found.
But: He sent me to the chief correspondent, *whom* I finally found.

Adjectives and Adverbs

These are the words that put color and size and shape and manner of doing things into our language — and, fortunately, they cause little grammatical difficulty.

A1 *Adjectives modify nouns or pronouns and may be used to describe, to tell number, and to show specific identity or quantity.*

The *large* desk   A *few* books   The *last* day of the month

A2 *Adverbs modify verbs, adjectives, or other adverbs and, in general terms, describe how, where, when, why, and to what extent.*

Type *quickly*   *Very* quickly done   A *gratifyingly* large response

Many adverbs end in *ly*, but this is not an infallible means of identification since a number of adverbs are indistinguishable from adjectives. For example, the long-standing debate of motorists as to whether it is correct for roadside signs to read "Drive slow" is grammatically inconclusive since *slow* is *both* an adverb and an adjective.

A2a *Do not substitute an adjective for an adverb to modify a verb.*

Wrong: He certainly treats her *different* from the rest of us.
Right: He certainly treats her *differently* from the rest of us.

Wrong: They want information *quick.*
Right: They want information *quickly.*

A2b *Be careful in the use of such adverbs as* scarcely *and* hardly *to avoid double negatives.*

Scarcely and *hardly* are negative in meaning as "I have scarcely any ambition" or "I hardly have a chance." They should not be used in combination with *not* or *no* because they form a double negative. Omit either the adverb or the negative in such sentences as these:

Wrong: We could *not hardly* be expected to accept these items for credit.
  Right: We could *hardly* be expected (or: We could *not* be expected) to accept these items for credit.
Wrong: That is the kind of error that can*not scarcely* occur twice.
  Right: That is the kind of error that can scarcely occur twice (or: cannot occur twice).

A3 *Use an adjective with verbs of the five senses* (taste, smell, feel, sound, appear, look, *and* be, *etc.*) *when the subject is referred to, an adverb when the verb is referred to.*

Notice the distinction in the following sentences:

He looks *ridiculous*. (*Adjective* describing *he.*)
He looks *intently* about him. (*Adverb* describing *looks.*)

It sounds *loud*. (*Adjective* modifying *it.*)
It sounds *carefully* planned. (*Adverb* modifying *planned.*)

He appears *strong*. (*Adjective* modifying *he.*)
He appears *rarely* at his office. (*Adverb* modifying verb *appear.*)

A4 *Comparision is the change in the forms of adjectives and adverbs to show a greater or smaller degree of the quality they indicate. There are three degrees of comparison—positive, comparative, superlative.*

Most adjectives and adverbs may be compared by adding *er* or *more* or *less* and *est* or *most* or *least* to the regular, or positive, form.

Positive	Comparative	Superlative
efficient	more efficient	most efficient
quick	quicker	quickest
capable	more capable	most capable
simple	less simple	least simple
able	abler	ablest
constructive	more constructive	most constructive

Some adjectives and adverbs are compared irregularly:

Positive	Comparative	Superlative
bad (adj.)	worse	worst
good (adj.)	better	best
well (adv.)	better	best

A4a *Use the comparative degree in comparing two things, persons, or actions—the superlative for three or more.*

On the informal level, we frequently say, "That's the best team on the field today" or "He was by far the best of the two speakers." In writing, however, accuracy demands a more logical use of these degrees. Hence we write:

Of the two men, he seemed to us to be the *more* qualified. (Not *most*)

This was the *most* difficult of all my assignments.

Of the two suggestions, we thought yours was the *better.*

This is the *best* of all the suggestions submitted by employees.

Certain purists place unnecessary emphasis on a few adjectives and adverbs which cannot be compared because their meaning is absolute. While these grammarians have logic on their side—with such words as *unique, endless, infinite, perfect, impossible, black,* etc.—popular usage ignores their reasoning. Such expressions as *most unique, more perfect*—the founding fathers attempted to found *a more perfect union*—are certainly acceptable in today's business writing. Business writers who wish to be very precise can acknowledge the logic of such situations by writing more *nearly* unique, more *nearly* perfect, an *almost* impossible task.

A4b *Use other following than in making comparisions with adjectives or adverbs.*

He is more efficient *than any* man in the office.

This is a sensible statement only if the "he" is not a member of the office staff; otherwise, the comparison should logically be:

He is more efficient *than any other man* in the office.

Wrong: This improvement makes our product better *than any.* (This construction, widely used in advertising, is logically absurb since it cannot be better than itself.)

Right: This improvement makes our product better *than any other.* (This constuction emphasizes what sales personnel want emphasized—your product is better than your competitor's products.)

Conjunctions and Prepositions

Conjunctions and prepositions are our joining words, the mortar which holds sentence parts together. In themselves, they offer no particular grammatical problems; but they are important in two major aspects of writing—the methods of punctuation and the principles of coordinating and subordinating sentence elements.

C1 *A conjunction links words, phrases, or clauses to other parts of the sentence and shows the relations between them.*

Conjunctions differ from prepositions in that they may introduce whole clauses (a group of words with subject and verb) and may indicate relative importance of ideas. Used properly, conjunctions may show that two ideas are of equal importance or that one is less important than the other.

C1a *Coordinating conjunctions join words or groups of words of equal importance. The most commonly used coordinating conjunctions are* and, but, for, or, *and* nor.

C1b *Subordinating conjunctions join to the sentence clauses of unequal importance:* since, because, if, although, when, where, how *are examples of subordinating conjunctions.*

C1c *Conjunctive adverbs are adverbs used as connectives. Examples are:* therefore, moreover, however, nevertheless, hence, thus.

C2 *Use coordinating and subordinating conjunctions to convey meanings and establish relationships precisely.*

By definition, conjunctions establish relationships of ideas. They should be used, therefore, with precision to be effective. There is nothing grammatically incorrect, for example, in a sentence like:

> This machine incorporates a revolutionary new principle, *and* it is based on three years of research.

This writer has two things to say about the machine, and he ties them together with a coordinating conjunction. Such a sentence indicates a solvenly process of thought because the two statements are probably not equally important. By subordinating conjunctions, we can show this relationship more precisely.

Because we spent three years on research, this machine incorporates a revolutionary new principle.

So that this machine could incorporate a revolutionary new principle, we spent three years on research.

Quite obviously, the circumstances will dictate which of these or other methods of expressing two facts is used. If the two ideas *are* of equal importance, the use of the coordinating conjunction would be correct.

C2a *Conjunctions usually indicate relationships of cause, comparison, condition, time, sequence, and contrast.*

To show a cause-and-effect relationship—*since, because, hence, thus, therefore, inasmuch as, so that, for that reason.*

To make comparison—*than, as if, as well as, like, similarly, although.*

To state conditions—*if, unless, except, provided that, under these circumstances, accordingly, or else.*

To show time sequence—*before, after, earlier, later, following, since, when, while, preceding, subsequent to.*

To show a sequence of ideas or facts—*first, second, finally, in conclusion, primarily, furthermore, moreover.*

To sum up—*thus far, up to now, hence, accordingly, finally.*

To show contrast—*however, on the contrary, on the other hand, by contrast, furthermore, not to mention, still less, still more.*

This is an elementary list; you can doubtless think of hundreds of other ways to express such relationships. The important principle is to see that your connectives express these relationships and your meaning as precisely as possible.

No teacher or reader of business writing needs to be told what is one of the chief faults of letters, reports, and memos. It is an endless succession of *and's, but's,* and *for's* reflecting an utter lack of subtle relationships or discrimination. Ask a child what he has been doing all day, and you expect an answer like: "I got up and I had my breakfast and then I got on the school bus and we shouted and sang and cheered and then we got to school . . ." and so on.

To avoid this monotonous level, learn to use conjunctions and conjunctive adverbs precisely to show shadings of thought and relative importance of facts and ideas. Study those which have been cited previously and use them in your writing when you are overworking *and* and *but* and *for.*

C3 *A preposition links a noun or pronoun to show its relationship to some other word in the sentence. Examples:* with, by, for, to, in, of, before, after, *etc. Prepositions also combine with other parts of speech in hundreds of idiomatic expressions like* accede to, comply with, desirous of, different from, agreeable to, *etc.*

C4 *In formal writing use* like *as a preposition or a verb, not as a conjunction.*

Many people use *like* as a conjunction in speech (He acts *like* he knows everything), but avoid its use in formal writing. Perhaps *like* will attain the status of *as*, a conjunction; at present, its use as a conjunction will grate on the nerves of many. It is interesting to note that Robert Gunning's *The Technique of Clear Writing* has a chapter titled "Write Like You Talk"; on the jacket of the book, the publishers have changed this to "Write As You Talk." Young writers in business will similarly play safe by using the preferred form below:

> *Not:* He always talks *like* he knows more than anyone else in the office.
> *Preferred:* He always talks *as if* he knows more than anyone else in the office.

> *Not:* He writes his reports in the impersonal style *like* he was instructed to do.
> *Preferred:* He writes his reports in the impersonal style *as* he was instructed to do.

You can test these easily by noting whether *like* introduces a group of words with subject and verb; if so, substitute *as* or *as if*. Notice that *like* is properly used as a preposition in these sentences:

> I did not know he would talk *like that.*
> He writes reports *like those* we recommend to our employees.

THE SENTENCE

By definition the sentence is a group of words that must express at least *one complete thought* or two or more *closely related thoughts*. The sentence is capable of standing alone and "making sense"; grammatically, this means that the sentence has a verb and its subject, expressed or understood.

Frequently, in conversation especially, we can convey thought without sentences:

> "Who will do the final report?"
> "Smith."
> "Your department?"
> "No. Elwyn Smith in Sales."

Furthermore, experienced business writers have learned to use sentence fragments or *elliptical statements*, as they are called, to good effect, particularly in sales letters and advertising copy:

You know the wonderful feeling that comes when you've finally completed a tough job? A sense of achievement. An air of satisfaction. A feeling of well-being.

All under one roof . . . Research. Art. Planning. Engineering. Construction.

Everything for one complete service. And all backed by 27 years of service. An organization of 213 professional men with creative ideas. To serve YOU.

This elliptical or fragmentary writing is effective for packing a number of facts or ideas in short space. It gives punch and forward movement, particularly in sales writing, but in the more formal types of business communication, fragmentary writing is undesirable and incorrect.

Structure

S1 *Avoid writing part of a sentence as if it were a complete thought or statement (the period fault).*

This is an important rule for writers in business, particularly for those who dictate. Some use their opening "sentences" as a warm-up period and dictate a clause or a phrase as if it were a complete idea; others merely add an incomplete thought in the form of a phrase or subordinate clause to what has been said before. These fragments can be corrected in two ways:

1. By connecting them to the preceding or following sentence if they logically belong there.

2. By recasting them to make complete sentences, usually by supplying a main subject or verb.

Notice how the following examples correct these faults:

Wrong: Referring to your letter of March 21. We will notify our dealer in Covington.
Right: Referring to your letter of March 21, we will notify our dealer in Covington. (Connecting the fragment to the following sentence; but see the discussion of this participial construction on pages 564 to 565.)

Wrong: As we agreed over the phone yesterday.
Right: As we agreed over the phone yesterday, the campaign will begin April 10.

Wrong: To confirm our agreement on November 12 at the Hotel Grandview.
Right: This will confirm our agreement on November 12 at the Hotel Grandview. (Supplying a subject and verb)

Wrong: *During* the sales period from Labor Day to Thanksgiving, we will introduce five new models. Each of these adaptable to color.

Right: During the sales period from Labor Day to Thanksgiving, we will introduce five new models, all of them adaptable to color.

Wrong: He had spent most of the month on the report evaluating personnel problems for the next five years. Which his supervisor thought good enough to transmit to the vice-president.

Right: He had spent most of the month on the report evaluating personnel problems for the next five years. His supervisor thought it was good enough to transmit to the vice-president.

Will it stand alone and make sense? This is the final test of the sentence. If not, correct the fragment by one of the two methods suggested.

S2 *Avoid putting two or more unrelated thoughts in the same sentence (the comma splice).*

This construction stems from sheer carelessness or lack of logic. It consists of connecting two unrelated sentences with a comma; correct it by replacing the comma with a period. If a logical relationship can be established between the thoughts, then the appropriate conjunction and punctuation should be used.

Wrong: The department had had a high accident rate, this was caused by several inexperienced employees who had not had their safety indoctrination.

Recast the whole statement to show a logical relationship:

Right: Because several inexperienced employees had not had their safety indoctrination, the department had had a high accident rate.

Wrong: Our employees stay with us over the years, the new stock purchase plan is an added incentive.

Right: Our employees stay with us over the years. The new stock purchase plan is an added incentive.

Wrong: As you requested, I forwarded the report to the Dallas office, the word then came back that the manager agreed with our conclusions.

Right: As you requested, I forwarded the report to the Dallas office. The word then came back that the manager agreed with our conclusions.

S3 *Avoid breaking ideas up into short, choppy sentences.*

Occasionally, this style can be used by skillful writers to obtain an effect:

He read our invitation. He visited the exhibit. He saw for himself the efficiency of the new design. And he ordered a year's supply then and there!

More frequently, these sentences sound choppy, childish, and thoughtless because they result from the writer's failure to organize closely related ideas into sentence units. Correct such constructions by putting ideas which logically belong together in the same sentence.

> *Choppy:* At that time, I first called it to your attention. You asked me to keep you informed. I wrote you again in March. The auditor arrived on April 2. The employee was found responsible. He was replaced on April 15.
>
> *Improved:* When I first called this to your attention, you asked me to keep you informed and so I wrote you again in March. After the auditor arrived on April 2, the employee was found responsible and was replaced on April 15.

S4 *Avoid long, rambling sentences with too many qualifying clauses and phrases.*

Such sentences frequently occur in reports; oftentimes, they stem from an admirable trait of mind—the desire to avoid saying something which is not always true and hence packing all kinds of qualifying phrases and clauses into one statement. This tendency can be corrected by putting the general statement into one sentence, the qualifers or exceptions into successive sentences. Frequently these sentences stem from less admirable traits—mental laziness and inability to organize; here, the only cure is to think about grouping ideas as logical sentence units which readers can grasp.

> *Unorganized:* We have made special efforts during April to bring our fleet of cars up to summer conditioning, which includes cleaning and painting, where that is necessary, but as you are aware, the heavy rains of late April have overcome some of these efforts and furthermore we had an unusually heavy number of road calls, totaling 87, for the month and this too hampered our efforts. (From the report of a transportation department)
>
> *Improved:* During April, we have made special efforts to bring our fleet of cars up to summer conditioning, which includes cleaning and painting wherever necessary. As you know, the heavy rains of late April hampered some of these efforts. Furthermore, an unusually heavy number of road calls—87 in all—limited our conditioning work.
>
> *Rambling:* The number of new unemployment claims, which, of course, definitely affect consumer buying power, dropped 400 in the municipal area from the previous week and in the suburbs dropped 211 from the high of 1,453 the previous two weeks, although the suburban high was affected by certain unusual conditions, and it would now appear, unless some very unexpected conditions arise which are not in this forecast, that the peak of unemployment claims for the first six months was reached during the week ending April 17. (From a market analysis report)

Improved: New unemployment claims dropped 400 in the municipal area from the previous week and 211 from a high of 1,453 in the suburbs the previous two weeks. The suburban high was affected by unusual conditions. Unless unexpected circumstances arise, the forecast is that the peak of unemployment claims for the first six months was reached during the week ending April 17. This will, of course, have definite—and beneficial—effects on consumer buying power.

Rambling: We try to supply our customers with the best merchandise and most economical service that is possible and this includes all brands of nationally advertised sporting goods, garden supplies, and hardware and a discount of 2 percent for cash payments within 10 days.

Improved: Our customers get the best in merchandise—nationally advertised brands of sporting goods, garden supplies, and hardware. And they get the most economical service, with added savings of 2 percent by paying cash within 10 days.

S5 *Avoid monotony and dullness for your reader by varying your sentence structure.*

Sentences can be classified as simple, complex, compound, and compound-complex according to their parts, or as loose, periodic, and balanced according to their overall structure. It is not within the province of this book to go into a detailed analysis of all these classifications. What is important is that business writers become conscious of the pattern of their sentences; if they tend to express most of their ideas in one monotonous pattern, a change of pattern will add to the reader's interest. Remember that you have three kinds of sentences to add variety to your style—loose, periodic, and balanced. Each of these is analyzed in the following three sections.

S5a *The loose sentence.*

Actually, most business writing consists of "loose" sentences. This is no derogatory term; it merely means that the sentence is organized in a normal pattern of subject, verb, and modifiers and that its essential meaning is disclosed before the end of the sentence. But because the loose sentence is so common, it lacks emphasis and strength.

We sent the order on August 12 by Railway Express as you had instructed.

The total seniority rating of each employee will then be posted in the department where the rating applies.

This report covers the operations of the purchasing department from August 1 to September 1, the first month of its activity under the plan of reorganization, which went into effect on July 15.

This is the normal pattern of sentence organization, and the great majority of sentences in almost any report, letter, or memorandum will necessarily be loose—subject, verb, modifiers. But when all your writing falls into this pattern, the result is dullness, monotony, and lack of interest.

S5b *The periodic sentence*

Change this basic pattern of the loose sentence by occasionally pushing a clause or phrase ahead of the main subject and verb.

> In accordance with the plan of reorganization effective July 15, this is my first report as head of the purchasing department.

> Unless a careful check is maintained at all times, these records of seniority ratings can cause difficulty and considerable discussion.

With this shift from normal loose order to a different arrangement, we force our reader to keep certain ideas in mind until the entire meaning is complete. Actually, without his recognizing it, we force his attention by holding him in suspense until the final meaning is clear. This is *the periodic sentence*, an arrangement which suspends meaning and builds to completion at the final word or group of words. Used judiciously, it adds considerable variety to style; readers of *Time*, the news magazine, will recognize it as "*Time* style":

> Last week, as it must to all men, to Joe Doakes of Koakesville, came death.

The periodic sentence is an effective method of breaking up the monotonous regularity of loose sentences. Business writers should learn to intersperse such sentence patterns occasionally. The technique is to hold back the main subject and verb until the end of the sentence, pushing the modifying clauses and phrases forward to the beginning. Notice that you have to read these sentences through to the last word before the meaning is complete.

> Thus at month's end, even though we discount most favorable factors and emphasize the few unfavorable ones, the immediate future looks good.

> To the good looks, attractive design, and low cost of this new unit, add our 31 years of experience.

> For those who do not face the realities of this situation, a danger of surplus exists.

S5c *The balanced sentence*

And finally, you can learn to write one other sentence pattern—the balanced sentence. This pattern should be used infrequently for emphasis because it has a contrived air which calls attention to itself. For most twentieth-century writers who seek a casual, informal style, the balanced sentence is a bit artificial. If you write advertising copy, however, this sentence pattern can be very useful. The balanced sentence uses a symmetrical arrangement of corresponding parts. Many of the world's most famous sayings have come in the form of the balanced sentence, a pattern which has made them memorable.

> I came; I saw; I conquered. (*Caesar*)

> Reading maketh a full man; conference a ready man; and writing an exact man. (*Bacon*)

> If I could save the Union without freeing any slave, I would do it; and if I could do it by freeing all the slaves, I would do it; and if I could save it by freeing some and leaving others alone, I would also do that. (*Lincoln*)

Notice the advertisers:

> Eye it; try it; buy it.

> Fasten it better and faster with Bostitch.

> How magical its refreshment, how welcome its sparkling goodness, how perfectly it goes with other foods.

> Better things for better living . . . through chemistry.

This is the essence of balanced sentences—putting parallel parts in balanced, symmetrical form. For the unusual occasion, for high-lighting an idea—such as the summary statement of a report or memo—for the sales letter or advertisement, it is a useful variant.

> The greater our efficiency, the lower the cost to you.

> By nature, he is carefree; by disposition, he is cheerful.

Logic and Consistency

L1 *Express parallel ideas in parallel form.*

This principle of parallelism can be applied to both the simplest and most intricate forms of expression. It is both a logical and stylistic device to help a reader. In its most elementary form, this principle is unnecessarily violated in such a sentence as:

> We are wholesalers for clothing for men, women, and *those who are under eighteen years of age.*

This is both sloppy expression and haphazard logic; in parallel form these elements would be expressed:

> We are wholesalers for clothing for men, women, teen-agers, and children.

To apply this principle, you should generally pair nouns with nouns, adjectives with adjectives, phrases with phrases, and clauses with clauses.

Not: This new product offers ease of operation, economy and *it is easily available.*
But: This new product offers ease of operation, economy, and *availability.*
Not: The manual gives instructions for operating the machine and *to adjust it.*
But: The manual gives instructions for operating the machine and *for adjusting it.*
Not: We will send you advertising material for increasing sales and *to acquaint your customers with our new products.*
But: We will send you advertising material for increasing sales and *for acquainting* your customers with our new products.

L1a *Repeat necessary words (article, conjunction, preposition, pronoun, auxiliary verb, etc.) when repetition is needed to make parallel structure clear.*

Not: We received a large order from him in September *and which* was increased in October.
But: We received a large order from him *which* he sent us in September *and which* he increased in October.

Whenever you use *and which, and who, and that,* you are linking two parts of a sentence which should be in parallel form. The best rule of thumb to apply to such expressions is to use *and which, and who, and that* only when they are preceded by another *which, who,* or *that* to which they are logically parallel. Notice the changes in the following sentences:

Not: This bill includes all charges through August 25 *and which* are subject to 2 percent discount within 10 days.
But: This bill includes all charges *which* were made through August 25 *and which* are subject to 2 percent discount within 10 days.

Not: The report reflects a great deal of research *and which* is all too rare.
But: This report reflects a great deal of research, *which* is all too rare.

Not: We found him a reliable employee *and who* has a high sense of integrity.
But: We found him to be a man *who* is a reliable employee *and who* has a high sense of integrity.

Not: This is a service of considerable value to typists *and that* many supervisors of stenographic departments have used.
But: This is a service *that* is of considerable value to typists *and that* many supervisors of stenographic departments have used.

L1b *Make certain that listed items which are parallel in thought are also parallel in form. Because lists are so widely used in business writing, particularly in reports, this principle should be scrupulously applied.*

Not: In this kind of analysis, three steps are always involved:
1. Scrutinize all the details carefully.
2. Eliminate all the unnecessary details.
3. A chart showing the flow of work should then be made.

But: In this kind of analysis, three steps are always involved:
1. Scrutinize all the details carefully.
2. Eliminate all the unnecessary details.
3. Make a chart showing the flow of work.

Not: When we wrote you previously, we requested you to send us the following:
1. A financial statement
2. A list of credit references
3. You were to obtain a letter of credit from a wholesale firm with which you have done business

But: When we wrote you previously, we requested you to send us the following:
1. A financial statement
2. A list of credit references
3. A letter of credit from a wholesale firm with which you have done business

Not: We appreciate your promptness in sending us the three items we requested— the questionnaire, the personnel evaluation blank, and *you are to be complimented* on the copy of Mr. Handy's speech.

But: We appreciate your promptness in sending us the three items we requested— the questionnaire, the personnel evaluation blank, and the copy of Mr. Handy's speech, on which you are to be complimented.

L2 *Do not unnecessarily shift the point of view within the sentence.*

When you express thoughts, facts, or information in sentence form, you necessarily take a *point of view*—that is, a relative position from which you view the events or from which you consider the subject discussed. You should, therefore, maintain one point of view in your writing unless there is good reason for change. This principle particularly applies within the individual sentence. We have already discussed unnecessary change of voice and tense (see verbs) as a major form of inconsistency. This construction occurs in such sentences as:

Inconsistent: The *writer* of this letter was educated in Texas and *New York City* has been his place of employment ever since. (Note the unnecessary shift of subject in the two clauses.)

Consistent: The writer of this letter was educated in Texas and has been employed in New York City ever since.

Inconsistent:	When *one* does a thorough job of gathering facts, *you* find that time passes rapidly. (Note the needless shift of person in the pronouns. *One* is third person, *you* second person. This shift is a bad habit of inexperienced writers.)
Consistent:	When *you* do a thorough job of gathering facts, *you* find that time passes rapidly.

or

Consistent and more formal:	When *one* does a thorough job of gathering facts, *he* finds that time passes rapidly.
Inconsistent:	We *received* this notification on April 2 and on April 4 we *arrive* there to find the plant shut down. (This shift in tense from past to present occurs chiefly in narratives and reports of accidents, safety accounts taken on the scene, and similar business communications.)
Consistent:	We *received* this notification on April 2 and on April 4 *arrived* there to find the plant shut down.
Inconsistent:	It was the opinion of the group that this should be done and I agreed. (This is unnecessary shifting from impersonal passive style to personalized active.)
Consistent:	The group thought this should be done, and I agreed.

Modifiers

Within the sentence, any word or phrase or clause which limits or qualifies the meaning of other parts of the sentence is a *modifier*. The rule governing all such elements can be stated simply:

M1 *Every modifer must have a word to modify and should be placed so that it is logically and naturally connected with the word it modifies.*

This principle points to the two central problems arising from modifiers: sometimes they have nothing to modify, sometimes they are placed too far from the element they modify to be recognizable as modifiers. The result can be ambiguity or absurdity.

A man bumped into me upon getting off the elevator. (Who is getting off?)

Upon getting off the elevator, the newsstand may be seen. (Does the newsstand get off the elevator?)

These are the methods used to correct mistakes which we think are good policy. (Methods or mistakes are good policy?)

You ought to have the knowledge which this reference book offers you at your fingertips. (Do you read Braille?)

M2 *Verbal phrases (participial, infinitive, gerund) or elliptical clauses which do not logically refer to some word in the sentence are said to "dangle."*

> Coming around the curve, the schoolhouse was seen.

Even if you change the word order, the schoolhouse is still coming around the curve. This is nonsensical; but you are being equally illogical when you use any of the following constructions in your letters and reports:

> Submitting these reviews of operations, the matter was referred elsewhere.

> Referring to your letter of March 25, the situation is being investigated.

> Reviewing the results of the Greenpoint Plant, the same conclusions were reached.

Writers of business letters, memos, and reports should be particularly careful about dangling modifiers. "Confirming your telephone conversation," "Referring to your memorandum of February 16," and "Thanking you for your cooperation" are frequent constructions that are encountered in business writing. In an earlier chapter, we have pointed out that these are weak expressions, ill-adapted for the beginning or ending of letters and memos. They can be avoided entirely in most instances, but since they are so deeply intrenched in the business vocabulary we can at least make them grammatically correct.

M2a *Correct dangling participles or infinitives (1) by making the doer of the action in the phrase the subject or (2) by changing the phrase to a subordinate clause.*

Not: Having shipped the order yesterday, our thanks are due you for your patience during this unavoidable delay.

But: Having shipped the order yesterday, we want to thank you for your patience during this unavoidable delay.

Not: To issue reports promptly, the duplicating group should be called.

But: To issue reports promptly, you should call the duplicating group.
When you want reports issued promptly, the duplicating group should be called.

Not: To obtain the utmost in comfort, the house should be insulated.

But: To obtain the utmost in comfort, you should insulate the house.
If you want to obtain the utmost in comfort, the house should be insulated.

M2b *Correct elliptical clauses by supplying the omitted words (subject or verb) or by supplying a subject which the elliptical clause can modify.*

Misleading: When ordered in large amounts, the transportation charges mount rapidly.

Correct: When this merchandise is ordered in large amounts, the transportation charges mount rapidly.

Misleading: While climbing the pole, the electricity was shut off.
Correct: While climbing the pole, the lineman shut off the electricity.
              While the lineman was climbing the pole, the electricity was shut off.

Misleading: When three years old, the move to larger quarters occurred.
Correct: When the company was three years old, it moved to larger quarters.

Misleading: When announced, the public will be urged to visit local dealers.
Correct: When the new prices are announced, the public will be urged to visit local dealers.

M3 *Place adverbs such as* only, almost, nearly, merely, also, scarcely, *and* even *near the word they modify.*

The idiom of popular speech has blurred much of the preciseness of meaning in such statements as:

He only won the fifth prize in the sales contest.

She only wanted to take her vacation in August. (Did she want to take her vacation only in August or is this *only* in the sense of an excuse for her action?)

These statements are perfectly appropriate in conversation where explanations can be made as needed. But careful business writers will watch the position of these words to see that a precise meaning is conveyed. It makes considerable difference, for instance, whether you say:

Our dealer is only open on Friday in the evening.
or
Our dealer is open in the evening only on Friday.

He had an accident in a company car almost at the township line.
or
He almost had an accident in a company car at the township line.

In these sentences, your meaning will determine the proper position of the modifier. If your dealer is open once during the week, he is "only open on Friday"; if, instead, he opens his store one evening a week, he opens "in the evening only on Friday."

Note the different connotations when these words are placed to modify different elements.

He even reported that there was a chance of malfeasance.
He reported that there was even a chance of malfeasance.

They just called about the conference which had finished.
They called about the conference which had just finished.

These are *merely* a few illustrations of how one word can affect your meaning in business writing; they also illustrate how *just* one word can change your meaning. *Only* by placing such words properly can you convey your precise meaning when you write.

M4 *Avoid placing a modifier so that it seems to modify either the words preceding or following it.*

The construction, known as the *squinting modifier*, can sometimes be corrected by punctuation; more frequently, however, a recasting of the sentence is needed.

Ambiguous: Since we accumulated more information by this method *in two weeks* we finished the report.

Clear: Since we accumulated more information by this method, we finished the report in two weeks.

Ambiguous: The machine she had been running *noisily* fell off the desk.

Clear: The machine she had been running fell off the desk with a great deal of noise.

Ambiguous: While he gained this experience *off and on* he went to night school.

Clear: While he gained this experience, he went to night school occasionally.

M5 *Avoid putting words between* to *and* the verb form of an infinitive *unless greater clarity and more natural expression result from doing so.*

This is the highly publicized "split infinitive" construction on which we commented earlier. It is actually a problem of misplaced modifiers. Common sense and the meaning to be conveyed should govern such constructions as these:

Not: We tried to quickly and economically issue reports.
Say: We tried to issue reports quickly and economically.

Not: To never own one is to completely miss one of life's satisfactions.
Say: Never to own one is to miss one of life's satisfactions completely.

PUNCTUATION

Over the years, a marked decrease has occurred in the amount of punctuation used in business writing as in other forms. One survey of the punctuation used in the editorial pages of the *New York Times* shows that the number of commas decreased almost 50 percent in 60 years. In letters, closed punctuation, which puts commas at the end of the lines and a period at the conclusion of the inside address, is now practically obsolete. It has been replaced by what is known as the *open form of punctuation*. The modern trend is to omit punctuation wherever it is not necessary for clarity; from that principle, open punctuation may be considered as the most up-to-date method.

How far to extend this functional approach to punctuating business letters still constitutes a problem, however, since usage has not completely crystallized. Business writers will find it helpful to think of punctuation as an aid to the reader rather than as marks to be strewn more or less at random. Punctuation has a functional use—making material more readable. Read these sentences:

> When the car is in the garage doors should be shut.
>
> On the day following the report was sent on to the manager.

To get their meaning, you'll have to read them at least twice and even then it will be very awkward. But suppose we insert one punctuation mark:

> When the car is in, the garage doors should be shut.
>
> On the day following, the report was sent on to the manager.

This is punctuation for clarity; and there is also a lot of punctuation which is simply conventional—a colon after the salutation of a business letter, but a comma after the salutation of a friendly letter, a period after Mr., a comma after a complimentary close. But conventional uses of punctuation make material more readable too, if only because readers have become accustomed to certain of these conventions.

You'll have to exercise judgment in punctuating reports and letters and memos; but your judgment will be better if you remember the following general tendencies:

1. Long sentences or long elements (like clauses or phrases) tend to require more punctuation than short ones.

2. Elements which interrupt the flow of a sentence require punctuation.

   > You knew that he was going. (Normal sentence order with no punctuation)
   >
   > You knew—did you not?—that he was going.
   >
   > You knew, of course, that he was going.

3. Elements which are out of the natural order of a sentence require punctuation. Natural order of the sentence consists of subject and modifiers—object or predicate noun and

modifiers. Notice that the following sentences are identical except for the order of parts and that the second sentence requires punctuation for that reason.

> We will take action when the report is turned in to the committee.

> When the report is turned in to the committee, we will take action.

In addition to these general tendencies, each of the major marks of punctuation indicates certain relationships and performs certain functions which should be kept in mind. These relationships and functions are explained in the rules which follow.

PU1 *The comma marks a rather close connection of parts, a slight pause for the reader. The most frequent uses of the comma are as follows:*

PU1a *Use a comma to separate two independent clauses connected by a coordinating conjunction (and, but, for, or not).*

> We greatly appreciate the interest you have shown in our methods, *and* we certainly wish we could comply with your request of October 15.

> The fact that the users of our products take the time to write us of their experiences is a source of gratification to us, *for* through such reports we get a valuable indication of how our appliances perform under conditions of everyday use.

> Our investigation showed that the Internal Auditing Section had recommended essentially the same changes, *and* we have collaborated with that section in making a joint recommendation to the executive vice-president.

When the two clauses are short and closely connected, the comma may be omitted.

> This is your responsibility and you must accept it as such.

> We appreciate your inquiry and you will see a demonstration of this equipment next Tuesday.

PU1b *Use a comma to separate words, phrases, or clauses in series.*

> This plan is designed to give you *more profit, easier payments,* and *wider selection of merchandise.*

> You will find him to be *cooperative, likable,* and *intelligent.*

Increasingly business writers omit the last comma between the next to the last and the last elements in such series when the meaning is unmistakably clear.

We have it available in small, medium and large sizes.

These reports are submitted on the last day of the week, month and quarter.

When there is any doubt that the meaning is clear, the comma should be placed before the conjunction. Notice the confusion that can result, particularly when the reader is unfamiliar with the subject, by dropping this last comma:

We received inquiries about this research from Smith and Jones, Johnson and Cohen and Black.

Is it Johnson and Cohen or Cohen and Black? Only proper placement of the final comma will indicate this unmistakably.

The comma is not necessary when each member of the series is joined to the others by a conjunction.

We sent the desks *and* the chairs *and* the files by express.

This applies to memos *and* reports *and* all forms of internal communication.

He will send the originals *or* the carbons *or* the new authorizations today.

PU1c *Use a comma to set off lengthy dependent elements preceding the main subject and verb.*

When you have seen all the features of this latest model, you will certainly want one.

At the time when we had originally scheduled the annual sales conference, a drop in consumers' purchasing power had occurred.

Since our offer of an adjustment did not seem satisfactory to you, we should like you to tell us just what you would regard as a fair settlement.

Where the elements are brief and closely connected to the rest of the sentence, the comma may be omitted.

Naturally you should expect better mileage.

In this instance no action is necessary.

By sheer coincidence both reports arrived in the same mail.

PU1d *Use commas to set off nonrestrictive clauses, introduced usually by* who, which, that, *or* where.

This rule requires careful differentiation between nonrestrictive clauses using commas and restrictive clauses requiring no commas. The simplest method is to read the sentence *without the clause;* if the meaning is changed radically, the clause is restrictive and needs no punctuation. Restrictive clauses limit or restrict meaning or pin down whatever they modify to a specific thing or things; nonrestrictive clauses usually supply an additional piece of information or add a comment about whatever they modify. Notice how the meaning is changed in the first sentence but not in the second when you read them without the clause:

A refrigerator *that gives 15 years of service* is properly designed. (Not *any* refrigerator but "a refrigerator that gives 15 years of service"; this is restrictive and requires no punctuation.)

A refrigerator, *which is a necessity to American housewives,* is a luxury in most parts of the world. (The clause here adds a comment or an additional piece of information but it does not limit or restrict the meaning of "a refrigerator.")

Notice that commas in nonrestrictive clauses *always come in pairs,* except when the clause ends the sentence. Many writers make the mistake of putting one comma at the beginning and none at the end of the clause. The following nonrestrictive clauses are correctly punctuated:

Mr. Gray, *who has been with us many years,* has earned an enviable reputation in our personnel department.

Our largest plant, *which is located in Columbus,* will be open for inspection this spring.

Our annual convention is held in New York City, *where our sales offices are located.*

Notice that the following clauses require no punctuation because they are clearly restrictive:

The man *who sold me this merchandise* is no longer associated with your company.

The order *that we received on October 15* was shipped on October 17.

Memos *which are sent to the stenographic department* must be received before 3:00 P.M. of the day they are to be typed.

PU1e *Use commas to set off parenthetical expressions and appositives.*

Many writers use commas as a kind of light parenthesis which gives less emphasis or marks a less abrupt interruption than the dash or parentheses themselves. Parenthetical expressions such as *of course, however, as you know,* and numerous others when placed so that they interrupt the normal flow of a sentence require two commas to set them off. Notice that here, too, the commas always come in pairs:

We knew, *of course*, that these prices would not prevail for a very long period.

On June 5 we reported, *as you will recall*, that this situation would call for careful handling.

The general conditions of the market, *as you will undoubtedly realize*, imposed definite limits on production.

The appositive can be informally defined as *another way of saying the same thing*, as in giving a man's title or citing his accomplishments briefly. It actually is a nonrestrictive element, as many teachers call it, and like the nonrestrictive clause requires commas. Because of the habitual use of titles, business writing requires an unusually large number of appositives.

We are sending Mr. Robert Evans, *our chief engineer*, to assist you.

Mr. Alexander Smith, *Director of Personnel of the Blank Company*, will conduct a seminar on "How to Evaluate Personnel."

The Executive Staff, *composed of Mr. E. C. Smith, Mr. P. W. Jones, and Mr. L. I. Johnson*, asked me to send these minutes of their meeting.

Our latest model, *the finest and most economical we have ever produced*, will be announced immediately after Labor Day.

PU1f *Use commas to punctuate the following conventional or routine situations.*

1. Following the complimentary close of a business letter:

    > Cordially yours,
    > Sincerely yours,
    > Yours very truly,

2. Separating geographical names, dates, and elements in addresses:

    Our nearest dealer is in Springfield, Missouri.

    This occurred on Friday, February 16, 1970.

    Please send it to Mr. John Chapman, 275 Park Drive, Cleveland, Ohio 44124.

    We will appreciate your forwarding this to the Standard Development Corporation, Kingston, N.Y. 12401. (Notice that no comma is used before the postal delivery zone: New York 10036, Omaha, Nebraska 68103.)

3.   Separating initials or titles following a person's name:

> This report was then sent on to Adams, F. W., Adams, T. H., and Baldwin.

> The certificate in the name of Frank X. Park, Jr., is listed as Frank X. Park, Sr., on our stock records.

> You might write to L. M. Bole, M.D., their industrial physician.

> Our alphabetical list of dealers shows him as Cohn, A. C., instead of Kohn, A. T.

PU2   *The semicolon can be regarded almost as a period within the sentence. It marks the end of one thought which is somewhat closely connected to the thought which follows. The most frequent uses of the semicolon are as follows:*

PU2a   *Use a semicolon to separate two independent clauses not connected by a coordinating conjunction.*

> We shall send your merchandise on March 25; this should arrive in ample time for your Easter sale.

> This new camera is not intended for novices; it was designed primarily for those whose knowledge and experience enable them to appreciate its greater versatility and finer craftsmanship.

> The report was submitted on time; the resulting action corrected the difficulty.

PU2b   *Use a semicolon to separate two independent clauses connected by conjunctive adverbs, such as* however, thus, hence, therefore, otherwise, consequently, moreover, *and similar words. (Notice that a comma follows these conjunctive adverbs.)*

> We know that you will like this new design; however, you may return any of this merchandise within 30 days.

> By placing your order now, you can be certain of delivery within 30 days; thus, you can assure your customers of an adequate supply of antifreeze this winter.

> We believe that this should be prevented in the future; therefore, we recommend that a thorough study of the causes be made.

> These words are also frequently used as parenthetical expressions requiring pairs of commas; writers should carefully distinguish between this parenthetical function and their function as connectives joining independent clauses.

We knew, *however,* that he would not complete the assignment. (parenthetical)
We knew that he would not complete the assignment; *however,* he was the only person who could start it by supplying the background. (conjunctive adverb)

He concluded, *therefore,* that you were not interested. (parenthetical)
He concluded that you were not interested; *therefore,* he looked elsewhere. (conjunctive adverb)

PU2c *Use a semicolon to separate two long or involved independent clauses with internal marks of punctuation.*

Even though such independent clauses are connected by coordinating conjunctions and would ordinarily require commas (PU1a), careful writers distinguish between the commas *within* clauses by using a heavier separator *between* the clauses.

This department wrote a series of 10 small advertisements, prepared slides, and drew graphs for the sales campaign; as suggested, we have placed heavy emphasis on electric fans, air-conditioning units, and water coolers in preparing this campaign.

When these changes are made, their cumulative effect will be to reduce our staff, our labor costs already being too high; and this reduction, which I mentioned to you last week, constitutes a major economy in this department.

PU3 *The colon marks a very close connection of parts; it notifies the reader that a list, an explanation, or closely related material will follow. The most frequent uses of the colon are:*

PU3a *Use a colon to introduce a formal list.*

There are three steps in this procedure:
1. Analyze the job carefully.
2. Eliminate unnecessary details.
3. Reduce operations to routine wherever possible.

These restrictions can be changed in any of the following instances: (1) required jury duty; (2) death in the immediate family of the employee; (3) illness of the employee; and (4) military service, such as the State Guard.

Three models will be shipped to you for display: 6W9—Portable, 17E2—Console, and 21N4—Commercial.

PU3b *Use a colon to introduce further explanation.*

> We should like to make a suggestion to help you: ship the damaged part to your nearest dealer, notify us when you have done this, and we will have a factory-trained expert at your dealer's to make the necessary repairs.

> The analysis shows that suburban buying habits are changing with the new housing: more land means increased demand for gardening equipment, functional architecture brings a trend to do-it-yourself merchandise, and greater distances make a second car a family necessity.

> We have it available in five colors: charcoal gray, maroon, off-white, dark green, and navy blue.

PU3c *Use a colon to punctuate certain routine or conventional situations.*

1. After the salutation of a business letter:

   Gentlemen:

   Dear Mr. Flemming:

2. Between hours and minutes in time:

   Employees must report at 8:30.

3. In introducing a formal quotation:

   We call your attention to the statement in your policy:
   This provision will remain valid under all conditions except military service, self-inflicted injuries, atomic attacks, or as is specified later, Act of God.

This use of the colon depends on the degree of formality and the length of the quotation. Many writers use a rule of thumb that quotations of more than four or five lines or about fifty words should be introduced by colons and be dropped down and indented to a new margin. Where the quotation is shorter, the writing more informal, a comma is used.

> He summed up his whole practice of human relations by saying, "Always talk to the guy."

> Maybe you've said to yourself, "I wish I could afford that kind of vacation." Well, now you can!

PU4 *The apostrophe indicates the possessive case of nouns and of indefinite pronouns (anybody's, everybody's) and tells the reader the precise point in a contraction where a letter or letters have been omitted. The most frequent uses of the apostrophe are:*

PU4a *Use an apostrophe to indicate the omission of letters in contractions.*

Can't, didn't, don't, we'll, you'll, I'd, '54

PU4b *Use an apostrophe to show possession.*

A company's location   A customer's statement   Companies' locations
Customers' statements

PU4c *Place the apostrophe properly.*

The real problem business writers face is not when to use the apostrophe to indicate possession but where to place it properly. The following principles should, therefore, be strictly observed:

1. Add an *'s* to form the possessive singular.

    A child's book   A company's location   A customer's statement

2. Add an *'s* to form the possessive plural of words which *do not* end in *s* in their plural form.

    Women's clothes   Children's books   Men's suits

3. Add only the apostrophe to plural nouns ending in *s*.

    The creditors' meeting   The directors' report   Three days' pay

4. Indicate possession in company names by placing *'s* after the last word or name only.

    Johnson and Johnson's new location
    The Universal Casting Company's products
    Green, Black, and White's service

5. Proper names ending in *s* or *z* add *'s* if the name is of one syllable; if it is a two-syllable name ending in *s* or *z*, only the apostrophe is required.
    One-syllable names ending in *s* or *z*:

    Keats's poems   Schwartz's clothes   Jones's report

    Two-syllable names ending in *s* or *z*:

    Dickens' novels   Landis' ideas   Hopkins' appointment

6. Personal pronouns require no apostrophe in the possessive. It should be noted, how-
    ever, that the form *it's* is a contraction for *it is.*

    The book is hers (yours, theirs, ours, etc.).

PU5 *Quotation marks are used to enclose direct quotations, to indicate borrowed
material, and words or phrases used in a special sense. Their most frequent uses
are:*

PU5a *Enclosing direct quotations.*

> At that time you wired us, "Send the goods immediately by express; John C.
> Worden, your city, will furnish credit information."
>
> Your letter of November 23 notified me of this change and said, "I will send you
> a payment by December 10."

PU5b *Placing quotation marks properly.*

Notice that commas and periods are always placed inside the final quotation
marks. Other marks of punctuation, like question marks and exclamation
points, are placed inside the quotations when they pertain only to the quoted
matter; outside when they belong to the whole sentence.

> At that time, I thought you said, "Can you maintain production at this rate over
> a long period?" (The question is asked here *within* the quoted material; hence,
> the question mark is inside the quotes.)
>
> What did you think when we wrote, "We have maintained our side of this con-
> tract"? (The question is asked in the material *outside* the quotes; hence, the ques-
> tion mark is outside.)

An increasing practice in reports, letters, and memos is to indent quoted
material inside the margins of the text. If this is done, *no quotation marks*
are needed. When reports, letters, or memos are double spaced, these quotations should be single spaced. (See PU3c for use of the comma or colon in introducing such quotations.)

```
We were, therefore, greatly interested in

the following statement he made about the

jargon that mars too much business writing:
```

```
      The very fact that business has become
      conscious of jargon is a hopeful sign.
      But much remains to be done.  In business
      writing, an amazing collection of strange,
      meaningless, trite, and pompous expres-
      sions has persisted chiefly because un-
      trained writers sit down to write with
      only the incoming correspondence and the
      hackneyed reports in the files to guide
      them.
```

PU5c *Use quotation marks to indicate special usage of a word or phrase or to en-close slang or technical words.*

This function of quotation marks is frequently abused by inexperienced writers in a quest for emphasis or humorous effect. Underlining the word or phrase is increasingly used in place of the quotes. Whichever practice is followed— quotes or underlining—use it sparingly and do it only at the first appearance of the word or phrase; after that no special treatment is required.

In the ratings, we think of this as "factual information"; actually, a very large element of human judgment and possible error enters this factual information.

Our search for the material was like those "who-dun-its."

She was so proud of her first letter until the supervisor called her attention to "Respectively yours."

In this sense, has he really "learned" anything?

PU6 *Use the end mark (period, question mark, or exclamation point) appropriate to the major intent and meaning of the sentence.*

PU6a *The period marks the end of a complete thought and a definite pause for the reader. It is used after ordinary declarative or imperative statements which are not intended to express strong feelings.*

Send the report as soon as possible.

He declared his intention to buy.

PU6b *The question mark is used at the end of a sentence intended as a direct ques-tion. Notice that questions can also consist of a single word.*

When did you say the report is due? Tomorrow?

Why did he write so tactlessly?

Do not use the question mark after an indirect quotation.

Not: He asked whether I would go?
But: He asked whether I would go.

The omission of question marks where they are required is generally caused by carelessness in rereading or revising written material. Since this mark of punctuation radically changes meaning, special care should be taken to see that it is used properly. Notice the difference in meaning in the following sentences, identical except for punctuation:

He wrote that report.

He wrote that report?

In so-called polite questions, there is an increasing tendency to omit the question mark in business writing:

Will you please send the signed copy as soon as possible.

Won't you please notify us of your change of address.

PU6c *The exclamation point is used to express surprise, strong emotion, command, or emphasis.*

Do it today!

Indeed I wish I could grant your request!

Let's start our planning at once!

In business writing, the exclamation point should not be overused. Particularly to be avoided are attempts to label humor or irony by the exclamation point as in these examples:

We told you we would get there firstest with the bestest line of merchandise!

If it weren't for people, we'd never make mistakes!

PU7 *Dashes, brackets, and parentheses may be used to set off certain types of parenthetical material.*

Since good business writing should reflect careful planning and organization, overuse of these marks of punctuation by business writers should be avoided; by their very definition, these marks indicate afterthoughts and, occasionally, irrelevant comments.

PU7a *The dash marks an abrupt shift; it tells the reader, "This is an afterthought, or this doesn't really belong here, or this requires special emphasis," the last being its most useful function in business writing. The chief uses of the dash are:*

1. To emphasize or contrast a short phrase or word.

    This new device they have developed is designed well, constructed sturdily—and priced far too high.

    He said that smoking was a useless, expensive, time-consuming habit—to which he was completely addicted.

    Report writers who report to readers with the same educational background are fortunate because their readers—and notice this phrase—speak the same language.

2. To indicate an interruption or an afterthought.

    We are writing the customer—and we should have said this in our previous letter—that the guarantee cannot be interpreted that way.

    The difficulty—as I think I reported to you—lies in the shortage of manpower.

    This man—you must remember him—would make an excellent reference to use for such a position.

PU7b *Brackets are generally used to set off inserted material which is extraneous or incidental to the text. Such insertions may be comments, explanations, or editorial corrections.*

    He reported that his research had preceded [Note] at a rapid rate.

    Be careful to write it re-creation [to distinguish it from recreation].

    Parentheses ( ) and brackets [ ] are often confused. Since most standard typewriters carry parentheses but not brackets, brackets must generally be inked in.

PU7c *Parentheses are generally used to enclose explanatory material or comments which may be helpful but not absolutely essential to the reader's understanding.*

    The discussion of accounting (see Book 2) was most helpful.

    If you have these in stock (they must be available now), please send them immediately.

The practice of enclosing figures in parentheses to repeat for accuracy is used infrequently in letters and reports today. Unless there is a special reason for doing so, do not write "He sent eleven dollars ($11.00)." Instead, write "He sent $11."

PU8 *The hyphen is a device which indicates that words or parts of a word belong together. Technically, it is more nearly a mark of spelling than of punctuation.*

Among the problems that plague business writers and typists is whether to use the hyphen in certain compound words and where to place it when an individual word is broken at the end of a line. In both situations, a good dictionary should be consulted, although even the best dictionaries differ about certain words. The status of compound words changes; *nevertheless*, for instance, has evolved from *never the less* through *never-the-less* to its present form. The following rules for the use of the hyphen are particularly useful for business writers:

PU8a *Use a hyphen to join words which form a compound adjective before a noun.*

We say "He is well known" but "He is a well-known man." (Well-known is here a compound adjective modifying a noun.) While this rule is not always strictly followed, precise writing such as technical reports, specifications, contracts, or procedures should follow it to the letter. Here are a few examples.

a 21-inch screen	longer-life wire
up-to-date merchandise	right-of-way statements
well-planned campaign	designed-for-comfort construction
better-than-average performance	copper-coated pipe
150-watt lamps	house-to-house survey
a middle-of-the-road policy	

PU8b *Use a hyphen to indicate the division of syllables in a word at the end of a line of typed or printed matter.*

Here, the dictionary is your only complete guide. But remember that words of one syllable (bought, sold) cannot be divided, that hyphenated words should be divided only at the hyphen (long-delayed *not* long-de-layed), and that it is pointless to divide a word just to set off one or two letters at the beginning or end of a word (divid-ed, e-lude).

PU8c *Use a hyphen to separate words or syllables in certain conventional situations.*

1.   With the prefixes *ex* and *self:* ex-president, ex-officer, self-focusing, self-determining.

2. When awkward doubling of vowels or tripling of consonants would result or when an awkward word would result:

> semi-independence   stall-less
> re-elect   pre-empt
> wall-like   re-enlist
> re-educate   anti-intellectual
> pre-engineered   anti-inflation
> co-worker (to avoid awkward word *coworker*)

3. With compound numbers from twenty-one to ninety-nine.

> Forty-seven men were sent.
>
> Twenty-seven dollars and seventy-three cents.

4. With words where repetition is avoided by indicating to the reader that the first word is incomplete.

> time- and labor-saving methods
> medium- and low-income groups
> upper- and middle-management categories

MECHANICS

Numbers

Like many other aspects of business writing, the practice of writing numbers has not been standardized. This is particularly unfortunate because numbers are so frequently used in letters, reports, and memorandums, and considerable savings could be effected if certain general principles were adopted to replace the haphazard methods now prevailing. The most authoritative attempt to achieve standarization is a Committee Report (Robert D. Hay, chairman) of the American Business Writing Association (December, 1952) titled "Standardization of Rules for Writing Numbers"; the following rules are based on this report, which recommends, as a general rule, that all numbers be expressed in figures when there are several numbers in a paragraph, a letter, or a report. To this general rule, the committee recommended the following modifications for readability and clarity in the use of numbers:

NU1 *Use the "rule of ten" and write out single numbers of ten or below and numbers divisible by ten up to one hundred. Hence*

We employed *nine* stenographers last year.

They invited *sixty* guests.

NU2 *If a sentence begins with a number, the number should be expressed in words.*

Forty people attended.

When this number is awkward to express in words, recast the sentence so that it begins with some other word.

Not: Three hundred and nineteen requests for the pamphlet were received.
But: We received 319 requests for the pamphlet.

NU2a *When numbers are expressed in words, as at the beginning of a sentence, use a hyphen to join compound numbers.*

Correct: Twenty-three, seventy-one, ninety-four.

NU2b *When a number standing first in the sentence is followed by another number to form an approximation, both numbers should be expressed in words.*

Not: Twenty or 25 days will be sufficient.
But: Twenty or twenty-five days will be sufficient.

NU3 *Use a consistent method to express numbers in a connected series or in related groups.*

NU3a *When a sentence contains one series of numbers, all numbers of the series should be expressed in figures.*

We have 9 dealers in Chicago, 11 in Detroit, and 23 in New York.

Nu3b *When a sentence contains two series of numbers, the numbers in one series should be expressed in words and the numbers in the other series should be expressed in figures.*

Five students scored 95 points; seventeen students scored 80 points; and eleven scored 75 points.

Two stocks moved to $115; seven went to $100; and four dropped to $87.50.

NU3c *Use a tabulation when more than two series of numbers are involved.*

Name of accountant	Daily rate	Number of working days	Total earnings
Barlow, Helen	$50	3	$150
Dickinson, A. J.	$35	2	$ 70
Oman, Charles	$40	1	$ 40

NU4 *When one number immediately precedes another number of different context, one number should be expressed in words, the other in figures.*

He ordered twenty-five 10 by 12 prints.

The specifications call for four 3-inch bolts.

You requested 350 two-way sockets.

NU5 *When large numerical expressions are used, set the digits off in groups of threes, from the right, by commas.*

3,975,000   15,000   49,172

The comma may be omitted for smaller numbers, although it may be included.

Correct: 1000 or 1,000   2917 or 2,917

NU6 *Amounts of money, generally speaking, should be expressed in figures.*

This is particularly true when a sentence, a paragraph, a letter, or a report mentions several different amounts of money. However, some questions invariably arise on how to use numbers in money amounts. The following practices are recommended.

1. When several amounts are written close together, all should be expressed in figures.

    Correct: The assets were $17,000; the liabilities were $3,000; and the net worth was $14,000.

2. When an amount of money consists of dollars and cents, the amount should always be expressed in figures. The dollar sign should precede the amount (unless in a tabulated column).

Correct: The invoice total was $50.51.

Correct: The bonds were sold at $999.50 each.

3. When an amount of money consists only of dollars, it should not be followed by a decimal point and a double zero. The double zero is not necessary, unless the amount is tabulated in a column which includes both dollars and cents.

Correct: The invoice total was $150.

Correct: $ 250.80

          200.00

          312.70

          286.50

      $1,050.00

When a series of money amounts contains mixed figures, all even figures should include the double zero for consistency.

Correct: The committee raised amounts of $15.00, $33.75, and $75.00 in the three rummage sales.

4. An amount should not be written in both figures and words. This procedure is acceptable only in legal documents and financial documents.

Correct: The check was for $57.

Correct: The total assets are $23,000.

5. An isolated amount of money of more than ten cents but less than one dollar should be expressed in figures.

Correct: The piggy bank yielded $.57.

Correct: The piggy bank yielded 57¢.

Correct: The piggy bank yielded 57 cents.

Correct: The piggy bank yielded nine cents.

6. An isolated amount of money in even dollars should be written in figures. When the even amount is ten dollars or less, it should be written in words.

Correct: The check was for $57.

Correct: The other check was for five dollars. (Assuming an isolated amount.)

7. When amounts of money are to be tabulated, care should be taken to align the numbers correctly. The right-hand digit of the largest amount governs the tabulation. All deci-

mals, commas, and dollar signs should be aligned properly. A dollar sign should be used both at the beginning of a column and at the end of a column after the underline. It should be set far enough to the left to take care of the longest amount.

Correct:	$ 50.00	*Correct:*	$1,000.50
	100.90	$5,000.00	
	1,100.10	475.00	
	10,133.10	————	
	————		5,475.50
	$11,384.10		$6,475.50
			1.00
			35.00
			————
			$6,511.50

NU7 *Miscellaneous. The following numbers should be expressed in figures:*

1. Dates:

Correct:	October 10, 1968	10 Oct 68 (Military)
	10th of October	Your letter of October 10 was most welcome.
	tenth of October	

2. Street numbers:

    Correct: 1503 Garland Street

3. Numerical names of streets:

    Correct: 110 First Street (All numerical street names under ten should be spelled out in accordance with the general rule of ten.)
    Correct: 110 69th Street
    Correct: 110 110th Street
    Correct: 110 110 Street

4. Numbered items such as page numbers, chapter numbers, figure numbers, table numbers, chart numbers, serial numbers, and telephone numbers:

Correct:	Page 10	*Correct:*	Chart X
	Chapter 10		Service Serial No. 01845283
	Chapter X		Policy No. V9109815
	Figure 8		Policy #V9109815
	Fig. 8		Claim No. 13189756
	Table X		File No. 2716
	Table 10		Telephone CA-7175
	Chart 10		Model No. 3223

5. Decimals:

> *Correct:*   10.25
> 3.1414
> .3535

6. Dimensions:

Correct:	8½ x 11 in.	*Correct:*	2 x 4 in.
	8½ by 11 in.		2 by 4 in.

7. Time:

Correct:	7 P.M.	*Correct:*	7:35 P.M.
	7 a.m.		7:35 p.m.
	seven o'clock		seven in the morning

8. Percentages:

Correct:	35%	*Correct:*	6%
	99.99%		6 percent
	0.09%		six percent ("isolated" figure only)

9. Fractions:

Correct:	$\frac{1}{32}$	one-half	110½ or 110.2
	$\frac{8}{64}$	two-thirds	
	$\frac{25}{64}$	one-fourth	
	$\frac{25}{100}$ or 0.25	three-fourths	

Capitalization

Inexperienced writers generally use too many capitals. A good general principle is to capitalize only when some specific convention requires it. The following rules indicate the conventional uses of capitalization which business writers should follow:

CA1 *Capitalize the first word of the salutation and of the complimentary close in the business letter.*

> Gentlemen: Sincerely yours,
> Dear Mr. Smith: Yours very truly,
> My dear Mr. Smith: Cordially yours,

CA2 *Capitalize the first word and all other important words in titles of books, reports, or business documents.*

The term *important words* is generally interpreted to mean all words except articles (a, an, the), prepositions, and conjunctions.

> A Report on the Last Quarterly Sales Conference
>
> An Analysis of Plant Operations for the Executive Committee
>
> *The Man in the Gray Flannel Suit*

CA3 *Capitalize proper names used to identify specific organizations, places, buildings, and the like.*

> the Warren Company   the Washington Monument
> the Chrysler Building   the Standard Corporation
> Times Square   the Modern Language Association

CA4 *Capitalize the first word of the following structural units:*

1. Complete sentences.
2. Fragments intended as units of expression.

   > What beauty! What economy!

3. Quotations, but only if the quotation is a complete statement.

   > Your letter of August 25 said, "Send the replacement part by air express."
   >
   > Your letter of August 25 said "good wishes for success" in a most gracious way.

4. Complete statements following a colon.

   > This experience has raised one major question: How can we cut these costs?

Do not use capital letters in the following instances:

1. *North, east, south,* and *west* except when they refer to a specific section.

   > He traveled west.
   >
   > We have relocated in the South and the Middle West.

2. General terms which do not identify a specific person, place, or thing.

   > a doctor (but Doctor C. E. Jones)

our president (but President C. E. Smith)

a high school education (but East High School)

a professor (but Professor Brown)

the city council (but the Centerville City Council)

his company (but the White Company)

my uncle (but my Uncle John)

3. The names of the seasons.

spring, winter, summer, fall, midwinter

4. Nouns used with numbers or figures.

page 57, type A, method 3

Exceptions to this are capitals in expressions like Table 3 and Figure 3 within a report, which may be used for emphasis; model numbers used within the company—Model 26; and trade names—Brillo, Verifax, and Anacin.

5. The first word of an indirect quotation.

Not: He reported that *He* would attend.
But: He reported that *he* would attend.

6. The names of studies when they are not used in the sense of specific courses.

history, calculus, engineering, accounting, forestry, agriculture, nursing

Use capitals when referring to specific courses.

History 101   Calculus 263

Remember, however, that names of nationality and language require capitals. Hence,

He studied history, English, calculus, and French.

Italics

Since typewriters, which produce the great majority of reports, letters, and memos, do not have italic type, the most common practice is to underline typewritten words which would be italicized in printed material.

IT1 *Use italics to indicate titles of books, newspapers, magazines, and reports.*

> He sent a copy of *A Report on Management Methods.*
>
> You will be interested in his book *Modern Communication in Business.*
>
> The advertisement appeared originally in *The New York Times.* (Note that this is the correct title—not the New York *Times.* Use titles exactly as they are given, and if the articles *the, a,* or *an* are part of the title, underline them.)

IT2 *Use italics to indicate foreign words or phrases.*

> His sales policy can best be described by the words *caveat emptor.*
>
> *Noblesse oblige* can be said to apply to the modern businessman.

IT3 *Use italics for a word, a letter, or a number referred to as such.*

> You should note the difference between *its* and *it's.*
>
> Because the *3's* and *5's* looked so much alike, we unfortunately misread the order.
>
> He never seemed to learn that there are three *l's* in *parallel.*

IT4 *Use italics to give special emphasis to a word or a group of words.*

For most business writers this statement about use of italics should be followed by a note of caution, for the tendency is to overuse italics and, hence, to diminish their effectiveness as a device for emphasis. In sales letters and sales material, however, italicized words and phrases can underscore key words if the underlining is used judiciously and sparingly.

> You can continue to have this service and *at the same low price.*
>
> Won't you call our dealer for a *free* estimate?
>
> This book is authoritative, complete, and, above all, *easy to understand.*
>
> His deadline for the report was June 4, but I did not receive it until *July 17.*

Footnotes and References

Many business writers shy away from the use of footnotes either because they do not know the proper form or because they think of them as being too pedantic or scholarly. Admittedly, footnotes are not used as frequently in business writing as in scholarly papers. One easy way for business writers to make reference to source materials is to incorporate the reference in the text itself by one of the following methods:

> As Stuart Chase says in *Power of Words* (New York, 1954), p. 173, "Good listening aids us in sizing up a person, a meeting, a line of argument."

or

> Stuart Chase in *Power of Words* (p. 178) comments, "A study of the remarkable communicating ability of honey bees shows that humans are not alone in possessing elaborate systems."*

How much reference there should be to publication dates, places, pages, and publishers' names should be governed entirely by the purpose and the reader. If a bibliography is attached, the material in the text can appropriately be cut to a mere mention of the author and title. As for the mechanics of setting up such references, a good rule of thumb is that quotations of less than four lines are spaced exactly like the rest of the text, with the same margins, and are enclosed in double quotation marks. Longer quotations are single-spaced, set off from the text by double spacing at top and bottom, and indented from the left-hand margin.

In long, formal reports and complex business documents, footnotes should be used, generally, for three purposes:

1. To cite the authority and evidence for statements, opinions, or quotations in the text
2. To make acknowledgments for assistance given or research done by others
3. To provide a place to define a term used in the text, to give additional information that does not fit into the text, or to explain in greater detail what has been referred to in the text

While practice varies considerably in different fields, the most common usage is to place footnotes at the bottom of the page on which the reference occurs. Hence, the typist must gauge her spacing carefully to provide room for the same number of footnotes as there are reference numbers within the text of that page. Footnotes should be single-spaced, should be numbered *consecutively* throughout the report or document; in other words, they should not be numbered 1, 2, 3 on page 4 and start 1, 2 on page 5. They may be set off from the text by a solid line from margin to margin, although this is not mandatory.

---

* Both quotations from Stuart Chase's *Power of Words* are reprinted by permission of the author and Harcourt, Brace & World, Inc.

F1 *Place footnotes properly and consistently in the text.*

In the text, the footnote should *follow* the passage to which it refers; for example, if the passage is a quotation, the reference should be placed at the end of the quotation and not after the author's name or the title of the book. This place in the text at which the footnote is introduced is marked by an Arabic numeral (1, 2, 3); Roman numerals (I, II, III) are not used for this purpose. In typed material, the footnote number is elevated slightly above the line but never a full space above it. While usage in business reports and documents has not completely crystallized, the most general practice now is to leave the number [1] without punctuation. The older practice of following it with a period [1.] or surrounding it with parentheses [(1)] or [(1.)] is not recommended. Whichever form is used, it should be used consistently throughout the document and in the references within the text as well as in the reference numbers at the bottom of the page.

Writers who prepare reports or articles for publication should always look at the magazine or journal to which they intend to submit their material and follow that publication's practice concerning the form and placement of footnotes. If you are in doubt about any of the many highly specialized problems which arise about footnotes, consult *The Modern Language Association Style Sheet* (you can obtain a copy for 75 cents from the Materials Center, MLA, 62 Fifth Avenue, New York, N.Y. 10011) or Kate L. Turabian's *A Manual for Writers of Term Papers, Theses, and Dissertations* (revised edition, The University of Chicago Press, 1955). While these definitive works tend to emphasize a more formal and scholarly pattern of footnoting than that customarily employed in business reports and documents, they can be relied on as completely authoritative.

F2 *Adopt a standard form of footnote style and be consistent in its use. Remember that a footnote is used to give the source of information.*

In writing footnotes, use the title page of the book you are citing as the source for the information contained. There is no need to repeat in the footnote any items, such as the author's name or the title, which have been supplied in the text. If you remember the purpose your report or document will serve and the kind of reader or readers, you can then select the appropriate items from the following list and arrange them in this order:

1. The name of the author in its normal order—not his last name first—followed by a comma. If the author's name is unknown, begin with the title; Anon. or Anonymous is not necessary except in alphabetical listings in bibliographies.

2. The title of the book, underlined or in capital letters if not underlined, followed by a comma.

3. What edition of the book you are citing, if it is not the first edition—for example, 4th ed.

4. These facts about the book, grouped within parentheses:
   a. The place of publication, followed by a comma.
   b. The year of publication, the last element within parentheses, so there is no punctuation. Place a comma outside the parenthesis.

5. The page number or numbers which you are citing, followed by a period—for example, p. 142. or pp. 147–148.

Typical footnotes would be arranged as follows:

Robert Gunning, *The Technique of Clear Writing* (New York, 1952), p. 74.

B. H. Weil, *The Technical Report*, 2d ed. (New York, 1954), pp. 21–27.

If the book has two or three authors, begin the footnote:

Gordon H. Mills and John A. Walter, *Technical Writing*, etc.

Glenn Leggett, C. David Mead, and William Charvat, *Prentice-Hall Handbook for Writers*, etc.

When the book contains a collection of articles, reports, or documents by different authors but edited by one individual:

Eldridge Peterson (ed.), *Advertiser's Annual*, etc.

When you refer to a report with no author given:

Annual Report of the American Management Association for the Year Ending December 31, 1963.

or

American Management Association *Annual Report for the Year Ending December 31, 1963.*

When you refer to articles in magazines, use the following form for the footnote:

1. The name of the author followed by a comma. The title comes first if the author's name is unknown.

2. The title of the article placed within quotation marks and with a comma *inside* the final quotation mark.

3. The name of the periodical, underlined and followed by a comma.

4. The date of the magazine—December 5, 1969—if it is comparatively recent; if it is a few years back, give the volume number in capital Roman numerals or Arabic numbers— XXV, February 16, 1960. Many magazines have abandoned the clumsy system of numbering volumes in Roman numerals; if you refer to such a magazine, your reference is vol. 25. The date of the magazine is followed by a comma.

5. The page number or numbers, followed by a period.

The footnote referring to a magazine article will conform to one of these examples:

Thomas H. Grainger, "The Emergency in Basic Science," *Saturday Review*, July 16, 1955, p. 11.

If no author is given:

"What Business Leaders See Ahead," *U.S. News and World Report*, January 27, 1956, pp. 24–25.

When you list the volume number of the periodical:

Virginia Parsons, "Testing Costs Money—Does It Pay?" *The Reporter of Direct Mail Advertising*, vol. 15, December, 1952, 20–23. (Notice that when the reference includes both volume and page number it is permissible to omit the abbreviations p. or pp.)

References to newspapers are made as follows:

Cleveland Plain Dealer, November 27, 1969, p. 13.
The New York Times, October 2, 1969, p. 42.
The Times (London), October 2, 1969, p. 12.

Notice that the name of the city is italicized when it is part of the title of the newspaper; otherwise, the place (London) is put in parentheses to avoid confusion with other newspapers of similar name.

References to letters, reports, minutes of committee meetings in company or individual files should contain names, titles, file numbers, dates, addresses, or any other information which is sufficient to identify them:

Minutes of the Monthly Meeting of the Cost Reduction Committee, October 22, 1970 (in the files of John C. Dunn, Secretary).

Letter from Mr. C. E. Woodley, 3907 East Auburn Street, Minneapolis, Minn. 55440 to N. M. Boland, Sales Manager, February 4, 1971.

Quarterly Report of the Personnel Department, July 10, 1970, p. 6 (in the files of the Department).

While they are not written materials, interviews constitute sources for many reports and formal documents in business. References to them are properly made in this form:

Interview with Charles F. Springer, Director of Business Information, The Los Angeles Chamber of Commerce, May 9, 1970.

Interview with Dr. Thomas Gresham, Coordinator of Research, The Blank Chemical Company, Warrington, West Virginia, June 10, 1970.

When sources are referred to more than once in the document or report, the footnotes following the first reference can be shortened. Two devices are then used:

Ibid. (for *ibidem*—"in the same place"). Use this when you refer to a source which is *the same as that in the footnote immediately preceding. Ibid.* is always underlined and followed by a period; it is capitalized only when it is the first word in the entry.

Op. cit. (for *opere citato*—"in the work cited"). Use this when you refer to a book or article already mentioned in a previous footnote *but when there are other references intervening. Op. cit.* replaces the title and facts of publication cited in the previous reference; it does not replace the author's name, since its meaning is "in the work cited."

These two useful devices are illustrated in the following:

¹ Sir Ernest Gowers, *Plain Words: Their ABC* (New York, 1955), p. 53.

² Stuart Chase, *Power of Words* (New York, 1954), pp. 262–264.

³ *Ibid.*, p. 282. [Refers to Chase's book.]

⁴ Gowers, *op. cit.*, pp. 95–97. [Refers to the same book as the first footnote.]

F3 *Use a consistent system in listing bibliographic entries, including sufficient information to serve your reader's purpose.*

Many reports and business documents require a list of sources used in their preparation. This bibliography, of course, contains an entry for each different source referred to in the footnotes as well as any other sources which may help the reader. Entries in the bibliography are arranged alphabetically by the first word of the title, disregarding the articles *the, a, an* (hence "The Cost of Planning" is alphabetized under *c*). For very long or complex reports and documents, bibliographic entries are sometimes classified according to type: books, magazine articles, business reports, and the like. When this classification is used, a separate heading—Books, Articles, Periodicals—should be supplied for each section of the bibliography and the items are then alphabetized within each section.

The first line of each entry is not indented; additional lines are indented the number of spaces used in paragraph indention throughout the report or document. Single spacing is used within each entry, double spacing between entries. The entry contains the same information as is used in the footnote except that it omits page references for books. Many report writers omit references to publishers in their footnotes and add this information to the other facts in the bibliography. Notice the arrangement in the following section of a bibliography containing books, articles, company reports, and newspaper references.

J. Bauer, "Logic and Language in Medical Writing," *Science*, vol. 117, December, 1953, pp. 40–41.

Cleveland Plain Dealer, November 27, 1956, p. 13.

Costs of Communicating, A Report by the Cost Analysis Division, available in Central Files.

Robert Gunning, *The Technique of Clear Writing*, New York: McGraw-Hill Book Company, 1952.

S. I. Hayakawa (ed.), *Language, Meaning and Maturity*, New York: Harper & Row, Publishers, Incorporated, 1954.

Minutes of the Monthly Meeting of the Executive Committee, June 30, 1956 (in the files of Henry W. Farr, Secretary).

Plain Letters, General Services Administration, Government Printing Office, Washington, D.C., 1955.

Charles E. Redfield, *Communication in Management*, Chicago: The University of Chicago Press, 1954.

"Speaking Can Be Easy . . . For Engineers, Too," Engineers Council for Professional Development, New York, 1952.

"The Strait Jacket," *Time*, February 13, 1956, p. 53.

Spelling

Most teachers have heard all the alibis pertaining to bad spelling. These excuses run the gamut from the optimistic "I'll have a secretary to correct any misspellings" to the fatalistic "I'm a hereditary bad speller and nobody can do anything about it." Perhaps too much emphasis has been placed on the horrors of poor spelling—although many "modern" schools seem to be offsetting this tendency by giving it no emphasis at all. Certainly there are more serious flaws in writing than misspellings; unclear, ambiguous, or meaningless constructions are far worse. But a misspelled word is something definite, something tangible for all who read to see. They may conclude that the error results from ignorance, from carelessness, or from inattention to detail. None of these conclusions will aid the business writer in his career or enhance the reputation of the company for which he works; and that is why misspelling should be avoided in memos, reports, and letters.

Correcting Errors in Spelling

How can this be done? First, you'll have to make up your mind that a working knowledge of correct spelling is important to your business career. Second, you can do these things:

1. Observe the arrangement of letters in words carefully. (When you don't, you write words like *thier, Britian, fourty, buisness,* and *similiar.*)
2. Watch your pronunciation. If you mispronounce a word, you will probably misspell it. (This produces *accidently* for *accidentally; maintainance* for *maintenance; dispite* for *despite; suprise* for *surprise.*)
3. Proofread your work carefully. Whether you submit written work to an instructor in college or sign material which you have dictated in business, you have a responsibility to see that it represents you at your best.

These instructions really add up to one—*use your dictionary constantly.* For anyone who writes, it is the one indispensable tool; for those who are unsure of their spelling, it is the only satisfactory answer since the "rules" of English spelling frequently have so many exceptions. You will do well, therefore, to look up each word about which you are uncertain and to keep a list of these words on which you can concentrate.

Twenty-five Words Most Frequently Misspelled

An exceedingly helpful and significant study made by Dean Thomas Clark Pollock of New York University, as reported in *College English* for November, 1954 (volume 16, pages 102 to 109), sheds considerable light on actual spelling errors. Dean Pollock collected reports from 599 college teachers of English in 52 colleges and universities on the 50 words these teachers found misspelled most frequently by college students. His analysis of these data shows that the majority of misspellings occur with a comparatively small number of words or word groups; in fact 9 percent of the different words or word groups in the study account for over half of all the misspellings of the total of 4,482 words or word groups the college teachers submitted to him. The conclusion which can logically be drawn from this exhaustive study is that college students can greatly improve their spelling by concentrating on a relatively small number of words or word groups.

Here are the 25 words and word groups which Dean Pollock's study revealed as being most frequently misspelled, along with specific suggestions for spelling them correctly or for using the proper form in the proper place:

1. *Their, they're, there*
   Their—possessive case of the pronoun *they.*
   They're—contraction for *they are.*
   There—an adverb meaning *in or at that place,* as "We sent the order *there* rather than delay delivery." Used also in sentences in which the verb comes before the subject: "*There* is hope of a quick solution."

2. *Too, to, two*
   Too—an adverb meaning *in addition* or *to an excessive extent or degree.*

   He *too* had difficulty organizing his reports.
   He used *too* many words.

   To—a preposition expressing motion or direction toward something.

   He sent it *to* the New York Office.
   We expressed our thanks *to* him.

   Two—a number: *two* people.

3. *Receive, receiving*
   Remember the rule: *i* before *e* except after *c*. Not all English words with *ei* or *ie* follow the rule, but rec*ei*ve and rec*ei*ving do.

4. *Exist, existence, existent*
   Memorize the exact sequence of letters in *exist* and remember that the other two forms are formed with *e*—existence not existance; existent not existant.

5. *Occur, occurred, occurring, occurrence*
   Remember the basic form *occur* and that any suffix added requires that the final *r* be doubled.

6. *Definite, definitely, definition, define*
   There is no *a* in any of these words and only one *f* in each of them. Most misspellings result from an attempt to spell the basic form as de*fi*nate. Pronounce it carefully and use the *i* before the *t* of the first three forms.

7. *Separate, separation*
   Remember the *a* (not *e*) which always follows *p* in these words.

8. *Believe, belief*
   These words also follow the *i* before *e* rule.

9. *Occasion*
   Two *c*'s and one *s*

10. *Lose, losing*
    Memorize *lose* and remember that the *e* drops out to form *losing*. These words should not be confused with *loose, loosing*, whose general meaning is *to free from bonds* or *not firm*, as "He got his hands loose" or "The loose papers in his briefcase."

11. *Write, writing, writer*
    The long *i* sound requires just one *t*; note the difference in pronunciation of *writer* and *written*.

12. *Description, describe*
    Always an *e* in the first syllable.

13. *Benefit, benefited, beneficial*
    Bene is Latin for "well" and your reader will regard you benevolently if you rigidly adhere to the Latin. *Benefited* is a bit tricky in requiring only one *t*.

14. *Precede*
    Misspellings of this word result from confusion with *proceed*, meaning *to move forward* or *to carry on an action*. *Precede* means *to go before in time or rank or importance*. You'll simply have to learn these spellings and meanings and then commit to memory the fact that *procedure*, a word used frequently in business writing, is a maverick in its spelling.

15. *Referring*
    Refer ends with one *r*, but the participle doubles the *r*. Since *referring* occurs frequently in business reports, letters, and memos, you should learn its spelling.

16. *Success, succeed, succession*
    Keep your attention on the two *c*'s which cause most of the trouble in spelling these words.

17. *Its, it's*
    Its—the possessive case of the pronoun *it*.

    > That report has proved *its* worth.
    > The machine was delivered without *its* fixtures.

    It's—a contraction of *it is*.

    > *It's* a pleasure to serve you.

    Contrary to written expressions of opinion by generations of college students, there is no word spelled *its'*!

18. *Privilege*
    The *i* before the *l* and the *e* after it are the trouble spots in this word.

19. *Environment*

Careless pronounciation causes most misspellings of this word—*enviorment* being the most frequent misspelling. Sound the word carefully, syllable by syllable—*en-vi-ron-ment*—and you can eliminate the major danger of misspelling.

20. *Personal, personnel*

Your *personal* hopes for attaining a career in business will probably start on the road to reality in a *personnel* office. Note that these two words are pronounced and spelled differently.

21. *Than, then*

Than—a conjunction used after an adjective or adverb in the comparative degree.

This is a better report *than* last year's was.

Occasionally it is a preposition followed by a noun or pronoun:

I joined the company earlier *than* John.

But as either part of speech, *than* always indicates some kind of comparison.
Then—an adverb indicating *at that time* or *soon afterward*.

He did not know *then* what he knows now.
We had to stop our research for a time and *then* we began again.

22. *Principle, principal*

These two words are really *three* in their functions, and to use them correctly you must know their functions and meanings.
Principle—can be used *only as a noun* meaning *an accepted or professed rule of action or conduct*.

These *principles* have been an integral part of our company's conduct of business.
He is a man of good *principles*.

Principal—can be used as an *adjective* or as a *noun*. As a noun, principal means *a governing official* such as the *principal* of a high school or *a capital sum* such as

He drew 4 percent interest on his *principal*.

As an adjective, principal means *chief, most important, first in rank, foremost*.

The *principal* parts of a verb
The *principal* reason for his action

Remember that only *principal* can be used as an adjective, that *principle* can be used only as a noun.

23. *Choose, chose, choice*

Choose is the present tense, *chose* is the past tense, and *choice* is a noun or adjective:

I hope you will *choose* our products.
He *chose* to take his vacation at Christmas.
He had a clear *choice*. (noun)
We sell *choice* merchandise. (adjective)

24. *Perform, performance*
Careful pronunciation will eliminate much of the possibility of error here. The word is not "*pre*form" but "*per*form."

25. *Similar*
Here, too, exact pronunciation will help; the most frequent misspelling is *similiar* which would have to be pronounced "sim-il-yar." The word is properly pronounced "sim-i-ler"—but remember, the last vowel is an *a*.

Three Hundred Words Frequently Misspelled in Business Writing

Use this list to check the accuracy of your spelling and keep a list of the words you misspell.

absence	bargain	confer
acceptable	believing	conference
accessories	beneficial	congratulate
accidentally	bookkeeper	conscientious
accommodate	bulletin	consensus
accompanying	bureau	controlled
accustom	calendar	convenience
achievement	canceled	correspondence
acknowledge	cancellation	correspondents
address	carburetor	corroborate
addressed	career	counsel
adequate	cashier	courteous
adjustment	changeable	courtesy
admirable	chargeable	creditor
advisable	chiefly	criticism
allotted	Cincinnati	criticize
all ready	clientele	decision
all right	collectible	deductible
already	column	deferred
analysis	commission	deficient
apologize	commitment	deficit
appreciation	committed	depreciation
appropriate	committee	desirable
approval	commodities	despite
argument	comparative	development
arrangement	competence	disappointment
assurance	competitive	discrepancy
athletic	complementary	dissatisfied
attendance	complimentary	distributor
authorize	concede	eligible
auxiliary	concession	embarrass
balance	conducive	enforceable

equipped	independent	occasionally
equitable	indispensable	offered
equivalent	inducement	official
erroneous	initiative	omission
evidently	inquiries	omitted
exaggerate	insolvency	opportunity
exceed	insurance	optimistic
exceptionally	intelligible	originate
exchangeable	intentionally	pamphlet
exorbitant	intercede	parallel
expenses	interchangeable	parliamentary
experience	interruption	particularly
explanation	irrelevant	permanent
extension	installation	permissible
extraordinary	invariable	permitting
familiar	jeopardize	perseverance
feasible	judgment	persistence
February	justifiable	planned
financial	labeled	possession
flexible	laboratory	precedence
forcible	legible	predominant
foreign	liable	preferable
forfeit	license	preference
formally	liquidation	preferred
formerly	livelihood	prejudice
forty	maintain	preparation
fulfill	maintenance	prevalent
fundamental	manageable	procedure
government	manufacturer	proceedings
grievance	mediocre	profited
guarantee	mercantile	progress
guaranty	merchandise	promissory
guidance	miniature	proportionate
handicapped	miscellaneous	purchasing
helpful	misspell	quantity
hesitancy	mortgage	questionnaire
hindrance	naturally	readjustment
humorous	necessary	receipt
hurriedly	negligible	receivable
illegible	neighbor	recipient
immediately	nineteenth	recommend
inadequate	ninety	reconcile
inaugurate	ninth	reducible
incidentally	noticeable	reference
inconvenience	obsolete	referred

register	substantiate	uncontrollable
regrettable	substitute	undoubtedly
reimbursement	successful	unforeseen
relief	superintendent	unnecessary
relieve	supersede	until
remittance	supervisor	usage
repetition	supplementary	using
representative	systematic	usually
requisition	tactfulness	vacancy
retroactive	technique	variety
salable	temperament	versatile
satisfactory	temporarily	vicinity
scarcity	tendency	visible
schedule	thoroughly	volume
secretary	transferable	warehouse
seize	transferred	warranted
serviceable	treasurer	Wednesday
significance	truly	welfare
specifically	twelfth	wholly
stationary	typical	witnessed
stationery	unanimous	writing
statute	unbelievable	written
subsidiary	unconscious	yield

Special Forms of Address and Salutation*

ADMIRAL, Full, Fleet

    Fleet Admiral John Jones   Dear Sir:
    Chief of Naval Operations   Dear Admiral Jones:

ALDERMAN

    Alderman John Jones   Dear Sir:
                                     Dear Alderman Jones:

AMBASSADOR

    His Excellency   Sir:
    The American Ambassador   Your Excellency:
    The American Embassy   Dear Mr. Ambassador:
    London, England
    The Honorable John Jones
    The American Ambassador

*Reprinted by permission of New York Life Insurance Company, from "It's the Style at New York Life."

AMBASSADOR (Foreign)

> His Excellency
> The Ambassador of the French
>   Republic
> Embassy of the French
>   Republic
> Washington, D.C.
> His Excellency
> Jean Longchamp
> Ambassador of the French
>   Republic

> Sir:
> Excellency:
> Your Excellency:

ARCHBISHOP

> Most Reverend John Jones

> Your Excellency:
> Your Grace:

ARCHDEACON

> The Venerable the Arch-
>   deacon of Philadelphia
> The Venerable John Jones
>   Archdeacon of Philadelphia

> Venerable Sir:
> My dear Archdeacon:

ASSEMBLYMAN

> The Honorable John Jones
> Member of Assembly
> Assemblyman John Jones

> Dear Sir:
> My dear Mr. Jones:
> Dear Mr. Jones:

ASSISTANT SECRETARY (Cabinet)

> The Assistant Secretary of
>   State
> The Honorable John Jones
>   Assistant Secretary of State

> Sir:
> Dear (My dear) Sir:
> My dear Mr. Jones:
> Dear Mr. Jones:
> (*Never* Mr. Secretary:)

ASSOCIATE JUSTICE OF THE SUPREME COURT

> The Honorable John Jones
> Associate Justice of the
>   Supreme Court
> The Honorable John Jones
> Justice, Supreme Court of the
>   United States
> Mr. John Jones
> United States Supreme Court

> Sir:
> Mr. Justice:
> Your Honor:
> My dear Mr. Justice:
> My dear Justice Jones:
> Dear Justice Jones:

ATTORNEY GENERAL
    (See Cabinet Officer)

BISHOP (Methodist)
    The Reverend Bishop John   Dear Sir:
      Jones   My dear Bishop Jones:
      Bishop of the Eastern Area   Dear Bishop Jones:

BISHOP (Protestant Episcopal)
    The Right Reverend John   Right Reverend and Dear Sir:
      Jones   My dear Bishop Jones:
      Bishop of Cleveland

BISHOP (Roman Catholic)
    The Most Reverend John   Your Excellency:
      Jones   My dear Bishop:
      Bishop of Baltimore
      The Most Reverend Bishop
      Jones

BRIGADIER GENERAL
    Brigadier General   Dear Sir:
    John Jones   Dear General Jones:

BROTHER (Religious)
    Brother John Jones   My dear Brother:
                             Dear Brother Jones:

CABINET OFFICER
    The Honorable the Secretary   Sir:
      of Agriculture (or State,   Dear Sir:
      Commerce, etc.)   Dear (My dear) Mr. Secretary:
                             (Postmaster General, Attorney
                             General)

CADET
    Cadet John Jones   Dear Sir:
                             Dear Cadet Jones:
                             Dear Mr. Jones:

CANON
    The Very Reverend Canon   Very Reverend Canon:
    John Jones   My dear (or Dear) Canon Jones:
    The Very Reverend John
      Canon Jones

CAPTAIN

Captain John Jones   Dear Sir:
United States Army (or Navy   Dear Captain Jones:
    or Marine Corps)

CARDINAL

His Eminence, John Cardinal   Your Eminence:
    Jones   My Lord Cardinal:
His Eminence Cardinal Jones   (to those of foreign countries)

CARDINAL (if also Archbishop)

His Eminence the Cardinal   Your Eminence:
Archbishop of Baltimore
His Eminence Cardinal Jones,
Archbishop of Baltimore

CHARGÉ D'AFFAIRES

The Chargé d'Affaires of   Sir:
    Mexico   Dear Sir:
Mr. José Gonzaga   My dear Mr. Gonzaga:
Chargé d'Affaires   (or use title, if there is one—
John Jones, Esquire   hereditary, military, or naval)
Chargé d'Affaires

CHIEF JUSTICE OF THE UNITED STATES

The Honorable John Jones   Sir:
Chief Justice of the Supreme   Mr. Chief Justice:
    Court of the United States   My dear Mr. Justice:
Chief Justice Jones   Dear Justice Jones:
United States Supreme Court
The Chief Justice of the
    United States

CHIEF OF POLICE

John Jones   Dear Sir:
Chief of Police   Dear Chief Jones:

CLERGYMAN

The Reverend John Jones   Reverend Sir:
Reverend Dr. John Jones   My dear Sir:
    (if Doctor of Divinity)   My dear Mr. Jones:
                                            Dear Mr. Jones:
                                            Dear Dr. Jones:

CLERK OF THE HOUSE (or Senate)

The Honorable John Jones   Dear Sir:
Clerk of the House (or   My dear Mr. Jones:
   Senate)   Dear Mr. Jones:

COLONEL

Colonel John Jones   Dear Sir:
United States Army (or   Dear Colonel Jones:
   Marine Corps)

COMMANDER

Commander John Jones   Dear Sir:
United States Navy   Dear Commander Jones:

COMMISSIONER OF A BUREAU

The Honorable John Jones   Sir:
Commissioner of the Bureau   Dear Sir:
   of Education   My dear Mr. Jones:
Department of Interior

CONGRESSMAN

The Honorable John Jones   Sir:
House of Representatives   Dear Sir:
The Honorable John Jones   My dear Congressman Jones:
Representative in Congress   Dear Representative Jones:
   (When away from Wash-   Dear Mr. Jones:
   ington)
Representative John Jones
House of Representatives

CONGRESSWOMAN

The Honorable Helen Smith   Dear Madam:
House of Representatives   Dear Representative Smith:
The Honorable Helen Smith   My dear Miss Smith:
Representative in Congress
   (When away from Wash-
   ington)

CONSUL

Mr. John Jones   Dear Sir:
Consul of the United States   Dear Mr. Consul:
   of America   My dear Mr. Jones:

CORPORAL

Corporal John Jones   Dear Sir:
United States Army (or   Dear Mr. Jones:
    United States Marine
    Corps)

DEAN (Ecclesiastical)

The Very Reverend the Dean   Sir:
    of St. Andrew's   Very Reverend Sir:
The Very Reverend Dean   Very Reverend Father:
    John Jones   (Roman Catholic)

DEAN (Graduate School or College)

Dean John Jones   Dear Sir:
School of Engineering   Dear Dean Jones:

DIPLOMAT

(See Ambassador, Chargé d'Affaires, Minister. For diplomats of lower rank, use the common form of address, unless they have military, naval, or hereditary titles.)

ENSIGN

Ensign J. J. Jones   Dear Sir:
United States Navy   Dear Mr. Jones:

ENVOY

(See Minister, Diplomat)

GENERAL

General John Jones   Sir:
United States Army   Dear Sir:
                                           Dear General Jones:

GOVERNOR

His Excellency   Your Excellency:
The Governor of Ohio   Sir:
The Honorable the Governor   Dear Sir:
    of Ohio   My dear Governor Jones:
The Honorable John Jones
    Governor of Ohio

JUDGE

The Honorable John Jones	Dear Sir:
United States District Judge	Dear Judge Jones:
The Honorable Helen Smith	Dear Madam:
Judge of the Circuit Court	Dear Judge Smith:

LAWYER

Mr. John Jones	Dear Sir:
Attorney at Law	My dear Mr. Jones:
	Dear Mr. Jones:

LIEUTENANT

Lieutenant John Jones	Dear Sir:
United States Army (or	Dear Mr. Jones:
Navy)	

(The salutation to an army officer below the rank of Captain should not refer to his title. Use Mr.)

LIEUTENANT COLONEL

Lieutenant Colonel John Jones	Dear Sir:
United States Army (or Ma-	Dear Colonel Jones:
rine Corps)	
(Omit the *Lieutenant* in the salutation)	

LIEUTENANT COMMANDER

Lieutenant Commander	Dear Sir:
John Jones	Dear Mr. Jones:
United States Navy	

(The salutation to a naval officer of or below the rank of Lieutenant Commander should not refer to his title. Use Mr.)

LIEUTENANT GENERAL

Lieutenant General John Jones	Dear Sir:
	Dear General Jones:
(Omit the *Lieutenant* in the salutation)	

LIEUTENANT GOVERNOR

The Honorable John Jones	Sir:
Lieutenant Governor of	Dear Sir:
Virginia	My dear Mr. Jones:

MAJOR

 Major John Jones   Dear Sir:
 United States Army   Dear Major Jones:

MAJOR GENERAL

 Major General John Jones   Dear Sir:
 United States Army   Dear General Jones:
 (Omit the *Major* in the salutation)

MAYOR

 The Mayor of the City of   Sir:
  Cleveland   Dear Sir:
 The Honorable John Jones   My dear Mr. Mayor:
 Mayor of the City of Cleve- Dear Mayor Jones:
  land

MIDSHIPMAN

 Midshipman J. J. Jones   Dear Sir:
 United States Navy   Dear Mr. Jones:

MINISTER (Diplomatic)

 The Spanish Minister   Your Excellency:
 The Spanish Legation   Sir:
 Washington, D.C.   My dear Mr. Minister:
 His Excellency John Jones
 Minister of the United States
  of America
 Madrid, Spain

MINISTER (Religious)

 (See Clergyman; Priest; Rabbi)

MONK

 (See Priest)

MONSIGNOR

 The Right Reverend   The Right Reverend and dear
 Monsignor John Jones   Monsignor:
            The Right Reverend Monsignor
             John Jones:
            My dear Monsignor Jones:

MOTHER SUPERIOR

The Reverend Mother Su-
perior
Convent of the Sacred Heart
Mother Mary Therese, Su-
perior
Convent of the Sacred Heart
Reverend Mother Mary
Therese
(Plus initials of the order)

Reverend Mother:
Dear Madam:
My dear Reverend Mother:
Dear Mother Mary Therese:

NUN

Sister Mary Therese

Reverend Sister:
Dear Sister Mary Therese:

POPE

His Holiness Pope Paul VI

Most Holy Father:
Your Holiness:

POSTMASTER GENERAL

(See Cabinet Officer)

PRESIDENT (College or University)

President John Jones
The Ohio State University
John Jones, LL.D.
President, New York Univer-
sity
(Use initials of only the
highest degree, unless in
different fields)
Very Reverend John Jones
Notre Dame University
(If a Catholic College)

Dear Sir:
My dear President Jones:

Very Reverend and dear Father:

PRESIDENT (State Senate)

The Honorable John Jones
President
The Senate of New Jersey

Sir:

PRESIDENT (United States Senate)

The Honorable the President   Sir:
   of the Senate of the United
   States
The Honorable John Jones
President of the Senate
Washington, D.C.

PRESIDENT OF THE UNITED STATES

The President of the United   Sir:
   States   My dear Mr. President:
The President   Dear Mr. President:
The White House

PRIEST (Roman Catholic)

The Reverend Father John   Reverend Father:
   Jones   Dear Father Jones:
   (Plus initials of the Order)

PRIEST (Episcopal)

Reverend John Jones   Dear Father Jones:

PROFESSOR

Mr. John Jones   Dear Sir:
Professor John Jones   Dear Professor Jones:
Dr. John Jones   Dear Dr. Jones:
   (If he holds a doctor's
   degree)
The Reverend Professor John   My dear Sir:
   Jones
The Reverend John Jones,
   D.D.
   (If he holds that degree)

RABBI

Rabbi John Jones   Reverend Sir:
The Reverend John Jones   Dear Sir:
Dr. John Jones   My dear Rabbi Jones:
                                 Dear Dr. Jones:

REPRESENTATIVE

(See Congressman)

SECRETARY OF AGRICULTURE, COMMERCE, DEFENSE, ETC.

    (See Cabinet Officer)

SECRETARY TO THE PRESIDENT

The Honorable John Jones	Sir:
Secretary to the President	Dear Sir:
The White House	Dear Mr. Jones:

SENATOR (United States or State)

Senator John Jones	Sir:
The Honorable John Jones	Dear Sir:
United States Senate	My dear Senator Jones:
The Honorable John Jones	Dear Senator Jones:
Senate of New York	

SERGEANT

Sergeant John Jones	Dear Sir:
U.S. Army (or U.S. Marine Corps)	Dear Mr. Jones:

SISTER OF RELIGIOUS ORDER

The Reverend Sister Mary Therese	My dear Sister:
Sister Mary Therese (Plus initials of Order)	Dear Sister Mary Therese:

SPEAKER OF THE HOUSE

The Honorable the Speaker	Dear Sir:
House of Representatives	My dear Mr. Speaker:
The Honorable John Jones	Dear Mr. Speaker:
Speaker of the House of Representatives	

UNDERSECRETARY OF STATE

The Undersecretary of State	Sir:
The Honorable John Jones	Dear Sir:
Undersecretary of State	My dear Mr. Jones:

VICE-CONSUL

    (Same form as Consul)

VICE PRESIDENT OF THE UNITED STATES

The Vice President	Sir:
Washington, D.C.	My dear Mr. Vice President:
The Honorable John Jones	Dear Mr. Vice President:
Vice President of the United	Dear Mr. Jones:
States	

Abbreviations for Names of States, Territories, and United States Possessions

The Post Office Department has authorized the following two-letter abbreviations for use with zip code numbers:

Alabama	AL	Montana	MT
Alaska	AK	Nebraska	NB
Arizona	AZ	Nevada	NV
Arkansas	AR	New Hampshire	NH
California	CA	New Jersey	NJ
Colorado	CO	New Mexico	NM
Connecticut	CT	New York	NY
Delaware	DE	North Carolina	NC
District of Columbia	DC	North Dakota	ND
Florida	FL	Ohio	OH
Georgia	GA	Oklahoma	OK
Guam	GU	Oregon	OR
Hawaii	HI	Pennsylvania	PA
Idaho	ID	Puerto Rico	PR
Illinois	IL	Rhode Island	RI
Indiana	IN	South Carolina	SC
Iowa	IA	South Dakota	SD
Kansas	KS	Tennessee	TN
Kentucky	KY	Texas	TX
Louisiana	LA	Utah	UT
Maine	ME	Vermont	VT
Maryland	MD	Virginia	VA
Massachusetts	MA	Virgin Islands	VI
Michigan	MI	Washington	WA
Minnesota	MN	West Virginia	WV
Mississippi	MS	Wisconsin	WI
Missouri	MO	Wyoming	WY

INDEX

KEY TO THE REFERENCE SECTION